The edition of *The Complete Works of Frances Ridley Havergal* has five parts:

Volume I *Behold Your King: The Complete Poetical Works of Frances Ridley Havergal*

Volume II *Whose I Am and Whom I Serve: Prose Works of Frances Ridley Havergal*

Volume III *Loving Messages for the Little Ones: Works for Children by Frances Ridley Havergal*

Volume IV *Love for Love: Frances Ridley Havergal: Memorials, Letters and Biographical Works*

Volume V *Songs of Truth and Love: Music by Frances Ridley Havergal and William Henry Havergal*

David L. Chalkley, Editor   Dr. Glen T. Wegge, Music Editor

Frances Ridley Havergal's formal education ended when she was 17, with one term at a young women's school in Düsseldorf, Germany, yet she was a true scholar all her life. Fluent in German and French and nearly so in Italian, she read and loved the Reformers in Latin, German, and French. Knowledge was never an end in itself, only a means to know better her Lord and Saviour and to help to bring others to know Him. The Bible was her only Book, and she studied the Hebrew and Greek texts of Scripture, memorized nearly all the New Testament and large portions of the Old Testament, and loved the Author with all her being.

Frances was brought to a saving knowledge of Christ when she was 14, and the rest of her life was consecrated to her Saviour, the Lord Jesus. Keenly aware of her own sinfulness and inability, her sole desire was to please and glorify Him alone. Very finely gifted, she was truly diligent with her gifts: her poetry is among the finest in the English language, after George Herbert; her prose works are deeply beneficial; a musician to the core, she left behind important compositions. Like her works, her life richly touched the ones near her and countless many who met or heard her. The Lord Jesus Christ was her alone, only beauty, and she glowed Him and His truth. Never wanting attention to herself, Frances' desire of her heart was for herself and for others to know her King, the Lord Jesus Christ. Her works are a gold-mine of help and enrichment. There is life in these pages: her works truly glorify the Lord, truly benefit His people, and powerfully reach those who do not yet know Him.

The Music of Frances Ridley Havergal by Glen T. Wegge, Ph.D.

This Companion Volume to the Havergal edition is a valuable presentation of F.R.H.'s scores, most or nearly all of F.R.H.'s scores very little if any at all seen, or even known of, for nearly a century. What a valuable body of music has been unknown for so long and is now made available to many. Dr. Wegge completed his Ph.D. in Music Theory at Indiana University at Bloomington, and his diligence and thoroughness in this volume are obvious. First an analysis of F.R.H.'s compositions is given, an essay that both addresses the most advanced musicians and also reaches those who are untrained in music; then all the extant scores that have been found are newly typeset, with complete texts for each score and extensive indices at the end of the book. This volume presents F.R.H.'s music in newly typeset scores diligently prepared by Dr. Wegge, and Volume V of the Havergal edition presents the scores in facsimile, the original 19th century scores. (The essay—a dissertation—analysing her scores is given the same both in this Companion Volume and in Volume V of the Havergal edition.)

Dr. Wegge is also preparing all of these scores for publication in performance folio editions.

Frances Ridley Havergal Trust   P.O. Box 649   Kirksville, Missouri 63501

Maria V. G. Havergal (1821–1887). This undated photograph (taken by Elliott & Fry in London) was the frontispiece of the original Nisbet edition of The Autobiography of Maria Vernon Graham Havergal.

WORKS

BY

Maria V. G. Havergal

Pleasant Fruits

Cripple Joseph

Autobiography of Maria Vernon Graham Havergal
Edited by J. Miriam Crane

Outlines of a Gentle Life

Memorials of Frances Ridley Havergal

Article on Great Campden House
Footprints of William Henry Havergal in Gloucester 1819–1822
The Last Week
Memoranda of a Tour with F.R.H. in 1876
Various Prefaces by M.V.G.H. to Books by Frances Ridley Havergal

First written about her sister Frances, this next statement is also true of Maria:

"Knowing her intense desire that Christ should be magnified, whether by her life or in her death, may it be to His glory that in these pages she, being dead, 'Yet speaketh!'"

Taken from the Edition of *The Complete Works of Frances Ridley Havergal*.

David L. Chalkley, Editor   Dr. Glen T. Wegge, Associate Editor

ISBN 978-1-937236-25-0   Library of Congress: 2011960054

Copyright © 2011 Frances Ridley Havergal Trust. All rights are reserved.

Frances Ridley Havergal Trust P.O. Box 649 Kirksville, Missouri 63501

Book cover by Sherry Goodwin and David Carter.

CONTENTS

	PAGE
Pleasant Fruits	1
Cripple Joseph	73
Autobiography of Maria Vernon Graham Havergal edited by J. Miriam Crane	95
Outlines of a Gentle Life	187
Memorials of Frances Ridley Havergal	243
Article on Great Campden House	365
The Last Week	376
Footprints of William Henry Havergal when Curate of Coaley, Gloucestershire, 1819–1822	389
Memoranda, by M.V.G.H., of a Tour in 1876 with Her Sister, F.R.H.	393
Prefaces by M.V.G.H. to books by Frances Ridley Havergal	402
Maria's Preface to *Kept for the Master's Use*, June 11, 1879	402
Maria's Preface to *Morning Stars*, September, 1879	402
Maria's Preface to *Under His Shadow The Last Poems of Frances Ridley Havergal*, November, 1879	402
Maria's Preface to *Memorials of Frances Ridley Havergal*, April, 1880	404
Maria's Preface to *Loyal Responses* with music, August, 1881	404
Maria's Preface to *Starlight Through the Shadows*, December 14, 1881	405
Maria's Prefatory Note to *Ben Brightboots and Other True Stories, Hymns and Music*, November 15, 1882	406
Maria's Preface to *Life Echoes*, September, 1883	406
Maria's Preface to *The Poetical Works of Frances Ridley Havergal*, likely the same year as the publication, 1884	407
Maria's Preface to *Letters by the Late Frances Ridley Havergal*, August 1885	409

LIST OF ILLUSTRATIONS

Maria Vernon Graham Havergal, undated photograph portrait with signature	ii
Hand-painted personal seal of Maria on a page of family members' seals	vi
Leaflet score, "A Worker's Prayer," words and music by F.R.H., published by J. & R. Parlane	3
Two acrostics on Giles Shaw by Maria V. G. Havergal, fair copy autographs in Maria's album of handcopied poems for Giles Shaw	4
Elizabeth Clay, photograph portrait, 1885	70
Poems by F.R.H. and W.H.H. in Maria's album of handcopied poems for Giles Shaw	71–72
F.R.H., sketch by T. J. Hughes, February, 1879	74
Photographs of Maria V. G. Havergal's gravestone	94
Jane Miriam (Havergal) Crane, portrait by Solomon Cole in 1845	96
Ellen Prestage Havergal, F.R.H., and Maria V. G. Havergal, photograph of the three sisters, 1854	98
Maria Havergal's appointment card for half an hour in Queen Anne's Room at Great Campden House	103
Maria's message card sent to missionaries of the Church Missionary Society, January, 1882	169
Marble epitaph of Jane Head Havergal, Maria's and F.R.H.'s mother	178
Published print, Wyre Hill Home Mission Schools, Bewdley	183
William Henry Havergal, photograph portrait, undated	184
Print portrait of W.H.H., the frontispiece of the original book *Records of the Life of the Rev. William Henry Havergal, M.A.*	185
Giles and Ellen Prestage (Havergal) Shaw, two photograph portraits, undated	186

Winterdyne, the home of Giles and Ellen Shaw, 19th century photograph	188
Ellen Prestage Shaw, two photographs, undated	190
Printed card, "The Perfect Satisfaction" (by unknown writer)	222
Frontispiece of *Outlines of a Gentle Life*, "Cedar Tree, Winterdyne"	237
F.R.H., photograph portrait (seated beside table with sewing basket, holding book with her left hand) February 1, 1879	238
Part of a manuscript letter by Maria V. G. Havergal	239
Astley Church and Rectory, drawn by Jane Miriam (Havergal) Crane	240
F.R.H., oval portrait by Solomon Cole in 1845	241
Part of I John 1 in F.R.H.'s Bible	242
Second view of Astley Church and Rectory drawn by Miriam Crane	246
Pages from the *Journal of Mercies for 1879*	316–318
F.R.H., manuscript list "Work for 1879 'If the Lord will.' "	319
Two pages from F.R.H.'s Bagster study Bible	362
Published leaflet poem, "Have you not a word for Jesus?" by F.R.H., and the placard pledge "Abstain from All Appearance of Evil." with her signature	363
Published print, Great Campden House	364
Published print, The Little School-Room at Great Campden House, 1820	368
Pages from F.R.H.'s Sunday School Register	369
Henwick House and Shareshill Parsonage, two homes where F.R.H. lived, drawn by Miriam Crane	371
F.R.H.'s manuscript of "Confidence"	372
F.R.H., oval portrait by T. J. Hughes, February, 1879	373
F.R.H., rough draft of verses in her handwriting, on an envelope	374
An In Memoriam card and an In Memoriam page "In Loving Memory of FRH"	375 & 388
Frontispiece of *The Last Week* published by James Nisbet & Co.	376
The home at the Mumbles near Swansea, Wales, where F.R.H. lived her last eight months and died	386
Manuscript score and signature of William Henry Havergal	389
Frontispiece of F.R.H.'s bound manuscript volume of Swiss Letters	393
F.R.H.'s hand-painted plaque of I John 1:7, "My own Text"	401
F.R.H., photograph portrait (standing and reading a smaller book) February 1, 1879	410

Maria wrote this in her Diary (see page 157 of this book): "January 1, 1883.— 'Jesus Christ, the Same yesterday, to-day, and for ever.' 'Able to subdue all things unto Himself'—just what I need. . . . Lord, open every life-page for me. Specially may I live to edit Fanny's letters for Thy glory." The Lord gave Maria her request. *Letters by the Late Frances Ridley Havergal* was published in 1885, and Maria lived until June 22, 1887.

This magnification is taken from the photograph by Elliott and Fry on February 1, 1879, when she was 42. The complete photograph is given on page 238 of this book.

Maria Vernon Graham Havergal (1821–1887) was a true servant of the Lord Jesus Christ. Very like-minded and like-hearted to her sister Frances Ridley Havergal, Maria glowed the Lord and His truth. When their widowed step-mother died in May, 1878, Frances was free to move, and she accepted Maria's invitation to come to live with her in Mumbles, near Swansea, Wales. Neither one knew that those would be the final eight months of Frances' life. Fifteen years old when her youngest sister was born, Maria was a genuinely devoted sister to F.R.H. and truly served Frances whenever they were together; and after her death Maria realized profoundly the value of—and was a diligent editor and publisher of—Frances' completed and uncompleted works. Her desire was the same as her sister's, the glory of the Lord, and help and benefit to others. The love of Christ defined and filled both ladies. Much of Maria's life's work was evangelism to impoverished or little-educated lost people who did not know the Saviour, especially women and children, both in England in Ireland.

Maria's own fine volume *Pleasant Fruits*, her *Autobiography*, and *Cripple Joseph* are rich works. Her edited books of Frances' poetry and prose and music disseminated and preserved the gold-mine left after her death. Maria's biography *Memorials of Frances Ridley Havergal* is as valuable as Frances' own prose, and the volume of *Letters by the Late Frances Ridley Havergal* (which Maria prayed to be able to complete) was the final book she published of Frances' writings. On Maria's gravestone is the inscription she asked to be written: "This is a faithful saying, and worthy of all acceptation, that Christ Jesus came into the world to save sinners, of whom I am chief." I Timothy 1:15. David Chalkley

> It became an increasing delight to me to visit the cottages, my swift walking taking me to many a lonely corner. I marvel now at my activities, and believe they sprang from love to God, and much delightful communing did I hold with the Lord Jesus on the wayside. He was more and more to me, and when my early retirement at night was smiled at, they little knew the delight of being alone with Jesus my Lord. [Maria, in her *Autobiography*, on page 109 of this book]

This was Maria's personal seal, hand-painted on a sheet with personal seals of other members of her family. Her seal shows the Dove pointing to and looking upon—with light shining upon—an opened Bible, the seal encircled by a locket of Maria's hair, all of that encircled by a beautifully hand-painted color wreath of flowers.

PLEASANT FRUITS

FROM

THE COTTAGE AND THE CLASS.

BY

MARIA V. G. HAVERGAL.

LONDON:
JAMES NISBET & CO., 21 BERNERS STREET.
1871.

"HATH NOT GOD
CHOSEN THE POOR OF THIS WORLD,
RICH IN FAITH, AND HEIRS OF THE KINGDOM
WHICH HE HATH PROMISED TO THEM
THAT LOVE HIM."

"BEING FILLED WITH
THE FRUITS OF RIGHTEOUSNESS,
WHICH ARE BY JESUS CHRIST, UNTO
THE GLORY AND PRAISE
OF GOD."

"WE BLESS
THY HOLY NAME
FOR ALL THY SERVANTS DEPARTED
THIS LIFE IN THY FAITH AND FEAR;
BESEECHING THEE TO GIVE US GRACE SO TO
FOLLOW THEIR GOOD EXAMPLES, THAT,
WITH THEM, WE MAY BE
PARTAKERS OF
THY HEAVENLY KINGDOM."

CONTENTS.

CHAP.		PAGE
I.	Almshouse Visits	5
II.	Walks and Talks	15
III.	Walks and Talks in Ireland	18
IV.	Lydia Watkins	26
V.	The Soil Prepared	29
VI.	George and Rhoda's Story	34
VII.	Susan Harris, or Fruit in Due Season	38
VIII.	Four Visits to Mary Hart	42
IX.	Early Fruit from an Irish School	44
X.	The Sister of "A Wise and Holy Child"	48
XI.	Visits to Men	54
XII.	Harry the Happy	58

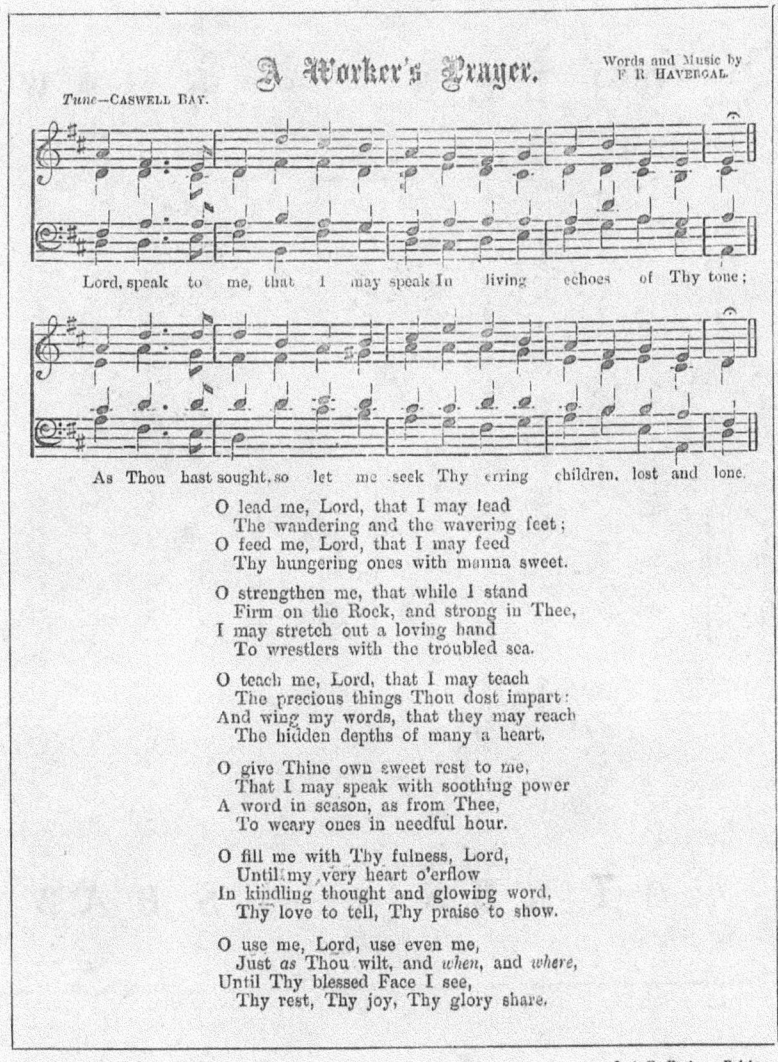

Maria knew and loved this hymn by F.R.H., which is truly done in Pleasant Fruits.

"The Lord will give Grace & Glory."

"Grace."

Grace be unto you and peace. *Phil. I. 2.*
I commend you to — the word of His Grace. *Acts XX. 32.*
Let us come boldly to the throne of grace. *Heb. IV. 16.*
Even so might grace reign through righteousness. *Rom. V. 21.*
See that ye abound in this grace. *2 Cor. VIII. 7.*

"Glory."

Shew me Thy glory — — — *Exodus XXXIII. 18.*
He might present it to Himself — a glorious Church. *Ep. V. 27.*
Afterward receive me to Glory. *Psalm LXXIII. 24.*
When the chief Shepherd shall appear ye shall receive a crown of glory.

For May 5. 1867.
M. V. G. H.

"The Lord will give Grace & Glory."

"Grace."

Grace, peace, and love be thine.
In words of Grace Divine.
Let every need by grace supplied,
Even His righteousness applied:
See that thy graces shine.

"Glory."

Shew him Thy glory, ever Thine,
His glorious Grant with Thee to shine;
After life's journey see Thy face,
With Glory crown the work of Grace!

For May 5. 1867.
M. V. G. H.

These are two poems written by Maria for her sister Ellen's husband, Giles Shaw, whose birthday was May 5. These two poems were written in a special album of poems (written by F.R.H., Ellen Prestage Shaw, and several other poets), all diligently and beautifully copied by Maria in a beautiful calligraphy, presented to Giles Shaw on May 5, 1867. This album had 172 pages of such fine penmanship, all copied by Maria, a labor of love. See also pages 71–72 of this book.

FRUITS OF THE VALLEY.

I.

ALMSHOUSE VISITS.

VERY refreshing and pleasant were the visits to the St. Nicholas Almshouses. It seemed like walking through a corn-field where the golden grain was ripe and ready for the sickle. The following gleanings from the sheaves now safely gathered in, may show the work of God's grace in ripening them for glory.

The Trinity Almshouses were founded in the days of Queen Elizabeth. They are a memorial of her visit to the "faithful city," a royal footprint not yet obliterated. A picture of the Queen still hangs over one of the old passage galleries. On Trinity Mondays, this faded and blackened portrait has fresh evergreens tied round it by the aged women. They loyally subscribe a few pence to gild the laurel leaves, and then indulge in a strong cup of tea, in memory of their good Queen Bess.

The dwelling-rooms are dry and comfortable, and there is a weekly allowance for the support of about fifteen women.

To many a hoary head, these almshouses have been a peaceable habitation and quiet resting-place, after life's rough and weary wanderings.

It is no use to hurry a visit here; there is so much to tell of the past, it is long before the present can be reached. Be "swift to hear," and let them tell the tale of life over and over again; for the patient listener will learn how the poor of this world are "rich in faith." And often deep teachings too will gush out from those who have long been sitting at Jesus' feet, and who are soon going to see Him face to face.

We will go up the narrow staircase and along the open gallery that leads to Ann's door. A box of mignonette smells sweetly, and there are pots of wallflowers and scarlet geraniums, while a fuchsia lives in a favourite old tea-pot. The room is clean and the old oak chairs bright. The chimney shelf contains quite a mosaic variety of curiosities, each having its tale of long ago. An easy chair covered with patchwork, is drawn out for the visitor, and Ann sits down in the old rocking chair, that had hushed many a little crying one.

Two or three morning talks must be given here as one. Ann shall tell her own tale.

"It was my husband's death that first brought me to know the Lord. He was very moral, and what people call a good liver. He was a mighty man for going to the Cathedral, and seldom missed. Sometimes I went too. I must say the music was heavenly there, but it never went farther than my ears. I suppose it was my ignorance, but it did seem strange to sing about being 'miserable sinners.'

"One night my husband saw the lights in a place of worship, and he turned in to listen. There was a two-edged sword to meet him there. He came home and said,—

"'Ann, I have been told to-night all things that ever I did, I am just a sinner, a condemned man.'

"Soon after his illness came on. I was taking him some gruel, and saw his face so full of grief. I said—

"'O Jim, what is the matter?'

"'Wife, I thought I had been an upright man, but the Lord has held up His glass for me to look in, and my sins seem like a great mountain. Oh, my soul, my soul, is it lost for ever? Kneel down, wife, and pray for me.'

"But I never prayed for myself, how could I for him?

"From that time the Bible was always in his hand, and it seemed to shine away his darkness. His time was not long. One evening he was leaning against me, and I saw from the change that came over his face, that the message was come for him to go. He sunk, and sunk, till his head rested on my knees. I said,—

"'O Jim, is the sin gone?'

"'Yes, wife, the mountain is gone, it's blood that took it away. I see a glorious hill now, it's there He calls me.'

"A few minutes more and he left me behind, and went to climb it.

"That trouble brought me to my knees. But I was longer wandering in the dark than my poor Jim, and I must have been further off too. One Sunday the 15th chapter of Luke was preached on, and it was a message to me. I came home thinking, 'Why should not I arise and go to my Father?' I put my two little ones to bed, and then I went on my knees. The thought came, how the blessed Jesus bowed His head on the cross, that He might fetch them back that were a great way off. I felt I must have Him to fetch me, for I could not stir a step as the prodigal did. For days I felt far, far off. One afternoon I left my needlework, though it was wanted at the shop, and I knelt a long, long time. The load that kept me far off was taken away, for my Saviour came to bring me home. All my grief was turned to joy, He helped me to give Him my rags, and He had got a best robe for me too. I could not praise my dear Saviour enough. I felt I could tell the whole world what He had done for my soul.

"My dear children were great comforts to me. My little girl brought me in a green bough from the hedge, saying—

"'Oh, mother, isn't God good, to send leaves on the bits of sticks.'

"It was a hard struggle to live, but I always had the assurance that the Lord would not let me want. Typhus fever came, and the children and I were all ill together. I pledged my clothes. One evening the medicine bottle was empty, and I knew we must have it filled. I made four journeys to get from my bed to the box. Jim's coat was left; it was very hard to touch that, but I knew he had got the white robe on, and would never be wanting it again. Before I opened the box I just knelt by it, and was saying, 'Thy will be done,' when a knock came at the door. Who should it be but a strange minister's servant! She said—

"'It's many years since I saw you, but I heard you were living in the town, and somehow it came over me to-day, I must go and find out where you lived.'

"So I left my Jim's coat in the box, and she soon saw our distress. She went back and told her master, and he sent her again with a basket of potatoes and cold meat. He was a good man, but never having a wife or children, he was not likely to know what fever was. I don't think parsons ever should be single; they can never feel for womankind, as those who have wife and children about them. So I thanked her, and said, that none of us could eat that now, and that I wouldn't be *covetous* and keep it from those that were well and hungry. So she went again, and came back with a one pound note and some eggs. Now, was not that the hand of the Lord?

"And I will tell you that was not the only time He heard my cry before I came to the Amen. Some time after this, we were very *drove*. It was breakfast time; my girl said,—

"'Mother, what do you put the kettle on for? there is no tea and no bread.'

"'Never mind, child, the hot water will warm us better than cold; and you and I will kneel down and tell our heavenly Father.'

"A rap at the door, and there was an errand-boy,—

"'My mistress has sent you two loaves of bread, because the baker's cart left her more than she wanted.'

"I just felt like Elijah. My Father knew I had no bread, and He saw my heart was too honest to send for what I could not pay for. Could I ever doubt Him again, when His blessed eye watched over my wants. Satan often came to tempt me when bread and work were short, but I had always this to silence him with. I can't read a word, but it is surprising what Scripture comes into my mind. My children read the Bible while I worked for them, and I learnt a good many passages. It is a long time since those days of troubles, but you see the Lord has led me all the way, and He won't leave me now. And then, He gave me this room, it will be the last I shall want till mine is ready in His mansions. I lie awake a long time, and then I pray to the Holy Spirit to bring me a verse, and He does. I know He does work on the mind, for I have proved it many years. Yes, He does speak, and I think He has brought me into this quiet corner, that I may have more time to listen. It is the voice to the heart that I love best now, and He does speak. I look round on the empty chairs sometimes, then I think of where they are sitting now, and that there will be no empty chairs in heaven. And my blessed Jesus comes so near me, and He fills all the room. Sometimes two or three of the Lord's people come in, and then we read and pray together. But I am never without His company, and that is the best of all. I was always fond of singing and in my poor way, I go through some hymns I know. But soon He will be teaching me, and how shall I sing then?"

Our next visit is to a dying one, Mrs. Amphlett. There is no mistaking who she means as she whispers, "Precious, precious!"

"What promise gives you comfort now?"

"Christ Jesus came into the world to save sinners—me, me."

After reading to her Psalm 23, she whispered,—

"No sting, no fear, no condemnation to them which are in Christ Jesus."

Some of her neighbours came in. She motioned to the one she loved best, Elizabeth Sherwood, to come near, saying, "Come in, thou child of God."

One of them saying, "Poor Mrs. A., I hope you will be better soon," she answered, "Don't call me poor, he who has Christ can't be poor; don't wish me to be better, dear; would you hinder me from my kingdom?"

The next visit was the last, one Sunday evening. Sweeter than the chiming bells were her farewell words. "Glory, glory" was her constant cry. Repeating to her Deuteronomy 33:27,

"Underneath are the everlasting arms," her full commentary was, "One arm is mercy, the other arm is love, and they are underneath *me*."

And yet she longed for more, not only to feel His arms, but to see Himself, and so she called, "Come, Lord Jesus, come quickly." And before that Sabbath closed to us, she passed away into the endless Sabbath above.

The next visit is far from being pleasant, were it not for the simple-minded talk of the old widow Evans, who is sitting there as nurse to poor Ann.

For many years Ann pretended to be a Protestant, and as such received the visits and alms of our Church. Lately she has declared that she has always believed in the Holy Catholic Church of Rome.

Ann. "It is a long time since you called, Miss, I thought you had forsaken me."

"The last time I came, you said you liked the priest's visits best, Ann; but I heard you were ill, and so called."

"Yes, I am ill; going as fast as I can go; O Lord, help me."

"Do you really want the Lord to help you, Ann, for you told me you thought the Virgin Mary could help you just as well?"

"Yes, I do say 'Hail Mary;' isn't hers a powerful name?"

"'There is nothing in the Bible about the name of Mary, but we read there that the Lord Jesus said, 'All power is given unto me in heaven and in earth.' Neither is there salvation in any other, for there is none other name under heaven given among men whereby we must be saved. And the Lord told His disciples, 'If ye shall ask anything in my name, I will do it.'"

Poor Ann seemed sleepy and did not answer, but her nurse, widow Evans, said,—

"Ay, that's the name. I am a poor ignorant sinner, but I know that Jesus is the only name they call in heaven, and it's enough for me. I am humbly thankful to you, Miss, for teaching me the only hymn I know,—

'How sweet the name of Jesus sounds.'

I haven't got it perfect, though I do put up my thumb for Shepherd, and the other names run on my fingers, but I haven't got my Tom, my jewel, to help me out with it now."

"I see that Ann is gone to sleep, Evans, so will you like to tell me about your poor Tom?"

"Yes, Miss, I do like to tell of him, for my heart is always talking about my Tom, my jewel. I never look up to the sky, but I think his shadow is among the clouds, but it's too far off for me to reach. I was quite a young girl at service when we lighted on one another, and our two hearts never came apart till his stopped beating.

"I was dairy-maid at P—— Court. My mistress was very notable in her dress; she turned the last maid away, because, when she gave her a new dress, she scauffed it all up into flounces, and she said she would never have such pomps and vanities in her kitchen.

"The first time I came down to go to market, mistress met me on the stairs. She had a mighty way of putting her hands behind her when she was pleased, and back they went,—

"'Well now, Betty, you do look nice. You can look the parson in the face when you say the Catechism in church, and get through the "pomps and vanities" with a clean conscience.'

"I had on a brown stuff, a Holland pinafore, and the bib full up to my chin. I had a close bonnet on, and asking your pardon, Miss, not like the bare-faced ones now-a-days. I have heard mine called a coal-scuttle shape. The biggest change in the world since my young days is the paltriness about dress. It all comes of young ladies going off to them long places, Paris for one, that's full of grandeur, and the first time they come back to their church, their bonnets are more thought of than the sermon. My poor mistress was the best fashioned dresser that ever I saw, though she had plenty of money to buy flounces. She had plenty of trouble too, for her husband died, and her two sons and her daughter all went melancholy like. She would not send them to the lunatics, but got some strait waistcoats to keep them in, comfortable like. Poor young things! it's well that the Lord's and a mother's heart loves their own, in or out of their senses. (I've heard that read at church, about the lunatics, that they were brought to Jesus.) They all died, and she and her money were left alone, till there came a man that *lighted* her."

"What do you mean, Evans?"

"Why, when a man marries a woman for her money, it's like a crow pouncing down on the corn, and lightening the stalks of their grain, till they are bare. It was a pity, for she hadn't her equal for neatness and notableness.

"I suppose it was my stuff gown that took Tom's fancy; anyway, he got very partial to me, and asked me if I could marry him.

"From our wedding-day never a cross word passed between us, for, if he said yes, I never said no. We rented a cottage on the mistress's farm. It was alongside of an orchard, and the apples grew thicker and bigger than the stars in the sky. I used to wonder if the apples that tempted Eve could be redder, till our parson said in a sermon he didn't think it was apples at all. But he didn't seem to know what it was, so I kept my own mind about it.

"Those were happy days with my poor Tom, my jewel. I can hear his whistle now; no one ever whistled like him. The larks might have took pattern by his tunes.

"For many years no trouble came to our door, but trouble is the right road to the kingdom, and so ours came—still I had my Tom. We were hand in hand, and parted all our troubles equal like. The mistress died; we had to leave our cottage, and one trouble came after another, till my poor Tom was taken from me. He was ill a long time with what they called the palsy. I used to comfort him with saying—

"'Tom, my jewel, it's the Lord Jesus shook hands with both your hands, and He's just left you a shaking token behind Him.'

"I can't bear to talk of that time, but I never knew till then there was one Name sweeter than my poor Tom's.

"I never was up to Tom in the learning. I am a poor ignorant creature and have no gifts like him, but I do pray for the Holy Spirit to enlighten me, and keep me in the right road. I go in the little back room there to think of His love and to cry at His feet.

"It's a help to me to come and nurse this poor neighbour, for I have only the parish pay. I do all I can for poor Mrs C——. I lay her as sweet as a violet every morning. I wish she hadn't left the right road, following them priests instead of the Lord Jesus Christ. I was here when our dear clergyman Mr. H—— called, and he laid it all before her as clear as a glass of water. I know it touched my heart and made the tears flow, to hear him discourse on our dear Saviour, and what a good priest He was. She's having a long sleep now, I hope you will call and reason with her about it."

"Did you enjoy the tea party at the schoolroom, Evans?"

"That I did, Miss, and we were treated just like kings and queens; and the music was so meritable. It illuminified me till I thought it brought the light of heaven down to us. I had only one thought—that I'd like to hear dear Miss Fanny and the ladies sing to me again in heaven, for then my Tom, my jewel, would be listening along with me."

Another of that evening's aged guests thus spoke of their feast on January 4th in the schoolroom—

"That was a pleasant evening; it was months since I had taken tea with any one. And as I watched them hobbling in on their crutches and sticks, I thought it was like bringing the prisoners out of the prison, and the hidden ones out of their holes and corners. It made me sink to the earth to think such vile wretched ones as we should be so remembered. But I traced all our enjoyment that evening to the overflowings of His love. He was the spring, for He put it in His people's heart to remember their poor neighbours.

"The crowning privilege was His presence. I summed up all that evening's enjoyment in three words 'God is love.'"

We pass on to another door and knock.

"Come in, come in. I am so glad you are come, for I was trying to find last Sunday's text and could not. It does so vex me that I can't remember my precious minister's sermons as I used to. I always take that verse in Solomon's Song, 'The voice of the turtle is heard in our land,' to mean the minister's voice in the sermons. I am sure ours is like the turtle dove's call. I've always found it good to sit under dear Mr. Havergal, many's the time he has fed my poor soul. I always look up to see who is going in the pulpit, and if it's not him my heart sinks. I know I ought to welcome all; but he never gives us dry crusts, and what he says comes so to my heart. My dear precious minister, how lively he comes among us, I know his step from any one's. I hope he will be the instrument to turn many to the Lord. I do pray for him; will you tell him so?"

"Indeed, I will, Surman, it is a great comfort to God's ministers to feel that their people pray for them. You seem very happy this morning."

"Yes, that I am, and I would not give up my happiness for all the world could give. Time was when I felt burdened, but now no heaviness stays with me, though of course it does rise sometimes."

"And what do you do with it?"

"I put it all on Christ; isn't He able to bear it? He has long carried my loads, takes them all on His dear self. And it's the same with temptations; the tempter can't go further than the length of his chain. My Saviour has long been my precious friend; it is many years I have walked with Him. I'll tell you what I would not to any stranger. What pleasant talks I have with my precious Saviour! He comes so near to me, and does manifest Himself in a way I can't tell you. May you know it yourself, my dear, and that will strengthen you to work for Him. Your work is not done, mine is; though I take every opportunity of speaking a word for Him."

"Have you often such opportunities?"

"I take all that comes, don't pick and choose them. The other day I got as far as where I could see a harvest field. A gentleman was standing there too, so I said—'I am thinking, Sir, how this field is like the day of judgment, when the Lord will come to gather the wheat into His barn, but He will burn up the chaff with unquenchable fire.' But he turned on his heel and went away. So I prayed for him and learnt the lesson for myself. I always did like looking at God's lessons up in the trees and down in the fields. Once I remember seeing a field of wheat, and bright scarlet poppies growing along with it. And the wind came and blew, and they all bent together, the wheat and the poppies. I thought that's just like believers and professors, growing together, bowing in the same worship, bending to the same God; some making a finer talk than a poor Christian, but the poppies won't be took up into the garner. But I am talking so long, Miss, and now I want the reading."

"What chapter shall we read, Surman?"

"I should like that one in the Song of Solomon, where he says, 'Arise, my love, and come away.'"

So verse by verse we read the 2d chapter of the Song of Solomon.

And this poor widow had the key to the Song of Songs, and very plain and sweet were her comments on each verse. And she spoke as one who, while she learnt, was also leaning on the Beloved.

Another time I asked her if she wanted any clothing.

"No, I want for nothing, the Lord provides for all my needs. I think I'm like Elijah fed by the ravens, for first one and then another neighbour brings me a bit. And your dear mother, she never forgets me, look what she made with her own hands; tell her she has my prayers, and tell her how I liked my precious minister's lovely sermon on Good Friday. He did explain to us about the cross of Jesus and His love in bearing it; it melted my heart quite. I can truly say my soul is profited by Mr. Havergal's preaching; my memory got so shallow that I'm glad to hear all I can."

When the Church Missionary Sermons were preached Surman always cheerfully gave her mite. She said,—

"I longed to put more in His plate, but I had only sixpence in my little store; I wished I had more to give Him, my dear God and Master. I wish all the poor blacks could know what a precious Saviour Christ is. I often think, Why did He choose and call me, when others are cut down in sin, and I, a rebel, brought to Him and saved with everlasting salvation. And to think of the end and of the glory coming to me then!"

Surman told me of a young friend in whose spiritual growth she took much interest.

"That dear child has called to see me again. It is quite wonderful how the Lord is teaching her. See how He waters His young plants. She said to me, 'I would sooner have both my arms chopped off, than lose my hope in Christ.'"

These "holy women" in the almshouse were often most helpful to young visitors, who were just beginning to seek the better part. There was such reality in what they said of the preciousness of the Lord Jesus as their living Saviour, the brother, friend, with whom they held sweet communion. It gave them opportunity to say a word in season, and I could tell of real blessing, real help Zionward, being the result of such visits. Often too, have their words cheered and encouraged me and taught me many a lesson, I learnt nowhere else so well.

Only one more visit must be recalled.

"Good morning, Surman, I am so glad to come and see you again."

"It does seem a long time since you went to Ireland; I thought I should never hear your knock at my door again. But here I am, still far from home, yet every night I think, Now it's one day nearer. And when I wake I think, There I've got over more of my journey without knowing it. I should like to know about their religion in Ireland; they don't think as we do."

"No, Surman, they do not keep to the lamp of God's word. Christ is not 'all' to them; it would make you sad to hear them talk of their trust in the Virgin and her intercessions for them. I will tell you what a Roman Catholic said to me, when I had been speaking to her about the Lord Jesus ever living to intercede for us.

"'That's not our belief, Miss, there's no help for us but through the Blessed Mother of God; wasn't she without spot or stain, and ordained for ages before to be the mother of God? Oh, Holy Mary, Queen of heaven, I adore thee. Didn't her Son say, 'All power is given to my mother in heaven and in earth?' isn't she pleading for me, and her Son daren't deny her anything? If it was not for her intercession, the wicked would be cut off, it's for her sake they are spared. I tell you, Miss, if an angel from heaven came and told me, the Holy Virgin wasn't at God's right hand interceding for me, I would not believe him. Sure the devils tremble at her name, she rules over the one half of heaven. God the Father is first, and Mary is next to Him. Oh, Holy Mary, I adore thee, I love thee, and I'll never trust in any other.'"

"Oh, dear, dear, poor thing! how could a woman save a woman? The Virgin never shed her blood, and so has no right to intercede."

"That is just it, Surman. St. Paul says (1 Timothy 2:5, 6), 'One mediator between God and man, the man Christ Jesus, Who gave Himself a ransom for all.' He who paid the ransom alone can plead it."

Surman.—"I wish I could tell her how Christ is my 'all in all,' my precious all. He is interceding for me, and there's my joy to be 'accepted in the beloved.' Then they don't rest on the promises as I do?"

"No, Surman, God's word is hid from them, and so they can't meditate in it day and night as you do. Were you thinking of any promise last night?"

"When I woke in the night, the thought woke with me how the Lord took Eve and 'brought her unto the man.' It seemed to me such a sweet resemblance of the Church being given to the Lord Jesus. I can't tell you how bright it pictured the Lord's love to me. How He chose me to be His, and then won't He come and fetch me home, and present me faultless before His throne? I have known what an earthly husband is, but there's none like my heavenly Husband. Yes, He is mine, He chose me from all eternity, and that's why I chose Him. Are we not bone of His bone, and flesh of His flesh, and doesn't He feed me daily with this life? Oh, what an arm I've found His to lean on. I shan't be always a weak creature here, grappling with the world, the flesh, and the devil. I shall get out of the enemy's gunshot soon. I can't see to read the chapter with you to-day, but I am ready for it."

The 26th of Isaiah was chosen; at the 4th verse, "Trust ye in the Lord for ever, for in the Lord Jehovah is everlasting strength," she remarked, "Yes, I have it, that's the Rock of Ages, Moses smote it, and 'that Rock was Christ.' And that stream flows on to me. I shall be drinking of it all my journey.

"You must ask my dear precious pastor to remember me in his prayers. What should we poor old women do without his visits? I know his step from the hundreds that go by my door. And please to thank dear Mrs. H—— for her kind present. Oh, what kind friends the Lord sends me!"

Would that such visits could be recorded of all the almshouse inmates! But it is ever the "few" from among the "many" that know the Lord. There were the self-righteous ones, who would reckon up many items of goodness. There were their good characters, and the good families they had lived in, their constant church goings, and their never doing any harm to their neighbours. They were very comfortable in their minds, and quite sure that such respectable, upright, good livers as themselves never need think of hell; besides, God was very merciful. It seemed like turning over and admiring their filthy rags, and heaping on one after another,—choosing rags, rejecting the King's wedding garment.

And there were others groping in the dark, yet thankful to hear of the light. One was most thankful for her young visitor's weekly call, and great were her lamentations if "our dear Miss F." was away. Ann would say, "I can't read myself, so she and her books are always welcome. I do grieve that I am no scholar, but I get to my prayers in my poor way. I pray that the Lord will enlighten me, and put His Holy Spirit in me,—that He will open my dark eyes, and save my sinful soul; it's all in my poor ignorant way, but it's sweet, too, to think of the blood spilt for me."

Passing by many doors, we knock at one on which might be written, "A disciple whom Jesus loves." The narrow staircase is clean, and the room is dustless. On the table, with green baize cover lies the well-worn Bible, the lamp to her path, and by it the spectacle-case, on which is worked, "Open thou mine eyes." A few flowers are in a glass, and some plants in the window-seat—all is order in this quiet room. Gladly we turn in hither, tired and discouraged, it may be, with the morning's work. It quite rests you to look at Elizabeth's calm, happy face. Her forehead is high, and her intelligent eye beams with the peace that "passeth all understanding." A crutch lies by her chair, for long ago her leg was amputated. It is always refreshing to sit down by Elizabeth, and listen and learn. Many of the deep things of God have been revealed to her by the Spirit. We can only scantily recall from imperfect notes some of her remarks on many passages of Scripture.

Deuteronomy 33:12, "The beloved of the Lord shall dwell in safety by him; and the Lord shall cover him all the day long, and he shall dwell between his shoulders."—"How large this promise is. I think believers are the exemplification of it, for they are the beloved of the Lord. Their dwelling-place implies such a nearness to the Lord, even to His heart; and then what a strong abiding place it must be on His shoulders. 'The government shall be on His shoulder,' and that also is where He lays the lost sheep. (Luke 15:5.) And all this blessedness is but commenced here; what will the reality be? The world may despise those who are so beloved of the Lord, but the world's scorn is the Christian's badge of honour."

Psalm 130:3, "If thou, Lord, shouldst mark iniquities, O Lord, *who* shall stand?"—"The Lord *did* mark it, but it was marked in our substitute. This is very comforting when the mind views its own deficiency and failings; not a thing I wish to do, but evil is present with me. Then I try to behold the life and obedience of my Saviour for me; not only dying, but living for me, obedient to the whole law for me. Then viewing His deity, I see the infinite worth of this obedience in my nature, as my kinsman. Therefore what He fulfilled in my nature, becomes my infinite righteousness. But there must be a full taking of Christ. The other night, when I was thinking of this, I said, 'Yea, Lord, I take all just as a beggar; I have nothing to bring to Thee; oh, let me lie the lowest, and yet take the fulness of Thy love.'"

January 1.—Elizabeth told me that her New Year's portion was, "Thou art the same;" remarking, "What a depth of infinite unchangeable comfort is here. The 'same,' His bosom ever the same for me to lean on. The 'same yesterday, and to-day, and for ever.' The 'same' in nature, in love, in faithfulness. Earthly friends are not always the 'same,' and sometimes, when you long for them most, they leave you. Like your dear father's going, it is such a bitter trial to me. I heard his step in our yard yesterday in all that pouring rain, and I thought, Your life is too precious to be out in such a wet day. I have found such rich gleanings while listening to his sermons, such soul-refreshing pastures; but though my earthly shepherd goes, Jesus is the 'same.'"

February 10.—"What passage of Scripture have you been thinking of, Elizabeth?" "For two or three days the words, 'He that hath seen me hath seen the Father' (John 14:9), have been a feast to me. I seemed to gain a glance into the mystery of the Godhead, the unity of the persons. The attributes of the Father revealed in the Son, the glory of the Father shining in the face of Jesus Christ; therefore, 'He that hath seen me hath seen the Father.' And this revealed unto us by the Spirit of truth. There is fathom upon fathom in the word. I seem to see one depth after another, and yet never reach the deepest. Oh, how all this is missed by those who only carelessly read through a chapter, without searching into its depths.

"Another word has struck me in Ephesians 1:22. 'Gave Him to be the Head over all things to the Church.' The word 'things' seemed to reveal to me so much of His providential headship. Things, that is, occurrences, minute arrangements, our everyday little things. He is the disposing Head of all things that affect His Church. Therefore my faith finds a resting place when I see all my little things are under His control. Often a little word seems to open to me the secrecy of His mind, and we know 'the secret of the Lord is with them that fear Him,' and to them He opens the secret treasures of His word."

Easter Monday.—Elizabeth looked happier than ever. She said, "I had such a breakfast, Easter morning. I woke very early, and these words came with power to my mind, 'I am the Resurrection and the Life.' 'The Life,' that is, my inner life here, (putting her hand on her heart). Dead once, but now alive in Christ, risen with Him. The knowledge of this seems to multiply all my mercies. I so enjoyed your dear father's sermon on Good Friday. (Genesis 22:18.) The Lamb the substitute for me. And he told us of all that was provided for the followers of the Lamb, the feast, the white robe, the living fountains of water. That same evening I had such an overwhelming sense of the dying love of the Lamb of God, I could only cover my face, as if gazing on the cross, and cry, 'Enough, enough; enough for justice, enough for Thee; Lord, enough for me.'"

Having introduced Elizabeth by these stray gleanings, we will now copy her Autobiography, which she had neatly written in two copy-books.

ELIZABETH'S AUTOBIOGRAPHY.

I was born in a village near Worcester. My parents brought me up to attend to the outward forms of religion. At an early age I went to service. I was moral and sedate, endeavouring by such conduct to gain the esteem of those I served in being faithful and honest. Previous to my afflictions I was looking forward for years to come with the prospect of much pleasure in life. But in a short time it pleased the Lord to disappoint my vain hopes, by visiting me with a painful lameness in my knee. One day I got my feet wet, and sat down with them so; a cold followed, and rheumatic pains. An abscess formed in my knee, and for months I lay ill. This was a great grief to me, and caused me to have hard thoughts of the Lord. Little did I then think that that affliction was to work for my good. I sought aid from many physicians, but all proved in vain. The lameness still increased, and in a few months I was compelled to leave my situation in hope that rest would do me good. I then had a dangerous attack of smallpox. I thought I was like Job, but I knew not the God of Job. The disease in my knee increased, and I lay in a most distressed state. It pleased God to direct His highly honoured servant, Rev. —— Lake, to visit me. This was in the year 1808. He read to me the third chapter of John, and spoke to me faithfully of the need of the new birth. I then related to him a long and dismal tale of my sufferings. His reply was, "If there was no sin there would be no sorrow." This caused the enmity of my heart to rise, and I thought, "Does he think me such a great sinner? He cannot know what a good character I have always borne." My life had been so precise and blameless that my proud heart revolted at being told I must be born again. My sickness continued, and my circumstances became so reduced that every mite of charity was welcomed. My kind clergyman called again and laid two shillings on my pillow. This convinced me that he had my welfare at heart, however sinful he deemed me, and that he had some motive for visiting me to which I was a stranger, and this softened me. Let this encourage visitors to the sick to go on showing kindness. He requested me to read John 3 and Romans 8. But I was determined I would not. He sent Christian friends to visit me, but I was so sullen and reserved, and so determined not to answer any question, that they conversed to each other. I was much surprised to hear these good people say that if they had what they deserved they would be in hell. I wondered what sort of characters these good people could be, and thought they must have committed some enormous crimes. Finding I was so reserved and sullen, these friends concluded there was no prospect of being useful to me, and gave up visiting me. But the Lord did not give me up. An aged Christian called upon me. My heart was opened to attend to what he said. He entered into the state of mankind by nature. He proved from Scripture that all had broken His holy law, in thought, word, and deed, and come short of the glory of God. He asked me what was man's chief end, and explained what it was to live for God's glory here and then enjoy Him for ever. I felt an utter stranger to the idea of living for God's glory. He then went on describing the state we were brought into by the fall, and clearly showed me what original sin was. And here my mountain of self-righteousness fell. I can compare my mind to a person suddenly opening the shutter of a dark room. I saw that I too was fallen, sinful, lost, on the brink of hell. Although I knew it not, that was being fulfilled, "When he is come, he will convince the world of sin." For, oh, what a discovery I had of my life and conduct in the sight of a holy God! Now I saw I had never done anything to the glory of God, but self was my highest object. I saw the exceeding darkness and wickedness of my heart, and where to look I knew not.

I had been praying for death to get rid of my pain, but now I felt terrified at the thought, and yet could see nothing else before me. I prayed as well as I could, and longed to see this friend again, but I was left of man, and from that time no human instrument had ought to do with the work. Necessity obliged me to go into the Infirmary, where I was visited no more. Blessed be the Lord, when He begins a good work He will perfect it.

The surgeon found he could do nothing to save my life but remove my limb. I sunk at the very idea of this, and feared I should die under the operation, and then hell would be my portion. I knew not where to look for comfort. But the Lord's tender mercies are over all His works, and the surgeon under whose care I was placed often gave me a word of comfort or instruction, though he knew not the state of my mind. The time drew near for the day of operation to be appointed, and on my surgeon saying, "Let me fix Monday," I burst into tears at the thought of dying. The surgeon was very sorry for me and put it off a day or two.

Bowed down and heavy laden, I opened my Bible and read that gracious invitation in Matthew 11:28, "Come unto me, all ye that are weary and heavy laden, and I will give you rest." I thought, My load is so very heavy, still there was the word, "Come unto me," and at last it reached my heart. I cried, Lord, help me to come, show me what it is to come. Then the Holy Spirit enabled me to cast my burden upon the Lord, which gave me a peace I never had before. Then I was led to meditate on the boundless love and compassion of the Lord Jesus, the Sinner's Friend. Another day I was in such a spirit of prayer I could find no words, and knew not how it was till I read Romans 8:26, "We know not what we should pray for as we ought, but the Spirit itself maketh intercession for us with groanings which cannot be uttered." I still had fear all was not right with me, remembering what my visitors often said, "You must be born again." As I had no one to instruct me, my only resource was to cry unto the Lord, my only Teacher, that He would show me what it was to be born again, and not suffer me to deceive myself. I read the 3d of St. John. When I read the verse, "The wind bloweth where it listeth, and thou hearest the sound thereof, but canst not tell whence it cometh or whither it goeth, so is every one that is born of the Spirit," this seemed so clear to me, that I was filled with joy and peace in believing, and said, "It is enough."

Instead of trembling at the sight of my surgeon, now I longed to see him, and felt ready for the operation. He appointed the next day. Oh! what a happy night I passed; promises of God's word came like a calm breeze to my mind. I longed for the morning to tell my doctor how willing I felt to go through it all. The nurse came to prepare me. I said, "Only cover my eyes." As I lay waiting to be carried to the operating room, I said to myself, "Is it possible I am so calm, so quiet, not a fear? surely it is the Lord." I was laid on the operating table. The operation lasted three-quarters of an hour, and was very severe, the amputation being far above the knee-joint (and no chloroform known then). I seemed lying in the arms of Jesus, as if He came between me and that sharp knife. I had so much of His presence that I was lifted up above my sufferings, painful though they were. I felt in the Lord's hands, willing that He should do with me what seemed good in His sight. How precious Jesus was to me in that trying hour I cannot find words to express. I saw clearly that all my sins were blotted out through His precious blood. I could not help exclaiming before the surgeons—

"Though my sins as mountains rise,
 And swell and rise to heaven,
Yet mercy is above the skies,
 And I shall be forgiven."

When I was laid again on my bed, I could not help singing—

"Such is Jesus,
Such is grace,
I long to see Him
Face to face."

During the succeeding night, though suffering much pain, my heart was lifted up with gratitude and praise to God for His boundless mercies to one so unworthy. When sufficiently recovered I left the infirmary. My much esteemed surgeon presented me with a Bible.

I returned to my parents in the country. Everything appeared new to me, and I felt a desire to tell every one to seek the Lord.

I had still much pain to suffer, and also some persecution, but the Lord was my refuge and strength. As soon as I was able I went to live in Worcester, and endeavoured to earn my living by needlework. How I longed for Sunday to come to hear the gospel. The first sermon I heard was by Mr. Lake, from Philippians 1:6, "Being confident of this very thing, that he which hath begun a good work in you will perform it until the day of Jesus Christ." This word seemed like a staff to lean upon, and has often been a comfort to me in dark seasons.

How good it is to go up to the house of the Lord, that He may teach us of His ways, and according to His word, "faith cometh by hearing." I cannot express how, when burdened with afflictions of mind and body, *the word* became a blessing to my soul. I found great comfort at this time in Psalm 7:10, "My defence is of God, who saveth the upright in heart." Truly I found the Lord faithful to His promise, "that they who wait upon the Lord shall renew their strength."

At times I was harassed with the thought, I had not been brought in the right way, not having experienced such convictions of sin as some others. This led me to cry, "Search me, O God, and know my thoughts, and see if there be any way of wickedness in me." The Lord was pleased to comfort me by Isaiah 27:8, "He stayeth his rough wind in the day of his east wind." He helped me to rest upon Him, and I proved the preciousness of His word, "Thou wilt keep him in perfect peace, whose mind is stayed on Thee, because he trusteth in Thee." When bereft of every earthly comfort, this verse was delightful to me, "Who shall lay anything to the charge of God's elect?" (Romans 8:33.)

Soon my happiness was to be mixed with a bitter cup. I had thought much of the words in 1 Peter 4:12, "Beloved, think it not strange concerning the fiery trial, which is to try you." I prayed much the Lord would prepare and make me willing for whatever trial He saw best for me. My surgeon informed me it was necessary for me to go into the infirmary again, to undergo a second operation. My greatest sorrow was in knowing I should be deprived of the ordinances of the Lord's house. I felt it a hard struggle till the words in Exodus 14:13 comforted me, "Stand still, and see the salvation of the Lord." Then I could say—

"O Lord, my best desires fulfil,
 And help me to resign
Life, health, and comfort to Thy will,
 And make Thy pleasure mine."

It proved needful that the operation should be performed. When passing through the waters the Lord was with me, and enabled me to repose in Him. During the amputation, and when the instrument pierced through my flesh, I was led to reflect on the sufferings of Christ. I dwelt on the wondrous transactions of Calvary; and, whether in the bitter draught, or the extreme pain, all reminded me of Him that was wounded for my transgressions. When He drank the bitter cup, He drank all the wrath of God for my sins. The joy unspeakable I then felt, words cannot express. It seemed almost too much for my weak body to bear.

For more than seven months I lay ill in the infirmary. During part of this time, I learnt another lesson. The Lord was pleased to hide His face from me. My bodily afflictions also increased, and, to all appearance, I was drawing near the gate of death, and I was left in darkness. It was suggested to my mind, all had been a delusion. Friends asked me how I was; my reply was, Christ is gone. Still I cried unto the Lord in my distress, and read my Bible. Often did I beg my attendant in the night to read to me the 54th chapter of Isaiah, as the 11th verse gave me a little comfort.

My distress increased and my sufferings also. I thought I was about to be launched into an unknown world, that I was the chief of sinners, and not a hope of mercy. I begged the nurse to fetch me some Christian friend. She did so; and I would say, for the encouragement of those who visit the sick, that the Lord was pleased to come with that visitor. My visitor patiently listened to all I had to say, and then answered, "The Lord is teaching you to walk by faith, and not by sight. Your salvation is Christ's finished work. He rests in His love to us, and would teach us poor needy sinners to stay ourselves on Him." She read to me the 6th chapter of Hebrews. Never shall I forget the preciousness of the 17th verse: "Wherein God, willing more abundantly to show unto the heirs of promise the immutability of his counsel, confirmed it by an oath: that by two immutable things, in which it was impossible for God to lie, we might have a strong consolation, who have fled for refuge to lay hold upon the hope set before us." In His great mercy, the Lord blessed this word, that it proved an anchor to my soul, both sure and steadfast.

For some time, I lay in a very weak state; for a fortnight I could take no food and had no sleep; even my doctor was astonished to see me live on from day to day. I revived a little, but all hope of doing anything more for me was given up, and when able I was removed to my parents. There I entered into the meaning of that Scripture, "From the end of the earth will I cry unto thee."

After a few months I recovered sufficiently to return to Worcester. Again I found the ministry of His Word most blessed. I learnt many lessons: the fallen guilt of my nature—the all-sufficiency and grace of the Lord Jesus—His imputed righteousness the covering for my naked guilty soul—that whether living or dying I was His.

At this time symptoms of dropsy appeared, and the complaint much increasing, change into the country was ordered me. The heart of one of His servants was inclined to receive me into his house. Here I had every comfort provided for me. Feeling my unworthiness, I reflected that all these mercies were laid up for me in my covenant Head, the Lord Jesus. I cannot describe the beauty I saw in that verse, (Hosea 2:19): "I will betroth thee unto me for ever, yea I will betroth thee unto me in righteousness, and in judgment, and in loving-kindness, and in mercies." What a blessing thus to enjoy the manifestations of His love, to sit at His feet and learn of Him.

January 1822.—I have this day proved so much of the tender compassion of that "Friend who sticketh closer than a brother," that I cannot help setting up this waymark. I had been overwhelmed with sorrow, so that I could not help weeping. Before I opened my Bible, the Lord applied this word with such power to my soul, that I sat down astonished with the suitability of His promises. Jeremiah 31:16: "Refrain thy voice from weeping and thine eyes from tears, for thy work shall be rewarded, saith the Lord." For a moment I could not tell where it was, but soon found it. I was so overcome with a sense of His loving kindness, that I fell at His feet to praise Him, casting all my care on Him. "O God, the Lord, the strength of my soul, thou hast covered my head in the day of battle." In this I discovered a covenant God, who is all my strength, and who is engaged to support, comfort, and shield me in every danger, and finally bring me through more than conqueror. I find it an unspeakable blessing to have a living Friend and Saviour, to whom I can tell all my wants. If I had all the angels of heaven, and all the saints upon earth, what would that be if I had not Jesus? Well may I say, "Whom have I in heaven but thee, and there is none upon earth that I desire beside thee."

January 1823.—Having experienced much of my Heavenly Father's care through the past year, I wish to put up another waymark. Many times has He appeared for me, when no other hand could help. Like the children of Israel, my way was shut up, and then He made a way for me, and gave drink to my needy soul. One time I remember being overpressed with difficulties, and pouring out my heart before Him, that one word Jehovah-Jireh gave me strong confidence, that whatever He saw best He would provide for me. Thus I have proved, through this year, that "the Lord is good, and a stronghold in the day of trouble."

January 1826.—*In the Infirmary.*—This has been a year of very great mercies and wonderful support. Often have enemies without impeded my journey heavenward, together with a poor, weak, afflicted body. But I have not sunk, because God was my support, and underneath were the everlasting arms. Thanks be to Him who has given me a daily victory. The changes I have passed through have taught me the uncertainty of all things here, that this is not my rest, but that there is a rest where sin and sorrow cannot enter. When the past year commenced, I was surrounded with Christian friends, and enjoying the privileges of the Lord's house. But it was the same love that laid His rod again upon me and bid me leave all these comforts and take up my abode in this hospital, where I am surrounded with poor fellow-sufferers. Alas! their chief concern seems to be to harden each other in sin. Never did I loathe vain conversation as now. What proofs do I see of the hardness of the human heart. Some repining under their pains, no fear of God before their eyes, others crying out under the pangs of a guilty conscience and the pains of death. Oh, how thankful I am, that amidst all these things the Lord Jesus is to me "the same yesterday, and to-day, and for ever!" I have indeed been brought by a way which I knew not, but by the right way to perfect peace and rest. For the last seven years I had been teaching some children in a little day-school, and was much attached to them and to the many kind friends who ministered to my wants. Now I was cut off from all these. His thoughts are not our thoughts, and though at first I was perplexed, this word silenced and comforted me, "The Lord is my shepherd, I shall not want."

January 18.—I am now entered upon another year of my heavenward pilgrimage. Never did I more feel my need of Jesus, never was He so precious to me as at this time, when completely shut out from all the means of grace and all intercourse with Christian friends. Sickness and disease are raging around me in these wards, but I have Christ for my refuge—my source of happiness—to whom I can tell all my wants. Since I wrote, last January, I returned home, and again went to the courts of the Lord, "sitting down under his shadow with great delight." Again I was in the midst of a Christian family. My heart was often filled with such praise for my mercies, that I could not sleep at night. But these comforts were of short duration, and my disease compelled me again to return to the infirmary. This was a dark cloud, because I had no word from the Lord. I could only watch and cry unto Him, who had hitherto prepared all things for me. My own weakness is so great, that I can only suffer as I am supported by Almighty power. He sees best to keep me in the dark. It is a trial of my faith, to cast out my anchor even in the dark, to throw myself upon Christ, believing that He sees me toiling in rowing. When it shall be for His glory, He will make known His will to me. It reconciles me to see so many ways in which I can be kind to my fellow sufferers and reason with them, and tell them of a refuge in the Sinner's Friend. It may be for this I am sent here, and if I may but glorify Thee, Thy will be done. O grant me Thy presence. Grant me strength to glorify Thee, day by day. Make me in any way conformable to Thee, whether by suffering, or by whatsoever Thou seest best for me. Let me not faint in the day of adversity.

The time drew near when I must again undergo a very sharp operation. I had a very great dread of it, but the goodness of the Lord again supported me. I had but faint hope of the means being successful, yet, if the Lord commanded it, I would go, as it were, with a "Nevertheless at thy word I will let down the net." Just at the crisis of the operation and my necessity, that verse, "He was wounded for our transgressions, he was bruised for our iniquities," was much comfort to me. I felt such a giving up of myself to Him that I lost sight of the pain. After this, every day seemed to increase my trials. Still, Jesus Christ is to me "the same yesterday, and to-day, and for ever." Yes, He supported me yesterday, He will not leave me to-day; so that I may boldly say, "The Lord is my helper." O precious Saviour! to me a compassionate high priest, touched with the feeling of my infirmities, knowing the weakness of my flesh "who in the days of his flesh, when he had offered up strong cryings and tears to him that was able to save him from death, and was heard in that he feared," didst Thou thus suffer and die for me? Oh, never may I drop a murmuring word under my sufferings. "He hath not despised nor abhorred the afflictions of the afflicted, but when he cried unto him he heard him."

January 1843.—Much of what I have related took place under very deep affliction. I have still much cause to praise the Lord for new mercies every day. I would again bear my humble testimony to the faithfulness and gracious care of my covenant God. Should the Lord's dealings with one of the greatest debtors encourage any under suffering, or should what I have written encourage those who visit the sick and needy not to be weary of their labours, that the Lord may be glorified, is my only motive.

Elizabeth Sherwood.

Trinity Almshouse.

There are some who doubt the authenticity of what is related in narrative tracts. They say, "I never heard poor people talk like that." Surely reading the above well-expressed and strictly copied autobiography is a convincing coincidence that such remarks in tracts are possible, and perfectly true.

It is also an illustration of the reality of the Holy Spirit's teaching the same truths both to the learned and the unlearned, to the noble and to the simple, to the Countess of Huntingdon, the Duchess of Gordon, or Elizabeth Sherwood in the almshouse.

But we must say farewell to the Trinity Almshouses.

It was a sad morning when we went round for the last time in February 1860. Whenever goodbye times shade our path, Elizabeth's parting words echo cheerily.

"How I shall miss you all! It has struck me that Christian friends are like shadows. There could be no shadow without the sun—there can be no friend without Jesus. Like a shadow, friends reflect something to me from the Lord Jesus, but they all flit by and pass away. And friends *must* pass by to leave one clear void for the Lord Jesus alone to fill. He must fill all things; so friends are flitting shadows, Jesus the never passing Light!"

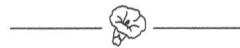

II.

WALKS AND TALKS.

To reach some distant districts we were most thankful for a ride. It was a good preparation for the day's work to drive up the long, steep hills, and there was time to enjoy the ever-widening, ever-varying views of forest, hill and valley. Sometimes a happy little party filled up the waggonette. They liked snatches of information about the dwellers in the cottages we rapidly passed, and they liked to peep into our tract bag, which also contained provision for the day, and tea, for which some widow's kettle would boil; and it was pleasant to hope, when our walks and talks were all over, and our night of death come, when no man can work, that those merry, bright-eyed children might then be ministering messengers in the haunts we loved so well. But we must leave the carriage, and turn into lonely lanes, over stiles, and through woods with mazy paths. These walks were indeed refreshing, away from street air, street noise, and street sin. In the scattered cottages dwelt many humble believers. Over their firesides and arm-chairs might be written, "In His hand are all the corners of the earth."

Visiting a cottage farm, round which cherry trees thickly grew, and touching even the door, the maid asked me to walk in. This was the third call without seeing any one, as baking, or churning, or dinner suggested it was wiser only to leave tracts. The aged master put out his hand, and as I took it, said,

"It warn't your good will that brought you here to-day!"

"Oh, yes, indeed it was."

"No, it warn't your will; it was Christ's will. Your'n His servant. He put it in your heart to come and see me. Sit you down, and welcome. Ever since you left those tracts, I've been praying the Lord would bless your work. And I know He will; you'll get some for His crown of glory out here."

"Thank you very much for your prayers. I am sure you would not pray for others if you did not know the Lord Jesus. May I ask what brought you to know Him?"

"'Cause I thought the devil would have me! It was the text of a sermon first made me think, 'Now is the accepted time; now is the day of salvation.' I felt I had not accepted pardon, and knew nothing of salvation. For three weeks I was in agony of mind, and could find no relief from the fright of being lost. One day I was at work in the fields, miserable, but still thinking over that text. In a moment I saw it—salvation for me, *now*, to-day. I could have jumped the hedge for joy. I threw down my spade. I must get on my knees and thank my Saviour. My heart filled with joy and love. I can't describe my happiness. I wanted nothing—nothing but Christ. This was many years ago. The Lord never gave me up, though I went backwards many a time. Like Peter, I followed Him too far off; but He comes nearer to me now—nearer than ever. Ay, through faith a man can do anything. It's 'Believe and live.' I see that in every page of the Gospel. And I take it, Miss, to believe Christ Himself is to have Christ in your heart. He says, and I believe Him, '*His Word is himself.*'"

And the old man laid his hand on the large Bible, identifying the written word with the personal Word. "The word of God is quick and powerful." (Hebrews 4:12.) "His name is called the Word of God." (Revelation 19:13.) "In the full assurance of faith," he exclaimed, "I shall go up with Him very soon. Yes, I shall hear *it* and go."

The ear that was waiting and watching for the Master's *voice* thought of no other "*it*."

Then he sent the maid to bring me a plate of cherries, and his sister who keeps house, brought me a glass of milk, as I refused all offers of cider or cowslip wine.

When I said good-bye, he blessed me, adding, "Come again very soon. He'll be with you and give you utterance to speak to poor sinners. He'll open their hearts for you."

When I called again, he had crept on his crutches to look at his sheep in the cherry orchard. After greeting, he remarked, "Christ knows all His sheep; He'll sort them; He'll take the sheep from the goats. That'll be a glorious time—one family, one fold. Christ knows all His sheep without marking them."

After getting back to his arm-chair, he told how happy he always was. "I am in Christ, and out of the devil's reach. Ah, I was in the devil's paw once. We're all alike. 'All have sinned and come short of His glory.' It's out of our power to save ourselves. It's when you feel Christ in your heart by the witness of the Spirit that makes you happy. It isn't only reading, but feeling His precious word in your soul; ah, that's the rejoicing of my heart."

"There are many sects and parties, I hear of them in my little corner; but it makes no odds what a man is called, *so that he's in Christ*."

One more visit to the Cherry Cottage. John had been ill with the "brown craturs," as his sister termed bronchitis. But, as ever, his happiness was overflowing, singing of the goodness of the Lord. He told me that when ill, he quite thought he was going to die, and he was only glad that the time was come. "All fear of death has long passed away. He's here, my blessed Jesus; He's good to me; I can bear anything with Him so near. He's all my study, my precious, precious Jesus."

His sister said, "It isn't only when he is awake, but when he's asleep, he's full of joy; he hoots out 'glory, glory,' and about 'my blessed Jesus.'"

"Yes," said the old man, "I'm always dreaming of Him; waking or sleeping, He's with me, and I'm happy. I can't describe the beauty of Jesus now; and what will He be when I see Him in glory? Ah! we shall see nothing in all heaven better than Jesus. That'll be the time up above. I was never much of a singer, but I *shall* sing then. Oh, my blessed Jesus!"

Truly does he realise what is possible for all believers likewise, "In whom though now ye see Him not, yet believing we rejoice with joy unspeakable, and full of glory."

A mile farther on were several cottages; each had its history. We select the most definite outline of early life given by one good woman:—

"I think it was very soon that I knew the love of Christ. I had great trials when a girl; we were thirteen in family, and bread was so dear. I remember wheat being twenty-seven shillings a bushel. We often suffered want, and I believe some of the little ones died from not having enough food. Calico at three-pence now was then one shilling a yard. It was war time, and I heard of the fight at Waterloo. I used to hear my mother praying—that made me think. Then I saw my little brothers and sisters lying cold and dead—that made me think more. The nearest school was nearly four miles away, but I went, Sundays and week-days. The good Rev. J. Cawood prayed with us, times and times. How well I remember him, patting our heads so kindly, and giving us pink sweeties. He was the first to start Sunday schools. I've heard when he was curate that he would be knocking at the doors before eight on Sundays to remind the mothers school would begin at nine. It pleased God to bless his teaching and praying. I was led to see myself nothing, nothing but a wretch and a sinner, but *all* I needed in Christ Jesus. That's the way I first went to Christ, and that's the way I go still, and He lays His hand on me and heals me. I often wake with Him, and lift up my heart and say, 'Oh, teach me; oh, speak to me.' This hymn often runs in my mind—

"'Oh, teach me more of Thy blest ways,
Thou holy Lamb of God,
And fix and root me in Thy grace
As one redeemed by blood.

"'Oh, tell me often of Thy love
Of all Thy grief and pain,

And let my heart with joy confess
That thence comes all my gain.'

"We are quite left alone here in this little wilderness, no visitor ever came till you and the other good lady called. It is so comfortable to see you come. Yet I'm not alone, for I do realise Him so near, that, like John, I seem to lean on His bosom. I see more and more what He has done for me, and that all our righteousness is as filthy rags. The book you lent me has been such a comfort." It was sermons on "The Matchless Beauty of Jesus" by our Campden House chaplain, Rev. J. Parker; and here in this out-of-the-world cottage was a king's daughter, one who could say, "My beloved is mine, and I am His." We sang some of her favourite hymns together, and then said good-bye.

Testimony to the value of early instruction was given me by a dying woman. Years ago she was in my father's Sunday school at Astley, and in E. P. H.'s class. I found her suffering with bronchial disease, and fast sinking. During an interval of relief she poured forth such praises for all the way that God had led her. She said, "All the verses and hymns I learnt when young are such a comfort to me now. We learnt the Gospel for the day, and Watts's Hymns in our class. After church and school, I never went off playing, as many of the children did. My parents were godly, and watched over me; they never let me go to fairs, or dances, or theatres. All I heard at school and church seemed to stick to me. Then I went to service. The last time I saw your dear father was on the common, he stopped me, gave me such kind advice. Oh, he was so loved, praise the Lord I had such a minister. But I never found true peace till some time after I had been in service. My mistress noticed how unhappy I looked, and told me she often found comfort by opening her Bible and reading a verse. I opened mine, and read, "Seek ye first the kingdom of God and his righteousness." That comforted me, and encouraged me to seek on. One evening I read the twentieth chapter of John, and how the Lord said, 'Behold my hands and my feet.' I can't tell how clear it all seemed to me then. Jesus died for me, His hands and feet pierced for me. Then I seemed to see all my sins lying like a great bunch at the foot of the cross, and by faith I saw them all cast on Jesus. I was so happy, I thought I must go home and tell mother to get her sins pardoned too. I went to ask mistress; she said, 'What's the matter, child?' 'I want to tell mother I've found Jesus and am happy.' This is years ago, and my Saviour has never left me. I have often been cold and wandering, but He's the same. I long, long to see Him, then I shall be like Him. I've one wish, and that is, if I could see my Sunday school teacher again." The wish was granted shortly before she entered into rest.

Another walk brought us to a cottage where most original talks amused and interested us. We won the poor woman's heart by bringing new ribbons to trim her wonderful bonnet. It really was a *bonnet*, in the coal-scuttle style of fifty years ago.

"Well, now, think of a lady touching my bonnet. Why, it looks better than new. Them strings be rich; shan't I lap it up for Sundays! Never no lady troubled herself to come to this cottage before, and to think of sewing for me! May the Lord return your kindness, I can't; but you'll see me crawl down to your door some day. Our parsnips are beauties, and you'll just boil some with your next bit of mutton, and think of me."

One evening I asked if she would like to tell me about her early life.

"That I should. You'll know me better then, and you'll find as I tells no lies; the truth's the truth. Years agone I was as gay as any one; never troubled about my soul. It's true I could read, but I'm just sure the Lord put the first thought into my head His own self. One day I was coming through that coppy (*i.e.*, coppice) yonder, from cutting heather for the besoms. I was alone, and the place was lone. A feeling came over me that my soul warn't safe. I trembled with the fear. I threw down the burden of heather and knelt under a tree. I always mark that tree now when I passes it. That was my first prayer to the Lord Jesus, and I asked Him to give me the Holy Spirit. Warn't it Him now that put it in my heart? warn't He a-saying, 'Seek and ye shall find?' I did find. I found Him, and I loved Him for wearing the thorns on His brow and bleeding for me; ay, and I love Him now. There's a hymn I want to learn perfect, 'I lay my sins on Jesus.' I do love a bit of singing. Please to let me sing you one of my hymns as I've puzzled over till I'se got *him* perfect.

"I suppose you want the tracts back. I'se many a spell over them. There's one book fits me beautiful, something for every day in it. Poor as I am, I w'dn't take the value of a gold sovereign for it.

"I wish I had had the headpiece on my shoulders twenty years agone that I'se got now, t'w'd have been happier for me.

"You sees, Miss, as I goes to church and you goes to church, but it don't sense the meaning in to me like. One night I was down for some errands in the town, and I see'd a crowd going in the schoolroom, says I, 'What's there?' 'A prayer meetin'.' So I went in. I never shan't forget her as read the Scriptures. I thought her the beautiful'st cratur, just like an hangel. I can't say as ever I see'd one; but you may depind on't, as good people be something similar. Mrs. F.'s prayer gave me a lift, and helped me on a good bit.

"I can't scrawl so far now, but I do get to Miss C.'s reading pretty regular. Some goes there, and some doesn't, and many's the word and the jeer at me from them as ain't in Jesus. I think it no disgrace to humble myself. I'm a poor sinner, and I says it. But it's worth all to catch hold of Jesus. I cares for nothing but Him now, and to get to my prayers, then I'm happy.

"You can't get on without prayer. I mind two or three children for their slaving mothers. You can't kneel down with them a worritting round you all day. Don't I long for them to be gone! I set the tea for my husband (he's such a beauty!), and I never pours out a cup till he comes; but often I wants my prayers the worst, and so leaves him and the tea, and goes off to the shed to my knees. I knows He gives me what I axes for. I'm like the woman as had the issue of blood, I came behind Him at first; now I've more faith, more hope. Ain't I happy! Don't you think as He helps me? I knows it. I'm under the frowns of the world, and such a poor object. Look at my poor legs! isn't it Him as helps me to scrawl to the readings. And I'm never terrified now, never fretched. If I haven't a bite of bread in the house, He knows it, and He sends it. Yes, I've great faith, I does believe in Him. When I'm weary with the toils of the day I gets His book; that's my comfort and my company. My husband's a trying at it too. He never worrits me, never axes, where have you been? Ah, he's the beauty of a husband!"

Perhaps some sister worker may say, "When are you going to tell us of discouraging walks and talks? Have you none of these?"

Oh, yes, we could fill volumes. Like every seed-sower, we meet with the stony ground, the thickets of thorny cares, and the rock which lacketh moisture. We could tell of half-opened doors and the uncivil reply. We could tell of almost trembling to take the message to some terrible drunkard, and how he has darted out through his back door, and so the opportunity seemed lost. We could tell of the sneering laugh and the coarse joke, as we turned away from trying to speak kindly but faithfully to some poor woman in the paths of sin. Yes, we could tell of visit after visit which seemed to bring no result, no success, no conversion, no melting of the heartlessness and indifference, which is more hopeless than even the downright attack and abuse of "all parsons and visitors and tracts." But our Master never fails us. He who endured the contradiction of sinners, He who was grieved with their hardness of heart and unbelief, can and does supply the needed wisdom, the soft answer, the exhaustless reply from "It is written." By singling out examples of good done by schools, visits, tracts, and, above all, by the ever-living lever of God's Word, which alone can raise the dead soul from its weight of sin and misery, all the praise and all the glory flows back to Him who alone giveth the increase. Go straight to your Master, dear sister, before every walk and talk, and remember it is His work, not yours, that the Lord is working *with you* both in the cottage of the drunkard, the blasphemer, and the stout-hearted ones, as well as in "ministering to the saints," and enjoying their heavenly conversation. Passing, as we must do, from the dwelling of the sinner to the believer, let us remember, "Such were some of you; but ye are washed, but ye are sanctified, but ye are justified in the name of the Lord Jesus, and by the Spirit of our God."

III.

WALKS AND TALKS IN IRELAND.

A LITTLE girl overtook me, and said, "Fine morning to you, Miss."

We walked together, and she told me about her father, who "went to Amerikey, and how she, and Mother, and Pat meant to follow him, some day, over the big say."

I asked if she could read?

"Sorra bit."

"Did you pray this morning?"

"I did. I said, 'Hail Mary' and 'Our Father.'"

"I am glad you know 'Our Father.' Can you tell me who it is that forgives us our trespasses?"

"Shure, an' it's the Blessed Virgin herself."

"But when you said 'Our Father,' who did you speak to? Now, just think a minute."

"I did spake to herself, jist. 'Thine, O Mary, is the kingdom, and the power, and the glory.'"

"Who taught you this?"

"His riverence, shure enough."

"Do you know who made this prayer?"

"Wasn't it the Lord Jesus Christ?"

"Quite right. And when He was a little baby, had the Virgin Mary any kingdom or any fine house to live in? Do you know where she laid Him?"

"In the manger."

"Yes, dear child, she had not even a cradle or a room at the inn. She never had any power on earth: we never read of her doing one wonderful thing. The Lord Jesus said in His last prayer, 'The glory which thou gavest me I have given them,' that is, to all His disciples, and to you and me; and when He went away He said, 'All power is given to me in heaven and in earth.' Now, I will read you the prayer just as the Lord Jesus said it for St. Peter to learn. Our trespasses mean breaking God's law, sinning against Him. As our sin is against God, so God only can forgive us. And He could not forgive us till the Lord Jesus had kept all the law for us; and, because of our trespasses, He died to bear our punishment. Did you ever hear this verse—'God, for Christ's sake, hath forgiven you?'"

The child looked up at me, laughed, and ran off, saying, "How do I know that?"

Further on, a young woman was sitting by the roadside crying. I said, "What is the matter?"

"Oh, my lady, I'm frightened; some fellows ran after me. I've got four miles more to go this lonesome road, and there's no one to take care of me."

"But I am on this lonely road, too, and I'm not frightened. I look up and know my Father in the sky is taking care of me, for Jesus Christ's sake. God's children are always safe under His eye and His care."

"Yes, Miss, but I'm under the order of the blessed scapular of the Virgin."

"Will you tell me what that means?"

The girl pulled a string off her neck and showed me a small square of gray cloth, with a cross marked on it in red silk.

"The priest blessed this and put the holy water on it, and if I wear it till I die, the Virgin is bound to come and release me when I've been an hour in purgatory."

What a cobweb hope! We had a long talk, and I tried to show her she was trusting in a lie, and that her very fright showed the Virgin was no help to her, and then set before her the glorious Gospel, which tells of a living Saviour and ever-present friend.

My next companion was a nice-looking widow woman. She listened attentively to some remarks, and then said, "My sins are a big weight, but, with the help of the Holy Mother of God, and through her powerful intercession, I'll be saved."

"But the Bible never once tells us that the Virgin does or can intercede. The Lord Jesus said, 'No man cometh unto the Father but by me.'"

"Oh, my dear lady, can He refuse His own blessed Mother?"

"Yes, He did. She came when He was preaching, and He would not leave off to go and speak to her."

"But wasn't she born a pure and holy Virgin?"

"No; for if she was, she would not have gone in the Temple to offer the turtle dove for her purification, according to the law of Moses; and if she was not a sinner, she would not have said, 'My spirit hath rejoiced in God, my Saviour.'"

"O ma'am, dear, didn't she go up with her body and soul into glory, and sit on the throne next to the Father? Isn't she all-powerful? No, as long as I live I'll put my trust in the blessed Mother of Heaven."

"The Lord says, 'Cursed is the man that trusteth in man.' Have you ever looked in your own Douay Bible to see if all you believe about the Virgin is true?"

"Oh, no, the priest won't let us read the Bible; it isn't for the likes of me, a poor, ignorant cratur, to dare to do that."

"Then your priest contradicts the Lord Jesus, who commanded us to 'search the Scriptures.' Let me just tell you from the Bible that the Virgin Mary is never once spoken of as an intercessor. Christ said, 'Whatsoever ye shall ask in *my name* I will give it you.' 'There is one God and one mediator between God and men, the man Christ Jesus.' And why that one? Because He 'gave himself a ransom for all.' Only He who paid the ransom could be the mediator. Did the Virgin shed her blood? Did the Apostles ever ask her to intercede for them?"

"Well, ma'am, dear, I have been brought up in this belief, and I'll never lave it. I have my trials and heart-sores heavy enough, heavy indeed."

"Then listen to these kind words of the Saviour, 'Come unto me, all ye that labour and are heavy laden, and I will give you rest.' See He did not say, 'Come to the Virgin,' but 'Come unto me.' You are weary, and your heaviest load is sin. The Lord Jesus bore that load on the cross, and it is such rest when we really believe our sins were laid on Him there."

There were tears in her eye as we parted.

Stopping at a lonely cabin, before I said a word on religion, the woman began to storm at me, probably from catching a glance of tracts. I sat quietly waiting for a lull.

"I can tell you what you are; you are not what I am, I was born in the one true holy Church, and in that I'm safe, and in that Church I'll die. You nor no one can be safe out of it. Ah, you tell me where your Church sprung from! You a born lady of larnin' (learning) and talent, an' I know you can't answer me that. I'm only jist a poor cratur in rags, but I know my Church is on the rock of St. Peter, and there's no movin' that. Don't tell me of the Bible. I have my holy director the priest, and he's inspired of God. I put all my trust in the holy Mother of God, and in all the angels and in all the saints. Isn't she next to God? Dare her Son refuse her? Ah, no! I'm in the Church, the true Church. I know what I'm sprung from, and you a born lady, don't. But I know what you're sprung from, Luther and Calvin, two divils! Don't get out your Bible, and don't talk to me of Christ as all your sort do, talk to me of the holy blessed Mother of God. O Mary, I adore thee!"

All this and more: I could only kindly say a word or two from the one book of truth, and left her.

In another cabin the woman willingly let me read some verses to her. She told me she had such fear she should never get to heaven at last. "How shall I ever earn it?"

"It is not our earning, the Lord Jesus earned it for us, and it is a free gift. His word says, 'The wages of sin is death, but the gift of God is eternal life.'"

"But shure, the blessed Virgin intercedes, and I can't be saved without her."

"But, my dear woman, God never once told us to pray to her, and when He taught His disciples to pray it was to our Father. He never named the Virgin."

"Oh, but He did put, 'Hail Mary, for thine is the kingdom, the power, and the glory.'"

She listened quietly to the truth, and seemed really anxious to find salvation. But when there is so much rubbish to clear away it takes long to find the hidden pearl, the one only Saviour. Often the opportunity of speaking to them never came back. Those who received my visits civilly the first time were afterwards either frightened to speak to me or abusive. They would go out of the cabin, stand on the road, call the hens or feed the pigs, not speaking a word, or even returning "good morning."

Their tenacity of belief in the Virgin, to the exclusion of the sufficiency of the Lord Jesus to save, is the most frequent and fatal error. To earn, to merit heaven by their own good works or suffering, is another dogma. A woman said to me,—

"Christ did suffer on the cross, but that wouldn't save me without sufferin' myself. The blessed martyrs had to die their death, or they wouldn't be in heaven this minute. If I don't have sufferin' here, I must in purgatory. And as for you, you scorn the holy Mother of God. Shure, she's just the same as God; she's next to Him on the throne. There *is* souls tumblin' into hell more than the stars of heaven, because they won't believe in the holy blessed Mother, the Queen of Heaven. Shure in the day of judgment won't her Son hold forth her glory?"

Reply seemed often like throwing a pebble to stop a waterfall; still the gospel is "the power of God unto salvation."

One morning a woman received me very civilly, and it was the second visit. As she allowed me to read before, I took out my Testament. She said,—

"You'll excuse me, Miss, dear, I'd like to hear more of your little book rale well, but I dar'n't; it's against our priest to hear or read any of your books; he forbids us."

"But he can't forbid you hearing the Bible, God's own Word?"

"No, I mustn't. I know nothing about the Bible. I never saw one, for it's not for the likes of us. I've got plenty of books and the general history of the Church. I ax your pardon, my lady, but didn't our Lord fix St. Peter's chair? Didn't He build the one true holy Church on St. Peter, and our holy Popes come straight from him."

"Yes, that is the great difference between our Churches; you build your Church on St. Peter, we build on the Lord Jesus Christ. St. Peter himself said, 'This is the stone, set at nought of you builders, which is become the head of the corner.' St. Peter said, 'Thou art the Christ, the Son of the living God,' and on this doctrine, this rock we build, for, 'Other foundation can no man lay, than that is laid, which is Christ Jesus.' Christ is the living stone, chosen of God, precious—see here it is in St. Peter's own letter."

The woman looked kindly at me, and said,—

"O acushla, won't you come into our true Church! You don't know all we believe, you don't know our ten commandments."

"O yes, I do, I really learnt them when I was a little girl. Will you say me the second?"

She said the third. I turned to the 20th chapter of Exodus, and showed her the commandment they altogether omit.

"Faix, I never heard a word of that before."

"Shall I tell you why your priests hide this command from you? Because it forbids what they teach you to do. The great God in heaven said, 'Thou shalt not make to thyself any graven image, nor the likeness of anything that is in heaven above or in the earth beneath, thou shalt not bow down to them.' Does not your Church make images and teach you to bow down to them and worship them?"

I do not give the woman's answer, as my notes fail me, but there was no denial of the fact that images are made, are set up, and that they do bow down before them while asking the intercessions of the saints they represent.

I asked her if she believed the words, "The Lamb of God which taketh away the sin of the world?" She said she did, but evidently put a different meaning to them.

"Oh, yes, He did take the sin away, glory be to His holy name; but shure I must follow Him by penance and confession, and good works, and I must ate His own body and blood our priest offers up on the altar."

Alas! whatever proof I gave her from Scripture, she replied—

"Well, acushla, yours must be the wrong Bible, but if ever

his riverence brings your sort into fashion I'll get one."

Poor thing, she was so kind in her way, and the big Irish love, that is always warm down in their heart's core, came gushing out between all our disagreements.

Another morning I called on a woman who had asked me to come again. I had happened to extract a thorn from her hand, which had given her pain some days. This had opened the way to speak of one who wore the crown of thorns for us. As I stood talking to her three or four boys threw lumps of dirt at me. The woman called to the mother of the boys to bid them leave off, but she took no notice. My poor friend then ordered them off. She was a kind-hearted creature, and most anxious to get me into her Church.

"Oh, lady, honey, don't be vexed with me for sayin' it, but shure unless you're baptized in our Holy Church you never can be saved. Oh, cushla machree, don't dispise the blessed Mother. Shure her Son won't do anything for you unless she axes Him. When we get safe into heaven won't we meet the blessed Mother first, houldin' the gates of glory open for us? and then won't we fall down on our two poor knees, avick, and thank her for bringin' us in? Now, wouldn't you just let me tell his riverence that you aint quite asy about your sowl, you that pulled the thorn out with your nice white hands. Oh, acushla, I'll never think of you without offerin' up a prayer for your sowl. Ah, if you'd only just let his riverence convert you, and get a sprinkle of the holy water, the love of the Virgin would *bile* up in your heart, and you could do it so asy, my darlint. I'd never brathe a word of it to any one, barrin' the priest himself—God bless him."

How could I but admire her loving zeal. She ever afterwards allowed me to speak the words of light and life, and, I believe, after many days, that they may be found bearing fruit.

When I turned away, the boys followed me with a pelting shower. Happily they were content with clods only; had they thought of stones, something more than my parasol must have been broken. I tried speaking kindly to them, which, being useless, there was no help for it but to walk quietly on, till a cottage came in sight, and then they ran off.

There was one little cabin where I always received a truly hearty "Cead mille failtha."[1]

"Oh, thin, don't stand knockin', for shure that's my own dear, sweet lady's voice. Come in, avick machree! Is it you've got married, that's it's this two long years I've been watin' for your shadow at my doore. Oh, acushla! Rosie drive thim hins out, they needn't be layin' their eggs in the bolster till my lady's gone! Shoo, shoo, now. There, look at the cratur's over her head an' under her feet, Rosie, Rosie clare thim out intirely, and clane the chair for the lady to sit down. It's your own chair, my lady dear; we riz the price of it, and got it purposely for yourself, for shure the likes of you shouldn't sit on the stools. Oh, but it's good luck and a blessin' come to me iver since your voice brought the music to me heart. Wasn't the cowld black earth (mud floor), me bed, and only the straw to soften it, acushla! Wasn't it you an' the darlint lady (Mrs. S.) that lifted me off it, an' put me on this fine comforting bed-stud, and didn't the life come back to me poor unfortunate bones. See, avourneen, I can move me hands an' me feet now with the help of your darlin' flannil, that's never wore out this months an' years.

"When I lay there in the corner on the cowld earth, an' often wished mysel' under it intirely, no priest ever crossed the thrashil' of the doore to see if I had a sowl or a body, but shure he didn't forget to send for his dues to my poor cabin, that hadn't the price of a windey (window) in it, nor as much as a chimley, let alone how it smoked me as dry as the herrin's. But shure the Lord sent me good friends, an' wasn't it them words of His that stuck to me heart, 'Come to me all ye that weary, an' be heavy laden, and I'll give you rest.' And I'll never change, with the help of God. The priest come wonst (once) when the Scriptur-reader was standin' there, an' says he, 'Which of us do you choose?' an' says he, 'if you choose that fellow and his book, I warn ye I'll not come when the death sweat's on ye, and, if I don't come, ye know well enough ye'll die out if the true Church an' be lost.' 'Sir,' says I, 'you never came to me till the Protestants did, they were me first friends, and they tould me the words that's claned and lightened my sowl intirely. It's their Bible I believe, and you needn't be throublin' about my sowl now, nor whin I'm dyin'. I've larnt where He says, 'Yea though I walk through the valley, etc.' No, me lady, I'll stick to the Great Priest, and His own blessed words! See, I can say all the verses for ye now, they come runnin' in my head like the clane fresh water arising in the little spring."

And then she repeated, with a few cabin variations, the 23d Psalm, the 14th of St. John, and many of the hundred mission texts.

Coming away I saw a woman following me till a turn in the lane. Where no one could see, she beckoned me to stop. I did not know her; indeed, I never asked any of their names, but she told me this:—

"Two years ago I met you on a lonesome road, you gave me two tracts, 'The Brazin Sarpint' and 'My God and Father.' I've worn thim tracts inch by inch away. The heart in my body often longs for a taste of His word, but I darn't let it be known. I never go to confession now, nor to mass aither. No one that is born of a woman will ever make me put my trust in any one but Him, Jesus the Lord, my Saviour. Haven't I looked to Him lifted up on the cross for me, an' He's haled my soul, glory be to His blessed and holy name for ever. I'm lonely and poor, my lady, but I tell my blessed Jesus all, and I pray day and night for His own good Spirit, and I hope I'll be would Himself some

---

[1] *Cead mille failtha* (Gaelic): a hundred thousand welcomes.

day. It troubles me greatly that I'm frightened to go to your church; perhaps I'll get stronger."

We walked together some distance and she joyfully took a Testament.

Another welcome awaited me from a very old woman, who had told me long ago how "she trembled to think of the fire of purgatory, and she didn't know how long she'd burn there, for she'd no son to pay for masses to get her out." And when I told her that God's word said nothing about purgatory, and asked her why she thought she must go there she told me that it was because of her sins. Then I read to her of Him who by Himself purged away our sins, that "the blood of Jesus Christ, His Son, cleanseth us from all sin," and other texts. She listened with her heart, saying, "Oh, that it might be so! Oh, what good words! Oh, can I come to Him now? I thought I never could do good works enough, and that I must burn in purgatory before I could get to Him."

It was to find out these trembling hidden ones, it was to tell of deliverance to the captives—to tell "the old, old, story of Jesus and His love"—to tell of the one living High Priest, ever willing, ever able to save to the uttermost all that come unto God by Him, which made it worth while to lose one's way and get home tired and late for dinner.

And if I now give examples of ignorance it is in pitying love, and the wish that it may open both ends of some purses for the fuller maintenance of that good old Irish Society, which sends forth valiant walkers and talkers, who, as one of them said to me, "go forth with the raal sword of the Spirit in their hands, and the burning love of the Lord Jesus in their hearts, to search out them He bought with His own blood."

Seeing quite a shelf full of books in a cabin one day I asked the owner if he had the best book in the world.

"O yes; I can show it to you," and he handed me "Lives of the Saints," by F. W. Faber.

'But this is not God's book, *His* must be the best."

"Ah, well, but you know Bibles are very dear. How could I rize five shillings for one? And besides I'm too ignorant to read it. St. Austin said he would not believe the Scripture without the authority of the Church, and so do I. I would believe nothing but what my Church says, not even the Bible. No, my lady, there's one true Church, and unless you're in that, and receive the sacraments, and do penance and good works, you'll be lost. Do you believe, Miss, that you ate the blessed body in your Church?"

"No, certainly not, for when the Lord Jesus first said to the disciples, 'Take eat, this is my body,' His body was there alive, standing before them. How could they eat His living body, it had not yet been offered on the cross? Besides, He ate the bread and drank the wine *with* the disciples; did He eat Himself?"

"Of course, He did, *the Lord received Himself, He ate Himself, and then told them to ate His body*, and I firmly believe that if I ate the body of Christ that's my salvation."

We had a long talk, but, like many others, he understood all mention of the blood of the Lord Jesus as referring entirely to the literal blood of Christ in the sacramental cup.

Another woman, who when a child had learnt Scripture in an Infant School, told me,—

"I'll never forget my verses and little hymns that her that's dead and gone up there first taught me. Didn't she send for us up to her own house and read what's stuck deep down in many a heart, an' 'ill never lave it, and didn't he come to see that we didn't forget her sweet words; the blessin' of the Lord rest on them she's left behind her."

In a lonely road I saw a girl carrying a chair, and presently a woman looking very ill sat down on it for rest. I stopped to ask kindly what was the matter, and spoke of the Lord Jesus. Without the remotest hint of controversy she began at me in this strain:—

"Don't spake to me, I know what you are; can't I see what's in your bag? Don't I know how your books run the Mother of God down; if there were five thousand women here this minute wouldn't she be the pure and holy one? How dar you born in sin say that she wasn't a pure holy Virgin? I'm sorry for the likes of you out of the true Church, goin' to a thousand hells where you'll be wantin' a drop of wather. Don't talk to me. I know a Protestant that went to a priest to ax him if he could be saved, and he told him what I now tell you, 'You're lost!'" and she laughed.

Poor thing, I waited till she left off, and then quietly answered her with a smooth pebble from my brook, and went on my way praying for her.

A widow asked me to read to her from my little book again. She said—

"My daughter and all the neighbours are agin your readin', and tell me I oughtn't to let you in, but I'm shure it's the truth you read, and I'll hear it. I may die soon, and it's all my thoughts and consarn to get my sins pardoned."

As I read she kept praying, "Lord, grant me that! Oh, that I may be worthy! Oh, that I may earn heaven! Isn't the Lord too vexed with me for all my past sins? But I do pray to the holy Mother of God to pardon me."

I took her hand, saying, "You know I love you."

"Yes, acushla, or you wouldn't have found me out; and I love you. And may the Lord speed you and send you your health."

"Thank you, I do love you, and I love your soul; so I want to tell you quite plainly it is not the Virgin Mary who can pardon you, for 'neither is there salvation in any other, there is none other name under heaven given among men, whereby we must be saved.' The Virgin never shed her blood for you, dear woman. Isn't the Lord Jesus the First and the Last. Didn't He save the thief on the Cross?"

"Yes, I do put Him first and foremost, but I was always tould to pray all to the holy Mother, for hasn't she power to intercede? O God, be merciful to me a sinner! Oh, do send me the right way. Oh, I'd go any way to get my sins wiped clane off."

After reading the good tidings and praying with her, she learnt off three or four texts, saying, "I'll think it all over when you're gone."

Once more I saw her, and the light was chasing away the darkness. God's own word had taken root amid the rubbish of early teaching. I took her an eye-shade, for which she was very grateful. Taking off my hat to read to her, she put her hand kindly on my head, saying, "The Lord love you." She listened very earnestly while I read the Bible to her, and she let me kneel and pray; and as I left her, she kept saying, "Lord Jesus, give me the water of life." And though in after visits her relatives would either lock the door, or stand and refuse admittance, I have not a doubt His Word was to her the power of God unto salvation.

Often kind efforts were made for my "convarsion," and it was touching to see the warm love gushing up for those Protestant friends who *showed* their faith by their works. "Yours can't be a very bad religion when it makes such men as Mr. S.," said one—ay, said many.

It may not be amiss to give verbatim some of their testimonies to Protestant love, which was a strong and unanswered evidence that if not in their "true Church," yet they surely had the true love of God and man in their hearts.

"Shure, and isn't it to his dure we fly when we're sick or sore, in want or distress? Isn't it his blankets that warms us the length of the long cowld winter, and isn't it his hand that's ever stretched with the kindness to us? Didn't he face the cholera, the cratur, and run with the hot bottles and the powders and the red flannel, everywhere he heard there was a poor sowl sick and sufferin'? Shure the ra'al love of God must be blazin' up in his heart, or he'd never feel for the poor as he does. And it's what I often think in myself that heaven would be a quare place intirely if he warn't there!

"And the good lady herself, Mrs. S. I mane, shure a more tinderer, kinder cratur' you couldn't find in the walls of the world. Let a poor body go to her dure when they may, isn't she always ready to see them and spake to them? She doesn't send the cowld message by the mouth of a sarvant. No, she comes to you her own self (ah, it's asy seen the ra'al true blood of a lady flows in her veins), and she axes you so kind-like to step into the beautiful illigant hall, that would dazzle your eyes to look at, and then she'd listen so quiet and patient-like to all our troubles and trials, and spake the feelin' words about the holy Saviour of the world, that the sound of her sweet voice, sayin' it so tinder, would bring the comfort into your breast. And she wouldn't stop at the good words aither, for she'd have a kind feel for your unfortunate body as well as your sowl, and her hand would be stretched with the can of sweet milk, and the arrowroot, and the drop of wine, and the beautiful fine broth, that you might carry home in the tail of your cloak without spillin' a drop of it, it would be so darlint thick. Ah! many an' many's the time the heart might drop down out of our bodies wid want an' weakness if it warn't for her goodness to us. May it all meet her at the gate of glory, an' may the blessin' an' binidiction of the heavenly Father be about her an' hers here an' hereafter!

"It's little use, avick machree, we'd have goin' to ax for help at the priests' dure, *they never have anything to give*; and it's mighty quare they'd look if you went to hear mass of a Sunday without droppin' your two or three pence into the money-box at the chapel dure. To tell you the truth, you'd have no business facin' them without it, for it's 'No money, no mass.'

"'Cast thy bread upon the waters, and it shall be found after many days,' might be written over that Protestant porch and illigant hall."

It was curious the effect which hymns or simple rhymes had upon Irish listeners; perhaps from their novelty, perhaps from the rhythm striking some unawakened chords within. I shall never forget the open mouths, the tears, the sobs, when reading to a gathering of Protestants and Romanists that heart-touching rhyme—

"Oh, why is little Willie dead?"[1]

The next morning a Romanist came to the hall door to beg I would read "Little Willie" again; it had sounded in her ears all the night, and she watched and wearied for the morning to hear the sweet words over again. When I began, down went the woman on her knees: "Shure them darlint words won't let me be sitting." She learnt the whole by heart.

Another of Mrs. S.'s "pinsioners" went to a friend, and she also read to her "Little Willie." She listened most attentively, and then said, "It's what I'm thinkin' in myself that the good lady that made that purty little *hemn*, must have lost a darlin' sweet babby herself, or she could never say the words so terrible feelin'.

"I felt a chokin' and a squeezin' in my bussum all the time you were readin' it, for didn't it bring back to my mim'ry my own poor little Paddy that was the pulse of my heart and the pride and the light of my eyes for three bright summers? But now, ah now! my fine bouchal bawee (fair boy) lies cowld and

---

[1] "Little Willie, the Infant-School Scholar." By Jennette Threlfall.

stiff in his coffin under the daisy-sod, ten long years come this Michaelmas. And though he's all that wary time gone from my arms, still the house to this day feels dead and desolate for the sound of his little foot, and the shout of his purty voice. Ah, wirrasthrue! he was *my* little Willie, the bird of my bussum! The light of heaven for ever to his sowl!"

But to resume our Walks and Talks. Sometimes they seemed pleased, yet frightened to see me again. I am writing of those who have passed away long ago, so that it cannot injure them to repeat their words. One said, "There now, God bless you, Miss, but don't be stayin' with me, for if my girl comes in and finds me talking to you there'll be such a row, and maybe hear of it a Sunday, when I wouldn't like to have your name put up. Not but what I like you to turn in to my poor bit of a place. I'm a poor ignorant cratur, how can I be saved, how can I ever earn it?"

"It's not earning at all, dear, it's God's free gift, because the Lord Jesus earned it for us. 'The wages of sin is death,' that's what you and I earned; but the Lord Jesus took our sin and took the wages for it too. Because He took our sin He was made a curse for us, and God paid to Him on the cross all the wages of our sins, and then, because He paid our debt, God gives us eternal life for His sake. Will you learn off this verse, and then you can think about it. (Romans 6:23.) You can't get out to work now, but your child does, and she brings home her earnings—her wages, and gives it to you. Now that loaf on the table, is it your earning or your child's gift? You take and eat it, though you did not earn it. So we poor sinners can earn nothing, merit nothing, deserve nothing; but our dear Lord and Saviour did the work for us, and on the cross said, 'It is finished.' He brings His earnings to us, His salvation, His atonement, His death for us; won't you take the earnings of Jesus Christ, pardon and peace, and life eternal? 'And this is the record, that God hath given to us eternal life, and this life is in his Son.'"

She thanked me and said, "It's clearer now, my dear."

Resting in a cottage, the woman, in answer to some remark, said, "But it's good works and charity to the poor that saves the sowl, Miss. There was a very rich man once, I've been tould, that was mighty bad and wicked intirely, the curse was ever and always on his tongue, and he never stretched his hand would anything to a poor body, barrin' three bare times in his whole life. Well, he was dying, and at the very gates of hell, when up comes St. Peter himself, would the kays of heaven in his hand, and says he, Haven't you done three charities in your life, my good man? Yis, says he, your honor's glory, I gave an ould coat wonst to a poor man, an' a stone if patateys to some orphants, the third good turn he couldn't remimber; but St. Peter, at any rate, up and said, thin and there, that for those three good works he'd let him off. Don't you believe it, Miss?"

It was a pleasant change to turn into a Protestant door. I remember visiting the father of a scholar, and he said, "I can tell you why, Miss, that the Roman Catholics don't read the Bible. They dare not! No; for the priests would rather keep them in the dark. They believe anything he says. If he told them that the Douay Bible was a lie, they would believe it. And yet the priests do nothing for them, not a mass for the dead, or the last rites for the dying, without their money's worth. I know many a one turned out of the chapel 'cause they brought nothing. Rich and poor pay money twice a-year to say masses to get the souls of their relatives out of purgatory. And I'll tell you how people remember the day that their relations die, because of going to pay up the mass-money; and some that you wouldn't think pay five pounds a-year for it." He told me about an orphan girl, a Protestant; her brother came and took her away from his care, pretending to be a Protestant. "When she went to live with him she soon found out his lie; he took all her books away, and burnt them and her Bible. Being ill she went to an hospital, and as she declared she would not live anywhere without a Bible, she got back to us."

A superior woman, married to a Romanist, said to me, "I know what Popery is. It's dreadful how much they make of the Virgin Mary; there's more preached about her than the blessed Saviour, and you'll see more images of her and the saints than of Him, and I often see them go and kneel down to her image. They put Christ aside. It is so deeply rooted in them, that I know many who would deny Christ altogether sooner than give up their belief in the Virgin. And you know they must tell the priest if a Protestant calls on them, or any tract or Bible given. They fear the priest more than God and firmly believe that if he doesn't absolve them, God won't. Oh, it's slavery! I tremble for my poor girls. Many's the sore beating their father's given them on Sunday for going to church or Sunday school. For four months my poor child kept away from church after a severe beating. One Saturday she went quite humbly to him and said, 'Father, please let me go to church to-morrow.' He said, 'I'll beat you if you do.' After praying about it, my child said, 'Mother, it is God's house, I must please Him first, and come what may I'll go to church.' I was sick at heart for her, but knew she was right, and the father had agreed that the girls should be Protestants. Her father saw her go out to church, but said nothing till she came back, and then followed her upstairs. I feared his beating her, and said to my boy, 'Won't you take your sister's part for once?' He ran up-stairs and stopped him saying, 'Father, it isn't fair, why should you beat her for going to her church, when mother's so good and works for me though I go to chapel, you'll never drive their hearts to chapel, father!' My poor husband, he doesn't know what he's hindering. He took all the children's prizes, and every Bible away, and locked them up. The poor children and I so longed for a Bible, and kind Mrs. S. lent us one. My girls opened the end of their bolster and slipped it in, so that it might not be seen, and when we knew father was safe at his work, we went up-stairs to read it. After some months, he made a second search and took this away. Now we go up to kind Mrs. S.'s, and read it there."

In answer to a girl rather boastfully telling me she was in the true Church, and was sure of getting the "last rites," I said, "Tell me, would you be glad to die to-night?"

"Glad to die!" she exclaimed, "shure, no one's ever glad to die, for they don't know where they're goin' after purgatory; but if I had a parlour, and a car to drive about on, I think I'd never ax to die. Well now, Miss, in your country did you ever see any one that wanted to die?"

"Yes, indeed, I could tell you of so many;" and then I told her of Emma Edwards and Lydia Watkins, and repeating the words that made them so glad and ready to go, I said to Biddy, "The same kind Jesus is calling you also; isn't He kind to want you to come to Him? Biddy, He says to you, 'Him that cometh unto Me, I will in no wise cast out.'" Her answer was, "Ah, now, but they are lovely words, and that's the truth."

A little baby having died, I called to see the grandmother who was mourning over the loss. She was anxious to improve the visit to *me*. I give some of her rapid words. "There's my darlint baby died this morning, but she wasn't too good for God. He makes them to take them, shure in my heart I wish I was would her to-day. No crown of goold u'd be worth what she's got. Ah, thin this is the wary world! No peace of mind in it from the queen to the beggar, and no salvation out of the true Church. Why, if my darlint hadn't got the sacrament of baptism she'd never have gone to heaven, never beheld the presence of God. She'd have gone to a separate place in hell where's there's no torment; an' what will you do, my dear, you're not in the one true Church? Why don't you follow our holy priests alaung? Shure all the angels in heaven isn't as pure and perfect as they are! They are Christ's successors, you must confess to them, and you must receive their absolution. O Mother of God, intercede for her! Thou art the Queen of heaven, pure and holy Virgin, immaculate without spot or stain. Didn't her Son give her all power in heaven and in earth, and isn't she plading for sinners, and shure her Son darn't deny her anything she axes. She commands God. An' if it wasn't for *her* intercession the wicked would be cut off; it's for the sake of the holy Mother of God you're spared. I tell you that if an angel came down straight from heaven and tould me that the Virgin wasn't at the right hand of God intercedin' this present minute, I wouldn't believe him. Shure the divil trimbles at the mintion of her blessed name. Doesn't she rule over the half of heaven. I know that God the Father is first, but *Mary is next to Him*, and them that don't believe this, do it for filthy lucre's sake. O Mary, pure, spotless, all-powerful, purtect me! O St. Joseph, St. Augustine, St. Bernard (and a dozen more) purtect me! I call on every saint I know every night and mornin' of my life, and I pray to every one of my dear childer gone to them, to pray for me."

To show that this woman and others did not wrongly quote what their Church teaches, I copy from authorised versions.

"Hail, Mary! Lady and Mistress of the world, to whom all power has been given both in heaven and earth."—(*Devotion to the Sacred Heart of Mary*, p. 205, approved of by Pope Pius IX.)

"In Mary, finally, we shall find life and eternal salvation."

"O Lady, . . . in heaven we have but *one advocate*, and that is thyself; thou *alone* art truly loving and anxious for our welfare.

"O great, exalted, and most glorious Lady, prostrate at the foot of thy throne, *we adore thee* from this valley of tears. We also *consecrate* ourselves to thy service. O Lady, change us from sinners into saints."—*Glories of Mary*, pp. 124, 158, 376, 377.

"Therefore, with the whole marrow of our hearts, with all the affections of our souls, let us worship this same Mary, because such is the will of Him who willed that we should have all through Mary."—LESSON 7, from *St. Bernard's Homily on the Nativity of B. V. Mary*.

We will finish our talks with the first visit, and the last, to a very poor, ragged, old woman. I saw her sitting at a cabin door, and the sad, sad look on her face told of a weary heart-load. I sat down by her, much to her surprise, and she said, "Well, no lady ever cared to spake to me, let alone sit in this poor place."

"I am sure you are very sad; what is it, dear?"

"It's the feelin' in mee heart, it's cold, and sore, and waery. I'd like to die out of it, but thin there's the fire waitin' for me, and who'd pay mass for a lone widdy? Who cares for the length I'll burn in purgatory?"

"Yes, some One does care for you, dear, One up there in the blue sky, and He knew that you and I would burn for ever, and He knew that you and I were sinful and lost. Just tell me, what makes you afraid you'll burn for ever?"

"Shure an' it's mee sins a waery load, and only the fire can burn them clane out of me."

"Yes, and my sins are a weary load too, dear, but no fire can burn them clean, no purgatory would take away one sin. The One who loves us is the Lord Jesus Christ, the Lamb of God, which taketh away the sin of the world."

"Can you tell me what the Lord Jesus did for us on the cross?"

"No; but He's hangin' in the chapel."

"He died to pay for our sins; you and I have got nothing to pay, and purgatory won't pay for it. Who has the money for saying the masses?"

"Shure, and his riverence tak's all he can get."

"Then you see the money does not go to the Lord Jesus at all. I will read to you just what He said to a poor sinful woman, who was sad and weary like you."

I read to her that priceless chapter, the 7th of St. Luke.

The woman drank it all in as the thirsty ground; she learnt off the verse, "And when they had *nothing to pay*, he frankly forgave them both."

Even then, that free salvation was largely believed by the weary one, and ever after, she clung to the one ray of light, which had pierced her gloom, that she had "nothing to pay," but Jesus had paid it all for her, that He had forgiven her all the debt, that His blood cleanseth from all sin.

We knelt down, and uninvited, a cripple boy who had been listening, came and knelt, and even a curly-headed Pat of three years old put up his hands, and it was sweet to hear them all saying, " for Jesus Christ's sake."

Some five years passed away, and I was told that "Granny was dying and wouldn't let the priest come to her."

I went. She was lying on a mattrass put on the table (a very usual alternative from the earth floor). The daughter said, "It's no use you're speaking to her, Miss; she knows no one, knows nothing, since she said, 'Don't send for the priest.'"

I knelt by her, took her hand, saying, "Do you know me, Grannie?"

The dying eyes opened, looked at me, and she said, "Know you? yes; and I'll love you for ever, for ever. When they had nothing to pay He frankly forgave them—forgave *me—me!*"

"He gathereth together the outcasts."

"He raiseth up the poor out of the dust, and lifteth the needy out of the dunghill, that he may set him with princes, even with the princes of his people."

"Praise ye the Lord."

IV.

LYDIA WATKINS.

THE following record is an instance of the entrance of God's Word giving light and understanding to a simple child:—

Lydia's mother was a widow, and night nurse in the Infirmary. Her daughter lived with an Aunt, and attended both Sunday and Day Schools. About the age of fourteen her health failed, and she was admitted as a patient under her mother's care. There were many lady visitors at the Infirmary, and the patients often spoke gratefully of their kind words, and how the books and tracts left by them cheered their weary hours. Nurse Woodward was a great help to such visitors, and would point out any one needing special attention. A frowning nurse would have been a hinderer, but she always welcomed those who came with their Master's Book and their Master's message. Dear old Nurse! many a pillow did she smooth, many a tired head leant on her, and many a word of comfort did she drop into dying ears. And we must just give here the record of a visit to Nurse when she was pensioned off and living in lodgings.

"There, now, it is you come back at last! and I've been a-worrying and a-praying for you, for fear you'd be lost on that sea. And when you went away, Father went too, and Mrs. Havergal; and you see you all seem like relations to me. You won't go away again? But I did hear Father's last sermon (Nurse never called *him* any other name); and I thought, there, now, he's going, and I shan't understand any one else till he comes back. I always knows what he means, and he speaks *out* like. Now, my dear, sit down; there's your chair; and, see, I've covered it with new chintz, ready for Father to sit on. You'll hear me my two Psalms. I keep spelling them over, fear I should forget."

Nurse was more than seventy-two years old when she first attempted reading. Among the many easy texts she knew by heart her favourite one was, "Fear not thou, worm Jacob."

One evening I found Nurse standing and looking at the moon through the chimneys opposite.

She told me that she always put that verse and the moon together. "That big, beautiful moon, hanging up so steady like," was made by Him that made the worms; and she was only a worm, and yet He made her as well as the moon. And He had done more for worms than for the moon: He had shed His blood to redeem them; then how could she fear? Dear Nursey! you are no longer a worm, but a citizen where there is "no need of the sun, neither of the moon to shine."

The patients all loved Nurse; how could they help it? One afternoon she asked me to go to a private ward. The young girl lying there was hopelessly ill. Her name was Lydia Watkins.

It was quite easy to talk to Lydia, for she said more than that disheartening "Yes, yes."

She had evidently been well taught at school, but had not an idea she was a sinner. She willingly found and read with me passages which tell of man's sin and man's danger. (It is generally wiser for visitors not to read *to* those they visit so much as *with* them.) We then read together the 15th chapter of St. Luke, with its threefold finger pointing to that word "Lost."

For many visits we read the Bible together, with earnest prayer that God the Holy Spirit would Himself teach her and make the words her light and her lamp. She always marked the verses, and said that she prayed over them. The first indication of the Holy Spirit's working in her by the word was her remark, "That verse about the lost sheep is like me. I never felt lost before, now I do, and afraid to die, and I can't pray right; but yet I do ask for the Holy Spirit to teach me."

The next visit, no one answered to the knock at Lydia's door. Opening it, the bed was empty. Nurse Woodward came to explain,—

"Don't be frightened, Miss, a fine thing has happened for Lydia. Yesterday a lady from Malvern came to go round the wards. She was a real lady, her own horses in the carriage, not but I can tell without that. I took her to see Lydia, and of course she was taken with her, and why not? isn't her dear face as pretty as ever any lady was born with, and hasn't she a heavenly look? The lady talked to Lydia, and she wasn't shy and foolish. When we came out, says she, 'Would change of air do that dear child any good, Nurse?' I said it might, and that her mother and the doctor could be asked. It was soon settled that she should go with her to Malvern for a few weeks, and that the lady would put her in clean lodgings. If you'll believe it, the lady took her away in her own carriage then and there. When I was packing her little things, she said, 'Nurse, be sure put my Bible in, and the "Young Cottager" the lady lent me, and tell her I shan't forget to read what she marked in my Bible.'"

Lydia returned in about six weeks. Malvern air had failed to check the cough and other symptoms of consumption. Her breath was shorter, and she was much thinner.

"How did you like Malvern?"

"Very much at first, and I went out in a chair every day, a good way up the hills. It was so pleasant, and the air blew so fresh, I thought I should get well."

"Were you comfortable?"

"Yes, the woman was very kind to me, but of course I missed poor mother, and there was no one like Nursey. The kind lady came very often, but after a fortnight she was obliged to leave Malvern, and then no one ever came to read with me."

"But I hope you read your Bible, dear?"

"Yes, I did, and prayed for God's Spirit to teach me. And the last verse you said to me, Miss, never left me, 'Him that cometh unto me I will in no wise cast out.' It seemed like Jesus calling me, and yet I couldn't come, couldn't get to Him, like little Jane did. I was so miserable, and hadn't that *feel* Jane had."

"What do you mean, dear, tell me?"

"I wanted to *feel* that my sins were forgiven, and I don't yet."

"It is not what you feel, dear child, but what the Lord Jesus says here in this Bible. Now look at His own words; here they are, 'Him that cometh'—not him that feels happy, or feels good, or feels forgiven—no, it is just Him that cometh, coming in your heart, because you want Jesus, because He says, Come—coming as you are, lost and sinful. None but God the Holy Ghost can draw you to the Lord Jesus, and help you really to come to Him. We will kneel down and ask that you may indeed come now."

After reading the latter part of the 7th chapter of St. Luke, I left her to His blessed teaching, believing that His word would bring her light and life. There is a point where man's work ends and God's begins.

Nurse met me the next day and said,—

"You'll find Lydia very happy, she says it's a verse that makes her so. She was very ill in the night, and her mother called me up to her. She took my hand, and told me she wasn't a bit afraid to go now, and that perhaps we'd go hand in hand to the gate of heaven. I can't tell you half she said, but that she was clinging to Jesus."

We went into the ward. Lydia was asleep, but presently awoke. Her first words were, "'Him that cometh to me I will in no wise cast out.' He has helped me to come."

Then she told how that and many other verses now made her quite happy. She thanked me for reading the Bible with her, and that now its light had come into her dark heart.

"Now I feel more afraid to live than die, for fear I should grieve my dear Saviour, I've been such a sinful child; isn't He good to take my sins away! I do want to see Him, indeed I do."

One Sunday, while listening to the church bells, she said,—

"I should like to go to church once more, but it will be better to go up and be close to Jesus always."

This hymn she liked very much:—

> "And is the Sabbath come,
>   And have we still a day,
> To mind our everlasting home,
>   To sing, and read, and pray?
>
> "Then let us up with speed,
>   The work is very great;
> And beg of God our soul to feed
>   With never dying meat.
>
> "That we may strengthened be
>   To walk the heavenly road;
> Until at last we come to Thee,
>   Oh everlasting God!
>
> "With Thee for e'er to spend,
>   With saints in perfect light,
> A Sabbath that shall have no end,
>   A day that has no night."
>
> —Anon.

Lydia said much that evening of God's mercy to her.

"How good He's been to me, an ignorant girl. I wasn't fit to be forgiven, I wasn't fit to come to Jesus, and yet He called me, the lost sheep. How good He was to let me come, and He did say to me, 'Him that cometh unto me I will in no wise cast out.' I'm as happy as little Jane, and know what that means now, 'Christ here and Christ there.'"

She asked if she was too young to receive the Lord's Supper, for she had been reading that the Lord Jesus said, "Do this in remembrance of me." She had thought much about it, and little Jane had wished it too. All that the Lord Jesus said was meant for her, because she did love Him, and He had died for her; mightn't she do what He told His disciples to do?

Lydia told all this to my dear mother, whom she loved very much, asking her to name her wish to Mr. Havergal.

She had not been confirmed, but was truly desirous "to remember the exceeding great love of her Lord and Saviour in thus dying for her."

His servant gladly welcomed such a guest to the Master's table.

One evening "two or three gathered together" in Lydia's room, her mother came, and we knelt by her bed, and ate of that bread, and drank of that cup.

"And Jesus stood in the midst, and saith unto them, Peace be unto you. And when He had so said, He showed unto them His hands and His side. Then were the disciples glad when they saw the Lord."

A few days after, Nurse sent to say Lydia was dying. She did not notice me when I came; she was looking up, and she said, as if one was very near her, "Dear Saviour, come, come, and fetch me!"

I can hardly write of what I saw. A light I had never seen before, a holy light, came down on her face again and again. One word only can express it, "Glory."

Once she looked at me, and said, "Him that cometh unto me I will in no wise cast out." And then, "Dear, dear mother, and dear nurse!"

Presently that glory shone on her again, and she said, "Nurse, make room for Him. The Lord Jesus is saying to me, Come. I do hear Him, and I am coming." Yes, He was come, fulfilling His promise, "I will come again, and receive you unto myself, that where I am, there ye may be also."

> "'Tis sweet to go! I would not stay
>   For ever in this house of clay,
> Here pain and languor are my lot,
>   But where I go, they enter not.
>
> "'Tis good to quit a world, where sin
>   Besets my path, and tempts within,
> To wear a robe of purity,
>   And see my Saviour eye to eye.
>
> "Lord Jesus, Thou hast bid me come,
>   Of all my hopes, Thou art the sum;
> One, one short pang, and I shall rest
>   For ever on my Saviour's breast."
>
> —Rev. W. Jowett.

V.

THE SOIL PREPARED.

WHILE writing these words, an illustration of them is passing in the field below. From the airy top of a summer house my eye glances on the distant Malvern hills, Woodbury and Abberley rise on the left, the church tower, woods, orchards in blossom spread around. Such a view! Would that all my weary sister-workers in crowded streets and close alleys could share its refreshment, and "rest awhile."

The field below is just prepared for the seed. The clearing, the ploughing, the preparing of the soil is all done, and the sower is now walking up and down, and from his basket scattering the seed.

And is it not so with the good seed of the Word of God? It takes root and brings forth fruit, only in the prepared—the good ground. The great Husbandman always prepares the soil. "So, then, neither is he that planteth anything, neither he that watereth; but God, that giveth the increase." "The preparation of the heart in man is of the Lord."

The same truth was forcibly told me by an Irish Scripture reader. Inquiring, whether he found it best to fix beforehand, what passage of Scripture to read in his daily rounds, he told me that, though he always carefully read over some chapter, he felt more anxious that the Lord would direct him *where* to sow the seed. "Every morning I pray the Lord to prepare the soil in some heart for the good seed. I do not know which heart it may be, but I trust that to my Master. So I go out, being quite sure His word will not return to Him void. That's why some listen, and I've had wonderful proofs that the Lord goes and works on the heart first, and then sends me with the seed."

That good man's sowing time was very short. His history may be shortly given. A few years ago a crowd gathered round a preacher in one of the back streets of Dublin. The preacher was discouraged by their apparent inattention and restlessness, and for many months knew not of the following result.

Within hearing stood a policeman keeping order. The seed was sown in his heart, he received it, he brought forth fruit.

Soon after illness came on, and he had leave to go to his native place. There the policeman told his old neighbours what great things the Lord had done for his soul. A tinker listened among others, and again and again he went to the sick policeman's cottage to hear the "old, old story," so new to him. He was a Romanist, but the entrance of God's word giveth light, and soon it chased away all the darkness, and the tinker was brought into His marvellous light. He could read, and soon got possession of a Bible. Soon he began to tell others the good news of salvation. For five years all his spare time was spent in going from cabin to cabin, speaking of Jesus Christ, the One Priest, the One Mediator, the One Sacrifice. And then the strong desire came, to give himself up, wholly and entirely, to the Lord's work. The result was (for this is mere outline), that the tinker was appointed by the Scripture Readers' Society to a mission post in Ireland. His labour was short, and the faithful servant was quickly called home to rest.

But his remark has often encouraged me amid the toil of unsuccessful labour. "Lord, what wilt Thou have me to do?" Direct me to those who are crying, "Come and help us." "Open Thou my lips" are the cries of His servants. And let His servants also cry, "Lord, open my ear to know Thy will." How useless is a deaf servant, toiling and hunting about his work, doing it his own way, heedless of the Master's voice, and so leaving undone the very work that would have brought him glory. Oh, to be swift to hear, and quick to see, our Master's work, to be ever ready in season, and out of season, to do His will!

The Scripture reader's advice cheered me one morning after completing a round of very disheartening visits. There was only one cottage more, and as new comers were there, the thought came, "Perhaps there is prepared ground here." And so it was. The stranger seemed pleased with the offer of tracts, adding, "Perhaps they will suit my case. I have had all these given me at times, and I have stitched them together," showing me quite a thick collection.

"And do none of these suit your case?"

"No, Miss, if you would please to listen, I feel a burden on me, a weight that, do what I will, I can't get rid of. I know that I am out of Christ, that my soul is not safe."

"And have you felt this long?"

"Not very. I have always kept to my church regular, and thought I had done no particular sin more than other people; but now I feel the worst of all—such a sinner. I can't even sleep at night, there is such a weight of sin on me."

"What first made you feel so? had you read or heard anything to alarm you?"

"Yes, one evening I read the chapter with this verse, ' How shall we escape, if we neglect so great salvation?' It seemed to stick to me, I had neglected it, it's too late to escape. I have thought so ever since, is it so?"

"Oh no, it is not too late to escape, that warning verse is to arouse you to flee from the wrath to come, and God's own word says, 'Now is the accepted time, now is the day of salvation.'"

"Well, Miss, I'll do all as ever I can, I would do anything to be saved."

"My friend, your doing will do nothing; the Lord Jesus has done all for your salvation. Your sins are like a debt; you have been trying to pay that debt yourself, but I trust God, the Holy Spirit, will teach you that you have nothing to pay, because His precious blood has paid it all. But will you find your Testament, and we will together read what the Lord Jesus said to a woman, who felt her sins a heavy debt as you do? He is the same kind Saviour still, and just what He said to her He says to all who come."

We read the seventh chapter of St. Luke's Gospel from verse 37, and afterwards earnestly prayed that God's Holy Spirit might teach her to believe His own word.

Again her visitor called, but found her in much the same state of mind, convinced of sin and longing for deliverance.

She said, "I cannot rest with this weight of sin on me, and if I think myself wicked, what must the great and holy God see me to be? I want an evidence, Miss, that He'll forgive me, how can I know it? I want the *feeling* He's forgiven me."

"My friend, you are looking for evidences and feelings in yourself, and you will never find them there. It is God's promises, God's word—those blessed words that the Lord Jesus said to all that are weary and heavy laden like you, that you must trust and believe. Have you read the chapters I marked for you?"

"Yes, I have, over and over, and I am so glad you put me upon reading. I kept waiting for some evidence to come in my mind, and I think God has sent you to make His way plainer to me. I told my husband how glad I was you came with the tracts, and advised me to read my Bible."

"And is sin still a burden to you?"

"Oh yes, and a heavy one, too."

Tears showed the reality. Again we opened our Bibles, praying for the Holy Spirit's teaching, while we read the comfortable words of the Lord Jesus to all who truly turn to Him, in Matthew 11:27–30.

But she shall tell herself how great things the Lord did for her, and how His word comforted her. It was some time before I called again, and finding her busy washing, said I would not come in.

"But I have so much to tell you, please do come in, I am so happy now. God's Holy Spirit *is* teaching me. I had been looking for evidences and a sign, and now I see that it is what Jesus said. When I read my Testament now, it seems as if He was talking to me in it, as if the Lord spoke it all to me like. As soon as I believed what Jesus said was to me, all my grief seemed gone. Every verse brings me comfort; it all seems new to me; and because it is written, I believe that 'this is a faithful saying, and worthy of all acceptation, that Christ Jesus came into the world to save sinners, of whom I am chief.' I had often heard that Jesus died; now I've got an interest in His death, it was for me. I have been meditating in particular on those words, 'It is finished,' and I see He did all, finished all for me. I am ashamed to think how blind I have been for years, trying to save myself, saying my prayers and trying to be good, but I was turning my back on Him. I can't thank and praise Him enough, that now He has forgiven all my sins. And I do thank Him for sending you to call on me."

Another time she related a remarkable escape:—"Since you called I was in great danger. I was winding up a bucket of water at the well, the chain got loose, and, in my fright, I let go the windlass; it struck me on the head, and I fell, senseless, all but down the well. It is seventy feet deep, and there I must have died; no one hardly comes by my door. I do not know how long I lay there, but at last I got into the house, and then fainted again. There was no one to come to me; if it had happened a few weeks ago, how frightened I should have been, but I felt 'the Lord is my helper.' Yes, I feel quite safe, the Lord loves me and I love Him, not that I love Him as I want to, and now I am so happy after prayer. I think 'He is the eternal God,' not changing like me. When I read His word, I feel there is no mixture in His promises, it is the Lord's word only. And wherever I open my Bible, it all seems such loving words, I can't pass one by like. How thankful I am that God sent you with the tracts that morning, and to point me to the Word. Will you please to look at this old book, it was my poor mother's. I have often seen her cry over it. There's one part on 'our loving Saviour,' you can see where her tears fell over and over again on this leaf. It is in 'Come to Jesus,' Newman Hall's. My mother died very happy. For a long time I feared to die, and trembled at the thought, now the fear is all gone."

Finding she had not read any Gospel through, I advised her to begin with St. Matthew. She was quite interested with the reason of all the hard names being put there. She said, "I often wondered how clergymen could read them any way, and I thought they were all the names of the children of Israel."

She remarked, on the words, "She shall bring forth a Son," "Because sin came by woman, so Christ came by a woman to put Satan lower and lower." We turned to Genesis 3:15, and Isaiah 7:14.

It is very seldom that the poor know how to use a reference Bible, and it is pleasant to see the interest it gives them to explain it, and show them how often the New Testament is the key to the Old.

Before my next visit, which was the last, clouds had arisen. She said, "I have had some dark temptations. How can such a sinner be saved? Am I His child? Then I go again to the Word, and I can't tell you, dear lady, what light comes to me from that. Every verse has so much in it, it seems as if the Holy Spirit took the light from the Word, and put it in my heart. It's an amazing thought that ever He should have enlightened me. I am a wonder to myself. A wonder that He woke me, for it was waking me from death. Yes, for years I was dead. Oh, how kind the Lord is to let His word come to me. I hope you'll point many others to the Word."

The last chapter we read together was the first message, which fell on "the soil prepared." "And when they had nothing to pay, he frankly forgave them both." "But he that received seed into the good ground is he that heareth the word, and understandeth it, which also beareth fruit." "Not by might nor by power, but by my Spirit, saith the Lord of Hosts."

Another instance of the soil being prepared, and therefore bringing forth good fruit, was the case of a young girl attending a night school and a Sunday class. The instruction there given by a diligent, but often discouraged teacher, rapidly grew up, and, in due season, ripened into pleasant fruit. Lizzie was one of the most regular attendants; however wet the night, however bright the Sunday afternoon, however few came through the rain, or resisted the enticement of Sunday strolling, Lizzie was always there. Beyond this, there was no hopeful indication; silently, deeply, the soil was prepared, and the seed sown by the means, though without the knowledge, of her teacher. Lizzie belonged to an unpromising family, with no home influence or example to help her. Visitors often overlook some "little one" of the Lord's flock in this naughty world, passing by the very door which they think hopeless, but where the Lord has work for them to do. During the absence and illness of her own teacher, Lizzie sent a message to say she was ill. I found she had a bad cough, and evidently some latent disease. During several visits nothing particular passed; she read with me a verse in turn (which ensures far more attention than reading *to* a person); she was silent and attentive.

One afternoon her mother said, "Oh, I am so glad you are come, Lizzie has been telling us all that she is so happy."

When I sat down by her bed, she said, "I am so happy, I've had such a happy afternoon, I've been with Jesus all the time. He took me with Him to a fountain, oh it was so beautiful, and He washed my feet."

I was silent, feeling it a difficulty—Was this mere feeling, or was the Holy Spirit showing her of Jesus? "Were you dozing, Lizzie?"

"No, I was wide awake; I did see Jesus and the fountain."

"It is only by faith, Lizzie, we can see the Lord Jesus here, but it is quite true there is a fountain. You have often sung the hymn at school, 'There is a fountain filled with blood.'"

Then we read together the thirteenth chapter of St. John, and Zechariah 13:1. We talked about it, as I wished to ascertain if she clearly distinguished between the literal fact of washing the feet, and the invisible washing of the soul in the blood of the Lord Jesus Christ. Her answers were simple and satisfactory, "Yes, I do believe that the Lord Jesus has washed my sins away; for a long time I have prayed, 'Wash me, and I shall be whiter than snow.'" Over and over she said, "Oh, I am so happy, Jesus has washed me." Thus, as a little child, she believed, and believing, she rejoiced with joy unspeakable.

Her deeply loved and absent teacher, who was ill and suffering, was often inquired for, and frequent reference made to what she had learnt in her school. A "Silent Comforter," belonging to that teacher, was hung on her bed, and left open at the verse, "The blood of Jesus Christ, his Son, cleanseth us from all sin." Lizzie voluntarily learnt all that page, and many others.

Reading to her Luke 15:1–7, and quoting, as a reference, "The Son of Man is come to seek and to save that which is lost," Lizzie said, "I like that verse; Miss W. read it to me yesterday, and I thought about it all night." One true sign of spiritual life was most evident in her thirst for and delight in God's Word. "As new born babes desire the sincere milk of the word," so did Lizzie.

Another indication was anxiety for the souls of others. Once, when I had prayed with her, and said "Amen," she said, earnestly, "If you are not tired, Miss, will you pray again, it never tires me. I like to pray to Him, and I want you to pray for my poor mother and father. Mother is very good to me, but I am afraid she hasn't come to Jesus. Do pray for them all." Very often was this wish repeated, and sometimes she would herself pray aloud for her parents, and sisters, and brothers, that they might all come to Jesus.

She spoke gratefully of her school. "Oh, that was a beautiful school. I did so love to go. I often cried if I couldn't go. Sometimes I have been the only one there on a fine Sunday afternoon, and it was so nice. I did love Miss C.'s teaching. If I get well, I shall like to go again to my school. It vexed me when, after she had been teaching us so beautiful, some of the girls would come out laughing and singing; it was a shame, how could they do it? Things that teacher said come back to me now and comfort me."

Doubtless, God's Holy Spirit accompanied that earnest teacher's work, and Lizzie was the first-fruits from a discouraging class.

Lizzie's answer to her visitor's inquiries was, "I lie and think of Jesus, and how He loves me, and I love Him."

"Yes, dear child, He loved you first. 'We love Him, because He first loved us.'"

She seemed to grasp that verse, and ever after held it fast; it was Lizzie's anchor. At this time she was very suffering, but rarely spoke of herself, unless questioned, and then would add,—

"Jesus is so good to me, He helps me to lie still. I like mother and all of them to leave me alone often, that I may think of Him. When I can't read, many verses I have learnt come in my mind and comfort me."

She was not at all shy, and would ask questions; such a welcome contrast to the constant "yes, yes," which visitors too often hear. This evening, she said,—

"Can you tell me how to pray more, I want to tell Jesus more, but I haven't got the gift to pray?"

"Prayer is *asking* and *telling*, dear child. Ask your heavenly Father for all you want through the Lord Jesus Christ. You need not use hard words or keep to collects. If you wanted to ask your father for something, you would not look in a book first to see how to say it. 'If ye shall ask anything in my name, I will do it.' Do you remember how often the disciples came and told the Lord Jesus what things had happened to them, told Him when they were afraid on the sea, told Him all their troubles. And so may you tell Jesus. Tell Him, when you feel impatient, tell Him when you can hardly bear the pain, tell Him that you love Him and want to love Him more, tell Him that you want your father and mother to love Him, tell Him, above all, that you want the Holy Spirit to teach you to pray. The Lord Jesus knew that we should not be able of ourselves to pray well, and so He promised the Holy Spirit should teach us how to pray and to help our infirmities. Shall we now pray together and tell the Lord Jesus we want the Holy Spirit to teach us both how to pray."

When leaving her, she said,

"Oh, I should like to go to Jesus to-night. I don't want to get well. It's a naughty world, I would rather go to Jesus, I should so love to go to Him."

One sultry evening in July, I found Lizzie very ill, and oppressed with heat. Some aromatic vinegar had been given me for mission use. I mixed some with water, and sponged her face and neck and hands. She kept saying, "Beautiful, beautiful." (This and Eau de Cologne is a most acceptable gift. A clean soft pocket handkerchief with the novelty of scent has often given more pleasure than would be supposed, and a little bottle left by the bedside is refreshing to the weary invalid in the close heavy atmosphere.) Then she said, "Please read to me about Jesus, I lies and thinks about Him, and how He loves me."

1 John 4:14 to end was read. She inquired affectionately for her absent teacher, saying, "If I am not spared to see Miss C., I shall meet her in heaven."

Then Lizzie asked me to sing; her favourite hymns were, "I heard the voice of Jesus say," to my father's tune "Evan," "There is a Happy Land," and "Oh, that will be joyful." It is often pleasant and resting to an invalid to sing softly to them, choosing their old familiar hymns and tunes. Old people especially, who may have been shut up for years from the house of the Lord, are always cheered to hear once more the glorious Te Deum chanted, or "My soul doth magnify the Lord." The Old Hundredth never fails to delight them, and many a feeble voice have I heard joining in the well-known tune. One aged sufferer quite clapped her hands the first time I sang for her, exclaiming, "Ah, that's it. The same as I sang when I was a girl. I couldn't start it by myself, please sing it again, again!"

"The Ministry of Song" has a practical verse which I have often seen realised:—

> "Sing at the cottage bedside,
>   They have no music there,
> And the voice of praise is silent
>   After the voice of prayer.
> Sing of the gentle Saviour
>   In the simplest hymns you know,
> And the pain-dimmed eye will brighten
>   As the soothing verses flow.
> Better than loudest plaudits
>   The murmured thanks of such,
> For the King will stoop to crown them
>   With His gracious 'Inasmuch.'"
>
> F. R. H.

July 14.—The intense heat was very trying to poor Lizzie; sponging and fanning much refreshed her. Her legs were swollen and painful, and for some time her right side had been paralysed, so that she was very helpless. She showed me some strawberries and cakes Mrs. F. had sent, but she owned the gift as His. "See how good the Lord Jesus is to me, He sent me all these nice things. I shouldn't have had them if He hadn't put it in her heart to send them."

Though no longer able to sing, she asked for a hymn, beating time with her thin hand, and looking so happy. Then she listened to the first chapter of the 1st of Peter. We dwelt especially on our being redeemed with the precious blood of Christ, and, therefore, He would keep what He had bought. Her cough was almost incessant, and with some difficulty she said,—

"Tell me what to say to the Lord Jesus, the last thing; I like to tell Him something before I go to sleep."

"Ask Him to fill you with the Holy Ghost, He so often told us to ask for the Holy Spirit."

And surely it was His teaching which filled her with holy longing to depart and be with Christ; again and again she said, "Oh, I long to go, when it's Jesus' time to tell me to come. I lie and wait for Him to say, 'Lizzie, come.' I should like to go to Jesus, I should, I should,' and the tears came.

July 20.—Lizzie seems kept in perfect peace and in the full assurance that the Lord Jesus loved her "first," that He had washed her whiter than snow, and that she was going to Him very soon. Again she spoke of her parents and her desire that they might be saved. Prayer that the Lord would open her mouth to speak to them, was specially answered, and other friends and neighbours said, "We can never forget what Lizzie said to us; she *was* happy." "She was full of Jesus," said one poor man.

July 21.—Before eight o'clock this morning, I went to say good-bye to Lizzie. She said, "I am so sorry you are going away. I shall miss you; but are you going to see my dear Miss C.?"

"No, dear child, but what message will you send?"

"My love, my kind love I mean, and I shall meet her in heaven. I am so glad I came to her school."

There was only time to pray and commend her to Him who first loved her, and would love her even unto the end. And her short journey was all but over, and home in sight. Kind visitors were daily with her, and they could tell of her joy and peace in believing.

One wrote, "Lizzie was too ill to speak much, but she said, 'Miss H. knows that Jesus loves me, and that I love Jesus.'" Another visitor, M.C., who had also been a most efficient and kind teacher in the night-school which Lizzie attended, now saw the quick ripening of the seed sown in tears. She took care that every little want was supplied, and once sent a messenger four miles to try and procure in July the invalid's wish for pork pie. This teacher relates that Lizzie's deathbed was most beautiful. "She never seemed to take in any fear, she was kept in such perfect peace, it was all 'Jesus.' If we asked her, Had she any fear of death? she seemed to wonder that any one could fear to go to Jesus. I remembered a most eminent Christian telling me on her deathbed she did not think any one could see Death without some fear, and that even an excellent clergyman, who had lived and laboured abundantly for Christ, had expressed a fear of death, and though that fear never came, for he died in his sleep, yet here was this dear child longing to go without any fear at all. Yes, it was beautiful to hear her say, 'It's all Jesus, Jesus.' Though she suffered very much and was often in great pain, yet she never complained, never talked about herself or her sufferings. The day that she died her own absent teacher, Miss C., had sent a letter to Lizzie. I went with it early, but as I could not go up stairs then, I called again, directly after morning church. She was dying, her hands and her feet were blue and cold, yet she looked so happy. I told her that Miss C. had sent her a letter; she listened to every word, never taking her eyes from me. I was afraid she would not understand the letter was hers, but as I put it near, her dying hand feebly tried to grasp it, and she whispered 'Mine.' When I had read it, I thought she would be too tired to hear the references read, but she wished me to go on. Her eyes looked brightly upward as I read to her Revelation 7:14. I said, 'Lizzie, you will soon have one of those white robes; and a crown, and no more poverty and pain;' she said most earnestly, 'Yes, oh yes.' Those little words seemed easier for her to get out. The last verse that I read to her was, 'The blood of Jesus Christ, His Son, cleanseth us from all sin.' Her dying message to her teacher Miss C. was, 'Give my best love to her and tell her that I shall meet her in—heaven.'

"She still looked happy, and never lost that smile and look of peace which I had always noticed. When I went away, she whispered, 'Good bye, God bless you.'"

THE TEACHER'S LETTER TO LIZZIE.

My dear Lizzie,—

I must write and tell you how very constantly I think of you on your bed of suffering. It grieves me more than I can say that I cannot be near you, but my comfort is to know that Jesus is with you, that He has washed you from all your sins and gathered you as His own lamb into His fold. You can tell to others now how true is what I have often said, that it is far better to have Jesus for your own Saviour and Friend, than all this world can give. The world can't help you now, dear Lizzie, can it? but Jesus has *saved* you, and He is with you every moment to help and comfort you in all your pain. Soon He will take you to that bright happy home He has gone to prepare for His own.

I have just been reading something about that blessed home in the seventh chapter of Revelation. Dear M.C. (who brings you this letter) will read it to you. It always makes me long so much to be there. Oh, how thankful we should be to that dear Saviour, who has suffered so much and died for us, that we might go there. In the 14th verse we are told who it is that will be there. "Those who have washed their robes and made them white in the blood of the Lamb. Therefore are they before the throne of God." So, dear Lizzie, if you have come to Jesus, as I believe you have, and He has washed you in His precious blood, as He does all who come to Him, then you have indeed cause to be happy, for you may be sure that He will be with you in the valley of the shadow of death, and carry you safely to His glorious home, where "there will be no more death, neither sorrow, nor crying, neither shall there be any more pain." (Revelation 21:14.)

It makes me very sad to think of not seeing you again in this world, but we must look forward to meeting in heaven, and you will be there to welcome me. Keep looking to Jesus, dear Lizzie, and remember always that He loves you and has washed you from your sins in His own blood, and He will never leave you.—Good bye. I am always your affectionate friend and teacher,

E.C.

During this last Sunday afternoon several came in to see Lizzie. To her clergyman she said, "I'm not afraid to die. I'm going to Jesus." She said as much as her strength would allow to one of her schoolfellows, begging her to "look to Jesus" and "try and follow Him."

Very often had she spoken to her father and mother, and again with dying breath she said, "Come to Jesus." Her mother says she was sensible and happy to the very last moment. She quietly fell asleep in Jesus, on Sunday evening, August 1, 1869, aged seventeen years.

"Therefore, my beloved brethren, be ye stedfast, unmoveable, always abounding in the work of the Lord, forasmuch as ye know that your labour is not in vain in the Lord."

VI.

GEORGE AND RHODA'S STORY.

GEORGE and Rhoda lived at Laney Green. She was his third wife. At the time that George told me his history, he was very infirm, seldom leaving his arm chair. He was a Wesleyan, but as long as he could walk, always came to church in the morning. He deeply valued the sermons preached there, and would remark, "That was a wonderful discourse, bless the Lord for such a light in the church."

George and Rhoda were always invited to the parsonage on New Year's Day, when all the old people and widows came to dinner. After dinner their pastor would sing and play some simple strain for them, and then leave his harmonium to younger fingers. It was pleasant to watch the effect of music on the aged guests, some beating time with their hands and feet, some motionless with delight and wonder as "Comfort ye," "O rest in the Lord," and "Whom having not seen, ye love," were sung for them. The scene might add another verse to "The Ministry of Song."

Then all joined in some well-known hymns, and the Worcestershire Christmas carol,

"How grand and how bright,
That wonderful night."

Rhoda's comment was, "'Tis wonderful! We can't play on that music, but up there we'll all have a golden harp a piece."

After the singing their pastor addressed them with words of comfort and warning. Then George was always the chosen spokesman, and rising, would make a hearty speech, with "thanks for all favours, and prayers for all blessings on their dear pastor and his partner." Her gifts of books and comforters closed the New Year's party. George was not able to come to our last gathering, he was weak and ill, and daily thought he was "just going over Jordan." And he longed to go, death had no terror for him, he knew he should then see Him face to face.

George had often told me scraps of his early life, and they were so interesting, that I took pencil and paper to note down his story more carefully. Wishing to divert his attention whilst arranging my papers, that he might not observe my reporting, I showed him a coloured print of Canterbury Cathedral in the "Sunday at Home." He wondered how ever such a big place could be built, or even thought of, and after examining it some time, said, "That is a grand place, but it's not so grand as this little fireside corner and my arm chair, for His glory shines here, that's the grandeur! it's Christ's presence makes a temple. Jacob had only one stone, and yet he said, 'This is the house of God and the gate of heaven.'" The old man shut up the book and told me of the many bright Sundays, when, in that little corner, the Lord drew near and was unto him "as a little sanctuary."

George was quite pleased to tell me his story, Rhoda was away, and he should not look at the clock so often, if his visitor would be pleased to sit a long time with him. His story shall be given without the interruption of the necessary remarks and questions, and as nearly as possible in his own words, saving the incommunicable Staffordshire dialect.

GEORGE'S STORY.

"It is many years ago since the Lord brought me out of darkness into His light. Better than forty years; and yet it all seems before me like as if it were yesterday. At that time I had the care of a team of horses, not on a farm, but for drawing goods or stones. I had good wages, but as I says, waggoners' money is like sodgers' money, it comes and it goes, and you're none the better for it. I was sadly too fond of drink; many's the time, to my shame, has it overcome me. I seldom went to church or chapel, for when a man's tied to a team he's little thought for Sunday. I've often gone forty miles on the Lord's day. My wife had more sense and headpiece than I had, and she came to this conclusion, 'George, if you won't give up that team and get a better master, I'll give up this house and go into lodgings, or go to service.' It put me about, and I didn't like her conclusion at all. But it fell out the master had words with me about the team, the first time for eight years, and he cursed me, so I left his service. We then came to live at Laney Green, with my father. Mother was dead, and badly he had used her, for he was a drunkard. The Green was an awful wicked place, it was notable for the poor wives being leathered and thwacked. Often I've heard the poor women's cries. One night my poor father came home drunk and began to leather my wife. Said I, 'If she's to be leathered, I'll do it myself.' So we soon left my father and took this cottage. It's true I was jeered at and called a woman's man, but I always found my wife's conclusions the best. It was a very dark place then, and my soul was darker still.

"One evening a child came round to all the houses, to tell us a missioner from Lunnun was coming, and there would be preaching that night. My wife said, 'Let us go;' and knowing her conclusions were always best, I said, 'Yes, we will.' We did go, and we were both caught that night. I can't tell which of us was caught first, but she told me her first prayer was, 'Lord, reach my husband,' and my first cry was, 'Lord, have mercy on my poor wicked father.' I shall never forget that night. The preacher was a home missioner, sent from London to Cannock and to go round some of the villages near. He was a Frenchman, but spoke as good English as any parson in a pulpit. He took his text from Mark 16:16: 'He that believeth and is baptized shall be saved; but he that believeth not shall be damned.' 'Oh,' said I, 'he's preaching to none but me, why that man knows all about my sins!' All my sins rose up before me, staring me in the face.

"I came away crying, 'God be merciful to me a sinner.' Soon after the missioner called on me; I said,—

"'Sir, it's no use your coming to me, I am too vile to be saved, I'm lost.'

"His answer was, 'The Lord has sent me to tell you quite different. "The Son of Man is come to seek and to save that which was lost."'

"I can never forget that man; when you've tasted the sweetness, you can't help loving the one that brings you the message. Since then the Lord has never suffered me to draw quite back, nor taken His Holy Spirit from me. He has always this gracious word for me, 'Fear not, thou worm Jacob.'"

Old George seemed tired, so we said good-bye, and went to hear the rest of his story another day, as follows:

"The missioner stayed a long time at Cannock. When he left, quite a stripling out of a Sunday school came to read chapters for me, as I was no scholar. Through thick and thin, snow and rain, did he come to his time, once a week. The old cottage in which we lived tumbled down, and then we came to live in this one. My poverty and other matters often cumbered me and threw me back, but the Lord never left me. He gave me grace to start afresh, whenever I backslided from Him. My wife was a much stouter Christian than I was. Satan could throw me down long before he could her, and I always acknowledged it. My first wife was a capital reader, better than my good little Rhoda there. I tell her she is as much at a loss for a letter as some ministers are over their words, when they can't express all they want to in the pulpit. Time went on, and my poor wife sickened and died. Almost the last talk we had was this, by her bedside. She said, 'George, I am going, but it's going home. I leave you with three children as can do for themselves, and three as can't. May God give you grace to train them aright; and, George, don't marry again till the children are grown up, it might bring discord.' I believe I promised her I would not. She died with a smile and a kiss.

"A fortnight after she was buried, I heard my wife's voice. I was lying awake about four o'clock. She called 'George, George!' I looked up, and she was leaning over me. It was her features somehow, and yet it was a glorified spirit. Ah, she was in a bloom! I've heard ministers speak of angels and glorified spirits in their sermons, and I have said to myself, 'You only get half-way to what a glorious spirit is, I've seen a deal more of one than you. I've seldom mentioned what she said. I tried to speak to her, but I heard a rustle, and she was gone.

"After my wife's death, I fetched my eldest girl home to take care of the house and children. Many were my trials but the Lord led me on.

"About six years after, I married again. I believe it was ordered for me. My second wife was a widow, and had been a schoolmistress. She was a scholar, and a truer churchwoman could not be found in Cannock. She was very sharp at the books, and a bit sharp in her temper too sometimes. The young stripling from the Sunday school was grown a man now. He still came to our cottage, and I got two or three benches for the neighbours to come in when he read and prayed. It might teach them not to leather their wives. Though my wife was such a scholar, she was brought in at one of these readings. I remember the evening. I was at work in the garden, and she called,—

"'George, George, come and put the benches and chairs for the reading to-night, I am too busy.'

"I went. She said, 'I wish the reading was over, I am dreading it.'

"'Indeed,' said I, 'why, it always rejoices me.'

"'Well, George, I must say that man seems to go on against me; he seems to think I am a sinner, worse than others.'

"I said nothing, but went up the road to meet him, and said, 'The battle's half won with my wife, don't give in, speak out in the Master's name.'

"He thanked me, and said he had been praying in particular for my wife.

"After all were gone, she cried a good deal. I said, 'What ails thee, wife?'

"Why, George, I see it now, I am the biggest sinner that ever was. For years I have read the Bible, and heard good sermons, but never till tonight did I see myself a sinner.'

"I have been trying to bring to my mind's eye the passage of Scripture that was read that night, but I can't. It was a quick work in her. Her temper mended uncommon. She was soon sent for. Hers was a happy, happy death. I sat watching by her when the last came. I said,—

"'Tell me how it is with you, for I see you are just entering in.'

"She heaved both her hands up, and said, 'Bless the Lord, all is well, all is well.'"

George's story must be unfinished. Rhoda's will supply the event of his third marriage. He is gone home at last, but I never heard how he passed through the valley. The verse that he loved so well, "Fear not, thou worm Jacob," is doubtless exchanged for the "Fear not, it is your Father's good pleasure to give you the kingdom."

RHODA'S STORY.

"My father and mother were very godly, and many a prayer they put up for their large family, that all might be led to know the Lord. My father had great faith that his prayer would be answered, even if he never lived to prove it. He believed none of us would be missing. Before he died, two of us were called in, but the most of us were outside still. The clergyman often visited him and I remember the last time he saw father's happy deathbed, he said, 'Oh, what a joyful death! it has preached me such a sermon!'

"My mother went to him and said, 'Is your soul steadfast still?'

"He took her hand and said, 'Ay, steadfast in the Lord, for He's kept me to the end. There are only a few more grains of sand in my hour-glass, they will soon run out, and then—I shall be with Jesus.'

"My father seemed sometimes overpowered with joy, and he seemed to look on death as the biggest joy. My poor mother lived a long time after his death. She died quite as safe, but in the midst of such agony and inflammation. She had a smile for Him when He called her, and I saw it too. I was crying by her bed; she said, 'Rhoda, don't cry for me, cry for yourself, and don't trifle any longer, get ready, child, for the Master. He's come, and I am ready.' That was her last word to me, but I did not heed it then. At the Sunday school many a call had come to me, but it all seemed lost upon me. My father's faith and my father's prayers weren't to be lost. I married; my husband was in the right road before me. It was a dream that alarmed me. I dreamt I saw my mother, and she said again to me, 'Don't trifle any longer, Rhoda, get ready for the Master.' An hangel was following her, and I thought he said, 'Now is the accepted time, now is the day of salvation.' With that, I woke. I knew it was only a dream. But that verse stuck to me. I woke my husband, and asked him to get up and pray for me. He did. The next Sunday the preacher gave out this text, 'Now is the accepted time, now is the day of salvation.' I thought, 'This is no dream now, this is the Lord calling me.'

"For many weeks I was very miserable, till one night, as I was on my knees, peace came. I can compare it to nothing else but a weight falling off. It's more than thirty years ago, but that lightsome day is clear before me. Ah, I thought then I should always be in that joyful mind. I was to be left, and proved and sifted, but the Lord smiled again and again. Yes, it was those words opened my eyes, 'Now is the accepted time;' I was quite in the dark before that.

"Father's prayer was answered for John next. I doated on that brother; when we were little, we were like two lambs together. His end was very sudden. He worked in a coal-pit. The last Sunday it seemed as if he knew he was going, and was getting all ready. He went to a prayer-meeting quite early, and when he came to breakfast he got his Bible. At dinner-time it was the same; at last his wife said:—

"'Why, John, what's come over thee? it's nothing but praying and reading to-day.'

"He said, 'I can't tell how it is, wife, but perhaps I mayn't be long here, and I would rather be praying while I can.'

"At nine o'clock the next morning he was killed in the pit. But his lamp was alight, and his loins girded, and so father had one more to meet him up there.

"My first husband and I lived very happy together some years. After his death troubles came thick, but my faith seemed to grow thick too. It seemed that when I told the Lord what I wanted, He put it in some one's heart to give it me. I had unknownst friends raised up. Bread didn't come to me in ricks and heaps, but my Father always sent enough. My son worked for me till he took an inflammation. I was in a strait then. I prayed and asked the Lord what to do. In the course of the day I thought I would go up to the hall. I was not unknown to them, but, of course, they didn't know my troubles. Next morning I took my youngest boy with me, he was very sickly too. I had been up to the house, but never went into so many rooms before. I was sent for into my lady's dressing-room. She was handsome, and so tall. Her little girl was by her, with her hair all down, like a shock of gold corn, and her colour like a rose.

"The lady asked me all about my affairs, as kind as if she were my equal. She spoke to me of better things, too, if I went to a place of worship, and if I had a Bible.

"I told her I had no Bible, and that I could not read.

"Then she sent her maid to take me to have something to eat, and I was to go to her again for the Bible. She said some one could read it to me. There it is, and there's her own 'M. V. G.' in it. It's almost wore out, but it's a lamp to my soul.

"When I went to the lady again for the Bible, it was in a room they called the library. It was stacked all round with books. I was quite struck with those stacks of books. There was another lady sitting there, she seemed weakly, but had such a heavenly smile. Those sisters were a pair! She noticed my little boy looking so pale, and went and picked a wonderful flower for him from some pots in the window. They said he was very thin, and asked if I ever gave him some arrowroot. I said it was unknownst to me. The lady sent for as much as two pounds of it, and, more than that, told me how to make it. It was the best medicine I ever gave the child, and it brought him round. There was one bit of advice the lady gave me. She said she was pleased to see me so clean and decent, that the patches on my gown were quite a credit to me, but she didn't like the bead trimming and flowers on my bonnet, that beads and patches didn't match very well. She said it so mild, I thanked her; and when I got in the lane, I sat down on a bank and pulled them off. To be sure I had put them on years before, thinking to please Daniel. Then I went on home, passing by the school-house the good lady had built in her own park for the poor children. It's been a fold for many a silly, straying lamb. My lady cared for the poor, because she cared for the Lord. Those good ladies have long gone to their rest, but they ain't forgot. You may see their writing in many a Bible besides mine, and old Hampton kept the marker in the very Psalm her hand put it to his dying day. I shall see them again, though, in the rooms of the Mansion, that will be better dressed than even the rooms at the hall.

"Some years after this my poor boy had an accident, and the doctor said it was impossible for him to live.

"'But, sir,' said I, 'I have prayed to the Lord for his life, and I have faith to believe he will live.'

"'Believe on,' he said, 'if you like.'

"I did believe on, and he did live, and is a comfort to me now.

"One day even my loaf was gone, and I really had not a penny to buy more. I had to go to H—— hall that day for an hospital ticket. I prayed before I went.

"The little girl I had seen so blooming by her mother's side was a lady now. She came to me, for she took after those noble ladies, and cared for the poor. She gave me the ticket. Then the housekeeper brought me a blanket and a sheet, which the lady sent for my sick boy. I could not help saying my heavenly Father must have told her that I wanted these worse than anything, for I had never mentioned it.

"I came away with these presents, but still I knew there was no bread at home. As I walked down Hilton Lane, under the tall trees, I heard the rooks talking away in the branches. I could not tell what they said, and yet it seemed as if they cawed, 'Fear not, consider the fowls of the air, your Father feeds them.' Just then I looked down and saw a piece of paper in the road. I took it up. There was one shilling and sixpence wrapped up. At first I thought why an hangel has dropped this for me, then I thought they've nothing to do with our money—it's sent someway by my Father, for I prayed to Him about my empty cupboard. Of course I asked if any one had lost it, but no one claimed it, so my prayers were more than answered.

"When I had been a widow some years, I lighted upon George. He was old, and wanted a nurse, and I wanted a fireside, and some one to care for me. So it seemed as if the Lord put us together to comfort one another on the last bit of the road home. We've been married seven years. George has got on faster to the kingdom than ever before. Affliction has rubbed down his temper. I can see the grace of God shining in him, and many happy hours we have together in our little cot. 'The Lord is with us, and He is enough!'"

VII.

SUSAN HARRIS; OR, "FRUIT IN DUE SEASON."

IT is sometimes pleasanter to look back on things past than to look on things present. As when journeying on some hot and dusty day we hardly enjoy the scenery, and glance weariedly even at shady nooks and cool brook-sides; but when home is reached, and the dust brushed off, we then recall the pleasantness we overlooked at the time. And so it is with many an effort to do good: we feel the toil and the fatigue, and the dust of discontent settles on our visit to the cottage, or the hour of teaching in the hot schoolroom. It may be years ere that dust is brushed away, and we see that even then "our labour was not in vain in the Lord."

It may refresh some patient Sunday-school teacher, who seems ever sowing and never reaping, here to recall the springing up of long hidden seed in a Sunday-school girl.

May the Lord Jesus bless this outline of the life and death of Susan Harris.

Let us look back some years ago, into the school-room of St. Nicholas, Worcester. It is Sunday afternoon, the sun is shining with July brightness, and though the room is spacious and airy, yet the little groups of learners seem restless from the sultry heat. It is a pleasant room, and the floor as clean and white as any man-of-war deck. This floor is certainly the idol of cleanliness with its good day-mistress, and both teachers and children have to learn and practise one well-taught lesson, "Scrape your shoes."

We will stand awhile by the first class of girls. They are very neatly dressed, and the school rule of "no flowers, no feathers, no finery," is well observed by both teacher and scholars. The expression of their countenances is very different. Mary so quiet, Ann an open English face, Matilda looks cold and proud, Anne-Maria thoughtless. The eldest is upwards of twenty, and seems an example of thoughtful attention. (Elizabeth remained in this class till her twenty-fifth birthday. She left a farewell gift of a neat box to keep the contributions of her class to the Church Missionary Society. A half-sovereign was added from her wages.) Among others we notice a pale-faced girl, with very plain and almost unpleasant expression. But her answers show that she thinks, and the Reference Bible in her hand is reward for good conduct. This is Susan Harris.

The teacher's eye glances round on her class, and she thinks, "How can I know my girls? how difficult to trace their hidden characters, save from the slight indications of their attention and answers." She longs to know in whom the seed of the Word may have taken root, or may be springing up; but all is hidden from her, so she remembers her father's word of encouragement at the last teachers' meeting, "The work is yours, success is God's."

Now we will listen to their careful well-trained reading, which even the good bishop, on their annual examination day, pronounced "excellent, first-rate." The fortieth chapter of Isaiah is the chosen portion. The teacher has taken much pains in the week in examining the passage and preparing her lesson. But somehow she fails to interest them; the class is restless, the teacher discouraged. The teacher pauses, that she may look up herself to the great Teacher—how that look refreshes her. The last verse is read—"But they that wait upon the Lord shall renew their strength; they shall mount up with wings as eagles, they shall run and not be weary, and they shall walk and not faint." From this she draws their attention to the natural history of the eagle; the strength of its wing, its upward flight, dwelling among the rocks, its piercing eye, meeting even the sunbeams. She speaks of the wings of faith bearing the soul upward, ever rising to things above, soaring among the heights of the Rock of Ages, and ever finding there "a place of defence, even the munitions of rocks." And then how faith is like that eagle's eye—how half-closed and dim the young eaglet's eye is, and then its gradual and strengthening clearness. So is the dimness of our faith, when the Lord Jesus first bids the spiritual eye "be opened." But as we gaze upon the Sun of Righteousness, the dimness clears away, and in "His light we see light." Thus, ever looking, ever rising, we shall at length pass into the land of light, where the wing of faith shall "rest in His love," and the eye shall "see the King in His beauty."

The lesson is over, and the teacher thinks "I have taught them nothing to-day; I have not even interested them; it is my fault, not theirs."

Wait, wait yourself, wearied teacher! trust more to the Spirit's teaching of your scholars; the dimness on their eyes may yet pass away, and the Sun of Righteousness arise on them with healing in His wings.

It is nearly four o'clock now. The school-room door opens, and their kind rector enters for his customary closing of the school. He goes round to every class, with a kindly word of refreshing to each teacher; and any refractory child is pointed out for admonition. The naughtiest spirit would melt under his gentle words and the hand so kindly laid on the shoulder.

He rings the bell, the teachers mark their class-books, and the Bibles are cleared away. Again the bell rings, all rise, and his silvery voice gives out and leads the hymn. The text word of his address is often taken from those unequalled hymns of Watts, or from the morning's text, or the subject of the school lesson for the day. The antiphonal questioning of boys and girls is quite spirited, the girls are so delighted to outdo the boys, and they generally succeed. With prayer the school began, with prayer it now closes.

The girls then walk out two and two, the boys meanwhile singing heartily "Hosanna to the Son." The first class of girls are privileged to walk home without joining the ranks. So the teacher's work is ended; she is wearied and dissatisfied with *herself*, but wisely resolves to take yet more pains with the preparation of the next Sunday's lesson. Ah! she little thought then, that the pale-faced girl Susan Harris went straight to the bedside of a young sufferer, and read to her the same fortieth chapter of Isaiah, and refreshed her by repeating much of what the teacher thought had all been said in vain. And when six years have passed, we shall find that afternoon's "dust of discontent" all brushed away, and that sultry hour's teaching recalled with pleasure.

Wearied, discouraged teachers! try more prayer, not only before your teaching, but *after* it. Return from your class and go and tell the Lord Jesus all that you have tried to say for Him. Plead for each child by name, your earnest cry will reach His ear, when it fails to reach their hearts. There is but one key that can unlock their hearts, but one hand that can turn that key. That key His word, that hand the wounded one, and that alone can open their hearts as Lydia's of old "to attend to the things spoken."

Some five years have passed away since that Sunday afternoon; we will follow the same teacher in her walk to the infirmary. This too is a school, even the sequel school of affliction. Many a bitter lesson is taught there; but how is the bitterness sweetened, when the scholar learns it of Him who said, "Take my yoke upon you and learn of me."

We will go to the upper women's ward. It is clean and well ventilated, and round the cheerful fires many convalescents are sitting. Nurse Woodward comes to meet us, with her motherly smile and warm pressing hand. "Well, Miss H., I be so glad you are come, I want you to tell the poor things all that I can't. It's little I know, but I want Jesus, and they ought to want Him too, for it's hard dying without a Saviour!"

We pass down the long rows of beds, with the many unknown sufferers, to one whose smile welcomes her teacher's visit. It is the quiet pale faced girl we saw in that Sunday class. Her countenance is much altered, peace and joy and hope have left a smile there we never saw before. Susan's Reference Bible is open by her, how worn it looks. A well-worn Bible is a good index of its owner. Susan takes it up and says, "My Bible is all my comfort now, it's so sweet to me. I hardly care to go to sleep for thinking of it, and the night never seems long, verse after verse feeds me with so many thoughts."

Many pleasant visits were paid to dear Susan, but no record was kept of them. A sister teacher of that class was more careful, and we give extracts from her notes. More than any other had this teacher led Susan to those still waters which now refreshed her in weary hours of suffering. Warmly did Susan love her gentle teacher, E. P. H. We give some of their conversations:—

Susan to her teacher, "I am so happy, I would rather be like this, than ever so well. Yesterday I was so ill and thought I was dying."

Teacher.—"And could you trust yourself in the hands of Jesus?"

Susan.—"Yes, quite so. He is such a Saviour, I could not be afraid. He is very precious to me, and I love to think of Him."

She then joined earnestly in what was said about sin, responding, "Oh yes, I think of my sins, there's no good dwelling in me."

Again Susan spoke of loving the Lord Jesus, and how her thoughts were raised to Him continually. "It seems as if I could think of nothing else; I look up to Him and feel He never will forsake me. The verse Miss H. last pointed out to me, 'Abide in me and I in you,' I have thought a great deal about."

Teacher.—"Are you not thankful, Susan, that the Lord Jesus has taught you thus to know and love Him?"

"Yes, I do thank Him, and I thank Him too for sending you to teach me; oh, I do thank you so Miss Ellen," and Susan grasped her hand.

The nurse told us that Susan was quite an example in the ward. There were many careless giddy ones, these she warned very kindly and would check the noisy talking which is so great an evil in most wards. Often she would get them to sit round her bed and read aloud, till her little strength was spent. One of the patients said, "I wish we were more like Susan, she never joins in the foolish talking, I wish we all followed her, she is a good girl, and sets us an example." "By their fruits ye shall know them."

After many weeks in the infirmary, Susan went home, she was not at all better, nor was any hope given of her recovery.

Susan lived at the corner of Cherry Tree Walk. It seemed strange that the long row of town houses with a high brick wall right before them, should get such a country name, but in the narrow garden behind, there really were cherry trees, and perhaps their snowy blossoms christened the walk as they fell. Susan's parents were very poor, and her father had only lately become a changed, and a church-going man. It had pleased

God to awake him by the preached word, and well did he love St. Nicholas' Church, where he first heard the message of peace. John was always in his little corner by the vestry door, and we often watched him going up the very last to the table of the Lord; the last there, perhaps not the last, when the Great Master seats his guests. John's words were very rough and simple, but so honest and warm. "I do love Mr. Havergal's sermons. I'll stick to him as long as I live." John always read and prayed with his wife and daughter before supper time. And when wife and daughter went to a better home and left John alone, he would call in his neighbours, "just to make two or three for the Lord to meet." They did, however, sometimes complain that "John's prayers were rather long, and that he pounded the chapter too much." But John was very real, and once when a visitor went up to his room and he did not hear her step or knock, through the open door she saw him on his knees, saying a long grace before his basin of broth and crust of bread.

His wife's name was Bridget, she was very quiet and civil, but not at all a comfort-maker for her husband and child. The ashes, the dust, the litter, seemed always undisturbed, and poor Susan sadly needed the cleanliness and tidy nursing, which in the poorest cottage can make a sick-room comfortable. And yet her mother loved her, and would watch by her day and night.

For many months Susan laid wasting away, her cough and weakness daily increasing. She had many visitors, and my dear father's quick step often stopped at her door. She often told me that "his prayers were such a comfort to her." "It's like heaven when he's praying with me. He always comes to do my soul good, and somehow his voice always comforts me. And then he asks me what I can fancy, and off he goes quickly and brings me something back so nice and relishing in his pockets. Often has he brought me an ice on a hot day." Ah, those pockets could tell kind tales of what they almost daily carried, marmalade, and patties, and potted meat, and best grocery to the sick and needy, and when choice flowers from O—— conservatory were sent to the rectory, he would always carry some away to sick-rooms.

Only One knew and counted all those "cups of cold water." At this time the loan of a water cushion from Miss N. was a great comfort to Susan. Not long before that same cushion had borne a gentle lady sufferer. Sweet Mary! the very smile of heaven had shone in her brilliant eye, and when the sleep of death spread over that sunny face, it lingered still in untold peacefulness. On that same cushion three young sufferers had found "beneath them the everlasting arms," and then passed away to lean for ever on Jesus Christ.

Susan told us that when she could not sleep at night she would light the candle and get her Bible, and that always refreshed her.

To her teacher, Miss E, Susan said, "I am proud of my Sunday-school, it's a blessed thing to go to one. I was at your school for eleven years, and do thank God for your teaching. I used to love to hear you, and try to ponder over it till the end of the week. You used to beg me to seek the Lord Jesus, and to pray for the Holy Spirit; and if you had not, perhaps I should have gone in wicked ways as many others did. It used to vex me if the girls did not attend at their class, I only wish I had attended better."

We will just glimpse at that other Sunday-school teacher, whom we left weary and discouraged that hot July afternoon. She is sitting by Susan's bed, and the poor, thin fingers are in the teacher's hand. Between the fits of coughing, Susan says—

"I was so ill all last night, and could get no sleep, as I laid awake one of the lessons you taught me at the Sunday-school all came back freshly to my mind. Do you remember explaining to us the fortieth chapter of Isaiah one Sunday?"

"No, dear Susan, I have quite forgotten it."

Susan.—"But I have not forgotten it, it was a very hot Sunday six years ago, and you told us a good deal about the eagle. When I went home that afternoon I thought so much of the lesson, and I went and read the chapter to a sick friend, and it did so comfort her. Last night those verses came to my mind, and a great deal of what you taught us about the wings and eye of faith, and it did so cheer me through the long night."

The teacher thanked God, and took courage.

One of Susan's thoughts will be pleasant for us to remember when the Sunday morning's clean and best clothes are put on. She said, "I often think, when mother changes me, and puts my clean things on, that I shall not want to change my robe of righteousness. That will be always clean and white, never soiled; I shall never want to put that off."

Sometimes, when too exhausted to speak much, she would say, "Just read, it's food to my soul." Another time she whispered, "I am nothing—nothing. Christ is *my* all; yes, He is all and in all. What should I do now without His promises? they comfort me."

Susan often spoke of a sister who died in consumption when she was about six years old. She taught her many hymns, and tried to tell her of the love of Jesus. Susan did not forget this, and often, as a very little child, wished to love God; and, in her prayers, "felt she was speaking to Him." But she always spoke of her Sunday-school teaching, as that which led her to the Lord Jesus.

To her most loved teacher, she said, "I do thank you very much, dear Miss Ellen, for all you've done for me. I often lie and think of what I might have been if I had had no school to go to. I might have gone astray, like many others, if God had not sent you to warn me Sunday after Sunday, and point out to us the narrow way. And what should I have done without all the Scripture I learnt there? When I lie awake at night it all comes back into my mind so sweet, and in the day, when I am too weak to hold my Bible, the verses come in my mind like food. I wish all my class would attend to it more, it's *after* they will want it."

Standing on the very edge of the world, to which so many cling, and for which so many live, Susan said of it, "This world! oh, it seems a very little thing to me now, just no more worth than this little room. I don't desire any more of it, the world is not worth living for. I would not give up my happiness, my hope, for worlds. My home is in heaven, and the Lord Jesus is *all* I want here or there."

December 22.—Her mother told the visitor that Susan sang a hymn in the night.

Susan.—"Yes, it was just as I woke the hymn came in my mind, 'I love my Jesus.' Always when I wake some text or hymn comes to my mind. I might have had trifling thoughts, but He sends me 'songs in the night.' And then I can't help singing, and it bears me up, and helps me to suffer the pain. I am very weak, dear teacher, but He holds me."

"Yes, Susan; and the hand that holds you is the pierced hand; it is the hand that will never loose yours; it is the hand from which none shall pluck you. As a poor old Scotch woman said, 'It's not my grip of Christ, but Christ's grip of me.'"

Her fellow-scholars often came to see Susan, bringing with them little kind presents. Many a lesson did they learn by that bedside, and very faithful was Susan's advice, especially to the careless ones. Referring to this, Susan said, "Mary and Ann were with me on Sunday, and they told me they had left the school. The Lord strengthened me to talk to them, and show them how wrong it was to give it up, and how much they could always be learning there. And I told them the comfort those Sunday lessons were to me *now*, and what I might have been without them."

Christmas-day came, and while Susan gladly remembered the good tidings echoing from Bethlehem, she rejoiced yet more in the hope of soon joining with angels and archangels, and all the company of heaven, in singing, "Glory to God in the highest."

To her teacher.—"This is my last Christmas-day, and it is the happiest I ever spent."

"Why, dear Susan?"

"I could not help crying for joy to think my next Christmas would be in heaven; that will be joyful, I shall be with Christ then. Oh, I would not give up this hope for worlds!"

From this time, Susan found much joy, as well as peace in believing. She was walking by the streams of that river which "makes glad the city of God."

Another day, Susan told her teacher of her increasing joy. "I was so happy all yesterday, Miss Ellen, I could scarcely contain myself. I was thinking of His love, the love of God in Christ, to me. Then I thought of a sermon your Papa preached on 1 John 4:16, 'And we have known and believed the love that God hath to us.' I have not forgotten it, though it was four years ago. The thoughts of God's love made me so happy, I wished the room was full of good Christians, that we might all be happy together, it seemed too much happiness to keep to myself."

Her mother said that Susan was suffering a great deal more now. Her answer was—

"Mother, dear, don't mind it so, I am quite willing to suffer this, and a great deal more, if He sees fit to send it me."

Teacher.—"I am glad, dear Susan, you are willing to suffer, rather than impatiently to wish to go."

Susan.—"I know it is all right and for a good purpose. He won't put on me more than I am able to bear."

Susan was too weak now to hold her Bible, but she would lay her thin hand on it, and ask all who came to read for her. The 8th chapter of the Romans and the 19th of St. John were her favourite passages. The good-bye whisper was often, "I am so happy—always happy now."

February 12.—A cold wintry day, with snow falling thickly. It was an effort for Susan's delicate teacher to brave the long walk through the storm, but she felt a strong impulse not to delay her visit. She found Susan very wearied and uncomfortable. Her teacher smoothed the tumbled pillows, and combed her tangled hair, and washed her face. This ministering refreshed poor Susan, who enjoyed being clean and neat, far more than her mother thought needful.

The teacher sat down by her now dying scholar, and as she wiped away the gathering death-drops on her face, she said—

"God shall wipe away all tears from your eyes, and it will be very soon now, dear Susan."

Susan.—"He will, He will. But my Saviour had no kind hand to do for Him what you have been doing for me. No one to do anything for Him as I have. I have pure water and nice things to refresh me, the Lord Jesus had none,—only that vinegar on the sponge."

Her teacher read to her, and they talked together of grace and glory. Long had she watched the fruits of grace springing up in her scholar's soul, and now the Holy Spirit had ripened them for glory. She lingered long by the bedside, it was not easy to loose the dying hand, that would never again hold hers so lovingly. But they parted, and Susan's last whisper, "Full of hope, dear teacher," seemed to give her a glance of the bright door just opening for her scholar.

That evening, the time came for Susan to rise on more than eagle's wings, and with glad flight to "mount up," even into His presence "with whom do live the spirits of them that depart hence in the Lord."

> "Then came a brighter season nigh
> When faith and hope shall cease,
> When love shall soar with eagle eye
> Above the splendours of the sky,
> To view Him face to face."
>
> Rev. J. East.

VIII.

FOUR VISITS TO MARY HART.

"And so, my dear lady, you would like to know something about poor Mary Hart. There must be a great many leaves in God's book, for I suppose there is a leaf for every child in His family. If I wrote the leaf of my life, it would be very blotted, but I like to think He writes it for me, and His hand wipes out the blots, and so it will be a clean page.

"I was always brought up in the fear of God, but it was the fear that kept me looking at a hedge of thorns. I lived with my aged grandmother. When I was about ten years old, she said it was time to shut the world out, and so she took to live in one little room, and said that I, her little Pollie, should wait on her. I wondered how grandmother was going to shut the world out, and was afraid she would keep the shutters up. I did not know then that the world was shut up in our hearts. Grandmother took to saying very long prayers, and I had to kneel by her quite upright all the time. It did not seem like coming close to a dear Father and telling Him just what I wanted, and just what I had done wrong, and then feeling glad He knew all; but I supposed grandmother wanted different things to what I, a little girl of ten years old did, and so the prayers did not seem long and hard to her. Afterwards, grandmother would open the large Bible on her round table, and I had to stand upright by her and read what the prayer-book put for every day. Then grandmother would shut her eyes such a long time; I supposed that was shutting the world out. I dared not stir, but oh, how naughty I felt. I longed that pussy would jump up on grandmother's knee, and that she might see how much happier pussy was playing about than her little Pollie, kneeling and standing so upright and so still.

"I cannot tell you all that happened to me, a great many leaves of my life won't open now. I am ninety-five years of age, and yet I am quite pure and hearty, and I am so happy, body, soul, and spirit. I have just had such a great blessing, my Lord has allowed me to sit at this little table, and He has given me sight to read two lovely chapters, the morning psalms, and a hymn. Oh, what a blessing! it's like meat and drink to me. The more I read, the more precious it is to me. I have no fear of Him now. I have got beyond the hedge of thorns, and am climbing the mountain to Zion's habitation, and He is guiding me. I can't kneel upright now as I did with grandmother, but my heart leans on Him, step to step.

"It is one and twenty years since I came to this nice room. It is a fine place, my dear, these almshouses. No more rent to think about, plenty of coals, found, and even warm blankets. Then I can have a nice bit of meat every day; and it is all from my heavenly Father. But I wonder sometimes, that almshouses are not built while the rich men are alive. I think it would please our Father better, if we did not keep the money in our purse till death comes, and makes us throw both purse and money away.

"I think it was in this room that the fear went out of my heart, and His love came flowing in like a river. It is a river, my dear, that never dries, it is always overflowing love. It was just in studying the Scriptures that His love and His light came. Every day brought me further from the hedge and nearer His arm. Yes, I knew what conversion of spirit was then. But it is the last ten years, that I have been with Him soul and body. I can't keep from Jesus a bit. Sometimes I ask myself, 'Is it wrong to be going to Him so often, to be calling so much on Him?' then that word comes, 'Call upon me; pour out your hearts before Him.'

"I am rather tired now, and if you will read me a chapter it will so rest me. But I want to tell you I am uncomfortable in not paying that penny a week to the missionaries; I had rather pay it, it is not much I can give to my dear Lord. Will you ask Miss Fanny to take to call again for it; besides I like her step on my floor, and the sun seems in her face, and she's always welcome to poor Mary Hart."

February 7.—"Is that you, my dear Miss H.? Well I have not been without thinking of you. It is so light this morning, I have been reading the Psalms and the lessons. How good my blessed Lord is to let me read, it makes me so happy, it is my great treasure. I was thinking how John in the vision had a book given him to eat, and though it was bitter at first it was so sweet after. So I read till I get to the honey; yes, it is sweet as honey to my throat, so smooth, so healing to every wound. On Saturdays I send for Mr. F. to find me the right Psalms and chapters for Sundays, for fear I have turned a leaf too much. I always look at the Epistle and Gospel too, because I know your dear father often chooses his text from something read at church. And then *I* seem to get a text, and it lasts me all the week.

"It is such joy when my dear Mr. Havergal comes to me, his prayers seem to lighten every load off me. He is like an earthly angel to me; ah, he does minister to me and many another.

"I have been trying to do without my nap after dinner, that I may have more time to read my dear Bible. My Saviour always comes with His word. Sometimes I feel a little dark, then I return to Jesus and he enlightens and enlivens me. He is with me, heart, soul, and body. It's glorious to feel this. Mine is a happy little home, for Jesus is with me, sleeping or waking. I go to bed at seven, but I don't go to sleep till after ten o'clock. That's my time for thinking of being with Jesus for ever. I seem to see it all, how I am laid in my shroud in my coffin, and then in the churchyard. Then I seem to see Jesus coming to take me to all my relations who are in glory, and I seem to see them led in green pastures and following the Lamb. Then I think how He will come down to the brink of the river for me too, and He will say, 'Poor Mary Hart, enter into the joy of thy Lord.' It won't be long perhaps—I seem to be in heaven every night, for the veil is not very dark between. Then I hear the church clock strike, and I up with my hands and think, 'One hour nearer my dear Saviour;' then He sends His dear sleep to my eyes. When I wake in the morning He is with me still. I am so happy, for my God is with me. I am just waiting for Him to call me. Sometimes I look at my windows, for the carriage wheels going by in the street make me think that *His* are long coming for me. And I say, 'Lord, pass not by this window, come in to poor Mary Hart, and take me away to sup with Thee in glory!' I often think I hear my Lord coming, even a rap at the door seems a token for me; when He does come, I shall like to open 'immediately.'

"I care less and less for the world, I find it is His love shuts it out of the heart. I used to like to sit at the window and look down the street, but never now. The world is so little to me, it is all like dross, now I have got the gold. You don't think I am deceiving myself, and that I could feel this joy if it was not His drawing me closer to Himself. Night and day it's nothing else with me but Jesus! it's all my cry, 'Come, Lord Jesus!'

"I think of Him as my all, He is in my all, and my all comes from Him. But though I am so joyful, I always come to Jesus as a sinner, ah, a lost sinner; I never let that slip. Sometimes Satan seems to rise against me, but I say, 'Get thee behind me, Satan,' and my Lord keeps him at a happy distance from me. I am happy, body, soul, and spirit, and soon I shall be for ever with my Lord.'

December 23.—"Who is it standing by my bed? my eyes are so dim, but I know your voice now. Blessings on you for coming to see poor Mary. I am still in the body, giving trouble to those who wait on me, but I am doing the work God has given me to finish. You wonder what work poor old useless Mary can do; my work is to wait patiently for my Saviour's call; just to lie here, till He comes for me. I am getting weaker and weaker. I have to ask when is it Sunday, and when is it Monday. I used to know when my happy Sundays came, I don't now, but it does not matter; it is all Sundays to me now.

"I can't read now, but I like to put my hand on my Bible and feel it near. And my Jesus is with me, heart, soul, and body. He is my support, my firm arm, that never gives way. I am so happy, I can only thank and thank Him.

"Will you read to me now? my ear is dull, but if I only get a word, I say, Ay, ay, that's mine, and it has been mine for years. I think you always choose me the sweetest texts, and they are mine and yours too.

"I like to feel your hand; let me hold it while you pray by me.

"Good-bye, and may God bless you. If we don't meet again here, the day will come when I shall come down the hill of Zion to meet you. And my Lord Jesus will be bringing you safe through the waters, safe from all the strife, and sin, and evil, and He will soon strip off you the last rags, and I shall see Him put the white robe on you. Ah, my dear, the Lord Jesus can do all this; that day will come, and 'He will do it.'"

December 27.—"I have had a long sleep. Have you sat by me long? You find poor Mary not gone yet; learning to wait the Lord's leisure. I am happier every day, for He lets me be happy. But it is His face I want to see; Himself, and no veil! He says to me, 'Wait my pleasure, wait my leisure, and at my holy time I will call for thee.' Sometimes I reflect if I do wrong in pressing to go; perhaps I should not say, 'Why tarriest Thou.' I, a poor, weak worm, not knowing what is right. But He knows all things—knows that I love Him. He won't have that down in His book against poor Mary Hart that she does not love Him. Dear Lamb of God! thou knowest that I love thee.

"I am very tired; the time will come when He will bathe our feet, and He will take a leaf from the tree of life; that's the plaister he is preparing for His pilgrim's tired feet. Ay, it is the Lamb in the midst of the throne will lead us, and we shan't be tired then.

"I want you to read the 22d chapter of Revelations—that's the sweetness.

"I often see it all pass before me. How I shall come to the river of Jordan to pass over; and then I seem to see that dear Lamb of God come down from Mount Zion, and His holy ones following Him like a flock. And they will come with Him to be ready to meet me, and they will all know poor Mary Hart's name, and will say, 'Come, come.'

"And then the Lord Jesus will come to my side of the river, to go through the waters with me; and then it will be glory, glory, for poor Mary Hart!"

IX.

EARLY FRUIT FROM AN IRISH SCHOOL.

HOW pleasant to watch a fruit-tree in the spring, covered with snowy blossoms. Some of the blossoms drop off and die away, but from others a tiny fruit springs. At first it is small, and green, and sour, but it is firmly in the branch. The life sap from the root flows even into that tiny fruit, and so it grows larger and larger. Many storms may shake the branch, and keen winds blow on it, but the fruit falls not; day after day the sun shines on it, till it becomes ripe and pleasant fruit—then the Master gathers it.

But many a child seems more like the blossom that falls, like the fruitless branch that withers away. There may be many blossoms in the Church that never yield living fruit in the Lord Jesus Christ. Unless the life sap of the Holy Spirit flows from the Lord Jesus into the heart, there will never be living branches, or ripened fruit.

The following is an account of three girls, who were indeed living branches, and so bore pleasant fruit.

They were brought up in one of the institutions, well known in Ireland as the Charter Schools. These schools are protected by Royal Charter, and give Protestant instruction and maintenance to many children, training them for service.

We must look back a few years, not into a schoolroom, but into a comfortable room at Celbridge Lodge. Lying on a bed, and looking very ill, is one of these—Mary M'Nally.

The kind friend who, for many years, taught at the school every Sunday evening, has given the orphan girl a home to die in. Sitting by her side is a delicate-looking girl Lucy Delamere. Mary has sent for her to speak to her schoolfellow about the Lord Jesus, knowing how precarious her health was. Another Charter School girl is standing by Eliza Lifford. She is there to wait upon Mary. Mary chose her because she could sing so well. Many were the hymns sung in that sick-room. Opposite Mary's bed a large printed text hangs, "My presence shall go with thee, and I will give thee rest;" and Mary could tell how near and bright that presence shone, how sweet to her that rest. Each of these three girls became ripened fruit. Of Mary M'Nally, her kind friend supplies the following remembrances.

"After Mary left the C—— school, she went into a situation in Dublin. Here the preaching of the Rev. M. Day was much blessed to her, and she clearly saw the way of salvation. From severe illness, she was obliged to leave, and knowing the kindness of her friends at the school, she came back to them.

The doctor advised her removal to the hospital in C——. In my visits to her there, I soon discovered she was one, indeed, taught of God. It was thought that she was then dying of consumption, but it pleased God to spare her a little longer, that her calm and cheerful piety might be better known among us to the praise of His own grace and glory. She became sufficiently well to assist herself, which she was always most anxious to do, having a sensitive reluctance of being burdensome to any one. The following autumn, she was again obliged to leave the service of Mrs. J——, of whose kindness she always most gratefully spoke. She returned to the school, till invited to come to my house, where she remained till her decease.

"It was a privilege to be with her and hear her testimony to the truth of all God's promises, and to witness in her the beauty and reality of true vital religion. May we follow her in the same path of simple confiding faith and trust in her God and Saviour, that we too may be cheered as she was, with the happy assurance of eternal glory in our dying moments.

"One night, a short time before her death, I found she had been suffering much from her cough and difficulty of breathing. She said, 'I have been so happy all day.' She was then much exhausted, but hearing her repeat something, I leaned down and heard her say, in a quiet solemn voice, 'Eye hath not seen, ear hath not heard, neither hath it entered into the heart of man to conceive the things which God hath prepared for them that love Him. No,' she continued, 'eye hath not seen; no, ear hath not heard; no, no, they cannot understand—the natural man receiveth it not, it is hid from them; but which God' (she added with great emphasis) '*hath* revealed unto us by His Spirit. Oh, yes, yes, He *hath* revealed it. Oh, that people did but know God in His real character, as revealed in Jesus Christ.'"

Mrs. H——, the housekeeper, who was most kind in waiting upon Mary, remembers many of her words.

One evening, some of the Charter school girls were standing round Mary. She said to them, "Seek the Lord Jesus while you are in health; oh, trust Him, and you will be safe. He will take care of you; see how richly He has provided for me. Don't put off seeking Jesus. I am tossed with pain and sickness, but then all my sins are laid on Jesus. I hope you will all prize Mr. S——'s Sunday evening class."

To Eliza Lifford she said, "I know you are a kind good-natured girl, but I want you to be more, I want you to find Christ."

Some of Mary's former fellow-servants from C—— House came to see her. When a servant there, Mary had even been a light-holder for Jesus. One of them, a German, wept over her, saying, "Oh, happy Mary, how I would like to feel like you!" Her answer was, "My Saviour will be your Saviour if you come to Him, He will not cast you out. But don't put it off—by His grace He led me early in life to seek Him. Remember, it is free grace that saves us; it is the freeness which makes the fulness." And then Mary put out her hands, as if she would show how He would encircle all who came to Him.

Mary's knowledge of Scripture was great, and whatever portion was begun to be repeated to her, she could always finish it. Even in her sleep she would repeat texts. She enjoyed singing, and among her favourite hymns were, "Jesus, lover of my soul," and "There is a fountain."

One morning she seemed very low. Mrs. H. said,

"You have had a bad night."

Mary. "Yes, I had a dark night, but Jesus is beyond the cloud."

Another day, Mrs. S. heard her coughing a good deal, and going to her, said,

"I am sorry to see you suffering so much."

She replied, "It is nothing, it is nothing; I have long intervals of rest, Jesus is very merciful to me. He had suffering, but I have mercy."

The last night came; she took hold of both Mrs. H.'s hands, saying, "This is the night that I am going to Jesus, lift up your heart for me." Almost her last words were, after taking a little water, "I shall soon be drinking of the water of life." She sank back—the ripened fruit was gathered, and Mary was safe in His garner above.

A fortnight before her death, she was arranging some little gifts of her books, when she told Mrs. H. she had six pounds in the savings' bank, which she wished given to the Charter School, as a testimony of the benefit she had received there. Premiums were given from this grateful bequest.

Of Lucy Delamere there is not much to tell. She was a very quiet girl. Mary often sent for her. She knew how sickly she was, and tried to lead her to know the Lord Jesus. Lucy was not ill long. She was nursed in the infirmary at the school. On Sunday evenings, after the class, Mr. S. visited her. Lucy never said a word, but she always listened attentively, and thanked him. Mr. S. particularly spoke to her of the necessity of reading the Scripture, with prayer for the Holy Spirit's teaching, and for self-application, not taking the promises generally, but for herself. As when reading the 53d of Isaiah, to say, "He was wounded for *my* transgressions, He was bruised for *my* iniquities."

After many visits, one Sunday evening, Mr. S. saw Lucy's countenance was so changed. It was beaming with joy. She exclaimed, "I am a brand plucked from the burning." Now I can say, "He was wounded for *my* transgressions, He was bruised for *my* iniquities."

Thus the Holy Spirit had taught Lucy the wonderful difference between *our* Saviour and *my* Saviour. Like Mary, Thomas, and St. Paul, she could now say, " My spirit hath rejoiced in

God *my* Saviour; *my* Lord and *my* God, Who loved *me*, and gave Himself for *me*."

Another promise of the Lord Jesus Lucy found quite true, "Your joy no man taketh from you." All who saw her noticed the glad look on her face. An old friend of the Institution went up to see her. He said, "Well, I have seen a sight to-day that well repays me for all the care and trouble I have given to the school. I went up into the infirmary, and there saw a happy, dying child, rejoicing in hope of the glory of God."

Other young visitors well remember her joyful look, and how she thanked them for the flowers they brought her.

The woman who nursed her remembered her with the greatest affection. She said of her—

"Lucy was a darlint to nurse. She was so even-tempered and gentle, just like a lamb, the crathur. An' she had such a thought for me, body and soul. Often she asked Miss B. to let me take a can of milk home for the childer. My poor jewel, it's one thing my eye never missed from her little table, an' that was her Bible, that never wanted the dust wiped off it. My darlint child knew I couldn't read, and that I wanted the good of the chapters as much as herself; and often she'd be saying so sweet and lovin'-like, 'Nurse, dear, let me read for you while I can.' You may think, my lady, I *don't* forget her. See, here's the keepsake she gave me, it's never left my pocket these long years. This was my lamb's little needlebook and thread case; it was lovely and clane when she gave it to me, but I liked the feel of it along with me always. These were her needles, and there's the ribbon, just as her bit of a hand left it. Oh, my dear child, how joyful she died. She is mouldering now; but if any one's soul is along with Christ, I'm sure it's Lucy honey's. I only wish I could die as *sure* as my sweet colleen did."

(The poor Nurse did die joyfully. She learnt to know and love Him, whom she called "My darlint Saviour, that spilt His heart's blood for me.")

Lucy did not linger long. Her joy was never taken from her. The young fruit was early ripened, and quickly gathered into that presence, where is "fulness of joy."

When Lucy was carried to the churchyard, her schoolfellows followed, and as they walked they sang, "When I can read my title clear," and other hymns, Eliza Lifford leading them.

When they came away from the graves of Mary and Lucy, they could not sing for tears. One verse might well be written there—

> "When from the dust of death I rise,
> To claim my mansion in the skies;
> E'en then shall this be all my plea,
> Jesus hath lived, hath died for *me*."

Some time after the death of Lucy, Eliza Lifford left the Charter School. She did not remain long in her situation. Then she tried to teach a little school, but that did not answer. She went to England, and nothing was heard of her for a long time. Illness came, and, being an orphan, there was no place but an hospital, and then the union, to be taken to. Now she grieved that she had not remained longer in her situations, and laid by a little. She wrote to her kind friends at the Lodge, and repeatedly had assistance.

The following letter was received by Mr. S. from a clerical visitor at the Union.

"When visiting the poorhouse hospital yesterday I promised one of the patients, Eliza Lifford, to let you know that she is drawing near the end of her earthly journey. She has a great desire to hear from you before she departs, or if you could see her.

"She is, and has been for a long and weary season, a great sufferer; but she is an example of faith and patience. My brother curate and myself have been deeply impressed with this, and are satisfied she is drawing supplies from the one only source of grace and strength," etc., etc. S. M. M.

In answer to this, a visitor went to find her out. It was not very easy to gain admittance, but at last the doors were all unlocked, and long stone steps led to the women's ward. What a bare, dreary looking place! rows of narrow beds and rows of pale miserable looking faces; sorrow and suffering seemed reigning there. The windows were high, nothing could they see, but the cold white walls. But they could not shut the sunshine out! that welcome visitor defies all bars.

The nurse pointed to one of the beds, saying, "That is Eliza Lifford." How changed, how emaciated, and yet a smile! She knew the visitor and burst into tears. It soothed her to be told that Mr. and Mrs. S. would soon come and see her. Then she poured out her lonely heart, that for four years had sorrowed on within those desolate walls.

"And shall I really see them again? Oh, then, the Lord has heard my prayers! I did not like to let them know where I was, but I did so long to hear their voice again. Mr. S. was a father to me, the fatherless; when I had no shelter he gave me one. It was there I waited on Mary M'Nally from our school. That time was like a little heaven below. It was hearing Mr. S. read chapters to Mary, and seeing her joy, that first made me think there was real comfort in religion. How I remember his reading the 12th of Hebrews, but I did not mind any of the promises then; now they are all so lovely to me. And then, a long time after that, when I was getting training lessons at the infant school, how kindly they supported me. Those were happy days, but my greatest treat was coming up to Miss F. H's little singing class in the drawing-room. That was music. We used to sing 'Jerusalem, my happy home,' and that's where I am fast going now. The doctors tell me, I am going as fast as I can, and I would not wish to be better or get well for all the world.

"I have found Him, I am in Christ. It is not long ago that I found Him—perhaps two or three years; it was not till He laid me low on a bed of pain. It was *in* His chastening that I found Him. 'Before I was afflicted I went astray.' I was wild and neglectful, I did not mind those lovely readings at the Charter School on Sunday evenings; since then I have longed to sit there again. Often I wished my school time was over, and fancied that I was too old to learn; oh, how foolish I was! And worse than that, I did not care to love and serve my Saviour. But,

"'Jesus sought me, when a stranger,
Wandering from the fold of God.'

"The Lord Jesus found me. I am washed and sanctified. I am going to Him; going to eternity, that *great rest*. I have not a fear, not a doubt.

"How kind of Mrs. S. to send me this nosegay of flowers, it's seldom flowers come into a ward. Lovely flowers! where I am going they don't want these.

"'There everlasting spring abides
And never-fading flowers.'"

And then her visitor begged she would tell her how she was, for not one word had she said about her evident sufferings, with her right arm quite useless and bound up in poultices.

Eliza.—"It is just like sores all over me; I think I am like Lazarus. There is not a bit of skin left on my back, and the hip bone is quite through. The knuckles of my hand are all raw too. I am a burden to myself and the poor woman that waits on me, for I cannot even turn. But it is all because He loves me, He is searching me in the furnace of affliction.

"It is four years since I came here, I think; but I hardly know how the time goes. All my books are gone but my dear Bible, the one Mr. S. gave me, that's on the shelf over my head. I can seldom turn a leaf to read, but the Holy Spirit brings many promises to my mind. How I wish I could just see Mr. and Mrs. S., and give them my blessing before I die. I do pray for them."

A month passed away, and again the visitor stood by Eliza, who said, "How good the Lord is to answer my prayers and send friends to see me. You are going over the Irish Sea, but I am going over the river of Jordan."

"And are you still suffering, Eliza?"

"Just the same; my sufferings are great, but then He is showing me miracles of His love. Oh, such love the Lord Jesus shows me! Is it not a miracle, filling me with His presence, so that there seems hardly room for an earthly friend to stand beside me? The ward looks desolate, but I am not; He comes so near me.

"I have seen dear Mr. S. since you were here. I tried to tell him of my neglect at the Charter School."

"Do you mean your neglect in learning the Scriptures, or your lessons, Eliza?"

"Oh, no! not neglect in head-learning. I got plenty of *head-premiums*, but it was heart neglect. I neglected His great salvation. It was not till I was laid on this hard bed of suffering, that I learnt God's Word in my heart. He put me in His school. But oh, I have learnt so little, and my mind seems so weak, I can't remember; often I can't even call a verse to mind. I was grieving over this to Mr. Shaw. He took my Bible and pointed out to me the promise in John 14:26: 'But the Comforter, which is the Holy Ghost, whom the Father will send in my name, He shall teach you all things and bring all things to your remembrance, whatsoever I have said unto you.'

"Since then, when I want a text, I ask the Holy Spirit to bring it to my mind, and He does. I never get any sleep but by the Word."

"What do you mean, Eliza?"

"You see, dear lady, sleep does not come natural to me, I am in such pain, and so restless, and so sore with my bones through the skin, I don't know how to lie. Then I ask the Holy Spirit to bring some verse to me, and He does, and then I put my hand under my poor back, and the verse composes me, and so I go to sleep on the Word. Last night my verse was Psalm 84:11, 'The Lord God is a sun and shield, the Lord will give grace and glory.' But I do so want teaching, I long for some one to come and teach me. There is some verse with 'needs be' in it. I have been trying to find it all the morning."

"It is in 1 Peter 1:6, Eliza. 'Though now for a season, if needs be, ye are in heaviness through manifold temptations.'"

Eliza.—"What does heaviness mean?"

"It means sorrow, being cast down, weighed down; a little child is called light-hearted, because it knows nothing of care or sorrow."

Eliza.—"Oh, I am just that. I am light-hearted; it's not heaviness, for my sins and sorrows are cast on Him. I never was so happy as I am now. I am hid in Christ; yes, I am in Christ."

Truly the fruit of the Spirit is "joy," "joy and peace in believing." It was a bright contrast to that dark foreground, the workhouse pallet, the hard bolster, the breakfast of dry bread and cold milk, the bare whitewashed walls, that unvarying horizon, the same pain, the same sores, the same unwilling attendance, the grudgingly given help, and yet amid all, a smile of joy, a hope which cast its anchor within the veil.

While the visitor was sitting by Eliza, two ladies came into the ward. Eliza said one of them was a new friend.

"For all the time I laid here only one lady ever came to see me, and she could not stay to read. It was reading and teaching I longed for, and so, because of my importunity, she asked this kind young lady to come and see me. Was it not an answer to prayer?"

Her friend came and sat down with them, and taking out her little Bible, said, "I will read you part of my morning chapter, Eliza, Exodus 17:5–7." And then there was searching into the hidden meaning of that smitten rock, that gushing water. "That rock was Christ." "The water that I shall give him shall be in him a well of water springing up into everlasting life." And when wilderness wanderings and wilderness thirstings are over, "The Lamb which is in the midst of the throne shall feed them and lead them unto living fountains of water."

After her friend was gone, Eliza spoke of the great attention and comfort she received from the ministrations of the chaplain, and another clergyman who came for him, Rev. S. M. M., and then Eliza asked her visitor to reach the hymn-book Mr. S. had lately brought her.

"Oh, how glad I was to get our hymn-book again, the same we sang from at the Charter School, the same I sang with Mary M'Nally and Lucy. Happy Sundays, happy class times, happy hymns; but it's all a shadow of what is coming!"

"I led the singing for years, but I *never* sang till now, that I cannot sing a note!"

A little while before the last shadows fled away, Eliza dictated this note to her kind friends at C. Lodge:

"I wish to return you my sincere and dying thanks and blessing for your kindness to me. I am most happy in my mind, and willing to depart this life when it will please the Lord to call me. I am still a great sufferer, but, thanks be to God, I believe my glass is nearly run. I had a letter from Miss H. about a month ago, which cheered my heart. The poor women in this ward do not forget to pray for her. I so enjoyed the tea you sent me, and it cheered their weak hearts too. I should be glad to know how my poor fellow-sufferer M. F. is, but I could not expect you to sit down and write to me. I do not forget Mr. S.'s last words to me. The Rev. Mr. M. is most kind and attentive to me, and gives me your kind assistance and messages. Kindest of friends, if possible, once more I would wish to see you. Wishing you all blessings, and many happy years, is the sincere prayer of your afflicted and humble servant, ELIZA LIFFORD."

A little while and one poor workhouse bed was empty, and one more came " to the spirits of just men made perfect."

And beneath the names of Mary, Lucy, and Eliza, may it now be written, "These were redeemed from among men, being the first-fruits unto God and to the Lamb."

X.

THE SISTER OF "A WISE AND HOLY CHILD."

(*Written for Children.*)

SOME years ago a memoir was published of "A Wise and Holy Child, or a short account of Elizabeth Edwards."[1] The children who read that book may like to hear about her sister Emma, and how she too obeyed the Saviour's call. Both dear sisters are now in glory, among the "spirits of the just made perfect." It would be a sweet and wonderful story if they could tell us about their home of joy and love, and we should like to listen to even the echo of the glad songs they hear, but now we can only look at the steps by which they reached it. They were young when the Lord Jesus called them to enter the narrow way which leadeth unto life. And the very same call comes to every child that has a Bible or a Bible teacher. You may think, "It is only my teacher who tells me to come to Jesus," but it is the Lord Jesus Himself who still speaks to you in His word, and

---

[1] Memoir of Elizabeth Edwards by Rev. W. H. Havergal, M.A.

says, "Strive to enter in at the strait gate. If you do not strive at once, every day will take you farther down the broad way that leads to destruction. Soon your heart will grow so deaf and hard, you will not hear the call of the Lord Jesus, or even wish to find that blessed way. Then, when it is too late, you will find you have missed the only safe road, and, though you may see the outside of the gate of the shining city, alas! it will be shut against you, and you will never enter in.

But it is not too late yet, and it may help you to begin that journey by hearing how the sister of the "Wise and Holy Child" did strive to enter in the strait gate, and how she found that wisdom's ways are pleasant, and all her paths are peace.

It is not very easy to talk to one's own pen and paper, so I will just make friends with the children who may read this, and think that I am talking to them about Emma Edwards. She was younger than Lizzie, a pretty child, with rosy face and dark blue eyes. If you had seen either of the two sweet sisters, you would have wished to know them. Emma's parents were not poor, and she had no hard work to do, though she was very useful in helping her mother in the shop.

Perhaps some of you do not like helping your mothers at all. Poor children are often very unwilling to get up in the morning when they are first called. They do not like learning to wash, and iron, and clean; they do not like learning to darn their father's stockings, or patch the little one's clothes. And ladies' children too are often quite cross if mamma asks them to do anything to help her; how seldom they *like* doing what she tells them, how seldom they say, "Can I help you, dear mamma?" Can we find a text in the Bible about doing what we don't like? Yes, here is one, "Children, obey your parents in all things." (Colossians 3:20.) "*All* things" must mean even those that you may not like doing at all. And of the children's great example it is said, "Even Christ pleased not Himself."

Emma's health was not very strong; she went to a good school, but the doctor said she must not learn many lessons. She also attended St. Nicholas' Sunday School. Her teacher loved her very much; she spoke of her as thoughtful and attentive, and her answers seemed to prove it. Still Emma did not care very much about religion, and her mother said, that though she was a dear good child to her, she wished she could see Emma caring more for her Bible and less about dress.

Emma deeply felt the death of her dear sister Lizzie, but four or five years had passed since then, and Emma was now nearly sixteen. Now, can you fancy yourself going with me to see Emma? for she is very ill. For many long weeks she has been suffering from some disease in the hip joint, which makes it agony to move. We shall find her home at the corner of a busy street, on the way to the station. We will pass through the shop, and now we are in the same room where I saw Lizzie die in her mother's arms. How very, very sad Emma looks as she lies on the sofa. Pain is not the secret of her sadness,—it is the thought of unforgiven sin and fear of death. For some time past poor Emma has been sorrowfully finding out, day by day, what a sinful heart she has. The doctor has told her mother she never can get well; Emma heard this, and her look of anguish was terrible indeed as she said, "I shall never, never go to heaven." Listen, now, as she says, "Oh, Miss H., what shall I do? I am so wicked, so sinful; I am not ready to die; indeed, I fear I shall go to hell."

Have you always felt so sinful, dear Emma?"

"Oh no, dear Miss H., for years I have never thought or really cared about it, but it is some weeks now that I have seen myself so sinful."

"And left to yourself, dear Emma, you never would have cared about it, but have slept on in sin and danger. Now, I do trust that it is God the Holy Spirit who is convincing you of your sin, and teaching you that your 'heart is deceitful above all things, and desperately wicked.'"

Emma.—"I find it is worse to bear sin than all my pain; often I lie awake in the night, crying and vexing about it."

"It is this burden of sin that the Lord Jesus bears away. Look back at Calvary, and 'behold the Lamb of God which taketh away the sin of the world.' It is *done*, dear child, 'the Lord *hath* laid on Him the iniquity of us all.' You are looking at your sin instead of looking at Him 'who was made sin for us, that we might be made the righteousness of God in Him.' It is such a blessed exchange, Emma, *your* sin was given to Jesus, and He will give you *His* righteousness. Then, in that righteousness, you are all fair and clean. Take your Bible, dear child, and let us find some of his own words. We will read 2 Corinthians 5:15–21. What comfort in the 18th verse, 'Who *hath* reconciled us to Himself by Jesus Christ.'"

Many such visits were paid to Emma, and still she spoke of sin as a heavy burden. Long ago the Lord Jesus had invited all who were weary and heavy laden to come to Him. There is no load so heavy as unforgiven sin. If we have not faith to see it cast into the depths of Christ's blood, it will, and must, cast us into the bottomless depths of fire everlasting. Poor Emma! she had not yet come to the Lord Jesus; but He saw her crying about her naughty heart, and, though she seemed to get no farther towards Him, He came nearer and nearer to her. And the very same promise that made so many glad in Judea and Galilee long ago, was soon to comfort Emma too.

My dear father often called to see Emma. Her mother said she would watch for his quick step, and longed for the time of his visits to come. Emma, especially, prized his Sunday evening visits on his way home from preaching at St. Nicholas. Once, when he was sent for after church to another invalid, she would not go to bed, but lay watching for him till after ten o'clock, knowing he never forgot to come.

For a long time Emma was "asking and seeking, and knocking." We do not always know exactly when we first find the Lord Jesus; we do not always see the gate of mercy opened. But Emma did; and it pleased the Lord Jesus to comfort her all at once. Just as He quickly said to the woman, who stood at His feet behind Him, weeping, "Thy sins are forgiven."

One Sunday in August Emma was in greater distress than ever. During the whole day she was in agony of mind. She told her mother it really seemed "as if Satan were trying to get hold of her, that she was going to hell, and that her sins deserved it." Her mother sent to tell my dear father of her distress. It was evening, the church bells were chiming, and the sweet sound was heard in the room of that weeping child. But in the courts above there was sweeter music still, even the joy of angels over one lost lamb found by the Shepherd. The Lord Jesus was even then drawing near to take poor Emma in His Shepherd-arm, and on His bosom to wipe away those sad tears, and turn her mourning into joy.

There were footsteps on Emma's staircase, the feet of one that brought "good tidings of peace." Her kind pastor stood by her, and was told her dark distress. With his gentle voice he repeated the words of Jesus, "Come unto me, all ye that labour, and are heavy laden, and I will give you rest." Then he knelt and prayed a long time, that she might *then* by faith "behold the Lamb of God, which taketh away the sin of the world," that she might *then* see the burden of her sin was laid on Him who was made sin for us. It was the prayer of faith, and, "while they were yet speaking," God heard and answered it. The Holy Spirit opened Emma's eye to look at Jesus, "wounded for her transgressions, bruised for her iniquities." And so the fearful weight was gone. She saw her sin laid upon Jesus, and believing, she rejoiced. Her kind pastor left her rejoicing in God her Saviour.

All this passed before church time. After the service we met her sister Leah, who said, "Do come and see Emma; she has been talking to us so sweetly, ever since Mr. H. left her. I never saw her so happy before, for she has been in such trouble of mind, quite despairing of ever going to heaven."

We found dear Emma altered indeed. A smile of peace was there; the sad look gone, and her eyes shone with a new gladness. As I leant to kiss her, she said—

"Oh, dear Miss H., I want to tell you all. You know how long I have felt such a sinner, and no hope that I should go to heaven. Now I do believe He has washed me from all my sins in His own blood. You often said those words to me, 'Him that cometh to me, I will in no wise cast out.' Now, I believe them. Yes, Jesus has helped me to come to Him; oh, it is so sweet to find Him."

"My sister E. is waiting below. Shall she come up stairs, Emma; she would like to see you?"

Emma.—"Oh, yes. I can speak to everybody now, and tell them I have found Jesus."

In replying to my sister, Emma said—

"Satan has been tempting me so, and to-day worse than ever, like the roaring lion ready to devour me. Oh, it is such agony when you feel as I have done, sinking into hell to be lost for ever. But while your dear Papa was praying with me all these fears went away; it seemed as if the Holy Spirit helped me to look at the Lord Jesus, and for the first time I saw that He died for my sins, and that His precious blood washed them all away."

"Do you wish to get better now, Emma?"

"Oh, no; I would not stay for all the world when the Lord Jesus comes for me. It will be all over then; all my sin and crying and pain gone—rest with Jesus for ever."

Her sister and friends were in the room, for she had been so ill and exhausted, she was thought dying.

Emma turned to them, saying, "Dear sisters, I want you to seek the Lord Jesus while you are in health. It will be a hard bed when you come to die, if you have not found Jesus."

We said good night to Emma, and promised to come again.

Emma.—"But perhaps I shall be seeing the Lord Jesus before then. I do hope He will come for me to-night."

But she was yet to wait for His coming "a little while," and show forth the praises of Him who had "called her out of darkness into His marvellous light." We will now try and tell you how Emma followed the Lord Jesus, through much pain and suffering, in patience, humility, and love. In patience. Only think what it must be to lie still for ten long months. It is not so bad to lie in bed if you can move about in it; but poor Emma had to bear sharp pain, and yet never move at all. No one knew till after her death how much she suffered, and how full she was of inward disease and sore wounds. She got very thin, so that the bones came through her skin, and yet she never fretted, but was patient still. Then she had leeches and blisters and medicine, and the noisy street made her head ache. Nor could she amuse herself with books or work, it seemed as if she could do nothing but bear the pain. Sometimes, when a little easier, Emma would thankfully say, "Oh, mother, thank God for this ease; what a mercy to be without pain for five minutes." Often her patient moan made her mother sad.

Dear children, how seldom you thank God for being well. For weeks and months and even years you do not know what five minutes pain is, and yet you do not really thank Him. And when in church we thank God for "our preservation, and all the blessings of this life," you are sleepy or talking, or letting your thoughts wander, and so you do not thank Him. Then when pain does come, how fretful and impatient you feel. And

Emma could not have been so uncomplaining, had not God the Holy Spirit taught her to be "patient in tribulations."

Emma also followed the Lord Jesus in humility. She remembered many of her past faults, and spoke very humbly of them. When the church bells chimed she would say, "Oh, mother! how very differently I should go to church now if I could. How differently I should try and pray there now, instead of thinking, as I used to, about other things, and how I should listen if I could only hear one more sermon!"

Emma had been fond of dress. She said that before she was ill, her clergyman met her and said, "Emma, don't love your bonnet and new dress too much, think more about the robe of righteousness your soul wants." Emma said, "I felt vexed with Mr. H. for saying this to me then, but now, these poor soiled sheets are more beautiful to me to lie in and know that Jesus loves me, than to wear the finest clothes I ever had."

Dear children, are you a little fond of smart dress, instead of choosing that which is neat and good, and according to that station of life in which it has pleased God to call you? The Lord Jesus said, "Take no thought, what you shall put on;" that is, no anxious thought—no trying to be finer than you can afford. Does that girl take "no thought," who teazes her mother to buy gay flowers for her bonnet, feathers for her hat, or some smart frock, that will not wash and wear? Would you like it to be thought of you, what I heard an old woman say to a girl, who had got scarlet flowers for the first time, "Why, child, you look as if your head was all a-fire!" In the Sunday school that Emma attended, both lady teachers and children observed the rule, "No feathers or flowers allowed." Let all children (and teachers too) choose for their pattern the lily of the valley, that neat hiding flower, that bends away from our gaze beneath its green leaves.

"Pretty lilies seem to be
Emblems of humility."

Another fruit of the Spirit which now ripened in Emma was love—love to God and love to those around her. Shall we listen to what she said one day to her mother as she kissed her? "Dear, dear mother, you have been a good mother to me, and I love you dearly, but now there is One I love better than all the world besides; yes, better than even you, dear mother!"

"Yes, my dear child, is it not Jesus you love best?"

Emma.—"Yes, it is Jesus, He is dearer to me than all the world besides."

When asked if she were happy, Emma said, "Yes, but I want to be happier still, for I want to love Jesus more and more."

She very much liked a hymn written by a clergyman, the Rev. Abdool-Messeeh. He had been a Mohammedan, and was converted to Christianity through the Rev. H. Martyn at Cawnpore. He sang it just before he died.

"Beloved Saviour, let not me
In Thy kind heart forgotten be.
Of all that decks the field or bower,
Thou art the fairest, sweetest flower.

"Youth's morn has fled, old age comes on,
But sin distracts my soul alone;
Beloved Saviour, let not me
In Thy kind heart forgotten be."

And now, Emma loved the people of God. She asked her mother not to let many friends come to see her, for she would rather talk to those who knew Christ.

Emma often said how much she loved her kind clergyman, Mr. Havergal and valued his visits. Once, while she seemed insensible, he stood by her for some time, and at length gently said, "Do you know me, Emma?" She opened her eyes and said, "Oh, yes! I shall always know *you*." She would fix her eyes on him and drink in all his words, often saying to her mother, when he was gone, "There is no one like Mr. H. I do love him so, and he always knows how to comfort me and what to pray for."

Her love for her mother was very great. Often in her pain, her cry would be, "My dear, dear, good mother, I love you so dearly!" Emma always seemed sorry to give her mother trouble in waiting on her, and would often beg her to lie down and take some rest. To her sisters, she was very affectionate and gentle, thanking them for all they did for her.

She also tried to show her love by thinking of and praying for missionaries toiling for God in distant lands. She had a missionary box, and would ask for it to be brought to her bedside, that she might slip some pence in, saying, "O mother, how often I forgot my missionary box when I was well; will God accept this from me now? I was a naughty girl to forget the poor heathen. Mother, you will keep my box, let it stand on the shelf when I am gone, and put a good many pennies in."

It was pleasant, also, to see Emma's thankfulness. When she felt a little better, she would say, "Thank God, thank God." When very thirsty, she would not drink till she had said, "Thank God for giving me this." Flowers always pleased her. I remember seeing her take out all the white flowers from a fresh nosegay, saying, "How white, how white! But I shall be whiter still some day, and never fade away like these flowers, when I have put on the robe washed white in the blood of the Lamb." This reminds me of some verses written by my father about flowers.

"Children, while you gather flowers,
Think how fleeting are your hours;
Think again, in Eden's bowers,
You may cull unfading flowers.

"Jesus is the sweetest flower;
　Give to Him each passing hour;
　He will then, in heavenly bower,
　Make you each His fadeless flower."
　　　　　　　　　　　　W. H. H.

Some weeks had passed away since that happy Sunday in August. Emma's fear and sadness had never once come back. She was now "looking unto Jesus." Looking at what He had done for her on Calvary, and looking at what He was doing for her at God's right hand. And those who look at the Lord Jesus will meet His eye looking down on them. She knew that He looked with pity on her pain. Looking, that He might guide her with His eye, and guard her from the Evil One. Looking on her with the light of His countenance, with the smile of His love. One evening, my father returned from visiting her, and said, "I have been seeing Emma Edwards. My visits there are always pleasant. Dear child, it seems with her that 'at evening time it shall be light.' In her little heart there seems waking up such peace and joy, like this beautiful sunset. Just now she has been saying to me, 'The Lord is very gracious to me. Last night I was in much dreadful pain, but Jesus seemed to whisper to me, Peace, peace, I am with thee.' She is suffering much with distressing oppression on her breath, and she told me she felt a great dread of being choked, and dying in a struggle for breath. But though she may suffer such paroxysms, they generally subside, and I told Emma I thought it would be God's will that she should die gently, just like her dear sister Lizzie."

There was one young visitor whom Emma loved very much. I cannot tell you much of what she used to say to her. But two or three days before Emma died, she took her hand and held it, saying, "Oh, Miss F., I am so very happy, so very happy! He is such a kind Jesus. I can hardly speak, yet it seems as if I could not be silent. I must tell you how kind and loving the Lord Jesus is to me. It seems such a wonder I should ever be saved, but He is such a kind Jesus, able to save even me. He has taken away all my fear of going to hell, and all my sad thoughts. I am quite sure now that He died for me, and that I am going to Him very soon." Emma's weary eyes closed, and she dozed a little while, still dreamily repeating, "Going to Him for ever,—to be—with Him,—how—how beautiful."

When she awoke, her watching friend kissed her sweet face. Emma took her hand again, saying, "I do love you very much, Miss Fanny. I wish you were coming to heaven with me now. I have always loved you, and I do not like leaving you behind, but you will come by and by. I am sure that Jesus loves us both." And then Emma whispered, "I was so very ill all last Saturday night, but it seemed as if the Lord Jesus came to me and made me so happy. And ever since He has kept me in perfect peace. He won't leave me again." F. then asked her what chapter she would like read. Emma chose the 14th chapter of St. John. Every verse seemed sweeter than honey to her, and she kept saying, "Oh that *is* sweet. Isn't that beautiful? Is not Jesus kind to leave such words for me?" Emma also spoke of the great dread she had felt of being choked when death came, adding, "But dear Mr. H. told me that I need not fear, for he thought I should die very gently; like my own sister Lizzie died on mother's lap, whist he was kneeling by her. I think the Lord must have put it into his heart to tell me so, for it gave me such comfort, and I have felt quite easy about dying ever since. I see now it will be like going to sleep—sleeping in Jesus."

Over and over again Emma said, "God bless you, dear Miss Fanny, I do love you so. Good-bye."

Emma's journey was nearly over. There was only one valley to pass through, and then she would reach the hill of Zion. We can watch her walking through the valley, but we cannot see her glad ascending of that holy hill, where now she rests for ever.

Sometimes the valley of death is very dark, and sometimes it is a lighted one, with only a soft shade resting on it. Just as if you were going to some beautiful mountain, you would have to pass through the valley first. If you set out early enough to reach it in daylight, the mountain would only softly shade the valley from the bright sunshine. But if you put off setting out, and so get to the valley at night, it would be a dark dark valley, with no light to show the way. There was a Sunday scholar who put off this journey to the beautiful hill of Zion. She was careless at school, whispering at church, and disobedient at home to her mother. Her teacher often begged her to follow the Lord Jesus Christ, and hear His kind voice, "Enter ye in at the strait gate." But still she walked on in the broad way of darkness and sin. So that dark walk brought her to the valley of death at night-time. Poor Ann! I stood by her bedside, and when her mother begged her to drink the medicine or she would die, she put her hands to her mouth and said, "I shan't." And then I saw her trembling with fear, so frightened to die. We begged her to pray to Jesus, but she said, "No! I don't want to pray, it is too late now." Nor would she listen to any reading of the Bible. The last words poor Ann kept saying were, "It is so dark, so dark; mother, mother, I am dying, and it's all dark; oh! I am going into the darkness!"

Oh, my children, will you, too, risk living in darkness, and dying in darkness? Will you risk putting off entering the narrow way? Will you risk getting to the valley of death, with no light to see the Shepherd-hand of Jesus; no ear to hear His voice saying, "Fear not, for I am with thee?" Will you risk seeing the dark, yet ever-burning pit opening for you at the end of the valley? Will you risk hearing Satan's lion-roar sounding nearer and nearer? Will you risk feeling, "It is too late to pray; I am lost for ever!" and then find yourself cast into outer darkness?

Jesus said, "I am the light of the world: he that followeth me shall not walk in darkness, but shall have the light of life." (John 8:12.) "Walk while ye have the light, lest darkness come upon you: for he that walketh in darkness knoweth not whither he goeth. While ye have light, believe in the light, that ye may be the children of light." (John 12:35, 36.)

When dear Emma reached this valley it was light. She was a child of light by closely following the Lord Jesus, the true, the only Light. He had Himself passed through this same valley of death. He found it dark, for there all the heavy clouds of our sin hid the light of His Father's countenance from Him. But as He there took all our sins away, so all the darkness passed away with them, and now His sin-forgiven children find it a lighted valley. Emma often said, "I fear no evil, for Thou art with me." "My heart and my flesh faileth me, but God is the strength of my heart and my portion for ever." For many hours she lay dying, suffering much from convulsive pain, and struggles for breath, But still she smiled sweetly, and would just whisper, "Happy, so happy."

> "Do you ask me for pleasure?
>   Come, lean on His breast,
> For there the sin-laden
>   And weary find rest.
> In the valley of death
>   You shall triumphing cry,
> If this be called dying,
>   How pleasant to die!"
> —M'Cheyne.

Very often she said, "Come, Lord Jesus, come quickly." She longed to be with Him, not that she might be out of her pain, but that she might be rid of sin, and see Him she loved face to face. If some one is coming to see you that you love very much indeed, do you not ask, "What time will he come?" and will you not run to the gate, or look out of the window, to see if the carriage is in sight? Just so. Emma longed to see Him whom, having not seen, she loved, and she knew, too, that He was coming to fetch her to His own glad home, to stay with Him for ever. Her mother told me it was wonderful to hear how many hymns and texts she repeated. One which her dear pastor, Mr. Havergal, said to her, was often on her lips—

> "Begone unbelief, my Saviour is near,
> And for my relief will surely appear."

The last verse she said very often—

> "Though painful at present,
> 'Twill cease before long;
> And then, oh how pleasant
> The conqueror's song."

Shall Emma tell you what she found the Lord Jesus to be to her then? "Oh! He is such a *kind* Jesus, *so* kind, and then He is *my* kind Jesus!" And when Emma said this, she was in great bodily misery, all earthly kindness was nothing to her; even her kind mother could not help her now, and often she went out of the room, because she could not bear to see her darling child in such agony. But her "kind Jesus" was drawing nearer and nearer, and His Spirit brought words of comfort from His written word to her mind. And the same hand, which long ago He had held open for the nails to be put in, and did not draw it back, was now holding Emma safely. "Neither shall any man pluck them out of my hand." (John 10:28.)

Her mother saw that Emma was just going to leave her, and she whispered—

"My dearest child, are you happy?"

"Oh yes, mother dear, I only wish I had breath to tell you *how* happy I am."

After kissing her mother, she put her hands together, saying, "Happy, happy for ever—for ever with my kind Jesus!" Then she tried to say the verse—

> "Though painful at present,
> 'Twill cease before long;
> And then, oh, how pleasant,
> The——."

But she did not finish that line, for she was really just going to begin that "conqueror's song," that would never end, to Him who had loved her, and had given her the victory. A few quiet breathings, one last smile, and Emma's spirit went away with that "kind Jesus," who would present her faultless before His Father's throne with exceeding joy.

May we not think of these two dear sisters, Lizzie and Emma, that they are together now among the spirits of the just made perfect, that together they behold His glory, that together they see their "kind, kind Jesus?"

Dear children, are you wishing to die like Emma and Lizzie, and be with them in heaven? Are you wishing you too could say, "My kind Jesus?" Then pray that God the Holy Spirit will teach you the first lesson Emma learnt, "I have sinned, I am lost and helpless." Perhaps you have never felt at all unhappy, never felt yourself to be a sinful child, never felt you were going to hell, as Emma did. This shows you that your soul is dead, asleep, and in great danger. A dead child cannot feel; a sleeping child sees not the flames round its curtains. Will you not listen to the kind voice of Jesus, *calling* you once more ere you wake in hell for ever? "Awake thou that sleepest, and arise from the dead, and Christ shall give thee light." (Ephesians 5:14.)

Do cry as Emma did, "Create in me a clean heart, O God." Do ask and seek and knock as she did, that God will give you His Holy Spirit to open your eyes to "behold the Lamb of God which taketh away the sin of the world." Then you will learn the same sweet lessons Emma did. You will *know* that the Lord Jesus has washed you in His precious blood. You will be quite sure that He loved you, and gave Himself for you. And you, too, will find out, as Emma did, how kind the Lord Jesus is. Every morning all your mercies will seem to drop out of His kind hand. As you walk along you will see His love in every bud and flower, and when you look at the far off blue sky you will think "There is my kind, kind Jesus." And then, too, you will feel that the Lord Jesus is always quite near to you; you shall find Him kind in watching you and keeping you from sin and Satan—kind in settling every thing that happens to you all through life—kind in drawing your heart nearer and nearer to His own, and showing you His everlasting loving-kindness—kind in teaching you to know His voice, speaking to you by His Spirit in the word. In the valley of death you will find Him, your kind Shepherd, coming very near, and saying, "Fear not, for I am with thee." And then what will it be *really* to see Him, and, amidst the songs and hallelujahs of heaven, to hear His own voice say, "It is I, your kind, kind Jesus!"

XI.

VISITS TO MEN.

WE have not many of these to record. A few stray gleanings from the deathbeds of those who are now in joy and felicity.

Among the occupants of Taylor's Lane Almshouses was Benbow Jones. He was a very happy old man, his lips overflowing with the grace of the present and the glory of the future.

He was fast sinking, or rather fast rising, to his rest. Asking him what he thought of Christ now, his answer was, "Precious, precious, precious! His boundless love fills my soul with joy unspeakable. I cannot utter the peace that pervades my soul. Here I am, waiting for His salvation. It's fifty or sixty years that I have known Him, and He will never, never leave me. He does not even let Satan buffet me. Let me tell you to keep close to Jesus; to whom else could you go? O precious Saviour! all Thy promises I have found to be Yea and Amen." His last Sunday came, he lay peacefully all the day, often saying, "How glorious, how glorious?" His last words were, "Riches, riches, riches!"

"Hath not God chosen the poor of this world rich in faith, and heirs of the Kingdom which he hath promised to them that love him?"

William Franklyn died in the Lord, aged sixty-six. The following dream is copied from his own writing. It happened when he was a young man, with no serious thoughts.

"I dreamt that Satan in human shape presented himself to me, and persuaded me to make away with my life. While thinking how I should put an end to myself, I looked on the right hand, and saw the Saviour clothed in white raiment. In an instant many precious promises of the Bible, which I had heedlessly learnt, seemed poured into my mind. Then I saw the glories of heaven, the company of angels, and I seemed to feast upon the glorious sight. It was as though I was out of the body, and the enjoyment, which I felt in that short space of time, seemed enough to repay me for all the sufferings of a lifetime. Then I seemed to return from this glorious sight to where Satan was still waiting for me. But during that time so much of the Bible seemed revealed to my mind that I was armed to reply to all that Satan said, and he had no power against me. He was in a great rage, and then showed me who he was. I saw on his left hand the bottomless pit, where was a great company, and their cries were beyond all I had ever imagined of torment and misery. I saw many whom I formerly knew. Satan left me, and I woke."

It was only a dream, but it had the effect of leading him to study the "more sure word" of God, and henceforth he followed Christ. He used to call his bedroom "my study, for here I study for heaven." His Bible was well-worn. He carefully listened to the sermons at St. Nicholas, and told me, "It is wonderful how they all come back to my mind in the week. Your father's preaching takes me into the depths of God's Word."

The quiet attentive worshipper was missed from his seat in church one Sunday, for he was called to "dwell in the house of the Lord for ever."

John Packman.

"Good morning, John; you look very ill to-day."

"Yes, Miss, I am weaker in body, but then I've no fear. My heart feels warm with the love of Christ. Sometimes, Miss, I wish I had more evidence that I am His child."

"The evidence is in His Word, John. You have just said that you love the Lord Jesus Christ, and here, in 1 John 4:19, it says, 'We love Him, because He first loved us.' Listen to this hymn—

"'And when I'm to die,
Receive me I'll cry;
For Jesus hath loved me,
I cannot tell why.'"

John.—"That is sweet; would you write it down for me, please. Perhaps it's selfish to want more evidence in myself, it would take the credit from Christ."

"You are right, John, all the credit and all the glory of our salvation belongs to the Lord Jesus alone."

"Could you please to tell me, Miss, what happens when the soul leaves the body? I've been thinking much about it."

"We will look in your Bible, John. The Lord Jesus said to the dying thief, 'To-day shalt thou be with me in paradise.' When Stephen was dying he saw the Lord Jesus, and cried, 'Lord Jesus, receive my spirit.' And St. Paul writes, 'Having a desire to depart and be with Christ, which is far better.' From these three verses we learn that the spirit is immediately received into the presence of the Lord Jesus, and that it is a conscious state of happiness, for it is 'far better.' If we love any one very much, it is just seeing them, consciously being with them, that we long for; and *the* joy of heaven is, that we 'shall be for ever with the Lord.'"

He turned to his young wife and little ones, saying, "These are my last care, but I can leave them all to God, He will provide."

John greatly valued my dear father's visits. How he felt his absence and illness shall be told from my dear mother's note-book:—

"While his people all rejoiced at his return, none so welcomed him as the sick. I remember John Packman's saying how he had prayed to be spared to see his dear minister again on earth, adding 'Then I could die happy.' He was spared, and cried with joy on his first visit, saying, 'Now my prayer is answered. I believe the Lord will soon call me home.' John said he wanted to thank him for all he had taught him, and to tell him that he had brought him to Christ. At this time my dear husband was very far from well, and it was with the greatest risk that he went in a fly to see him. On the second visit John sent for all his relatives to come upstairs. He spoke earnestly and faithfully to them, telling them to listen to Mr. H.'s warnings in time, and not wait till sickness came. He then asked his minister if he thought he could live many hours, or if he might die before he could visit him again. He told him that most likely he would die before the morning light, and so it proved. When prayer was going to be offered, seeing that his father and brother would not stir, John said, 'Kneel; oh, do kneel, and pray now.' As Mr. H. left the room John lifted up his hands, blessing him, and cautioning all to listen to and follow him, for he was a holy man of God, and none like him.

"Some time after John's happy death, his grateful wife told what otherwise we should never have known. She said that Mr. Havergal noticed that her husband seemed to have some trouble on his mind, but could not find out what it was. 'When we came downstairs Mr. H. asked me what John's trouble was. I showed him a heavy coal bill unpaid, that lay like a weight on John's mind. Mr. H. took and wrote his name on it, and said that he would pay it clear off. He went away. I ran up to show John, and when he saw 'W. H. H.' on the bill, he said, 'That is a God-sent thought, that was my last trouble; God bless that righteous man.' From that time I never heard him say anything but 'I shall soon reach my long and happy rest,' and 'Patience, heaven! patience, heaven!' It was just as Mr. H. said, he went to his rest before daylight came, saying, 'Lord Jesus, receive my spirit.'"

"Mr. Hill the Churchman."

This was the well-known name of the beadle of St. Nicholas Church some years ago. He was a remarkably handsome old man, and in his official costume of scarlet and black velvets was quite a picture. An artist's sketch of him still hangs in my father's study.

The outline of his consistent life shall be taken from part of the sermon preached the Sunday after his death, May 12, 1850, by Rev. W. H. Havergal. Psalm 84:10, "I had rather be a doorkeeper in the house of my God, than to dwell in the tents of wickedness."

"What the original speaker of these words was willing to be, Richard Hill was. For thirty years he was the doorkeeper of this house of God. He loved his office, because he loved his God. He was respected in it, and was a goodly ornament to it, for he was not only a handsome old man, but a good old man, and an everlasting instrument of good to many in this parish. A week ago he ended his office, and was taken, I doubt not, to a higher office in the better Temple above. There was nothing very extraordinary in the character of our venerable beadle, neither would I represent it as perfect. But there is enough in it to warrant his minister testifying his respect for him, and to present some parts of his character as eminently worthy of the imitation of you and of me. It is plain that a genuine love for the house of God must be grounded on a genuine love for God Himself, as well as every ordinance of His house, which is intended to draw us to Him, to make us like Him, and to comfort us in Him. Such love to God, and consequently such love to His house, was for many years the prevailing affection of our late beadle. It was, too, in this very house of God that the lamp of that affection was first, consciously to himself, kindled in his heart. The short-lived ministry of that excellent and venerated servant of Christ, the Rev. John Greig, was, as he told me, the means of arousing him to a sense of sin, and to a knowledge of the Saviour. But though he always attributed his spiritual conversion to the agency of Mr. Greig's preaching, he has frequently told me that, after Mr. Greig's death, he grew careless. He recollected many things to lament in his walk and conversation.

"It is plain from our text that the Psalmist, who was willing to be a doorkeeper in the house of his God, was not only a man of a loving heart, but of an humble spirit. He not only loved God as his God, but felt that it would be an honour and blessedness to serve Him in even the meanest capacity. He would rather be a doorkeeper in His house than excluded from it. Unless we feel a covenant interest in God, as our God in Christ Jesus the Saviour, we never shall have the heart to say what the Psalmist did. Think of a king being willing to leave his throne, and turn porter to the tabernacle, rather than never attend the tabernacle at all. Have we the faith, the love, the humility of the Psalmist? Eminently indeed is an humble spirit requisite for acceptable worship in the house of God. They whom He chooses, and causes to approach unto Him, are they who feel their infinite unworthiness of Him, and, as to their original position, their immeasurable distance from Him. 'To this man will I look, even to him that is poor and of a contrite spirit, and trembleth at my word.' (Isaiah 66:2.)

"To our late beadle it was, of course, no humiliation to fill the office which he held, honourably to himself, and usefully to the parish. It appears that, on the erection of the galleries, Richard Hill was in a temporary way appointed to superintend admission to them. This was before 1820. He was then, and had been for some years, one of the watchmen of the parish. At the beginning of that year he was violently assaulted by a party of ruffians, who all but deprived him of life. Compensation was made to him by the parish. In consequence of what he suffered in the service of the parish, and from being considered in every respect a fit and proper person, he was in 1820 appointed beadle of this church. From all that I can hear it has seldom been the lot of a man in his standing to be so generally approved and respected as he has been. He was a peaceful neighbour, and a pattern of a husband. All his fellow officials, too, very highly esteemed him.

"My friends, you who, in the providence of God, are called to perform duties of service, no matter of what degree, how honourable to the character of a man is it, for such things as these to be said of him when he ends his service, or ends his days! But what is of far greater consequence, how honourable is it to the religion of that God who has given him grace to persevere in well-doing unto the end. It matters little what is the state of life in which it pleases God to call us, so that we do but glorify Him in it. Adorning the doctrine of God our Saviour in all things, is said of servants especially, and not of Christians generally, as is frequently quoted from Titus 2:9, 10.

But here I would acknowledge for him that he was fully sensible of many deficiencies and errors in himself. I have heard him complain of being too apt to mind others, without duly minding himself. To one individual, who said to him, when hearing a similar complaint, 'But, Hill, did you not love your Bible, and love going to church?' he replied, 'Oh, yes, but I did not make it my business. I always loved my church, and for these forty years have regularly attended it; but then, when service was over, it often was like done with, and my thoughts would go roving about.'

"But let us notice here that the Psalmist's love of God's house, the humility of his heart, and his hatred of wickedness, all originated in that spiritual renewal of his nature, which the Holy Ghost alone can accomplish. Left to ourselves, we never should love either God or His house; there would be no humility in our hearts, nor any holiness in our lives. To be otherwise than we originally are can be effected only by that Spirit, who is the sole source of grace and power to man. All good dispositions and desires proceed from the operations of God's Spirit. Accordingly, when a man loves the things of God, and finds his chief delight in them, it is because the Spirit of God has made him a new creature in Christ Jesus. Then it is that the word of God, the day of God, the house of God, become the meat and drink of the child of God. All these great changes and fruits of the Spirit gradually became more and more discernible in Richard Hill. He was visited with severe illnesses within the last dozen years, which seem to have been greatly blessed to him. In nothing was their effect more discernible than in his constant and humble efforts to be a blessing to others. I speak advisedly in saying that, for many years, no man was a greater blessing to this parish than was its beadle, Richard Hill. He was the constant visitant of the sick poor. Long before the name Scripture-reader came into use, he was one. Making more minute inquiries since his death, I find fact upon fact to prove that he was the means of many a true conversion. Among other testimonies, old George Vaughan always attributed much to his visits. It was the occupation of his leisure hours to read and pray and converse with those who could not come to the house of God for instruction. He was generally known among our better sort of poor as 'Mr. Hill the Churchman.' And would that we had many more such Churchmen; men who will talk for their Church, and pray and live for their Church, in all the evangelical purity of its doctrine and sanctity of its discipline. But the religion of our doorkeeper, 'the Churchman,' was not a mere Church religion, it was a vital heart religion, nourished by union to Christ, and thriving where it always ought to thrive, first and fairest, at home. After his second marriage he made a point to have family prayers, and this was made the beginning of great blessing to his wife. She died about six years ago. An eye and ear witness has told me that the manner in which he used to read to her and pray with her, during her last illness, was really beautiful as well as touching. She used to say, 'I ought to be the happiest woman in the world, because I have the best husband in it. He cares for my soul, and leads me to heaven like a little child.'

"Oh, what a pattern is this to many a husband, and how well will it be for all husbands and all wives, even among the poor, to follow that part of it which relates to family prayer.

"Last year the good old man was attacked with alarming illness. A visitor remembers reading to him the 8th chapter of Romans. Pausing at the 6th verse, 'To be spiritually-minded is life and peace,' he said, 'Oh, that peace, I enjoy it now, and shall enjoy it for ever, for ever.' At the 15th verse he repeated, 'Abba Father, *my* blessed, blessed Father.' More than once I surely thought he was entering the valley of death, but the Lord and Giver of Life called him back from it, and spared him for another year. This was a most blessed season of spiritual growth to him.

"But ere I remark further respecting it, let me recur to a circumstance, which, though known to some, may be heard by all now, and possibly by one, whom of all others I could wish to hear it. One day while the aged sufferer was in a deep slumber from the effects of medicine, some heartless person slipped into his room and stole from his bolster all the money he possessed. The amount, about twelve or fifteen shillings, was soon made up to him; but his money was stolen. Not one living on the premises was suspected, but some one else was. Should that unhappy person be present, let me tell him, that money will be as fire in his pocket, and let me exhort him, for his soul's sake, to repent him truly of his sin, and then to return the money either openly or secretly to myself, for the benefit of the little orphan daughter whom the sufferer has, with many anxious fears, left behind.

"The illness to which I have been referring was counted by him the greatest mercy of his life. Respecting it, he said, 'I desire never to forget the Lord's goodness in sending me that illness last summer. I seem as if I had wasted all my life before that; it looks like a barren vineyard. Oh, what a mercy that the Lord did not cut me down, such an unprofitable servant! Oh, how my sins rose up before me! For a few days and nights they seemed like flames burning me up, because I had been so vile and wicked before my God.' Yes, dear friends, it generally is the case that at some time or other true penitents, though they know their pardon in Christ Jesus, are taught to feel by God's Spirit, that sin is an evil and bitter thing.

"Another time he said to a visitor, who was leaving Worcester, 'I don't think I shall live to see you again, but as the Lord in heaven pleases, it will be best. My times are in His hands, and His blessed will be done. My race is nearly run. My pains are often very great, but never too great. It's best I should have them, they make me think of my sins and of Him who suffered for them on the cross. Oh, how can I ever thank him enough!'

"A relative just then came in; but such was the stream of his words that he seemed as if he could not stay from speaking of his Master, and of his longing desire to be made meet for his heavenly home. He added, 'I want to serve the Lord with all my heart, not to speak of any one else, only to win Christ and be found in Him.' In this way, and much more might be told you, did the Lord show that he was fast ripening His aged servant for the garner of His glory. He rallied sufficiently to do as he usually had done in the house of his God, but as he one Sunday said to me, it was under an impression that he should not do it much longer. And so it proved, the final attack of his malady came. He was conscious that the time of his departure was at hand. He had but one care on his dying bed, and that was for his little girl, the child of his old age. The thought of leaving her an orphan, only nine years old, and for whom he had nothing to leave but his blessing, did touch the heart of the kind old man. If any other heart should be touched for the child, I shall be but too glad to receive any offerings their hand can afford to bestow. As he lay gradually sinking, about three days before he died, it was said to him, 'Your flesh and heart are failing.' 'Yes, but the Lord is my portion, He supports me.' With clasped hands and bright smile he exclaimed, 'I am waiting for that joyful call, "come away, come away." Oh, how glorious for the Lord to bid me come up to Him from this world of sin and misery!'

" Far more might be told you, but let this suffice, for I cannot trust myself publicly to tell it."

But what the preacher did not say may now be written. Often did the old man speak of the pleasure and comfort the visits of this beloved pastor gave him. Blessing on blessing did he pour out for him and his family.

One day he pointed to a little round table, saying, "Oh, what a pleasure it is to me when Mr. Havergal kneels there, it's like heaven begun below, and that's where I've long knelt and felt my Saviour so near, He meets me there."

"Do you often feel the Lord's presence, Hill?"

"Oh, yes, He is always with me day and night. I've no fears now. Death can't fright me. I shall not be afraid to go this night. Blessed be His holy name, I know I shall drop into the Lord's hand. He has led me safely all through the wilderness, and I shall soon be safe in all His glory. Blessed be His name. He has washed all my sins away. All my trust is in Christ. He is my hope. He has drawn me to Him, how can I ever thank him enough for all He has done for me, a poor miserable sinner, I want to be always praising."

"Oh, what a blessed, blessed time it will be to meet my beloved Saviour, that shed His precious blood for such a vile sinner! It won't be long till He takes me to His glorious kingdom for ever. My strength and my heart faileth, but God is the strength of my heart and my portion for ever."

When he entered the last valley only the shadow of death was there, and he saw the other side of shining light. And as he looked he said, "Oh, what a glorious ascent up that heavenly hill!" His parting words were a legacy of blessing, "The Lord bless my dear minister, and dear Mrs. H., and all his family; the Lord in heaven for evermore bless him. Amen, and Amen."

When the next Sabbath morning came, the doorkeeper of God's earthly house ascended to dwell in the house of the Lord for ever.

He died, May 5, 1850, in the seventy-ninth year of his age.

Some time after his death the following letter was sent by his son to his valued teacher, Mrs. H.:—

Dear Teacher,—

It is almost with shame I take my pen in hand to answer your letter, after delaying it for so long a time. Methinks I shall never forget the sermon preached on my father's life and death by Mr. Havergal. Happy shall I be, when my existence is no more, to have the same tale told of me, as of my dear father. I assure you, teacher, it was a great trial to part with so good and kind a father, Never could any child have had a better father, and to part with him was almost heartbreaking. But yet, in the midst of all this trouble, there is consolation, for it is only for a time we have parted, if I can but take the same way and path he took, and our Saviour prepared for us to walk in. I suppose my little sister will enter the school next Sunday. I hope she will be a good child.

Would you look to her yourself a little, as she is very young to be left in this wicked world without a parent? Teach her to look to Him, who is a Father to the orphan. Please to send me word how she conducts herself. Remember me to all the boys in the first class. I do hope they will pay attention to what they hear. I wish I had done so. I was often naughty when not found out. Often other boys have got into disgrace, when I have been the sole cause of it. Tell them not to follow my example. If there is any boy I have so injured, I humbly implore forgiveness, and I hope he will forgive. Accept what I write, and remember me kindly to Mr. Havergal, and believe me, your grateful scholar,

T. H.

XII.

HARRY THE HAPPY.

"WHERE shall you be set down, ma'am?" said the porter, as he shut the door of our cab at a busy railway station.

"At the Union Workhouse, please."

On arriving there, the doorkeeper looked at our order for admission to see Joseph Henry Ford in the male bedridden ward.

He asked, "Have you anything about you to take him?"

"Yes, here are some mince pies, and a bag of apples and oranges."

With a kind smile the man unwillingly added, "But, ladies, have you any wine or spirits?"

"Oh, no; I am a teetotaler."

"All right, Miss. Will you sit down in the waiting-room, as it is my duty to ask the master's leave for your bag to go in?"

He soon returned with permission. We followed him through a large hall, strewn with faded evergreens and paper decorations now taken down, as Christmas time was past. He left us as we entered the men's ward.

It was spacious and lofty, almost like the nave of a church, with a double row of iron pillars. Down the centre of the room a wooden partition divided four parallel rows of iron bedsteads. There were about seventy beds, and, as in the porches of Bethesda, "In these lay a great multitude of impotent folk, of blind, halt, withered." And He, who is still "moved with compassion," sees them lie, and knows how long they have been in that case.

The friend who accompanied me had long known, and often visited, Harry Ford. His letters to her had interested me so much, that I had occasionally written to him, and friends had sent through me stamps, and books, and tracts. Passing between the long rows of beds, I should certainly have stopped at his without my friend's saying, "This is Harry." That happy face, that peaceful smile, that hand on an open Bible—that was "Harry the Happy."

While my friend talked to him, I looked at Harry's surroundings. Suffering faces and uncurtained beds were seen; groans here, impatient words there, and incoherent ravings from a man past his hundredth year, were heard. No fireside corner, no high-backed chair and patchwork cushion, no purring cat, no singing kettle, no black tea-pot, no tray with two cups and saucers, no wife to look at, gray-haired and wrinkled, yet dearer than even when the promise was made, " to love and to cherish, till death us do part." "What God hath joined together, let not man put asunder," seems unheeded by Poor-Law legislators. The only echoes left of home are the click, click of the clock, and the chiming of Sunday bells. Still, in justice, it must be admitted that the beds were clean and comfortable, and the ward well warmed by hot water pipes and thoroughly ventilated. The quality of the food was good; the sameness of diet the only complaint. Who would not tire of fat mutton every day, and tea made in a copper?

At the head of every bed, were some shelves for their few books and belongings. Harry produced from his a pot of workhouse marmalade.

"This is the way to make the most of an orange, Miss! I cut it, rind and all, in very thin slices, put it in a jar with a little water and a sprinkle of sugar, and then a spoonful quiets my cough in the night."

"How did you keep Christmas, Harry?"

He opened his Bible, and laid his hand on it, saying, "*I had this*."

"Did you see any holly or ivy?"

"No Miss, I heard there was some in the hall, but none came in here."

"See I have brought you some, Harry, and I will tie it round the iron pillar. Flowers are scarce now, so I could only get a nosegay of herbs. I gathered some thyme, marjoram, and sage; perhaps you remember them growing in your mother's garden?"

"Well, now, that is kind! I haven't seen a bit of sage for years, that *is* homelike!

"But please, Miss, to look at what I made for my Christmas decoration. Last summer you sent me a sprig of cedar, myrtle, box, and a passion flower. They often brought His word to my mind, 'He shall grow like a cedar in Lebanon.' 'Instead of the thorn shall come up the fir tree, and instead of the briar shall come up the myrtle tree.'

"I dried them all, and here they are tied round this little paper garland. We are not allowed nails, but the master kindly allowed me one to hang it over my bed, and the picture you sent me of the mission room on Wyre Hill. That picture gives me work to do, praying work for all the people who go there. I try to do some little work for the Lord here; when my breath allows me, I read aloud to the poor men. Only a few care for it. It is one of my great trials, the bad language I hear, and their carelessness about their souls; not a thought about eternity. There was a dreadful death only last week. A man was always cursing and swearing; one night he was cursing till he went to sleep, and in the morning was found dead in his bed. It made me feel His amazing grace to me, to call me out of darkness into His marvellous light,"

"And are you generally happy, Harry?"

"Oh, yes, though sometimes not quite so bright as others, but then I always have the witness of the Spirit within that I am a child of God, that I am an heir of God, a joint-heir with Christ.

"No words can express the happiness which flows from this."

"Have you any visitors, Harry, besides kind Miss B.?"

"Yes, a few, and our chaplain is a very kind man, and has such a beautiful voice, he has just been reading and praying in the ward."

"Are you fond of music, Harry?"

"Very; years ago I played fairly on the violin."

"I will lend you this musical box, Harry; my sister brought it me from Switzerland to please the poor sick people I visit. I hope to come again in a month, and you shall keep it till then."

"Oh, thank you! I have heard no music since I came in here."

"Are you suffering much, Harry?"

"I am quite helpless from the dislocation of my hip, and I always suffer more or less with bronchitis."

"Would you like this warm comforter and these muffatees Miss B. has knitted for you?"

"No, thank you, I must not take them; for we have orders to take off any bit of flannel for the night, and I should only miss them then."

So unwillingly we brought them away.

Just then a singular incident occurred; an old man in the next bed, hearing me addressed by name, called out, "Havigail, Havigail; why, that was the name of our parson years ago, he turned the parish upside down. *He* was the man as could preach, and put a stop to sin!"

We were soon friends and talking over old times and places, and the good seed my dear father sowed nearly fifty years ago. The old man proved to be the son of Betty Dalley, and brother of our worthy Astley schoolmistress. He spoke of Harry as his best friend in the ward, and that he had led him to seek the Shepherd from whom he had gone far astray.

It was now time to leave the ward. A friend had supplied me with five shillings for Harry. I laid it in his hand. Tears were his answer, and then, "Oh, the goodness of my God! I can only pray for this unknown friend."

Harry's history shall now be given, as related in his letters to my friend and myself. They are faithfully copied, the spelling being singularly correct.

To Miss B——.

Male Bed-ridden Ward,
Midnight, 1868.

Dear Christian Friend,—

I promised to send you a few lines, and now all being still, is a good time for me to write. We always have the gas on at night, which makes it comfortable, as I can read when I am awake, the gas being nearly over my head. I often think of you and all others when you are fast asleep. Oh, what a blessing it is that our poor body is watched over, when the image of death is on us. These are the seasons for me, when all is quiet and still, surrounded as I am by those who, like myself, are often racked with strong pains, and have no kind friends to converse with and comfort us. You would think such times very hard, and so it is, as far as earthly comforters go. It is sweet to hear the voice of a friend at your bedside, and receive a little nourishing food, such as the poor body often requires.

But how much more sweet to hear the voice of our Best Friend calling us to listen to Him, to hear His word of consolation, and to receive from Him food for our precious souls, and His promise assuring us that He will soon come for us and take us to Himself. There we shall be for ever free from all pain and sorrow, and live for ever in the realms of glory. All our pains will be over, we shall have no more restless nights or troublesome days; all will be one clear everlasting day, a day we shall ever spend in praise and glory to Him who liveth and reigneth for ever, ever. The Lord in mercy look down on the poor dear souls, who are at this time led away by the spirit of Popery. It is a time for us to look up and pray for the ingathering of the flock, that we may see the Church of Christ flourish and become strong,— that we may see the strongholds of Satan broken down and scattered to the winds, that we may see those who are now in the way to hell, brought to walk in the way to glory. Dear friend, receive the following lines from your poor pensioner. It is many a day since I have done such before, and now all being still, I thought you might be a little pleased with poor Harry, although I do not pride myself, or think myself at all clever for all that.

> These lines, my friend, I now indite,
> Although it is past twelve at night,
> I mean the enemy to fight,
>   While on my way to glory.
>
> My captain Jesus on ahead,
> Who rose triumphant from the dead;
> By Him alone my soul is led,
>   To win my way to glory.
>
> All hail our Jesus, glorious name!
> Who always was and is the same,
> Who from heaven to earth once came,
>   To raise our souls to glory.
>
> Rejoice, my friends, we will obey
> This heavenly call from day to day,
> And for our fellow-creatures pray,
>   That they may seek for glory.
>
> Oh, that we may live to see
> Many to our Saviour flee,
> Escape eternal misery,
>   And seek for endless glory.
>
> Our time on earth may not be long,
> Oh, may we join the blood-bought throng;
> And learn to sing the heavenly song,
>   The saints now sing in glory.

J. H. Ford.

To Miss B——.

Dear Friend,—

… I will now tell you a little of my history. I was born near Penzance; the Rev. C. De Le Grice was our clergyman. My happy lot was to be blest with pious parents, and they did all that lay in their power to set a good example to their family. We had the Scripture read, and family worship twice every day. Very often, when my beloved father went to his room, he would take me with him, and there he prayed for us. I remember well his tears and prayers when sad tidings have been brought of the death of a brother in a foreign land, and then again of another, and another. We were thirteen in family; I was the youngest, and a great favourite with all my brothers and sisters. I had many advantages given me to become, what we may call, a good boy, and so become a good man; but, like most other children, I was sometimes rather too self-willed, and no doubt had too much of my own way; yet I always loved my parents most dearly, and my brothers and sisters. To pass by my childhood, when about eleven years of age, I wanted to go to sea, as all my brothers were sailors, and I wanted to see foreign countries as they did. Nothing would do for me, but to sea I would go. At last I was permitted to go a voyage with a dear friend of my father's. It was Christmas time, and they hoped the winter voyage would sicken me; instead of that it made me more hardened, and I liked it well. But then I was only cabin boy, and knew nothing of the dangers to come. Years rolled on, and many were the dangers I had to encounter. I often thought of my parents, and prayed the Lord to preserve me to see them again. I knew they were praying for me and my brothers. I remembered well how my dear father would always pray for all who "go down to the sea in ships, that do business in great waters." Now my parents had many and heavy troubles. First, I had one brother who fell from the mast, and was all but dead when taken up. He lived about six months in an hospital—this happened in America. Another brother fell and was killed, never spoke, but was taken up dead—that was in Sydney, New South Wales. There was about two years between these troubles, then two sisters died, about five and six years old. Another poor brother had his skull broken by a stone thrown by a bricklayer; it was not intended, but it hit him, and he only lived a few weeks. A few months after another brother was ripped up by a wild cow. Here was sorrow upon sorrow. My dear parents and two sisters were almost heartbroken, yet all bowed and said, "The Lord's will be done." I was young and felt it much, but it soon went off; I was among sailors, and had no time to grieve. After a few years a dear brother, eighteen years of age, and six of the crew, were all drowned. Here was another heavy trial; and scarcely got over, when a brother, a dear pious one, died with the yellow fever in Africa. Then my dear father was laid down with a paralytic stroke, and my dear mother suffered from the tic doloreux. She often lost her reason; but, even when raging, would cry, "Patience, patience, Jesus, Jesus!" She died; and such a happy end! For several days all her pains left her, and we, who saw her, could rejoice with her, and rejoice when she went to her Father and our Father. But I should have told you of myself being broken up before this. My dear mother was alive when I was hurt, (fell from the mast and broke the thigh, and other injuries); and, dear soul, how she did take me round the neck and kiss me, and oh, the agony she was in for me. When my bones were set, she came to me to nourish and comfort me. After my dear mother's death my sisters died one by one, only father and me left together; at last poor father died, and here am I left alone; (no, I should not have said so), I am not alone, I have a friend or two left, you know; but, above all, I have a Friend round about me, One who is with me at all times. He cares for me asleep and awake.

And now let me say, with a joyful heart, with praise to my great Deliverer, "Let the saints be joyful in glory: let them sing aloud upon their beds." (Psalm 149.) And I am on my bed singing praise in my heart to the Lord. For the present, dear friend, adieu.—Yours, etc.,

J. H. F.

To Miss H——.

Dear Sister in Christ,—

... You wish to know about my conversion. I had dear pious parents, they did all they could to bring us all up in the fear of the Lord; their prayers and tears are fulfilled, I humbly hope, in my being led to put my whole trust in Christ for my salvation. I was, as all poor sinners, going the downward road to destruction. I think my first conviction of being a sinner lost for ever was thirty-four years since, when on a voyage to India, and crossing the line; it thundered, lightened, rained, and blew so tremendous, that I trembled greatly. I went below and thought, Well, I cannot escape to a place of safety. I prayed the Lord to look on me and help me to put my trust in Him, to deliver us from the storm, and bring us in safety to the land again. I remember I lost all my fear and trembling, and felt such a calm within as I cannot describe.

We lost our mizen mast and fore yard, the sails were split, and there was much damage, but we arrived safe to land. The Lord be praised for all His mercies in preserving me in the midst of storms and dangers on the deep, and His watchful and tender care in withholding me from the many snares laid for me by those who professed to be my friends on the land. I have had strong temptations to follow the thoughtless and gay to places of amusement, and to such places as I would not mention, but thank God for His watchful care in keeping me from the snares of the wicked. At that time I was looking more at my good works, than at the finished work of the Lord Jesus. Up to the age of twenty-three or four I was a self-righteous Pharisee. I was in London, and at a chapel, but I do not know the name, nor did I ever inquire, but I heard a sermon from the 21st verse of the thirtieth chapter of Isaiah, "This is the way, walk ye in it." I was led from that time to search the Bible more, and pray for the Lord's blessing and His Spirit to direct and lead me in the right way, till, at length, I was enabled to cast all my care on Him, who, by His own almighty arm, "brought salvation, and of the people there was none with Him." So it pleased God to reveal Christ in me as the only hope of glory. May the happiness of our souls daily arise from the Holy Spirit revealing Christ unto us. My cough is very troublesome to me at times, but the Lord be praised for enabling me to bear His chastisement, and may I, through grace, be kept by His almighty power to His everlasting kingdom. The Lord bless and comfort you all, and may it please Him to prosper His work in your hands. You may work for a long time before you find that which you desire. But be not discouraged, you will find your labour is not in vain, the Lord in His own time will own and bless His work. Go on, and fear not the enemy, he is chained, he cannot harm thee, the Lord is with thee to bless. May the comfortable communion of the blessed Spirit lead us daily to praise and glorify our heavenly Father, through Jesus Christ, our Lord and Saviour. Amen. I remain, your humble servant and well-wisher,

J. H. F.

To Miss H——.

My Dear Friend,—

With much pleasure I send you these few lines, with my sincere thanks for your kind present, and especially the books and your sister's hymns. I do not know which delights me most. "Faith and Reason" is very good. "All Your Need" is truly delightful. I can say, from experience, the Lord has supplied all my need so far through life, and I doubt not but He ever will supply me out of the fulness of His treasures. The riches of His grace are inexhaustible, His promises shall all be fulfilled in due time. Often when I knew not how I was to get a morsel of bread, and knew not where to go, I have felt sick at heart, and have been afraid to make my wants known to any one, the Lord has been my guide to direct me to the place where I have found relief. I will just tell you an instance. Some four or five years since, one Tuesday afternoon, after I had been all the morning going from street to street, calling from door to door, but could sell nothing, I felt very weak and tired. I sat down to rest me, with my box by my side, full of thought. A lady, with a little boy, passed by. I heard the child say, "Oh, mamma, look at that poor man!" I looked up, and, a few yards off, I saw them stopping, and then the dear child came running to me with sixpence. I was then in Highfield Road. Here was a supply for me; there was threepence for my lodgings, and threepence for some bread and tea. Then I called at one house in that road, it was No. 17, and I was asked into the kitchen. Shortly the lady came to me, and two of her little daughters. I was ordered something to eat, and the cook was ordered to give me the remainder to take with me, so that I had bread and meat for two days, and two shillings to put in my pocket. I need not tell you what I felt at having such a present, and my thanks to Him who directed my steps to that door in particular. So have I ever found the Lord to supply all my need in all temporals, and I am sure He will also bestow on me all I need for my comfort in all my affliction. He will not leave me comfortless, He will be with me in all my sickness to cheer me, and raise my weary, sinking spirits by sweetly smiling and saying, "It is I, be not afraid; I will never leave thee, nor forsake thee." Many times I have found it hard. I have left my lodgings in a morning and gone for two or three miles without selling anything, and have been a whole day and not sold a pennyworth, yet I never despaired. I knew well the Lord would provide. I did all I could, and then was sure the Lord would send me relief from some quarter, and I always found it. I could tell of the many times I called on a dear friend ever ready to help me, but I feared to put too much on her good nature, but she always gave me sufficient for my present wants. So the dear Lord provided me with all my need from day to day; and what more do I want? Why, I am in want daily. I want to be in all things more and more like my Jesus. I want to lay my head on His breast, to give this poor heart to Him, to look to Him daily, hourly, and abide by Him truly and faithfully unto the end, looking forward for the time of my departure, when He shall take me to the mansions on high. I was pleased with the "Passion Flower," and "Myrtle," and "Cedar," you sent me, and have made these few lines.—

Believe me, with Christian respects, yours in the Lord,

J. H. F.

THE PASSION FLOWER.

When I beheld the passion flower,
I thought upon the solemn hour
When on the ground Christ prostrate lay,
And prayed in such great agony.
He to His Father thus did say,
"Let this cup from me pass away;"
Yet "not my will, but thine be done."
So said God's well-beloved Son.

Oh, garden of Gethsemane!
Often may I be found in thee,
Led by the Spirit to adore
Him, who the sin of sinners bore;
Oh may I often there be found,
With Christ who lay upon the ground;
By grace, through faith, believing see
He drank the passion cup for me!

J. H. F.

To Miss B——.

Male Bed-ridden Ward.

Dear Friend,—

With a thankful heart I now write these few lines thanking you for your great kindness in remembering me, one who has not the least claim on you, that you should be so very kind. It is the Lord's doing, to Him be all the praise for His putting it into your heart to give me a part of your substance, to enable me to get a few little things I should not have here, but for His love in remembering me through you. I am much better than when you last heard from me, I take no medicine, nothing but what I get in from out. Some candied horehound with a few biscuits, and have had a few smoked herrings, with a bit of ham now and then. When your letter came to me I was without any stamps, and out of all, so I see the hand of our Lord in it. "I will never leave thee, nor forsake thee."

Oh, the heart, the heart, the wicked evil heart, if left for a moment to itself, what a conflict, how soon the dark clouds spread themselves abroad and cast down the poor soul, if but for a moment our dear Friend hides his face from us! When it pleaseth the Lord to dispel the dark clouds and shine forth again, what rejoicing once more, and a fresh supply of grace to waft us onward to our heavenly home! You will remember giving me a little book, about three years since, "Sunlight in the Heart." There are some nice lines in it—

"The gloomiest soul is not all gloom,
　The saddest heart is not all sadness;
And sweetly o'er the darkest doom
　There shines some lingering beam of gladness."

As you say, the work of grace is all His own, so all the comforts we receive are from the Lord. His ways in dealing with us are mysterious, we are not able to comprehend His ways; but this we know, all things are working for our everlasting good. As the poet says—

"Though dark be my way,
　Since He is my guide,
'Tis mine to obey,
　'Tis His to provide;
Though cisterns be broken
　And creatures all fail,
The word He has spoken
　Shall surely prevail."

Dear friend and sister in Christ, He will never leave us, He will for ever keep us near Him; "as the Father loveth me, even so have I loved you." May we be kept by His Holy Spirit, and strengthened by His love, to walk in His ways, and at last hear His heavenly voice saying, "Come up higher." The Lord bless you in all your works and ways, and go with you to bless you in your mission of love to poor sinners, and comfort your heart at all times. Remember me in your prayers, and the Lord hear you at all times, and may all we do be to the glory of His holy name. Amen—Yours in Christ,

J. H. F.

To Miss B———.

Dear Friend,—

. . . I have suffered much in body, the pains have been severe from my head to my toes, oh, such pain! But our Father enabled me to bear all without a murmur or so much as a groan, no not so much as to disturb those next to me; although they knew I was not well, they little thought what I was enduring at the time. Dear friend, what cause of rejoicing and thankfulness, I could scarcely think it possible for one to feel such acute pains and be so quiet and peaceful, but what cannot our dear Father perform? I have been recovering these last two or three days, but am very weak and cannot sit upright yet, but hope I may *if it so please My Heavenly Nurse,* who has made my bed in all my affliction, and is by me to comfort me by night and by day. This is a very trying month to me. It is no use asking the doctor to alter my diet (fat mutton); I have heard many ask him, but he has never done it. . . . I hope my good friend Mrs. B. is better; may the Lord give her patience to endure her affliction, knowing it shall all work for good. Not one pang more or less than is our lot to bear, and then, oh, then, the perfect joy to be felt for everlasting! No more pain or sighing, no more grief, no, nothing but everlasting joys and felicity, for ever enjoying the smiles of our risen Lord and Saviour. Dear friend, may the Lord bless and comfort you all with His holy presence, and give both you and me to taste more of His love day by day; may we be kept by His almighty power, and may His Holy Spirit ever keep our minds in peace. The grace of our Lord Jesus Christ be with us all. Amen, Amen—Yours in Christ,

J. H. F.

To Miss B———.

Dear Friend,—

I was happy to hear from you, and truly thankful for the supply of stamps, although I was not run out of the last I received from you. But the joy I ever feel to have a line from you I cannot express. I am not now as I once was, I cannot go up to the house of God to hear His word and worship with His people, and I have no one but yourself to send me a word of encouragement by the way, so that a line from you cheers my poor heart. Often do I long for the postman's voice about the beginning of the month, not for the sake of receiving any amount of stamps to get me a few little things for the poor body, but to think and feel I am not alone in the world, that I have a few dear friends who are led to take an interest in me. It is a blessed truth indeed, "by this shall all men know that ye are my disciples, if ye have love one to another." "Love is the fulfilling of the law." What is more pleasing to parents, than to see their children living together in love? May we through grace be led to pray for one another, that we may grow in grace, and see and hear of the work of the Lord prospering in the churches. I trust the Lord will enable me to pray daily, for all who go forth on errands of love to poor souls, that they may be refreshed by His presence, and the work of the Lord abundantly prosper in their hands. We have no strength of our own, we can do nothing of ourselves, but in Him all fulness dwells. Christ must be our all. Be not discouraged, my dear friend, you also will reap a joyful harvest. Look up! you are labouring for a good Master, go on with your labour, and when it is finished, He will call you to Him and give you your wages. I am as well in body as I could expect. I am slowly decaying, my flesh is going off me, there will be enough for the worms to devour; never mind the poor body, I rejoice in hope of a glorious resurrection, when body and soul will be reunited to live for ever in the kingdom of glory.

J. H. F.

To Miss H———.

Dear Christian Friend,—

My dear friend Miss B. has been to see me, and it refreshed me. I see the goodness of the Lord in giving me kind friends to cheer me by the way. I am alone in the world, that is, I have no relative to send or to come to me; my only cousins are in China and Australia. But I have Christ to commune with, and He is pleased to give me a few of His own dear children to minister to my little wants, such as I should not have in this workhouse.

On the 6th of September last, the postman brought me an envelope; inside there was half a sheet of blank paper, with half-a-crown's worth of stamps and the little book, "Mountains of bread." I am not so poor as Ann, who had no bread or money to get any on the coming day. My bread is sure, yet it brought to my mind the word of our dear and heavenly Father, "I will never leave thee nor forsake thee." "Bread shall be given thee, and thy water shall be sure." I know nothing of the friend who sent it me, the post-mark is Wolverhampton, but I know no one there, and none of my kind friends have been there. The Lord knows, and may He bless the giver abundantly in their soul, and bring them at last to live with Him for ever. Dear friend, it makes me very sad, when I look around me here, to see so many on their beds, and not one do I ever hear inquiring, What shall I do to be saved? I hear them often blaspheme that holy name, and when I speak to them about it, I am abused and am called a fanatic, hypocrite, and all kind of names. I bear it all with patience, and pray for them when they are asleep. You told me you see hundreds every day going the broad way; I know it must depress your spirit, but still hold fast the plough. Paul may plant, and Apollos may water, but God giveth the increase. Yesterday a man here died suddenly, and never did I hear him once say, "Lord, have mercy on me." Certainly we do not know the thoughts of men, but it is a solemn thing to think of. Another poor fellow, who has laid on the bed next to mine ever since I have been in this ward, died on Saturday. He had been paralysed, and could not speak. He was fearfully convulsed, and his struggles at the last were fearful. I hope I shall never witness the like again. I am still a poor sinner, and have nothing to trust to but my Saviour, and what more do I want, nothing, nothing! having Him I possess all. I have the promise of everlasting life, and "He is faithful that promised," and will also perform. Let us rejoice, and endeavour in all our conversation to praise and glorify our Saviour Christ, helping and assisting each other in our prayers, that the Spirit of our Father may be our guide while travelling through life, and be our great support in the last moment. Then to be conveyed to mansions prepared for us in glory. I told the wardsman last night, if he should be here and see me die, to say, "There lies a poor sinner, who died believing in Christ, and trusting alone in the atonement made by Him. Oh, the love of God to us poor sinners, and the obedience of Christ to the will of the Father, to lay down His life for us, while we were sinning against Him! How great His love no tongue can tell, then let us love Him, with all our heart, and soul, and strength. May the blessing of the three-one Jehovah be with us evermore.—I remain, your brother in Christ,

J. H. F.

P.S.—Let us pray earnestly for the Lord to uphold the church in these awful troublesome times. May He strengthen and cause His dear ministers to fight boldly in the strength of the Lord, and take the devil by his horns and throw him overboard, that he may swim back to the pope and tell him he can do nothing in old England. I think of His mercy in delivering me from the power of darkness, how great His love to me a poor atom of earth, a weak worthless worm. I send you some verses I made on "The Tree," and "The Beggar;" there are so many better able than me, that I feel ashamed to send them, but trust they will please you.

J. H. Ford.

Harry's hymns are given untouched. Less perfect rhyme and rhythm may be found in the writings of some recognised poets.

Harry had but One Teacher. "Who teacheth like Him?"

THE TREE.

O fruitful tree, beneath whose shade
   I sit me down to rest;
No beast of prey can near me come,
   Although they oft molest.

Its branches spread both far and wide,
   It shelters all who come;
Millions are now beneath its boughs,
   And still there yet is room.

This tree is beautiful and fair,
   We all may freely eat;
The King's command is, "Give to all,"
   'Tis his delight to treat.

Beneath the shadow of this tree,
   I rest me day and night;
In eating of its goodly fruit,
   Is my poor soul's delight.

If once you taste this precious fruit,
   Your soul will crave for more;
Oh, come, dear friends, and freely eat,
   Come now, both rich and poor.

Ye naked, come, just as ye are,
   It matters not how vile;
The Master of the fruit will greet
   You with a loving smile.

Come, lame and blind, all in distress,
   Shelter beneath this tree;
You there will find a sure relief,
   From all your misery.

Joseph Henry Ford.

THE BEGGAR.

I go a begging every day,
   I want to get a store;
I do feel such a craving,
   I'm always wanting more.

Who would not be a beggar
   To get a little food,
When he is sure of something,
   That something very good.

For my own part I wonder
   Why some do feel so shy,
And rather than go beg a bit,
   Would sooner pine and die.

I'm not like that, but tell ye
   I love to beg my bit,
And many a rich morsel
   I oftentimes do get.

Why should not others join me?
   I see no reason why,
There is enough for every one
   If they would only try.

I go to beg of Jesus,
   The starving sinner's Friend,
He always does my wants supply,
   And will do to the end.

I know He will give nothing
   But what is good indeed,
To all who come unto Him,
   And tell Him what they need.

Oh, come, no longer look so sad,
   Come, knock at mercy's door;
Ask, and receive His precious gift,
   As thousands have before.

The lovely Jesus bids thee come,
   He waits thy soul to bless,

Come and be clothed, as all His Saints,
  In perfect righteousness.

J. H. F.

ONCE AND NO MORE.

Once and no more the Saviour bled,
Once and no more His blood was shed;
Once Jesus suffered on the tree
To save such guilty souls as me.

Once did He bow His sacred head,
Once was He numbered with the dead,
He rose again triumphantly,
And lives and offers life to me.

Rejoice, my soul, though wretched, vile,
Thy Saviour deigns on thee to smile,
And loving saith, "Come unto me,"
And have at once salvation free.

True, once the sacrifice was made,
That once the debt of sin was paid;
My captive soul was then set free,
And so I had my liberty.

This is good news to all below,
News that should make our hearts o'erflow
With love and gratitude to God,
Who sealed our pardon with His blood.

J. H. F.

WHY CHRIST DIED.

  Do you ask the reason why
Jesus Christ came down to die,
Why He left His Father's throne,
Why He left His heavenly home,
Why He took our nature up,
Why He drank the bitter cup,
Why He to His Father cried,
Why on Calvary He died,
Why He in the tomb did lie,
Why He rose and went on high,
Why He sits at God's right hand
  In yon bright and happy land?
Listen, dear friends, God's Word doth tell
It was to save our souls from hell;
That we might live with Him above,
And be partakers of His love.
This then is the reason why
Jesus Christ came down to die.

J. H. F.

I went unto my Jesus, and told Him all my grief,
He looked and smiled upon me, and came to my relief;
He bid me come when hungry, and not to stop away,
"O come and drink when thirsty," I know I hear Him say.

Then let me live on Jesus, the true and living Bread,
Drink from the flowing fountain, for Jesus is the Head;
O may I live on Jesus, and blossom as the rose,
And flourish as the lily, that in the valley grows.

J. H. F.

TO THE MISSION ON WYRE HILL.

I often turn my head and see
A little picture sent to me,
And think of those who oft repair
To offer praise, and worship there.

The Mission Room on Wyre Hill
May God in His rich mercy fill
With praying souls, saved by His grace
Out of the once lost, ruined race.

My heart responds with those who meet
To welcome you to Jesu's feet,
And train you in the narrow way
That leads to everlasting day.

May those dear souls who do attend,
Find there the sinner's dearest Friend,
Jesus, who died on Calvary,
To save and set the guilty free.

Ye who are poor and in distress
Come and exchange your ragged dress,
Throw off your filthy rags straightway;
Wash and be clean without delay.

My fellow sinner, only think
How near you are unto the brink
Of the great world of mystery,
Where you and I shall shortly be.

If you've not thought, begin to-day;
For life to Jesus, haste away;
He loves to hear the sinner cry,
He bids you come, why will you die?

Now, come, my friends, and do not fear,
You'll find a kindly welcome there;
He'll clothe you, feed you, give you rest,
And number you among the blest.

Farewell, my friends on Wyre Hill,
May God your Mission room well fill,
And spare your lives to bless the day
You first met there to praise and pray.

Joseph Henry Ford,
Bed-ridden Ward.

  As eagles on the rocks do build
   And rise toward the sun,
  So may we build on Christ the Rock,
   The strong and holy One.

  The eagle keeps the sun in view
   As she doth upward fly;
  So may we keep our Jesus Christ
   In faith's apiring eye.
J. H. F.

Dear Lamb of God, how great Thy love
To leave Thy shining courts above,
To ransom such a worm as I
When by the law condemned to die;
When my destruction seemed so near
In my behalf Thou didst appear;
Stern justice Thou didst satisfy,
And set my soul at liberty;
My Jesus did to me draw near,
And bid my soul be of good cheer;
I need not therefore be dismayed,
He says, " 'Tis I, be not afraid!"
His Holy Spirit is my guide,
My wants by Him are all supplied;
No gift or grace will He withhold,
So doth His word to me unfold;
He near me is from day to day,
And strengthens me upon the way;
Then shall I not contented be
Since Christ is such a Friend to me?
The hour will shortly come when I
Shall see Him coming down the sky;
Then freed from all my deadly foes,
Secure from sin and all its woes,
Shall mount aloft and ever be
With Christ to all eternity!
J. H. F.

THE STAR.

"There shall come a star out of Jacob."—Numbers 24:17.

  Behold! behold! the glorious star
   That shone upon the earth,
  The morn the herald angel came
   And told of Jesu's birth.

  A manger was the lowly cot
   Of heaven's brightest gem,
  Behold, my soul, in that bright star
   The Babe of Bethlehem!

  O blessed morn that star appeared
   And brought the news to men!
  That holy Child that was to come
   Was born in Bethlehem.

  But now He reigns in heaven so high,
   The King of kings is He;
  All nations of the earth shall soon
   Before Him bow the knee.

  That glorious star that shone so bright
   Now guides us on our way
  That leads to heaven, our resting-place
   Of bright eternal day.

  Jesus, be Thou my guiding star,
   In all I say or do;
  Let all my conversation prove
   I am a Christian true.

  O let no glittering star of earth
   Delude my soul from Thee,
  Or wicked thoughts disturb my mind;
   Be Thou my all to me.

  And when my course is run below,
   Then may I joyful rise,
  And see that once bright glorious star
   In heaven beyond the skies.

  There to behold Him on the throne
   In starry majesty,
  And join to sing His praises there
   To all eternity.

December 25. J. H. F.

"SO WILL I COMFORT THEE."

  Help, Lord! to my relief draw nigh,
  And listen to my humble cry;
  My soul, my all, I yield to Thee;
   Come, holy Jesu, comfort me!

  Whene'er temptations me assail
  O let them not o'er me prevail;
  Bid Thou the wily tempter flee,
   And let Thy Spirit comfort me.

  When gloomy thoughts within me rise,
  And hide Thy presence from my eyes,
  Dispel the gloom and let me see
   Thou still art near to comfort me.

  I daily, hourly, need Thy care
  To guide me while I sojourn here;
  O guard my soul, and ever be
   A constant comforter to me.

  When through the vale of death I go,
  Protect me from the daring foe;
  I there shall stand in need of Thee
   To be a comforter to me.

Then when my spirit takes its flight
   To the bright world of heavenly light;
There shall I ever worship Thee,
   Who didst on earth "so comfort me!"

J. H. F.

"REMEMBER ME."

I nothing have, I nothing am,
   My all I draw from Thee;
Thou dear atoning, bleeding Lamb,
   In love remember me.

While on my bed I helpless lie,
   Whate'er my lot may be,
Still this shall ever be my cry,
   Dear Lord, remember me.

My sins they are a heavy sum,
   I do confess to Thee;
The Spirit and the Bride say, Come!
   O then remember me!

Whate'er may be my future state
   I leave, O Lord, to Thee;
I still will knock at mercy's gate,
   And cry, "Remember me."

J. H. F.

"SEARCH ME."

Am I in earnest, O my God,
   In seeking Thy dear face?
And do I earnestly look up
   To Thee and pray for grace,
To keep me in the narrow way
   That leads my soul to Thee,
And strive with all my soul and might
   From every sin to flee?
O search my heart, and try me, Lord;
   What is amiss forgive,
And send Thy Holy Spirit down;
   Thy grace unto me give.
O let me not deceive myself,
   Nor trust my treacherous heart,
But look to Jesus Christ alone,
   Who takes the sinner's part.
O let me daily walk with Thee,
   Rejoicing in Thy love,
And patient wait till Thou shalt say,
   Come live with me above.

J. H. F.

"YE ARE OF MORE VALUE THAN MANY SPARROWS."

The pretty little sparrows, which
   I see in yonder trees,
Not one can fall unto the ground
   Unless the Father please.

Thou, O my soul, more value art
   Than many sparrows be,
For Jesus Christ hath told thee so,
   As in His word we see.

The very hairs upon thy head
   All numbered are by Him,
And every thought that's in thy heart,
   Yea, all that dwells within.

All that I think, or say, or do,
   Is open to His sight;
Nought can escape His watchful eye,
   In day or darkest night.

O let me then be careful how
   I spend my time while here,
That all I think, or say, or do,
   Be done with godly fear.

J. H. F.

"FIGHT THE GOOD FIGHT OF FAITH."

1 Timothy 6:12.

I'm on the battle field,
   My foes stand thick around;
I must not, dare not, yield,
   But firmly stand my ground.

Though weak, yet I am strong,
   Made so by grace divine;
I know, too, that ere long,
   The victory will be mine.

The Lord is my defence,
   To shield me from the foe;
'Tis He will drive him hence,
   Down to the shades below.

I think how Jesus bled,
   To cleanse my soul from sin,
And by that blood He shed,
   The victory I shall win.

Then when the battle's o'er,
   I shall have rest and peace;
For ever, evermore,
   My joy will never cease.

Farewell, farewell to all,
   My glass will soon run down;
Then shall I hear His call,
   To wear the conqueror's crown.

Angels and saints will be
   My loved companions there,
I shall my Jesus see,
   And in His glory share.

Oh, haste that happy day,
   My Jesus, heavenly King,
When I shall be alway
   With Thee in heaven shut in.

J. H. F.

Thy mercies, O my God,
   Demand a song from me;
But for my Saviour's blood,
   Oh, whither could I flee?

Jesus, no name but thine
   Could free my soul from sin;
Sweet Spirit, all divine,
   Come, make me pure within.

Thou hast prepared Thy throne,
   High in the heavens above;
And reignest King thereon,
   Thou God of endless love.

Oh, let Thy Spirit come,
   And dwell within my heart;
Bid evil thoughts begone,
   And wickedness depart.

Then shall my soul look up,
   And praise Thy holy name,
And take salvation's cup,
   With praises for the same.

My soul, my all I give,
   With cheerfulness to Thee;
Who died that I might live,
   In heaven Thy face to see.

J. H. F.

AS YOU GO.

Fear not, 'tis thy Beloved's voice,
He calls and bids thee to rejoice,
In Christ God put thy sins away,
And he upholds thee every day,
        As you go.

Oh, thou loved one, be not weary,
Tho' the road be rough and dreary;
Onward press in Jesu's name,
And His matchless love proclaim,
        As you go.

Stay not, nor cast a look behind,
Keep thy Beloved in thy mind;
The way with diligence pursue,
And ever keep His cross in view,
        As you go.

Fear not Satan or his roaring,
Let thy mind be upward soaring
To the blest haven of repose,
Though earth and hell thy way oppose,
        As you go.

Oh, thou loved one, be not weary,
Can the road be rough and dreary?
Is not thy Beloved near thee,
By the way to guide and cheer thee,
        As you go?

Put away all fear and sorrow,
Do not tarry till to-morrow,
Now's the time thy love to show,
To Him who loves thee here below,
        As you go.

When time with thee shall be no more,
And thou shalt land on yonder shore;
Peace, love, and joy, and lasting rest,
Will be thy portion with the blest,
        Where you go.

J. H. F.

MY BIRTHDAY, AGE 54.

"Through Thee have I been holden up ever since I was born."
—Psalm 71:6.

Awake, my soul, this morn to praise,
   My Saviour, Christ the Lord;
With joyful heart thy voice now raise,
   And Jesus be adored.

Angels now listen while I sing,
   This little song of praise
To Christ my Saviour, Priest, and King.
   In low and humble lays.

The sweetest name that e'er was known,
   The loveliest and the best,
Now pleads before His Father's throne,
   For all His people's rest.

He shed His blood, oh, wondrous love!
    He died that I should live,
To praise Him in His courts above,
    And glory to Him give.

Praise Him, ye saints that dwell on earth,
    And I will praise Him too;
With joyful heart and holy mirth,
    I'll sing His praise below.

We all can sing and say much more,
    Than angels ever could;
For on the cross our sins He bore,
    And cleansed us by His blood.

Oh, rich, oh, precious blood divine,
    Peace-speaking blood to me;
To beautify this soul of mine,
    'Twas shed on Calvary.

Praise, praise to God's beloved Son,
    All praise to Him be given;
Praise to the holy Three in one,
    All praise in earth and heaven.
                  Alleluia!

March 14th, 1870.   J.H.F.

Only once more have I seen Harry. He was asleep when I went to his bedside, but soon roused. It was Saturday afternoon, and it was pleasant to see clean towels and handkerchiefs brought round to each patient. All had on a flannel dressing-gown, and the room was comfortably warm.

He told me he had begun reading Genesis with the New Year. That morning he had read the 49th chapter. He said, "When I read the 25th[1] verse, 'Joseph is a fruitful bough, from thence is the shepherd, the stone of Israel,' Christ darted into my heart in a way I cannot express. I had been searching for Christ all through Joseph's history, the type is so clearly of Him. I had often read this chapter, but never till this morning did I find it sweeter than honey.

"No one can tell what this sweetness is but those in whom Christ dwells, and to whom the Holy Spirit reveals it. I can't find words to express my happiness in Him.

"Sometimes I get a gloomy hour, but not often; and as light is sweeter after darkness, day brighter after night, so I find the shining of God's countenance after a withdrawal.

"I am often amazed that He, the great and Almighty God, should manifest Himself to me, a speck, an atom, just sinful dust and ashes. It is such marvellous love, so boundless, that throughout eternity it will be exhaustless."

"Do you remember sending me some of your verses, Harry? Would you have any objection to my printing some of them? God might bless them, if we prayed it might be for His glory."

Harry.—"Print my poor things? certainly I never had such a thought, never! But if He would bless my poor pen, oh, I should so like to fetch Him a little glory."

"Let us think and pray about it, Harry; bring your hymns like Mary brought her alabaster box to Jesu's feet.

"Now tell me how you liked the musical box?"

"Oh, it *has* been a treat! Every evening I wound it up, and all in the ward would be quiet then, and liked it so much. Here it is, quite safe."

"I have brought you this glass harmonicon, Harry, and a cheap concertina, it only cost one shilling and sixpence, but I thought you might like it, as you said you were fond of music. I wonder if you would like a flute better?"

"I have no breath for that now, Miss, but when I was a lad many's the time I've taken my flute and violin to bed with me, and woke the house with it in the morning. I used to copy out scores of anthems and chants; your father's name was well known to me as a musician. I should like to have some notes of his music here. I can tell anything by note."

"Worcester Chant" was well known to Harry, and so we sang it softly together. His last remark was in answer to this question, "What does music suggest to you, Harry?"

"That for which there is no comparison, the voice of the Lord Jesus in His word, in this Bible, *that* is living music now. But no earthly music can compare or give any idea of that which ear hath not heard. Music will be the voice of the Lord Jesus, and I shall hear it in the Upper Temple, in the Holy of Holies."

Verily he is, "Harry the Happy."

"Happy is he that hath the God of Jacob for his help; whose hope is in the Lord his God."

GOD MY COMPANION.

Oh, may I daily walk with God,
    And be submissive to His rod,
And daily wash in Jesu's blood,
        With God for my Companion.

Since I from sin and Satan flee,
    And Jesu's blood was shed for me;
How can I then unhappy be,
        With God my true Companion?

When with my heart to Him I cry,
    He doth my every want supply,
And no good thing will He deny;
        He is my best Companion.

Should friends forsake me in distress,
    He will not leave me comfortless;

---

[1] This is found in the 22nd and 24th verses of Genesis 49.

With humble joy I do confess,
    He is my sole Companion.

The powers of hell I need not fear,
Although with hellish rage they tear;
My God is ever by and near,
    Oh, what a great Companion!

And when through death's dark vale I go,
The river threatening to o'erflow,
I shall in safety be led through,
    By Him, my dear Companion.

When landed on that heavenly shore,
Where sin and sorrow are no more,
To meet with those that went before,
    And there, with my Companion.

What everlasting songs of praise,
In that blest place our hearts will raise,
Through never, never ending days,
    To God our great Companion!

Joseph Henry Ford,
Bed-ridden Ward.

Portrait of Elizabeth Clay in 1885. She worked with Maria in Bewdley, Worcestershire, for ten years, and she was a very close friend of F.R.H. from their time as classmates in 1851 until Frances died in 1879. See pages 135–140 of this book. Elizabeth labored in a very rural part of India, in very difficult circumstances, among the poorest women, and decades later she wanted to remain on the field till her death, but her health required her to leave and return to England. F.R.H. would have readily, gladly joined her in India, if her own health had not been so fragile and she were able.

Deut. xxxiii. 25.

As thy Days thy strength shall be,
This should be enough for thee;
He, who knows thy frame, will spare
Burdens more than thou canst bear.

When thy Days are veiled in night,
Christ shall give thee heavenly light.
Seem they wearisome and long?
Yet in Him shalt thou be strong.

Cold and wintry though they prove,
Thine the sunshine of His love;
Or with fervid heat oppressed,
'Neath His shadow thou shalt rest.

When thy days on earth are past,
Christ shall call thee home at last,
His redeeming love to praise,
"Who hath strengthened all thy days."

F.R.H.

Rest in the Lord.

Psalm xxxvii. 7.

"Rest in the Lord!" Sweet word of truth,
A word for age, a word for youth,
A word for all the weary world,
A banner-word by love unfurled.

Then cease, ye wearied ones of earth,
To slave for pleasure, gain, or mirth:
Cast down your load of vanities,
And welcome God's realities."

"Rest in the Lord!" Sweet word of grace,
To all the Saviour's new-born race;
'Tis music, light, and balm to them,
An hourly-guiding apothegm.

Then, Lord of rest, we rest in Thee,
For all our daily destiny;

Two more pages from Maria's album of handcopied poems for Giles Shaw. See page 4 of this book. The second poem begun on this page is completed on the next one, 72.

Our mighty guilt, our grief, our care,
We cast, (strange act!) on Thee to bear.

For Thou, dear Lamb of God, wast slain,
To bear each load, and ease each pain;
And now Thy Blood and righteousness
Are rocks of rest in all distress.

And when at last we fall on sleep,
Nor heart shall throb, nor eye shall weep;
Then, blessed Saviour, let it be,
That Thou shalt write, "They rest in Me!"

Rev'd. W. H. Havergal.

Henry Martyn's Last Words.

I sat 'neath the orchard's refreshing retreat,
And thought with sweet comfort & peace,
"Though no hand may cherish, tho' no voice may greet,

"His arm is my pillow, His Word is my feast."

And musing I said, "When shall time cease to be,
And the bliss of eternity gladden my breast?"
For I thought of my sin & the world's misery,
And I longed to depart where the weary find rest.

"And when (still I said) shall the new earth & heavens
Where righteousness dwelleth in glory appear?
For there no defilement, nor sins hated leaven,
Nor sorrow, nor sighing, shall ever come near.

"No wickedness there shall debase or destroy;
And innate corruption for ever shall cease:
Oh rapturous vision! O fulness of joy!
The cross-bearing pilgrim shall reign there in peace."

Rev'd. W. H. Havergal.
Astley Rectory 1827.

Besides poems by William Henry Havergal and three of his daughters, F.R.H., Maria, and Ellen (Giles' wife), Maria copied poems by Anne R. Cousin (the complete poem "Last Words of Samuel Rutherford"), H. F. Lyte, Horatius Bonar, Augustus Montague Toplady, William Cowper, John Newton, Charlotte Elliott, George Herbert, and several others.

CRIPPLE JOSEPH:

A Story of Grace.

BY

MARIA V. G. HAVERGAL.

ALL PROFITS TO THE HAVERGAL HALL PROTESTANT SCHOOLS, LIMERICK.

LONDON:
JAMES NISBET & CO., 21 BERNERS STREET.
1887.

CONTENTS.

Introduction	75
Journals and Letters	77
Hymns	84
Fragments in Pencil	90

This drawing was almost surely a sketch by T. J. Hughes before his beautiful portrait found on page 373 of this book. The address written below the sketch, 2 Elm Row, Hampstead (London), was Hughes' address. See her sister Maria's comment on page 239 of this book.

INTRODUCTION.

THE Psalmist speaks of God's "hidden ones;" their names, their history, their faith and patience in tribulation, all wrapped up in the folds of obscurity. Hidden awhile perchance from man, but not hidden to Him who telleth the number of the stars and careth for the sparrows; and in the day when the King makes up His jewels, many a lonely and hidden gem shall be safely found in His casket.

Such a hidden one was Joseph Harrison till the following letter led to the unfolding of his history:—

To the Rev. CHARLES BULLOCK.

I humbly write enclosing one shilling for the Frances Ridley Havergal Memorial Missionary Fund. It is a poor invalid's humble mite. I will, with your permission, relate the circumstances under which it is sent. I have been afflicted more than nine years. A friend sent me *Royal Commandments* (F. R. H.). This book is indeed a joy and comfort to my soul, and I read my daily commandment with a pure happiness, and each day gain a renewal of strength from *My King*. The portions for the tenth and eighteenth days have been an especial blessing to me. The book is very dear to me. I most willingly deny myself some little necessity that I may contribute to the fund.

JOSEPH HARRISON,
82 DUKE STREET, BIRMINGHAM.

[See page 367, *Memorials*, F. R. H., page 351 of this book.]

This letter was afterwards sent to me by Mr. Bullock, and I requested a friend in Birmingham to visit Joseph, and tell me of his circumstances. Her answer was, "It is worth any journey to see his beaming face, and though Joseph is enduring much suffering and privation, he is indeed rejoicing in his King."

Subsequently it was my great privilege to visit him from time to time. After his death his Bible was sent to me, diligently marked throughout, and the words, "joy, love, comfort," in pencil, recur again and again under the promises he found so precious. His shorthand exercises, a book of outline drawings, MS. books, and a large couvrette he worked for me, as a grateful offering, prove his industry. One book he filled with passages from Scripture, proving the divinity of the Lord Jesus, was sent to me with his Journal and hymns. Knowing Joseph's strong desire to bear witness to the Godhead of the Lord Jesus, and how clearly he saw the errors of the Unitarian doctrine in which he had been brought up, and knowing how he wished his little history and hymns might bring even one ray of glory to his Saviour God, is the reason for the publication of these pages.

Joseph's clearer faith and joy so originated in reading the books of my beloved sister, Frances Ridley Havergal, that I wish to entwine their memories, and therefore propose to devote all proceeds of this book to the noble work carried on in the Memorial Havergal Hall Schools, Limerick.

It is with pleasure I receive my publishers', Messrs. Nisbet's, unsought assurance that they contribute their share of profit also.

This Havergal Hall was formerly a Masonic building—one of the rooms seats a thousand. The Irish Society and the Rev. Canon Gregg advanced the money for its purchase, and proposed it should constitute a memorial to F. R. H. for her loving labours for the Irish Society. Gradually the purchase has been refunded by those who value her writings.

Canon Gregg has also laid out a considerable sum on the building, and he is the devoted and responsible manager of the schools held therein. Not only are many (some orphan) children supported, clothed, and trained in our most holy and scriptural faith, but several classes for the instruction of adults are held. The members of the Y. W. C. A. also meet in this hall, numbering 260 members, and the Misses Gregg conduct various classes for them. As there is *no* endowment for all this good work, and the Irish supporters are suffering from the distressful landlord difficulties, I cannot but commend these schools to the sympathy and support of English friends. (The fullest information will be given by the Rev. J. F. Gregg, St. George's Street, Limerick.)

May I describe one room and its sacred mementos of my beloved sister? Messrs. Elliot and Fry presented an enlarged and coloured photograph portrait of F. R. H.; this is enwreathed with ferns and wild roses (her favourite flower) painted by Helga von Cramm. Around this are photos of her birthplace and tomb, and many of her hymns in large print. Beneath stands a cabinet, designed by our brother, the Rev. Francis T. Havergal; it is carved from his old church oak, and the Winterdyne cedar tree. This cabinet contains the whole of F. R. H.'s writings in prose and poetry, also all her musical compositions, and her hymn tunes and chants in *Songs of Grace and Glory*, with many of the illustrated cards so widely known. I have also added translations of many of her works, and of her Memoir in French, German, Swedish, and Dutch. Eventually I hope copies will be sent of translations of these already published in Bengali, Indu, Tamil, Singhalese, Malayalim, Telegu, Japanese, and some of her hymns in the Benga dialect, Central Africa.

Reverting to the history of Joseph Harrison, the following pages will testify to the marvellous joy that supported him in much suffering. His faith was unswerving when once the truth of the Godhead of Christ shone into his soul, and consciously did he rejoice in the assurance that his passport for glory was signed by the blood of the Lamb.

May Joseph's words and hymns prove one prelude chord to the final and glorious anthem of the upper choir: "Blessing, and honour, and glory, and power, be unto Him that sitteth upon the throne, and unto the Lamb for ever and ever;" for "He is LORD of Lords and KING of Kings!"

Maria V. G. Havergal.

1887.

ANTICIPATIONS.

(*Written at Day-dawn,* May 29, 1880.)

"Until the day break and the shadows flee away."
—Song of Solomon 2:17.

Shadows so darkening,
Dream-like are passing,
Deserts so dreary,
Footfall most weary,
Lonely night weeping,
Vigil watch keeping,
Achings so trying,
Teardrop and sighing,
Shadows unveiling,
Mists fleeing away,
Changing to day!

Shadows no longer!
Day-dawning yonder,
Sweet voices calling,
Sister's chant falling,
Palm branches waving,
Stormy clouds breaking.
Welcome! sweet morning,
Glory-light dawning,
Haven is nearing,
No breakers fearing;
Gaining the strand
Safe, safe to land!

Thus I pass yonder,
Lost in sweet wonder,
Praising and soaring,
Always adoring,
Raiment all snow-white,
Blood-washed and sun-bright;
In Christ victorious,
Visions so glorious!
Hushed on His breast,
There shall I rest;
Shadows all past,
Daybreak at last!

Maria V. G. H.

These are four of the emblems on various covers of books by Frances Ridley Havergal published by James Nisbet & Co. The harp was Frances' personal emblem. Nisbet was her primary publisher while she lived and after she died, and they did exceptionally fine productions of her books. If an item by F.R.H. was published by Nisbet, the Nisbet edition is nearly always definitive.

JOURNALS AND LETTERS.

THE following Journal and Letters by Joseph Harrison relate his simple history.

I will only describe my first visit to his humble home, 82 Duke Street, Birmingham. The narrow staircase ascended, his mother opened the door into Joseph's lowly room. He was lying on a small and seemingly uncomfortable bed, a table near with a well-used Bible, and several of my dear sister's books. Such a happy, happy face looked at me, a stranger; but when I said, "I am Frances Ridley Havergal's sister," his smile was beaming. Joseph told me of the comfort my dear sister's books had been to him. I inquired *where* he first saw them? It seems that during his stay in the Convalescent Hospital at Ventnor, a kind colonel visited the wards, and lent or gave F. R. H.'s books. To one patient, a friend of Joseph's, he gave *Loyal Responses*, but Joseph did not *then* notice the book. But his friend died, and when dying spoke of the comfort he found in her hymns. Joseph returned home, and soon a wish woke up in his heart to know more about those hymns. He wrote to the colonel, asking the favour of a copy of the *Loyal Responses*. The colonel replied he had not one, but sent *Royal Commandments*.

Joseph remarked, "I was not ready for *Loyal Responses*; I had not yet received God's command to believe on the name of His Son Jesus Christ as my Saviour God."

Reading the *Royal Commandments* was to Joseph the unveiling of the Lord Jesus to his soul. I then listened to the story of his sufferings, and marvelled at his joyful patience under them. Far more did I marvel as he told me of his exceeding joy in the Lord, and those bright manifestations of his Saviour's presence he so constantly and vividly realized.

I noticed his hard paillasse. Paillasses are one of our English mistakes! straw hammered down instead of the Swiss method of loose hay, chaff, or even dried leaves that can be shaken up comfortably.

When I returned at night to my three soft mattresses, how could I enjoy them, and Joseph on that hard paillasse?

My patent for mattresses is to have the hair put loosely in the tick so that it can be shaken up daily into a delightful springy cushion, reminding one of purple heather seats on mountain or hillside. No, I could not enjoy my mattresses till one of them was packed up for Joey. My nurse, M. Farrington, went with me and took it, and my nephew's dressing-gown was a welcome addition, in which Joey said he "felt like a duke!" (It is just possible some spare mattresses may be shaken up into this patent, and may bring ease and sleep to some poor invalid.) Another visit I took a life-sized coloured crayon of my beloved sister, the valued gift of Messrs. Elliot and Fry, who hereby brought me back a glimpse of the bright original. It is singular that I thus gratified Joseph's wish without knowing how much he longed to see my sister's face *once*. This portrait gives her golden hair, but not *the* sunny smile—no artist could catch *that*. When I placed the portrait before Joseph, he exclaimed, "Ah, how lovely! what a smile! what a luxury you have brought me!" The glimpse seemed to satisfy him, and as I took it away he spoke of seeing and knowing her in the brightness to come.

We turn now to his Journal.

JOURNAL.

February 3, 1880.—(A day never to be forgotten by me.) I received, through the post, a copy of *Royal Commandments*, by F. R. Havergal, from a kind colonel at Ventnor, now my very dear brother in the Lord.

Till then I knew not anything of F. R. H., only seeing her books in the hospital. This book was the very thing I wanted. God had ordained it, I am sure. It came to remove the veil from my eyes, to give me light, to give to me my precious, precious Saviour. I read on daily in *Royal Commandments*, having new and sweet joy every day. I had been walking in darkness, yet staying on my God for more than twelve years. The chapter for the 10th Day, "Trusting in Darkness" (see Isaiah 50:10), brought me much joy, and on reaching Day 18th, "Our Work in God's Hand," the veil was removed (see Appendix). I saw things as I had never seen them before. I was filled with joy and happiness unspeakable. I felt I must write to F. R. H., and tell her the joy she had given me, and thank her. I wrote to the publisher, Nisbet, asking him to forward my letter enclosed; but I received my letter back, and a note to say F. R. H. *was dead*.

I felt I had lost a dear *sister*, for so I had learnt to think of her. I opened the February number of *Home Words*, 1880, and there saw a picture of her burying-place, Astley, Worcestershire. The remarkable feature is, that though I had had *Home Words* to read more than twelve months, I hardly ever opened it, and had not noticed about F. R. H. in it. My heavenly Father had made it so, that He may now make my joy full. Two hours after I knew of her death, I felt somewhat calmer, for I knew she was in heaven, and so I began to write some verses, and finished them some days after.

ON HEARING OF THE DEATH OF F. R. H.

February 20, 1880.

Thou hast gone to thy rest, sweet disciple of Christ,
    Thy writing and work is all o'er;
Thou hast shown unto thousands the pearl of great price,
    O blest be thy name evermore!

Thou hast entered the joy that never shall end,
    Thy labour of love is well done;
The race of thy life was so run to the end,
    Thou the crown of the victor hast won.

Thou art sleeping in peace, sweet disciple of love,
    Thy watching and waiting is o'er,
Now a guest with the Bridegroom in heaven above,
    Pure happiness thine evermore.

Now thy songs to the Saviour re-echo above,
    Made perfect in word and in praise;
And thy worship of Him, the King of thy love,
    Thou wilt ever adoringly raise.

Sing on in thy joy richest praise to this King,
    The wondrous, eternal "I Am,"
Of His grand love and mercy, make heaven to ring,
    Sing sweetly, sing "Worthy the Lamb!"

J. H.

February 25, 1880.—The more I think of it, the more do I find that "God moves in a mysterious way, His wonders to perform." For had I read much of *Home Words*, I should never have written to thank F. R. H. for the joy she had given me, in that she had made me to know and feel that I had a PERSONAL SAVIOUR who NOW was doing ALL things needful for me, and that I should not have to WAIT till I got to heaven before I could be HAPPY in HIM!

Who can tell my joy in my knowing that my dear, *dear* SAVIOUR was WITH ME,—*keeping me*,—that HE was about me NOW, and that I may breathe His very presence into my soul; that poor weary soul which for so many years had been seeking Him, battling midst doubts and fears in the *dark*; now all was LIGHT! all was JOY! Oh, bliss unspeakable!

Soon after this I sent the letter I had written to F. R. H. to the editor of *Home Words*, asking if there should be any sisters of F. R. H. to forward it, as it might cheer and comfort them to know that their sister's works had given such joy to a poor invalid. The Rev. C. Bullock kindly sent my letter to them, and he also sent me his book, *Within the Palace Gates*.

I little knew the joys my heavenly Father had prepared for me,—that now I was to have such friends, who would give me such happiness, as I never had had before. From my childhood I had attended a Unitarian place of worship. For some years I had felt a need of a *personal* Saviour, as I knew I was a guilty sinner, and that I deserved eternal death. I longed—oh, how deeply!—to be saved; yet though I went to chapel, expecting to hear the glad tidings, I came away empty and dejected. I must say that, from my weak state of health, I could not always attend chapel, and so may have missed such a sermon. I had no one to advise me what to do. In 1879, I was weaning myself from that congregation, for I wanted to go to a place of worship to hear of Christ as the Saviour of the world, to hear about Jesus Christ and Him crucified. And now I was to have my faith tried very very greatly. I forsook the Unitarian Chapel, and that same December I was laid up with an illness nearly unto death; and our family, through illness and want of employment, were reduced to very great straits. Were I to tell all, it would seem a fable. I nearly sank through want; but my dear Lord gave me strength to hold fast my confidence, and in His own way He kept me, making His words very precious, as in the following hymn:—

THY WORDS.

Lord Jesus, make Thy words my strength,
    Be Thou at my right hand;
Then though temptations struggle long,
    In Thee I firmly stand.

Lord Jesus, make Thy words my joy
    In dark affliction's hour;
When giant troubles press me hard,
    They are my refuge tower.

Lord Jesus, make Thy words my guide
    Along life's thorny way;
When I Thy words sincerely trust,
    My feet shall never stray.

Lord Jesus, make Thy words my peace,
    When strife doth rage around;
Sweet oil of comfort, pure are they,
    For every troubled wound.

Lord Jesus, make Thy words my rock
    Whereon my faith shall build;
Though tempests wild around me beat,
    I stand with calmness filled.

Lord Jesus, make Thy words a power,
    To draw all men to Thee;

With true repentance make them lay
    Their sins at Calvary.

Thy Words *are* Life, Strength, Joy, and Help,
    A Guide to me and all;
Rod, Peace, and Rock, a Power to save,
    A perfect All in All!

J. H.

When I had left my bed some weeks, my Unitarian friends allowed me a pint of milk daily. I felt thankful for this, for though I had not, nay, would not send them word of my illness, yet when they offered kindness, I could not but accept it with thankfulness.

"Oh that they would preach salvation in Christ Jesus! for there is none other name under heaven given among men whereby we must be saved."

Can any one wonder at my joy, now that the Lord had revealed Himself to me in *Royal Commandments?* It was, and is, simply joy unspeakable.

I had long prayed that He would give living food for my spirit, and then food for my body. He had thus given me the first portion of my prayer, and now He was about fulfilling the latter portion, in making for me new friends. True and faithful is He! Now I exclaim—knowing and feeling its truth to the depths—"There hath not failed one word of all His good promise."

SING PRAISES!

No tongue on earth can tell His worth,
    Who died on Calvary.
In purest love He shed His blood,
    To make the whole world free.

Worthy the Lamb! One with I Am,
    In joy the angels sing;
They tell it out, with mighty shout,
    Which makes the Heavens to ring.

Worthy the Lamb! echoes below,
    In feeble human voice;
But when above, with burning love,
    We'll shout it and rejoice.

March 31, 1880.—To-day I received a gift of F. R. H.'s books from my very dear friend and sister in the Lord, Miss Havergal. I read in *Under His Shadow, Free to Serve*; my poor heart was wonderfully affected by it. Among the books was *Morning Stars, or Names of Christ for His Little Ones.* I read the Prefatory Note and Preface. There was something in the Preface which greatly interested me, and through it I wrote some verses,—"Seek." I was also greatly touched by the simple Prefatory Note of M. V. G. H. I little dreamt that the Lord would give me the great joy to speak to this dear friend "face to face;" yet so He did, and oh, what joy did that day bring me! I felt I had been with one of His ambassadors. When thinking of this and all His tender mercies unto me, a poor sinful creature, I can but say with David, "Bless the Lord, O my soul; and all that is within me, bless His holy name."

To M. V. G. H.

April 1880.

MY DEAR FRIEND,—

I have received the books of Miss F. R. H., and, oh, what treasures! It would be one of the most difficult tasks to say which I liked best. They are mines of treasures, leading me to God's *own* Treasury. I shall not attempt to thank you, 'tis useless. God bless you, I love you; there, that's all!

Opening *Under His Shadow,* I read *Free to Serve*; my heart filled to overflowing while I was reading them.

April 12, 1880.—I received through post from Plymouth a large volume of Goodwin's *Exposition, Ephesians and Revelation.* It was accompanied by a letter, which contained a well of sweet comfort in Christ to my soul. This letter was very specially blessed to me, for that day my youngest brother was very ill, it seemed even unto death. Here I was, lying ill in bed also, and my blessed Lord had given me another friend to take his place (my brother was twenty-four weeks in hospital, and returned convalescent, thank God for His mercy, to me—God is love). I never think of this day without my heart being filled with joyful thankfulness to my dear Lord for His giving me my new and dear brother, through Miss Havergal writing about me. Psalm 133 is so beautifully true. "In my distress I called upon the Lord: my cry came before Him, even in His holy temple, even into His ears." Psalm 18:6, and Psalm 89:52, "Blessed be the Lord for evermore, Amen and Amen!"

While reading in Goodwin, page 417, my mind was powerfully worked upon. It wonderfully shows forth the rich mercy and love of God; and I thought how utterly unable infidels were to stand against such marvellous loving-kindness as these glorious truths set forth.

I thought much about an infidel named Bradlaugh, and feel sure if he and his friends would read Goodwin they must cry for forgiveness; and after they have come and tasted and seen that God is *good,* they would build upon the Rock, Jesus Christ, and surely find, "Blessed is the man that trusteth in Him."

ON THE WORKS OF GOODWIN.

What! say that Infidels shall flourish, while the Lord
Shall give such men as Goodwin, writer grand!
Nay! pierce them with Thy Spirit, as a sword,
Oh, bring them to Thyself, with strong and mighty hand.

O Goodwin! would that Infidels thy works would read;
Then surely shall they taste and see the Lord is good.
Then would they find God's Word a lamp of light,
And dread e'en one look back to error's fearful night.

Rich treasures, Goodwin's works for searching minds,
Yielding true wealth from God's own boundless store,
Treasures laid up in heaven, we safely find
New life, new joy in Christ, henceforth and evermore.

O Word of God! most true, most grand and great,
Revealing Christ, *my* Christ, unto my longing soul;
Who shed His life-blood, ransom rich and free,
Bearing my curse, dying instead of me.

J. H.

Before I knew the Lord Jesus to be my Lord and *my God*, I had often read through the Psalms as a matter of duty, and when coming to the 119th, always thought, "What a long psalm! it will take such a time to read that one." Alas! my heart was not right then, I did not see Christ in the Psalms. Now I read this psalm with a new and sweet joy. I picked out all the verses with reference to "the Word," and I thought "the Word" must be Jesus. So I applied each verse thus to my heart, and it gave me the very sweetest joy, and made the psalm very *precious* to me. Ah! my poor heart was right now. Again and again I turned to this psalm to enjoy my joy in Jesus as *the* Word; once, while turning over the leaves of my Bible to find it, I suddenly thought of the "White Stone." While searching in the Revelation to find it, I read about the "new name" written in the stone—through reading that I wrote the following lines,[1] and am sure the poem is my reward for my love to Jesus and changed feelings, all glory be to Him!

(*Last Page in Journal.*)

April 24, 1882.—It was on the 12th of December that I took to my bed with one of my serious illnesses. I began to sing to my Saviour through reading Miss Havergal's books, on December 19, 1879, and my *first word* was Jesus.

> "Jesus, Thou Thy life didst give,
> Thine own life, that I might live."

And now I have reached April 1882. My passage through the fire has been severe, but now through God's merciful blessing I am able to leave my bed for an hour or two. But before doing so I wrote the following piece, "Jesus!"[2] My heart rejoiced that my dear Saviour had given me "songs in the night." I thought as I *began* with "Jesus!" my first and my last word should be

---

[1] See hymn, "Write Down my Name," p. 46. [See page 85 of this book.]

[2] See hymn, "Jesus," p. 57. [See pages 88–89 of this book.]

Jesus! I was filled with a calm holy joy. "Bless the Lord, O my soul; and all that is within me, bless His holy name."

JOSEPH HARRISON.

LETTERS TO M. V. G. H.

February 21, 1882.

Text for to-day: "The Father himself loveth you."
"Bearing about in the body the dying of the Lord Jesus."

DEAR FRIEND AND SISTER,—

I was greatly rejoiced to see your handwriting on the wrapper this morning, and have much joy in the contents,—I must specially mention the beautiful card, "And he shall serve Him for ever." You will be pleased to know that the pains are better; my kind surgeon has given me a medicine that has very greatly relieved me. Through the warm clothes sent by your cousins I am not so pinched up.

Last Saturday was the second anniversary of my dear, dear Lord Jesus revealing Himself to *me* as my Saviour; oh, the light, joy, and peace which was then and has ever since been mine! Surely the 18th day of F. R. H.'s *Royal Commandments* was greatly blessed by the Holy Spirit to me; yea, I am sure the writer was filled with the Spirit while writing it.

It had been my intention to tell you how my Lord brought me out of darkness into His own pure light and joy, giving me His own sweet peace and rest from my trouble and sorrow, but my pains would not allow me. Yet I was blessed and permitted to tell it out at a prayer meeting this week, etc.—Your humble servant in the dear Lord.

God bless you. "God is love."

J. H.

October 31, 1882.

Text for to-day: "Be of good courage, all ye that hope in the Lord. Rejoice evermore."

. . . I must write, that you may rejoice with me in a very blessed *gift*. But first a word about your hair bed. I sleep sounder, longer, and am altogether more refreshed by lying on it. This I know will make you glad, and I prize it very much, and the soft pillow you sent me from Keswick.

Now about this gift. You know how the hard plaster of Paris jackets hurt my spine, and how the surgical instruments in the Orthopaedic Hospital could not be adapted to me, it clipt and cramped me so. This was a trouble to me, and seemed to cast a shade over my future physical life.

You, dear sister, prayed that our dear Lord would lighten my pain; and now see His blessed answer. While thinking it over, He has opened my eyes to see the kind of support that would suit me. So I take the *idea* as His special gift. (Then follow the details.) A young cabinet maker is doing it for me, and from a rough sample; it will support me beautifully. Are not the ways of our dear Lord wonderful? Surely he can *do* when all else fails.

God bless you. "God is love."

J. Harrison.

POST CARDS.

January 11, 1883.

Text for to-day: "Ye are the light of the world."—Matthew 5:14.

"The God of hope fill you with all joy and peace in believing."— Romans 15:13.

Dear Friend in Jesus,—

I have received all safely, and thank you very much indeed. The glass lid of the pretty box to keep all my papers in was broken. I have so much joy in the Lord Jesus, through His holy grace and loving mercy—through trusting Him for much, and letting Him *do* entirely for me. You know I am so weak and dependent. With loving prayers for yourself and all.—Your servant and brother in Christ Jesus.

God bless you. "God is love."

J. H.

Text for to-day: "He that shall come will come, and will not tarry."

"The Lord will give grace and glory."

Dear Friend and Sister in the Lord,—

I have been in much communion with our dear Lord Jesus about you, and I hope you will rest from literary work till after Christmas, even though you should feel remarkably well, which I believe you will do. You must rest, rest, rest! and take it as a very special holiday from Himself. I have prayed, and do pray, Him to work mightily for you, that nothing of His shall fall to the ground; or suffer loss, but receive greater blessing instead.—Yours in humble Christian love.

God bless you. "God is love."

J. H.

82 Duke Street, Birmingham,
January 10, 1883.

Text for to-day: "I know that thou canst do everything."—Job 42:2.

"As the Father hath loved me, so have I loved you."— John 15:9.[1]

My Dear Friend and Sister in Jesus,—

I hope this letter will find you in improved health; I feel really anxious about you. I seem to think you are so tired and exhausted. I pray daily, yea, and often for you; and while praying to our dear and precious Lord Jesus about you, the following picture passed before me. It seemed as though our Lord was a Shepherd, and the sheep were following Him home to the fold. You were with them; but oh! so tired, such pain and distress, to keep up with the rest! The loving Shepherd saw you, and tenderly said to you,—

"Let my sheep rest. I will sit down by you, and be with you." (This, as it were, to comfort and assure you.) He therefore sat down on a grassy mound, and you lay down to rest—but only for a little while; for, breaking away, you again struggled after the other sheep that were nearing the fold. Again, you were so very distressed, it was quite painful, and the kind Shepherd tenderly said,—

"Come, do rest with me, I will be with you."

This time you lay down, and laid your head upon His breast. His arms were about you, and your rest was perfect and complete,—so happy, too, and no further breaking away. All things seemed full of holy peace, joy, comfort, and rest, that, as I saw this in my mind's eye, I felt happy about you, and loved our dear Saviour and Shepherd. Surely He is with you, loving you tenderly! Has my dear sister been breaking away, doing *her* will? I have prayed about this, and asked our dear Lord Jesus to guide you.

I truly hope all is well, and that all indeed is to the glory of God in Christ Jesus, our precious Redeemer and Saviour.

I am getting a little stronger, but cannot sit up every day. I safely received your sister's book, *My King*, for which I thank you very much. I seem to love your sister, though I knew her not in the flesh. Her writings help me more and more. That you may be mightily blessed throughout the New Year, to the glory of God in Jesus, is the sincerest prayer of your brother in the Lord.

God bless you. "God is love."

J. H.

P.S.—I thank you very much for the lovely box from Africa. I never had bride-cake sent me before. May our dear Lord bless His missionary servants, and may He give them many precious souls is my daily prayer. Yea, I pray for all connected with you.[2]

J. H.

February 22, 1883.

"I am thy Shield."

Dear Friend and Sister in Jesus,—

Most joyfully received your kind letter, nice fresh butter, flowers, etc. Have been full of pain and weariness, but to-day feel better.

Most certainly I will pray for the Unitarian minister, that our Lord Jesus will open his eyes and give him light to see Him as his Saviour, Lord, and *God*. You see the Unitarians say that our dear Lord Jesus is our Guide, Teacher, and Example, showing us how we may live and serve our heavenly Father; but that Jesus gave Himself for us, suffered death's penalty, offering Himself in our stead, and is indeed Substitute, and our Saviour, is quite out of their theology. At least I found it so, to my grief, the years I attended chapel.

I am so glad you are going to send *My King* to ——, and may I humbly suggest you will please send him *Kept*. We will pray about it, and if he cannot agree with all that is therein, how Christ is for us, it

---

[1] This *parable* was singularly *true* of M. V. G. H's restlessness through pressure of letters.

[2] This refers to my sending Joseph a tiny box of wedding-cake from Zanzibar. My dear missionary niece, Amy (Havergal) Downes Shaw, little thought how many prayers were offered for her by this invalid!

He took much interest in the detail of Rev. A. D. Shaw's work at Kisulitini, East Africa.

must touch his heart, and with our dear Lord's blessing take the veil away.

After much prayer for you, I seem to think the next month will be brightly blessed by our Lord to you, and you will have some special work for Him. Now you must work and *rest*; you must not be restless, while your head and hands are quite still,—know that Christ's power is working *in* you and *for* you to His glory; so you must be content to rest as well as work. David said, "I have behaved and quieted myself as a child." Surely you will quiet yourself too. When the soul rests in the Lord entirely, the day opens with sweet and holy communion in prayer and *reading with the* Lord Jesus.

Then finish your literary work for Him at 10 A.M., with short silent prayer for His holy blessing on it. Then exercise and visiting. In the afternoon some rest and sleep,—get in the cosiest position possible, and shut your eyes,—this rests the poor head. Afternoon letters strictly brief (!!??). Then prayer and praise and rests for the night. All this is for Jesus! and all will be well done, if one talent is not made to suffer for another! The Lord bless you.

You say your poor forehead burns and aches from all the letters and writing,—do try a fourfold wet cloth and flannel over it, turning it now and then.

In Christian love and gratefulness, and earnest prayer.

God bless you. "God is love."

J. H.

April 24, 1883.

Text for today: "Wash me throughly from mine iniquity."—Psalm 51:2.

"Be of good cheer."—Matthew 9:2.

DEAR SISTER IN JESUS,—

I really am anxious to know how your health is, and your poor thumb, that has been so long useless. That no *evil* has befallen you, I feel sure, for you are in the *safe* keeping of your dear and precious Lord Jesus. But physical pain may have overtaken you, though mind, it is all to His glory!

Oh, what a joy to me to see your bright face again! and well, and happy, and *resting*. I must underline that last word, though the whole is from my heart. Do you know, I think that poor, bad thumb (out of joint) has been purposely given you for the glory of our Lord Jesus Christ. That it is all for His glory is my sincerest prayer. Till my spirit and self-will was thoroughly broken, there was no one more struggling and restless than myself. I used to feel that I could do, must *do*, I would be *doing*, so that I have even made myself seriously ill with fresh abscesses through it. Often did I repeat this—though it was to struggle to earn my living. I was not happy through this trial; but oh, when I saw that it was the Lord's *will* I should *not* work (made plain to me by continued affliction and weakness), I humbly and truly said, "Thy will be done." 'Twas hard at first, yet only thus was I, could I, yea, can I, be happy in Jesus. To suffer His will has become easier and easier, bringing me yet greater happiness with it. "Bless the Lord, O my soul; and all that is within me, bless His holy name."

With loving, sincere prayers, yours faithfully.

God bless you. "God is love."

J. H.

April 26, 1883.

Text for to-day: "Fruitful in every good word and work."—Colossians 1:10.

"Lo, I am with you always."—Matthew 28:20.

MY DEAR, DEAR SISTER IN JESUS,—

Oh, how I wish I could bear your pain for you! I should be so happy were this possible. I am so sorry about the accident to your foot, and hope bran poultice will strengthen it. I do hope your thumb will be well soon. I have prayed long and earnestly to our dear Lord Jesus about your nerve suffering. I have asked His holy guidance and blessing on what I send you (a registered box of morphia lozenges, which I did *not* take). I hope He will bless them to you, for they have been blessed to me.

I pray earnestly that I may be a comfort to you; may the Lord bless me so to be. Now I must tell you about the honey and potted meat,— quite a choice of luxuries, for we can never buy the like, or nice butter. The honey is truly delightful; oh, how I enjoyed my breakfast with it, quite a rich treat! May the Lord keep, comfort, guard, and bless you; may He lift up the light of His countenance upon you, and give you peace, is the earnest, sincere prayer of your humble servant.

God bless you. "God is love."

J. H.

May 25, 1883.

Text for today: "Their iniquities will I remember no more."—Hebrews 8:12.

"Saved in the Lord with an everlasting salvation."— Isaiah 45:17.

DEAR FRIEND AND SISTER IN JESUS,—

I was greatly rejoiced yesterday in receiving your beautiful gift of a melodion, with flowers, butter, tracts, etc. God bless you. I do hope going to the Mumbles with that good nurse Mary F. will make you quite well.

You sent me just before Christmas an almanac—the British Workman's,—it is nailed on my bedroom wall. The text for May 9 was, "Ask what I shall give thee." I turned and placed my hand on my Bible, and prayed, "O God, let my life be lived in holy service to Thy glory in Christ Jesus. Amen." Through the day I thought several times of the text, and in the middle of the night the following hymn was given me. I wanted to write it down, but remembered I had but little candle—not enough. I should like to dedicate it to you :—

Matthew 5:16.

O make my light a shining light,
My works, to good works be,
That men may see, and in delight
Give glory unto Thee.

O give, dear Lord, a full delight
To walk in all Thy ways;
Let me not faint, lend of Thy might,
A strength for all my days.

O make Thy word a lamp of light
   Unto my weary feet;
Then I with strength can walk upright,
   And all my troubles meet.

O make Thy word a shining light,
   To guide me in Thy path;
Then though with sorrow ends the night,
   A joy the morning hath.

O Jesu, of the world the Light,
   Let me abide in Thee;
Abide in me in glory bright,
   Through all eternity!

O give me light, and make my light
   In purity to shine;
It will indeed be heavenly bright,
   Because, dear Lord, 'tis Thine!

(*His last note.*)
June 20, 1883.

Text for to-day: "He bare the sins of many."—Isaiah 53:12.

"Certainly I will be with thee."— Exodus 3:12.

MY DEAR SISTER IN JESUS,—

It is a great joy to me to be enabled again to write you. 'Tis a blessing indeed from our dear Lord Jesus. Since I last wrote you I have been very near the gates of heaven. There has been no fear or agitation, but a quiet, firm, and simple trust; for I know that my heavenly Father, who gave me my precious Saviour, will not deny the life hereafter: through blessed Jesus, NO FEAR, NO FEAR of death. The day after I wrote I had a serious relapse, and felt myself to be dying. I grew cold, my throat swelled, my breath began to rattle, and I had symptoms of cholera. My prayer was, "O my God, if this shall be the call home, or if it shall be deferred a little longer, let my death or my life be all to *Thy* glory in Christ Jesus, my precious Saviour. Amen."

I was now mercifully shown what to do, and the Lord made me to remember that Dr. J. Collis Brown's chlorodyne was for cholera. I at once had some procured. I took it, and it at once stopped all the bad symptoms— glory be to God!

But the strain to buy the necessary little extras to tempt my appetite is really more than my dear mother, though all willing, can do. Could you please send a little help, for I am sure you would rather I asked you than remain silent and suffer longer. We are indeed really poor; for through the past six winters my stepfather has been out of work, and this kept us down, together with the sickness at our house; so you will see how very joyful I have been to receive your kind gifts, for, oh, at times my food has been so poor! I have *not* mentioned this before, but I know you will forgive me. With love and gratefulness.

J. HARRISON.

God bless you. "God is love."

Every note and card ended with this benediction, and Joseph's golden seal, "God is love."

The next letter was from Joseph's mother.

82 DUKE STREET, BIRMINGHAM,
July 17, 1883.

MY dear son Joseph wished me to let you know when death had taken place. He passed away at ten minutes to six last night, and was happy to receive his Lord Jesus. His end was peace; he had a very happy deathbed. One of the days he said to me, "I wonder what Miss Havergal is doing now." I return you many sincere thanks for all the helps that you have done for my dear son Joseph. Poor fellow, he stood in need of all. Please thank your sister Mrs. S. for the nice butter and flowers often sent him. I will return the music box (melodion) you gave him: he played a little in bed up to the last fortnight. Wishing you all the health, and God's blessed goodness to rest on you and your family, and I hope we shall all meet in heaven.—Your humble servant,

HARRIET BREWSTER.

The mother wrote again,

July 18, 1883.

I THOUGHT I would not send too soon, as I know you have got too much to think about. Poor Joe often told me you work too hard with your brain. He often spoke of you, and thanked God for sending such an angel (*sic*) as you are; and he said, "God bless her for all she has done for us all." The week before he died, he said he would not change places with a worldly man if he had the finest mansion he ever saw. Joe often said, "Mother, read Miss Havergal's books every day;" I have, and always found comfort in them. The readings is beautiful, it helps any one out of trouble; there is always something fresh to be found in them.

Poor Joe did want to see his brother Jim, and said, "Mother, I have been praying to God if it was His will I am ready to go now, and if He please, I should like to live to see my brother come back from Australia." But Jim cannot be here till the end of August. We do miss poor Joe; although he was such a sufferer, he always had a comforting word for us when we were in trouble, and often said, "Mother, lay all your cares on the Lord Jesus, and He will help you through." (My second husband has been so good to Joe.)

HARRIET BREWSTER.

The last scrap of Joseph's writing was this. "Early morn. The Lord our Righteousness, Lord Our RIGHTEOUSNESS. Blessed be thou of the Lord. The Lord bless thee."

What blessed signification in those capital letters! Written on the very threshold of the King's palace. They reveal to us Joseph's safe passport, and safe trust in the righteousness of Christ; and so having on the wedding garment, to him was granted an abundant entrance into the everlasting kingdom of our Lord Jesus Christ.

Memorial Card.

JOSEPH HARRISON,

The beloved son of

WILLIAM AND HARRIET HARRISON,

Departed this life, July 16, 1883, in the 29th year of his age.

Buried in the New Cemetery, Hockley, Birmingham.

WHY DO YOU WEEP?

Why do you weep?
I am falling asleep,
  And Jesus my Shepherd
Is watching His sheep;
  His arm is beneath me,
His eye is above—
  His Spirit within me
Says, "Rest in my love."

  With blood I have bought thee,
And washed thee from sin;
  With care I have brought thee,
My fold to be in.

  Refreshed by still waters,
In green pastures led,
  Thy day has gone by,
I am making thy bed.

  There calmly repose,
While the shades gather round,
  I lay as thou liest,
And hallowed the ground.
  And fear not, confiding
Thy spirit to me;
  Sweet peace in my presence
Its portion shall be!

  Nor long shalt thou wait
For the sound of my voice,
  To rouse thee from slumber
And bid thee rejoice;
  The dawn of that morning,
Unclouded, is near,
  When robed in His glory
Thy God shall appear;
  Then thou shall arise,
In His image to shine,
  And filled with His fulness,
Say, "All things are mine!"

NOTE.—This hymn, and sweet music to accompany it, was composed by John Lockey, of High Wycombe, 1848. It was one of Joseph's favourite hymns.

HYMNS.

WOUNDED IN MY TENT.

LYING wounded in my tent,
Crippled form and sorely bent,
Yet quite happy though in pain,
Jesus in my soul doth reign.

Though sad troubles falling fast,
Thick as snow, with wintry blast,
Chill my frame with icy cold,
Still my heart on Christ doth hold.

Though my spine in pieces break
Through my flesh *their* way to make,
Till with pain I'm nearly blind,
I in Jesus comfort find.

Though my brain, through thinking long,
Is with tightest tension strung,
Grievous though the chastening be,
Still I know He loveth me.

When I see my sins as ink,
Deepest black, my heart doth sink;
When I know that I must die,
Still, oh still, I joyful lie.

On the cross I look and see
Life through all eternity;
Jesus *died*, yea, shed His blood,
That my soul should *live* above.

These words, "Lying wounded in my tent," came to my mind through something the Rev. C. Leach said to me.

All the words are physically and, yes (standing in Christ, my precious Saviour, I dare humbly say it), morally true. I have had spinal curvature for ten years; and I have had abscesses in the spine, and undergone many surgical operations. Both of my hips are diseased, so that pieces of bone come away from them and the spine. My deformity and illness is no pain of mind to me. The 3rd verse of Psalm 100: "Know ye that the Lord He *is* God; it is He that hath made us, and not we ourselves; we are His people, and the sheep of His pasture," makes me quite *satisfied*. I have a calm, joyful assurance that "whom the Lord loveth He chasteneth, and scourgeth every son whom He receiveth" (Hebrews 12.6). The latter part of the verse makes me quite happy—the scourging and chastening which all sons receive, being bodily affliction, may be grievous; but we do know that in one way or other the chastening is for the good of our souls, by our dear Lord God. If we will but see it, affliction will make clear to our view how deep for us is the *love* of God; and that indeed "all things shall work together for good to them that love God" (Romans 8:28).

WRITE DOWN MY NAME!

O Lamb of God! write down my name
   In Thy fair book of life;
Make me to bow and worship Thee,
   In this and endless life.

Thy Father's name writ on my brow,
   Give me the joy to know;
Then live the life, to follow Thee,
   Wherever Thou shalt go;

Let not the Beast of blasphemy
   Have place by me to stand;
Oh, keep his name and number from
   My forehead and my hand.

Give me the power to overcome,
   And from the Tree of Life
Find fruit to eat, and leaves to heal,
   And strength for every strife.

Thy hidden manna give to me,
   And grant Thine own "white stone,"
With new and precious name thereon:
   Let that name be Thine own.

In patience let me "keep Thy word,"
   Kept from the tempter's power;
Give me the strength to keep my crown,
   Through every trying hour.

And in the temple of my God
   May I a pillar stand.
Lord, sup with me, and I with Thee,
   Amidst Thy bridal band.

Clothed in Thy righteous, spotless robe,
   Washed in Thy precious blood;
Through tribulation great and long,
   I haste to joys above.

Now, may I stand and sing God's praise,
   Yea, Jesu's praise and Thine;
Worthy the Lamb, One with I AM,
   Most glorious King Divine.

My name *is* there! I see it shine,
   Writ by His hand of love;
Lord Jesus come! for Thou *art* mine,
   Thy breast my rest above!

                      J.H.

April 19 — I read in F. R. H.'s *Morning Stars, or the Names of Christ for His Little Ones*. The chapter on "The Lord our Righteousness" had a marvellous effect on me; I was filled with wonderful emotion, and could scarcely contain myself to finish it. Soon after I wrote the following piece:—

THE LORD OUR RIGHTEOUSNESS.

My righteousness, my righteousness,
   Be Thou, my Lord, to me!
Give me the sight to see *my* works
   As filthy rags to be.

Clothe me with Thine own spotless robe,
   Before my God to stand;
Then shall I sing Thy praise for aye,
   With all the angel band.

Clothe me with Thine own spotless robe,
   Call me to Thine own feast;

Give me the place long kept for me,
   Although that place be *least*.

Clothe me with Thine own raiment white,
   That I may live in Thee,
In endless light and glory bright,
   Through all eternity.

Our RIGHTEOUSNESS, OUR RIGHTEOUSNESS,
   O blessed Trinity!
Of Father, Son, and Holy Ghost,
   Now, and for ever be! Amen.

                              J. H.

IN THE WORLD IS TRIBULATION.

OFTENTIMES I am sad and weary,
   Full of very trying pain;
In the world is tribulation,
   But in Christ sweet rest I gain.

Through much pain I feel quite happy,
   'Tis the chastening of my Lord;
He supports, and so He draws me
   To Himself with loving cord.

O dear Jesu, love and keep me
   To the end of all, I pray;
In Thine own arms take and keep me
   With Thyself, through endless day.

Though the road is rough and rugged,
   He will smooth it with His hand;
And through *all* will safely keep me,
   Till before His face I stand.

I am faithless, He is faithful;
   I am weary, He is rest;
O my Saviour, how I love Thee!
   I can't speak, I feel so blest!

NOTE by J. H.—For upwards of a week I had hardly any sleep or rest from pain. One morning I was lying nice and cosy, when the first verse flowed through my mind. I felt loth to sit up and write it, but it came louder and louder, so I wrote it, and then the other verses flowed through my mind—wearying pain was forgotten, and the last two lines tell how I felt.

EMMANUEL.

GRAND name, which pierces through the night
Of sorrow with a glorious light;
All grief is changèd into joy,
Christ gives fine gold without alloy.

Sweet name of mercy, love, and light,
Which cometh with a gentle might,
To take away all grief and pain,
And in our hearts forever reign.

Rich name, which tells the boundless love
That brought Emmanuel from above,
A ruined world from death to save,
And promise life beyond the grave.

JOY AND COMFORT IN PAIN.

CAN I murmur at rich blessings,
   Given to me in disguise,
By a kind and loving Father,
   Purely good, and "only wise"?

No! for they, O joy, do make me
   More to lean on Jesu's breast,
There to find the sweetest comfort,
   Holiest joy and perfect rest.

O my God, how can I thank Thee
   For such wondrous love to me!
Take my all, and in Christ Jesus,
   Let it to Thy glory be.

(Flowed through my mind when suffering intense pain.)

"LET BROTHERLY LOVE CONTINUE."

I CANNOT speak my Saviour's love,
   He is so very good to me;
Across the waste, He as the dove
   Brings peaceful olive leaf to me.

When filled with sorrow, grief, and pain,
   I feel that I must surely die;
A holy calm through Him I gain;
   He gently whispers, "I am nigh."

He comes with healing in His wings,
   And binds with love my wounded heart;
His hand removeth all that stings,
   And gracious ease He doth impart.

Then though my brother treat me vile,
   Shall words of vengeance be my cry?
Nay, Jesus bless him with Thy smile,
   And save him lest his soul should die.

O Jesus, give my brother life,
   And sweetest health in Thee;
Make him and me to leave all strife,
   And only think of pleasing Thee.

O brothers, let our hearts unite
  In bonds of brotherhood and love!
Let us agree as in His sight,
  Till comes pure harmony above!

HUMBLY PRAY, AND FULLY TRUST.

Trust your Lord with perfect trust,
  Take to Him your every care;
With their weight you would be crushed;
  He alone has strength to bear.

Do not worrit (baneful state)!
  Leave your troubles at His feet;
Run through doubt with sword of faith,
  Victor you will be complete.

While you worry, sure you must
  Ever feel a want of ease;
Humbly pray, and fully trust,
  Then you will your Saviour please.

Now be happy and content;
  Bright and cheerful onward run,
For Jehovah's aid is lent,
  And your Saviour's rest is won.

THINE ALONE.

Thine alone, dear Lord, I pray
Thou wilt never let me stray
Far from Thee, my only Way;
  Jesus, keep me Thine.

Thine alone though I be poor,
Greatest poverty endure,
Make me of Thy love feel sure;
  Jesus, keep me Thine.

Thine alone, if I have wealth
Many friends, and robust health,
Leave me not unto myself;
  Jesus, keep me Thine.

Thine alone, Lord, I implore,
When affliction tries me sore,
Balm of comfort thou wilt pour;
  Jesus keep me Thine.

Thine alone, O lead me out
Of all evil, fear, and doubt;
Make my faith in Thee be stout;
  Jesus keep me Thine.

Thine alone, no want for me,
All my need supplied in Thee;
Through all time, eternity,
  Jesus keep me Thine.

HOPE ON, HOPE ON!

Think not because the sky is dark,
  And storm doth rage with fury wild,
Thou art not safe within His ark;
  Hope on, hope on, my little child!

The storm may come but for thy good,
  To show how great thy Maker's love;
It proves He *can*, who said He *would*,
  In safety keep thee through the flood.

The tree of Hope to thee He gave,
  And planted it within thy breast;
Then pluck away all doubt and fear,
  And dwell in peaceful, happy rest.

Water this tree with waters blest,
  For faith and hope in Christ are they;
Beneath its shade you'll find it best
  In peace to pass each gladsome day,

Then fill thy heart with heavenly joy,
  Take Hope, work hard to prove thy faith,
With smiles thy Saviour standeth by,
  New strength for thee He doth create.

Hope on, hope on! though trials great
  As mountains do appear in view,
Jesus will bear their crushing weight,
  Because His name is Faithful, True.

FRAGMENTS.

With my heart full of emotion,
Simple faith, and true devotion,
Safely resting on the ocean
Of thy love, I pray to be.

Lord make my eye so single be,
Full of Thy light, that I may see
In perfect truth Thy love for me,
In all things, Lord, I pray.

Give me a tongue to truly speak
Thy love to all within my reach;
And may my speech be bold, yet meek,
Thy glory always may I seek.

Just take the Lord unto your heart,
    And give to Him your every care;
New love, new strength, He will impart,
    And *all* your trouble He will bear.

He comes with healing in His wings,
    And binds with love my broken heart;
His holiest joys He always brings,
    Which for the world I would not part.

TO MY DEAR NURSE, SARAH BLAND, ON HER BIRTHDAY.

Nursie, may your little Joey
    Wish you peace and lasting joy,
Health and strength, and simple wisdom,
    And content without alloy.

Joey greets you on your birthday,
    Blessèd be thou of the Lord;
In our ward, oh may He let thee
    Shed His holy light abroad.

Sometimes earthly sorrow makes us
    Weary, sad, and full of pain,
Oft you see us crushed and helpless,
    Bound as with a cruel chain.

While we thus are filled with sorrow,
    And our burdens hard to bear,
Jesus comes to seek and save us,
    Showing forth His loving care.

Yes, on wings of healing gentle,
    All our wounds he maketh whole;
Rending down our veil of darkness,
    While true light shines in our soul.

Nursie, may you love and serve Him,
    Bidding sad ones look above,
To a perfect Friend for all times,
    Mighty, gentle, full of love.

Filled with light and love for Jesus,
    I would have thee, Nursie dear,
Happy, bright, with joy and gladness,
    Shining as the noonday clear.

Living, working thus for Jesus,
    He will live and work in you,
Changing sorrow into blessing,
    Truly making "all things new."

"ASK WHAT I SHALL GIVE THEE."
1 Kings 3:5.

Lord Jesus, I do ask Thee, grant
    To me my soul's desire,
My heart the altar, do Thou make
    Thy love its living fire.

And may my every thought and deed,
    Lit by this holy flame,
Shine forth in purity divine,
    To glorify Thy name.

Make all my words sweet comfort, Lord,
    Indited by Thy love,
To bring lost, wandering souls to Thee,
    For endless life above.

Make me a blessing unto all,
    Dear Lord, where'er I be;
May many hearts unite to sing
    Sweet praises unto Thee.

Thus would I live in love and praise,
    And unto Thee would bring
My every friend, yea, all the world,
    My Saviour and my King.

JESUS.

Who can give me joy for grief?
    Jesus, blessed Jesus.
Who from sorrow, sweet relief?
    Jesus, blessed Jesus.

Who will change my heart so vile?
    Jesus, blessed Jesus.
Who on me so mean will smile?
    Jesus, blessed Jesus.

Who will change my strife for peace?
    Jesus, blessed Jesus.
Who from passions strong release?
    Jesus, blessed Jesus.

Who will always be my guide?
    Jesus, blessed Jesus.
Who will never leave my side?
    Jesus, blessed Jesus.

Who will always be my Friend?
    Jesus, blessed Jesus.
Who will keep me to the end?
    Jesus, blessed Jesus.

Who will wash away my sin?
    Jesus, blessed Jesus.
Who will give me life divine?
    Jesus, blessed Jesus.

Who doth stand, my great High Priest?
    Jesus, blessed Jesus.
The mighty God, the Prince of Peace?
    Jesus, blessed Jesus.

COUPLETS.

"Learning long before your teaching,
Listening long before your preaching,
Suffering before you sing."
"For there are long slow overtures before such bursts of song,
Much tension unconfessed, much training and much teaching
Compressed, concentrated in ever-flowing store."
Zenith.—F. R. H.

I thought much of these beautiful lines, and one day, while musing, I wrote in couplets how God had dealt with *me*. (If "couplets" does not sound suitable, perhaps some kind friend would suggest a better name.)
    J. H.

Many teachings to instil
In my heart His blessed will.

Many chastenings it requires,
Till my heart His will desires.

Suffering pain before I taste
Of His sweet and holy grace.

Fighting sin, ah! many an hour,
Only conquering by His power.

Battling long with doubting mind,
Till a perfect faith I find.

Feeling faint and hungry quite,
Till I eat the bread of life.

Wandering, lost, and inly blind,
Home and sight in Him I find.

Often leaving His bright way,
Still my Shepherd is my stay.

Though in sin I often slide,
Still he calls me to His side.

He doth lift me with His hand,
Then in Him I firmly stand.

Though I am so very vile,
He doth bless me with His smile.

All His ways for me are best,
In them only am I blest.

Every shaft is barbed with love,
Teaching me to look above.

All His chastenings well I need,
Else on ashes I should feed.

Saviour! make me pure and bright,
Ever walking in Thy light.

Cleanse me with Thy precious blood,
Fit me for Thy home above.

I can rest secure in Thee,
For Thy love surroundeth me.

Jesu! Saviour, on me pour
Thy sweet Spirit evermore.

SONG TO MY SAVIOUR, LORD AND GOD

Give me a tongue to sing Thy praise,
    Both morning, noonday, and at night;
With thankful heart my voice upraise,
    To sing Thy mercy and Thy might.

Great is Thy glory Lord on high,
    The heavens indeed are but Thy throne
Yet Thou wilt hear the lost one's cry,
    And make Thy heaven his heavenly home.

Man's cry for mercy Thou wilt hear,
    When doubting, sinking 'neath his guilt,
Christ's answer comes, "Be of good cheer,
    To save thy soul my blood was spilt."

O Lord my God, I am a worm,
    Through sin made guilty in Thy sight;
But Thou dost call me to return,
    And live with Thee in glory bright.

O Lord God, how great Thy love,
    In might and mercy none like Thee,
That Thou shouldst take lost man above,
    To live with Thee eternally.

Lord Jesus, make me pure and free,
    To sing Thy mercy, might, and love;
Make me to lose myself in Thee,
    To find an endless life above.

FRAGMENTS IN PENCIL.

"Little Joe's Address to Unitarians."

WILL ye listen, Unitarian friends? "There is none other name under heaven given among men whereby we must be saved" (Acts 4:12). Nothing unholy is allowed to approach God; "We have all sinned and come short of the glory of God" (Romans 3:23). Therefore we *are* unholy, and unable to bear His glorious light, the glorious searching light of His holy countenance. Jesus Christ, the only-begotten, well-beloved Son, one with God, "I and my Father are one" (John 10:30), came down from heaven, dwelt among men, suffered and died that we might live. Christ shed His precious blood, the holy sacrifice, the holy for the unholy, the righteous for the unrighteous. His "precious blood" is a living fount, in which we must wash our filthy rags, whereby they will become robes of righteousness, made white (holy) in the blood of the Lamb.

Will ye listen to the parable in Matthew 22:2: "The kingdom of heaven is like unto a certain king which made a marriage for his son (vers. 11–13). And when the king came in to see the guests, he saw there a man which had not on a wedding garment. And he said unto him, Friend, how camest thou in hither, not having a wedding garment? And he was speechless. Then said the king to his servants, Bind him hand and foot, and take him away, and cast him into outer darkness; there shall be weeping and gnashing of teeth."

We are all unholy unless we are made holy through Him and by Him, who left the glory of heaven and its unspeakable joys to live among us in sorrow and grief, and at last offer up His life for us in our stead, thereby offering a perfect sacrifice for our sins, and providing a perfect robe of righteousness in which *alone* we can stand before God.

Truly in the world is tribulation; but let us listen to the gracious words of our Saviour, "But be of good cheer, I have overcome the world;" and again, "Come unto me, all ye that labour and are heavy laden, and I will give you rest" (Matthew 11:28).

How wonderful, that our blessed and beloved Lord and Saviour came down from heaven to be lifted up on the cross, "that whosoever believeth in Him should not perish, but have eternal life" (John 3:15). Again, "Now ye are clean through the word which I have spoken unto you. Abide in me, and I in you" (John 15:3, 4). "The Spirit and the Bride say, Come; and let him that is athirst come; and whosoever will, let him take of the water of life freely" (Revelation 22:17). Jesus saith it. Oh, may we all come to Him, and abide in Him, and so have eternal life. "He shall save His people from their sins." God hath spoken it; therefore ye must believe.

May God add His blessing!

Little Joe.

March 11, 1880.

The Love of our Saviour.

Who can speak it? Who can think it? None. It is in truth a "love which passeth knowledge." That it should be possible for One to leave the glories of heaven, with its purity, grandeur, and joys unspeakable, for the sorrows of the world, with its filth, paltriness, and misery, is in truth something more than we can conceive. He came as light to those in darkness, a Saviour to the lost, a joy to the sorrowful, a rest to the weary, a life to the dead. He came to take away our unholiness, and give us His holiness, to make us (who are unclean and spotted with the leprosy of sin, and unfit to stand in the presence of the holy God) altogether new creatures, giving us His holy garment of righteousness wherein to stand in the presence of God. All this and much more—more than the tongue can speak—has He done for me, for you, for all! Oh, how our hearts should go out to Him with the fulness of the purest love! Oh, how we should bow down and worship Him in reverence and awe! Oh, how we should strive to please Him, and do that which is pleasing in His sight! But, alas! what do we do? Do we take Him in, giving Him a place in our hearts, our home, our table, asking His blessing on all we do? Do we seek to do "all things" pleasing in His sight? do we ask Him to lend us of His strength to keep us in all temptations and trials? Alas, alas! our heart of hearts must answer no. Do we not rather shut Him out, and (by our actions) drive His holy presence from among us! Do we not rather refuse Him a place of shelter in our hearts, in that we feel not the deepest sorrow and love for Him who lived such a life of profound grief for our sakes to give us joy? Oh, what a love is Christ's for us! Nay more, He is continually calling us who are so unworthy to come to Him. He knows our trouble, anxiety, grief, and, yes, our wicked state, yet He sweetly says, Come unto me, and I will give you rest. Listen then to what He lovingly says to us, whom sin and Satan are trying to destroy, "I am come that they might have *life*, and that they might have it more abundantly." Not simple life, but life abundantly for ever. And this is not all; having made us clean by the word which He has so lovingly spoken to us, He says, "Abide in me, and I in you;" what love is this, that Jesus Christ, the Saviour of the world, will live in us! Who can measure love like this? And as if to make our assurance still more sure, He says, "Him that cometh to me I will in no wise cast out." After this, His crowning assurance, can we refuse any longer to go to Him? Why, He is waiting to give us eternal life (John 10:28).

Let us think of His cruel death—reviled, stripped, buffeted, spit upon, crowned with thorns, led from hall to hall, then amid murderers and malefactors lifted on the cross with driven nails, left there to thirst, and agonize, and die. And then, oh mountain upon mountain of love, while suffering unspeakable agonies, He cries in unspeakable love, "Father, forgive them, for they know not what they do." Surely a flood of love was poured out on all the world in these words—words that all who rest upon shall surely live. Look once more—"One of the soldiers with a spear pierced His side, and forthwith came thereout blood and water." Blood poured out, blood spilt for you and for me. It is now and ever will be a living fount where we may wash away our sin and become holy unto the Lord. When we thus see Jesus on the cross, the good Shepherd laying down His life for the sheep, are we not drawn with golden chains of love towards Him? Do we not hear His sweet voice saying, "Dost thou believe on the Son of God?" and shall we not fall down, and worshipping say, "Lord, I believe; Lord, save, or I perish;" and immediately He answers, "I will," and gently stooping down, with all the tenderness of a father, taketh us by the hand, saying, "Son, I say unto thee, Arise." May God add His blessing for Jesus Christ's sake.

March 22, 1880.

Tenth Day. —"Royal Commandments."

F. R. H.

(So blessed to J. H.)

TRUSTING IN DARKNESS.

"Who is among you that feareth the Lord, that obeyeth the voice of His servant, that walketh in darkness, and hath no light? let him trust in the name of the Lord, and stay himself upon his God."

Before we take this peace and strength-giving precept, with its enfolded promise to ourselves, let us examine ourselves as to the conditions: fear of the Lord, and obedience to the voice of His servant. They are very dear. If we are not casting off fear, if we have this "beginning of wisdom," this perhaps not sufficiently recognised "treasure," the fear of the Lord, and if we have sincerity of purpose about obeying the voice of His servant, and are not persisting in some known and wilful disobedience which causes a different kind of darkness, the darkness that blindeth our eyes, then we are called to listen to all the comfort of this commandment.

"Let him trust in the name of the Lord." What name? "The Lord, the Lord God, merciful and gracious, long-suffering, and abundant in goodness and truth, keeping mercy for thousands, forgiving iniquity and transgression and sin." What name? "Wonderful, Counsellor, the Mighty God, the Everlasting Father, the Prince of Peace." What name? Just this, Jesus! But how can we trust in what we do not much consider? Trust needs a very broad and strong foundation for its repose; it cannot poise itself on an inverted pyramid. But if we walk about that foundation, and go round about it, and mark well the bulwarks, we shall put ourselves in the way of realizing what reason we have to trust.

Is it dark now, dear friend? Will you, as a little child, simply do what I ask you this morning? Take this *Name* of the Lord, in all its varied fulness, "shut thy door," and kneel down without hurry. Then, asking first the Spirit's promised help, pray over every separate part of it, as so beautifully revealed for our comfort. And as you take up each word in petition, tell the Lord that you *will*, you *do* trust that, even though you cannot see or feel all the preciousness of it.

Trusting in the name of the Lord, the triune Jehovah,—Father, Saviour, Comforter,—will lead you on, not perhaps to any great radiance of light as yet, but to staying upon your God; for, mark the added pronoun, first only *the* Lord, then "*his* God." Both the trusting and staying may be at first in the dark, but they will not be always in the dark. He that believeth on Him shall not abide in darkness. Unto him "there ariseth light in the darkness." But the promises are progressive: we must follow the Light as soon as we see it, for "he that followeth Me, shall not walk in darkness."

But, meanwhile, even the trusting and staying shall be blessed, for "blessed are they that have not seen, and yet have believed." "Blessed are all they that put their trust in Him;" and "all" of course includes you. There may be very much unconscious blessing apart from sensible light and joy. The visible, light-bearing rays of the spectrum are not the whole beam. It is not they which make the plant grow; it is the dark rays, with their mysterious, unseen vibrations, that bring heat and chemical power.

The first conscious blessing is not linked with even the trust, but with the "staying," which grows out of it. "Thou wilt keep him in perfect peace whose mind is stayed on Thee: because he trusteth in Thee." Then again, the staying, and the certainly resulting, because absolutely promised peace, lead on to fuller and more settled trust: "Trust ye in the Lord for ever."

How we do love a little child that nestles up to us from its cot in a dark room and kisses the hand that it cannot see, and pours out all sorts of little confidences, which it did not tell in the broad daylight! Do we not fondle it with a special gush of affection? However much we loved the little thing before, we think we love it more than ever! When the Father's little children come to Him in the dark, and simply believe His assurance that He is there, although they cannot see, will He be less loving, less kind and tender?

> "I cannot hear Thy voice, Lord,
>   But Thou dost hear my cry;
> I cling to Thine assurance,
>   That Thou art ever nigh.
>
> I know that Thou art faithful,
>   I trust, but cannot see,
> That it is still the right way,
>   By which Thou leadest me."

Eighteenth Day. — "Royal Commandments."

OUR WORKS IN GOD'S HAND.

"Commit thy works unto the Lord."

Suppose an angel were sent down to tell us this morning that he was commissioned to take all our work under his charge to-day, that we might just be easy about it, because he would undertake it, and his excellent strength and wisdom would make it all prosper a great deal more than ours, how extremely foolish it would be not to avail ourselves of such superhuman help! What a holiday it would seem, if we accepted the offer, as we went about our business with the angel beside us! what a day of privilege and progress! and how we should thank God for the extraordinary relief His kindness had sent!

Far higher is our privilege this day; not merely permitted, but pressed upon us by Royal Commandment, "Commit thy works unto Jehovah!" Yet this is but the third strand of a golden cord, which is strong enough (if yielded to) to draw us up out of all the miry clay of the "pit of noise," where the voices of fear and anxiety and distrust make such a weary din. We are to commit the keeping of our souls to Him; then we shall be ready for the command to commit our way unto Him, and then our works. Then, having obeyed, we may exchange the less confident expression, "Unto God would I commit my cause," for the bright assurance, "I am persuaded that He is able to keep that which I *have* committed unto Him." *Of course* He is!

Not an angel, but Jehovah, bids us this day commit our works to Him. It is not approving the idea, nor thinking about it, nor even asking Him to take them, that is here commanded, but committing them: a definite act of soul, a real transaction with our Lord. Suppose you have an interview with another worker, and, having had a distinct understanding as to what you wish him to undertake for you. You verbally and explicitly transfer to him the management and responsibility of some work. You are not actually in sight of it, you have no tangible objects to hand over, you might do it in a dark room, but the transaction is real. The burden of the work is no longer upon you, if only you have confidence in the one to whom you have committed it. And if you have the further confidence that he is considerably more capable than yourself, and can do it all a great deal better, you are not only relieved, but rejoiced. Just such a definite transaction does our Lord bid us make with Him this morning. Will you do it? Will you not, before venturing away from your quiet early hour, "commit thy works" to Him definitely, the special things you have to do to-day, and the unforeseen work which He may add in the course of it?

And then leave it with Him! You would not have the bad taste to keep on fidgeting about it to the friend who had kindly undertaken your work for you! If we would only apply the commonest rules of human courtesy and confidence to our intercourse with our Divine Master! Leave details and results all and together with Him. You see when you have committed it to Him, your works *are* in the hand of God. Really in His hand! and where else would you wish them to be? Would you like to have them back in your own? Do you think His grasp is not firm enough, or the hollow of His hand not large enough to hold your little bits of work quite securely? Even if He tries your faith a little, and you seem to have laboured in vain, and spent your strength for nought, cannot you trust your "own Master" enough to add, "Yet *surely* my judgment is with the Lord, and my work with my God"? Especially as He says, "Thou art my servant, in whom I *will* be glorified;" by which "Ye *know* that your labour is not in vain in the Lord."

That for the past work. For the present, "I will direct their work in truth." And for all our future work, a singular shining in the eastern horizon: "Mine elect shall long enjoy the work of their hands."

> Distrust thyself, but trust His strength,
>   In Him thou shalt be strong;
> His weakest ones may learn at length,
>   A daily triumph song.
>
> Distrust thyself, but trust His love;
>   Rest in its changeless glow:
> And life or death shall only prove
>   Its everlasting flow.

Distrust thyself, but trust alone,
  In Him for all—for ever!
And joyously thy heart shall own,
  That Jesus faileth never.

       F. R. Havergal.

"WILL YE NOT COME?"

LUCIUS.
              Words and Music by
              F. R. Havergal.

Will ye not come to Him for *life?*
  Why will ye die, oh why?
He gave His life for you, for you!
The gift is free, the word is true!
Will ye not come? Oh, why will ye die?

Refrain, after any or each verse.
  Will ye not come? Will ye not come,
    Will ye not come to Him, to Him?
  Oh, come, come, come to Him!
Come unto Jesus, oh, come for *life.*

Will ye not come to Him for *peace,*
  Peace through His cross alone?
He shed His precious blood for you;
The gift is free, the word is true!
He is our Peace—Oh, is He your own?
    Will yet not come, etc. . . . for *peace?*

Will ye not come to Him for *rest?*
  All that are weary, come:
The rest He gives is deep and true,
'Tis offered now, 'tis offered you:
Rest in His love, and rest in His home.
    Will ye not come, etc. . . . for *rest?*

Will ye not come to Him for *joy?*
  Will ye not come for this?
He laid His joys aside for you,
To give you joy, so sweet, so true!
Sorrowing heart, oh, drink of the bliss!
    Will ye not come, etc. . . . for *joy?*

Will ye not come to Him for *love,*
  Love that can fill the heart?
Exceeding great, exceeding free!
He loveth you, He loveth me!
Will ye not come? Why stand ye apart?
    Will ye not come, etc. . . . for *love?*

Will ye not come to Him for ALL?
  Will ye not "taste and see?"
He waits to give it all to you,
The gifts are free, the words are true:
Jesus hath said it, "Come unto Me!"
    Will ye not come, etc. . . . to Him?

Nothing to Pay

Words and Music by Frances Ridley Havergal

Nothing to pay! Ah, nothing to pay!
Never a word of excuse to say!
Year after year thou hast filled the score,
Owing thy Lord still more and more.
    Hear the voice of Jesus say,
"Verily thou hast nothing to pay!
Ruined, lost art thou, and yet
I forgave thee all that debt."

Nothing to pay! the debt is so great,
What will you do with the awful weight?
How shall the way of escape be made?
Nothing to pay! yet it must be paid!
    Hear the voice of Jesus say,
"Verily thou hast nothing to pay!
All has been put to My account,
I have paid the full amount."

Nothing to pay! yes, nothing to pay!
Jesus has cleared all the debt away;
Blotted it out with His bleeding hand!
Free and forgiven and loved you stand.
    Hear the voice of Jesus say,
"Verily thou hast nothing to pay!
Paid is the debt, and the debtor free!
Now I ask *thee*, lovest thou Me?"

The front and back of the gravestone of Maria Vernon Graham Havergal, photographed by David Marlow in 2009.

In the family vault in Astley Churchyard, William Henry Havergal was buried in 1870, his second wife Caroline Anne Cooke was buried in 1878, Frances Ridley Havergal was buried in 1879, and Maria Vernon Graham Havergal was buried in 1887. (See page 160, Maria's diary entry for November 19, 1885.) As there was no room for an epitaph for Maria on the family gravestone, a separate gravestone was made for her and placed near the family vault, engraved with these words:

Maria Vernon Graham Havergal / Born at Coaley Gloucestershire / Nov 15 1822 [This was a mistake: Maria was born November 15, 1821.] / Died June 22 1887

This is a faithful saying and worthy / of all acceptation, that Christ Jesus / came into the world to save sinners / of whom I am chief. I. Tim. I.15.

THE AUTOBIOGRAPHY

OF

MARIA VERNON GRAHAM HAVERGAL.

With Journals and Letters.

Edited by her Sister,

J. MIRIAM CRANE,

AUTHOR OF "RECORDS OF THE LIFE OF THE REV. WM. H. HAVERGAL, M.A."

"Ye read her story,
Take home the lesson with a spirit-smile;
Darkness and mystery a little while,
Then—light and glory,
And ministry 'mid saint and seraph band,
And service of high praise in the eternal land!"
—F. R. Havergal.

LONDON:
JAMES NISBET & CO., 21, BERNERS ST.
1887.

H. S. Wright
with kind regards from
The Compiler. Decr 1888.

This inscription to H. S. Wright was found in a copy of this Autobiography of Maria. The "Compiler" was Maria's oldest sister, Jane Miriam (Havergal) Crane (1817–1898).

Jane Miriam (Havergal) Crane (1817–1898). This portrait was painted by Solomon Cole in 1845.

Miriam Crane was the first of the six children of William Henry and Jane Head Havergal, four years older than Maria and nineteen years older than the sixth child, Frances Ridley Havergal. Miriam wrote the biography of her father, *Records of the Life of the Rev. William Henry Havergal, M.A.* (London: Home Words Publishing Office, 1882); she compiled and edited *Swiss Letters and Alpine Poems* by Frances Ridley Havergal (London: James Nisbet & Co., 1881); she gathered and published *Streamlets of Song for the Young*, a posthumous volume of poetry by F.R.H. (London: Nisbet & Co., 1887); and she edited *The Autobiography of Maria Vernon Graham Havergal* (London: Nisbet & Co., 1887). Nineteen when Frances was born, she tutored her from the age of two-and-a-half; she lived nineteen years after Frances' death. Miriam was a genuine disciple and a very gifted lady herself; she was a finely gifted artist, and a poet, though very few of her paintings and poems have been found. After her husband Henry Crane's death, she travelled extensively in Europe, and wrote a manuscript book, *Wanderings of a Widow*, never published. She and her three sisters, Maria, Ellen, and Frances, were all like-minded and like-hearted, but no memorial account was written—or at least has not been found—of Miriam, a true daughter of the King.

PREFACE.

IT seems fitting that some record should be made of the writer of the "Memorials" of our gifted sister, which has attained such an unusual circulation; the biographer herself having also written other pleasant pages, and being well known as an active and faithful Christian worker.

And this my dear sister, Maria V. G. Havergal, herself felt, when two years ago she asked me to promise to write her life, in the event of her decease. I declined doing so, as I then thought it unlikely that I should be the survivor.

Last year, when she felt the seeds of death again springing up within her, the request was renewed. I then advised her to write an Autobiography, saying it would probably be more edifying, and certainly more amusing than anything I could write. Hence the present volume, which I feel sure will be welcomed by many known and unknown friends.

As the Autobiography is by no means consecutive, I have added Journals and Letters, which supply some of the missing links, and outline her ceaseless activities. Miss Clay, who for ten years was her devoted fellow-labourer in Bewdley, has kindly contributed a notice of that period.

I need not dwell on my sister's affectionate, sympathetic, generous, and energetic character, as her own records fully reveal it.

She exemplified in her life the epitome of St. James, "Pure religion and undefiled before God and the Father is this, to visit the fatherless and widows in their affliction, and to keep himself unspotted from the world." To use her own expression, it was "the one passion" of her life to visit the sick and needy, relieving not only their temporal but their spiritual necessities. By holding forth the Word of life, the glorious gospel of the only Redeemer, she was the means of turning many to righteousness, who with her will shine in the heavenly kingdom "as the stars for ever and ever."

J. MIRIAM CRANE.

WESTON-SUPER-MARE,
  October 1887.

CONTENTS.

CHAP.		PAGE
I.	Early Days.	99
II.	School Life.	102
III.	Home Life After School.	107
IV.	Records of My Mother, 1846–1848.	112
V.	The Sisters' Home at the Mumbles.	114
VI.	Suffering and Support.	119
VII.	From Sidmouth to Wales.	122
VIII.	Various Instances of God's Impulses in My Life.	130

	PAGE
Ten Years in Bewdley. By Miss Elizabeth Clay.	135
Extracts from Miss S. Head's Journal Respecting M. V. G. H.'s Stay in the Lake District.	141
Journal of a Visit to Aix-les-Bains and Switzerland in 1882.	142
Diaries from 1883 to 1887.	157
The Havergal Album.	162
Letters from M. V. G. Havergal.	163
Closing Scenes. By J. M. Crane.	172
Extracts from Letters of Sympathy to M. V. G. H.'s Sister, J. M. C.	177
Poetry. By M. V. G. H.	179

Three close sisters. This photograph of Ellen Prestage Havergal (later Mrs. Giles Shaw) on the left, Maria Vernon Graham Havergal on the right, and Frances Ridley Havergal in the middle, was taken in 1854. That year Ellen turned 31 (February 19), Frances turned 18 (December 14), and Maria turned 33 (November 15).

THE AUTOBIOGRAPHY

OF

MARIA V. G. HAVERGAL.

CHAPTER I.

EARLY DAYS.

"Surely goodness and mercy shall follow me all the days of my life."—Psalm 23:6.

"We have turned every one to his own way."—Isaiah 53:6.

"Goodness and mercy," and our "own way," are the epitome of my life. The days of that life are closing, and it is toward eveningtide—the shadows are merging into a sunset glow. Looking backwards from the home-height nearly gained, the evening radiancy lights up the pathway—the windings, the by-ways, the short cuts, the snares, the pitfalls, and all the mistakes of my "own way." And again—I see the golden line of God's everlasting, ever overruling love; I see the "right paths" in which He has safely led me, and the goodness and mercy which has surely followed me. And now, tarrying as it were in the land of Beulah, I desire to write down recollections of the past; and may all I write be to the praise of the glory of His grace!

My greatest spiritual mercy has been the experience of God's everlasting love. "Yea, I have loved thee with an everlasting love; therefore with loving-kindness have I drawn thee" (Jeremiah 31:3). My greatest temporal mercy was having wise, loving, holy parents, whose training has been a life-long fence; but I too often chose my own way, and long delayed giving up my will wholly to the Lord.

Our Church collect exactly expresses the desire that would have saved many a mistake:—"O God, forasmuch as without Thee we are not able to please Thee, mercifully grant that Thy Holy Spirit may in *all things* direct and rule our hearts."

Still I can, and do humbly and heartily, as one of His unworthy servants, join in the thanksgiving:—"We bless Thee for our creation, preservation, and all the blessings of this life, but above all for Thine inestimable love in the redemption of the world by our Lord Jesus Christ, for the means of grace and for the hope of glory."

I was born at Coaley Vicarage in Gloucestershire on November 15, 1821, being the third child of the Rev. William H. Havergal and his wife, Jane. I was christened on March 19 by the Rev. Jeremiah Smith, author of two volumes of sermons and some family prayers. When still an infant, my father left this sole charge for Astley, Worcestershire. I never revisited my birthplace till after his death in 1870. My father's footprints shone out clearly after fifty years. Their record I wrote for my father's Memoir by my Sister Miriam, chap. 4.[1] My vivid realization of original sin was singular when at fifty years old I gazed on the window of the room where I was born and the churchyard gate through which I was carried to my baptism. Certainly my own childish memories prove that *I* was not regenerated in baptism.

---

[1] Chap. 4 of *Records of the Life of the Rev. William H. Havergal,* by his daughter, J. Miriam Crane, published at *Home Words* Office, 7 Paternoster Square. [See pages 373–376 of this book.]

In my Coaley rambles I met the old man who remembered my father at the Vicarage, and he told me of his liberality when a poor curate. "You feature your father uncommon, Miss! Well, he was a good-giving and good-living man. Ah, yes! I remember when you were born. Master sent me late at night some nine or ten miles to fetch your nurse. Says he, What's your charge, James?—Anything, sir.—There's six shillings. Well, that was handsome and no mistake! Ah, the folks did fill the church then, and this lane was full of gigs and carts awaiting on Sundays. He told us plain out, of Christ, and just how a man could get to glory; and he was a musicianer, such a fine voice to be sure. Why, he made tunes in his headpiece, and made a new hymn-book."

My first remembrance at Astley Rectory was suffering, when about two years old; it was night, and I remember being frightened with some leeches applied by an old Betty! and longing to get to my loving mother's arms. Yes, I remember the nursing and the rocking chair (still existing at Winterdyne); and far more do I remember the loving, lovely face of my mother.

My next distinct memory was faith. I may have been four years old when I broke a large pane in the dining-room window. I was alone. I can see now the black horse-hair sofa where I knelt down crying, "Please, God, mend the window!" Then, still kneeling, I looked back, verily expecting to see it done! Again I prayed, fearing the punishment when found out. I do not think that getting no answer disturbed my childish faith, for I was not punished.

My Sunday memories stand out most clearly from six years old. We then wore green silk bonnets and pretty pink gingham frocks with fine cambric frills, plaited by our ironer, Ann Lane. At eight o'clock the church tenor bell rang out.

Punctually at a quarter-past eight all assembled for prayers, the youngest child sitting on father's knee. He always read a Sunday Psalm, *i.e.* having some reference to holy worship. Then he gave the child on his knee the Church missionary plate; this was carried round for pence and half-pence; and joy when a visitor's shilling brightened the coppers! And then my father prayed for God's blessing on the missionaries and the heathen. (His first sermon for the Church Missionary Society was in 1825, and the record of his Church Missionary Society sermons and speeches as a pioneer in Devon, Cornwall, and Yorkshire are full of interest.) The money on the plate was changed into silver, and put in the missionary box, which often yielded four or five pounds per annum.

I was too young to go to the Sunday school like my eldest sister Miriam did, but to sit by dear mother at church was considered a treat and not a bore. Even the Sunday dinner had example in its arrangement. Beef and chickens, roasted on Saturday, potatoes, apple tart, and custard, all prepared then. So the maids went to church comfortably twice as we did. (A very homely parenthesis to mistresses!—Do see that no dishes are washed up on Sunday. Early rising on Monday sets all straight.) Oh that lodgers in pleasant seaside holidays would "*consider* their ways" and abstain from hot dinners and suppers, which make poor maidens say, "Oh, there is no Sunday for us all the season!" On Sunday afternoons we might sit in the pleasant garden, under the yew trees, or in the shrubbery where the arbutus and evergreens hid us cosily. The churchyard, too, had its little hiding-places, behind the tombs; and there we sometimes stood and watched the open graves and the coffins put in—those mysteries to little minds, wisely dispelled by our mother taking us to see some child in its happy sleep of death; and so the thought of "Jesus hushing the sick child to sleep, and that there would be no medicine and no doctors in heaven, and only sweet songs and happy days," took away all fear of dying. Four o'clock in the summer was our "happy time" with mother—Bible texts said over, Dr. Watts' *Divine and Moral Songs,* or Ann Taylor's unsurpassed *Hymns for Infant Minds.* Wholesome divinity therein! crumbs of sweet comfort that have fed me all my journey, ever and anon chiming their gospel truths. I can say those books, now, from end to end!

When older, collects, catechism, and the epistle or gospel learnt, and some of the morning sermon talked over. After tea, service at six; then the garden walk, and supper from gooseberry and currant trees, and milk from Lily and Rose, our dear cows; and as the holy light faded, our mother's good-night words and prayer, forgotten maybe, but tiny seeds sown *for ever*—that Sunday *was* a happy, pleasant day, "*the* best of all the seven."

One hymn in mother's Bible I have never seen elsewhere—it was given her by the Rev. John East of Bath:—

> "And is the Sabbath come?
> And have we still a day
> To mind our everlasting home,
> To sing, and read, and pray?
>
> Then let us up with speed,
> The work is very great;
> And beg of God our souls to feed
> With never-dying meat.
>
> That we may strengthened be
> To run the heavenly road,
> Until at last we come to Thee,
> Our Saviour and our God.
>
> Ever with Thee to spend,
> With saints in perfect light,
> A Sabbath that shall never end,
> A day that has no night."

Mother's large Bible always lay on the table in her room. Often I wondered why at five o'clock every afternoon she went into her room and locked the door till nearly tea-time at six. At last I tried the door, and it was not locked,—mother was reading her Bible! That made me think more of the Bible than ever before.

A few incidents from my fifth to my ninth year, recalling my parents' training and my happy Astley days, still present themselves to my mind.

Our little week-day lessons were taken by dear mother, except when tall sister Miriam came from school for her holidays. How clever we thought her, and what pains she took with our writing! My brother Henry went to school; so gentle sister Ellen, my junior, was my dearly loved companion. We were very different: "Good little Ellen," or "Papa's harmless dove," just describes her. Even then she would tastefully dress her dolls and quietly amuse herself; while my restless activity fed the poultry and hushed the chickens to sleep under my hand. I had sundry pets, including nests of field-mice, and I even loved the toad that always came for bread and butter at tea-time. Busily gardening, helping mother sow the seeds in our garden-beds, in which the dear old larkspur, bachelor's button, Canterbury bells, and marigolds grew happily together; and the old York and Lancaster, the cinnamon, and China roses,—not tied martyr-like to stakes, but twining with honeysuckle and jessamine.

And even then mother taught us useful ways; we could beat the eggs for cakes and custards, and strip the fruit for pies, and pare the apples for those "Astley apple turn-overs" I never see now. We were taught to care for the poor people, and fill their cans with milk or broth, and take little baskets of pudding to sick folk. Not often, but sometimes, we went with father on his visits of comfort, and we saw how kindly he shook hands, how gentle his ways, and then he felt the invalid's pulse and saw about the medicine, for he was skilful, and the parish doctor thanked him for saving him visits; and then he read to them Bible comfort, and prayed! Even the cats and dogs knew his step, and many a paper of game or little bones has he taken to some poor Betty or Molly's cat!

My father's early rising and his punctuality are stereotyped in all our ways and likings. Our home-call bell went with the clock, and our meals came to a minute, which saved both temper and time. Order and neatness reigned in our rooms; father's large desk was a wonder when he sometimes opened the inner lid. I can see it now: the box with "sacramental alms," the nook for memorandums, the box of jujubes for Sundays; the wonderful sensitive fish and some C.M.S. curiosities were shown us at times,

I cannot remember any good thoughts when a child; there was no spark of love or holy desire, not even a wish to go to heaven. For a child's soul is either dead or alive, either quickened by God's Spirit or asleep in original sin. Natural amiability and even obedience to parents may exist without any grace. My first conscious impression was one Sunday night, after Ellen and I were in bed. My mother came and sat down by us and spoke with tender earnestness of God, of Christ, of heaven, of hell,—her words I forget, but they roused me, and I cried, and felt "Mamma and Ellen love God and are quite sure to go to heaven, but I am not fit! I can't love God a bit."

When six years old, a great event came—going to visit Grandmother Havergal at High Wycombe. Places then were secured days before, in the day or night coach, from Worcester to London, a twelve hours' journey. Father took me; the yellow post-chaise and a postilion in blue came from the "Hundred House" for the eleven miles' drive, the coach leaving at 6 P.M. The six horses up Broadway Hill impressed me; still more the moon shining through a wood, and I thought the trees were running from us. At Oxford, the midnight supper and the guard's horn hurry us to our places, and then a nap on father's arm till the horn awoke me at the "Red Lion," Wycombe, about 3 A.M.

My Wycombe memories are pleasant, and I soon loved my wise and holy grandmother, whom my father called "the pole star of his life."

Grandmother was an early riser, so was I. From six to seven she always sat by a round table with a green baize cloth, near the window, reading her Bible. I would run off and peep again—"Why ever did grandmother shut her eyes? Was she sleepy?" so I asked. "I am meditating,—run away and play." "Meditating" was not in my spelling-book, and old Nanny did not know. One day grandmother told me all about it; so I thought God must be very near her, when she reads all those Psalms and chapters, and that "meditation" was their talk together afterwards.

I looked in some brown books with red leather backs,—*Hervey's Meditations,* but the words were too hard.

Father did not stay long,—he left some large books, for all her life grandmother was a great reader. She gave me lessons in French, and told me of her school-life in a French convent, and when the Revolution came, about her escape in an open boat from Calais. The Lady Abbess and the Sisters came to England. Her letters were beautiful, and had much of the spirit of the Port Royalists. But it was the convent life that strengthened grandmother in the Protestant faith; she had seen the reality, and so detested what our Church calls "blasphemous fables and dangerous deceits." I was quite sure I never would pray to a woman, and how could the Virgin Mary hear all over the world! It was so kind of Jesus to die for me, and as I could not find out the Virgin ever did that or anything else for me, I decided I would never be a Roman Catholic.

My early Protestant notions were confirmed in after life by residence in Ireland and France.

On Sunday my grandmother left early to superintend the church Sunday school. She was one of the first Sunday-school teachers in England, and was punctually at her post by 9 A.M., till her seventy-second year! She was the honoured friend of the Rev. Charles Bradley, that "prince of sermon-writers"; and as the dozen and more little B.'s came into this troublesome world, the senior babies were trotted off to her care for some days! The successor, Rev. G. W., also needed the same nursery relief; and I remember well seeing grandmother packing fowls and ham into a large basket for the curate's table. (Why should not a Saturday's basket always find its way to all our good working curates from squires and well-to-do people?)

Nanny was the very type of the good old domestic,—living sixty years in the family, and retiring with a pension into an almshouse. Nanny talked to me about "Master William," then my father, and how he was called "curly rosy Willie Havergal." One of those curls is by me, and singularly matches the curls of his daughter Frances (though his hair became dark). Nanny told me "the naughtiest thing Master Willie ever did, was taking the cat to bed!" Also how wonderfully the same Willie played on the big organ at Wycombe Church.

A chamber organ was grandpapa H.'s amusement, and my chief memory of him is, his singing and playing on it; and then his pennies for me to buy gingerbread on market days. I thought "Alderman Havergal" sounded grand. Once he drove me in a gig to Windsor. My memory must be good, for I could describe it all: the silver drawing-room and tables, and the flags in St. George's Chapel, impressed me most, and there I first heard a real anthem, and "very heavenly" was my childish verdict.

That Wycombe visit was repeated, and led to frequent correspondence with my honoured grandmother, whose wise judgment in all things was a very bulwark to me in after life.

Returning home, a governess, Miss Bulgin, was the next event. Of course sister Ellen was good; she always was! and I tried to be so, and she gave me two prizes for good conduct,— Thomson's *Seasons* and Johnson's *Rasselas.*

My governess was truly happy and kindly treated, and father helped her in her old age. How very *little* makes sunshine in the life of a governess!

My sister Miriam was then at Great Campden House, Kensington. My father said, "I cannot give you fortunes, but I can give you good educations." Her school tales riveted me, and to find that Signor Guazzaroni taught the young Princess Victoria Italian, and then came to Great Campden House and gave lessons to *my* sister, seemed wonderful.

CHAPTER II.

SCHOOL LIFE.

IN August 1833, when nearly twelve years old, I joined my sister Miriam at Great Campden House. From a quiet country rectory to a London school with from sixty to eighty girls, was a change.

(I have written a description of my life there, and it was printed in the *Sunday at Home* in 1863.[1] I received many kind letters from old Campdenites and the Dowager Countess of Carnarvon, thanking me for my notice of the lovely Juliana Howard.)

[1] See pages 364–368 of this book.

Some further details occur to me. One excellent idea was, offering as a privilege a quiet half-hour's retirement to any pupil who really wished for such time to read and pray. It was unobtrusively done,—a pencil note, laid on our dear Madame Teed's table, ensured an interview in her room—a very sanctum, a holy place where the Good Shepherd often met and folded the little ones. If our desire seemed sincere, our name, the hour and the name of the room, was entered on a card, and kept in our Bibles as our passport to quietly leaving the schoolrooms. Mine is extant—

> MARIA HAVERGAL,
>
> 11½ to 12 o'clock.
>
> QUEEN ANNE'S ROOM.
>
> ---
>
> "Grow in Grace."

This was principally for the senior girls, the younger ones had "happy times" with one or other of the teachers or elder girls.

The plan of motherhood was good,—the elder girls taking kindly charge of the preparation of lessons, and the conduct of two or three little ones. My sister Miriam was mother to Charlotte Long (Mrs. Howard of Greystoke Castle), M. A. Jessop, and myself.

Our studies were more simple than in these days of brain-pressing torture! Our repetition lessons were heard before breakfast, in the summer at seven, when we walked up and down the broad gravel walk, by the side of our various teachers, repeating Magnall's Questions, Guy's Geography, Lindley Murray's Grammar, and once a week repetition of poetry. Cowper's *Task*, Wordsworth and Milton, and scraps from Shakespeare. We brought a variety in the "Oxford Prize Poems," containing Bishop Heber's *Palestine,* and Mrs. Hemans' and also Miss Emra's poems. Eighty lines was an average task. I remember a sensation, where it was reported to Madame, that Miriam Havergal repeated five hundred lines and Maria three hundred, faultlessly, one morning. Often Miss Stewart would say, "Maria, I shall hear your repetition last, for a *bonne bouche.*" In winter we made these repetitions walking up and down the long schoolrooms, and so got warm for prayers at eight. Breakfast over, came our morning walk, from nine to ten. Our wide gravel walk, the terrace by Queen Anne's Chapel, a shady wood in summer, and our little gardens were sufficient variety. The elder girls were taken twice a week to walk in Kensington Gardens, or to the gravel pits, Notting Hill, which was then waste, unbuilt ground. In these walks, English might be spoken, the only exception to our French conversation the whole half-year. We dined at two, and after dinner had an hour or more in the garden.

Why do not professors give peripatetic classes in the pure air our Father *means* us to breathe? Why do not governesses foresee the healthy impetus of a turn out of the schoolroom in the midst of morning lessons, opening all windows? Twenty minutes would sweep away the cobwebs of listlessness and ill-temper, and more real work would be done. Rainy days were never doleful, forms and tables were cleared away for a good hour's exercise of games or drill; quick martial music gave zest to our jumping steps, for which I and others got awards for doing heartily.

The religious instruction given us by Madame was of no ordinary standard. Short pointed remarks and questions at our morning and evening prayers, weekly Bible classes on consecutive subjects—types and prophecies, comparing the Old and the New Testament, the Articles of our Church, with Scripture references thoroughly learnt—chapter and verse always given, so that a *real* Campdenite would be her own concordance! Thankfully do I bear testimony to the value in after-life of all Scripture committed to memory. It was a crucial test, repeating to Madame those chapters in Exodus 25 to 32 about the taches and loops and sockets of silver; and the elder class will remember failing in the almonds and knops and branches, and Madame's dignified exit with the only two lights, leaving us to repentance in the dark!

Far deeper were Madame's appeals to our consciences; vividly did she set forth the way of salvation. Most winningly has she put her arms round me, when admitted to her own room, and told me of Jesus' love, that He was calling me, that He first loved me; but no answering chord was touched in my still sleeping heart. Others of my age " believed in Jesus," and that unmistakeable smile was theirs. I wonder if the promised sealing in the forehead (Revelation 7:3) means outwardly that restful smile God's children wear? I had now been nearly twelve months at school; sister Miriam had left, taking first prizes in the first classes and the annual silver medal from Mons. De Rivière, the drawing master.

I was fairly forward in my classes, and always got marks for repetitions. Though I had no musical execution, I remember my music teacher bidding other girls notice M. H.'s "soft touch," and how well she played chords for twelve years old.

In December 1836, when the arrangement for the home journey came, I was sent to my cousin Mrs. Usborne, in London, first. There I found my loving Aunt Stratton, and in the pretty drawing-room, my aunt and cousin told me of the wonderful home secret! A sweet baby sister had come on December 14th—a little sister! and the new pulse of love awoke that eternity will never exhaust. I was fifteen, and brother Frank, the youngest, was seven years old; so the novelty was exceedingly sweet.

I remember her christening day; the fine cambric cap, worked by Miss Ridley, and a wee relic of her christening robe, are among the treasures in my large F. R. H. album. The Rev. John Cawood—that standard-bearer of gospel and Protestant truth for fifty years at Bewdley—received her into Christ's Church. Her godfather, Rev. W. H. Ridley, was not present, or Lucy Emra, but her other godmother, Elizabeth Cawood, held the babe. It is remarkable that this godmother said (when F. was but a child), "F. R. H. is an angel now, what will she be in heaven? and I believe she will DIE SINGING," as indeed she did!

My dear father at this time was still suffering from the effects of an accident, and music was his alleviation. Long before the little one could speak, she would coo in time with the nursery rhymes that brother Frank actually sang before he was a year old. Our father's arms and shoulders were their first music-stool, and there they sang his melodies to "Twinkle, twinkle, little star," "Thank you, pretty cow," and others. And so our first and last memories of our darling sister are those of happy song.

[*Note.*—The next pages describing our sister Ellen's school life are omitted, as they are identical with those published this spring in *Outlines of a Gentle Life*. J. Nisbet & Co.—EDITOR, J. M. C.]

My love of the Beautiful nearly led me into scrapes. It was against rule to leave the schoolroom; but having once seen some beautiful portraits in the drawing-room, I stole in for another look. But one face haunted me, that of Lady Juliana Howard (a former pupil), and I risked the forbidden *entrée* to gaze on my ideal. I thought she must be in heaven, or she would not be painted; so Lady Juliana must be among the angels.

Another ungratified wish was to discover the secret "Cats' Gallery," which some of the elder girls had seen. Visions of purring pussies and kittens; whole baskets of them must surely live there. Audaciously I ventured up to the fifth storey, to find only a gallery of chests of drawers and our home boxes—no pussies at all! I noticed some mysterious-looking green baize doors, but did not venture to try them. Of these more anon.

It was October 1834 when we noticed one and another of our schoolfellows disappeared, also a governess. One morning I felt sick and hot, and my teacher told me to lie still till Lizzie came. Lizzie was the lady's-maid, and the confidante of all the headaches. Duly at 11 A.M. Lizzie and a waiter of black doses and little crusts of bread came into the schoolroom, administering the same to all complainers.

Lizzie came to me and looked serious, and said, "Doctor Merriman is coming soon." Pleasant name and pleasant doctor! His visit over, Lizzie and a housemaid came and wrapped me in blankets, and carried me up through the veritable "Cats' Gallery!" The baize doors opened, and I found myself in an inner room, in the whitest of beds, and there I saw the missing schoolfellows,—a pleasant introduction to the scarlet fever hospital!

Never, while memory lasts, shall I forget what followed. An hour passed, when my dear, kind Mrs. Teed came in with a tumbler of deliciously-cold raspberry vinegar and water. She sat down by me, and spoke so tenderly, not much, but asked, "Does my little Maria believe on the Lord Jesus Christ?" Alas! I answered. "Yes;" and it was not a sudden or excusable "Yes." For some days I had planned, "If Mrs. Teed asks me again, 'Do you believe?' I shall say 'Yes;' it will please her so."

"But, Maria, is there any verse that helps you really to believe on Jesus?"

"Yes; 'Christ Jesus came into the world to save sinners.'" Alas! all this was pre-arranged by me, just to deceive my kind teacher, and so get more thought of by her. With a loving smile she left me, deceived by my false profession. When that dear friend came again she brought a little tract, "Poor Joseph," a half-witted man, who chanced to hear Dr. Calamy preach from those words I had claimed (1 Timothy 1:15): "Joseph is a sinner—Christ Jesus came into the world to save sinners—why not poor Joseph?" I said nothing, and I clearly remember that never again had I anything to say, nor had I any of the happy feelings that naturally ooze out when believing is a reality. As I got better, a dull remorse came; but I was not brave enough to own my fault. All those sweet counsels and prayers were listlessly heard. Jesus Christ was nothing to me. I had not believed in Him, hence I did not even care to hear about Him.

Soon pretty pink three-cornered notes came upstairs from my class-mates: "We are so glad you believe in Jesus; is it not very, very happy to find such a Saviour?" and then they sent me strings of promises that would have shone as pearls had my eyes been opened.

My dear parents were informed of my happy confession, *alias* a deceitful veil, which thickened more and more darkly around me. (I perfectly exonerate dear Mrs. Teed; the Lord alone knoweth what is in man.) When convalescent, I returned home. I remember the thoughtful niceties for my journey, but the parting prayer fell unheeded. Mrs. Teed's farewell gift was a morocco pocket Testament. On the first page she wrote indelible words: "A shepherd IS a keeper of his sheep." Simple words! but to me a life-long legacy. I have read them at sea when the fog-bell was ringing, and hushed the trembling passengers at midnight; in wild, lonely Irish bogs, when tracked by priest or spy; on Swiss mountains, when I have recklessly lost the track; or in lonely châlets, with thunder crashing and lightning piercing the pines,—those words were always a power. It was long before I found their scripture place, in Jeremiah.

But when first given to me I heeded them not. Reaching home I forgot the past, and being still weak I was nursed and petted. Dear Mrs. Teed wrote me a lovely letter, which referred to my supposed happiness in being a child of God.

I showed the letter to Miriam. She wisely and gravely told me that she could not discover any good change, and that she "had never seen me read my Bible." It was quite true, and no test is so sure as feeding on or neglecting God's holy Word. St. Peter gives the same test: "As new-born babes, desire the sincere milk of the word, that ye may grow thereby" (1 Peter 2:2). The analogy is perfect. "Being born again, not of corruptible seed, but of incorruptible, by the Word of God, which liveth and abideth for ever." "How ye are clean through the word which I have spoken unto you" (John 15:3). The same word becoming by the Holy Spirit's power the invisible seed and germ of new and spiritual life in the soul, it follows that the life must be nourished and increased by the same means—the Word. "Man shall not live by bread only, but by every word that proceedeth out of the mouth of God" (Matthew 4:4). Our Lord confirms this: "The words that I speak unto you, they are spirit and they are life;" and in His last prayer, "I have given them Thy word" (John 17:14). Hence with children, or giants in the faith, who grumble at their experience and moan over their shortcomings, the question comes—are you honestly "desiring," "searching," meditating on holy Scripture pure and simple?

No special occurrence marks the next few months, till my return to Campden House. It was delightful to return, for I deeply loved and reverenced Mrs. Teed, and also had many school friends. Being good-natured, I often helped some to whom our Church Articles and Scripture references, and also our chronology lessons, were rather a trouble. No books but Bibles were allowed in our bedrooms, and this prevented any early study, but *vivâ voce* coaching did help my friends. Three of us had the privilege of a bedroom without a teacher in it, and we had permission to speak, the wise rule of "Not one word in your rooms" being enforced in the larger bedrooms, such as Queen Anne's Room, Queen Anne's Chapel, and the Long Room, where watchful teachers ensured quiet and order.

How I admired some of our companions! Annette Maria Francisca Celestina, with her Spanish loveliness; the dark Russian, Sophia; some fair West Indians; and then four charming daughters of Lady C. L. came, in their novel Swiss hats. The Layards from Ceylon, and Scotch and Irish, gave variety to our nationalities.

Madame Teed's piercing eyes were most character-discriminating, and the *on dit* "Madame is an angel and a witch" often proved true. Of course some of the gay girls did not love her, did not like the "education for heaven" as well as for earth; but doubtless in the last great gathering, many a gem from Campden will be found in the Lord's casket of jewels.

The time of the confirmation came, and I was a candidate. Sincerely and humbly did I crave that it might be a time of blessing to my soul. I had no assurance of forgiveness, only hazy hopes and dreamy satisfaction. The "hungering and thirsting" for Christ, the delight in His word, the thrill at His name, the real pleasure in holy conversation in our prayer unions, were wanting. My replies, my confirmation papers, were all satisfactory, and also my interview with our good chaplain. Well I remember his wise and holy counsel, as I walked by him in the garden. It is strange, that even then, confession of my deceitful profession *never* occurred to me. I am thankful I did not again make any false statements, so it was taken for granted I was all right. Long ago I had tearfully asked forgiveness for all my sins, and one wish, one good desire was in my heart—the fruit of God's everlasting love—that in confirmation I might indeed be confirmed by God the Holy Ghost.

Large old-fashioned carriages took us to St. James' Church, Paddington—no veils or caps were usual then—only plain white dresses and capes, so there was nothing to distract our attention (as the almost bridal attire must now-a-days). The high pews effectually screened us, and I remember most earnestly praying for God's Spirit, and very heartily saying "I do." As I walked up the long aisle to the holy table and knelt there, the one cry arose, "Give me now the Holy Spirit. Oh do, do." And so God's everlasting love drew me then (the unworthiest of all there) nearer than ever before. Returning to Campden House, in the long silent drive, unmistakeably the Spirit brought to me with assuring words, "My beloved is mine, and I am His." My first communion was in the Rev. C. Smalley's Church, Bayswater. I have no distinct remembrance of it, but for years my sacramental times were tearful longings, intense hungerings after Christ, rather than the joyful experience of many. So, even now, I look back on my communions with the Lord Jesus in His word, rather than at His table, as the most vividly precious seasons.

At one period Campden House was noted for its dancing, the Princess Victoria's master giving lessons; and the breaking-up dancing soirées gave opportunity for the graceful ones to enhance the popularity of the school with the noble of our land.

But the time came when the Lord arrested the principal herself; I cannot distinctly record her conversion, but it was a most complete passing from death unto life—old things passing away, all things becoming new. The test of this new life was the consequent anxiety for the salvation of her pupils, and the determination to put away the accomplishment which was the charm and attraction of her school; because she saw the lurking evil, and that dancing well must lead into the world's bypaths. It was at the risk of breaking up the school, but the brave plunge brought its full reward. For a time numbers lessened, but a reflex tide of popularity with high-minded parents set in, and God gave the brighter blessing of many young feet choosing for themselves the paths of pleasantness and peace, and finding in Christ the abundance of joy and those life-satisfying pleasures, which end in His presence, where there is fulness of joy.

For it is not giving up, it is getting; it is not self-denial to please the Beloved of your soul. A betrothed one joyfully foregoes any pursuit that would risk the loss of her engagement ring or the smile of approval.

Oh that parents and the principals of schools saw this matter in the light of eternity! The very fact that "my governess did approve—she was a Christian—so it can be no harm to dance," has been the life-hinge into the world's vestibule; whereas the simple fact, "My parents and my governess did not approve, and I really cannot do it to the glory of God; I should not like to die in the ball-room," becomes a safeguard. "Thanks; I never learnt dancing," sets many a fair foot free from the luring snare.

Our deportment, our walking, our constant curtseys, and our calisthenics, taught by the same Mr. Jenkins, were sufficient guard against clumsy ways and lazy postures.

Occasionally we were all invited in turn to breakfast with Mrs. and Miss Teed. I have copied from a large MS. book, by C. Bosanquet, many of the quaint, spicy, yet profitable remarks of Mrs. Teed at these times.

Then the good Rev. James Parker, our domestic chaplain, held noble sway over his young charge, Bible classes, confirmation preparations, communicants' instruction, were all helpful. His sermons, with their four divisions and maybe eight or nine "little heads" under each, were good memory pegs, and helped us in our Sunday sermon writing. That has been a life-help to me, so without shorthand I could faithfully give fair reports of any sermon till sixty-three years old.

It is sadly that I record the way in which God's everlasting love led me to deep penitence and real humblings, more than a year after that deceitful profession of belief in Jesus. Of course my dear governess believed me, and so treated me as a child of God. I think I was really a favourite with her, for my outward obedience and my accurate lessons and replies in divinity. Doubtless, I was the last girl in the school she could suspect of any breach of God's laws; so when some cake was missed from the drawing-room, it distressed and pained her exceedingly. "The fool hath said in his heart, There is no God," "The eyes of the Lord *are* in every place," was solemnly dwelt upon at prayers. Again my naughty audacity in gazing on portraits and the beautiful things in the drawing-room, was the step into the horrible fall of purloining her cake; this time Lizzie was on the watch. That evening I was summoned to the dear place, where such tender love, such holy pleadings had gone up for me; and now I stood as the culprit. Wisely and faithfully she drew me to confession; even now I can see that dear face grieved to the quick—grieved most that one who had so professed should so grievously have fallen. She pictured the grief to my dear and holy parents—the disappointment to the teachers that I could no longer be trusted, that my high place in her esteem was gone. Wisely she spared me the shame of punishment before the whole school, but some special marks of favour were withdrawn. And then the sin against the Lord, the grieving Him. I do not think I then or for years realized clearly that first false step in profession, so Mrs. Teed dealt with me as a tempted, fallen child of God—that I had listened to the devil and forsaken Christ.

My privilege of going alone was still mine, and then I could sob and cry and confess to Jesus, all the sins which now glared out on my soul. The rest of that half-year was a very sorrowful time, and I believe God's Spirit showed me the evil of my own heart. Still it never occurred to me to tell Mrs. Teed of that deceit. But I loved my friend increasingly. I remember watching for the first rose to blossom in my garden for her—and then writing with it a pencil note "that I was so unworthy, but I am your loving, sorrowful child, Maria."

My conviction of sin was deepened by a solemn warning. One of our schoolfellows was taken ill, M. L., the only child of parents who most reluctantly parted with their beloved for this her first half-year. Her recovery was prayed for. The elder girls joined in fervent supplication for the life of her soul. One midnight we heard carriage wheels, and next day the elder ones knew that London doctors came. In those days there were no large printed texts. The dying child needed a living Saviour—Jesus only. "The Father sent the Son to be the Saviour of the world," was written large and clear, and the card soon put where Mary could see its glad message. And Mrs. Teed's believing prayer was that by His own word, life and light would shine into the child's heart. "He that heareth my word and believeth on Him that sent me hath everlasting life," became the Lord's own "verily," His own "Talitha cumi;" and so in the twilight the glad, unasked-for confession came. "Mary *wants* a Saviour—Jesus my Saviour—God sent Jesus to save me. Yes, it is all true; all mine." The parents had come, and again the dying child pointed to the text, and with touching eagerness begged her father to believe also. Again God sealed those words, and the hitherto unawakened ear heard and believed. With all the agony of farewell to their only one came the new joy that Jesus was precious to them also, and as the pearly gate opened for her, so would it also for them. Silently all knelt round her dying bed, silently did One more draw nearer and nearer, even the Saviour of the world, completing His work by receiving her unto Himself, His shepherd arm safely gathering and carrying her home on His bosom. The "shoulder" for the straying sheep—the "bosom" for the folded lamb.

I might recall many more answers to Mrs. Teed's believing prayer and trust in the efficacy of God's own word. In some cases her dear scholars returned to homes with no sympathy, but rather opposition. To these she counselled obedience and cheerful home piety. One, who was prevented from further intercourse with her friend, sent the assuring message, "Although my house be not so with God, yet hath He made with me an everlasting covenant, ordered in all things and sure."

Mrs. Teed's influence over me was salutary and lifelong. Her own departure (5th January 1858) was a true sunset in calm radiancy, stedfast faith, and joyful anticipation, based on the atoning blood. Her dying words were, "I am fast going home; but I find the blood of Jesus *my all-sufficient suffciency!*"

And now on the 17th of June 1838 I bade farewell to Campden House; farewell to the royal rooms and chapel, and terraces and walks; farewell to the holy teachings, prayers, and songs; farewell to my ever most revered, most beloved friend on earth; farewell to clever teachers and masters; farewell to those eighty-five schoolfellows of girlish beauty and loving ways; farewell to the Campden chorus, whose echo ever lingers,—

> "Glory, honour, praise, and power,
> Be unto the Lamb for ever;
> Jesus Christ in our Redeemer,
> Hallelujah, praise the Lord!"

CHAPTER III.

HOME LIFE AFTER SCHOOL.

GOD'S "everlasting love" might be the shining motto of those happy days. Shielded from even ordinary temptations, but enjoying intensely all the charms of our beautiful neighbourhood; with a father never too strict, never too indulgent; with a mother teaching us thrifty elegance in our dress, and self-helping habits, order and cheerfulness,—a truly merry and happy household were we.

My bedroom had white dimity hangings, and pretty pink ruchings from mother's tasteful hand, a table for my desk, and the queer assortment of books I revelled in; the window trellised with a vine; below was mother's garden, with a few flower-beds and the grassy bank, a light railing only dividing it from the churchyard; and the little fir-tree, planted by father, that *now* stands sentinel over that holy resting grave of my nearest and dearest (with just room for *Maria* also!). Beyond was an undulating meadow, fringed with firs and elms, and the road leading down to the steep Toot hill. Away valleys and slopes, rising to Yarron, an Elizabethan farm, and the twin round hills, surmounting the lime quarries; beyond these the Abberley range, and Woodbury, with its fir-tree crown and ancient British encampment. To the south the Church Bank, or, as we called it, the Adders' Bank, where once young Lord Louth, finding two large specimens, brought them alive, with Irish innocence of reptiles, to my father, fortunately gripping them by the neck. The Adders' Bank is a steep declivity, with a rippling brook below. By an old tree-plank we crossed into Glashampton Park, still skirted by the snowdrop wood and daffodil and narcissus beds. Only the large stables are left, where lived Widow Sayce and her pretty tabbies. From my window I could just see the magnificent elms that root in the foundation ruins of a once noble house, all burnt to ashes on the eve of its completion! It is a digression, but the Glashampton story has a shining of God's ways, and how He brings good out of evil.

Long before my father came to Astley it was, at great cost, enlarged and beautified. It had a picture gallery for valuable paintings, which were still in the packing-cases, and so were saved. A large organ was rescued, which by a singular coincidence was afterwards in my father's church of St. Nicholas, Worcester. A feast was given to the workmen, and in the after-carousal ashes from a pipe set fire to shavings, and the whole mansion was totally destroyed, and never rebuilt. A print of the old house is in Nash's *Worcestershire*. Soon after, as the Rev. D. J. Cookes, the new proprietor and restorer, was surveying the smoking ruins, he saw one of the carpenters sitting on some planks reading a Greek book. Naturally surprised, a conversation followed, in which Mr. Cookes learned that his name was John Lee, that all his tools had been burnt in the fire, that as a boy he was at school in Shropshire, was apprenticed to a carpenter, and that Archdeacon Corbett, discovering his talent for languages, had himself instructed him in Latin and Greek. The apparently accidental burning of his tools was the circumstance which determined him to pursue more exclusively his classical studies, and he became master of the Bowdler Schools, near Shrewsbury, and afterwards entered the university of Cambridge, where he became the distinguished Professor Lee.

Back to my window! It was a July Sunday evening, soon after my home-coming, and the afternoon had been rather sleepily spent. The bells were chiming for evening service, and I looked out on the people assembling, and standing by the graves here and there, the living and the dead; the silence of those graves, the hum of the living voices above them flashed on me the solemn thought, that every one standing there, and I too, must lie dead and silent also. And a very glimpse of eternity, of the reality of heaven and hell as real places, where each one of us must be for ever, burnt in me a new and powerful desire to help some at least to find the Lord Jesus I trusted in, I knew dear father preached faithfully; I knew dear mother, though in feeble health, visited the poor. (Never forgotten were her words in old Molly's house, "We are saved only by the blood and through the merits of Jesus Christ.") I knew that sister Miriam taught the first class in the Sunday school, and covered tracts and lent them; but I had never done a thing, I had never spoken of Jesus, and when He came in His glory, might He not say, "Ye visited me not." *That* was the spring, of what I may humbly say became the very passion of my life, visiting not only the nearer cottages, but scouring over unfrequented fields with tracts and my dear Campden Testament, speaking (feebly of course) of and for Jesus Christ my Lord.

A class of girls was given me, and most diligently did I prepare the Sunday lesson, first studying the subject and consulting Scott and Matthew Henry's Commentaries, and then writing down every word of what I intended to say! (Some of these "Lessons for the Little Ones" I sent up anonymously to a magazine, and they were printed with commendation.)

On Sunday, in the summer afternoons, all the forms were carried to our orchard and lawn, and those open-air times led me always to adopt the same when superintendent of larger schools. We gave two tea treats—summer and winter; it may help some country vicar to carry out the Astley plan. It was the custom for every resident, or farmer, to send a cake once a year; this divided the expense fairly with the rector. Scripture texts were given for punctuality and good lessons; kept in the scholar's little bags, a dozen when learned perfectly were exchanged for a penny ticket. At school treats, these again were changed into Bibles, Testaments, prayer-books, and the few children's books then extant. The great event of our ecclesiastical year (excepting the festivals) was our Church Missionary Sunday. My dear father records that the first C.M.S. sermon at Astley was preached by the Rev. John Davies, of St. Clement's, Worcester, in 1823. Finding that the Astley Wake was a time of influx to the parish, my father wisely made that Sunday attractive by some stranger preaching for the C.M.S., with special hymns and lively tunes of his own composition. (See *Records of W. H. H.*, p. 135.[1]) All our missionary boxes were opened; and very interesting it is to look back on the names of the cottagers and their monthly or quarterly pence.

Our missionary interest was further enlivened by the meetings at Bewdley and Worcester; seldom any dull, prosy speeches there! Of course we thought our father's eloquence supreme; his musical voice and lively anecdotes, and the graceful wave of his white hand, were followed by more cheers than for others.

I was just eighteen when an invitation came to dear grandmother's, with the delightful prospect of staying at Oxford and seeing my brother Henry at New College. Dear mother went with me for wardrobe replenishings to Worcester; she chose a white straw bonnet, with pink and white watered ribbon, and some delicate pinky flowers were shown. We never wore flowers—we wished to be examples in our Sunday school; but how I begged for these and got them! Then at Scott's, how I teazed for a gay pink muslin! but mother wisely chose me a soft dove cashmere, and a neat *mousseline de laine*. Arrived at Wycombe, my pink flowers did not escape grandmother's eye; I think just then I had a turn at pomps and vanities, and received some attentions from a schoolfellow's sailor brother. The Oxford Commemoration was near, and my visit at Wycombe nearly past, but not profitably. I contrived to get a white muslin dress, with white satin trimmings, made unknown to grandmother, and Aunt Mary lent me a splendid black lace shawl. I could write pages of my Oxford visit, staying with the Vice-Principal of St. Edmund's Hall (where my father graduated in 1816, and two of his grandsons did so in 1882 and 1886). I went to breakfasts and soirées, and to see the Bodleian and up to Great Ben of Oxford, and under the great bell, received compliments and bows, "*that* is not the only *belle* we see," etc. And one discreet old Astley friend at an evening reception whispered, "Miss Havergal, don't mind all that is said to you. Mr. G. compliments every one." That sobered me, and the unsatisfying reaction set in; there was no real pleasure in the chat and laugh, and amid all the real interest of the Commemoration Day, thoughts of better joy stole in. I think the exquisite music in New College Chapel was my greatest delight; it thrilled through me, and then, as ever, I liked to shut my eyes, that melody alone might possess my whole being.

On my return, dear Astley home ways seemed sweeter than ever; the exceeding beauty of our walks, the botanical treasures, and in the lime-kilns hammering for fossils, was a change.

---

[1] *Records of the Life of the Rev. William Henry Havergal, M.A.* by Jane Miriam Crane (London: James Nisbet & Co., 1880), original book page 135, pages 617–618 of Volume IV of the Havergal edition.

I was a great reader. I liked having half-a-dozen books going,—great volumes of Calvin, Flavel, Pearson on the Creed; Hooker's Ecclesiastical Works, in 7 volumes; Newton on Prophecy, and all the Reformation Series; Bishop Jewel's folios; Jeremy Taylor and Gurnall's Christian Armour. The Homilies I knew well, and wish they were not out of sight now. Then there was Calmet's Bible Dictionary, and Scott and Henry. For higher reading, Belzoni's Travels, Robertson's America, Hume and Smollett's History of England, in close print. I never read novels, and so enjoyed sound wholesome food. I always thank my father for his express wish on that subject, and so when in after visits I saw them, not even a wish came to me. Once I did, as a trial, read one, to see if I could close the book and go with appetite to other studies. No. I felt the whirlpool of imagination stirred, but the dreamy mawkishness and unreality disgusted me. Often in travelling, books and *Punch* have been offered me. Two words always settle that—" give account;" so I would rather not read what I could not give account of.

With all the charms of our Astley life one was wanting—friends of our own age. The arrival of Mr. and Mrs. T. S. L., and one son and several daughters, at Astley Hall, supplied the void. The eldest, H., became my most valued friend; she was older and far in advance of my faith and knowledge. We studied the Bible together, we read and then talked over our abstracts of various authors, and our repetition of poetry kept us in practice. My love for her was enthusiastic—her footsteps even sent a thrill through me! Together we systematically visited the cottages, some far away; and she and her sisters in after years were valuable teachers in the Sunday school. My friend was an especial help to me in sacramental seasons. I loved Christ, and longed for more than the outward form. I wanted deeper communion with my Saviour. Oh how diligently I examined myself, how tearfully I read over the story of His cross and passion! and often I would go in our quiet chancel on the weekday to seek the Lord. The church standing close to our garden was rarely locked, and often in the summer I have been in it by five o'clock to secure early prayer. And yet I always came away from the Sacrament unsatisfied, and often so tearfully that I had to get off from dinner and ask for bread and milk in my room. I see now the Lord was teaching me not to place undue or exclusive value on any means of grace, and I have found the most vivid and exquisite manifestations of Himself and His exceeding love may be on the lone mountain or in the still chamber of suffering.

Dear H.'s friendship continued after her happy marriage with the excellent Rev. S. R. W. I wish some record had been kept of her pattern life as wife, mother, and devoted parish worker. My father had the greatest esteem for her, and she appreciated his teaching, and carefully did she keep notes of his Astley sermons. Mysteriously was this valuable mother suddenly called from her eight little ones; but in the glory all life-enigmas are solved.

But dear H. E. L. was not married while we were at our dear and much regretted Astley, and she was one of my sister M.'s bridesmaids from our next and temporary home, Henwick House. This was in the parish of Hallow, where my father awaited his promised succession to a living in Worcester. We had a large garden and long terrace (shortened since) overlooking the Severn. And what happy evenings we had of song and music when we were all at home! our then little darling Fan joining with wondrous facility. Her fairy form and golden curls seem flitting now amid the home scenes that rise and fall, and pass away in the dimming past.

Then came the first flight from our home nest—our eldest sister Miriam's marriage. Truly her father's daughter—clever, generous, and noble; her artistic etchings and sketches, and her descriptive verses, deserve a passing mention. It was very pleasant that her beautiful home should be Astley parish, and the boon Oakhampton was to all of us, and dear F. especially, no words can tell.

[*Note.*—The EDITOR allows *part* of the sisterly panegyric to remain, as showing how M. V. G. H. followed the precept, " in honour preferring one another."]

About this time a desire arose that God would really rule my life, and I think too rigid and ascetic ideas possessed me, also a turn of High Churchism. I fasted no end, and believe my health was much injured by it; besides, I regret the almost untruthfulness of my excuses for being absent from meals. On Sunday, as I taught in a far-off Sunday school, I often gave my sandwich dinner away, partly from good-nature, partly from supposed merit. In my dress, too, I tried to deny myself in every possible way—wishing to give to the poor the cost of silk dresses, etc.; it was the looking away from Christ, substituting works for His exceeding love, and His one final and for ever sufficient work of our redemption.

My father gave me a ring of rubies, but once I was touched by some missionary details, and having but little pocket-money, I put my ring on the plate. I never had another ring till, four years after my dear sister's death, I received a letter from the north of Scotland, saying that a dying girl had taken off her ring, and wished it might be sold for the F. R. H. Memorial Fund, for it was her books that had led her to Christ. I telegraphed back that I would redeem the ring.

It became an increasing delight to me to visit the cottages, my swift walking taking me to many a lonely corner. I marvel now at my activities, and believe they sprang from love to God, and much delightful communing did I hold with the Lord Jesus on the wayside. He was more and more to me, and when my early retirement at night was smiled at, they little knew the delight of being alone with Jesus my Lord.

In 1843, I paid a visit to some kind and holy friends in Bath. The Rev. John East was my father's college friend, and his church of St. Michael was at once his life-work and his tomb. I returned much refreshed to my parish duties with many new resolutions.

In the summer of 1844, my dear father took me to Scotland with a friend, who had suffered from an engagement being broken off. Untwine any clasping tendril, how helplessly torn the blossoms lie—the beautiful Augusta! it seemed strange indeed any one could forsake her.

We were favoured in travelling with my father, his pleasant talks and that invisible sympathy that tears not open lattice-grief, and withal that alluring to the truer love of a patient Saviour, waiting for the torn blossom to revive under His healing smile.

To me it was all novelty—the steamer, the sea, Ailsa Craig, and the beauties of the Highland lochs and mountains,—all seemed the opening of a new page in God's beautiful lesson-book.

How unconsciously we carry out God's purposes—how the travelling day chosen for one's own convenience may be the crossing of another's pathway in need of our sympathy! I was watching the sunset at sea, and the crested waves parting in foam against our steamer, when I saw the distressed face of a foreigner, who failed to make the captain understand her rapid questions in very broken English. She sat down lonely and sad; I offered to be interpreter, and so get the information wanted. She had friends in the island of Arran, but where or how to reach them she knew not. We, too, were bound for Arran, but must sleep at Ardrossan. I told my father that the Swiss stranger was evidently in difficulty; so he arranged to frank[1] her there, and she went with us to our hotel.

The next day I was deeply interested in her history, but however could she find her Genevan school friends with no clue but Arran? We landed at Lamlash, and we went in search of lodgings, Mdlle. following us.

All at once I saw two graceful girls approaching, and the cry, "My friends! my friends!" was the happy result. Of course they called to thank us for our attention to their friend, and we joined in rambles to Loch Ranza and Goatfell. The elder became Augusta's friend; only two years passed, and both met on another and more shining shore. The younger charmed me with her intellect and grace, and some twenty years after she married into our family!

Andrienne Vignier subsequently visited us, and by her tender nursing of my beloved mother, and in other ways, proved a friend in trouble. Her history ought to be written in full,—a brief outline must suffice.

An only child of Protestant parents, their castle and estate could not be inherited by her, but passed to the brother's son. He was a Roman Catholic, and from childhood was Andrienne's ardent lover. Owing to an accident when ten years old, Andrienne was taken to Italy for spinal treatment. There every effort was made to induce the child to abjure her Protestant notions. She described to me the endeavour to frighten her; after some brave refusal, she was told evil spirits would come for her if she were not in the true Church. And phosphoric outlines of horrible forms were made to pass before her on the wall as she lay in bed. All in vain! Then she was taken one evening into the chapel to confess; refusing to do so (I only wish I could repeat her clever answers), she was locked up all night alone in the chapel. The morning found the brave child firmer than ever; and when the priest told her he should go to heaven, but she must be lost for ever, she exclaimed, "If you will be in heaven, I never wish to go."

Years went on till her coming of age was to decide the choice—to be a loved wife and a countess in the castle of her ancestors, or to earn her bread as a governess in a strange land. No dogma, no obstinacy ruled here; in the strong, firm persuasion that Roman Catholic doctrines could not be proved by Holy Scripture, and that as they detract from the glory of Jesus Christ and substitute the merits of Virgin and saints, this true follower of Christ counted all things but loss, and literally gave up lover, house, and lands for His name's sake. It was soon after this that I met her in that singular way.

Once again, after the trial of loneliness, the count tried again. She was walking with her pupils (Augusta's sisters, for I had introduced her to Norton), when an Italian greyhound ran caressingly to her. She knew then its master was not far distant. Two interviews followed, not only with herself, but her English friends; but when Jesus Christ *is* a reality in the heart, we must be more than conquerors.

Her later path was one of wonderful ministry; not only in England, but away in Naples, noble deeds could be told of her generous rescue of some in distress. Andrienne gave me a singular detail of her assisting two escaped nuns, and their revelations strongly confirmed my Protestant faith. I will not give particulars, as I did not write them then. Brave Andrienne! when the Son of man comes in His glory, your name and your confession of faith shall be confessed by Him, and His smile will be your eternal compensation.

It was during this visit to Scotland that my father became acquainted with Dr. Laurie, of Monckton Manse, to whom he dedicated a lovely melody to "Burns's Prayer." This had a piano accompaniment, and is the original air from which the popular tune "Evan" was afterwards taken by Dr. Lowell Mason. When visiting my father, Dr. Mason was charmed with his singing it, and requested a copy. Turning to Frank, my father told him to give his copy to the Doctor, who took it to America. He wrote for permission to shorten the air to a C. M.

---

[1] A "frank" was a notice on an envelope in the place of a stamp, and a government frank signified—declared—free postage. This verb "frank" apparently means that this lady would be freely delivered—taken—to her friends' address.

hymn tune. My father did not think it in strict ecclesiastical style, and would not allow his name to appear; hence it got published with his initial H. only, and, appearing in Dr. Mason's collection, soon got his name instead of my father's.

Would that more had heard my father's exquisite touch and extemporized fugues and harmonies—waves of melody, now richest chords, then gentlest adagios. His voice was sweet and clear, and his long-sustained shake would hush us completely.

My brother Henry also had musical talent, and his chants and tunes deserve to be better known. His set of Christmas Carols, both words and music, are extremely bright and varied. It is not many have built two organs, and he was master of several musical instruments. His power in architectural drawing was also considerable, and when he was sub-librarian at the Bodleian, he made an illuminated catalogue of the music, which so delighted Dean Gaisford that he made him a present of £50, and it is preserved among the treasures of Christ Church Library, Oxford. My brother Frank also built his own organ, a very sweet one, on which his daughters play, and the youngest extemporizes beautifully.

In 1845, the Bishop of Worcester gave my father the important living of St. Nicholas, Worcester. It was a great change from the freedom of country life to the centre of a town, with all the responsibilities and activities of a large parish. It was overwhelming even to walk through the alleys and courts and ins and outs of the Butts; but my resolve came to know them all. Very delightful were our visits to the four sets of almshouses; so many dear pilgrims in them just waiting to cross over. Some of their histories I have written in *Pleasant Fruits,* and I often picture their different surroundings now in the spirit-state of joy and felicity. It is sometimes my indulgence to recall the names of all God's saints I have known, and as it were rejoice in their exceeding joy.

But it was not among saints only the Master called,—house-to-house visits, finding out lodgers and hidden ones, the heart-aching ones, whom it did ease only to tell it all out. To listen is a great point in visiting; it opens the barred door, which all one's pious remarks will not.

I remember pausing at every door for a look upward for wisdom, and, wherever possible, I read God's Word; proposing that they too would read verse about, awoke more attention. If the mother could not read, then let her children take turns; to read to and talk *at* people is almost useless. In cold and heat, snow and rain, I plodded on for hours daily. Occasionally a country walk with my dear little sister was a treat. Poor child, it was not a happy time for her, and I often regret many an omission that would have brightened her path. As elder sister, I was too exacting of what *ought* to be done, and was more of John the Baptist than the tender, loving Saviour. Memory recalls so much for regret in the home-life, while outwardly I was supposed to be all that was energetic and good. Elder sisters have so much in their power, and, oh, that daily I had striven to make every one happy! In the parish it was all very well, and there I do think I was loved. My knowledge of the hundreds of poor, the names of every man, woman, and child, was a great help to my father, especially in the yearly distribution of the church gifts.

The Sunday school under my dear father's supervision became a model. Punctually as the clock struck half-past nine, he gave out the hymn; no waiting ever. The boys' school had been disorderly, so my father tried the new plan of the teachers being all ladies, and it answered admirably. Many of the elder lads turned out well, and several former scholars have come in after life to look at my father's portrait, and tell how they loved him, and how advice and kindly teaching had been golden in their effects on them. One of my scholars was a very clever lad, and I gave him lessons in the evenings and sent him to a night-school. When leaving St. Nicholas, I commended him to Miss Breay's excellent teaching, and to her he owed his future progress. It was pleasant to receive a letter from my old scholar, asking my earnest prayers on his ordination, and saying, that though he could not recall any exact words, " It was your angel touch on my shoulder that became the call to a holy life," His mother told me that on Sunday evenings he would come home from church and lie silent and absorbed on the hearth-rug. Asking his thoughts—"Mother, when I am a man, I should like to preach like dear Mr. Havergal, and stand in his pulpit." The wish was realized.

Several of our dear scholars died in the Lord; my father's beautiful account of "A wise and holy Child" might well be reprinted. I supplied him with notes of her conversations, and I do prize the fact that it was our *own* sweet mother's remarks on the hymn she gave out in the Sunday school, that bore fruit in Elizabeth Edwards' life and happy death. My mother's health failed soon after we came to St. Nicholas, but not till she was known and loved, and I may say admired, as I remember noticing when she went in the High Sheriff's State carriage to the cathedral at the time my father was chaplain to his Astley friend, T. S. Lea.

My dear father was now in the very zenith of his labours, preaching, and popularity. His church was densely crowded; the hearty congregation, singing to his own tunes and chants, testified to their genius, while his house-to-house visitation, with cheery loving words, ensured the affection of his people. I remember how much his visits were appreciated by the families of our tradesmen; to some of the younger ones, especially at their confirmation time, he became much blessed.

CHAPTER IV.

1846–1848.

DURING the illness of my dear mother, I kept an account of many remarks and conversations. As the mother of Frances Ridley Havergal, surely these records ought not to be folded up in the oblivion of the past. They may strengthen the faith and patience of some who may likewise be called to endure the inevitable sufferings of that dire and unmanageable disease—cancer. A large MS. book is lying by me; it is impossible to copy it as it is, and my own aching arm warns me to hasten in whatever I write, so I will make some extracts only. I believe the prayers and holy example of our sweet mother were the spring of untold blessing to her children; and now that the fourth generation are rising, it is right they should know something of Jane Havergal. I was myself but a tiny child when I was shown a window pane, with "lovely Jane Head" indelibly written on it.

I have a long letter from an eminent Christian, written to my mother when quite a girl. It was in answer to her own statement of difficulties, which really proved how deep and true was the work of grace in her soul, and also referring to the time of her conversion. My dear mother told me what follows. "When I was about twelve years old, a good lady, Mrs. K., took much interest in me, and when I went to visit some friends in London, her advice kept me firm in refusing to go to a dancing party. I also remember, when visiting my eldest sister at her pretty home, that I took Scott's Commentary to my room and delighted in reading it. Indeed, from a child, my dear mother taught me to love my Bible, and I can remember always securing quiet time for reading." This love for her Bible was her shining way-mark through life. Her knowledge and love of hymns was great, and her voice was sweet and true. As a curate's and rector's wife, she admirably guided the home details. The cottagers loved her, and when we left Astley Rectory in 1841, a solid silver cake basket was presented to her by the parishioners. Her health failed soon after my father took the Rectory of St. Nicholas, Worcester; but one of her school addresses bore special fruit, as may be read in the little memoir of "A wise and holy Child."

The intense love of her youngest child Frances for her mother, and the deep grief, told with such force in F.'s "Four happy days," reveal the secret influence, that bore such a wealth of after-fruit in her child's life and words. And the very same Bible promises were precious alike to mother and child, the very same hymns were chosen by them in dying hours, and fully has the early prayer been answered—

"Bring me, oh bring me to Thy house of light,
That there with my loved mother I may dwell,
And e'er rejoicing in Thy presence bright,
May praise Thy love, who doest all things well."
F. R. H.

November 1846.—My mother was so ill that her absent children were sent for, and my Aunt Stratton came. Brother Henry was the first to arrive, and kneeling by her, with her hand on his soft hair, she said, "There is nothing like loving the Lord Jesus, He is indeed precious—such a Saviour! I think that ever since I was sixteen years old, I have really loved Him, but not of myself, it is God's free mercy that gave me the least spark of living grace; no merit, no righteousness in me."

Directing something to be done orderly, mother added, "What order there will be in heaven!" When taking food, "The bread of life is mine, I shall soon be admitted to the marriage supper of the Lamb." To my father, "I hope I am safe; nothing of my own to trust in, all vile and worthless, nothing to be satisfied with in myself, the merits and righteousness of Christ are my only trust. In the night it was as if the heavens were open to me, and, like Stephen, I saw Jesus interceding for me." When we were all watching around, my mother said, "Dear children, few mothers are so blessed as I am in you—it is God's love." By her wish, it was arranged that we should join with her in commemorating the death of Christ. Previously, she contrasted our service with that of extreme unction. "Of what avail could that be—enough for me that I am complete in Christ. I seem to see those words emblazoned in shining light, 'It is finished,' the whole work of redemption completed for me." (Years after, her child wrote, "It is finished" is the central word of eternity!) Calling Fanny, she told her to go and change her frock. "You are going to see us receive the Sacrament, darling; if you live to grow up, I hope you will understand it, and partake of its inward grace; never forget you first saw it in your dying mother's room. It is the emblem of Christ's love in dying for you—for me."

Some hours afterwards, my mother said how much she enjoyed the time. "Oh yes, I have so *much* comfort, Christ is all in all to me. I find Him faithful to all His promises; in Him they are indeed 'Yea and Amen.'" Then we all sang hymns, and she told us what comfort she often found in repeating them and texts of Scripture. My brother Henry especially ministered to her in repeating Scripture and playing hymn tunes in the next room. His godfather, Rev. John East, she often spoke of. "Our intimacy has been a great earthly blessing—such a man of God! dear Henry, may his prayers for you be abundantly answered." My mother's thankfulness was ever rising. "My breakfast—how new are God's mercies every morning, I feel them in everything."

Saying I feared I did not do all I should for her comfort, she replied, "Dear Maria, I am abundantly satisfied with all your care; I often think of poor creatures who have no one to minister to them as I have."

To Aunt S.: "I have often thought of that text, 'Daughter, be of good cheer, thy sins are forgiven thee;' I too may touch the hem of His garment and shall be whole. Will you repeat 'How sweet the name of Jesus sounds'?" Then Henry repeated "In this world of sin and sorrow." "Yes, that hymn has often comforted me; Henry, you sing it, and I will try and join."

Often have I lamented my inability to speak to others, and repeating hymns has helped me to express my feelings.

Then mother chose these to be sung: "O Zion, when I think of thee," "O God, our strength in ages past," "There is a land," "In vain my fancy strives to paint," "Whence those unusual bursts of joy," saying, "*That* is just the song for *me!*"

But the danger passed, and our mother was again able to join us occasionally. On Sundays it was her delight to follow the congregation in the church services. One of her windows in St. Nicholas' Rectory opened close to the church, so that the reading and singing could be heard. And she remarked how much enjoyment she gained by knowing the same Scripture was read by our Church throughout the world, and thereby enjoying the communion of saints, though alone in her sick-room. My father too always told her his texts and the outlines of his sermons.

Our sister Miriam's visits from Oakhampton with flowers and fruit were a great enjoyment; and these were shared with many a cottage invalid, dear father carrying them.

In August 1847, my mother was able to go for change on Rainbow Hill. The refreshing air and view of the Malvern Hills were very pleasant. Once I stood with her at early dawn, and as we watched the mist rolling away, she said, "Soon will all my shadows flee away, and the bright morning of eternity dawn for me." Again, "Think of the distance between a holy God and sinful man—such a chasm! but all is filled up, bridged over with redeeming love. But there must be a great change in the natural heart, or it could not enjoy the pleasures at God's right hand." Another time, reading 1 Peter 1:8, "Whom having not seen ye love," etc., our mother said, "I had glimpses of that in the night, and rejoiced with joy unspeakable and full of glory—so, so happy!" Returning to St. Nicholas' Rectory (it is taken down now), she could again closely join in the services, and even heard my father's voice in the pulpit. Afterwards she remarked, "I think preachers need so much prayer that God's Holy Spirit will accompany their word, and that God may speak through them."

September 1, 1847.—One of her daughters asked, "Do you ever wish or pray to get better?"

"Oh no, I pray to be prepared for worse pain than this, for I do not know what God is preparing for me. But what God orders must be best,—all is quite right, all suffering is for my good. I do not shrink from pain; if that is God's will, I could bear more, and pass through all the fiery trial appointed for me. Patience is so often mentioned in Scripture, so it must be necessary for His people."

That night mother exclaimed, "How beautiful!" "What is beautiful?" "The hill of Zion, and Dr. Watts' hymn, 'Come ye that love the Lord' gives me such happy thoughts. Then I have been thinking of the lovely gardens at Oakhampton, and that dear little Miriam, and how I long she may walk with me in the golden streets. Yes, I do get happy moments even in pain, and see my Saviour almost as if face to face."

January, 1848.—Calling dear Fanny to her side, her mother said, "Now you see dear mamma on her dying bed,—you too will come to die, how will you feel then if you are not safe in Christ? I am more anxious about you than your sisters, because I hope their hearts are fixed on God their Saviour. Always remember it would be my greatest pleasure to see you loving heavenly things. When you are tempted to do wrong, pray to the Holy Spirit to guide you. Nothing but the precious blood of Christ can make you lovely in God's sight. It is my heart's desire that you may be saved with His everlasting salvation. Now say that hymn, 'Life is the time to serve the Lord,' and often think about it."

After some very intense pain, our dear mother said, "What am I that God should take notice of me, even to afflict me! Oh, why should He thus care to purify me, why should He thus love me?

> 'Oh to grace how great a debtor,
> Daily I'm constrained to be!'

Yes, grace, free grace, will ever be my song. Precious Saviour, sanctify me, prepare me to see Thee face to face. Oh that it may please Thee speedily to deliver me from the burden of this sinful and suffering flesh."

June 1848.—Dear mother said, "I am in the depths of misery; if I had been told what pain I had to go through, I should not have believed it possible that I could bear it. Oh, I hope you will sing and rejoice for me when I am gone; the very bells should all ring for me then! There must be no mourning for me when I am delivered from sin and sorrow. All things will be ready, and I shall be summoned to the marriage supper of the Lamb."

June 20.—As sister Miriam and her husband were supporting her, she said, at intervals, "Oh, these bitter, bitter pains! but I know the Lord's mercy will not fail me. Christ has done all for my salvation, nothing else could give me comfort now. My Saviour is my strength and my song. It is so wonderful that my fear of death is quite gone, and I have only a longing desire to die. Oh, why tarriest Thou?" Dear papa said, "My dear, I think you have not many days now to wait for Him." She replied, "Oh, praised be His name! How glorious to know that I shall soon see Him who was pierced for me!" That evening she was easier, and listened with enjoyment while Miriam played some hymns—"Come let us join our cheerful songs," etc., and little Miriam sang to her, "Come to that happy land."

After this time her words were very few, but full of holy peace. Sometimes she exclaimed, "My Saviour! Come, Lord Jesus, come quickly."

In perfect peace our beloved mother passed away on the evening of July 5, 1848.

CHAPTER V.

THE SISTERS' HOME AT THE MUMBLES.

October 1878.

ARRIVED at Park Villa, Caswell Road, and found our thirty-two packages of home books, pictures, plate, and china had arrived.

The next evening my dear sister Frances came unexpectedly, and no room was ready for her. Her first words were, "I am so glad to get to you, Marie!" She was very weary and exhausted after giving Bible addresses at Plymouth, and much pleasant intercourse with strangers. She spoke of her visit to "B. M." as a very intellectual treat. The elegant surroundings there were a strong contrast to the carpetless bare rooms not yet ready here. Her spirit of content with any lack of things tasteful, though so consonant to her refined nature, struck me much.

Never grumbling, but brightly setting things in order with little elegant contrivances; making the most of what she had, her hands seemed a fairy wand in transforming bare rooms and walls. "Give me American cloth, bright nails, and a hammer, and you will see, Marie!" So our rough packing-boxes were made into music-stands and tidies. How I wish F. R. H. could have been photographed as the merry carpenter! deftly dovetailing and contriving. We could not get help at first, and so we two nailed down her study carpet; and good Tucker unpacked Frances' dear study table and the Astley arm-chair, and the little couch from Pyrmont Villa, and Davie and Johnnie carried up the books, the remnants of our father's and her own library. It was strange how my darling counselled me not to bring *many* of our pretty home things,—"it will only cumber us, Marie." But I was determined her study should be cosy, and have blue damask curtains to match the blue chair coverings.

And now she could freely invite her friends or the villagers to her study; and many a Nicodemus crept up there and unburdened the sorrows or the awakening difficulties in their souls, finding Christ, or entering into the full blessedness of true, whole-hearted consecration to the King. If F. R. H.'s study walls could speak, what *messages* of love, what words of holy, tender pleadings would they unseal!

By seven o'clock my sister would begin her "One hour with Jesus," and then the half-hour till our morning prayer-bell rang was one of her freshest thought times. We carried out our early home punctuality to the minute, and also our early retiring for the night.

In these lodgings, as elsewhere, and following dear father's example, we invited the household to daily prayer. When other visitors came, intimation of the same was given, so that often our parlour was full. My sister played and led the hymn, and then came verse by verse reading. She always liked me to throw out any thought or comment, giving us herself some deep findings from her own spoils in the Word.

Then at our breakfast, the sun shining through the bow-window made our tent seem pitched like Judah's, "towards the sun-rising."

Often my darling would rub her hands, crying, "What emancipation! it is jolly! I had no idea it would be such fun living with you, Marie!" The breakfast parlour was my room, containing dear father's bust, and Astley Church, and St. Nicholas. A picture of convolvuli and marguerites and ferns, enwreathing brightly "Joy cometh in the Morning," was painted for F. by dear Florence M. Photographs of sister Miriam's home and conservatories, and her Constance's wedding group—then brackets by dear nephews, and flowers were everywhere.

But the postwoman's step and knock disturbed our talks, and my sister would come in, both arms full of letters, with their too often postal burdens, that frittered away the precious health and time, which, but for them, would have written volumes more of rich legacies of thought. For my sister always attended to letters first, answering if possible by return, and often doing exceeding kindness to strangers in answering their various requests.

At noon a run to our cliffs. Once she wanted to watch the moment of the highest tidal wave—the wind was furious. Presently she turned towards me—"Marie! I am faint." I laid myself on the grass, and drew her on me, as it was damp. How ill she looked! I had some warm lozenges with me, and by and by she recovered. Very slowly did I get her home. Even then F. unselfishly said, "I have spoilt your watching those grand waves—Marie, you will be better without me!" Little did she know how tear-graven those words echo even now in 1886. "Better without me,"—ah, I would exchange anything to have my darling!

Another day she and I strolled on the cliff, and down into Caswell Bay. I left her sitting on a seat, that she might be quiet, and turned upwards. Presently a stranger came up the road, and sat down by her. What followed I did not know till three years after my sister's death. Going into a Mumbles shop, the mistress exclaimed, "Then it *was* Miss Frances I saw!" "What do you mean?" "Oh, miss, it is three years ago—I had landed from a sailing-boat in the bay, and sat down very tired. The lady was singing a hymn so softly by herself. Then she spoke to me—oh, so sweetly, of Jesus, and the joy of trusting Him; and she was pleased I knew Him too. Just then she heard a call. I looked up and saw you, miss, far on; and the dear lady just bent and gave me a gentle kiss on my forehead, saying, 'My sister is calling me—good-bye.' I never knew who it was till now I know you are Miss H. and she that angel."

Another day we had taken donkeys to Bishoptown valley, and dismissed them at the school and church. In the churchyard a mother was crying while putting flowers on her daughter's grave. I do not know all that F. said to her, but she gently placed her hand on her shoulder with "Think of the meeting, not of the parting!" Simple but inexhaustible comfort! instead of our thoughts dwelling on the last looks and words and coffin and funeral day, rather looking on—on to the sure meeting, the loving welcome home in the many mansions, where we have been long waited for, "Beside the crystal sea, I wait for thee."

Another incident of her walks I give in the "Memorials" when she met old John in his threadbare coat. He has shown me the very spot, far down the steep cliff, and how she got a stake of wood, and bidding John put his burden of wood down, passed the stake through, and lifting one end she helped to tug it up the cliff, and then called Davie to conclude it through the village, for she would not do things to be looked at.

The winter was severely cold, but my sister bravely visited every house both in Newton and many of the Mumbles cottages with almanacs and books. I have the hammer and nail box she carried to put them up.

The village school was her untiring delight—singing with them, and giving Bible-class lessons, and then finally made the offer of a new Bible to each who repeated perfectly the fifty-third chapter of Isaiah.

It was much impressed on me to get to the Union Workhouse, standing far up the hill of Ceyfan Bryn. I did not know the way, but thought by sleeping at the Gower Hotel I could walk there and back the next day. So I laid in packages of gingers and peppermints, and tea, and books, and tracts. But snow fell, and it was far too deep to risk unknown paths. Still I longed to get there somehow. I was told a 'bus left Swansea at 5 P.M., and thereby I could cross the moor, arrive at the hotel at 8 P.M., and so in the morning visit the Union. It was a weary wait till the 'bus started at six from Swansea, whither I went by train. A deserted wife and her children were my companions, and a man. Soon the driver stopped. "All please to walk up this pitch"—icy indeed; then in again, rattling over the wild moor, the moonbeams on the snow and the desolation—I might have been in Switzerland! and enjoyed it accordingly, quieting the children with gingerbread. The man listened respectfully to the snow lessons that sparkled around. Nine o'clock P.M., and we drove up to the Gower Hotel. "Can you give me a quiet room, please?" and seeing the look at my late appearance, added, "I am a clergyman's daughter, and am going to visit the Union." "Pray, step in, ma'am—it's a bitter night. Very sorry, but we have no rooms in the winter." "Can you tell me of one in a farmhouse? If it was summer, I could sleep in the hay!" "No, miss, nothing at all. You had best go on in the 'bus to the inn at Reynolstone." But the 'bus was gone! and I stood roofless under the stars and on the ice! Then the woman directed me to a Mrs. Jenkins, where once the curate lodged. That was hopeful; and off I tramped merry enough, but very cold. Soon I heard running behind me, and a lassie who exclaimed, "I could not catch you. Mistress sent me after you to show you the cottage." "That is kind. What is your name?" "Mary Tucker." And so my little guide turned out to be niece to our good landlord at Park Villa. Knocking at Mrs. J.'s door, the very picture of a Welsh wifie, trim and clean, appeared, when I repeated my only certificate, that I was a clergyman's daughter going to the poorhouse, and nowhere to sleep! "Come in, come in!" were welcome words at 10 P.M. Such a fireside, and such a white cosy bedroom all ready. After thawing, such tingling pain and fever came on, I thought I never should move again. While getting my supper, a knock at the door. "Please, have you got any raspberry vinegar?" "No, indeed—good-night." That question struck me; some one must be very ill, someone might be dying—might, oh, might *this* not be the answer to that strange impulse to brave such a journey? Enquiring, I found that a lady *was* very ill in a mill near; that she was come from Bath to die near her old Gower home. Much I prayed that night that if *this* was to be my King's errand, the door might be opened for me. So I called next day, explaining how accidentally I heard of the illness. Readily was I shown upstairs. The unmistakeable shadow of death had fallen on the sufferer with cancer, and all its attendant suffering. She thanked me warmly, listened eagerly, and seemed just to need the voice in the wilderness to clear away the fear and doubt; she wanted the finger to point to the Lamb of God—to the atoning blood which cleanseth from all sin. (I did *not* take notes, so I make up no conversations.) Just as my visit was ended, worthy Philip G. drove up with a sack of corn. Depositing that at the mill, he gave me a seat, for he was going as guardian to my ultimatum, the Union.

It is a wondrous view from the Union windows: below, the Needles Bay with the three Aiguille rocks; through the trees the church tower; away to the right, Oxwich Bay with its sweep of sand; and to the north, the summit of Ceyfan Bryn, from whence you see the peculiar boot-shaped promontory of Gower.

Gwyn's introduction secured me the entrance to all the wards. Dear old pilgrims, some in the land of Beulah, some groping in by-paths. Old blind Nanny was specially happy with hot butter toast and tea! and she assured me the Union was "almost like heaven! Jesus Christ loved her, and she could sing to Him now." One lonely man's history was sad indeed—a clergyman's son. My impression was he had been wronged, and his rightful mother's property wrested from him.

I saw many proofs of how much comfort is utterly in the hands of the master and matron. Here the home-made bread and butter, the currant cake I saw in the orphans' bags on their way to school; and going into the kitchen, the matron showed me the potato scones she was frying in dripping—"Such a treat in the wards, miss. I never sell my perquisites; and if it's cold-meat dinner, I make warm gravy and put it on their potatoes; it's a pleasure to make the most of their food for them." Matrons and masters may live a noble life of unseen ministries of love, or they may screw down to desperation the helpless ones, whose cry reaches only One, who will avenge. Workhouses have ever been a special visiting interest; and many a tale could I have written years ago of histories told to me.

After three or four hours among the wards, the mistress gave me refreshment, and then I mounted Gwyn's trap for the drive home. He waited while I called again on the dying one—the life fast ebbing out into the deep ocean of eternity. Surely the clinging clasp would be met in the strong hand that is never shortened that it cannot save.

Often again in spring days did I revisit Ceyfan Bryn. Once I went down to Puldy, and up by High Pennard, and so over the cliffs—a lonely ramble of hours—till I met a Welsh shepherd. Offering him a book, his answer was, "I think *you* love my Lord."

"Yes; how glad I am you can say 'my'!"

He looked intelligent, and his remark was forcible. "Did you ever notice in the Gospels, that our Lord was never *present at* a deathbed!—He saw the bier, He stood by the damsel and the grave of Lazarus; but *death could not face the Lord of Life!*" Naming this to my sister F., she pondered it, and not long before her departure referred to it, also saying, "It *is* true, and our Lord's words, 'If a man keep my saying, he shall never see death,' confirm it. The believer will *so see* Jesus that he cannot see death at all! isn't that splendid!" To her this was soon a glorious reality; her eyes verily met the King's coming unto her, and so death was left behind her—not even a shadow dimming that bright tryst.

The winter was most severe, and my alpenstock was useful in the icy lanes. I can't think now how I took the almanacs to every cottage in far-off villages. Returning one day, I passed a farmhouse of the better class, with a drive up and a porch. I was tired out, but hurried up to the door. "Ask your mistress if you may take these almanacs" (I always bid servants ask leave). A pleasant kindly person came out and said, "Certainly, and I should like one for the parlour. May I ask your name?"

"I do not think you can know it; we are strangers; but it is Havergal."

"Havergal! why, that's the name of that good curate in Gloucestershire my old uncle is always talking about."

"It must be my father, then, for he was curate at Coaley in Gloucestershire, fifty years ago."

"Coaley!" said my new friend, "why, that's my birthplace!"

"And mine too; so we must shake hands." So, in the far-off Gower, that ice-cold day, the loved name of my father, remembered and revered, warmed me thoroughly. I often called afterwards, and heard glowing memories of his early labours in the Lord.

One more coincidence arising from that wintry visit. Many weeks after, when my beloved sister was dying, a stranger then visiting at this farm called asking to see me. Reluctantly I went down, and there stood R. Kingscote of Kingscote, once my father's pupil at Astley, whom I had not seen since I was "little Maria," and now he was a veteran in the King's service. He spoke most warmly of my father. I asked him to pray with me, for I was sorely troubled. It was soothing, and his farewell words often come back to me with the King's power: "*Nothing can break our relationship!*" *i.e.* once in Christ, God is our Father, Christ our Brother, for ever and ever.

Another freezing day I went a long round, praying some work might turn up. In a lonely farm I was told of a dying farmer at some distance, and the information that "he didn't see his danger, body or soul," led me to earnest prayer. The lanes were slippery and all ice-bound; but my sister had taught me the firm heel-stepping on glaciers, and I delighted in the keen air. Certainly my brisk powers of walking have been unusual; in Ireland I was called "the walking lady," as my father was called the "lithomest man in England." I found Thomas Jones far on in consumption, without a glimmer of light for the valley. He asked me to come again, and again the Holy Spirit, the Lord and giver of life, blessed the words of Jesus: "The entrance of Thy words giveth light"; "He that heareth my word and believeth on Him that sent me hath everlasting life" (John 5:24). O blessed grammar! O joy-giving present tenses! It is a marvellous, ever-perpetual "now!"

Thomas sent for me when dying, to thank me for bringing him to Christ, and died in sure hope.

Christmas Day, 1878.—My sister was very ill, and yet she arranged on a tray presents for all in the house, and she sent Mary with warm cuffs and comforters to many cottages. It was the first Christmas without singing my dear father's carol, "How grand and how bright!"

Dear Frances and I had some time before returned the call of an aged and saintly pilgrim—a clergyman's daughter living in retirement. Her carpetless floor caught Frances' attention. She consulted with me how to send a warm carpet as a Christmas gift, and so we managed that it should surprise her. Very sweet was that brief intercourse, now resumed for ever.

Towards the end of January 1879, dear Frances went to London. I plaited some fine tulle ruchings, which suited her well, and how pleased she was, saying, "That will do if I go to the Duchess of ———." I entreated her to get a sealskin jacket. "I never had one, Marie; I will think about it." Dear sister, instead of getting the needed sealskin, she bought two fur cloaks and made presents of them, and just got a plain cloth jacket for herself. All through life she ever gave to others rather than supply her own wants.

Dear Frances was absent three weeks in London. Many saw her, and it was the last time. She told me of her shaking hands with Rev. E. H. Bickersteth, as she so admired his hymns, and poem "Yesterday, to-day, and for ever." And fifty years ago his honoured father and ours travelled together on Church missionary pioneering work.

One morning she went unwillingly to be photographed. She was cold and weary, and always regarded it "as resignation to torture." Messrs. Elliott & Fry were most painstaking, but no ray could transfer her radiant expression. Mr. Fry treasures the basket and crochet she held. The standing pose, with her large Bible, I think is the best.

Frances told me of a very pressing offer of marriage in that London visit, and how difficult it was to shake off the "pure and holy love laid at her feet."

In writing her Memoir I did not allude to several such proposals all through her life, or the one secret disappointment which gives a minor in some of her poems. But I may now say my sister bravely and unreservedly severed a correspondence and friendship which, though it scathed her heart, brought her into the fullest joy of being henceforth "only for Jesus." This bitter fruit yielded an afterwards of exceeding sweetness, and enabled her to counsel others who were tempted with the golden chain of matrimony under the delusion that they might win their beloved one to Christ. "Only in the Lord" was my sister's safe rule and practice.

During our evenings in the last spring, dear F. told me many incidents I could not print in the Memoir, so I shall only record some as bearing on her life-story. At this time she was revising the proofs of *Life Mosaic,* and when the copies came down, with their Alpine illustrations and artistic borders, F. exclaimed, "Oh, I should so like to send one to the Princess Beatrice! You know, Marie, I so specially pray for her." Then F. told me of an incident that led to this loyal wish coming to pass.

During a previous visit to London, Frances was invited to an amateur musical evening. Some classical music was rendered, and F. was especially riveted by the finished singing of an Italian lady. Presently my sister was invited, last of all, to the piano. True to her resolve, "Let me sing only, always, for my King," she chose a song of Handel's. Then the hostess gracefully pressed for one of her own compositions, so she sang, "Whom having not seen ye love." She always sang so rejoicingly the words, "Though now ye see Him not, yet believing ye rejoice," up the scale of joy—she knows better now—and then the deep adoring thrill, "With joy unspeakable and full of glory." The rooms were hushed, and then the Italian stranger, with tears in her eyes, sought her as she left the piano, with "Miss Havergal, I envy you; your words and face tell me you have something I have not." I may not write more detail, but this lady knew well the Princess Beatrice. And as pleasant correspondence followed this interview, F. ventured to express her longing for *Life Mosaic* to reach the Royal Princess, and it was graciously accepted, and Her Royal Highness's autograph was written beneath her charmingly sensible face, and sent to my sister, with a pleasant assurance that H.R.H. Princess Beatrice admired her poetry. In my sister's desk there still lies, where she placed it, the Royal portrait. Here again this explains the entry in F.'s "Journal of Mercies"—"For reaching the Princess Beatrice."

Long after my beloved sister had passed beyond the reach of praise, we were gratified to see an extract from our sister's lines on "September" enwreathed by the same Princess with heather and autumnal leaves in her artistic Birthday Book.

So that test of singing only sacred words brought about this pleasant Royal favour to the truly loyal singer for her King.

Another anecdote I must veil as to names and locality.

My sister was requested to call on some young ladies who had come for the season of hunting and balls. The call was followed by a walk, and then an invitation to luncheon. She went prayerfully, and it was well. There she found a clever, dashing stranger, who launched a severely critical attack on religion in general, asking my sister her opinion of theatres and plays and operas, and then ridiculing her replies. The sneer was not even covert, and never had F. been so painfully and ungenerously quizzed. She quietly endured it; the host seemed perplexed. The mother was an invalid, and not present. The ordeal over, my sister was invited to visit the invalid mother, and there she found an eager listener as she told of the peace in Jesus, the utter rest for the world's weary ones.

Then the ladies proposed a walk, which F. would have declined, but the host said, "I shall have the pleasure of walking with Miss H.," so further attack was checkmated.

Frances had just returned from abroad, and had visited the fortifications at Belfort and other Franco-German places. She gave a lively description of these, and also showed her accurate knowledge of fortification, which extremely amazed and delighted the courteous general.

But the lady's attack left F. but one course; she wrote a polite note that she would not again call, and could only remain their silent and sincere friend.

Some months after, F. received a note of apology and distress for the pain given her. Without giving details, I will say that my sister was blessed to all the family; and that general knelt with F., and gave his allegiance to her King, and the invalid's welcome to my sister's visits was a pleasant "afterwards."

Once when she was about to converse with a clergyman, she said, "Marie, when an hour is up, come in." There was F., her hand waving, and I just caught this characteristic end of her talk, "Oh, why don't you preach the gospel of Christ?" Answer, "My congregation are well educated and well acquainted with the truths of salvation; if they were Zulus, I should preach differently." F., "Then I will be a Zulu next Sunday, and just preach at me!" To her delight, a real gospel sermon was the result.

My sister strongly believed in the power of intercessory prayer, and gave me this glimpse. "Conversations are no use without prayer. There was Mrs. ——, whom I specially wanted to attend our Young Women's Christian Association meeting. The night before, I prayed for her only, till very late, that the Lord would graciously reveal Himself to her, and that she might receive the full blessing. Next day I saw her come in. I was asked to take one of the prayers. I prayed, believing that there was one kneeling among us, waiting and desiring to receive the blessing. I pleaded that the Lord would then give it her in all its fulness, that He had promised they who asked should receive, and I believed Him. When we rose from our knees, Mrs. —— just turned towards me, and her face was simply transfigured. I saw the answer was given. We had no conversation till some days after; she then told me of the fulness of her joy and peace in Christ Jesus Himself."

Doubtless many young ambassadors in Christ's Church are even now reaping the legacy of those mighty intercessions. And yet my sister could sympathize with those whose prayers seem unanswered; and after her death I found a book with many initials only, and this clue, "Unanswered petitions"; and a longer list of initials with "That these may be fully consecrated." But every such burden was cast on her Lord. I copy one of our talks.

"Do you think, Marie, that this simile holds good: that when we *first* cast our burdens on the Lord, He cuts the strings that bind it on, then if we gave a leap it would all slide off; if we don't, it sticks, and on we go, toiling up hill,—I mean if we just thanked and praised at once, and believed the Lord took the burden, it really would be gone?"

Marie. "Were you thinking of the burden of sin?"

Frances. "Yes, or of any other trial, aggravations,—things one can't bear."

M. "If the Lord carries *us,* then He carries our burdens too."

F. "Ah, there our 'Little Pillow' for last night comes in. 'I will carry you,'—how safely, how tenderly a child is carried, it does not *see* the way!"

M. "Is not carrying His first and last act—the lost sheep carried on the shoulder—the departing spirit carried to His bosom; so He bringeth them to the haven."

F. "Yes, but perhaps the winds won't carry the vessel in just the tack one expects."

My sister's needlework was most rapid and perfect. She would say, "People never give me credit for needlework! I do like getting a whole pile of socks to mend when I visit busy mothers; and at the missionary working-parties it amused me to see my plain sewing handed round!"

Then how delicious Fan's touch on the pianette she bought specially for me! Sometimes rapid waves of melody, rising, falling, ebbing into softest ripple, then full glorious chords, so reminding me of dear father's harmonies. Often she sang for me her recitative and air to the words in Isaiah 12: "And in that day thou shalt say, O Lord, I will praise Thee: though Thou wast angry with me, Thine anger is turned away, and Thou comfortedest me." Then a brilliant, "Behold, God is my salvation; I will trust, and not be afraid,"—the very shout of a victor. But the third verse, "Therefore with joy shall ye draw water out of the wells of salvation," was real water music, the notes seemed sparkles of water dropping gladly, and the illusion was so perfect that one's soul seemed refreshingly sprayed with joy! Alas! that priceless manuscript is lost. Frances had written it all down within a few days of her death. I believe my sister told me she had sent it to some critic. I have inquired and searched vainly for this " my lost chord." The melody floats through and through me still, yet strangely I cannot sing it. Dear Cecilia is the only one who remembers somewhat of its melody.

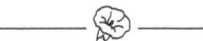

CHAPTER VI.

SUFFERING AND SUPPORT.

IN May 1884 circumstances led me to visit the Old Rectory, Cavendish, Suffolk. Dear Nurse Carveley invited me to be her guest for a few days. She had prepared for me such tasteful rooms, with photographs and hymns of my dear sister Frances everywhere. The Old Rectory is a charming boarding-home for ladies, Mrs. Green supplying most liberally every comfort. I remained here some weeks, much enjoying the quiet, and also the pleasant society of other ladies. It has a large garden, shady walks, and a delightful abundance of garden fruit, which we gathered at any time. Mr. Green conducted family prayers, and the order and punctuality suited me. It was a time of preparation for a sudden page in my life, which more than any other proved the faithfulness and loving-kindness of my Lord. It is to glorify Him that I testify how, in minutest need as well as greater, His strength was sufficient for the day. My health was variable, occasional sickness and weakness; but still I could walk far, and was in good spirits and able to amuse the guests with accounts of my walks and talks in Ireland and Switzerland, and on Sundays giving simple Bible talks after hymn-singing and prayer.

It was Sunday night when, preparing for rest, I quite suddenly felt a large hard substance extending under my right arm. The conviction flashed upon me—"This is cancer." I trembled a little, but knelt down and simply prayed my Lord that, if it was so, I might glorify Him, and patiently bear all that might be coming. It was a solemn night, with thoughts of eternity nearing, and oh, the peace of resting one's whole self on the word of Jesus, on His precious blood! In the morning, kind Mrs. G. tearfully confirmed my idea, but I decided at once that I would not distress my dear sisters or friends, and only wrote to my doctor. His answer was reassuring,—I might be mistaken, and of course he reserved opinion till he saw me. I was positively lighthearted, for had I not committed the whole burden to the Lord? I was anxious to finish writing out the journal and hymns of my cripple friend, Joseph Harrison. For I alone had the MS., and so it would be my fault if his little candle was not set on the candlestick. Many other papers and bequests I arranged; and I remember the very day before I was going to my doctor, Frances S. writing to say she was waiting for *my* preface to the second volume of F. R. H.'s Poetical Works, which she was arranging for me. Prefaces ought to be pith. As this was my tenth, it was a little difficult to prepare, especially as I was not at all well.

The next day Mrs. G., Miss A., and Mrs. R. kindly came with me as far as Cambridge. I had asked my dear friend Mrs. Snepp to let me stay at Perry Villa, so as not to go near my sister's. Perry Villa is full of holy remembrances. There my dear sister Frances was often the honoured guest, and her memory mingles with much labour unto the Lord, whether in classes, choir, or joint editing of *Songs of Grace and Glory* with good Mr. Snepp. "Many a hymn Miss Frances has written there," said the maid. "Ah, she was loved!"

It was soothing to me to wander in the lovely garden and the shady walk to church, and I could rejoice for them—the holy sleepers—now spirit-free and serving their Lord with songs of glory only.

I had arranged for my nurse, M. Farrington, to meet me at Dr. Malins'. He told me I was looking in very much better health. "And now, doctor, you must tell me candidly what is the matter." He looked grave, sat down silently, then most feelingly said, "It is stone cancer, and not a shadow of escape from this conclusion."

"So I thought; what do you advise?"

"Only two courses—operation, or, if it runs on, certain death."

"Now, doctor, why can't you do it at once, this afternoon, and so save my friends?"

"Impossible; you don't know what an operation involves, and you would like to have a sister with you."

"Oh, dear, no! Mrs. Crane is abroad, and as to making my gentle sister Ellen suffer for me, oh never, never! Mary is quite enough, and you know He whom I trust in will be with me."

"It is absolutely necessary your friends should know. I will write to-night."

Promising to secure suitable apartments for nurse and self, we left Dr. M., and I returned to Perry Villa. Heaven seemed nearer! the very clouds looked chariots, and oh, might it be I was really going beyond them. Sunday was the perfection of rest and enjoyment, and I talked with the maidens on the garden-seats with their Bibles. Monday a telegram, shortly followed by kind Mr. Shaw and dear Ellen. It was the worst of all to distress her; but I think she was relieved and astonished at my good spirits and strength.

Tuesday night, July 22.—Drove to the lodgings, laden with flowers, fruits, and luxuries, from kind Mrs. S. Such a happy thought stole over me as I went into my new room; there I should be shut in with Jesus!

Arranging the exquisite flowers was a great pleasure, and unpacking many a token of dear ones at Winterdyne. I slept fairly well, and quite enjoyed my breakfast. Sweet promises floated around me, and not a flutter of fear; verily it was the enfolding of His wing. Presently Dr. M. came in, and asked if he could do anything for me. I said "Yes; will you kneel down with me?" I just committed myself into God's hand, asked for quietness, and that I might glorify Him; for skill to my doctors; and then, "Thy will be done" came gladly from my heart. My doctor's reverent "O Lord, grant this, for Jesus Christ's sake, Amen," was a sustaining clench to me. He left me. I prepared and stamped a telegram for Winterdyne. I opened my dear Bible; my eye rested on Hosea 2:19, "I will betroth thee unto Me for ever; yea, I will betroth thee unto Me in righteousness, and in judgment, and in loving-kindness, and in mercies."

What could be sweeter! This then was a second betrothal time to my Lord "in judgment," quite as needful as the long ago time of first love. Love, all love and faithfulness, and His strong arm closed around me as the doctor opened the door and said, "All is ready." Resolutely I inhaled the ether, the inevitable suffocation feel was conquered, and then all was silence and darkness for three-quarters of an hour. Then the waking up—"Mary, when will it be over?" "It's all done; see, you are nicely in bed, and doctors gone." Then came the consciousness of utter weakness and helplessness. But truly, not one thing had failed me—not one word of all His good promises had been unfulfilled to me; and now underneath were the everlasting arms, in a manner only those know who have felt them.

I did not know till some weeks after how graciously God had answered my prayer, that I might glorify Him before the doctors. I had placed on the wall the identical card which my dear sister Frances called "My own text,"—"The blood of Jesus Christ His Son cleanseth us from all sin." My nurse said to me, "Before you were conscious of speaking at all, you preached a splendid sermon on the blood of Jesus Christ."

The next few days passed in excessive weakness, and the sultry weather was against me. But I believe my teetotalism of sixteen years greatly contributed to my recovery. A friend of mine who was operated on, and kept up afterwards with brandy and milk and opiates, could hardly walk on two sticks at the end of ten months, whereas in three months I was walking to the top of Malvern Hill. Of course I had a specially skilful doctor, and I shall always gratefully recall his unremitting care and his truthful candour, when I have asked him as to the probable issue of symptoms. I do respect a doctor who can say, "I never let my patients die in the dark," or who will say, "This is a glimpse into eternity." I do think it is so wise and kind when the medical eye sees a fellow-traveller nearing eternity to tell them plainly. The secret fear and dread of death may be there, and false hopes of life may lead them to defer the momentous looking into their soul's safety till it is too late—too late for ever and ever.

Nothing could exceed the devoted and unceasing watchfulness of my dear nurse. With all my attempts to conceal my wakefulness, I never could deceive her. I rarely slept after four, and used to watch the sun's finger of light moving on the opposite wall. One almost remarkable source of comfort was the distinctness with which I recalled dear Frances' singing and playing. Every chord and note, both of accompaniment and words, sounded softly around. Sometimes it was Handel's "Comfort ye," "Rejoice greatly," or "He shall feed His flock." Sometimes it was her own melodies. Often when she had sung, "When thou passest through the waters I will be with thee," I had said, "Fan, dear, I only hope you will sing that to me when I am dying." Now I heard it all again, and her thrilling emphasis on the word "*I*," and then those lovely soothing chords hushing down every ripple in death's river, and the last chord changing as it surely will some day, into the first touch of heavenly harpings.

This was not continuous, and the notes came unexpectedly; perhaps when I was trying to look at a verse or two and wearily closing my Bible, then her recitative, "Who are kept by the power of God through faith unto salvation, wherein ye greatly rejoice, though now for a season, if need be, ye are in heaviness through manifold temptations," would come with irresistible power, passing through all her minor chords and changing into the melodious major key of "Whom having *not* seen ye love"; but now for *her*, the negative is all left out, it is to her the fullest bliss of *seeing* Him face to face! And so my sister's ministry of song flows on, and the wish of her heart is fulfilled, "With my song will I praise Him."

In this illness I learnt the value of having committed much Scripture to memory; for now I could not dig into the mine of gold, but all my store of previous diggings were a safe and shining store. It *is* marvellous how the word of the Lord speaks to one's inmost soul, supplying its every need.

It was strange indeed for me to lose the power of standing and walking, and be thankful for the first lifting on to the sofa. But as soon as I was told I might, I vigorously made effort to regain the unused power. Your own will and resolution has much to do with the regaining strength—one can try! one can shuffle and creep along by chairs, and merrily determine not to give way. I remember when dear Mrs. Snepp's carriage came to take me a first drive, to go downstairs it was the same as some precipitous glacier. How strange the world looked, after seeing four walls only; how exquisite the flowers and grassy banks in the People's Park! If ever I keep a carriage, shall it not minister as this one did to me? And what kindly ministries flew to me—such boxes of flowers, such jellies and grapes and peaches! Late one evening, when very feverish and thirsty, my doctor's little Lina came with most exquisite peaches in such a pretty box, with "To be taken immediately."

Then dear ones from Winterdyne came with all the little *homey* things I used to like there. So the Lord cared for me, and in five weeks I was able to travel to dear Winterdyne.

Long after I had left Mrs. L.'s apartments, where she had shown me most Christian and considerate attentions, she told me how remarkably my operation had nerved her for a far worse one soon after. I can give her words: "I often wondered why the Lord sent you to my house. Other invalids had come and gone, but you were to teach me a lesson. I stood on the staircase when Dr. M. opened your door, and said, 'All is ready'; and never can I forget your calm, stately march into that slaughter-room. I saw the support the Lord gave you, and three months after it gave me great encouragement; and I also received help and comfort from the Lord in my time of trouble, and my soul was filled with joy unspeakable."

September 1884.—Set out alone for West Malvern, disregarding entreaties to take an attendant. It has been one of my mercies not to be dependent on others, and solitude intensifies my enjoyment of hills and cloud-land. Telling the driver to take me to Mount Pleasant, I decided on the cheerful rooms. I could not use my right arm freely, and so the mistress unpacked a hamper and saw my name. She quietly said, "You have forgotten me, but I knew your face directly. Your father, Mr. Havergal, often called me to hold his hymn-book and tell him the words (after he lost his sight) in St. Nicholas Sunday school!" Of course, I remembered her name, and my frequent visits to her mother, and the musical talents of her brother. So again and again my father's dear name has been my herald from north to south.

Family prayers were reverently announced, and I joined them. An aged lady attracted me, and in a few days I was told Miss C. would like me to come in her cosy room. That opened the way to mutual and loving intercourse. Dear aged pilgrim! her tale of ninety years was the record of God's love; but the deepest humility tinged all her reflections, and the deepest adoration her anticipations of the coming glory. She said to me, "Every morning I look out early and see the trees shining in the early dawn, and I like to begin praising my Lord with the little birds. And I think it can't be long before He comes in His glory and in His wonderful, wonderful love; He won't forget me, the least and most unworthy of His people. And I can never thank Him enough for sending *you*—your voice is so distinct, I always hear you, and my deafness often shuts me out from friends' conversations. It is a long time since one of the Lord's servants was so permitted to comfort me. I had a very dear friend, a Polish count, who from persecution in his own land came to reside here. His Bible readings and teachings were such a help to me. We always went straight to the Bible, and then straight to the Lord, and that's the surest, quickest comfort." Once I took her some grapes and fruit, and it seemed she had been "so longing for a little dessert," but would not expend on herself. She was greatly interested in my tales of East Africa, and my brave missionary Archie, and Amy's work there. Unasked she gave me half-a-crown to help build the new church at Rabai, whose stones Archie had quarried out under the burning sun. I believe *that* half-crown lies with our Queen's coins in the foundation-stone. And months after, when I wrote and told her of little Havergal Shaw, she sent another half-crown for his baby hand to give at the opening of his father's church. His photograph was sent her, and many a prayer ascended over it. Very strongly she hoped their little son would always be called Havergal, and live to be a missionary.

I really felt parting with my aged friend, and her words, "My heart has been sighing for you, my darling, and now it is farewell, but we shall surely meet in His kingdom." (I visited her again in 1885, and on June 11, 1886, she passed into the glory so long watched for.)

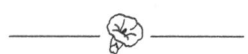

CHAPTER VII.

FROM SIDMOUTH TO WALES.

I LEFT Sidmouth June 1, 1886. The previous month was one of daily pressure—letters came, interviews were wanted, applications made for all kinds of information or charities. Of course, it is delightful to receive constant testimonies of my darling sister's work, and the blessing on every line she has written is so wonderful, but the labour of replying is very great. I had brought down to Sidmouth piles of my old diaries and MS. books, hoping to arrange them and to have dear sister Miriam's valuable oversight; but there they are untouched, and no one else can know their dates and plans.

Most pleasant were my closing calls on my kind friends at Sidmouth. And oh, what a comfort it was to have my Bible at hand, and thus read the Word, and then with prayer commend each to the Lord's safe keeping!

I cannot describe the comfort and privilege of attending the All-Saints' services. The orderly conducting of the whole was so like my own dear father's cheery churchmanship, with nothing to irritate or distract the eye; none of those excessive decorations that always seem to me desecrations of God's temple, bringing in Pagan offerings or Romish rites. Oh, the comfort of saying one's own Amen! and with reverent and lowly voice asking for His mercy, instead of hurried intonings and irreverent scrambles. Then the Rev. R. B. M.'s thoughtful, logical, scriptural sermons, suggestive food that you *must* think about and be the better for. No Christless sermons, but truths radiating to Him the centre,—Christ first, Christ last, Christ all in all. And I freely say my Church privileges at All-Saints revived and cemented my love for the dear old Church of England, which did get shocks and shakes from her unfaithful pastors and un-Protestant innovations.

The evening communions there were indeed a visit to the upper room and a quiet entering into the King's banquet and the King's own presence. Very strongly do I hold to the individual act of taking the bread, not having it laid in my hand. For as guilty Adam was forbidden to take—to eat—to live; so Christ my Lord reversed that prohibition, and said, "*Take—eat—live,*"—so I delight to put forth my hand and obediently *take* it. And then I liked our Lord's words being said *once* to each table in holy sweet silence; for who can prove our Lord kept on repeating them to the apostles as often so wearisomely done?

Farewell, All-Saints, both pastor and pastorine, with your faithful, loving labours; may rich blessing descend on all, so that after many days fruit may abound to the praise and glory of God.

I left Sidmouth for temporary lodgings at Edgbaston—joined by dear cousin H. H.

June 2.—Dr. Malins called; I had not seen him or any doctor since November, and wished to know candidly my present state and the possible duration of life. At the end of our interview he said gravely, but in his own kind way, "The disease has not made the progress I expected. Your general health is improved, but notwithstanding all this, the goal is in view." Yes, your goal is in view, and you are hastening to it now. Was it not like catching the sound of the Astley church bells, as so often I had done when nearing home!

Dr. Malins approved of my going to Mid Wales and try bracing air with my good cousin H. H. If ever travellers were told where to pitch their tent, we were. I did not know even the name of the place Nurse F. had passed through in 1883. I guessed at Lanwrtyd Wells just before starting, and could not even pronounce it right. The 'bus landed us in a field, and the stepping-stones over the stream to Dolgoy were almost impassable (a stranger told us there were rooms). Cousin bravely jumped through the spray, and soon returned with Catherine the strong, who helped me over to quiet rustic lodgings. Oh such foldings of hills and mountain breezes, and here we tarried thankfully.

Park Villa, Caswell Road, July 9, 1886.—The prayer of months is answered! In past days of weariness and sickness, it seemed an impossibility I could revisit our dear Welsh nest, and I had honestly given up all self-will about it, leaving the wish in His dear hand.

The driver of the waggonette was the first to welcome me at the station. "Why, P., I never put my name to the order!" "No, miss, but I knew your writing, and very glad to see you back among us." *There* was a trophy of God's grace and temperance! When I had an evangelist and a tent for three weeks on the Mumbles sands in 1882, P. was one I especially prayed for; and, thank God, in my sister's study he signed her temperance book, with three of his sons, and after I left every one of his family did so. And he has stood firm five years now, and at Swansea I had the pleasure of seeing him bring his wife up for the blue ribbon. He became valiant, and many a coachman has he won over; yes, and gentlemen too, who would tempt him with the old "tip and treat," have themselves paused at his stedfast "No, thanks, I have something better now." During our drive he told me of his eldest son's death in the Brazils, and so another of my sister's band has, I trust, passed into rest.

It was a glorious evening, the lighthouse standing picturesquely in the blue sea, and every cliff and point bringing back memories of 1879.

And now I am writing in her room! it was a gracious message the Lord whispered to me as I first entered it, "*Thine* eyes shall see the King in His beauty." I was on the very spot where her eyes first visibly met the King's—where her joyous, loving welcome to Him was, "Oh—oh—He—He is come." I can't describe that faint, dying, thrilling tone of exquisite satisfaction; it returns to me with the smile and that wondrous musical "He"—and then her life ebbing away in melody and love. Yes, and she has beheld the land that is very far off or (margin) the land of "far distances," so expressive of those wondrous spirit flights into distances of glory! But the message was, "*Thine* eyes"—*mine* too—all dim and veiled now—"shall see" the same King; and again as I knelt by her bed, the promise came to me too, "Rejoice greatly, O daughter of Zion; behold, thy King cometh unto thee,"—not only going *to* Him, but He coming *to* and for His sin-forgiven one. So He comforted me. I remembered once talking over this verse with dear F., and she said, "Marie, that shall be a chapter in *My King*, and you have made a royal contribution to it. I ought to put 'M. V. G. H.' under it." (See chapter 6, p. 24,[1] "Thy King cometh unto thee!") [Volume II of the Havergal edition, pages 25–26]

It is pleasant to find good and abiding fruit of my sister's work here, though seven years have passed. I will just daily jot down exactly what is said about her.

Returning from our favourite walk, by the fields to the old chimneys, where the sea view is gained at once, and the nook in the cliff to the right, where we sat riveted with the MS. of Prout's *Never Say Die,* I met the father of Fred P. Enquiring for him, the father said, "If your sister had lived, she would have brought a blessing to every one, she had such a way with her. Lads don't take to every one, but I do believe they would have given their life for her. In course she didn't go on with a thing for a few hours like, but she brought it to an end; the lads loved her so, and just saw into what she did; and Miss F. in course could make them do anything."

Calling on deaf Mrs. P., she kissed my hand. I showed her F.'s photograph, which she wanted to put in her bosom and keep. One visit before this, she saw the tears in my eyes, and said, "Vexing, vexing for *her!* She's happy; she would not come back for a thousand worlds—*there's no moaning among her singing!* Pretty creature! I did like to see her shake her pretty curls. She come and come when my hip was broken, and brought me pudding and tea and gingerbread. Look! here's Miss Frances' own roll of texts; she put a nail and hung it up before me; and the last time she brought a posy of primroses—my dear Miss Frances! Here's the warm cuffs she made for Christmas; I keep them rolled up."

July 23, 1886.—The anniversary again of God's goodness and support in 1884. I was singularly happy that I was able this morning to minister to a sick woman operated on yesterday. So I knew how to refresh her; and she always says it was my going with a hot bottle and flannels that saved her life previously. Often had I prayed in my days of helplessness, that if raised up, it might be to minister to others; so the Welsh

---

[1] *My King* by F.R.H. (London: James Nisbet & Co., 1877), original book page 24, pages 25–26 of Volume II of the Havergal edition.

woman's thanks mingle with this sentence from dear Amy in Africa, "Dear Aunt Maria; our hearts are full of love for you; it always does us good even to think of and talk about you. If you are spared for nothing else, you certainly are to comfort and encourage your missionary Africans."

And on this anniversary evening I have reached Llandilo! The elder class of lads in the Sunday school prayed nearly a year that I might come and teach them once more. It is truly in weakness and inability even to prepare a lesson, save what I did on the hillside days ago. So I trust the Lord will prepare me by this utter self-emptiness, and that I may just bring His message, not mine at all.

Tuesday, July 26.—It is all past now, my pleasant Llandilo visit.

After a restless night, to find I could not rise on Sunday morning threw me on the promise, "As thy days, thy strength shall be;" and I knew I should be better by two o'clock. Dry bread and gruel dinner! The boys' teacher had arranged I should meet the class in the open air, as I could not stand the hot schoolroom. It was not far to a quiet hill crowned with shady trees and dry grass in Dynevor Park. I was there first to select the most comfortable place, and welcome the dear lads as they came smiling up. We had a general talk first, even touching on politics, as their teacher told me they enquired what Miss H.'s views were on Gladstone and Disestablishment. As I had lived in Ireland, I gave them a few facts of what Popery *is,* and what it will do if ever in the ascendant. I knew Maynooth, and could speak of the unfairness of robbing the Irish Protestant Church to enrich that. I could tell them of the loyal Bible lovers in Ulster who would be driven to desperation. I pictured our churches and cathedrals desecrated by secularists and infidels. No Church means no Queen, no God! no peace, no order. The example of our Lord in paying tribute to Caesar rivets the question of obeying the powers that be. In Old Testament times certainly, Church and State were cemented by God.

Then we came to their own welfare, and my thanks for their many messages and letters, and their photographs. For these I had brought my own, and gave them round with some of dear F.'s books. It is always best to leave nothing secular till afterwards. We knelt in prayer that the power of God's Holy Spirit might descend on each of us. John 15 was our portion, dwelling on being in or out of Christ, being a dead or living branch, the possibility of being a dead branch in Christ's Church, and mistaking that for living union with Him. We may be ecclesiastical branches, baptized, confirmed, communicants, and yet never *in* Christ. The evidence of life being sap flowing, fruit bearing, so the living branch has the Spirit's life and the Spirit's fruits. (See Galatians 5:22.) What blessed safety and nearness when *in* Christ!

And I testified to what I had found Jesus Christ to be to me, and what I knew He was to some of them, and how to each that loving voice now said (Revelation 3:20), "If *any* man hear my voice, I will come in to him," etc. Then I asked them to sing a hymn in Welsh. After prayer, a silent waiting for God's Spirit, and it seemed an opportunity for renewed yielding of ourselves to the Loving One, who was so manifestly with us.

"In full and glad surrender,
We give ourselves to Thee.
O Son of God, who loved us,
We will be Thine alone;
And all we have and all we are
Shall henceforth be Thine own."

As I was first on the woody height, it may be I shall be first at a better and holier trysting-place, and watch them safely crossing the river, and resting on His holy hill. Amen and Amen.

[*Note.*—See F. R. H.'s poem on the "Col de Balm."]

Not long after, I received from Edward H. Davies, one in the class, a large crayon likeness of myself, with indications of latent talent if not genius.

Monday morning, I was off by nine to visit Johnnie Howells. Kneeling down by his chair, I said, "Johnnie, who is it?" "It is my friend." Dear little cripple, it was worth a good deal to fetch that happy smile on your pale face. He was eager to repeat all the texts and hymns remembered for two years. And we sang again, "Jesus loves me, this I know," to my father's tune. "Johnnie must come and dine with me if mother can manage it." He was a dear little guest, and over and over he said, "My dinner is beautiful." Before he went away we had a happy time; and I felt assured this was one of Christ's own lambs. "Tell me, Johnnie, would you like to get quite well and grow a tall man, or would you rather go to the Lord Jesus?" "I would rather go and see the Lord Jesus." "So would I, Johnnie, dear; and I think we are both going soon. It will be nice to see His face." When the mother came for him, she said he had one wish, he so wanted to have my likeness! "And if you please, miss, we have been saving money to have our Johnnie's likeness taken for you; but I am afraid it will cost four shillings." "Well, Mrs. Howells, suppose Johnnie and I are taken together! You take him now to the photographer; I am leaving in two hours." It was quite interesting to fix Johnnie and his crutch on an easy-chair, and to see his astonished looks at the surroundings. His dear little face came out beautifully, with the King's smile on it. The photographer was quite interested; and we sang his hymn again. Johnnie was carried down to his chair; and as I stooped to say good-bye, he said, "May we meet in heaven." Last Christmas I sent a warm scarlet jacket, an accordion, a scrap-book, and one shilling to Johnnie Howells, North Bank, Llandilo. I wonder who will do it next?

[*Note.*—John Howells died in the next month, August 1886.]

I returned to Lanwrtyd Wells. The surroundings of hills and mountains, lanes fringed with ferns, shady woods, where many of these pages have been written, quiet nooks where often I have found amid the sparkles of the morning dew and the early song of birds much sweet soul-rest, and enjoyed soul-outpourings with the Invisible.

The quiet and rest at Dolgoy improved my general health wonderfully. The weather was fine, and often I went out with my writing for some shady seat. How strange with all the life and energy I felt, with the ability to jump over stiles and climb high and higher, and yet to know by that hot inward monitor that my doctor's words must be true, and the goal was in view! Thoughts came as rapidly as the clouds, whose changeful beauty ever soothed me. How seldom you see even *one* in a crowd ever looking up! Clouds have been one of my mercies; their speechless lessons, reflecting light, painting earth's landscapes with those veilings of blue or bright shiftings of light and shade. Clouds are the dust of His feet, as well as His chariot. And what marvellous words have come through cloud-veilings, whether on Sinai or in the mystic Shechinah! But none more marvellous than those when the Lord entered the clouds on Mount Olivet. Contrast that mount of victory with the mount of temptation,—Satan showing Him all the kingdoms of this world, and the glory of them, with the vauntful lie, "All these things will I give thee;" and so in the final moment of victory our Lord recalls that Tempter's assault, and quenches it for ever with His Kingly assertion, "All power is given unto me in heaven and in earth."

The mother of some of F.'s brightest "temperance officers" told me that "the last time that Miss Frances called on me, I was very low about my eldest son, who had just joined the volunteers, and I was afraid of the company it would get him into, and she told me to pray on and trust on that God would answer prayer, and she knelt with me by that sofa, miss—I can't forget it—and her prayer is answered; my boy after that was different, and took no delight in bad company. Miss Frances had such a loving way, I always thank God I knew her."

Mrs. W. told me that "once Miss Frances stopped more than an hour over my Willie—she wanted to get him to Christ; it cut my heart, and I never, never did hear it put so how the Lord suffered in His love. Miss F. seemed to see Him on the cross straight before her." "And has Willie kept on?" "Yes, miss, I do believe it, and the first time he went in the vessel to France, the captain gave them all 'treat money' to go ashore. Willie would not touch a drop, and instead he bought mother a present, and if you please he brought a bottle of the best lavender scent. He said, 'I can't give it Miss Frances, she's gone, but I can give it her sister.'" Certainly that scent is fragrant to me!

I called at L.'s, the last cottage my sister went to. The son William, for whom she stitched the paper bag for tracts to take to sea, had sunstroke, and the poor fellow is in the asylum. I was glad to hear that even in delirium he asked for his Bible and sang hymns. This affliction may be a safe road to the kingdom. His father spoke with tears of my sister. "If ever there was an angel among us, it was Miss Frances! I was bad out and out till she came; and didn't she shake hands so friendly—I never shed more tears than for her, and little Ben is as firm as a rock. A man held brandy water to him and a knife, and said he would cut his throat if he didn't drink it, but Ben kept his pledge."

Even when my sister went by the tram her words flew home. A young artist sent her apple blossoms painted on china, as a remembrance of her bringing Christ to her on the tram-car.

Our old friends Mr. and Mrs. L. met me. "Never, never can I forget her beautiful spirit, and that gleam on her face—so sunny and yet always a distant look, as if she saw farther than we did."

One of Frances' constant attendants at her Bible reading described her standing and her face so earnest, "and no one ever did play music like Miss F.; she touched up the notes sharp, and brought such a sound out of them, and her voice—I hear it now—no, no one ever sang like Miss F.!"

July 16th.—It is pleasant that Mr. and Mrs. Tucker, and Davie and Johnnie, come up to prayers as in F.'s time. Mrs. T. said, "I often see Miss F. as she used to stand by her piano in the readings, and she spoke so earnest, every word seems printed, and she made it all so clear, and her hand waving up and then turning to the references, and she did like us all to have Bibles and follow her; she was a blessing in my house."

Hearing that Mrs. G., our postwoman, was very ill, I went down to the far end of Mumbles to see her. She was in bed with incessant cough, and so emaciated. I will just quote her words as I gave her Frances' photograph to look at: "Yes, that's my dear, dear Miss Frances. Out of the hundreds of visitors I've taken letters to—no one like her—she was *my one!* I can see her now, with her beautiful hair so smooth, and once she said, 'You think I can do nothing but write! but you shall see me sew; look at this white body I have made.'

"She did work hard; twenty and six-and-twenty letters a day, and rolls besides; she worked hard, I know, but always that beautiful smile; and when I didn't bring so many letters, *you* would be so delighted and say, 'Now she will have a little holiday!'"

I asked, "Do you remember the last words Miss F. said to you?" "Yes, 'I am waiting by the gates to enter in!' I saw her four times in that illness, and she was always happy in her pain; and oh, how she wanted to go to Jesus. She said, 'He won't deceive me this time.' And now I am going too. I am a very great sinner, but Jesus died for me. I do, *do* trust Him, and He has sent His beautiful smile to me; don't I look happy? I am so contented; and are you happy, dear Miss Havergal? Yes, you are not altered a bit, Jesus is with you, and we shall not meet again here—but there." I asked her what I should ask the Lord to do for her. "Oh, to wash me and keep me in the precious blood. Stand one minute, I want to see your face; yes, it's happy, happy! and we shall meet very soon." So, with the "*Gloria*" and "Worthy is the Lamb that was slain and hath redeemed us to God by His blood," I knelt and commended her to the God of all grace.

She then touchingly reminded me of my dear brother Frank, and all he did that week in June 1879. "I can't forget meeting your brother on the road; he wanted the plate for that dear coffin. It was registered, and he said, 'There, you shall be the first to see it!' So he opened the Baroness's parcel—hadn't she painted the roses and forget-me-nots beautiful, and how quickly; then there were some of Miss F.'s last words, 'There hath not failed one word of all His good promise.'"

I told her this plate was photographed and printed in the book *The Last Week;* so I sent it down to her the next day. I could not but recall how strongly F. felt for all "Postal Burdens," and the employment of so many on Sunday. I am so grieved that some of my sister's temperance lads, now fine young men, are getting robbed of their Sundays. Some leave their homes here at 4.30 p.m. to catch the train to Swansea for office work, and then off with the mail train to Gloucester—sorting letters and delivering bags all Sunday evening, while we are enjoying holy worship. Then leaving Gloucester at 2 a.m. and on till 7. Very well these summer nights, but, oh, what in the freezing winds! Staunch soldiers not to get alcohol then! O nieces and nephews of F. R. H., you at least will not receive or send letters on Sunday! thus robbing thousands of their God-given rest. It is true the trains go, but my letters going in them make me a partaker of the national sin. Never shall I forget a dying postman say, "Government has paid me for my time, but who will pay me for my soul!"

I do rejoice that one dear nephew followed his grandfather's example and worked nobly against the tide, till he won hundreds of signatures, and so secured the postmen Sunday rest.

Really my revisit here seems a continuous shower of friendship and flowers! Such roses, choice in their bloom and foldings,—what hand folds like the Creator? And the thought came that the same Hand will one day fold up the out-stretched heavens—"As a vesture shalt Thou fold them up." All this Saturday have friends come to the sacred study, and all my sympathies have been drawn out in the various trials told me. Thank God for giving me a word in season, and enabling me to kneel again and again and commit the burdens to Him. And I seem to be speaking in the light of a near eternity, and so to testify to each of the reality and preciousness of Christ to me. To one dear friend I said, "You used to call in 1879; my sister did not see you, but she said, 'Marie, have you been faithful to Miss ——?' 'No.' But when that dear voice was hushed, I told my friend of this and said, 'Now I shall always get the Bible and have prayer when you call.'"

Even after nine o'clock, such an elegant basket of flowers and peaches seemed a climax; but there was deep sorrow in the kind donor's face, and so we knelt—for Jesus of Bethany is the same to sorrowing hearts now as then.

The Lord sent me sleep, for I had been on the stretch all day, and it is just marvellous how I forget the hot consumings within, and smile and enjoy everything far more than in the days of my exceeding health and strength. And then I awoke on what will be my last Sunday in this dear room, with the words, "I shall be satisfied when I awake after Thy likeness." The *same* words that hushed me the moment of my sister's awaking in glory. "Thy likeness"; yes, Thine image shall again shine in place of the defaced impression. "We shall be like Him, *for* we shall see Him as He is." Dear father used to say that was a spiritual photography by the Son of Righteousness's appearance to the rising saints, instantaneously producing His glorious likeness.

Both my dear father and sister did *not* hold the popular *pre*-millennial views, and the more I read the more clearly does Scripture seem to point to one final coming again of Christ in glory at the day of judgment. Christ's promise is, "Lo! I am with you always, even to the end of the world." All admit this is an invisible present presence, and, taking the words as they stand, point to that same presence *to the end* of all things. The pre-millennial view also does away with the glorious outpouring of the Spirit, and the restoring of the Jews, and their being the great converters of the heathen world. It seems all a golden chain to me, a spiritual millennium, a time of special manifestations of Christ. But, oh dear, how can this curseful earth be fit for His blessed feet till the consumings "of the elements," and after the final judgment! *Then* comes *down* the New Jerusalem to the *new* world out of the ashes of the old; then the saints are caught up to be for ever with the Lord; then no confusing of Gog and Magog wars,—all is over with the *one* final advent of Christ—never to return. And the pre-millennialists so wrongly put away the thought of death. "Oh no, *I* shall not die, my Lord will come." And I know where some most eminent saints have had a cloudy death-bed from indulging in this false hope, and their doctor says, "You *are* dying!" and so the fallacious hope of rising in the clouds is a mistake, and for the moment it shakes their faith. Only a moment, for Jesus as surely comes to the bedside as in the air. To me it is all one—

"to die is gain," to pass through the valley is as momentary and as gloriously light as if through the air.

"But this I do find—we two are so joined,
He'll *not* be in glory, and leave me behind!'"

I remember my sister F., with her exceeding common sense, ending a long discussion by many strong pre-millennialists—*all* differing widely,—"I think, when our dear Lord does come, not one of you will be able to say, 'There, *I* told you it would be so!'"

Of course both she and I believe and rejoice in the fact of His coming, as she wrote, "Thou *art* coming, O my Saviour;" but the time, the how, the when, we leave where the Lord left it. "Of *that* day and that hour knoweth no man, neither the Son, but the Father."

And I do think these dear students of prophecy map out their own views and hopes, and twist Scripture to support it. Also, they teach so much of a *coming* Saviour, that they overlook the joyful reality of His presence *now*. *I* so look forward to my body's quiet rest in the grave, and the spirit's entrance into bliss, unfettered with return to earth.

But it is time for prayers, and Mr. and Mrs. Tucker, and Davie and Johnnie, and some dear little lodgers and maids, are in F.'s study. We read the last chapter in the Revelation, with that lift into the world above, and the throne and the Lamb. Always the *Lamb*—in that world of glory every ray, every song, every smile, must all radiate back to Calvary's cross, where the Lamb slain procured the joys unspeakable and eternal. And then I bid them mark, in verse 17, the threefold call,—the "Come" to whosoever will.

Some stay to sing at Frances' harp-piano her words and music, "I am trusting Thee, Lord Jesus." Breakfast over, a group of dear children are announced, and books I had given are brought for inscriptions; and again I give them words from the Word of Life, and we all kneel and in that consecrated place tell Jesus we do all wish to be washed whiter than snow, and we will say, "Jesus, I *do* trust Thee, trust without a doubt." And we sing dear Frances' melody to those words on the same harp-piano her hands used to touch.

It is not time for service yet. There are those peaches; how they would refresh the dying post-woman! So I pack them in a basket with flowers, and a copy of *The Last Week,* that has the floral inscription Mrs. G. wished to see. Little George can take the wee basket without hindering his being in time for church. This gives me opportunity for a talk with his worthy mother, and she pours out that secret heart-consuming grief—the trial of suspense—when month after month brings no letter from her husband in the far-off land. "You will pray for him, dear Miss Havergal? I have so longed to tell you! I can bear it better now, and I shall feel you are praying with me." We take the burden to the Lord. And it seems laid upon me to find some gold that will enable her to provide some little furnishings, so that she can let a room. To miss the father's monthly supply is a trial. Ah, dear! the sorest hearts rarely complain.

Ten minutes to spare! so away to dear deaf P.'s cottage. How Spirit-taught she is! His voice reaching the life-long silences, and she smiles and points to her dear Miss Frances' text-roll. "She put it on the nail there, just where I could see it; she never forgot me." But I make signs that I am going to chapel. She answers, "Miss F. always went to church." So do I when Jesus Christ is preached, and now failing strength will not allow of the long steep walk.

Dear P. sits by me in the little chapel, and I turn up all the sermon references for her, and I should like to hear the commentary that lights them to her mind.

I walk home with cousin and the kindest of ladies, whose gentle presence is ever a charm to me. Just when tired and reaching Park Villa, there is a row of maidens, smiling and curt-seying, Can they know *me?* Yes; it is my dear old Bishopstown class, come by mistake for three o'clock! Such a walk, and two hours' wait! I had provided plenty of buns, and a meat-pie; raspberry jam was quickly sent by kind Mrs. Holme, so a repast was spread. And then Captain H. brought a large basket of gooseberries, "See, girls, how God cares for you in all this, from strangers." Yes, truly, "Love is of God," whence all goodness flows.

Making enquiries for absentees, I find two of my class are sleeping. Ah, teacher! no voice reaches the coffin. Now, now, now! is the lesson for me. Thankfully do I hear that both Ellen and Ann spoke of trust in Jesus, and going without fear to the better land.

Our quiet room seemed favourable for close questioning. I should never, never teach them again, and that each might really be "in Christ" was my heart's longing. The quiet, stedfast confession of faith and trust came from each. We read John 17, that prayer of holy keeping,—the prayer that still goes on within the veil, the prayer that must prevail. Verse 24, that grand "*Father, I will.*" All through Christ's earthly ministry, the Father's will, the Father's work, seems first; but now Christ claims His divine sovereignty, and in sight of His completed atonement and ransom price, gives promise of His glory. Lord Jesus, Thou hast kept nothing for Thyself! Thy love shares all. What earthly monarch likes his throne to be halved? Thou givest Thyself, Thy life, death, kingdom, throne, and glory! The listening disciples had seen Thy weariness, Thy marred face, and soon in the garden's shade would see the sweat, like great drops of blood; they would see their Master's face with no beauty, and the bruising of the serpent's heel in the death pallor; they would bind it in the death-clothes. But can, oh! can they forget this triumphant "I will"?—"that they also whom Thou hast given me may behold my glory." And for me remains this glorious "behold." When the shadows are past, I shall, I must, behold Thee in Thy glory. Amen.

With farewell love my dear class left me, and I felt each was in the Lord's safe keeping.

I had been on the stretch for seven hours, so I did not go to evening service. It was getting late, when two strangers were shown in dear F.'s study, apologizing for intrusion. The youngest said just this: "I had such a longing to see you once more, Miss H. I must thank you for what you said to me two years ago. It was your last Sunday at Bishopstown School, and you spoke to me in the churchyard, entreating me to take up the work you were leaving. I cannot tell you the blessing that school has been to me. It was the beginning of my own learning of Jesus and finding in Him all grace, and then wisdom to teach. You will never know the blessing you were to all Bishopstown, nor how that school has prospered from your labours there. You began it all, and if you knew how the children love you, and love to talk of you! Now Mr. T. superintends, and lately I was struck to see the attention of his first class—young men of 24 to 25, eagerly drinking in the words spoken; and the dear girls in your class who died were safe in Jesus." I could but say, "Lord Jesus, I thank Thee!" And in the twilight followed touching disclosings of the briars, difficulty, and temptation in the young disciple's path, and my heart's sympathy flowed out as I counselled her to give up all for Jesus,—that "only in the Lord" was imperative, but would bring the King's compensating "I also for thee." Prayer again, just where my sister so often found the King's ear. "Farewell!" with a golden after-light on Caswell Bay. "So shall thine afterward be, O Lord!"

Supper, and exhausted. Cousin saying, "You shall see no one else." How restorative hot bread and milk!—unfailing to me these eighteen years of teetotalism.

But a knock, and Loney: "If you please, could you come in the kitchen?" I did not feel tired now! and what a dozen or more of smiling, loving faces are come to say good-bye! The Lord gave me words. Had I not in many a sick hour asked Him to let me testify once more of what Jesus was to me?—of His strong arm, strong love, and how the precious blood was a peace-bringing passport, when the golden gate seemed near? As I cannot remember *exactly*, I will write nothing of my farewell. But again all sang her Caswell song of trust and triumph in death.

Very gracious was the sleep sent; once on my pillow, my strength was gone. Never mind! such a happy, happy Sunday!

Such a good night and waking promises for grace and strength sufficient for the day, which I felt would be a keen severance from all the surroundings of my beloved sister's last days on earth.

I looked on the pictures and texts I had placed in holy memoriam. Over the last pillow, her hymn in large type, "I take this pain, Lord Jesus, from Thine own hand." Also the hymn she sang to her tune "Hermas." Over the mantelpiece her large card, "Our motto, For Jesus' sake only;" and beneath it her photograph. Over the toilette the words, with white lilies and ferns, "With Christ, which is far better," and two coloured texts, the gift of brother Henry's widow, and other of F.'s hymns.

Just as I was a little sad came the ministry of cats!—which I as firmly believe in as of angels. Enter old pussy, the mother of our Dot and Trot in 1879. Every morning she had come purring and loving as of old; but to-day she would not touch the milk, and restlessly departed. Up again, bringing me her new little kitten Dot, and off again for Trot the second, laying them in the safe, dear old place. Faithful pussy! thank you, thank you. Would that we Christians purred and praised more! And your kitties are the *fac-similes* of those that loving hands here caressed and petted.

I *must* record another strange cat-ministry. It was at Winterdyne in 1879–80. I was in the quiet, far-up north room, where I had written nearly all the Memoir of F. R. H., with hundreds of letters to read and choose from. I was writing the last pages, and scalding tears came uncontrollably as I endeavoured to picture that holy death scene, that sweet song, that radiant look, that tender, tender entreaty, "O don't disappoint me, any of you!"—as if her glory would be marred if one were absent. No wonder the tears blinded me, when through the door ajar stole in the fine cat Ginger. It jumped on my shoulders and literally, gently and purringly, licked the falling tears away. That soft loving purring was a ministry; and had not my own dear father, as well as Frances, loved Ginger too? And so I laid my pen down and let Ginger purr and soothe me.

But I must keep to this Monday, July 26, 1886—probably my last day in Caswell Bay. From the study windows the bays were blue under the clear sky, and Ceyfan Bryn looked tempting to ascend.

Within the surroundings are changed. F.'s study table, with drawers intact, her neat desk, her bookstand just as she left it, the arm-chair she wrote in,—these are all now transferred to Winterdyne. Only her harp-piano and my father's music-stool, and a little chair and table remain. And all her pictures are safely cared for. But it has been my pleasure to leave speaking mottoes on the walls. An enlarged photograph, which gives her "massive forehead" and holy smile, seemed to be so lonely. The thought flashed, "Why not let all Frances' dear ones surround her?" So I put a bracket for flowers beneath the large portrait. To the left, a chromo of our lovely mother with her child's verses, "My mother's last request." Then dear father and sister Miriam, brothers Henry and Frank. By gentle sister Ellen I placed her good husband, and last myself.

On the other side of dear Frances I placed the group of dear brother Henry's widow and their seven children; Amy with her African boys' class, and Archie with his converts; also the photographs from his "Leopard" story, with little Havergal sitting on its skin. On another wall were arranged Astley Churchyard and the quiet tomb; the Consecration Hymn, "A Worker's Prayer," "Do what Thou wilt," etc. etc.

Again the rising sadness of the last look around was dispelled by the ministry of flowers and fruit brought by kind Captain H. How kindness does help one!

August 22, 1886.—Restless and feverish last night. In vain I tried to lie still. Two or three times I knelt, confessing sin that rose before me; and as I cried, "Father, I have sinned, I am not worthy to be called Thy son," His answering tenderness came afresh to me. For if our part of the parable be true, God's part must be also. Then I asked to glorify Him by lying patiently awake, or to send me sleep. God's sleep comes to me by soft shadowy lights passing before my eyes, and sometimes my mother's or sisters' faces, then fair flowers that are new to me, all in soft celestial light, and this invariably hushes me off into sleep.

But last night, after prayer for God's teaching by the Holy Spirit, the story of the faithful three in Nebuchadnezzar's fiery furnace came to me vividly. Perhaps as the flames of the furnace rose fiercely, God's word of promise, "When thou walkest through the fire, thou shalt not be burned," were forcibly applied to their shrinking hearts. Then, instantaneously, the very presence of the Son of God, and thus the miraculous transmuting of fiery flame into crystalline coolness. How splendidly this proves the divinity and omnipresence of our Lord, even before His incarnation! What manifestations of His love and sympathy and power might they not have rejoiced in! One could wish to know their mysterious intercourse. How truly He is Lord over every element, wind and wave, air and flame! Doubtless our holy martyrs experienced somewhat of the same miraculous presence, exchanged for the all-glorious reality of Himself as the flames became His chariot "paved with love."

And thus the aged Polycarp refused support at the stake: "Leave me as I am; for He that hath granted me to endure the fire will grant me also to remain at the stake unmoved, without the help of nails." And when the fire was kindled, it is recorded that the flames touched him not. A high wind wreathed the flames into a triumphal arch around the victorious confessor of Christ, and there he stood unconsumed,—fulfilment of His Master's promise, "Neither shall the flame kindle upon thee." The executioner's dagger swiftly releasing the martyr's spirit, according to his prayer, "I bless Thee that Thou hast granted me this day and hour to receive a portion amongst the number of martyrs in the cup of Thy Christ, unto resurrection of eternal life, both of soul and body, in the incorruptibility of the Holy Spirit."

I wish that Foxe's *Book of Martyrs* were more read, and those glorious confessions and professions of faith in Holy Scripture, as so well recorded in the Parker Society's lives of our Reformers, pages once so familiar to me. But in the world to come, what unfoldings there will be of God's faithful keeping of His promise in the very letter as well as spirit!

The talks in eternity will be all of His goodness and faithfulness, and it will be delicious to hear His praises, with no mingling of sighs.

After thinking of this I slept, and seemed to hear Fanny singing her hymn—

"Is it for me, dear Saviour,
Thy glory and Thy rest?
For me, so weak and sinful,
O shall I thus be blest?"

And then I dreamt of her deep humility and abhorrence of any self-perfection, and I awoke up on God's own Sabbath, strengthened and assured that for all the future I need fear no evil, for "Thou art with me, Thy rod and Thy staff they comfort me."

"Upon Thy Word I rest,
Each pilgrim day,
This golden staff is best,
For all the way.
What Jesus Christ hath spoken,
Cannot be broken."—F. R. H.

August 24.—Some of my thoughts and prayers last night exactly correspond with those of my dear niece, A. E. S., expressed in her note received to-day; so I copy them. "It does seem so strange why God should send *you* all this dreadful pain; truly His ways are not our ways, and I can trust Him only to do what is best for you, though I cannot see the wherefore, and I do ask Him constantly to spare you as much pain as is possible, and to strengthen and uphold you with His right hand ('and so face to face') through it all; that His sweet presence may so engross you that the pain may be forgotten, and that you may lose yourself in the ocean of His love." The last words I read in Frances' room were hers,—

"'Jesus only!' In the glory,
When the shadows all are flown,
Seeing Him in all His beauty,
Satisfied with Him alone;
May we join the ransomed throng.
'Jesus only'—all our song!"

'Farewell to kind motherly Mrs. Tucker and worthy husband. One tap on my father's barometer and away.

Something impelled me to go into a cottage near, where Myles was converted by *Never Say Die,* and long after went safe home, saying, "What steps up to the gate." I was startled to find little Ethel apparently dying—only time to kneel at Jesus' feet for her, and point to His cleansing blood.

In Newton school just rapid words of His love, and a prayer and promise left, to speak, maybe, in years to come, "Hold Thou me up, and I shall be safe." "I will uphold thee with the *right* hand of my righteousness" (Isaiah 41:10). "I the Lord thy God will hold thy *right* hand," ver. 13. How splendid F. R. H.'s inference—"*therefore* face to face!"

But for these dear trots, simple words of the safe holding of His hand—the dear red hand that was wounded with the nails before it could wipe out every sin of those it holds, or as my little rhyme runs:—

> "O how good is Jesus!
>   May He hold my hand,
> And at last receive me
>   To the better land."

I asked dear worthy Mrs. M. to let them sing the other sweet words, and so I slipped away. As I passed by the school boundary wall, I remembered how Frances arranged all the school there to sing for Sankey, "Safe in the arms of Jesus," and then how she jumped in their carriage, and at the bottom of the hill answered Sankey's "We shall meet again," by waving her hand skyward and saying, "If not here, in the bright city there!"

The door of L.'s cottage was open; there sat brave Ben, who valiantly keeps his pledge. The mother told me that poor William was no better, but that he read his Bible and a book I had sent him. So that was the last cottage call. The waggonette came up, passing the last bank, and the exquisite view of the little vessels moored in the blue waters beneath. I felt convinced it *was* my very last look, but no matter! "So He bringeth them to the haven, where they would be;" and just then a butterfly rose on glad wing, and I thanked God for pleasant days at Caswell, and pleasant hopes of soaring far beyond those cliffs and bays.

CHAPTER VIII.

VARIOUS INSTANCES OF GOD'S IMPULSES IN MY LIFE.

GOD'S impulses may generally be distinguished from our own, and prompt obedience is safest. If Philip had not "*run,*" he would have missed the eunuch! During my work in Bewdley, I tried *not* to get up early on Sunday mornings. There was the steep walk to Wyre Hill, to open school at 9.30 A.M. Often standing the whole time, and if teaching the gallery of little ones, needing much liveliness and action. Dear little dots, I did love teaching them, and, whenever possible, took them outside the school. Then there was the walk to Ribbesford Church, over so many stiles, that singing of hymns was a great help to order. Sitting with the school at church, and then the avenue walk home; dinner, and up again to open P.M. school, play and lead singing, give closing address, and *vivâ voce* examination of boys and girls. I found it answer to keep one class behind in rotation for a short, loving, personal talk about "Jesus only," and thereby getting to know more of the dear children. And when fatal fever broke out, some of them when dying repeated texts and hymns, and spoke of Jesus and His love. At one time I also took the harmonium at the evening church service, then a visit or two in the almshouses, *my* land of Beulah; so no wonder I did not try to get up early! But Whitsunday morning I awoke soon after 4 A.M. with the unusual impulse to go at once to P. B., an elder scholar, seriously ill. I rose and stole noiselessly downstairs, and through the quiet streets. P.'s house door was open, and her mother came down, telling me that ever since two o'clock her child had begged I might be sent for.

The shadow of death had fallen, and distressing was her cry, "O teacher, am I safe? Oh, if I am lost after all." No church, no sacramental grace sets safe stepping-stones for the soul's last footing. Christ only, His promise only, can guide through the cold waters. Softly repeating the comfortable words of our Saviour Christ and, slowly too, giving time for the soul to grasp them, then silent prayer, then the familiar hymn,—

> "I heard the voice of Jesus say,
>   'Come unto me and rest,'"—

and comfort came. I had brought a fan and *eau-de-Cologne*, and after using them she seemed easy and refreshed. And now the shadows were passing, the Shepherd was come, and she heard and knew His voice. "Just as the clock struck seven, leaning on my arm was exchanged for Jesus' strong arm, swiftly receiving her unto Himself,—

> "Do you ask me for pleasure,
>   Come, lean on my breast,
> For there the sin-laden
>   And weary find rest.
> In the valley of death
>   You shall joyfully cry,
> 'If this be called dying,
>   'Tis pleasant to die!'"
>
> —M'Cheyne

When at West Malvern, I was purchasing some niceties to send a great sufferer, and telling Mrs. L. about her, she said, "I have a lodger recovering from cancer, and I have been praying so that God would send some one to comfort her." It is pleasant to be a personal Amen! This led to many visits to Mrs. H. My heart ached for her; she was incessantly in pain, and could hardly walk. I persuaded her to diminish and gradually give up all stimulants and opiates, and she did so, thereby improving in general health. And I believe *this* had come between her soul and Christ, for she was walking in darkness and despondency. Every day I spent a little time with her, sending the nurse to my breezy haunts meanwhile. God's Word became the light to her path, and it was beautiful to watch the entrance of the Sun of Righteousness, when the dark shutters of unbelief were unbarred. Still I was not quite happy about her, recovery was hopeless, and it became a weight of responsibility to be her only visitor. Just then a dear Rev. nephew came for two nights only. I told him the case, and with her consent he called. I left them and walked up and down the road in the twilight, praying that God's Holy Spirit would bless his message.

Yes, that *was* the meeting moment of her soul with Christ, the transfer of her sins to the Substitute, and as A. said, she then consciously grasped the promises that led her into the joy of peace and pardon.

To comfort and encourage her was delightful work, and joyfully she confessed, "Jesus is my precious Saviour." She died the following spring in much suffering, but in much joy.

Sometimes the work was not pleasant. One Saturday evening after ten o'clock, I was led to visit a dying man, with some nourishment for the night. Turning up a sad street of public-houses, I was just in time to rescue one of my Sunday scholars (twelve years old); her drunken mother was literally beating her head against a wall. "My poor child, why is this?" "Mother is beating me because I won't go in with her to drink." This explained the sad, weary look I often noticed on Sundays. I took her to sleep at her grandmother's; that led me to pass the door of a fine young husband in my night class. There he stood, breaking every dish, and all the pretty crockery lay in bits on the floor. The wife, with baby's forehead bleeding from its drunken father's blow, stood crying in the street. I saw her safely to her mother's, who herself knew what it was to take refuge in a pig-sty. No wonder I am a strong teetotaller, and nothing is so convincing as to be able to say, "See, I have tried it myself, and even when ordered brandy medically, I have just turned it out and taken hot water and ginger."

Another strange impulse was the almost positive conviction that seemed given me of people living in hidden sin. Once I was riding a pony in unfrequented lanes, and took a narrow turning which led me to two cottages. Women and children were in both. Fastening the pony to the gate, I knocked at the first door, and was civilly asked to sit down while getting some tracts out of my bag. Then, asking God's guidance, I opened my Testament at John 4. When I read the verse, "He whom thou now hast is not thy husband," I looked at the woman and exclaimed, "You must forgive me if I am wrong; I am a perfect stranger; I never heard of you or these cottages, but I think you are not married, and just living here to hide your sin. You cannot hide it from God, and He has sent me to tell you so. Let me be your friend, won't you?" The woman started, covered her face, saying, "You are right." I do not remember more sufficiently to write it down, but paid many more visits.

Once I had taken lodgings in a secluded farmhouse in Devon, with such a nice mother and daughters, and the cleanest of rooms. Going down to breakfast the first morning, the large sash window was closed. As I put my hand to unbolt the upper part, it suddenly fell, dragging my thumb and fingers between the sashes. The pain was intense; I am not given to fainting or fear, but was glad to lie down. I stopped the bleeding, but saw my right thumb was twisted wrong. Wet bandages, lying still, and not writing of the mishap, followed. Three or four days after, I heard of a dying girl, and went to visit her; she was all right—trusting, and not trying. Just then a doctor called, who from Christian sympathy occasionally came a very long drive to see her. I asked would he look at my thumb;

he commended my treatment and pasteboard splints. Offering him a book and leaflets, he looked at the name. "Oh, I have had the great pleasure of meeting this lady. Do you know F. R. H.?" That was pleasant in this outside place, and this was in 1874, before many of her books were published.

Patience and splints were my holiday lesson—still I could walk, and visited every cottage. Once I went miles through lanes and moorland with no vestige of houses, till I saw a white cottage, and smoke out of the chimney, which brought a vision of tea-kettle and tea-pot. It was comfortably furnished, many books and little elegancies not often found in cottages. I produced my groceries—I generally carried some—and was welcomed to the tea-pot. Only general conversation passed. The woman told me of her son in the Midland Counties, whom I had seen.

We are told that the disciples returned and told Jesus all things that befell them. That has often encouraged me to tell my Master of walks and talks, and so some new guidance has followed. Thus, whenever I thought of that pretty lone cottage, an uncomfortable suspicion arose. I tried to stifle it as very uncharitable, but that revealing verse at Samaria's well would speak, and impelled me to take the long walk again. I remember praying that if the Lord had really any message for me to deliver, the woman might be at home. Yes, the door was open; she looked constrained and surprised to see me again. At once I told her frankly, but kindly, how unaccountably I was impressed with the fear that sin had come between her and God, for she had spoken of early faith and love. I told her how painful it was to me thus to intrude on a stranger, but I knew how tenderly the Good Shepherd followed the sheep if wandering in the mire of forbidden sin. I then knelt down and asked God, for Christ's sake, to show us both any hidden sin against His pure and holy law. Tears were in my eyes as I spoke to the still silent woman; then she unburdened the sad story, which I cannot write. Once again I called, and the man being at home, God gave me courage openly to remonstrate and show it was possible to repent and retrieve this sad life.

Going to another part of Devon, I took lodgings on very high ground. Resting half-way up the hill, a young carpenter was passing by, to whom I spoke. No mistake about his colours. He told me an instance of presence of mind as the result of looking up. He was fast asleep one midnight, but his mother, a godly woman, had sat up reading her Bible, but on carrying the paraffin lamp into her bedroom she upset it, and was enveloped in flames; her cries aroused the husband, who seemed powerless; the son awoke with the cry of fire; he looked to his Lord, and going to his mother's room saw the wave of fire just reaching the bed-clothes. He threw the blankets over his mother and extinguished her flames, and quick as thought threw all his Sunday clothes on and stamped the fire out! and though only in his night attire and flames all around him, he was mercifully preserved. All night he applied oil, and soothed the poor mother, who was frightfully burnt. She was removed to the hospital, and the son asked me to visit her. And the little ministry to her led to my making friends with the nurse, whose cheery countenance was most attractive. She came from Mildmay, that great pulse of love to God and man. Nurse told me of the sad loss of her purse on the journey, containing not only money, but a valuable locket and keepsakes. Another day she told me somewhat of her early history and living in Hereford; so I asked, "Did you happen to know the Rev. F. T. Havergal?" Oh yes, he was the kindest and best of friends to me, temporally and spiritually. It was pleasant to hear of my dear brother so very far away, and how generously he had helped her. So this encouraged me to show her my thumb, and she improved my bandages. After three or four opinions, I finally went up to Hutton, the bone-setter in London, and he instantly discovered the wrist was out of joint, and as instantly twisted my thumb into place. Poor thumb! it had hard lessons once and again. An aged man with a sore leg and no one to dress it regularly, seemed a little bit of work. For a month I went daily, and then got my own thumb poisoned. Real pain and sleepless nights followed, but they were times of refreshing too, and I had a most vivid sense of leaning where St. John did.

Once again, years after my thumb was out of joint, when little able to bear it, a dying woman had sent for me, and as the carriage was going into K. first, I went for the drive and shopping. Just as the carriage door was shutting, my thumb got in for a squeeze, and I saw and felt it was out of place again. Still I told the coachman to set me down at poor Mrs. S.'s, and as heavy snow came on I bade him take the horses home. I went upstairs, the woman opened her eyes, saying, "Miss Havergal, you have deceived me, it's too late now, I am a lost soul, the flames have been round me already." She closed her eyes, and I knelt down, overcome with her words and my own pain. Silently I pleaded for the poor creature, and tried to recall what I could have said to deceive her. An hour passed, when she roused, and with fearful earnestness said, "You told me of Jesus, but you did not tell me of my sins and this hell that is begun; don't I see the pit; don't I see the devil? Too late, too late; I am lost, lost." "Lost!" O Saviour, Thy foreseeing love provided for this cry from a soul hovering over the blackness of darkness.

No time for talk or reasoning now, only God's living word could reach that sinking soul: "The Son of man is come to seek and to save that which was lost." This I repeated slowly, again and again, with that other life line, "The blood of Jesus Christ His Son cleanseth us from all sin." The woman looked at me more calmly, and I said, "Mrs. S., let us come straight to the Lord Jesus." She repeated a simple prayer after me, and was again unconscious. Two hours had passed, the snow was deepening; I had two miles to walk, with my thumb in pain. But I went round to my walking nurse and arranged for her to go and stay the night with the poor creature, knowing she would point to the one Saviour. The poor woman lived a week; I was only able to go once more. That death-bed taught me that sin was sin—hell was hell. The woman was not in my district, but I had accidentally met her, and had spoken of Christ, not of sin and its wages.

"And He must needs go through Samaria" may also be the clue to some of His servants' journeyings. The Good Shepherd's eye still searches in the wilderness for the lost and straying, and so He impels the errand feet to take this or that turning. When visiting my dear sister Ellen in Ireland, my walking power was often graciously used. There were many lovely carriage drives, which served as pioneer observation of lonely cabins, to be visited on foot. I cannot tell of much result, but know that God's word and message reached many. When welcomed, I gladly returned again and again. One widow told me, years after my first call, that her husband took all the portions and little books given him to the workhouse, and hid them in his razor bag, reading them when possible. Another aged woman, whom I found in great horror of going to purgatory, saying, "Och, and I must be burning for ever; shure a lone widdy has no one to pay masses to release me." If ever our Queen's reprieve brought joy in a condemned cell, far more did the grand reprieve and free pardon through the blood of Christ unlock the binding chain of Rome and set her soul free.

Sometimes they seemed afraid to ask me into their cabins, but would follow me a little way, and then, sitting down amid the purple heather, listen to the story of love. I wonder now at those long rambles, when rejoicing in the flush of health; truly did I say, "Thou makest my feet like hind's feet." Resting and singing awhile, with hat thrown off, on a moor-side, a girl crept cautiously to the other side of the hedge, watching my movements, so I hailed her, "Shure an' I thought it was an angel!" She sat down and we had a long talk, for by listening first one wins confidence, and without arguing they soon disclose their belief and trust in the Virgin, clinging to her mediation with the Son, praying to her, adoring her equally with God. I know this is smoothed over in England, but I could give hundreds of conversations, proving the absolute trust for salvation in the Virgin Mary: e.g., "Well, I'll trust to the blessed Virgin to the last minute, and I'll die in her blessed arms; she's got the power in heaven and earth. There, my lady, look at this blessed picture—there's the real ladder to glory—isn't the mother of God helping them safe up, and them on Christ's ladder a tumblin' into hell?"

Of course the priests heard of these rambles, not that they ever visited the poor, unless sent for the last viaticum. Nor could I ever find the same friendly and fatherly visits which our working clergy delight in.

A woman suffering with cancer thankfully received my visits. While reading a chapter, another woman rushed in, "O acushla, run, run, Father W.'s coming down the lane, and I am never the one to see me darlint lady under his anger—run, run!" I told her I was not going to run, and should like to speak to Father W.

Enter Father W. with courteous bow.

"Miss Havergal, I presume." I bowed assent.

Father W. "Allow me to enquire why you are visiting one of my flock?"

"Certainly, her husband works for my brother-in-law, and she has thanked me for my visits."

Father W. "Your intentions may be more than mere charity; you cannot possibly know the doctrines of our holy and true Catholic Church without instruction. Willingly will I give you such instructions at my own house (seeing my wonder), or I can meet you at your sister's."

"Thanks, I have the Douay Bible, Missal, and Catechisms, and I have read more than you imagine."

Father W. "Then why do you go about teaching doctrines contrary to the Catholic Church?"

Handing him my open Testament, "God's word is what I read, God's word my rule of faith and doctrine, and holy Scriptures are able to make wise unto salvation." Then looking at his pale, worn countenance, "O Father W., you go to the dying, and instead of pointing to Jesus only, bidding them 'behold the Lamb of God,' instead of teaching them, 'Neither is there salvation in any other,' instead of teaching the merits and intercession of Jesus Christ, you distract the dying gaze to Virgin, Saints, and Sacraments,—there it is in this Missal." And I spoke tenderly too of the preciousness of Christ for him and for me.

He listened and paused, and then finding I declined all interviews, he rose and poured out the most cutting, satirical, withering condemnation of my Church and my profession, adding that henceforth my footsteps would be closely watched, and that my visits would be prohibited next Sunday.

I listened in silence, rose and bowed, simply saying, "May God bless you, Father W.," and left.

I never mentioned this interview lest my friends should check me, or be uncomfortable at my long walks. Certainly I got a pelting of stones once or twice, and when I saw the priest's horse in the distance I have taken another lane, but I never found any other hindrance, and many portions of God's pure word were safely given.

Some five Irish miles away, beneath a railway-arched crossing, there were three dwellings. I should never have discovered them, but met an aged woman in a field; she looked so very sad, and just a few kind words seemed pleasant to her. She asked me to come and rest—just two stools in the barest of cabins. And the withered hand seemed groping in the dark towards the living Hand coming down to hers. Poor old granny; the dear red Hand to wipe out the sin that burdened was just what she wanted. Surely it was the impulse of God's love that led me to that corner. Again I went; the neighbours next door rejecting my visits, and a growling dog was rather unpleasant. Thankfully she listened and learnt off a verse each time. Another day came, a strong now or never impulse. I was not well, not equal to the long walk, and there was to be an infant school treat that day. Fortunately I heard the carriage was going near the bridge; it was an effort to bid the coachman set me down, but now or never was irresistible. Never did I regret it; that was my last visit and my last walk, in Ireland! Cheering was her evident grasping of the Hand, from which none can ever pluck away—God's word was the power unto salvation, and in that safe keeping I expect to meet her in the kingdom. And my dear Master took care of me, for, most unexpectedly, a friend's carriage passed on returning, and took me up. The next morning I was very ill, and never saw cabin friends again. When able, I was carried down to the carriage for drives, and lying there bade silent farewell to my former haunts; and then returned to England, never to revisit Ireland.

Workhouses are a special opportunity of ministry, and even a casual visit, when waiting for trains, has been God's impulse to carry His message of love.

In 1870, when visiting my birthplace, Coaley, I found some of my father's old parishioners were in the Dursley Union. How their faces lighted up at the mention of his name,—the young curate they loved so well. As I was leaving the men's ward, an aged man with earnestness said, "May I ask *you* one question?"

"Quite fair, Richard, for I have asked many."

"Is Jesus Christ precious to *your* soul?"

Wise and searching question! how it thrilled to one's deeper self. Often have I passed my lesson on, and so old Richard's question reached many an ear in railway or drawing-room or cottage.

Passing into the women's ward for a general address, I was interested in R., a cripple girl, and left her the *Dayspring* Magazine and other books. Three years after, she wrote, having found my address in one of them, so I continued to post her the Magazines. Three years, and she wrote again, from a workhouse in Derbyshire. She had been visiting a sister, who one day turned her out in the street, literally stript and starving, because she had reproved her for drunkenness and worse sin. Kind neighbours took her in, but could only pass her on to the workhouse. She had one longing wish, which was, "Oh that I could get back to Dursley, and see father again; but the guardians won't pay my fare." I wrote comfortingly, and told her to pray about it, and meanwhile be industrious.

Health took me to Buxton, and looking in *Bradshaw* for my return journey, I found I could wait three hours in ——, and visit R.'s workhouse. The master and mistress spoke well of her, so she was sent for. As she told me of her longing to see her father, and how she prayed to get to him, the sudden impulse came. "Take her to-day." So I told R. to kneel down and we would tell our Father in heaven all about it. I then went to the master. "Can I take R. to-day? I shall send her to her father." "Oh, certainly, if you choose to be responsible." Still two hours to wait, so I asked, "Can I go in the sick wards while R. gets ready?" "Oh yes, it's not the visiting day, but there are two cases—dying." "Dying." One was a negress, with thick curls, and the poor thing grasped my hand tight, for the solemn loneliness of death was creeping over her. She knew something of Christ, and was just ready for the King's message of free pardon, "Nothing to pay," for His blood had paid all her debt. And as I knelt with the two dying ones, surely the Lord heard their cry, the same Lord Jesus so ready to forgive. Poor woman! how she kissed my hand and blessed the Lord for all His love!

R. was ready; all her belongings on her! She was very lame. I had sent for a fly, but it never came. I rushed towards the town, saw a waggonette standing at a spirit shop. "Driver, can you take me to the station?" "It's private, miss, but you can ask master in there." "Do pardon me, I am anxious to catch the train with a lame Union orphan; could you possibly oblige a clergyman's daughter?" "Oh, certainly; give my man your orders." I looked at his glass, looked at him. "*That* often leads to unquenchable thirst; there is living water, Christ gives it—oh so satisfying! From my heart I thank you for kindness to the orphan," and offering a nice book, I bowed and left. R. was hoisted up, and as we drove rapidly off, her look was enough. A kind porter, seeing my dilemma at the long steps, put us in the lift, and soon after we reached Birmingham. "He that hath two coats" opened my carpet bag, and her wretched boots were exchanged for spare ones, with a little packet of necessaries. I telegraphed to her father, put R. in charge of a kind-looking Sister of Mercy, and father and child met at last. He only lived two years,—a little colportage work of Bibles, and F. R. H.'s books helped him. One evening he was at a prayer-meeting and prayed; in a few hours all was over, and the gate entered. R. was comforted; she had two happy years, and saw father die in peace.

TEN YEARS IN BEWDLEY.

It was during the summer of 1867 that Maria and Frances Havergal paid a visit to Morecambe Bay, and invited me to join them in order to talk over a home missionary effort which had been laid upon their hearts. In consequence of their brother-in-law, Mr. Shaw, having settled at Winterdyne, near Bewdley, they had become with him and Mrs. Shaw deeply interested in the spiritual condition of the neighbourhood. At that time in the large and scattered parish in which Winterdyne is situated, regular schools and district visitors were unknown. No lay efforts were being made for the good of the people, except in one corner, called Wyre Hill, where a native of the place, Miss Pountney, having herself been brought to a knowledge of the Lord under very unfavourable circumstances of life, desired to make Him known to her poorer neighbours. She devoted her spare hours to doing what she could, and taught of God, and through the instrumentality of books which came in her way, she gathered the women around her for a mother's meeting; the children were collected in a cottage and taught on Sundays, and older ones were instructed in a night-school in the same place.

This quiet but true work was carried on more or less for several years, but about the time that Mr. Shaw came to Winterdyne, the health of the earnest worker failed, and it was feared that it must be given up. Maria Havergal was at that time watching for God's guidance. Her father having just retired from his active labours, and settled with Mrs. Havergal in the well-worked town of Leamington, no longer needing her help, she felt herself called to a more distinct mission sphere. This seemed to be the call for which she was waiting, and the autumn found her settled in Bewdley in company with a younger helper, who had loved and looked up to her from childhood; and who has ever felt it a great privilege to have been associated with her in the work.[1]

Miss Havergal's first object was to aid and strengthen the work already established on Wyre Hill, but at the same time house-to-house visiting was immediately set on foot. The entire parish of Ribbesford was explored, and divided for covenience into districts, in which every house was included, not omitting the public-houses, of which there were an unusual number. The farmers' wives nearly always welcomed the loan of a helpful book, and amongst the poor a selection of tracts, or pictorial papers sewn together, were regularly circulated and exchanged. This naturally opened the way to conversation, and wherever there was opportunity a portion of the Bible was read.

Such visits being an entirely new thing, at first occasioned great surprise; they could not understand their object. The people, however, soon learned to regard her as their friend, and in cases of sickness she was constantly sent for.

It was her rule from the beginning that she and her fellow-helper should always visit separately, and take up different branches of the work. By this means much more could be accomplished, and kind and willing helpers arose by degrees who could give a portion of their time to assist in the night-schools for boys, factory girls, the mother's meeting, or other efforts.

Extracts from a manuscript book written to interest friends during the second and third years of her Bewdley life, will give the best idea of her work at that period. It is much to be regretted that an earlier book, known to have been filled, cannot be found, and that in her later years at Bewdley she did not write such accounts.

This second book was begun at the close of 1868, when dark clouds had for a time obscured the early promise of the mission, which M. V. G. H. recounts as follows:—

"No journey without a hill, no sky without a cloud, no work without failure.

"For a year and a half our work had gone on smoothly. A large new mission-room had been built, and opened by the Bishop of Hereford. The Sunday and day schools had multiplied threefold. Perhaps a little pride crept in as the new superintendent saw new and rigid rules resulting in new order and new diligence. One rule relating to the expulsion of feathers and flowers, which was ruthlessly enforced on the little wearers of real red cocks' tails, etc., brought about an outside improvement. Compensation was offered by the promise, 'Bring your hats to Park Lane; they shall all be cleaned and nicely trimmed.' This brought an extensive millinery trade, not very profitable! Very much to the credit of the Rector's daughter and teacher of the first class of girls, she cheerfully volunteered that most valuable of all aid—example. Forthwith the great girls set the same example to the more tenacious feathery tribe below.

"It was pleasant to see the large numbers arranged in the spacious well-ventilated room, and there were no more casualties of broken forms, or restless children who must stand because they could not sit. It was pleasant to begin a Wyre Hill Church Missionary Association with the help of pictures, large as life, lent from dear old Shareshill schools. . . .

---

[1] Miss Elizabeth Clay, the writer of this paper.

"We are first sketching the sunshine before the storm. The attendance of elder boys and young men was especially good. These were allowed to walk first by themselves to church, instead of two and two with boys and girls down to five years old. It is always well to spare occasion for the sneer and laugh at young men's attendance at any class.

"The night-school was flourishing. Poor lads! it was wonderful why they came at all. The average had walked six or seven miles, besides standing at their work all day, either in the Kidderminster factories or the distant coppices, etc. Half-past four o'clock A.M. all the week round is early rising. And yet they came, and their fun, which it is not wise altogether to repress in a voluntary school. From 7.30 till 9 P.M. writing, arithmetic, and reading went on. Then singing, which was greatly improved by the very good harmonium. A few verses, a few questions, and one thought to take home, and then all knelt. Rising we sing, 'Praise God from whom all blessings flow.' Then wishing to set an example of manners, I bow to them all, with 'Good-night, boys,' answered by antiphonal chorus. Lanterns were lighted by the more fortunate ones, and for the boys living at Park End, full two miles away through woods and over streams, it was certainly desirable at 9.15 P.M.

"Sometimes a boy would stop behind for another word from the teacher. One evening a bright open face seemed sad and cloudy. As the boy lingered, I said, 'What is the matter, W.?' 'Please, miss, I have had a loss this evening, and I am frightened to tell father and mother.' 'What is it?' 'It is my mason's rule; I dropped it coming back from work, and that made me late at school. I had walked seven miles from my master's, and mother leaves me a crust and cup of tea at Mrs. Aston's close by the school here, as I live too far off to get home. So I went without that, and I went a long way back to look for it, but it's no use. They are bad off at home, and I am only apprentice, and so don't get much yet.' 'I am very sorry for your loss, W., and I am glad you told me, because I want to be your friend as well as your teacher. I am pleased to tell you how much your quiet orderly behaviour helps me. On Sunday our lesson was about three lost things, the *lost sheep*, the *lost silver*, the *lost son*. But every one was *found*. You have lost your tool, but you have given up looking for it, so it will never be found. Is not this different to that Friend who is looking, "*until* He find it"? The Lord Jesus not only looks but finds. Is He not looking for you?' 'I hope so, miss, I think a great deal more about Him than I used to. What you said a few Sundays ago helped me to bear my master's unkindness; he swears at me so, it's so hard to bear. You told us how the Lord was with Joseph when a servant lad, and how He would be with us too.' We had more nice talk as he walked with me down the hill. It was an allowable pleasure to give the unasked-for help towards another tool, and perhaps it will fasten the thought how the Shepherd looks until He find it."

It was about this time that, stirred up by the extra drinking which preceded a contested election, the workers began Temperance work. Miss Havergal thus mentions her first attempt in the boys' night-school:—

"Another evening the teetotal principle was set before them. A bright medal and some attractive cards and Band of Hope almanac were examined, and details listened to."

(These details related to the very successful Gospel Temperance work of Miss Breay in Worcester, and of Miss Crockett in the neighbouring parish at Bewdley.)

"Then a white blank book was produced, called Register of the Wyre Hill Temperance Society. Of course the pledge was solemnly read and signed first by myself. About thirteen boys came forward and signed also. Some of the boys would not, because when they had colds, 'rosemary and cider were such a cure.' Others said, 'Father drinks and mother, why should not we?' Still thirteen names in the white book gave a ray of sunshine. Then came the storm. I had overheard whispers at the writing desk, 'There's a treat to-night; mother is going to the ——, and lots of women, to drink.' Leaving the school later than usual, the clock struck half-past nine as we came near our lodgings. Suddenly I said to my faithful helper, Miss C., 'I will go to the —— and see if it is true about these treats, and if our own poor mothers really do go. Let us see for ourselves who do drink, then we shall know who deceive us and who are innocent.' We went on silently, prayerfully, that God would give us wisdom for this hour.

"In the court-yard several women were standing, some we knew and begged them to go home. They assured us they were come to look for their husbands in the men's drinking room. 'Which is the women's room?' 'There, miss.' I tried the door, it was locked. Knocking was vain, but I determined to get in, so waited till a man came up with a tankard of ale. He knocked and shouted through the keyhole, 'Here's your ale.' The door opened, and I followed closely in. Whispering to Miss C., 'Soyez tranquille, pas un mot,'[1] we entered the room. There were women, wives and mothers, some nursing infants even as the poison cup was quaffed. Between forty and fifty women were sitting or standing, or stamping round a blazing fire. Overhead were the tramping feet of drunkards, and their shouts and cheers mingled with the shriller voices below. I stood quietly watching what was going on, turning my face aside. Several men came in and began dancing with a young woman. I looked at them and said calmly, 'This is not your room, please to go out.' Some knew me, and they all went away. The fearful scene was intensified to us because the woman foremost in warming the ale over the fire, and then loudly enticing all to 'drink away,' was a Wyre Hill mother, one who not long before had been very ill, and then professed deep contrition and tearful desire to hear of Christ and holiness. Some had slunk under the table, but were identified by coarse remarks, as 'Mrs. B.'s a-saying her prayers under the table.' They shouted, they screamed, they stamped, they jumped up and down. Two or three songs were being sung; the language of one chorus rolled as waves of burning pitch on my ear.

"But it was no use to stand there. I whispered, 'E., tell me the names of all of our women, your eyes are better than mine.' On the back of a temperance reward card did I pencil the dark list. Then I spoke to a few near me, begging them to go home. One was a sister whose brother had died only a fortnight before, and sad to say the young widow, the mother, the sisters, all were here. Also a girl whose mother had only just died. A few did go, but others were unmoved. The noise grew louder as a fresh tankard came in. Just then a stout woman jumped up and said, 'I'll give you a song.' 'No,' I said, 'you must hear me.' I bolted the door and stood with my back to it facing the whole crew. Taking out my little Testament, I raised it saying, 'I

---

[1] French: "Be quiet, not a word."

am come here as your friend, and, because I am your friend, I warn you. Many of you know me, but there is One Eye in this room who knows every one of you. And every one of you will give account to God. Is this the place for wives and mothers? This Testament shall tell you what God says about drunkards.' I turned to Galatians 5:2; 1 Corinthians 6:10, etc.; 2 Corinthians 5:10.

"There was perfect quiet as I read, but only a tempest lull. Angry voices cried, 'I am not drunk. I can do as I like.' Argument was no use there. The warning given, we left the room. . . . .

"Not only at the —— but in twenty-eight other public-houses were these nights of drunkenness going on—men, women, and even children constantly enticed to sin. One night in particular some of our night-school lads drank till they lay sick in the streets all night, their mothers coming to them at early morning to send them off to their work. Not only was it drunkenness, but other dark results— quarrelling, swearing, fighting, parents upbraiding their children, children their parents. A nice girl in Miss C.'s night-school said, 'I am ashamed of my mother; she is always drunk now.' One of my best night-school lads had gone quietly to bed, when his mother returned at midnight, drunk to infuriation, and turned him out of the house."

But we will turn away from this dark cloud which for a time lay so heavily on the Mission (hindering and even breaking up classes and meetings), to brighter scenes. Miss Havergal's account of conversations in the two farthest districts, three and four miles from Bewdley, to which she and her helper usually started together, each visiting one of them alternately, will doubtless interest many.

"Lye Head and Bliss Gate are the names of our two farthest districts. To reach them we often had the loan of an Irish car, which set us down fresh for our work, after which a leisurely walk back through lanes and coppices was pleasant.

"Taking away the negative, I find it well to act on the positive maxim, 'If any man work, he shall eat.' Consequently, we generally stored lunch with our tracts and books. But I found it gave great delight to one humble friend to boil the kettle and fry some cottage ham, taking care she should be the gainer. As she partook of our London tea she exclaimed, 'Well, this is comfortable, to eat and drink together, and what will it be up there?' Our visits here were always refreshing; the poor cottagers in their scattered homes, far from the street sins of Bewdley, seemed to be a simpler, purer type. Lye Head is a lonely place, containing only a few cottages and small farms; but the view is lovely, a sweep of forest, hills rising far beyond, and the foreground of apple and cherry orchards and heather and gorse patches. Our first visits were quite a phenomenon, it was such an unheard-of event for ladies to bring tracts to their doors. 'Not had a tract for years, miss, unless they give them out at the chapel or we pick one up on the road.' 'What brings you here, and who do you belong to?' was the evident expression of their faces. Showing them our Testaments and tracts, and assuring them that the rector knew us, was always a satisfactory introduction; and a few words of the great love of the Lord Jesus, who had healed our sin-diseased souls, and that therefore we longed for them to come and touch Him too, would often unlock the ready heart-response of these simple cottage believers. 'In His hand are all the corners of the earth' might be written over many an arm-chair in the fireside corners of Lye Head and Bliss Gate.

"Visiting one cottage farm with cherry trees thickly round, even to the door, a little maid asked me to walk in and see the master. He was aged and infirm, and could not leave his arm-chair. I had called two or three times before, but either dinner or churning or baking had prevented my going in, and I had only tracts. He put out his hand, and, as I took it, said, 'It warn't your goodwill that brought you here to-day.' 'Oh yes, it was. I have walked three miles to come and see you.' 'No, it warn't your will; it was Christ's will! You're His servant, and so He put it in your heart to come and see me. Sit you down, and welcome. Ever since you left those tracts I've been praying the Lord would bless your work out here, and I know He will. You'll get some for His crown of glory at Lye Head.'

"'Thank you so much for praying. I am sure you could not pray for others if you did not know the Lord Jesus. What brought you to know Him?' ''Cause I thought the devil would have me! It was the text of a sermon first made me think, "Now is the accepted time, now is the day of salvation." I felt I had not accepted pardon, and knew nothing of salvation. For three weeks I was in agony of mind and could find no relief from the fright of being lost. One day I was at work in the field, miserable, but still thinking over that text. In a moment I saw it. I believed salvation was for me, *now*, to-day. I could have jumped the hedge for joy. I threw down my spade. I couldn't work. I wanted to get on my knees and thank my Saviour, for my heart was full of joy and love. I can't describe my happiness. I wanted nothing else but Christ. This was many years ago. The Lord never gave me up, though I went backwards many a time, and, like Peter, followed Him too far off. But He comes nearer to me now than ever. Through faith a man can do anything. It's believe and live. I see that in every page of the Gospel, and I think, miss, it's believing Christ Himself. The best way to explain it is—have Christ in your heart. I shall go up with Him very soon; yes, I shall hear it and go.'

"Then he showed me his large Bible, and asked me to read a chapter, and his explanation was so simple and fresh. When I said good-bye, he said, 'Come again very soon. He'll be with you and give you utterance to speak for the benefit of poor sinners. It is He that opens the heart.'

"My next visit was after the sudden death of his niece, who lived close by. Her first baby died when three days old, and in about three weeks, just as the young mother was dressing to come downstairs for the first time, she fell, turned black in the face, and died before any help could be obtained. It is very solemn to a visitor to find that one so lately spoken to is gone for ever, and where? Vainly we try to recall the last words spoken. Was I faithful? Did I point to the Lamb of God? Did I read and pray with her? Oh, how often can we only humbly cry, 'Deliver me from blood-guiltiness, O God.' The old man had got on his crutches into his little fields to look at his sheep. 'He'll sort them, take the sheep from the goats. That'll be a glorious time—one family, one fold. Christ knows all His sheep without marking them.' After getting to his easy-chair he told me how happy he was. 'I am in Christ, and so out of the devil's reach. Ah, I was in the devil's paw once; all alike—all have sinned and come short of His glory. It's out of our power to save ourselves. It's when you can feel Him in your heart that makes you happy. There are many sects and parties, but it makes no odds what a man is called, so that He is in Christ.'

"April 1, 1870.—Long had we waited for weather for our distant work. Keen wind and rain at last rolled away, and April came with a smile on her face. A merry party of little nieces and nephews waited for us in the waggonette near our lodgings, and soon we were on our way, thankful the horses could take us up the long, steep hills, and set us down untired for our visiting. One young visitor we left at her newly-chosen district. With twenty-one districts, Miss C. and myself were most thankful for any subtraction of work. Our rector's daughter takes another. I found S. very much worse; he had been ill with bronchitis, or the 'brown creatur' as I hear it called. Dear old man! his happiness was quite overflowing. He said, 'All fear has long passed away. He's here, my blessed Jesus. He is good to me. I can bear anything with Him so near. He's all my study, precious, precious Jesus.' His old sister said, 'It isn't only when he is awake, but when he's asleep, he hoots out, "Glory, glory, glory," and about his blessed Jesus.' S. 'Yes, I'm always dreaming of Him, but waking or sleeping I'm happy. I can't describe the beauty of Jesus now, and what will He be when I see Him in glory! Ah, we shall see nothing in all heaven better than Jesus. That'll be the time up above. I'll sing glory then. Oh, the blessed Jesus!' I left him where he seems to dwell, just on the threshold, looking through the door, and rejoicing in hope of the glory of God.

"Another warm welcome always greeted us at Mrs. J. O.'s. Without any questioning, she began telling me of her early history. 'I think it was very soon that I knew the love of Christ. I had great trials as a girl; we were thirteen in family, and bread was so dear. I remember wheat being twenty-five and twenty-seven shillings a bushel. We really were lost for want. I believe some of the little ones died from not having enough food. Calico that I get for threepence now was then a shilling a yard. It was about the war time, and the Waterloo fight, that I used to hear my mother praying, that made me think. And then when I saw my little brothers and sisters lying dead and cold, that made me think more. Then I went three miles and a half to Mr. Cawood's school in Bewdley. Mr. Cawood prayed with us times and times. Ah, I remember it. I was led to see myself nothing, nothing but a wretch, nothing but sinfulness in me, but *all* help in Christ Jesus. That's the way to go to Christ, and He will still lay His hand on me and heal me. I often wake with Him, and I lift up my heart and say, "Oh, teach me; Oh, speak to me." This hymn is often running in my mind:—

"O teach me more of Thy blest ways,
Thou Holy Lamb of God;
And fix and root me in Thy grace,
As one redeemed by blood.

O tell me often of Thy love,
Of all Thy grief and pain;
And let my heart with joy confess
That thence comes all my gain."

She continued, 'We are quite left alone here in this little wilderness. No one ever came to see us till you and the other good lady called. Oh, it is so comfortable to see you come. But yet I am not alone, for I do realize Him so near. Like John, I seem to lean on His bosom. I see more and more what He has done for me. "All our righteousness is as filthy rags." I enjoy Him more and more, and soon I shall be like Him and see Him as He is.'

"Another visit she told me she had been very ill, but so happy. 'The book you lent me was such a comfort to me. I have read it twice through, but can't spare it yet.' It was sermons by my old revered school clergyman, the Rev. J. Parker. 'The matchless beauty of Jesus.' And here in this out-of-the-world cottage was one who could say, 'Yes, He is altogether lovely *to me,* the chief among ten thousand. He is precious, and He is mine.' I asked her if we should sing and pray together. It was so pleasant to hear her voice joining in the old hymn, 'How sweet the name of Jesus sounds.'"

Visits to another country district Miss Havergal has thus recorded:—

"One pleasant walk brought us to a district which we had to name afresh. It went by a fearful name suggestive of murder, 'The bloody Hole.' And yet such a lovely little dell; the lane fringed with ferns and flowers, and only a few cottages which no visitors had ever reached. Mrs. B.'s heart was quite won by her visitor offering to retrim the faded bonnet. It was of wonderful dimensions—a real bonnet in the coal-scuttle style of fifty years ago. It was amusing to hear her ejaculations as new bows and strings were sewn on. 'To think of a lady touching my bonnet! Why, it looks as good as new. Shan't it be lapped up for Sundays.' Her thanks were followed by the offer of some eggs, which being declined she would bring some of her parsnips. 'The next time you boils a bit of mutton, miss, please to put in my parsnips, and think of me. Never no lady troubled about me before, and I hope the Lord will return your kindness better than I can.'

"One evening she told me her little history. 'I'ud not tell any stories—the truth's the truth. Years agone I was as gay as any one; never troubled about my soul. I am quite sure as the Lord put the first thought into me Hisself. One day I was going to the coppice to cut heather for besoms. I was alone and in a very lone place. A feeling came over me that I was not safe. I thought something might happen, and I felt so trembling and frightened. I put down the burden of wood, and knelt down under a tree. I often pass the tree now. That was my first prayer in earnest to the Lord Jesus Christ. I axed Him to give me His Holy Spirit. He put the prayer in my heart, and from then I took to seek the Lord. He says, "Seek, and ye shall find;" yes, and I have found peace and comfort in the Lord. I love Him for wearing the crown on His brow, ay, that I do. I want you to lend me the hymn you sing at the reading, miss, "I lay my sins on Jesus." I must get him perfect. I love a bit of singing. Be you come for the tracts, miss?' 'Yes; will you like a book this time?' 'I should; I've had many spells at t'other. What a-many years I lived here, and no one ever came! You know, miss, I go to church, and you goes to church, but it doesn't cense it into me like. And there's Miss C. Her's a good cratur; warn't she a great friend! She is good. She used to say, "Now, do come to Jesus!" Ah, poor thing! I am hurt about her suffering so, but her's very stedfast. If it warn't for you ladies, we poor souls might live and die and be lost for ever, for what any one else cares. There are some as ain't in Jesus as makes remarks; but I think it's no disgrace to humble myself and say, "Well, I am a poor sinner." My husband's a-trying at it too. Ah, it's to catch hold of Jesus! I cares for nothing—nothing in this world now. When I can get to my prayers, then I'm happy. I mind two or three children all day, and you can't pray with them about you. Then my husband comes home, and I leave him to his prayers, and I go for mine to be alone with Him. You can't go on without prayer. Then I feels happy; I don't know what I wants, but He does. Warn't the thunder very serious? it makes my narves go cold. But I'm not afraid; no, I've got a Protector. It's all His blessed handiworks. If I had the head on my shoulders twenty years ago that I have now, 't would have been happy!'

"Another evening I found Mrs. B. full of delight with a new book just given her. 'He's fitted me out beautiful. Look at this book! something for every day. Oh, its lovely! Poor as I am, I wouldn't take a gold sovereign for it. Ah, I am a deal happier than I used to be, though I am under the frowns of the world and such a poor object (from skin disease). Don't you think as He helps me? I know He does give me what I axes for. I am like the woman as had the issue of blood. I comes behind Him at first; now I have more faith, more hopes; I do believe Him, and I am never terrified now, nor fretched, nor put out. If I haven't a bite of bread in the house it don't vex me now, for He knows when to send it. He watches over me. Yes, I've great faith. I does believe Him. If ever I am weary with the toils of the day, I gets His book and reads; that's my comfort. And my husband never worries me. Ah, he's *the beauty!* He never controls, never axes where have you been! Yes he is a beauty of a husband!

"Another evening I called at a widow's house to change the tract. She was out, but her son, aged about twenty, was reading the Bible. I knew that he was a total abstainer, and, better still, a real convert. 'You look very happy, John.' 'Yes, indeed; but I warn't used to think as I do now. The world and the things of the world took all my thoughts. I often grieve now to think how I gave all my attention to what I now hate. I was more for pleasure—not a drunkard. I never went the lengths some do, but my mind was full of races and gambling. Oh, how miserable I was when brought to see my state by nature! It was in attending Miss Crockett's meetings I began to think, "What am I living for? and what is eternity? If it has no end, all that I am sowing now must be reaped then in misery." It was eight or nine months before settled peace came. I can't get on without prayer; it seems as if I can't leave off when I begin, the Lord Jesus seems so near me. A sermon I heard from Mr. Fletcher in Dowles Church was a great comfort to me. As he was preaching, it seemed to burst in on my heart the new life there was in Christ. Oh, if wicked folk could but see what there was in Him! But I didn't either. I should have carried on a few years, and got harder and blinder; but He caught me in the right time. When I am at my mason's work, I get solid thoughts; all our building is vain unless we are building on the chief cornerstone. If I hear a text I puzzle over it, and I think the Holy Spirit works in me by the Word. I quite wonder sometimes how I mortally hate the things and pleasures I used to love. I can't bear to hear them mentioned even. Before, I used to listen to sin; now, I broil at it, I get away from it. And oh, how sweet it is when the Scripture fills my heart with thoughts of Jesus!'"

Sundays were always very busy days. Twice up the steep hill to Wyre Hill and back, to morning and afternoon School as superintendent, was no trifle, and in addition there was usually the walk with the children to church after morning school. Yet, that the devoted labourer found opportunity for extra work also, the following account will show:—

"Sunday evening work. This is necessarily very scanty,—just calling on two or three sick people, or looking after stray lads from the Sunday school, and generally ending in a visit to J. H., to see if he is sober. One Sunday evening a kind helper from Winterdyne, Miss E., accompanied me to try and stir up the absentees from the first class boys to start again. We met a group of four; all promised to come. Up, up the uneven, stony path of Sandy Bank to a boy who in the week had been caught by machinery at his factory. A word there; then to some mothers who were thankful to have their Charlies and Johns looked after. 'Will you come and see H.?' 'Who is he?' replied my companion. 'It is the poor man who has so often broken the pledge; he came drunk to Mr. B.'s temperance meeting, and said he had spent five shillings that day in drink. He took the pledge next day, kept it three months, got a good suit of clothes, went to Miss Crockett's meetings, and then alas! fell. This is the door.' H., in very old dirty clothes, is sitting with a Testament and book on the table. Really not any chairs for visitors. 'Good evening, H. How is it with you?' 'Very bad, miss; very bad.' 'Have you been drinking?' 'Not to-day, but I was all the week nearly.' 'But why do you do it, H.? You are very miserable, are you not?' 'Yes, that's right enough; but it's company, you see—it entices a man on.' 'You trust in your own strength, H. You have never really come to the Lord Jesus, who would give you grace against this sin.' 'I often think I will, and I get reading.' 'Have you been to the service?' 'No; I couldn't go in these clothes.' 'But where's your nice new suit?' 'Oh, they are gone.' 'To the pawn?' 'No; I parted with them for nothing as you may say; let 'em go for five shillings a-Tuesday.' 'And I suppose they cost you thirty shillings.' 'Yes, and more. I wasn't in my senses like, and so threw them up for the drink.' Miss E. then spoke kind words to beg and encourage him to return; to come now—'to come just as he was to Him who waits to receive sinners.' Prayer followed, and then we went home under the starlit sky, praying that poor H. may yet be one for whom there shall be joy in the world beyond the stars.

"A contrast to this visit was one last Sunday evening. Coming out of church, Miss E. said, 'Do let us go and see H. again.' Miss C., ever ready for any work, said she would accompany her; so I went to an invalid out of our district. She had long been suffering, long rejoicing, long waiting. I found her in an easy-chair, with a blanket round her, suffering from extreme bronchial oppression of breath and restlessness. An interval of relief came, and she poured forth such praises. Long years ago she had been in my dear father's Astley Sunday school, in my sister Ellen's class. It would encourage Sunday-school teachers to hear her testimony. 'Oh, the comfort the hymns and the verses I learnt are to me now! I remember one Sunday morning I could not say my hymn and gospel, and did not like to go to school. My parents were godly; you remember that? Well, father called me and helped me, and heard me say the lessons. Then he took me to church, and put me with the children. After church and school

I never went off playing as many did. What I learnt seemed to stick to me, and kept me from ever going to fairs, or dances, or theatres. I went to service, and the last time I saw your dear father was coming from the place. I met him on Astley Common, and you were with him, and he stopped and talked to me, and gave me such good advice. Oh, he was loved! and it's so wonderful some of his family come to see me now. Praise the Lord! After that I went to the service of a Mrs. C.; such a good woman. At this time I was very unhappy about my sins. I was often afraid to go to sleep at night, thinking I should wake in endless torment. One day I opened my Bible at "Seek ye first the kingdom of God and His righteousness." That comforted me, and I thought I will seek on. One day I was reading John 20, and how the Lord said, "Behold my hands and my feet." Oh, I can't tell how clear it all seemed then. Jesus died for me; His hands and His feet were pierced for me. I seemed to see all my sins lying like a great bunch at the foot of His cross, and by faith I was enabled to cast them all on Jesus. Oh, I was so happy! And my Saviour has never left me; no, He will never forsake me. I have often been cold and wandering, but He is the same. Oh, I long to see Him, and I shall be 'like Him.' Afterwards we read the 8th of Romans, and then I sang a hymn, which the poor invalid much enjoyed. Before going, I told her the great privilege we all had of hearing the gospel so plainly set forth by Mr. L. (at some evangelistic services); that he asked this question, 'Where are your sins?' With unhesitating confidence her answer was, 'I have cast them all on the Lord Jesus, and He has taken them all away.'

"But there is the same Spirit, the same Teacher for all God's sons and daughters, and therefore all learn the same lessons.

'I am a poor sinner, and nothing at all,
But Jesus Christ is my all in all.'"

During the later years at Bewdley, when the lodgings of the first three years had been exchanged for a house rather further from the rougher districts, Miss Havergal's practice was to devote a portion of Sunday evening to the almshouses near at hand, visiting especially the sick and infirm who were cut off from public worship, and who greatly valued her ministrations.

The progress of years brought various changes in the details of work, but the foregoing extracts will give an idea of the spirit which pervaded all, and are fuller than letters which contain the chief, if not the only record of her work in subsequent years. Some accounts may, however, be found in her well-known book, *Pleasant Fruits from the Cottage and the Class.*

Reference has already been made to life-size missionary pictures which were exhibited in the Wyre Hill Sunday school. The interest thus awakened was deepened in the summer of 1870 by a visit from Miss Neele, of the C. M. S., which led to the support of two little girls in the Agarpara Orphanage, one of them by the Sunday school. Later on, Miss Havergal interested by her pen other children in different places, and by this means and other efforts, another orphan was supported in the Ludhiana School, then under Miss Jerrom's care.

Although circumstances obliged her to give up regular work at Bewdley in 1877, yet whenever she stayed at Winterdyne it was her habit, so far as she was able, to visit old friends amongst the poor. This explains an interesting fact which has just come to light, and which illustrates how wonderfully God uses His willing instruments, often quite unconsciously to themselves. A worker in Bewdley says that about a year and a half ago a woman from Bliss Gate came to her, begging to know where she could find Miss Havergal, as her husband wanted to see her, and no clergyman or any one else would do. He was then very ill, and died happily, but wanted to tell Miss Havergal that, accidentally hearing her voice praying at the bedside of a sick child through an open window while he was in the garden, was the *turning-point in his life,* and he longed for the same sweet voice beside his own dying bed. Miss Havergal was then ill and far away, and probably never heard here of this result of her faithful labours.

This brief memorial of an important period of her life must surely impress every reader with her faithfulness and devotedness. Truly she was a bright example. Although she never ignored the bodily needs of the people, and might often be seen carrying soup or other food to the houses of the sick and poor, renewing the hats of the Sunday-school girls, and helping the poor in innumerable ways, yet her supreme object was to win souls for Christ. For this she was "instant in season, out of season," watching for opportunities, and faithful in using them, never sparing herself, "stedfast, immovable, always abounding in the work of the Lord;" and we know that her "labour was not in vain in the Lord."

Elizabeth Clay.

EXTRACTS FROM MISS S. HEAD'S JOURNAL.

RESPECTING M. V. G. H.'S STAY IN THE LAKE DISTRICT.

By the kind providence of our God, I was invited by my very dear cousin, Maria Havergal, to join her at the English lakes.

August 12, 1880.—On arriving at Keswick I spied dear M. looking out for me, and to my surprise she was lame. She had not told me that she had had a narrow escape from a serious accident after parting with her brother at Hereford. She gave me a sweet welcome, and we proceeded to the charmingly-situated hotel where she was staying till she could get rooms, the town being full on account of the Keswick Conference, which had just closed.

August 13.—M. planned a row on Lake Derwentwater, and a young man staying in the hotel, with whom she had had a little intercourse, proved a good knight-errant. For two hours we rowed about this most beautiful of the lakes; mountains bound it on all sides, forcibly reminding us, as dear M. said, of that descriptive verse of the sweet Psalmist of Israel, "As the mountains are round about Jerusalem, so the Lord is round about His people."

August 14.—Dear M. being still lame, we rowed again on the lake with a dear Irish girl, M. F., mentioned in F. R. H.'s *Memorials,* and her ministering friend, Miss Ward J., who has a rich voice, and as we glided along she started some hymns in which we all joined, thus greatly heightening our enjoyment.

August 15.—Sunday. A bright, hot day. Canon Battersby preached from 2 Corinthians 4:7: "We have this treasure in earthen vessels," etc. He very touchingly alluded to the sad drowning of the Rev. H. Wright in Coniston Lake on the previous Friday. This devoted servant of God preached his last sermon at Keswick on Sunday, called on M. on Monday, attended an evening meeting, and proceeded to Coniston on Tuesday, and on Friday while bathing with his sons he was seized with cramp and drowned. Bishop Ryle preached in the evening on the death of Mr. Wright, whom he had known from a boy, and whose loss is so great to the Church Missionary Society. While I was at church, dear M. addressed the ostlers and stablemen under a tree; she said they listened most attentively. At night, three of the maid-servants went to her room to have a talk about their state. Though sorely needing rest, she seems unable to resist the opportunity of winning souls to Jesus.

August 17.—Moved with M. into lodgings.

August 19.—Rowed to Lodore Falls, landed, and M. sat on a mossy stone while her three nephews, who arrived two days before, ascended by the Falls. I went by an easier route as high as I could, and had a superb view, though the mountain-tops were veiled. Later we called at the Rectory and received a kind and pastoral welcome, and at eight went to hear the wonderful musical rock-stones.

August 20.—Excursion to Ulleswater, and the next day the nephews to Skiddaw.

[*Note.*—These and other excursions are not described, as M. V. G. H. could not join in them from her lameness.]

August 21.—In the evening we sat in the churchyard. I knitted while M. talked in her own sweet way. I am so glad we came to our quiet lodgings, for she was getting very weary; hotel life is restless, and her intense yearnings to bring souls to Jesus was a perpetual strain. For three consecutive nights the young people came and knocked at her door for spiritual talks.

August 22.—My second Sunday at the lakes. Family prayers at 9 o'clock, M. playing a hymn, then a Sabbath Psalm read verse by verse, our good landlady and servant joining, and dear M. prayed so nicely. Then we all went to church, morning and evening, enjoying the services and Canon Battersby's preaching. After evening service we sat on Castle Hill and enjoyed the lovely prospect of mountains and Lake Derwentwater, the sun setting in glorious majesty on one side, the moon rising in calm beauty on the other, the clouds fleeting, and the moon gradually as it were surmounting and leaving them all behind,—a comforting emblem of the Church, and therefore of each individual member being brought safely through all obstacles and shadowy difficulties until safely reaching the home that we long for.

August 23.—M. roused us all up at 6 A.M. with a proposition that we should start as early as possible for an ascent of Helvellyn. So we had prayers at 7.15, and the young men engaged a waggonette for the day. We drove to Wythburn, at the foot of Helvellyn, and finding there that Mr. F., of Eaton Square, was going to Grasmere, M. proposed that he should go with us there, and then our party go on to the lake. It was very lovely all the way; two small hills were pointed out called the Lion and the Lamb from their resemblance, and another like a young lady playing on a piano. During our drive we met a carriage, and Mr. F. recognised three of the ladies, who proved to be very dear Worcestershire friends of M.'s. They flew to her with open arms, and we went to their lovely summer home called The Hollens (this is the old Saxon word for hollies). It was then settled that the nephews should return and ascend Helvellyn, while M. and I remained quietly with her friends. M. calls them "the Doves," as when she first saw them they were all dressed in dove-like silk, with white satin cap ribbons. After luncheon they took us to see a cottage in their grounds, and dear M. then engaged it for a fortnight, so we go on September 1. She was wanting when her nephews left to move to a quiet spot; she is getting known at Keswick, and many call from all parts, and she often looks so weary. In the evening we drove back to Wythburn, where we took up the nephews, and returned to Keswick, having exceedingly enjoyed our adventure.

August 26.—Just as day was breaking, I could see as I lay the sun peeping from behind the mountains, and watched till the earth was flooded with his rays; then I got up and was on Castle Hill by 6.45. On returning to breakfast at 8.30, I found that M. had been before me, descending by a different route; so we did not meet. She is now busy editing *Life Chords,* some of her sister's poems, illustrated by the

Baroness Helga von Cramm. M. and I went to an evening prayer-meeting. Canon B. spoke very forcibly on the abiding union in Christ. I do feel very thankful for this real help to spiritual life. Our Father is so good in providing rich pastures in the wilderness.

August 28.—Another intensely hot day; one of our party, the Rev. J. E. R., left for London; he is one of the Rev. Webb Peploe's curates; we shall miss him, but our young men's sisters, A. M. S. and A. E. S., arrived in the evening.

August 31.—M. called us up at 6 A.M., proposing as it was such a gloriously clear morning to go in the churchyard, asking us to take our Bibles and "say our prayers" there. Alice and I obeyed the summons, and certainly the mountains were exquisite in the early morning. It was a great scramble to get W. off, as he had fixed to leave by the early coach. This was the day we had arranged to move to Grasmere, and as we drove away lowering clouds made the grand mountains look a deep purple. One very fine effect was a rainbow on the side of one,—the prismatic colours were very visible. It was raining fast when we arrived at our cottage, called Hollens Lodge.

September 2.—A glorious morning after the rain, so M. proposed a little mountaineering. We went up a near hill, and were rewarded for the toilsome ascent by marvellously beautiful views. We spied six lakes and three tarns, and nestling far below, the village of Grasmere with its picturesque church, looking like a lovely miniature set in a vividly green framework. At one of the tarns we met five little girls going to bathe. Of course, dear M. had a sweet little talk with them about learning God's mountain lessons, and they are to call tomorrow for *Morning Bells* and *Little Pillows*. In the evening M. went to see her friends "the Doves."

September 3.—Our kind friends took us in their carriage to Ambleside. We passed Southey's house, and on through ever-varying beauties to Rydal Mount, and had permission to go into Wordsworth's garden and the summer-house where he most frequently wrote. After seeing Ambleside, we drove quite a different way back by the enchanting little Loughrigg tarn, dear M. exclaiming and I re-echoing, How beautiful! and how good God is to let us see all this!

September 5.—Sunday. Dear M. very poorly and restless, and could not go to church, but she did not lose anything,—a disappointing service. In the evening we passed the church; M. looked in and accosted the verger, saying, "I am so sorry, so sorry." Said he, "What for, ma'am?" She replied, "To see this cross and candlesticks and flowers; I am a Protestant, and we have no business with these symbols in our church; it is breaking the second commandment, 'Thou shalt not make to thyself any graven image, etc. Thou shalt not bow down to them.'" He answered, "The teaching is not amiss, and people need not look at the things"; but she maintained that it was decidedly wrong.

September 12.—Sunday. My last day at Hollens Lodge opened brightly. I went to church alone in the morning, and with M. to hear the catechizing in the afternoon, and in the evening we attended a drawing-room meeting at the Hollens; it was a real communion of saints—most refreshing.

September 13.—We left Grasmere for Ambleside, steamed down the graceful Lake Windermere, thence by rail to Furness Abbey, and the next day I bade adieu to the lakes and mountains, thanking our Father for this wondrous recruiting of mental and physical power.

[*Note*.—Many more expeditions were made before September 13, but as no more of M. V. G. H.'s sayings were recorded, the accounts are not copied here.]

JOURNAL OF A VISIT TO AIX-LES-BAINS AND SWITZERLAND IN 1882.

"That instant."—LUKE 2:38.

"THAT instant" seems one of life's hinges, the opening or shutting of events totally new to us, but proving that our moments, our steps, "even" as the "hairs of our head," are all counted and ordered beforehand by our loving Father.

So with the aged Anna, that temple worshipper and watcher. The key-note of her life-long yearning seems given—that she was "looking for Redemption." And so when God's "instant," the fulness of time, was come, the Redeemer visibly entered the temple of this His fallen world, and in "due time" was manifested in the temple at Jerusalem.

By the Holy Ghost, Simeon came "that instant" into the temple, took in reverent arms Immanuel. Then came the golden "instant" of Anna's life; she came, she saw, she believed, she praised, and henceforth "spake of Him." Forgotten all her weary vigils—her dim, yearning lookings; the Christ was born, the Redeemer had come to His people, and she saw and rejoiced!

It seems a "come down" to choose this superscription, "that instant," for things that happened during a few weeks' stay in Switzerland. Yet the words did often flit through my mind, when God's tender overrulings consciously hovered over our steps. May it be *only* for His glory!

May 25, 1882.—Left London with my niece, Alice E. S., reaching Dover in clouds and rain and rough waves. From Calais we proceeded to Paris, and at 9 P.M. reached 77 Avenue Wagram; welcomed by our Champéry friend Margaret C. And the last time I saw her! darling F. stood waving her hand, at Pension Schonfels, in 1876.

Miss Leigh was absent, but her manifold organizations seemed all alive and beating time truly. Many histories were written in the numerous faces that flitted past me the next morning, and some spoke of my sister F., and the blessing her books were to them; and it *was* a little "afterward" to me, to be told that my *Memorials* of her had helped and taught them.

Miss G. not only told me of the liftings she received by F.'s works, but the marvellous power some of her thoughts have had with infidels. She gave me particulars of one most learned man who was staggered by the genius, the master thought of F.'s argument in her *Thoughts of God*.

I was much impressed with the utter self-denial of Miss Leigh's lady workers. Dear Margaret C., for instance, did not seem to have one hour to call her own—seven classes weekly, ten hours' readiness to interview the hundreds of applicants for advice, situations, sympathy or help, and listening to the sad and weary—investigating the tangled threads of many a young life.

And all this in an atmosphere of ceaseless clang and direful din night and day. We never slept one night in Paris, though Avenue Wagram is called quiet; so we rushed gladly away by night train to Dijon. A young Italian lady and lovely child were with us—such beautiful eyes! And when her darling was cozily tucked up for the night, we *saw* God's lesson in that mother's watchful eye and care. They were going to Naples, a forty-eight hours' journey. It was pleasant to have her gentle response to a few words, and after speaking of Jesus and His great love, the Italian kissed my hand so gracefully.

About 3 A.M. we left the train for a few hours' rest at Dijon; how the faint dawn and utter calm reminded me of 1876, when dear F. was with me, and we were shown to the same rooms in the Jura Hotel. Left Dijon at 1 P.M. for Aix-les-Bains, and ought to have arrived 8 P.M., but it was nearly 11 P.M. when we reached Aix.

We had written for rooms at the "Hotel de la Paix." We saw on the platform a solitary figure, evidently not knowing what to do; so I spoke, and she said it was too late to go to some friends, and would be glad to follow us to our hotel. While Alice and I were enjoying tea and chicken, we wondered if the stranger had like fare. So I went on a voyage of discovery *au troisième,* and as usual hit the right door. "No, she lunched at one, and would now take some water!" Soon Alice and I stole up the staircase, for our fowl had wings to spare. We met again occasionally, and Medora C. told us she was a special correspondent of some Herald, both in poetry and prose. From the far West she seemed to have wandered to Paris, and then to Aix, to find an artist friend, who, however, had left.

Sunday began as we laid down; but truly no outward calm, no Sabbath at Aix, only an hour's quiet; then tramp, tramp, and before four, workmen and carpenters' hammerings and sawings and shoutings were incessant. Alas! we were just opposite a theatre and casino. The little English Church was overflowing, so I brought chairs from our hotel and sat in the open air. Medora came and looked over my hymn-book. It was rather a comfortable service. Again but little sleep; so by 4 A.M. on Monday I was off to the high outskirts of the town to reconnoitre for more peaceable quarters. I wandered far and high, every one was astir, at least the natives. No lodgings to be found, but at "that instant" I met a woman resting her bundle, so I chatted awhile. She looked sad, and told me she had just said adieu to her husband and two dear little ones. He could not work, so she was going to Lyons to get in an hotel, and earn for them. I had no books with me, but said, "If you will come to my hotel, I will give you one at 9 o'clock." She hesitated, so I said, "Will you come with me, then, now?" "Oh yes;" so we had a long talk, and passing by the image of the Virgin, gave me the right to protest. I *always* do, and find it answers to speak boldly against trusting to any one but Jesus. She sat down at the hotel while I wrote her name in F.'s *L'Invitation Royale;* it was delightful to send one to Lyons. Of course I helped her for the journey.

After breakfast Alice and I took a carriage in search, and found quiet rooms at the Châlet Lubini—paying a franc a day for service; which service, I soon found, must be mainly my own. However, I made our table pretty with vine leaves and flowers under a shady tree. Only one day's civility! no "service" evidently for us, and the third morning I found the breakfast plates locked up, and the teapot! and all our belongings poked into a small cupboard, and madame was hard, and I told her ladies never did what I was obliged to do there, especially as I paid her own terms—seven francs per day for two very small bedrooms, no salon, and no food. I was so very poorly also, and felt altogether cast down. Madame even grumbled at our garden-table. However, I got *a* plate for Alice, and said no more to her. I thought of One for whom there was so often " no room." It always answers to tell Jesus *first.* Then, at "that instant," I remembered the night before our doctor met us coming from the Baths, and desired us to walk a longer way back, and that *en passant* I had just seen a lovely villa, with roses and arches and orange trees—a very Eden. I went straight there, and Madame de Lille came in her dressing-gown and night-cap. It was evident it was very first-class, and soon she told me only duchesses, countesses, and even pashas came there—sixty and seventy francs per day for a suite of rooms. I told her exactly how it was,—for the first time in my life I had found *in*civility; the abstraction of the plates and teapot seemed to touch her, and furthermore she frankly informed me she "liked my face very much!" so then I opened my brooch, and she was so taken with my father's *distingué* features, that she at once offered me two rooms for eleven francs daily, and our meals would be served in a pretty vestibule, but on rainy days in a *salle à manger.* I said I would bring my niece to see them.

I was so glad not to tell Alice of the cloud till the *"instant"* guidance had come with it. So we went, and were treated most courteously then, and during the whole of our stay. The rooms were charming. The garden of little terraces and slopes covered with flowers and roses climbing up the tulip and lime trees; roses growing as nature meant them to, not tied like martyrs to stakes, our stiff English way. Such arbours and trellises of Virginian creepers; many orange and lemon trees; in the distance, the blue lake of Bourget, and above the "Deut du Chat;" and to the left, far heights that caught the sunset glow, and shone in true Swiss rose-tint.

We observed that madame never went to mass, and spoke very liberally of our Church. One day she told us that she was brought up a strict Catholic, with the greatest reverence for the holy Fathers. But when travelling with her parents, and at a large *table d'hôte,* in a town where some mission services were being held, three of the priests sat together, and were enlivening themselves and others with details of all the confessional secrets poured out to them that day. Joking at what seemed to her so sacred; this, and their indulgence in wine, etc., so utterly disgusted her, that she never went either to confession or chapel again for forty years. "But," she added, "I must send for them *once*—when I am dying, for the last sacraments." I pleaded that, with the Lord Jesus for her Priest, she would not need this. "Ah, but then I should not be buried in the Church." We had many talks, and once she knelt down with me and prayed for the Holy Spirit's teaching. Amen and Amen.

One of the excursions is to "Les Innocents," about three miles away. We went by diligence, June 21st, part of the way, or rather, being over-crowded, had a nice carriage, sharing it with an old priest, with such a sad, weary look. He told us of his wanderings in America, England, etc., and now he was come for the end of his days at the Monastery of the Haute Coombe. "So," I said, "you are quite a pilgrim; it is so happy to be Zion's pilgrim, and the New Jerusalem in sight." "Ah yes, yes, but we do not know." So I took out my Bible and said how precious that guidebook was,—more precious still *Jesus Himself;* and told him of F.'s joyful sure hope in life and death. He accepted her French leaflets, placing them in the leaves of his missal, but the end of the chestnut avenue was come, and we left the carriage for our walk. I do hope I shall get to that monastery some day. After a toiling hot walk we reached one of the establishments where the Angora rabbits are kept in large numbers, for the sake of their soft fur. This fur is pulled from them, the motherly dame showing us how to do it, and assuring us they liked it. Some were pure white, others dark slate colour. The fur is twisted on a primitive wheel.

Then we tried to follow the guide-book, and did at last stand on a railway bridge, overlooking the Lake Bourget. But my pen will never give an idea of that glorious revelation of pure and perfect sky-reflections—here azure, there opaline, and again deep ruby shimmerings on the lake; while the steep banks of the "Deut du Chat" seemed microscopically clear, in the bluest of blue shadings.

Returning, we were tired and hungry, and so sat down under the shady trees of a little roadside restaurant for bread and milk. Presently Alice said, "Auntie, I see some one very ill inside the door." I asked the daughter if any one was ill? "Oh yes, my mother has been ill for some years; she can seldom come downstairs." So it was *an* "instant," for if Alice had not seen her I might never have had the privilege of speaking to one of God's hidden ones. Instantly I found the right ring—that indescribable *something,* that shine of Christ's own love and light. And as I repeated my little stock of God's promises in French, I was delighted to find her taking the verses up, and repeating them without me. Thus she knew John 14:6, John 3:16, 1 John 1:7, and others. Then I lifted my heart for what else to repeat, and it was singular that when I repeated John 10:27, 28, 29, that seemed just *the* comfort she needed. For the fear *had* come. I will quote her words. "Would Jesus hold her *always?* How, when death came? Sometimes she had no fear; again it came, for she was almost blind and could not read, and no one ever came to speak of Jesus, *my dear Jesus,* as you, the kind stranger, do. Ah yes, these are good, good words. And when I was a child at school, the first words I ever learnt are these that you say to me to-day. Ah yes, then I learnt the gospels and the epistles, and all my life those good, good words have come to me again and again. They are God's words, and so they cannot die. Ah, why do they not teach them now?

It is wrong, so wrong; the children never learn them now, and how can they find the good Jesus if they don't know His good words by heart? In my long dark nights the good words of God come again to me, and now you repeat the same. God must have sent you!" etc.

She was *so* thankful when I knelt and came with her to the Good Shepherd. I left her rejoicing in His promise, "None shall pluck them out of my hand." Dear old Constance! would that the School Board Bible extinguishers had learnt your logic!

It was pleasant to post her a Testament and F. R. H.'s French books.

Then we explored one of the oldest castles in France, quite deserted, only cats and chickens about in the dark entrance-hall. We had to hurry back, taking short cuts through vineyards, to catch our return diligence, and verily we were but just an "*instant*" in time. After our three hours' excursion, and the sun just grilling, we were thankful to ride back.

We were extremely interested in the gardener and his wife, the *cuisinière,* at Villa Bel Air. They were Vaudois, and, as they said, "Protestante and Evangélique." They had formerly a little farm, six cows and some goats, and dear little ones—Ida and Albert. The good man signed a bond for his friend, and in time creditors came for his little all, "thus smarting for his suretyship." All was sold up, the children left with the grandparents, and husband and wife obliged to go into service. And *French* service and *servitude* is different indeed from English. On Sunday, cleaning and gardening went on; it did so jar one's own happy rest to see this good man at work, raking all the gravel, paths and clipping the trees. Often he said, "There is no rest for us; it is not like this in Switzerland." I saw his poor wife Jenni crying, and asking why,—"because she had not once been allowed to go to church, though Félice was allowed to go to mass at 5 A.M."

Whereupon I made little Sunday parables to madame, describing the happy rest the English servants had, particularizing on Sundays at Oakhampton and Winterdyne; the idea of the gardeners and coachman, etc., sitting down on morocco chairs and round the dining-room table, by 9.30 A.M., with their masters and Bibles, was a forcible contrast. Anyway, it so far hit the mark that the next Sunday Emil was allowed to church at noon. The succeeding Sabbath he and Jenni and Félice were sent out for a walk.

June 16th.—By train to Chambéry, fifty miles, to visit Challes, whose sulphurous springs are very famous. Several omnibuses were waiting; Alice chose an open one with a canopy fringed like a great parasol; this took us to the "Hotel d'Angleterre," and it was the very nicest of all, and here we camped for a long day. I was washing my hands in an upper corridor, when a door opened to let loose a boy, who had evidently longed for the same. His mother saw me, and bowed and spoke in French. I answered we were strangers just come for the day.

"Would I not come in and rest in her room?"

After a few quite general remarks, the lady said in English, "You *are* Miss Havergal. For a fortnight I have been trying to find you in Aix. At last I asked Dr. Cazalis, and he said you were at Villa Bel Air, and I was coming to call. Your sister's writings have been such, such comfort to me, also to an invalid friend; indeed, the Bible and F. R. H.'s books were the only ones she read."

I found M. Watson had instructed this Mrs. Parry to seek me out! Her opening the door "that instant" was the missing clue.

Alice went with me roving among boulders and flowers; a splendid dark red orchis, with spurs three inches long, was quite new to me. Returning, I felt wistful for one bit of work, and speered about vainly, till on the stairs a scrub-maiden, all in the rough, but with wavy hair and soft dark violet eyes, stopped and eagerly took some cards. She told me she was from Italia, far from her mother. She knew French, and learnt off a text and a prayer. Her name was "Jacinth," and why shall I not hope to meet her again within the city whose foundations are garnished with "jacinth" and precious stones.

Tuesday, June 27.—Left Aix at 7.45 A.M. for Geneva.

The route was a succession of lovely surprises, by the shores of that exquisite Lake Bourget. The Rhone was on the other side, as we left it roaring through boulders, with woods and heights and valleys smiling far and near.

Arrived at Geneva soon after 10 A.M., we deposited our baggage on a convenient stage, whence our steamer for Chillon would leave at 1.20. We took a carriage to drive round the city. Beautiful Geneva! with the rushing Rhone of deepest blue.

We went into the cathedral, and saw Calvin's chair. Many footfalls seemed to me still echoing in those aisles—my godmother's, Mrs. Vernon Graham—and how I wished I could go to her tomb at Petit Sacconnex! Then I remembered how sister Miriam and that happy party were there in 1869; and now darling Minnie and Fanny have met for ever in the temple above. And one older memory still; my own dear father once stood there, and I knew how his grand Protestant heart would thank God for the Reformation truths rooted there and remaining still. And others that stood with dear papa are all gone—gone! It was saddening, but the sun-ray stole in, bringing the cheer, "Jesus Christ, the same yesterday, to-day, and for ever."

We had prayed for guidance that morning, so of course it was given; and in one case, our turning up the right-hand street, and not the left, led to a singular "instant." We passed some musical-box manufactories, but being hungry we thought we would find a restaurant first, and out of many chose one facing a very large music-box manufactory. Lunch despatched, we went in, asking permission to hear one or two of the boxes play, but said that we should *not* be purchasers. Chairs were politely placed, and at "that instant" a party entered for the same purpose. I did not look at the gentleman and his wife and two sons, being absorbed in the novel adjuncts to our ordinary musical-boxes. One had two combs, producing the double effect of violin and piano. Another, sweeter still, gave a harp accompaniment. After a time the gentleman said, "Have you any sacred music? these are all secular airs." "Yes, we have Sankey's." Turning to me, the man snapped his fingers, saying, "Sankey's music is weak—it is nothing." I said, "Still there is a marvellous power in Sankey's tunes. I grant you that the harmonies are weak, but they move the masses in England." "Ah, ah! you mean those revival services. As for that, they are all humbug. I am a Jew. I have been in London, and you Christians will spend hundreds to turn one of us from the faith of our forefathers—that execrable Society!—and you let your poor starve. Give me a religion that feeds men's bodies!"

I answered, "Granted there are poor, but with many it is their vice and their drunkenness, and our English charities provide abundantly for the deserving."

"Ah, yes," he said; "but what is the use of your grand excitement meetings?"

I said, "What is the use of your making all this lovely music if no one comes to admire and hear it? We Christians know the music of the name of Jesus, the Saviour, and we know He is preparing celestial music; so we do want all these poor, wretched ones to come and share it with us, and often Sankey's songs induce them to learn the way to heaven."

"Ah! you are sincere, I daresay; but it is nothing to me, and Sankey's music *is poor!*" (The party meanwhile had gone into the next saloon.)

"Well," I said, "wait till you hear Sankey sing; that is magnificent!" Before this I said to Alice, "*Was* that Sankey?" I thought she said "No," and being short-sighted thought no more of it, till a shopman came to the irate Jew, saying, "Hush! that is Mr. Sankey himself!"

I rushed into the next room to Mr. Sankey, and he advanced with—"Maria Havergal!" He gave me a chair, for "that darling Frances" was all that I could say, as the last time we met she was with us in full health and vigour, standing with the children of Newton School, leading and singing with them "Safe in the arms of Jesus" as Mr. and Mrs. Sankey's carriage passed by, after their pleasant visit to us at the Mumbles, April 1879. And then Mr. Sankey got out to thank them, and to shake hands with old Mrs. Barry, his washer-woman. Dear Fanny then jumped in the carriage, and went a short way, leaving them at the bottom of that steep pitch, that cold east bank, where not long after her glory warrant reached her in that singular rain-cloud. Sankey told me how bright and young she looked, and when he said, "We'll meet again," she said, "Yes; if not here, in the bright city there!" and her upward finger and waving handkerchief was his last sight of F. R. H.

It was comforting to hear from him and dear Mrs. Sankey of so much blessing from her words and the Memoir, which seemed specially useful to young converts. But my time was passing, and it was well that Alice reminded me we had only a quarter of an hour to find our steamer and embark.

The day was perfect for our lake views, and the clear waters reflected the blue sky. It was not till nearly 6 P.M. that we neared the landing pier at Chillon, and found, as I had arranged, our faithful maid, M. Farrington, waiting for me.

I was more interested than I expected in the interior of the Castle of Chillon, and we saw that curious flickering on the ceiling of Bonnivard's prison, the reflection of the movements of the ripples on the lake, which Fanny so well describes in *Swiss Letters,* and no other traveller seems to have noticed. One could not help hoping those same reflected sun-rays may have cheered the heart-hopeless prisoners with thoughts of Him, the Light of Light.

The audience-chamber of the Duke of Savoy and the bedroom of the Duchess stirred up olden memories of troublous times.

Thursday, July 29.—To Vernayaz, passing Mouthey, where dear Fanny and I took the diligence for Chambéry in 1876. All *so* familiar; all the same, except that sunny presence.

At Vernayaz we took a mountain carriage for the steep zigzag road which winds up the very face of rock and precipice. How the pines root in fissures and crevices! and how the boulders in their glorious boldness jut in and out, hiding the tenderest ferns and mosses creeping far out of reach!

> Wise little mosses! surely you creep
> Over the boulders grand and steep
> Brave little mosses! your song I would sing,
> Firm on the rock I evermore cling.
> —M. V. G. H.

The route was far more grand than I remembered it,—ravines and gorges, heights and depths, that just cannot be described; and silent praise for all these works of the Lord—great and marvellous—seemed the only outlet possible.

We passed so many well-known haunts. Fanny's favourite walks and seats, and the pines where we spent our church time on Sundays—even the very rose trees with their dark red flowers recalled the past. It was pleasant to be recognised by Valérie Loufât at the "Pension du Mont Blanc," at Fins Hauts; and the old mother was specially warm in welcoming me back. "Here are the same rooms, mademoiselle!" Yes, there it was, that little bare pine closet—the simplest bed and solitary chair that Fanny occupied. I wondered, as I often do, at her extreme content with the barest necessities of life around her, and her merry adaptativeness to what would be unendurable to many. And yet few had more elegant tastes.

Deep love for her memory dwells in Fins Hauts,—and to see the people kiss her photographs! More than that, I found the truths she had taught and sung were firmly rooted. The mother's "Bien sûr" followed all the promises I read with her; and the father's response was also satisfactory. Both the following days were wet; so we only had a beautiful gleam or two.

Sunday brought sunshine, and Alice went with me to the high walk where we could see Mont Blanc.

I hoped a few could come for a Bible reading; but no notice being given, it was a failure. In the afternoon I went among the châlets, and found the old friend, who at once remembered me and our talk about the one "bon bâton." Several came out of their châlets, and brought chairs, so there was a little seed-sowing, and the children took cards and verses home.

After tea, I passed some ladies, and offered F.'s leaflets. They at once exclaimed, "Oh, they are *dear* Miss Havergal's!" They were from Lausanne, and knew all her books well.

"Katrine," the priest's servant, was much on my mind; and finding she was still there, I went to speak to her; but the priest himself opened the door, and said she was gone to Salvans that evening.

I said it would have been pleasant to see her. "Possibly he remembered my coming for the loan of his Bible six years ago, and his correcting the hymn which I now offered him in print." Yes, he did remember; but he must beg me not to distribute them in the village. He said, "It is not the doctrine of our Church." So I pointed to the lines, "Tous mes moments, tous mes jours Seront pour Toi!" etc. "Is not that your faith?" "Yes; but you despise good works—you think nothing of them." I said, "Excuse me—see this line, 'Que je vive et que je meure, Seulement pour Toi!' What can be better than every moment given to Jesus Christ?" "Ah, yes; but you place no merit in it." "Certainly not!" and turning to Titus 3:5, I read St. Paul's verdict.

We talked some time, quietly, the priest looking at all the references I turned up. I told him of F.'s happy death, singing as she crossed the river, and that "the blood of Jesus Christ, His Son, cleanseth us from all sin," was her only confidence in death, as it had been in her life. He said much that was truth, and admitted that when he came to die, if no priest were near, he should make his act of contrition to God only; and so we parted, he accepting F.'s "Seulement pour Toi," and "Sans Christ." (Her "Invitation Royale" went by post some time before.)

Monday, we left Fins Hauts, an hour's easy walk down to Châtelard, where carriages pass for Tête Noire, or Chamouni. The Hotel Royal there is kept by Frederic Loufât, Valérie's brother. Six years ago he was master of the Couronne at Argentière, where we passed a fortnight. It was touching to see that man's feeling for Fanny—with tears telling me all he remembered of her, and the impression indelibly left. He had seen much sorrow. His first-born son died in a few weeks. He said, "Oh, how I grieved! I could not say, God's will be done. Then we had another beautiful boy, and I said, 'O God, it is Thy child!' And when in eight months it sickened, I never prayed for its life, only 'God's will be done;' and so He sent for my little one. Again, a most lovely boy was given us for eighteen months only. God took it. I cried, but I did only say, 'It is the Lord's will;' and I knew how very safe it would ever be." This simple submission was surely good fruit.

The wife's remembrance of Fanny was even more distinct and almost wonderful,—how she kissed the photograph! Some time after, in the most earnest way she implored me to spare her one for her treasure. I do not like to repeat all her soul confidences, but gladly did she accept my proposal to go up-stairs that we might quietly seek the Lord, and verily I believe it was a time of finding and trusting. Most encouraged was I when she told me that some simple words I had said to her six years ago had followed her almost daily. Of course I had forgotten them; but she said that when I went to say good-bye in her room, I spoke of the one Saviour—the one hope as so sure and sufficient, and, pointing to my alpenstock, said, "One good staff is enough."

Thus one passing word was blessed. May this encourage fellow-travellers.

We had to wait *five* hours there before a carriage passed which could take us on to Chamouni; but I could not regret the delay. And singular to relate, on coming again in three days, I found poor Madame Loufât seriously ill, and in such agony, that I could only sit by her, and say a word or two. So I was thankful I had taken the "instant," given on Monday for that prayer. Her husband seemed so tender to her, and I am glad they have one little boy living.

In our carriage to Argentière were some most lively French girls. The road was very steep. Alice walked much, but I could not. We passed the terrible bridge where a year ago, as a carriage was passing, it gave way, and the travellers were dashed in the strong current beneath, among the boulders. The father, mother, and daughter were drowned. No trace of the poor girl was found till lately her hair was discovered. The driver was saved, but went quite mad from the terrible scene.

Not very far on the same road we came to a bridge which from rains needed repair, and one plank was gone. All got off the carriage except the driver and I, so the French girls said, "Vous n'avez jamais peur." This opened the way for speaking of the joyful confidence of a good hope in Christ.

Before arriving at Argentière, we all had to walk down the very steep hill; and my young French companion was truly interested about dear Fanny's happy death. That she had no fear *then* seemed marvellous to her,—or that she could really be "happy" when the doctor said she could not live. They all seemed quite pleased with some leaflets. They went on to Chamouni; but we stopped at the Couronne at Argentière. I found my way to the same bedrooms as in 1876. It was nearly 7 P.M. when our repast was over. I was tired, but knew it was my only "instant" to find a girl I had been much interested in. So Alice and I started towards the rocky nest of châlets. The path seemed very steep now, though I thought nothing of it then. The rose colour was on Mont Blanc. It seemed but yesterday since Fanny and I saw so many golden sunsets. But Marie Carrière was in my mind; and just as I wondered how to reach her, I saw three boys some way off, and hailed them, "Do you know Marie Carrière?" "Oh, yes, yes!" "Then will you tell her, her friend the English lady is come again, and is waiting here to see her." Off they ran, and in ten minutes Marie came bounding down the rocks, and was indeed glad to see me.

It was her own brother to whom I gave the message. Curious he should have been there the "instant" I needed some one to take it. For the rose colour had paled, and twilight was fast coming. Marie sat by me on a boulder, and we went over the precious promises I longed should be good seed. Then she walked with me to the hotel for a French Testament and a little present. It was almost dark, and I did not see a gentleman there till the waiter came. I don't know *why*, but I said, "Possibly you want your supper, so I will not hinder the waiter." The stranger said (in French), "Thanks, I am quite exhausted, as I have tasted nothing since morning." We chatted till his supper came—only a jug of milk and dry bread! Then I ordered my bread and milk, and, turning to the traveller, said, "You seem like me, in the Land of Promise!" He replied in English, "You may do it from *choice*—mine is from *necessity*; for the last three months I have taken nothing else, and only twice a day. For five or six years I have been travelling about as an evangelist. I go in these valleys among unfrequented châlets. I preach wherever I can. Sometimes I sell New Testaments and portions; but my stock is exhausted." I said it would be pleasant if he would accept some of my stock to disperse, and went and brought him a selection, including F.'s "Sans Christ" and "L'Invitation Royale," and some English leaflets. The moment he saw her name, he exclaimed, "Ah, I know that blessed life!—no other books have taught me like F. R. H.'s. They are so Scriptural; they seem inspired." Of course I told him she was my sister. He thanked me, and was extremely interested in seeing her photographs.

Without any request, he told me that some years ago he was curate to Rev. A. Dallas; knew Mr. Cory and other clergymen. He gave some very singular instances of God's providing for him. Some time before, he was at Geneva, and after paying his lodging, on Sunday morning found himself without francs or food. He walked through several streets (not knowing any one), and was singularly impelled to knock at the door of a fine-looking pension. It was opened by an old servant of a cousin. At once she recognised him, and begged him to walk in! Food and lodging followed. Another Sunday he was breakfastless, and thought he would see if there was any prayer-meeting, and seeing a lady with her Bible, enquired. She led the way, and being too soon, a person fell into conversation with him and invited him to lunch. He was a grocer. Finding Mr. Amersley was an evangelist, he gave him twenty francs, and thus, he said, "My need was supplied in answer to my prayer, as I walked hungrily up and down the streets." I suggested that if he worked with some society he would not come into so great straits; but he said, "He walked as the Lord led him, and so far had been much blessed." He told me sometimes it was very difficult to get a hearing, that he met such bigotry and superstition. I told him how often it was my prayer that God would order my steps; and specially that morning had I asked to be let do something for Jesus my Lord, and so I should think it a privilege if he would accept help as from the Lord. So I wrapped up thirty francs, rejoicing I had returned to the room "that instant," or I never should have met this worker.

Tuesday, August 4.—Alice and I started on mules at 6 A.M. for the Col de Balm. Our guide was so intelligent and pleasant. I found he was Pierre Devouassoud, cousin to Joseph Devouassoud, Fanny's favourite guide in 1869 and 1873. Because Joseph was just sixty, his name was taken off the list of guides; so that though equally competent, he lost many chances. I sent Fanny's little Memoir in French, "Le beau Départ," and her "Invitation Royale."

And now I was really going up the Col de Balm, but not with my former strength when I *always* walked. The air was deliciously cool and clear; we seemed to have everything perfect—sunshine, blue above and beneath, the flowers in their smiles, away, Mont Blanc in whiteness, the dark rocks jutting into the Rhone valley with their pine fringe, and even the far distant Oberland range all visible. Our guide said we could not have had a finer day. But we were not on wings, and poor Alice could not enjoy the jolting mule, the path was so torn up by late heavy rains. When at last I stood on the very summit, Fanny's lines came rushing over me, "Sunshine and silence on the Col de Balm!" etc.

> "Not vain the same fond cry if first I stand
>   Upon the mountain of our God and long,
>   Even in the glory, and with His new song
> Upon my lips, that *you* should come and share
> The bliss of heaven, imperfect still till *all* are there."

I do believe in ministries of nature; so often the passing of butterfly wings, the song of bird, the happy hum in grassland have soothed away some bitter moment. And so, just now when *her name* came with overpowering dearness to my lips, I saw two birds, one chirping feebly at the foot of the cross on the mound above us, the other on the very height, singing such a joyous song, and by and by the poor little chirper joined it, and both flew away *together* singing. Thus may it be!

We returned to Argentière, and after four hours' rest went to Chamouni. Two priests were in our carriage; one was intelligent and pleasant. We had a tussle of course; it is firm arguing when St. Paul is on one side (Romans 5:1). We started at 6 A.M. the next day, in brilliant sunshine, and so saw all in crystal dew and morning brightness, and returned from the Mer de Glace before 10 A.M., and just as we gained the hotel down came soaking rain, through which numbers of tourists came in drenched. Fires were lighted in both salons. We waited till two o'clock, and then dismissed our guide, and resolved to stay for the night. It was so cold; but then we were dry, and I was sympathizing with some fellow-travellers less fortunate, when one of the ladies suddenly said, "You *are* Miss Havergal! When I saw you talking to my friends, and you left to make some enquiry for us, I said to one, 'Do you know who you were speaking to?' I am convinced it is Miss H. from her likeness to the portrait in the Memoir." Of course I assured her how grievous that woodcut is, and was glad to show them a better likeness of my sweet one. The next morning came, the rain was gone, the clear shining come. So with a real "thank God," we rose early, and got back to our very comfortable hotel, the Union. Again in our descent the clear atmosphere revealed all the beauty of Mont Blanc and the attendant Aiguilles. Our farewell look at the Aiguille du Dru was through pines—very towers of strength and beauty, and a light cloud beneath seemed to be the only wing that could ever scale its inaccessible heights.

I was almost sorry to be told that one, and one person only, had ever climbed there—that was the guide who won an English bride in another perilous ascent. Pierre told me they were "très brave," and are still together making grand ascents. Their children, a boy and girl, will have good training. We saw the pretty villa built by the lady. In the afternoon we went to look through the large telescope towards Mont Blanc. I wished specially to look at the Grands-Mulets, because dear Fanny was there in 1873. It was very singular that we should have chosen the instant when a lady and her guides were very near it. The telescope had tracked her all day, and now we saw them all. Alice saw her fall in the snow, then bravely on till we saw her step into the same châlet which F. had rejoiced in gaining. Then the telescope was turned to show us some of the crevasses and marvellous blocks of ice, and also the points of some of the Aiguilles. The gallery of Loppé's pictures was open, and we quite enjoyed seeing sunrises and sunsets else unattainable.

Friday, July 7.—As neither of us had strength for the usual excursions, it seemed wiser to hasten back to Chillon, where we had left our heavy trunks. Again a fine day, and we had a comfortable carriage and pair to take us through the Tête Noire to Martigny. Our farewell looks at Mont Blanc and those shining heights just brought the vivid impression to me, that the next time I saw them, it might be looking down! We lunched at the hotel half-way through the pass, and there I remember F.'s meeting some young girls she had previously sighted, and how eagerly they seized upon her for more help. So she asked me to go quietly on and wait till her work was done. Quite an hour passed till I saw her springing along to the boulders where I waited, and then, however did we toil up to the Forclaz! and then I saw the rough "auberge" where we slept the night, just that Fanny might again talk to the poor woman she remembered three years before. And then our early rapid walk down, down those endless zigzags to the road for the great St. Bernard. Delicious days!

And now I was doing all this in a carriage! At Martigny we rested and dined at Hotel Mont Blanc, partly because I wished another talk with a special of mine, the diligence conductor—such a nice fellow.

It was 9.30 P.M. as we reached our Hotel d'Angleterre at Chillon. *Just* as we entered it down came the thunderstorm which we had watched hurrying over, and the lightning on the lake was very grand. And the next day, Saturday, came drenching showers. In the intervals I ventured by steamer to Vevey to find out Monsieur Caille. It was pleasant to see F. R. H.'s books in his shop. Asking for one, he said, "If you will come in this room you will see *all* Miss Havergal's works, and I am just writing a letter to her sister about the translation of the Memoir." I said, "Your letter need not be finished, I am the sister!" He was very pleased, and I saw the translations of many of F.'s books I did not know of before, as "Jésus et Ses Dons," "Une heure avec Jésus," "Celui à qui nous avons affaire," "Les choses précieuses."[1]

He asked me about reproducing the portrait of F. in the French translation of the Memorials, but I begged him *not*, as it gives a most unpleasant idea to strangers of her sunny self! He told me that Madame Duy was a most clever translator, and it was by his wish she had applied to me about it. I had previously asked Mademoiselle Tabarié to translate it, and believe she has far more spiritual sympathies, but as she declined, and is throwing all her mind into "Kept," I must trust it will be fairly done.

Instead of pushing on, we took a good rest till Monday. Sunday was very rainy, and though dressed for church it was impossible to go. In the afternoon I had a little Bible and

---

[1] "Jésus et Ses Dons" ("Jesus and His Gifts," likely *Royal Bounty*); "Une heure avec Jésus" ("One Hour with Jesus"); "Celui à qui nous avons affaire" ("Him with Whom We Have to Do"); "Les choses précieuses" ("Precious Things," a poem by F. R. H.)

music lesson with the five children of the hotel; it was pretty to hear even the wee ones sing "Seulement pour Toi," and repeat texts (on their fingers, my infant class way).

August 10, Monday.—We left Chillon at 8.20 A.M. for Lausanne, Fribourg, Berne, down Lake Thun to Interlachen, Lauterbrunnen, and up to Pension Wengen. I arranged to take M. Farrington with us, that she might see some of her dear Miss Fanny's favourite haunts. She has been attending a painfully interesting case in the neighbourhood. We stopped at Fribourg to hear the organ that F. so well describes in "Swiss Letters." We were half an hour too soon; a large school of country children came in, and a great many strangers. It was painful to see the irreverent way in which some knelt, and while rapidly moving their lips, stared in our faces. Some again were devout. I had secured a programme, the only one, and so handed it to others. Some English ladies were in the next row before us, and with the programme I handed some of F.'s leaflets and her "Seulement pour Toi." Afterwards they followed us out of the cathedral, and were certain it was M. V. G. H., and gave such an outpour of all the blessing the Memoir and F. R. H.'s books had been to them. One of the ladies had seen her at Mildmay, and said she was so impressed with her bright sunny face. I was afterwards accosted by a young lady saying, "I must speak to you, Miss Havergal; could you spare me one of those leaflets?" And then she tearfully told me how she longed for F. R. H.'s full trust. It was my privilege to encourage her with the thought that God's promises were as rich and as sure for her as for F., and told her the verse that so often comforts me: "God is able to make all grace abound towards you" (2 Corinthians 9:8). And then that Jesus was the same, the very same for her.

But to go back to the organ; yes, it was thrilling and singular in effect. A fugue of Bach's, and then that delicious minuet in Handel's "Sampson" was succeeded by "The Invocation." In this the "vox humana" seems to accompany in most human tones. I never heard anything that so gave me the idea of *ceaseless,* pitying intercession, pleading with depth of love that would not be denied. Ah! one hardly fathoms that Jesus is ever living, is ever interceding. The "Tempest" was very curious, but not quite so delusive as at Lucerne, where I involuntarily said, "It really *is* raining!" and we both preferred the distant chords and voices singing a hymn tune after the lightning and thunder. But both the organ and organist at Fribourg seemed infinitely superior to those at Lucerne.

By 3.20 we were again *en route* for Berne. My *vis-à-vis* was a Spanish gentleman from Malaga, who gave me much interesting information generally, and specially about Pastor Fliedner's evangelical work in Madrid. He was taking his boy to school in Germany, who, though only ten years old, could speak English and French fluently.

Approaching Berne I thought I must treat ourselves to the Bernerhof, so that from the roof we might hope to see a repetition of Fanny's first sunrise on snow mountains. The evening was stormy, but we went down the long arcades to the Bear Garden.

August 11.—Awake before dawn, and with M. Farrington watched all the snow peaks flushing into rose, and thoughts of *that* daybreak came back to us, when we watched for *her,* all shadows fleeing away. Afterwards Alice joined us on that most enjoyable Bernerhof roof.

Berne is a bright clean city, and the older part so quaint and strange. We left in sunshine, but immediately clouds and rain pursued us, and we could only see the dim outlines of the Niessen and Beatenberg from the Lake of Thun. Just as we landed it was fair, and on reaching Interlachen we proceeded in an open carriage to Lauterbrunnen. I told them how in 1876 F. and I with our knapsacks rushed on, and how swiftly she steered me to a little pension at Gsteigwyler. And then we passed the steep path to Eisenfluh, from whence Helga painted her marvellous "Moonlight on the Jungfrau," and where F. and I had quite an adventure in the kind widow's little châlet. It is one of the grandest drives beneath the bastion rocks of the Hunnenfluh, and then to get into real snow peeps, and be actually near the long far-viewed Jungfrau; and the Stauback was in full force from the heavy rain. At the Stauback Hotel we watched a merry party of fourteen school girls mounting on horses for the Wengern Alps and Grindelvald. But life and *death* strangely flash together. Just before reaching Lauterbrunnen, Alice noticed several men and women down by the side of the torrent, and now we were told they had just discovered the bodies of a young man and woman who had accidentally fallen in two nights before, and were drowned.

August 12.—M. Farrington returned to Chillon, and Alice and I proceeded up the steep zigzags for Pension Wengen. Enquiring of my mule-driver for the good old widow Lauener, I thought he said she was dead, and I began rejoicing for her, knowing how she longed even in 1876 for her departure. So I was exceedingly astonished, when reaching the door of her châlet, to see her dear old face smiling a welcome; and the guide told me we must dismount, and not proceed to Pension Wengen as I had arranged, as it was quite full; so I dismissed our porters. Alice meanwhile went in to survey our châlet quarters, and returned with, "Auntie, two ladies have put flowers and fruit for you, and Aunt Fanny's photograph; guess who they are?"

Instantly I guessed M. Fay, though I had not heard of or from her for three months; and so it was! Our devoted Irish friend of 1856! turned up in Switzerland, and her ministering angel, Miss M. L. W. Jackson. And it *was* a pleasant surprise to be cared for in a strange land. And that dear mother Lauener, whom I had been picturing in the spirit-land, came feeling my feet, and brought her own wonderfully warm slippers; and oh, how she spoke of "Fraulein Fannie, my dear, my beloved one!" The rain fell in torrents just as we were safely housed, making us again thankful for another "instant" of God's care over us. We were in rather stuffy quarters, so we were glad to move to the Pension Alpenrose, kept by a daughter of Madame Lauener, a pine-wood habitation, so clean, with most comfortable beds and pillows. The view from our windows much the same as at Pension Wengen, the Jungfrau and its dove-winged Silverhorn, the Breithorn, and other real snow peaks; while behind us were the singularly varied juttings of the Lanberhorn and Männlichen. The walks in all directions reveal endless varieties of Swiss landscape. The society there was extremely agreeable, and we enjoyed (what is rarely found) family worship every evening. In one salon, Pastor Fiesch, from Paris, gave a French *culte*, while in the other saloon a German pastor assembled his countrymen. It was so pleasant, when our French *cantiques* were over, to hear the slower chords of the German chorales from the next room. Soon after our evening meal was the time chosen, and afterwards nearly all united in amusing innocent games.

It is so seldom that any one cares the least about *my* soul, that I was extremely grateful when the good Judge Niebuhr invited me to join an English reading at 5 P.M. on Sunday. He had looked so wise and grave, we were rather terrified at him, while his wife had charmed every one with her sweetness, and withal she was an invalid. I have seldom seen such a lovable creature, and did not wonder at the grave man's tenderness for his "little one." The book he read from was by Alexander Jukes, on "The New Man and the Eternal Life." It is full of deep teaching, which made one feel far behind, and yet it braced the desire to attain also such clear and realized perception of the "Verilys of Jesus Christ." It was pleasant to find dear F.'s name and books well known, and that her Memoir also had been read. Several travellers called on me, just because of my name. Two from Dresden gave me much interesting information regarding the Luisenstift there, where education on the highest Christian basis is given to the aristocratic families, with strict discipline, and very simple fare, such as would rather astonish our English girls. And at Dresden dear F.'s name and teaching are also known. The directress spoke English fluently, while the English teacher, Miss B., turned out to be niece of our clergyman at Leamington. Fanny's life seems to show to many the practical possibilities of holiness. While at the Pension Alpenrose, my friend Miss Jackson received a letter from that most fragrant friend, Miss Nugent, saying, "Every Swiss view that precious Fanny saw has a deep sacredness for me, and a glory touch." Yes, truly it was so.

At the Pension Wengen, Lauener told me he never should forget his first sight of F. R. H. in her straw hat, and in all the bloom of health and vivacity. He took me into his bureau, and there was F.'s photograph side by side with her guide Hans (Lauener's brother). Both are now resting on the height of heights.

Saturday, July 16.—An expedition to the Wengern Alp, the Schideck, and the Lauberhorn. Alice accompanied Miss J. and M. F. I had not strength for it, and so took charge of the blind lady, whose singular desire to *see* Switzerland was gratified by this same ministering M. L. W. J. Truly she is a valiant woman to steer two invalids for fourteen months amid all the difficulties of Swiss railways and roads. About two o'clock I saw a commotion in the porch of the pension, and Lauener waving tablecloths as he discovered through a telescope our travellers had arrived on the heights. I knew it all, and again that panorama of snow peak and glacier passed before me, and dear Fanny's joyous song as she stood there. The good *mère* Lauener said the sweetest things about F.; that "now her robe was whiter than snow, her song changed to the new anthem; yes, she was singing always, always now; that the Lord Christ could not do without her harp and her voice in His choir." She was so delighted with the translation of F.'s "Kept" in German (by Fraulein Mousterburg, published by Spittler of Bâle). What seemed to touch every one was the fact of her singing when dying, and the joy with which she welcomed the news that she could not recover.

After more than a fortnight's stay at Alpenrose, we left by Dr. Cazalis' advice, to take a second course of baths at Aix. Sunday was our last day. The morning service in the salon was well attended. I felt I should never again assemble with them on earth, and our intercourse had been so pleasant, and so many histories and life-stories had been told me by one and another, that I felt quite attached to these foreign friends. There sat good Pastor Fiesch and his pleasant wife; the young doctor (a brilliant musician) at the piano; ladies from Geneva—one in black who had lost her husband, son, and daughter; their miniatures are most lovely. Her voice was marvellously flexible and powerful; indeed, I was struck with this in all the foreign singers. Then there was Alice's special friend Helène, whose beautiful young sister had married the good Count Bernstorff. He only saw her once in Berlin—her first re-union—an introduction sought—all followed *en suite*. Then there was her aunt, from whom we received many kind attentions, and her brother. Then an English friend, Miss Hall, who knew Ceci's friends. A grave German pastor who leads a mission itinerating life, and his most polite little boy, who knew how to take his hat off! Then there was a nice young lady and her *fiancé* from Zurich. Also, a Mademoiselle Pestalozzi—related to the well-known school improver. And above all, there was Judge Niebuhr, and that most gentle wife.

My headache was so bad, I had to keep upstairs most of the day; but that gave me a better opportunity for prayer, with two or three in my room. It was a very rainy Sunday, and we could not tell till we awoke on Monday if it was possible to travel. But again, the sunshine was our index to go forward; and so we left Wengen soon after 6 A.M. I placed cards of adieu and little souvenirs of books on every plate for our friends when they came down to déjeuner. And their kindly response gave me much pleasure, and their names will not easily be forgotten.

Madame Fenz and the good domestiques gave us fervent farewells, especially one Emilie, whose pleasant "à votre service, madame," was quite winning. I was obliged to submit to the ignominy of a *chaise à porteur!* down to Lauterbrunnen. I who walked up and down and to Mürren, eight or nine hours at a time, easily in 1876! By post diligence to Interlachen to see the Giesbach Falls, and slept at Brienz. Off early, Tuesday, August 1, for the Brunig Pass to Lucerne. It was a splendid day, and we were exceptionally comfortable in a carriage and pair, a stranger who sat on the box sharing the expense.

The Brunig Pass! Fanny describes it, and so I will not attempt to do so, but earnestly commend it to all who can pass by that glorious scene of height and depths—precipices, pines, and limes, and all mountain and forest beauty mingled endlessly. The carriage brought us to Alpnach, one of the arms of Lake Lucerne, where the steamer was waiting. It would be better to do Lucerne before the Bernese Oberland, which seems to dwarf these mountains. We found the Schwan Hotel most comfortable and moderate. At 6.30 P.M. we went to hear the great organ, which is far better than the organist, and there was nothing that thrilled you as at Fribourg.

Wednesday, August 2.—The day brightened, and we thoroughly enjoyed the succession of surprises as we steamed into the windings of the lake down to Fluellen.

Thursday, August 3.—By rail through Berne to Geneva and Lausanne. Slept at Hotel Gibbon. In the morning, I was pleased to find F. R. H.'s books in a shop, and was told there was a good demand for them. Instead of taking the train all the way to Aix, I thought it pleasanter to go down the lake to Geneva and change there. Again we had the bluest blue on that lovely lake. Geneva was all *en fête* and gay with flags, and intensely hot; but we had not long to wait, and Alice secured plenty of greengages for our journey. Certainly the fruit is abundant, and at Aix also the market is well supplied. Peaches in great quantities, six for 2d. Enormous and juicy pears for 1d. or 1½d. each. At our *table d' hôte* fruit is plentifully supplied both at the half-past ten breakfast and the 6 P.M. dinner. It was a little disappointing to have to return to Aix, but as our doctor begged us to do so, it seemed right, and the line "Anywhere with Jesus" chimed ever and anon. We arrived at Aix on Friday, August 4, and took rooms at the Hotel d'Angleterre.

August 8.—Feeling a little better, it was pleasant to begin again some walks and talks with my French tracts, leaflets, and New Testaments.

New milk and bread was brought to me by 6 A.M., and then the shadow of the great hills was a protection from the heat of the sun during the early part of my walks. Then the cool morning air, the dew on the flowers, and the utter quiet, were most delightful. My first visit was to the village of Challes by an upward lane, with houses of the most wretched and filthy aspect, and the inevitable dunghills close to the doors. The state of litter and filth is indescribable, and the inner apartments, with few exceptions, were untidy and miserable. No flower-border, no kitchen garden, no trim shelves with plates and glasses, no arm-chair for the father, only the barest forms or stools. It seems hopeless to attempt anything, but the sure seed of God's word *can* root even here.

I had made one friend out of this village—Marie, a little maiden who used to drive her mother's cows at 4 A.M. to some high pastures near our hotel. We had chatted often, and Marie had learnt several verses for me in the Testament I gave her, and while I sat under the chestnut trees Marie would repeat them. She begged me to go and see her home. Some women were washing at the village pump, so I enquired from them where Marie lived. They use neither tubs nor hot water—every woman brings a plank, which she fixes into the wide trough of water flowing from the pipe. On this wood the articles are beaten, rolled, and screwed in a most noisy way. How they come clean I can't understand. When I came up, all the washing ceased, and a few kind words were well received; then other women came out, and I had a good opportunity of speaking of Jesus, the Way, the Truth, the Life, and of the living water He offered, and of the cleansing no soap and water could ever effect, ending with that precious promise, 1 John 1:7.

Then I found my little friend Marie Duisit. Her mother welcomed me, but I never saw such a yard of litter and filth. Plenty of hay, two cows, pigs and chickens. The house had been two hundred years in their family, as the blackened stone testified; but to sit down inside was simply impossible; and though the room was large, it was very dark. So we sat on logs, and two or three neighbours came near while I began to read from a Testament, but handed it to Marie, thinking the mother would be gratified, and then I could ask Marie to read the same again. Saying good-bye, one of the women asked me for tracts. I don't know why, but I said, "Oh, I should like to come to your house, may I?" It was curious that out of two dozen women, I was led to ask this of the only one who had a sick daughter. The woman steered me past rather unsafe treadings in that dunghill maze (I tried to forget Dr. Cazalis and what he would say), and went into her house, which was of a more tidy appearance than the last. She opened the door into the bedroom, darkened with the clothes of the whole family hanging thickly all round the walls; and as the four-post bed hangings were of endless garments, I could not at first see that there were three beds, and on one a pale-faced girl, Jeannette Noirey.

Though extremely astonished (for there are no lady or district visitors in France), she was pleasant and chatty, and soon told me all her sad history. Both knees were swollen and powerless from rheumatic stiffness, and for three years she had been laid up, with only a rare limping on two crutches into the outer world. It was nice to kneel down and tell Jesus for her all her need, and then I asked her to repeat with me a few simple words to Jesus. Then I sang (a very free translation!) Fanny's hymn, "I am trusting Thee, Lord Jesus."

I was glad I had some peaches to give her, and Mrs. Grimké's pretty text cards. Jeannette entreated me to come again, and I did so several times, and gave her knitting materials; and to my joy she accepted a French Bible as my farewell gift. Leaving Jeannette, I went up the village, leaving tracts at or under every door, till my bag was empty. The next morning I took a longer walk, over a bridge, with mountains on either side. I thought I saw a short cut through a vineyard, and so took it, spying some houses in the distance. The path in the vineyard came to an end; just then a woman weeding the vines appeared, and she directed me up a stony bit, which led again into the road. She came with me a little way, and then pointing to some large iron gates said, "My old mother lives there." I certainly should not have ventured through what seemed a private drive; it led to an ancient stone farm-house, with massive doors, and all the appearance of warlike defence, now in utter untidiness. Jessamine and Virginian creepers were twining long wreaths round the old windows and doorway. Beds were airing as usual, either thrown half-way out of the window or on the farm blocks. A nice old woman bade me sit down. It was all news to her that there was "nothing, nothing to pay," no merit of ours wanted when Jesus had paid all our debt. Luke 7 was read. Then she told me to go in the garden. Evidently once dainty feet had trod the lawns and long terraces with thickly trellised vines. The view was extensive; below, the church and village of St. Jeoire (that seemed a map for my next day's work); far away, the Dent du Nivoli and the Grande Chartreuse. I sat down and roughly sketched the outline. The old woman brought me some milk, and told me that Mademoiselle who owned this farm was out, and that herself and her sons and daughters also lived here. I enquired about this Mdlle., and left word that the English lady was much obliged for seeing the garden, and that I hoped for the pleasure of seeing her next time. The next and the next time came, but Mdlle. was always engaged, so I could only leave two or three books. But though Mdlle.'s door was shut, another wider one opened in the large old courtyard, where the springing water coming through a very ancient stone structure, with a wide circular trough, was a *pro bono* washing resort.

I reached it before seven one morning, at the very "instant" needful for a talk. Some eight or nine women had just finished their breakfast, seated on clumps of wood and pine planks, and smilingly asked me to rest myself. It is so easy to ask a few kind questions, and to admire their beautiful country and the vines; and then the running water, so free, so cleansing, suggests lessons of life. I asked leave to read some of the Lord Jesus' own words, first telling them I was going to shut my eyes and ask the Holy Spirit to teach us, and would they not do the same? This morning the words came so easily, for had I not asked my King to open my lips for Him? But as I met the eyes of those quiet listeners, a rushing tenderness for their precious souls to find this Saviour *now* came over me. They saw my tears for them, and were deeply moved. "Ah! the poor lady does care for us."

Most willingly did they all kneel down with me on the pine planks. Afterwards I spoke to those that seemed impressed, and a week after found out one or two in their own homes.

After this happy time, I went on to a few houses, but no one was at home. I had just one book left, the pretty French book for children called "Le beau Départ de F. R. Havergal," giving the account of her bright going home. I pressed on and came to a large schoolhouse; all was silent, but looking up I saw a little girl's face at an upper window. Wishing to get at her, I enquired "where the road led to?" whereupon she ran downstairs and invited me into the empty schoolroom. Her father was the teacher, but it was a holiday. Taking out my little book, I told her it was about my own dear sister, and as her name was Françoise too, she looked interested. This led on to the story of "My own text," and I found the words in my French Testament, and asked Françoise to read them and to the end of the chapter. She was a most intelligent child; it was only a passing talk; but as she repeated over and over for me two or three passages of the Word that will never pass away, I thanked God that I saw her little head at the window the "instant" of my passing by.

August 16.—To the village of Challes again. Saw Marie and Jeannette. Passed by the boys' school, where several were assembling. I knew it was useless to give my books there, and so went on, praying that some might be disposed to follow me. Soon one and another came round me while I was speaking to some women and giving tracts. One woman said, "This is a good lady; I have seen her before, and she only tells about Jesus Christ." The women cleared off, and about thirty or forty boys gathered. I sat against a wall and asked them to make a *demi-lune* around. The idea of a half-moon took, and soon I had a three-deep circle. I spoke of the Lord Jesus as looking down *then,* loving them, calling them, telling them He was the way to the bright city up in the blue sky above us, and how He wanted little soldiers; but the great devil wanted them too; and how the good Captain had fought the devil for us and got the victory, and so the way was quite clear to come over to Jesus Christ's side. And the first thing the Captain did was to wash His little soldiers white in the blood He shed long ago when He got the victory. And then I got two texts learnt in chorus, and then came my bag of books, and Mr. Spier's French leaflets were all eagerly caught by the little fellows and carefully put in their book satchels. All this just in the very "instant" before the school bell rang. Later or earlier I should have lost this delightful seed-sowing. Often I met people going to market who gladly took books. Perpetually did my prayer for guidance get answered, some awkward dirty lane leading to some lonely house where God's message was wanted. One poor lame creature was actually with her naked feet sitting close to a dunghill, her yellow sickly face telling its tale of suffering. My heart seemed drawn to her, and even the sympathy of my poor words seemed a little cheer. I should not write all this, but I do want to encourage travellers abroad to go out into the holes and corners around. And it is so sweet to keep asking the Master to direct, and all comes so much easier when we do so. I often got catechized as to our Protestant religion, and always good-temperedly gave them an outline. Many were astonished at our belief in Father, Son, and Spirit, and that we were baptized. I *never* shrank from plainly showing them the truths of vital difference to their errors. It is well to learn off such verses as prove Christ is the only Mediator and Intercessor, that He never told us to ask in the name of Mary. (John 14:6, 13, 14.) That He said, "It is finished," so we have "nothing to pay." Also, I found our creed in French very useful to repeat. It is well always to speak *kindly* of the Virgin Mary—that she is happy in heaven because she trusted in God *her Saviour;* that she would not have called Jesus *her* Saviour if she had no sins to be saved from. So, being a sinner, I can't *trust* in her, that I hope to see her in heaven by and by, but that she never did *do* anything for me, and that Jesus *did,* and so all the glory is His, and His only.

Sunday, August 20.—On two previous Sundays Alice and I had early church in some shady corner, as no service of any kind was going on; and certainly we Church of England people can hold communion better by having a Liturgy, and value Psalms and Lessons, which seems a sweet link when in a strange and godless land. But this Sunday I told Alice we would have church in the evening. The village of St. Jeoire was to be my Sunday service. I was off at 6.30 A.M.—my way a very straight road, but with glorious mountains always in sight. I had never been there—a long straight village, houses on either side. I saw the first door open, and an old woman, who looked friendly, so I asked to rest, and told her where I had walked from, and why I came. She could not read at all, but gladly listened and learnt off two texts, a neighbour joining. Then she said, "Don't you go to the next door, but to the next after; they are very pious there." It was the post-officer's home, and four or five charming maidens were just ready for mass. The mother looked at my books, and was the first and only one who said she did not care for them. I made no way there at all. The next door was the village shop, all open, and people buying. The woman was superior, asked me to sit down, and soon guessing I was a Protestant, catechized me well on doctrine and practice. God's written Word is the best sword. She accepted two or three books, and I left. The street seemed turning out as the bell for mass was tolling, so I thought it wiser to turn aside up a lane and let the people pass on. Such neat-looking girls, how I yearned over them! Well, they would all find a F. R. H. leaflet or portion or text card under their doors on return! Up the lane, large stone farmhouses, and there I left tracts; then guided, I came to a nest of houses, more cleanly; and of the few not at mass was one of my friends at the old fountain. She was so glad to see me, and in a moment gave me some milk from the pail just brought in. I had a long rest there, and then we asked a few to join us in the farmyard, men, boys, and women, and I had a good time. Then I went to other houses, returning to St. Jeoire down that lovely lane. I put leaflets here and there, knowing quite a stream of people would be returning from mass from far-off villages. Passing the door I was told not to go in, I thought I would, and found almost the best opening of all. The Word was *heard* gladly, and my last New Testament received, and also I directed some leaflets for the woman's daughter in Paris. Looking in again on the old woman I first visited, I found her on her knees; she had not forgotten the prayer I had taught her, or the promise. I arranged with a girl to go and read to her, who was singularly open and most anxious to hear further. I had met her in the week, and her very sweet little sister Georgine, minding their cows one evening, and told them I was so sorry I had no leaflets. The next evening we went that way again, and far away they saw us, and scampered to meet us—three or four such dear children. We noticed their very pretty curtsey, so different to the English bob. Certainly the very poorest have the *politesse* we greatly lack. I had told Marie I would come and see her at St. Jeoire on Sunday morning, and so she had posted her sisters along the road to conduct me. Marie was preparing to be a schoolmistress two years before, when she was seized with typhoid fever, and was most dangerously ill, and she was still delicate. I am sure there had been the work of grace, with such real love for Jesus, and apparently trust, and when speaking of God's Spirit Marie said, "I *did* receive the Holy Ghost when I was confirmed." Her face was so peaceful, and somehow I felt that secret intimate fellowship of spirit with her when kneeling before the Lord. I visited her again. We had frank discussion on our points of difference; but Marie spoke very differently to many, and I believe to her Jesus Christ was first and last. She accepted all the books I could find, and gave me her address. She was *so* eager for books, and promised to give all she could spare in the village. So this is a future opening for posting books and leaflets.

As I rapidly returned to the hotel for eleven o'clock breakfast, I could not but rejoice in the strength given me for that early morning's work, and commended each and all to the God of all grace, that His Word might not return unto Him void.

I could fill pages with interesting remembrances of the many I talked with at our *table d'hôte*. It always answers to be polite and easy, and a little sympathy often unlocked many a confidence, and led the way to speak of Jesus, my King. Then it was a little wedge to offer a parting souvenir of F. R. H.'s "Royal Invitation" in French. One young priest looked fearfully ill; his chiselled features and superior bearing were attractive. Another young priest and two most gentlemanly youths were with him. They did not mix with the others, and I never got beyond a word or two at table, till one day, when I had not been well enough to appear, and was sitting in the garden, they all passed (bowing of course); but the priest stopped, and most courteously enquired for my health. And then I said, "Now let me ask how you are? I have not quite courage to talk at table to those far off, but I have often sympathized for your ill-health." Yes, he was ill; it was the will of God. He had travelled much—twice to the Holy Land, Egypt, etc. Then again he earnestly hoped my health would improve. I said, "It may for a little time, but I know, Mons. L'Abbé, my days cannot be long, nor do I wish them to be; to depart and be with Christ is far better. It is so glorious to have that blessed hope." He said, "Very true; but might it not be a little selfish to wish to depart, so long as we could serve God or be of use, as I see you are, to your niece, and as I am trying to be to my dear nephews here."

This led to further pleasant talk. One day when I went in the salon I found him with F. R. H.'s books (which I always put on the table), and the younger priest said he knew a little English, and had been trying to read the Memoir. They had both read the few proof pages of Madame Duy's translation. On leaving Challes both priests accepted F. R. H.'s "Royal Invitation" and the smaller books from Caille's. Another well-to-do couple (my neighbours at table) grew from unreachable coldness to most warm and friendly intercourse, ending in the lady's freely talking to me, and coming to my room for prayer. She told me she had a pious mother who was praying and weeping for her; but for herself this world was enough. It was singular how she seemed to prize F.'s books. Another, a young mother, was in deep mourning for her only child, and alas! her one thought was, "God is so cruel, so hard; He should not have given her to me only to take away!" It is most difficult to talk wisely; the clue in such cases is the perfect felicity and happiness of the little ones in heaven, and let us take heed to get there too. I do believe in nurseries in heaven, and that every tiny vessel will perfectly reflect the Saviour's likeness. And I could envy them in *one* thing—they never sinned and grieved the Saviour. "Forgiven much" may bring the "much love;" but shall we ever forget wounding and grieving Jesus?

I must not forget an incident when returning from a visit to our doctor. It is about ten miles by rail from Aix to Chambéry. The train was very full, and at the last moment we were put in a first class. A pleasant lady looked extremely wearied and dusted, and she told me that through mistake at that ever-provoking Dijon they had been pushed into a slow train, and so had been twelve hours longer *en route*—forty-eight hours without rest—and her husband, an Italian, was returning from England quite ill. She had lived thirty years in Italy, and as Florence is extremely hot in the summer, they had tried our English temperature, but the constant rain and damp had only increased his illness. Just a word or two about the "right way and the Guide who never takes us a wrong turn" was pleasantly received. I had none of F.'s leaflets, but offered another. The lady opened her travelling handbag, saying, "That is the book that daily teaches me." The "Memorials of F. R. H."! I could not help saying, "My darling sister!" "Is it possible? What a privilege to meet you! I do thank you for telling me." Then she whispered to me that her lady companion opposite was a Socinian. Would I give any detail about F. that would be useful to her? Rapidly I told of F.'s rejoicing in Christ as her King; that her joy in life was the clear, deep, conscious need of a divine atonement; that it needed the blood of God's own Son to atone for sin against God, and the infinite ransom was secured by the precious blood. I told of F.'s joyful security; that her dying passport was the blood (1 John 1:7); how she whispered, "Bring my own text," and said, "Jesus covers all." And then that marvellous meeting with her King! The glad welcome in face and eye and failing speech—to me more like the soft cooing of a dove. "Oh, He is come—come! My King, *you are come!*" And then her song to Him—we only caught the first note—"He!" No more for us; but with Him she sings for evermore and evermore. The train stopped at Chambéry. Madame Martini handed me her card, and I promised to post some of F.'s books.

By Dr. Cazalis' advice we again returned to Aix, that Alice might try another course of baths. It was difficult to get rooms. We heard of visitors even sleeping in the omnibus! and of many going to Geneva, failing accommodation. We were thankful to get rooms at the Maison Chabert, near the baths. It was lively at our *table d'hôte*, forty-five filling two tables. We found our places set near some very pleasant ladies. Madame Testenoire, with a most benevolent smile, and Madame Fontaine de Bonnerive, with her daughter Magdaleine, was a perfect fountain of vivacity. I never listened to such sparkling descriptions of places and things. Also her lively actions—fingers, hands, arms in endless motion emphasizing her words. She was certainly clever, and one evening she most bravely parried the infidel ideas of her next neighbour. Poor man, how I did pity him! gambling every night and day. Once I sat next him, and he asked if I never took wine. I told him why—that I denied myself for the benefit of a large class of youths. This led on to his saying he believed only in a Deity. I found our conversation was attracting notice, but words seemed given me of what I found Jesus to be to me. I wrote him a letter before leaving, and gave him F.'s "Royal Invitation" in French.

A new arrival, a very delicate young man of most *distingué* appearance, sat in silence, because the stiff old militaire from Paris in the next chair did not bow or speak to him. So we drifted into smiles and bows and a few words. I said to Alice, "I believe he is of the best family of any." Poor fellow, how he gambled; and then he disappeared for three days, being too ill to get up. It stirred my compassion. Who cared for his soul? His mother was dead, and so no loving words from her could reach him. It was not till the last night or two I had an opportunity. After dinner, all stood about in the ancient courtyard chatting, and so in the twilight I got courage for a few words. He took it so gratefully. "Ah, madame, I see you pray that sinners may be converted." So that was the wedge that helped me to write him a farewell letter, with a Testament and F.'s books. Shall I ever see Monsieur le Viscomte d'Epiollaz again?

Trying to get morocco Bibles for some of my friends led to the discovery that Bibles were not to be bought in Aix. All the booksellers informed me, "Bibles are not read in Aix; you will only find one at the priest's. But we have one copy in four large volumes, for 200 francs!" Happily at the Scotch Presbyterian Asile Evangélique they kept the cheap Testaments, and of these I gave largely.

The fruit and poultry market was a grand place to "sow seed." It was held under the lime trees from 4 A.M. till 7.30. Of course I did not throw them away, but used to pray for some opening. By giving a tract or a leaflet to one peasant, others would gather round me and listen to the story of Jesus, the only Saviour and Mediator. Then hands would stretch out for my supply. The last morning I had to replenish my basket. One dear woman was most importunate for a Bible, and waited patiently while I went for one.

One day we went on the Lake Bourget in the steamer, which daily gives excursions for three or four hours. We landed at the Monastery of the Haute Coombe, where there is a most splendid chapel, with the monuments of the Kings and Dukes of Savoie. We followed the stream of sightseers, and were received by two Jesuit monks in brown serge costume. One party went to the left, one to the right. Such a series of grilles and bats and bolts—every tomb locked in! Really I felt nervous—one seemed so doubly locked in. Brother Frank would have been in raptures with the exquisite carvings and tracery; but I kept seeing *one* weary face—the monk I met in the carriage two months before when going to Les Innocents.

I said to Alice, "Do you mind my leaving you? I must find out that monk we met." Alice laughed, but I went up to our Jesuit guide and said I much wished to see one of their order who spoke English—was very tall and ill. "Ah, c'est Mons. le Supérieur." Go and knock, indicating my route. I felt rather audacious, but proceeded. My knock brought a porter, and then a whisper travelled on from one to another, "Une dame Anglaise désire voir Mons. le Supérieur." I was conducted through stone corridors, and a door was unlocked into the reception-room, and I was locked in. (I never do like locks.) It was barely furnished, but some paintings on the walls of saintly faces set me musing. The door opened, and a most stately form, arrayed in white flannel robes with blue silk facings and cordons, appeared. Yes, it was the weary face. I said, "Do you remember me in the carriage going to Les Innocents?" "Oh yes, very well." "You looked so ill and weary, I came to enquire after your health." He was very gracious—seemed touched that any one should care for him. He told me he was so ill, and that he had fasted that day. "Oh," I said, "why fast? why not rejoice in the liberty wherewith Christ makes His people free? If He has done the work, no need for our additions. Oh now, do get some good beef tea!" "Ah, yes; but we have a bad cook, and we get only *bouillon* and bad bread, but the fruit is good." I cannot remember all that passed. He told me that he had three converts from London staying with him for instruction. Of course I had no intention of being instructed. It helped me much to tell him of Fanny's happy faith in life and death, and that led to sending him her Memoir and other of her books, which I have no doubt he will read.

[*Note.*—With this very characteristic and amusing episode M. V. G. H.'s account of her tour in Switzerland and Savoie abruptly ends.]

DIARIES

FROM 1883 TO 1887.

January 1, 1883.—"Jesus Christ, the same yesterday, to-day, and for ever." "Able to subdue all things unto Himself"—just what I need. Left my sister M. after a visit of a month at Oakhampton. A page shut. Lord, open every life-page for me. Specially may I live to edit Fanny's letters for Thy glory.

January 2.—Whence came disorder? How one gets topsy-turvy; in vain I try to keep all in order. So, spiritually, yet I find gravitation to Christ as my centre.

Sunday, January 7.—I awoke with Psalm 84:7, "Every one of them in Zion appeareth before God," so none will be left behind. Rather depressed, and restrained in prayer. Took a class and felt helped. In the evening, the thought, "I have Jesus," gladdened me.

January 9.—Fine, and had a good time at Wyre Hill, and at G. S.'s evening meeting. He gave a very sweet address on Acts 4:12, and the sevenfold names of Christ.

Sunday, February 18.—Helped with Ellen's boys at ten, and class of girls at three. I did long for even one soul to Christ. Messages from Thee is my cry. I got one for myself in speaking of John 5:24, "hath everlasting life,"—a positive assurance.

February 19.—"The God of my mercies shall prevent me." What comforts I have even in my bedroom! Very restless at night, and nerves upset. The feverishness is so trying, but I tell Jesus all as I never did before, and He whispers comfort.

April 12.—Ella B. told me how Fanny's "Memorials" brought her to Jesus; it seemed a harvest-sheaf after all my tears. Felt very ill, but wrote the preface to "Lilies and Shamrocks." My pulse and heart beat so fast; is it my journey speeding nigh the last step? Such a sweet quiet in Jesus came over me, and I fell asleep at His feet.

June 3.—At Caswell Bay. Darling Fanny's birthday into glory. She is present with her Lord, and her words come to me—

"Praising Him too, waiting for you."

Went on the cliffs in the evening alone; I often sing and praise the Lamb there; I did long to hear His still small voice.

June 18.—Hon. C. H. and wife from Halifax, Nova Scotia, came to see Fanny's rooms. He said all her books are so read and blessed in Canada.

June 23.—Read of dear A. S.'s privations in Africa so nobly borne; let me pray more for all missionary workers. Felt much humbled, but the worse I am the more wonder of His grace to come down to my depths. So pleased the lodgers like my taking family prayers.

July 21.—Left The Mumbles for Llandilo; found "upper room" lodgings ready—did thank God for all mercies.

Sunday, July 22.—Distressed to find the old heart wanderings even in God's holy temple, and after all His purging; quite ashamed.

July 24.—J. E. R.'s wedding day. May all the bridegroom emblems be realized—

"And seat us where Thy marriage song
Shall never, never cease."

August 1.—Made a trip to Llandovery; seemed sent to comfort a poor woman. Lovely weather; next day sat in the park, and talked of the past to M. F.

August 27.—Left Llandilo, and arrived at Avon Villa, Keynsham; next day cousin S. H. arrived—a noble enduring Christian, and the day after sister Miriam came, to my delight and comfort.

Sunday, September 2.—Did rejoice that dear W. preached Christ fully; lovely sermon from Song of Solomon 2:14.

September 5.—Felt cross about callers, but shook it off, and some seemed very sweet Christians.

September 7.—Had a first-rate time at Chewton School with the dear children on the miracle of the leper. I walked marvellously; felt my old talent of legs, but afterwards very poorly.

September 16.—Rev. James Hannington, missionary from Central Africa, preached twice, and gave a graphic account of his sufferings. He told me about assisting at niece Amy's marriage at Zanzibar. At 3 P.M. addressed M. E.'s cottage gathering of twenty-two on "Nothing to pay" (Luke 7:42). It came with new force to myself; and verse 44, "He turned to the woman." Ah, He never turns away. What will it be when He first turns His radiant face on me! On Monday addressed the almshouse women.

Sunday, September 23.—Took Miss E.'s servants' class; spoke on "Walk in the light," and "Walk with me in white."

September 23.—Left Keynsham with sister M. for 35 Upper Belgrave Road, Clifton; very poorly, did not sleep.

October 2.—To Clifton Conference with M. Rev. T. Greaves—a grand address on the Sonship of Christ, and met Pastor Don Luiz Rodriguez, and his sweet English wife.

October 8.—Moved to nice clean rooms at Cote Bank, Westbury-on-Trym, where sister Ellen came to see us.

October 30.—The famous Isabella Bird, now Mrs. Bishop, called, and lent us her last book, "The Golden Chersonese."

November 1.—We spent a pleasant afternoon at Hillside, the lovely home of the widow of brother Frank's godfather, H. V. T.

November 3.—Dear sister M. left me for Boddington Manor, and then to go abroad with J. and A. Had a cry till L. brought a kitten up, which comforted me!

November 15.—Did not think I should ever live to see this date. A sweet message at church from Rev. T. Greaves, "Be still" (Psalm 46.). Just suitable for my restless, unquiet spirit. Lord Jesus, tired of self and all, I come and lay me down on Thy bosom, believing I shall be more than conqueror through "Him that loved us."

December 3.—Left Westbury, and arrived at Winterdyne.

December 21.—Addressed the Bewdley Grammar School boys on 1 John 4:14, and prayed that one might be a missionary. Told them of E. Clay's work in the Punjaub, and gave C. M. S. publications to all.

Christmas Day.—Awoke at midnight, and had comforting thoughts about "Emmanuel," that He was man to understand my loneliness, and God to fill the gaps and void. Sometimes a sleepless night is God's special lesson-time; heard all the hours strike till four. The point brought vividly to my mind was my life failure in not referring all little details to God's will. Lord, what wilt Thou have me to do? It is a comfort to me to remember, "It is God that worketh in you to will and to do."

December 29.—Damp and misty. Smallpox is on the increase; it is the only thing I have dreaded all my life. Thank God I am feeling quieter and not hurrying so. He is teaching me.

Sunday, December 30.—Felt concerned about Mrs. W.'s soul, and P.M. started off to see her. O Holy Spirit, show her sin and self! Met several dear "nowhere" lads; spoke to them. Had prayer at B.'s. Now, for myself, I just go to the Fountain with all my Sabbath sins, Sabbath self-pleasing, etc. Lord Jesus, wash me; and forgive all even unto sixty-one years, that life ended I may see Thee and begin the life that has no end.

January 1, 1884.—"Emmanuel" was much in my mind for the new year. That name was revealed, not imagined—"with us," who are so straying from Him.

January 14.—Have been ill since January 2, when I went to W.'s, and foolishly put carriage windows open, and so got a chill.

January 26.—Prayed much for guidance in giving money; have helped some laid on my mind. Lord, every farthing is Thine, teach me how to give. Heard dear M. is ill at Mentone, but know she is in Thy dear hand.

February 24.—Have had much writing lately, and consequently many restless nights. When praying this evening, the promise came so forcibly, "Ye shall ask what ye will, and it shall be done unto you;" so I prayed for P. W., that the power of the Spirit might come on him while preaching.

Sunday, March 2.—Took Ellen's class very badly,—taught them more about Satan than Christ.

March 3.—Made a mistake, telegrammed without prayer, and so regretted it after. Not happy; of course Jesus can't bless what I do without Him.

Sunday, March 9.—Took M. C.'s class. Spoke on Matthew 25. The muffled peal rang out for J. J. I could hardly speak for crying, but entreated the girls to accept the spotless robe, and to see to their lamps. His last words were, "Blessed Saviour."

April 3 to 5.—Went to Birmingham; saw some King's daughters; one ill for twenty years said, "The arms that uphold the universe are stretched out for me, and are underneath me." I so enjoyed the intense delight of pleasing Jesus in these visits, but was very poorly afterwards. Oh, may I live to print dear Fanny's letters!

June 12.—Left Bewdley; saw W. and E. at Oxford. Oh, may they be ambassadors for Christ, and not for the Church only! Arrived at the Old Rectory, Cavendish.

June 19.—Dear Nurse C. left; she has so kindly ministered to me; Lord say, "Inasmuch," etc.

[Note.—The interval between this date and the next is described in the Autobiography.]

Sunday, December 14, 1884.—This is dear Fanny's birthday. Felt her loss so keenly; well, but her gain is great. I most regret not oftener seeking her help for my own soul, and not giving her more pleasures, as I could have done. Took F.'s class P.M., and was much helped. John 13:8 came to me for myself; Jesus came to Peter, so He comes near to wash me. Have been very restless and sleepless of late.

Christmas Day.—Sunshine all day. Had my church with Miss W. and poor R. Went in to G. P.; his face was shining more than mine. I said, "G., have you a bit of comfort for *me?*" (for I was feeling low and as if I had to be always talking and comforting others). In three words quite a thrill of joy came to me through this poor fellow saying, "Jesus loves you." Truly it unveiled the heart of Jesus to me. It is now evening, and I have been looking in Fanny's own Bible, at her Christmas marks. Now she sees the King, not in swaddling clothes, but in His full beauty. I daresay she has heard the same song that Gabriel sang.

December 31.—Awoke anxious to write letters and give cheques more entirely all for Jesus. Went to see sick people for G. S. Lord Jesus, Thou art ever the same; be the same to me and all my dear ones as to F. Yes, I will trust and rejoice in Thee and in the fountain opened for all my sins of 1884.

Sunday, January 4, 1885.—What shall I render unto the Lord for all His benefits? Bless the Lord, O my soul, and forget them not. Spared, chastened, strengthened, less restless sleeplessness, more certain trust, more desire to please my dear Lord in all little details. Went to Ribbesford Church and to the Lord's table with F. and Ella B. Song of Solomon 2:4.

January 28.—Saw Dr. M. yesterday, who says there is no return of the disease. Left Birmingham and arrived at Willie's home, Lynchmere, close to Hertford. Was helped to witness for Jesus in the train.

January 30.—Took some Swiss milk from a faulty tin; very sick and ill, half-poisoned. Dr. S. said if I had not had sense and drank three quarts hot water it would have been serious. Felt strangely happy in cramp and burning tongue. What if the wings were coming!

February 3.—Dear sister M. arrived from Montreux to stay with me while W. and B. are at Pau.

February 26.—Went too long a walk by Bengeo with M., who was taken ill after it. P.S.—She continued ill nearly two months.

May 1.—M. has helped me to correct the proofs of Fanny's "Letters." So thankful they are done, for I fear my disease is returning. It must be " the footsteps of the end." Jesus is the end, so for myself I would rather go.

May 8.—I am making a little tour; said good-bye to Amy and Archie and little Havergal at Home Lodge.

May 25.—At Caswell Bay. A trying day taking down all Fanny's pretty things; but it is clearly right, and I prayed to give away what I ought.

May 30.—Finally left dear F.'s "nest" for Llandilo. The last minute gave thanks on her piano, the Gloria, to our father's chant "Worcester;" then F.'s last song, "Jesus, I will trust Thee," to her tune "Hermas," and my whole self did trust.

Llandilo, Sunday, May 31.—Took the first class boys at the church Sunday-school; such dear lads. One said, "We remember your *texes* two years ago." In the evening I took cripple J. a hair-cushion I had made for him.

June 1.—Left 2 Bank Terrace, Llandilo, for Birmingham.

June 2.—Saw Dr. M. He confirmed my opinion that cancer was re-forming; but I felt quite happy and fearless. On to Winterdyne. On no account shall I tell my sisters, to distress them. Nieces so kind and ministering. Tired out and had a sleepless night.

June 6.—"Set thine house in order." Up at five sorting old letters; such heaps of thankful ones, but best to burn them.

June 11.—Returned to M. at Hertford.

July 1.—Went with M. to Claxton-on-Sea for a fortnight at Lansdowne House; from thence for a night to the Old Rectory, Cavendish.

July 15.—Left Claxton for Hertford. Too late for the train, but M. was in and went on, and I was led to visit a lonely house while waiting, and found a dear fellow-sufferer, one of Christ's hidden ones. With tears she said, "I shall kneel down and thank God for your visit."

July 23.—The first anniversary of my operation, when the Lord so unspeakably upheld me. I felt very ill, but told Him I was willing to suffer again. One's deep sense of sin makes His love seem so wonderful. I confessed all to Jesus my Saviour, and do utterly trust Him, so human, yet so divine. Oh that I could give Him joy! Oh that He will work in me that which is well-pleasing in His sight!

July 27.—Went for the last time to the dear girls at Christ's Hospital. Gave them one word to think of, "Kept," also Christ's prayer.

July 28.—Took the Y. W. C. A. meeting. Spoke on the type of the Brazen Serpent; was much helped, there was the hush of His presence; still I got no personal interviews afterwards.

Mrs. Abel S. called—a sweet sealed Christian. So very poorly, was quite unable to go to church on Sunday.

August 7.—Sister M. and I left Hertford; she for Boddington Manor, I to Birmingham.

August 8.—Awoke so ill I could hardly get up. Went to Dr. M. and asked him how long I might live. He said a year, or two perhaps. This was a relief for M.'s sake, and to find I could return to her. Went to Winterdyne.

August 21.—Left Winterdyne. Shall I ever see it again, and all those kind ones? Willie and his sweet B. and Alfred had been there. A remark of his about God's clasping my hand was very sweet. May he be much used by the Master, and his ministry come with power. A cloud came over me; can it be possible, after all, the Lord Jesus won't own me? To die mistaken—how awful! Met Elizabeth Clay, and came on to West Malvern (Downes).

August 28.—Dear Frank came yesterday. Drove with E. C. to Malvern Wells, where I remember being when a child, and remember the lovely views and walks. My early undutifulness presses upon me.

August 30, Sunday.—E.'s conversation so heavenly and interesting about her Indian work, I felt ashamed of my deadness.

September 1.—Left Malvern to live at Sidmouth with Miriam. We had engaged No. 4 Fortfield Terrace. Dear Willie met us.

September 2.—A storm and gale. Very wretched all day. May I be purified from so much dross. What should I do without 1 John 1:7?

September 3.—A lovely day. Some comfortable teachings. A little bit of work has turned up.

September 6, Sunday.—Went with M. to All Saints. Most thankful for Reformation service and Gospel sermon on

Galatians 5:18, from Rev. R. B. M.

September 22.—Drove with Ellen and Giles, and walked up the West Cliff. I had been thinking in the night of "Him that overcometh," etc., and so had they!

September 25.—Walked up the East Cliff; saw the seagulls flying. How soon shall I be flying? Certainly F. has the best of it up there! Felt great longing to be always obeying Jesus.

October 11, Sunday.—Went to see B. B. as often. Evening text was Psalm 27:4—a sweet time. Walked home with Lady R., and enjoyed the fellowship of saints.

October 20.—Walked for two hours on Mutter Moor. Dear E. Clay left England; felt it a great wrench.

October 22.—Walked two and a half hours up Peak Hill and over moorlands; I do so enjoy utter stillness and no presence but the Lord's.

October 25. —To church with M. and John H. C.; a powerful sermon on "We would see Jesus," and the closing hymn began with the same words. Such a happy hush in the night though feeling ill; I had direct comfort leaving all to Jesus, and went to sleep like resting on His hand.

November 10.—Went to Birmingham to see Dr. Malins, and on to Winterdyne.

November 17.—Walked with Mr. and Mrs. Storrs, and rejoiced in my ability to race; quick walking is such a delight to me; a bright hoar-frost.

November 19.—Went with F. H. and W. B. to plant roses and daisies round Fanny's grave. I always picture that vault as her robing room for glory, and that I may be the first to see her rise in His beauty and dear papa. (There is room for me in the grave.)

November 25.—Left dear Winterdyne; slept at the Old Manor House, Keynsham, to see my new great-niece, C. H. S., and returned to Sidmouth on the 28th.

November 29, Sunday.—I rested A.M., but went to church P.M. Did not enjoy the pre-millenarian teaching; it does not seem to help one in the knowledge of Christ. To die is much surer for me anyway, and quite as happy.

December 3.—I gave an address to the Zenana Working Party on A. D. Shaw and wife's missionary work in East Africa. I was so ill, I was scarcely able to go, and left early, but quite enjoyed speaking for our Missionary King. I have so enjoyed the glorious sunsets lately.

December 20.—Leonard B.'s ordination day; I prayed the Lord Jesus to really call and ordain him to Himself, to clothe him with His righteousness, anoint him sevenfold.

December 31.—Awoke early. That verse, "Thou art mine," was so comforting all day in very trying sickness. I feel such a strong desire really to please my King in all I do, and write, and give. These are the last words I am ever likely to write on a December 31, so my last look is and will be to Jesus, and my last hope is in Him; His blood cleanses from all sin. I know I am in His dear hand, and hope God will keep me brave and bright, so that I may not distress my dear sisters. Lord, I thank Thee for all the lessons Thou hast taught me in this illness.

January 7, 1886.—Splendid frosty day. The sunset and afterglow quite Swiss. From three to five at Zenana drawing-room meeting. I spoke on our Lord's question, "What wilt thou that I shall do unto thee?"—the New Year application of it, His willingness and ability to do all we need through the new year. Let our answer be, "Do Thou for me." Has Jesus ever really done anything for us? "I—unto thee"—close contact. Then I gave an account of E. Clay's warm reception at Jhandiala and Ajuala, and the illuminations in her honour. Then I read Amy S.'s letter from Kisulutini about the foundation of their church being laid. I do excessively enjoy addressing. It would be grand to preach in St. Paul's.

January 8.—Very much pressed with letters. Strangers write, "I have a strong impulse to write to you." Ought I not then to accept this postal burden as work for my King? He knows I do often put my right hand in His. I am glad the promise in Isaiah 41:13 is to the "right hand," because it is the hand that holds the pen. Burnt a heap of letters, all of thanks for my parcels. I should not like to get their "inasmuch," and not the King's.

January 15.—Wrote an answer to Count Bernstorff, giving permission for F. R. H.'s "Letters" to be translated into German, and they were only published in December! Is not this the Lord's seal in thus sending them to high places? It quite cheered me.

January 16.—Sleep is a peculiar mercy to me. Often my restlessness is soothed by some hymn of dear Fanny's. I seem to hear her singing every note, and so her ministry of song is not yet finished. "When thou passest through the waters" comes to me often. I remember saying, O Fanny, I hope you will sing that to me when I am dying. It may be the memory of that air will come floating to me then.

January 29.—I feel sure my life will not be long; it is literally "dying daily" since the shadow fell on me. I could only cry, Lord Jesus, come for me; and the hush came, "I will come again and receive you unto myself." That whole passage, John 14:1–3, is to me full of comfort as to death, not millennial coming, confirmed by St. Stephen quoting our Lord's own word, "Receive my spirit." I believe "I will come again" refers primarily to Christ's coming to and for each disciple who then heard Him, and for each of the countless multitudes since.

February 2.—Began copying out Jos. Harrison's verses; but writing and my world-wide correspondence gives me restless nights. Visited a sick woman, and wish she would care for her soul as much as for her cough. Looked at the clouds; they have a soothing influence on me. It is curious how seldom I see any one looking up on God's ever-changing panorama.

February 8.—Have been thinking of John 17:11, 12. "Kept," what an unassailable security! "A shepherd is a keeper of his sheep" was written in dear Mrs. Teed's gift-Testament to me. What a shield those words have proved! I have hugged them in storms and danger, in Irish bogs and sea fogs; and I shall be kept at His feet till I can look up and thank my Keeper for ever. I took M.'s advice, and so was *kept* from writing a letter to-day that might not have honoured God. Yesterday took Miss A.'s class on missionary subjects. Let me intercede more for the dear labourers in foreign lands.

February 9.—A very troubled day, a case of "they wrest my words," and yet I did pray before writing what did the mischief. Sister M. very kind; wish I had taken her advice. It is as a Christian I am grieved, but I see no remedy but bearing it patiently. "In weakness made strong,"—how exactly the Lord's promises dovetail into our needs! Not one thing hath failed; never has He said more than He means.

February 18.—Took Mrs. M.'s mother's meeting; spoke on "To you that believe He is precious." Christ is precious in Himself and in what He is to us. It is singular that an African bishop when dying slowly spelt the word p r e c i o u s, while an aged man in Dursley workhouse startled me in 1870 with " Miss, *is* Jesus precious to your soul?" Could not sleep at night till the old hymn came as a lullaby, "Can a woman's tender care," etc. I feel as if I could welcome pain if the Lord Jesus comes nearer. O Saviour, what Thou hast been to me no words can express.

April 3.—Such a good night, thank God! The hymn, "He gave me back the bond," was very sweet to me; it reminds me of two lines a dear old saint told me she once heard—

"He smiled and showed His bleeding side,
And then He smiled again."

I like to think of Jesus as "exceeding glad." At His table I felt His blood so precious, as I so specially need its cleansing power.

April 5.—Dear M. so ill; one can only trust it is God's way, and so must be the right way. And as before a royal feast every vessel is separately polished and brightened, so the dear Lord takes us up one by one into His hand. He who is pure must and will purify.

April 6.—F. A. S. came for a visit—quite a comfort. Rather troubled to-day; yes, "the lip of truth" is not always mine; the sad stumble grieved me till I knelt before the Lord.

April 24.—On the Mutter Moor with dear Frances, the air so free and refreshing. Dr. M. answered my letter for advice; as to the inevitable pain—

"The strength to bear it calmly
Thou wilt command."

[*Note.*—There are no more entries in the Diary for five months, but they are described in the Autobiography.]

Winterdyne, November 11.—Not inclined to get up to breakfast, but I prayed, Lord, make me brave, and so jumped up. *N.B.*—Is it truthful to do this, to hide all from dear Ellen? but I cannot bear to distress her. So tired at night, got into bed without kneeling down; saw Gethsemane in my dreams, and Jesus kneeling in agony, and I thought He came to my bedside and told me it was *for me.*

November 14.—Blessed Sunday! because there is no post-bag. Taught dear A.'s class and played the harmonium, but it hurt me to do so.

November 15.—My 65th birthday. The realization of original sin always comes up on this day; but with that the exceeding preciousness of the cleansing blood. Went to the alms-houses; it always so refreshes me; it is a bit of revisiting the old times when E. Clay was here.

November 19.—M. C. kindly ministered to a real need. Went to some sick in Bewdley. Wonderful how I can race about!

November 20.—Off to Wyre Hill. I read the Bible to the people always, if possible, and get them to read verse by verse; that makes us more one. Think God helped me to testify plainly of His love.

December 4, Sunday.—Mr. S. being at Cheltenham with Ellen, I took his men's class at 9.30; went over Revelation 3:17 to end. Walked to church and stayed to the Lord's Table. Took A.'s class P.M., but felt no power with them, not having prepared properly.

December 10.—When walking out I met and spoke to a respectable widow; she asked, "Can you tell me if Miss Clay and Miss Havergal are alive?" I said, "Miss Clay is in India, and I am Miss H." She looked at me and said, "You are not the Miss Havergal who used to come and read and pray with me in —— Road?" "No; I do not remember you; it must have been my sister Frances; she had fair curls," etc. "Yes; that's the one!" Seeing her again to enquire, I found that dear Fanny had much comforted her. So after many days fruit is found.

December 12, Sunday.—Tired, and had some pain; wondered how I could take Ellen's class, but God helped me. The word "endure" is so strengthening, for it implies suffering to be borne. Christ *endured* the cross "for the joy set before Him." Let me look at the coming joy!

[*Note.*—This is the last entry for 1886. Particulars of some of the remaining days are in M. V. G. H.'s *Outlines of a Gentle Life,* which was published in the spring of 1887.]

January 1, 1887.—How much has happened since I last wrote in a diary! Dear sister Ellen gone to glory, and so my fear of being a burden to her is gone; her gentle heart will never be distressed at seeing any of us suffer and die. I rejoice now that I hid from her how much I was suffering; often I prayed to be brave that she might not guess. How little dross she had! She was walking closely with God, and so had no need of the furnace fires as I have.

I do so look back on her gentle life, and how patiently she bore remarks made even in fun against herself. I think she suffered more from timidity than most knew, that she was often longing to speak for Jesus, and did so, sometimes with fear. She loved to put others first; she always gave the best seat in the carriage to me; she would avoid ringing bells just to save the servants trouble. I believe no one but God knew her self-denying ways in dress and everything. I can only rejoice for her that she is spared the crushing sorrow of widowhood, and I know the burden Winterdyne must have been to her alone.

February 3.—Came to sister Miriam at Edingworth, Weston-super-Mare.

March 14.—I see one reason why my life is spared—to see dear E. Clay again, but she has not an idea of my state. I have saved her eighteen months' sorrow by not alluding to it in letters.

March 18.—I do so wish to die here; it would so save them all at Winterdyne; to be a burden to those dear nieces is my dread, but I have put it in God's hands.

March 20, Sunday.—Not out all day. At the time of Holy Communion I got a piece of bread and some water, and went through the service. Christ can feed me if lawfully kept from public ordinances.

March 27, Sunday.—Too suffering to go to church. Felt glad so many are praising Jesus in the height, and that Fanny is singing to Him. I had a cry for dear sweet Ellen; but oh! her joy and rest! Lord Jesus, I thank Thee.

March 30, Wednesday.—Went to Mr. Hunt's church. Subject—The Righteousness of Christ. (Romans 3:22.) So clear, it swept away every cobweb of self-righteousness; the Holy Spirit made it most comforting. I went over the sermon in the night, and was glad to have this best robe put upon me; every scrap of mine is filthy rags. The real nearness of Christ is my help; as He walked with the children in the fiery furnace, so He is with me now. He is true, true!

April 2.—It is real pain now, I can hardly crawl to the near seats, but felt as content as when roaming and climbing the hill-tops. It is a great pleasure to recall Swiss journeys now, but the everlasting hills are nearer and nearer.

April 3, Palm Sunday.—Walked with M. to church; a faithful sermon. I prayed Jesus to bless dear Ellen's Memoirs to be given away to-day. Oh bless it to souls! I wrote it in much pain, and but for M.'s help in revision it could not have been out so soon.

April 10, Easter Day.—My very last here, the next at His feet. I am enabled to cry, "Not my will, but Thine, be done." His dear hand really upholds me; in the long nights the Holy Spirit teaches as never before.

April 25.—Dear Nurse Farrington came; such an untold comfort. I have deep views of sin; Lord Jesus, show every page of my life, and pass Thy bleeding hand to cover every stain. Oh precious blood! I do trust it for my passport.

April 27.—Mr. Hunt called, and so comforted me with his faithful loving words.

April 30, Saturday.—My pulse is 120, but Jesus has the key of death. O come, unlock the door, that I may fly away and see Thee!

[*Note.*—This is the last of the very few entries in 1887.]

THE HAVERGAL ALBUM.

From the "C. M. S. Gleaner" of January 1887.

A VERY interesting gift has lately been made to the Church Missionary Society by Miss Maria V. G. Havergal. It consists of several long-cherished memorials of her father and of her sister F. R. H.

The late Rev. W. H. Havergal (beloved as a pastor, and well known as a musical composer) was an earnest and untiring advocate of the missionary cause sixty years ago, when its friends were fewer, and its work little known; and with the example of her father before her, it is not to be wondered at, that while still young, his daughter Frances spoke of the C. M. S. as her favourite Society. Her affection for it ever grew and increased; she loved it, spoke for it, wrote for it, and when anxious to devote to the Lord's work what she possessed in the shape of jewelry, it was to the hands of this Society that she entrusted the offering.

Most of the interesting memorials sent by Miss Havergal are gathered together in a beautiful album, carefully and tastefully arranged by her own hand. In it may be seen the portraits of her father and mother, with likenesses of her beloved sister F. R. H., taken at different periods of her bright and blessed career, interspersed with appropriate texts. In it may be seen the original MS. notes of sermons preached and speeches made by Mr. Havergal on many a tour on behalf of the Society, enclosed in envelopes neatly gummed on to the pages, and also the hymn sheets prepared by him, and containing often his own compositions for use at the Anniversary C. M. S. Services in his own church. In it may be seen pictures of Winterdyne, the beautiful residence on the banks of the Severn, where F. R. H. dwelt for some time with her sister and her brother-in-law, Mr. Giles Shaw, showing the room where she composed and sang for the first time her inspiriting hymn, "Tell it out!" These, with some autograph letters, etc., are followed by photographs of a beloved niece of F. R. H., with her husband, the Rev. A. D. Shaw, now a C. M. S. missionary in East Africa, and some photographs taken by the latter illustrative of missionary work; also by the portrait of F. R. H.'s friend, Miss Elizabeth Clay, labouring among the women of India, with notices of the Village Mission inaugurated by her. The Album rightly closes with the portrait of her who, in much weakness, has gone through the labour of compiling it, and has presented it to the Society.

Together with the Album, Miss Havergal has given an MS. book of her sister Frances, containing the original copies of some of her well-known poems, and also cases of sermons by her father. Among the trophies of the work done by the grace of God, through the instrumentality of the Church Missionary Society, these memorials of some of its most devoted friends and labourers at home will hold an honoured place. May the remembrance of their zeal and whole-heartedness be the means of stirring up many to increased and prayerful effort in the great work of sending and bringing the gospel to the heathen!

S.G.S.

LETTERS FROM M. V. G. HAVERGAL.

To Miss L. H. Ludlam.

MALVERN HOUSE, LLANDUDNO,
Sept. 6, 1858.

... Lately, my dear father preached one of the special sermons in the nave of our Cathedral to such a mass of hearers, and we are told that his voice was more distinctly heard than any one's, even than the Bishop of Oxford's. His text was Acts 5:20: "Go, stand and speak in the temple to the people, all the words of this life." So appropriate! and "the words of this life" were explained as the glorious life-giving truths of the Gospel. Fanny said it was a wonderful sermon, and he went flowing on with such animation and eloquence. Poor child, she is too proud of her father. Well, I prayed that some jewels might be added to the Redeemer's crown by it. Fan was so delighted, because, previously, a chant and a long anthem of his were splendidly given by the choir.

F. is very full of the Irish Society, and is made secretary to it in Worcester; it sends Irish Bibles, etc., to the Irish-speaking population. Mr. Shaw labours so for it, but the Spirit's teaching is needed to drink in its lessons of love. To realize "this is my Beloved, and He is mine," and "I am all fair in His sight," is what I glimpse sometimes, and long for more of His immediate teaching.

It is not reading others' sweet thoughts of Christ, but one's own heart that must know His preciousness, and my hand must touch the hem of His garment. There seem to be such unknown depths in His love, as A. Newton calls it, "the ocean-fulness of His love;" and yet how content we are with a drop, a taste, when He bids us "drink abundantly, O beloved." I feel Him near on these mountain-tops where Miriam and I roam. There is a quiet mountain church, where, as we chant "The sea is His, and He made it," the waves mingle their praise.

To the same.

CELBRIDGE LODGE, DUBLIN,
AUG. 25, 1861.

You must tell me soon how it has been faring with you this summer. Your dear mother is still His waiting one; but though the chariot wheels tarry, it will come, and then, as a dying Scripture reader said, "My Master's chariot is come, and oh, I find it so easy!"

Fanny is now at Oakhampton, enjoying the loveliness of Astley. She is not composing at all, it gave her such headaches. I saw a gentleman in Scotland, who said she was the first living poetess, and that her contributions to *Good Words* were eagerly sought. Dr. Macleod, the editor, besides a cheque, sent her copies of all his works, some 12 or 15 volumes. She plays so beautifully.

I wish I could give you good news of Ireland. About here the people are forbidden to listen, not only to the Bible, but to what any Protestant may say. The Scripture reader says even violence is sometimes offered him. There is a secret committee in every place to watch their neighbours, and report any visit or Protestant doings. It is not the people's fault, they would gladly hear, but the priests forbid.

Ellen's is a very well ordered household. We have singing at family worship, and the little ones come in, but baby being only a few months old has sometimes to be dismissed with her commentary! They are wonderfully obedient children. I believe it is a criterion of an obedient child to go to bed without roaring, and the same with medicine. One of little F.'s pretty questions was, "Auntie, when they have sung the 'new song,' what will they sing next?"

To the same.

SHARESHILL VICARAGE,
SEPT. 4, [1863.]

Thank you for a deeply interesting letter, forwarded to me in Ireland some time ago. I know that you are daily feeling the loss of your excellent brother, and yet every day brings you nearer to the happy reunion. Oh, Lucy, how many a sister would envy your sure hope of your brother's glory! It is so delightful to know he lived in the Lord and died in Him. Just contrast your last meeting with him on earth with your next above. You on your sick-bed, he, wearied and worn, and neither able to relieve the other. Then think of meeting where the inhabitant shall not say, I am sick, and where the sister spirit shall recognise the glorified brother, enjoying that greater degree of glory the faithful minister enters into. I do not like to imagine beyond what revelation discloses, and the books now read on the employments of heaven seem to me puerile in the extreme.

My niece, M.L. Crane, went with me to Ireland. She is the sweetest girl I know, and was much admired, and the cottagers would say, "Isn't she a jewel! look at her eyes, and the bloom on her cheeks," etc. etc. Ellen and her husband do much good. Their home is quite the "House Beautiful," where pilgrims come and tarry awhile. I got about among the cabins a little, saw the hens laying their eggs on the nest by the bolster, and the cow or the pig sharing the bedroom. The worship of the Virgin is far before that of the Saviour of the world. There are three Jesuits, and I have no doubt my visits are reported. Often the poor things would say, "Oh, Miss, we should like to hear you read, but dare not, we should have to do penance." They have no idea that Christ can save them without the Virgin. They have a book called the *Glories of Mary*, in which her name is constantly put instead of His; *e.g.,* "Mary so loved the world that she gave her only," etc. Also in the Lord's prayer, "Thine, O Mary, is the kingdom and the power," etc. One man said to me, "The Bible is a dead letter; there are more souls sent to damnation by your Bible reading than anything else." Awful, is it not? I could write sheets of what I hear and see.

You ask for Fanny, she sparkles away. She sent such a sweet tale to Nelson the publisher, called "Katinka, a story from Russia," and most curiously the MS. is lost. And now farewell. May He who changes not be gladness in your hearts. May the comfort of His Spirit revive my dear friends, and make each more meet for the inheritance of the saints in light.

To an Invalid Aunt.

LANSDOWNE CRESCENT, WORCESTER,
APRIL 22, 1859.

Perhaps the enclosed lines on "Beautiful Zion" may refresh you in your weary hours. M.'s children have learnt it, and sing it so prettily. They give me a glimpse of the beauties waiting for me. Your way, my dear Aunt, has been rough, but it is the "right way," and the end shall be to enter into the gates of

"Beautiful Zion that I love,
Beautiful city built above,"

The past season of our Saviour's suffering must have been very precious to you. He bore our griefs, and in all our affliction He is afflicted. His aching brow and pierced hand can feel for and sustain the tried sufferer. Jesus would not even receive anything to dull or alleviate the pain. Oh the depths of the sympathy of Jesus!—sympathy with you, dear Aunt. Oh, look up and say,—

"For soon will recompense His smile
The sufferings of this little while."

I trust this hope is yours, and this is an anchor cast within the veil. Who can cut the chain that fastens our souls to Jesus, the "Rock of Ages"? "No condemnation" to them who are in Christ. "Who shall separate us from the love of God in Christ Jesus?"

A poor Christian, bedridden for twenty-five years, is just released. She was willing for His will to be done in her, and now she is with her dear Lord. The twelfth of Hebrews and the eighth of Romans were her favourite portions. . . .

One of my almshouse women was so filled with the dying love of Jesus on Good Friday, she could only look at His cross and say, "Enough for justice; enough for God; enough for me!"

To the same.

SHARESHILL VICARAGE,
AUG. 27, 1860.

I wish you could see our pretty home, and especially how the people crowd to church. Some farmers come twice a-day who seldom came once before. I hope many will really be stirred up to attend to the soul. One old man is very amusing. The first time I met him he said, "Is your father the new parson I hear so much talk of? Well, he had need come among these dry bones. The Lord can work by whom He will: it was by a primitive woman the light came to me. Thirty years ago that. Ah, she was a woman! She went to try and convert the schools at Wolverhampton, and the master was so angry with her, he said he would put her in the stocks; but he didn't though, for after all, he took her to church and married her! I have a mighty notion of you women, and whenever you have a word of exhortation you're welcome to come to my cot. . . ."

It is indeed trying for you to wait so long at the very door of heaven; but the Lord Jesus has the key, and when He opens, all our earthly chains will fall off, and, like Peter, we shall pass through the prison wards and enter into the city. The promise I send you is, "Thine eyes shall see the King in His beauty." I send you Fanny's lines on that, they are published in *Good Words*.

To the Girls of the Charter School at Celbridge, Co. Kildare.

CROMER, NORFOLK,
SEPT. 26, 1867.

MY DEAR GIRLS,—

Do not think that I have forgotten you and the pleasant Sunday evenings when you used to sit so still and answer me so nicely. I should like to walk round and speak to every one again, but my letter must do that; and what should I say to you? I think it would be, "Dear child, are you *in* Christ? Have you come to Him?" I trust some *can* say, "Yes, I have come, and I am so happy, and I do believe what Jesus says, 'Him that cometh unto me, I will in no wise cast out.'" To such I would say, 1 John 2:12–28. To those who are still away from Jesus, outside of His happy fold, let me say, "What are you waiting for? Come, for Jesus calls you; come, for all things are ready! and come *now*, before the door is shut." Think what it will be, to be shut out from the Lord Jesus for ever! Do not forget the little prayer we used to say together, "Lord, open Thou mine eyes, that I may behold wondrous things out of Thy law." Fill me with the Holy Ghost, for Jesus Christ's sake. Amen.

If you look at the maps, you can see the long journey I have had this summer. From Bewdley down to Guildford, then to Great Malvern and its beautiful hills, then up to Morecambe Bay, Kendal and Keswick. There I saw our highest mountains, Scafell and Helvellyn, and the lakes of Windermere and Derwentwater. One remarkable rock is called the Lion and the Lamb, and it looks just like them; another rock resembles an organ and a lady playing at it.

The rocks teach us many lessons: "Lead me to the rock that is higher than I;" "The Lord is my rock;" "The shadow of a great rock in a weary land." Find out the chapter. Now look at the map again. From Morecambe through Lancaster, Crewe, Birmingham, Rugby, Peterborough, Ely, and Norwich to Cromer. Here I am sitting, and from my window I see the grand white waves rolling in. On the sands are sea-weeds, crimson and scarlet, but they fade so soon; put what I send you in a basin of water. Cromer is quite on a promontory,— sea to the north, east, and south; and it is the only place in England where the sun both rises and sets in the sea. How I wish you were all here!

I saw the lifeboat go out one day, and also I saw the life-lines or ropes that they send to a ship if it is sinking. The waves are so high no boat could go to it, no arm long enough to help. So they keep long ropes ready, and if a ship goes on the rocks they fasten the rope to a rocket and shoot it out to the ship; the sailors catch hold of the rope, then along the rope they slide. A life-preserver or sea-escape is a round belt of air, which a man puts round his waist, and there is a sort of sack below it to keep his feet steady. Only one at a time can come in, and they must trust the one rope; then the sailors on shore pull the rope in, and the poor sailor is safe. I thought, "How shall we escape if we neglect so great salvation?" Ah! if you were sinking in the deep waves, how you would watch the only rope, the only life-escape coming to you, and how eagerly would you get into it! "Neither is there salvation in any other, for there is none other name whereby we must be saved."

The beautiful desk you gave Mr. Shaw stands in the drawing-room at Winterdyne. I was quite astonished to see my name in the address.

Farewell, my dear children, and may God the Holy Spirit guide you to that happy land where we shall meet for ever.

Give my love to Miss Kavanagh and her sister, and with my love believe me,—

Your sincere friend,

MARIA V. G. HAVERGAL.

HARLECH, July 8, 1872.

DEAR SISTERS AND LISTENERS,—

So far safe and well in our pleasant wanderings, thanks to God! When we reached Dolgelly we found comfortable rooms, and, after tea, went to the lovely Torrent Walk. There was a marvellous sunset, Cader Idris resplendent. Our landlady has a brother—a missionary in Bengal. When he decided to go out, a brother minister said to him, "I know a young lady who has wished to take up mission work ever since she was a child." He went that day to see her, and soon married her, of course.

At 7 A.M. next day, we set out for the Precipice Walk, but made a detour up a craggy peak with a most repaying result. We camped on the heather for two hours, and then returned to the track. Fanny exclaimed, "This is quite *à la Suisse!*" for the rain had crumbled the path away at the steepest slant of the rock. We *were* glad of our alpenstocks, and did not reach Dolgelly till 5 o'clock. After tea I heard bells chiming, and found the old church open for service. Alas! there was so much of the outward—vases of artificial flowers and crosses. No wonder the church empties and the meetings fill. Next day we took the train to Barmouth Junction, and then walked. F. said the "Rhine is not prettier in many places." We took a great dislike to Barmouth, there seemed no air, and the sands were loose and dusty. So we resolved to go on to Harlech. We soon found three rooms high up, near Pen-y-garth, just the thing. Fanny found a low stool for sitting in her window; she is quite content if she can sit and look at the sea; she is first-rate in being pleased and satisfied with things as they are. She thinks the air bracing, and likes the shelves and arm-chairs in the rocks near us, and the old castle and the distant views beyond it. Sunday was a pouring wet day, but I enjoyed its rest. The weather is clearing to-day, and we are going for a long evening on the sands. We do thank our heavenly Father for allowing us such rest and leisure.

To the same.

HARLECH, July 13, 1872.

"He led them on safely," and pleasantly too, I may thankfully add. Our lodgings are comfortable, barring the crossest child I ever knew. It never purrs, which teaches me how our heavenly Father must weary with His un-purring children. Tuesday we took a climb up the peak above the Tallysanna road, and had to get over some stone walls. I had a tumble to humble me. F. beats me by her peculiar agility. Wednesday morning we started in a spring butter cart. The gleeful old woman goes to the mountain farms to collect butter. She also gets butter-mugs of 60 or 70 lbs. for winter use. This cart took us six miles, to near Cwm Bachyan Lake, with its frowning rocks above, and the long pine-wood walk, with the rushing stream, charmed F. We saw two tourist lads, evidently astray; they gladly came up to us, and together we went up the Roman steps, very curious indeed. The lads went on their twenty-mile walk, and we camped and lunched, and then went to sleep on the heather. At three we started back, and reached the rose-covered farm, where Frances and Alice slept in that thunderstorm night. Here we made signs for tea, and had the half-yards of bread, and the butter was so delicious! A baby was in the cradle, and the fifteen olive-branches (or hindrances, I was going to say) were all at home, and working in the fields and dairy. We so regret they knew no English. We walked back to Harlech by eight. Fanny looks well, and actually condescends to like what she eats, and says she sleeps splendidly. Tuesday, we went down to the shore to bathe, where it is quite lonely,—no need of bathing women and machines,—but, alas! a whole herd of black cattle forestalled us; they raced into the sea, dashing into the waves as high as their backs; they then walked along in the sea, and finally went back to their pasture. I was not aware of their sea-bathing instinct. Cows always keep F. within bound, they are her policemen, and she is rather glad to keep near me and out of their beat. Yesterday evening I did some needlework on the rocks, and read the first newspaper we have seen for a week!

We both agreed to have another quiet Sunday, and not push on in the rain,—health and strength being our main object in coming here.

To an Invalid Aunt.

LLANBERIS,
JULY 19 AND 20, 1872.

. . . Sunday morning we went to the Welsh service, it was too far to go five and a half miles to the English. In the evening I took tracts to some of my old friends. Then a girl knocked at our door, and said, "Please, I am Lydia; I come three miles to see you." I found it was the girl I gave my hat to on condition she would go to the Sunday school, so I had her in; her broken English was very amusing. I was asked to call again on the poor young widow whose husband was buried last week. Her mother-in-law spoke broken English, but in such a forcible way. She said to me, "I can't talk English, but I come ever to one verse, there I conquer, 'The blood of Jesus Christ His Son cleanseth us from all sin.' Satan can't face the blood,—I lose him there."

Monday we left Harlech for Port Madoc, such a lovely road, under great rocks and past little lakes and a river, till we came to Pont Aberglaslyn. After lunch, on we went to Beddgelert, an eight miles' walk. Neither of us felt tired, and it was such a charming evening. I proposed going on instead of sleeping there, but first we had tea at such a clean blacksmith's; I mean the wife was clean! [*N.B.* The way is, carry your tea and sugar, go to any shop for a threepenny loaf, send for new milk, get eggs boiled, and you have a capital tea. You constantly see in Welsh windows: "Hot water and carpets! 3d. each for attendance."] You cannot think how we enjoyed the Naut Gwynaut Lake, and Snowdon looked grand. We were glad to spy the lonely mountain inn, Pen-y-Guryd, after our sixteen miles' walk. Tuesday we were off by eight to go up Moel Siabod, a mountain that painters frequent. *Black* says, "The ascent is difficult, guides can be engaged." Of course we set all this at defiance. It would be as likely as if Johnnie Crane took Nanna with him riding! There is no beaten track at all; we walked two hours, then rested, and in less than another hour we were on the top, with a grand view. After a nap on the heather, we descended on the other side to Capel Curig, and, after a lunch, we started back for our inn at Pen-y-Guryd. This was our first extravagance; but meals and bed and all extras only came to 4s. each the first night, and 5s. each the roast-beef night, including bed and meat breakfast. Wednesday was lovely, so we started at eight, going up the steepest and grandest side of Snowdon by a zig-zag path. We arrived safely at the top about noon. We had a clear, grand view in the sunshine, and we did thank God for letting us see His handiworks. I am so pleased that Switzerland has not spoiled Fanny's enjoyment in Wales, she constantly exclaims how delighted she is. . . . About two we began to descend, for clouds had veiled the summit, but it was lovely to see them drifting and clearing. I had written to secure rooms with my cottage friend at Llanberis, as we came down that side. We were a little stiff the next day, but I wish you could see how well F. looks. We decide to stay here till Saturday the 27th, reaching home (please God) on Monday.

Fanny is well, and so useful in the schools and parish, and her heart is quite set upon Christ; she has been drawn by His love.

We all join in much love to you, dear Aunt, and be sure I pray for you; and Jesus says, "Fear not, I will never leave thee, nor forsake thee."

To a Friend.

A plain question shall have a plain answer. "Pleasant Fruits" are strictly facts, not outlines filled up. For twenty-five years I have kept a blank note-book in my District-bag, and noted at the time, *i.e.* immediately after, anything striking in a person's words, see p. 115.[1] The only exceptions are when my notes failed me, though the outlines were fact.

Dear old Mary! her sweet, simple words flowed like poetry. Out of hundreds—I might say thousands—of visits, I selected such as seemed to me to show God's work, not mine, that so the glory might be His who only made me a messenger. Often have I wondered myself at my poor friend's outpourings.

I could not vouch for every word of my answers, and have given texts in full to make them more clear. Where possible, I give their histories without the breaks of my remarks and questions. I have avoided living subjects, except Elizabeth Sherwood, who is eighty-four, and one or two on the verge perhaps of eternity, who appeared so humble and true.

In re-copying my notes, I pruned away, as I hoped, all self-touches. In p. 91[2] I touch as lightly as possible on what was a marvellous radiance, a transfiguration glory, which I longed for some infidel to see. My present work is a mission chiefly on Wyre Hill, Bewdley, under the rector, in a parish of 2000, with Miss Elizabeth Clay. Our walks extend four miles. Some account of it has been published in *The Ladies' Scriptural Magazine* for May, June, and July 1870, signed M. V. G. H. "Not unto us, but unto Thy name be all the glory."

To Miss M. C.

Ael-y-don Terrace, Barmouth.

Just to tell you the thoughts yours and F. M.'s loving presents brought to me. The lilies whispered directly, "I am the lily of the valleys," and He said by them, I am going with you, I am your lily,—your clothing of purity and humility. And I had lately wished so to go really down, down in His valleys, and take the lowest place again while listening to all those addresses. And as I shut my eyes wearily, the rumble of the train resolved into quite a musical chorus to the old Scotch tune (French) and the Scotch paraphrase,—

"The Lord's my Shepherd, I'll not want,
 He makes me down to lie
In pastures green; He leadeth me
 The quiet waters by";

and all on through the Psalm.

Rough farmers' voices awoke me, so I asked the one nearest to smell the lilies, and he said, "I never see them growed before: where do they grow?" Then another said, after my remark about who was the lily of the valleys, "Can you tell me why it says, 'I am the Rose of Sharon'?" That helped me to speak of the red rose, the crimson blood, and the white robe of purity. Then I gave one a lily, and he put it so carefully in his button-hole, and said, "I'll keep the remembrance of it as long as I live."

They left at Shrewsbury, and then I opened the scent-bottle, which brought my own father's love back, for he always brought us some from abroad. I had to wait two hours at Ruabon, and found out some of God's hidden ones in the almshouses. One said, "I am in the fold, and I am quite, quite sure I am going to Him."

At Barmouth, Miss Jones was waiting for me, with flowers on the table, and the pretty little things I like to see. Then I opened your box, and so enjoyed the love first, and the sweeties after, the jam and the cake, etc. But I can't think why you thought of all this for my journey—no one else had. And the thought came, Why do they love me? and then I felt it was in Him who loves us both.

To a Friend.

... You see my sister F.'s books are not about religion, but about the Lord Jesus as a personal living Saviour. It is an actual revelation of Himself in one's own soul, which is so unmistakeable that no one has an idea of the joy till the Holy Spirit teaches it. Then comes that bright, happy communion with Him which is worth all else. Of course outsiders cannot understand it, but to all comes His loving royal call, "Come unto Me." Reading the Bible with the expectation of finding One we know not, gives intensity to our search. That some do not know, do not even care, does not alter the great facts of revelation; the great fact that the soul is spiritually dead and so needs conversion—a literal new life, even a new creation (2 Corinthians 5:17); and that without this, Christ's "Verily, he cannot enter the kingdom of God," must come true. I know there are many to whom this inner joyous life is a sealed enigma. I wish such could see, as I have seen, the two classes of death-beds. Death is the great unveiler, no forms or rites avail then. Yes, I have heard the young and beautiful exclaim in agony, "Oh, what madness to live for this world!" Another said, "Oh, I have been deceived, I am lost, I am lost, there is no hope now!" and no prayers or promises gave any comfort. Then the contrast to see, yes, see a visible glory descend on the dying one, not only on my darling sister, who literally never saw death, but only her King, and most surely He came Himself, and her triumphant "Oh, He is come!" was it not the sealing of her holy life? Was it not to strengthen you and me to live the life of faith which so many ignore? This is my special message to you—"Rooted in Him;" and just as the tiny root sucks up the moisture, so the soul that is in Christ has the life-giving streams of His Holy Spirit. "In Me"—nothing short of this brings peace or joy. And, so to speak, with an out and out venture, an entire yielding of your very self to Jesus, a very grasping of that dear hand, so long and so lovingly stretched to save you, the Holy Spirit opening your eyes to see your pardoning Lord, and your ears to hear His precious promises (John 6:34); then full, sweet joy, union, and communion will be yours. "Now ye are clean, through the word I have spoken unto you."

To the same.

It is so strengthening to know that the work of grace in our souls will surely be carried on, making us more like Jesus Himself,—that this happy life of trusting Jesus about everything, asking what He wills about everything, will go on in dark days as well as in bright ones. And the source of all this is the love of God in Christ, and this is an everlasting, endless fountain, whose fulness will flow into your heart and mine, until we see Him face to face. I was thinking of His promise that the Holy Spirit should " take of the things of Christ and

---

[1] *Pleasant Fruits* by Maria V. G. Havergal, original book page 115, page 34 of this book.
[2] *Pleasant Fruits*, original book page 91, page 28 of this book.

show them unto us," and I found how little I knew of this showing; just like a little child, who impatiently turns over the pages of his picture book, and learns nothing, sees only half its beauties, till he lets his teacher show him page by page; so I did cry, "Show me the things of Christ," and very soon the showing came of His love, in washing me in His own blood.

I shall never write to you on a 29th of February again. Is it not solemn? In eternity I shall be waiting for you to come through the golden gates.

The love of Jesus is such a reality to me in almost constant suffering;—that He is mine, is near as if His very arms held me, and the promises are such a comfort.

Farewell. Meet me, washed white in the blood of the Lamb.—Yours till then,

M. V. G. H.

To her Brother's Twin Boys.

The Mumbles, 1879.

Dear Willie and Ethelbert,—

I was much pleased with both of your nice, kind letters. You told me not to answer; but I feel sure Aunt Fanny would have done so. In many things she has left me such a good example, and it was just because she was always trying to follow the Lord Jesus Christ.

I have found an old letter about you both which says, "I have not at this moment any wish so great as that the services at the Tent may be the Lord's own call to them. My father's own grandsons, the elder bearing his own name, W. H. H. Oh, do pray fervently for them! I do hope they will be wholly the Lord's."

You are right, Willie dear, in noticing how God's Holy Spirit taught her even from a child.

You would be really proud if you read half the letters I do, about her blessed influence even among the literary and learned men. One writes, "Her poems are almost Miltonic, and of marvellous sweetness and power." Another, "A more lovely life was never known." A Unitarian writes to me, that since reading "My King," he has left his false doctrines and loves the Lord Jesus.

But I must not stay. I have such headaches, and such heaps of letters. But I think pocket-money is always short at the end of term, so I just send you 5s. each. Aunt Maria does love her dear nephews, though not able to come and see them yet awhile. You need not answer, for I am leaving Wales.

To Miss E.M.

The Mumbles, October 25, 1880.

I am still under letter interdict, and still constantly disobedient; but what can I do? With constant appeals to my sympathy, and countless requests, I must respond. I do want *all* my letters now to be real work for Jesus. So may He give me words *for you*.

And the message was in Ezekiel 11:16 the day you left home: "Yet will I be to them as a little sanctuary in the countries *where* they shall come." Of course that is Jesus Himself, *with you*. Now a sanctuary is a place to abide in, so see that you abide in Jesus. A friend of F. R. H.'s writes to me about this continuous living *in* Jesus,—stepping out of yourself into Him, and it is the *present* tense, "To *whom coming*," 1 Peter 2:4, just as continuously as "cleanseth." Now, dear E., I wish I were quite sure that you are *in* Jesus. I know you *love* Him, desire Him, but there is more. In Him, then, would flow the sweet conscious reality that Jesus *is* with you as your living, loving Head.

My darling would say, "Whatever are you waiting for?" Simply at once take the step, and believe that by the Holy Spirit's power, as you look up and say, "My Lord and my God," as surely Jesus meets your cry, and says, "Fear not," (why?) "I *have* redeemed *thee; thou art Mine*." Did you see in Ezekiel 16:8 that baby allegory, "Thou *becamest* Mine"? and then, in ver. 60, after all the wanderings and forgettings on our part, He says, "I will remember;" and compare with Jeremiah 2:2 and F.'s "Dost Thou indeed remember *me!* Just *me*, the last and least."

Now, two words to sum up—"sanctuary," "Mine."

To the same.

The King is so good. He is altogether lovely. Do keep tight hold of His promises, dear; they are sure. His forgiveness is so specially sweet to me just now. Look at the horizon of *unlimitable* pardon, "as far as the east is from the west! so far . . ." is it not delicious? "Free and forgiven, and loved, you stand."

To Mr. Eugene Stock.

The Mumbles, April 20, 1881.

Yours just come to the "Welsh Nest." I longed to get here after work in my brother's parish, and I do think there was real blessing to some of the gloomy ones; it's odd how some will stick in the ditch! One poor body exclaimed, "My husband always *fathoms* it out to me after he comes from church, but you have lightened me most of all!" Another: "Well, Miss, I've puzzled it over, and I sees it clear now, and I do trust to Jesus." So, many thanks for your real service to Miss Clay; she is a real live missionary. A more humble and devoted spirit I never saw. Her prayers are up to Moses's almost; she must get Amens. She wrote from her tent; had had crowds of women clasping her hand, and saying, "Come, come again." Miss C. says no Biblewoman can live alone in an entirely heathen place without the protection of a husband. She has already found a good Christian, and her blind husband, who have begun work.

I never opened your *Gleaner* till a very weary day, and was vexed with a Holy Cross Guild man. I had to be civil, and to be candid. Didn't I give it him!

To the same.

The Mumbles, January 2, 1882.

Thanks; I carried the C. M. S. Almanacs three miles Sunday morning, through such a gale of rain, to the Sunday school where I work—often alone, for no other lady will trudge as I do. A splendid class of boys, who are keen for Mission news, for Archibald Shaw taught them two Sundays, and left a footprint. I had to return and jump into bed, and there spent my New Year's Day. How delightfully you organize the Almanac texts!

My New Year's wish for you is, that you may be the King's penholder.—

Yours in the same work, a few notches lower,

M. V. G. H.

To the same.

THE MUMBLES, 15th December 1881.

Thanks for your sister's thoughtful book, so well worked out and in.

You printed my name once *sans* permission, so I have done the same for you! See preface to *Starlight*. That is the seventh preface I have written, and I had to kneel at Fanny's sofa to ask the King for the words. Now see one of my ideas—" Aunt Maria's ideas," they are called.

Starlight has F. R. H.'s "Marching Orders" in it, and other sweet last words, so I wish to send a copy to all your missionaries, masculine and feminine. How shall I do it? Shall copies be sent to Salisbury House, or addresses to Nisbet? Of course I pay post either way. It will be so delightful to send a King's gleam all round the world. How many hundred copies will it take? I shall also send copies to Islington College. I do thank God for giving me the *idea* to print "Tell it out," with the music, as a prelude to F.'s " Marching Orders;" and after them I give one of my dear father's missionary hymns. All *this* idea came out of a tiff with Sankey! He asked leave to print a mutilated hash of "Tell it out," omitting all the 8-line words and music for this line of his own, " Let the song *ne'er* cease! " And I fear old Eve was in me, and I said "No, it must go as F. R. H. wrote it, or not at all." Then I felt sorry I did not let even a bad version of it go, and then I thought to put it in *Starlight,* and telegraphed just in time.

NOTE.—[From the *C. M. S. Intelligencer* for February 1882.] "Starlight through the Shadows," by the late Frances Ridley Havergal (London: J. Nisbet & Co.), is primarily " a daily book for invalids," planned by the lamented authoress as a special work for 1879, but not finished when " the Master's home call" came for her in the summer of that year, and now published just as she left it. With it are bound up some outlines of addresses prepared for her classes and meetings of young women and others, which are indeed beautifully suggestive; and also the stirring papers entitled " Marching Orders," which she wrote for the *C. M. Gleaner* in that same last year of her life. It will interest our readers to hear that Miss Maria V. G. Havergal, to whom the whole Church of Christ is already so deeply indebted for the Memoir of her sister, and who has now edited this posthumous production of that sister's facile and gracious pen, has presented 500 copies of " Starlight through the Shadows" to the Church Missionary Society, to be sent (at her own expense) to all the Society's missionaries, and to the native clergy acquainted with English. That they will value a gift so generously given, we are sure; and we know that they cannot please the donor better than by teaching to all the Native congregations and schools, Frances Havergal's missionary hymn, "Tell it out," which is prefixed, with its proper tune, to the papers on "Marching Orders" in this volume.

The message sent to each missionary:—

FROM
FRANCES RIDLEY HAVERGAL'S SISTER
(MARIA V. G. H.)
To the Missionaries of the Church Missionary Society.

MAY THE "STARLIGHT" OF HIS PROMISES, AND THE SUNLIGHT OF HIS PRESENCE, CHEER AND BRIGHTEN YOUR PATHWAY.

F. R. H.'s STUDY,
CASWELL BAY, NEAR SWANSEA.
January, 1882

To the same.

LYNCHMERE, HERTFORD,
June 14, 1885.

You are a reality now, instead of C. M. S. essence! I am thankful you gave me a C. M. S. blessing on the steps of that House Beautiful. The dome of St. Paul's photographed itself on my mind, and with it the thought that soon we shall be standing where there is no temple, no veil, no shadows, and the nations gathered there by the C. M. S. workers, *home* workers as well as the out-stations.

And I never said "Thank you!" but I do mean it heartily; your Bible studies make me wish to be young again, and teach. You do compress your thoughts admirably, and compressed thought expands with brain digestion. I like your chapter on the Ladder, and the "Lucky Fellow" chapter is quite a hit. The book seems to amuse me, not wrongfully, but racily. I am much better,—not near the Land of Beulah.

To Mrs. Matthews.

February 27, 1882.

I try to answer by return of post, else I get so oppressed and sleepless with postal pressure; but since Christmas health is returning, by God's mercy.

Ah, yes, I know all about it, and better still, Jesus knows. I will just tell you two or three things that comforted me, and may they be His whisper to you. I am sure He loves you by this " setting apart." " Make straight in the desert a highway for our God." So in the desert of loneliness, the unfilled place, the desert aching comes. It is His voice, " Comfort ye," etc. God will fill the empty places left by our dear ones.

One does so go back to lost days and moments. Often when grief seemed unbearable, the simple words, " Hush me, Lord Jesus," have brought His human tenderness so near.

I am selecting more poems of Fanny's for print; also, if well enough, treasures of her letters. For some reasons, I did not in the "Memorials" fully show her severe home discipline after papa's death, but think I shall now.

My dear friend, just lie still in Jesus, and take F.'s words, "More grace, and for you."

Excuse more, writing is so bad for me, and letters come from all over the world!

To the same.

Your husband's illness is a sore trial, but your dear Lord is watching you and your dear one in the furnace. "I will take away all thy tin." Dear F. said that is our fair appearances,—tin is so like silver, but must all be purged away. The dear Hand does it all, the same that plucks us as brands out of the burning. Zechariah 3:3–7 is such a sweet connection with John 10:27, 28. Once plucked out, we shall never be plucked away out of the dear Hand. Ah! that Hand felt the scorching flame for us.

To her Brother.

2 Bank Terrace, Llandilo,
August 6, 1883.

I did not think I should live to write this date again, and send you every loving wish. Truly both you and I have daily reminders that we live on the edge of eternity. More and more it seems to me the one great life business is to make our calling and election sure. I suppose that means, to see that we have effectually received and obeyed God's call, and by the evident signs of the Holy Spirit working in us, making God's secret purpose of election sure in our own case. I like what an old woman said, "I was so bad I could not have chosen God, if He had not chosen me." "According as He hath chosen us in Him, that we should be holy and without blame before Him in love." And yet with this high standard, I am sure I can only take the publican's place, and cry, "God be merciful to me a sinner;" and if it were not for the abundant pardon, I should have no hope. "Forgiven until now" is such a nice verse, and as F. put it,—

> "O precious blood! Lord, let it rest on me;
> I ask not only pardon from my King,
> But cleansing from my Priest; I come to Thee
>   Just as I came at first,
>   A sinful, helpless thing."

I am sorry to hear some one has said that Fanny's works were unsound. I do most seriously challenge and deny this statement. I could copy written proof to the contrary, from bishops, priests, and deacons, besides professors and reviewers. There has hardly been a Church Congress or Conference since her death, but her name has been mentioned with the deepest respect, and her works spoken of as "unrivalled manuals of Christian literature," also as "a complete body of divinity." A very eminent man said her "Thoughts of God" rose to Miltonic grandeur; while the testimony even of some Roman Catholics is striking, and how they read her books!

Because of her high standard of holy living, which she carried out most literally, and her high standard of spirit life, some may object, but there is no truth that has not been assailed; and I do say that there is not one sentence in F.'s books that can be proved unsound by Holy Scripture or the Thirty-nine Articles. Mind, I do not think that any manuals of devotion, any comments on the Bible, should do away with our own daily search of God's Word. How her words have been blessed in leading others to the same holy, happy life, is simply miraculous, and eternity alone can reveal it. I must stop, but I do wish —— to read what I say.

Since coming here I am better, and it is quieter than at The Mumbles; I cannot stand noise. I fear this very damp, misty weather tries you, and I am so sorry for the hay here, so much is still out. Give my love all round, from your sister,

Maria.

To Mrs. F. B. Grant.

Winterdyne, 21st Jan. 1884.

We were all glad to receive such good accounts of your welcome home, and certainly, like a good wife, you write more of your husband than yourself. There is much advantage in having simple village people, and I have no doubt they will thankfully receive your pastoral visits. May you both come to them in the fulness of the blessing of the gospel of Christ. We love that old word "gospel," don't we?—God's good news to the lost and perishing; and realizing for myself what it was to be lost, makes one rejoice and cling to salvation and the precious blood that cleanses and atones. I so often find poor people listen when I tell them of dear Fanny's own text, 1 John 1:7, and how she clung to it to the last.

I am pleased you told me your need of her books, and request you to do so always. I now send some cases in blue of her prose and poetry.

So sorry for all your detentions and trouble. Still the King's word must come true, "Nevertheless afterward it yieldeth the peaceable fruit of righteousness,"—"*it*" singular number; so, separate little afterwards, till the one grand "afterward" dawneth. Is not the Lord good to scrape away our "tin"? So much of my services I thought silver, were only tin, so the cleansing blood is more and more precious.

I like your lines on the little ones and on holding firm. I keep up, down to breakfast, and open my window at four or five.

To a Godson, L. B.

Winterdyne, April 1, 1884.

I wish we could have a little talk instead of this letter. You may be sure I am thinking about you as the day comes near when you will promise what I once promised for you.

Think much of the inward grace promised you, even the gift of God's Holy Spirit. No outward form has grace in it, and I do so hope you are quite clear about Baptism as being the outward rite of admission into Christ's visible Church, so that you need to be born again of the Spirit, so as by that new birth to be united by faith to the Lord Jesus Christ.

It is just a real definite transaction between your soul and the Lord Jesus,—you coming to Him, you telling Him you do desire to be His child, His soldier, and offering your heart for the blessed Spirit to come in and dwell with you—in you. And as surely as you say honestly, Lord Jesus, take me, wash me, sanctify me, so surely He does His part. He confirms you; the Bishop is only the visible hand. Yes, the very hand of the Lord Jesus will surely then descend in blessing you, and shedding in your heart the Holy Ghost to strengthen and keep you.

I know there must be many temptations and difficulties; even some around you may hinder you. But cheer up; if you choose Christ, He will stand by you,—yes, quite near to you, His poor little soldier. And, L., I feel sure the Lord Jesus speaks to those who listen; I mean some promise, some verse out of the Bible, comes to our heart as just what we want, some text that helps us at the minute. I hope to send you and your brother a book, and some cards my sister F. wrote, and also some for you to give any of your schoolfellows.

To her Eldest Sister at St. Moritz in the Engadine, the day before her operation in Birmingham.

July 1884.

Dearest M.,—

I do specially want you to be quite happy about what you have just heard—will take place before this reaches you. I am so wonderfully strengthened and supported. I have slept better than ever every night since Dr. M. told me. Do not make the slightest change in your winter plans even if I do not go on favourably; you are best among God's solitudes. Last night I had a most comfortable view of the gladness it must be to the Lord Jesus to have borne death in our place, instead of us. It came from feeling so glad that this inherited disease has come to me, instead of any of my dear sisters; it is nice to be a scape-goat, and you see I have natural courage to bear without the least fear. Also, with such a doctor and nurse, I want my dear sisters to see that it is wiser and better for me and them not to have any one else. Dr. M. has taken rooms at No. 9 Francis Road, Edgbaston, and Mrs. L. knew about F. R. H., and is delighted to have me! I shall be well looked after. Now, please think of me in the Land of Beulah, just resting in the King's arbour, and there from His own hand to receive the chastening for my profit; and I know whom I have believed, and just rest on the precious blood to cleanse and gladden me now and ever.—

Your loving

Maria.

To J. and S. H.

3rd Nov. 1884.

It was impossible to answer your query till to-day. E. Clay has taken her passage again conditionally on the 25th. She has been brave indeed, intinerating to 274 new villages, over bridgeless rivers and sandy holes in unmade roads. She carries her mattress and cooking utensils; and, as she often saw dirty hands put dirty sweetmeats in the milk, her goat goes along with her, and its little kid on the top of the bullock-cart. Fancy her going with only a blind Scripture reader and his wife to quite new places, and she wishes to visit 1500 villages! She goes to the head Baboo and gets leave to see his wife, and then into minor courts. She has already built two churches and two houses. She has never received any salary, and only has her conveyance expenses paid in India, not her passage money. She belongs to the Church of England Zenana Society, in close connection with the C. M. S. She still suffers from deafness and roaring noises in her head, but is better, and is just waiting God's will. I trust she will yet go.

I have been like a carpet-bag, squeezing in more than it will hold, but nothing to your crowded duties. I know how desolate your evenings must be; but, O happy mother! safe for ever on the other side with the Lord. I hope you keep up, like dear, good pilgrims, hastening "onwards and upwards."

To J. and S. H.

December 1884.

Thanks for your love on Nov. 15, and the mittens. Oh, S., what fine stitches! I do wear them, and prefer black.

"Precious faith" gets tried; poor tired ones, your time to "sit still" will come. I never saw before the origin of reserved seats! It is St. Peter's idea, 1 Peter 1:4, "reserved in heaven for you," *you* individually, so no one else shall or can sit in your reserved seat. You hold the ticket, 1 John 1:7; the blood is the passport. As the stewards pass you up and up, oh! what will it be to pass up the shining ranks and see the seated, rested dear ones, and sit down with them in our reserved seats there!

To Miss W.

Feb. 9, 1886.

Your note is indeed a treasure, dear friend, and how singularly the Lord is answering the prayer!

I am often thinking of you, and know all is well; the Lord will strengthen her on the bed of languishing, and make all her bed. And now you have reached that sweet word "carry;" because you are helpless, He must be carrying you step by step nearer home. And then the "I,"—even I will carry you, not trusting any one else to do that soul-carrying.

I do rejoice you have tender human hands to minister to you, and I know true love moves them. How different to a rich invalid lady I hear of, who has positively suffered from a cruel though highly-paid nurse.

Just my love,—the card is done by a dear invalid.

To Miss E. M.

Sidmouth, March 29th, 1886.

The times are very dark, one really does not know what comes next; only the Lord reigns, and He will put the crooked straight. What comfort there is in Isaiah 40:1, 2, 3. I hope you are encouraging yourself, dear, *in* the Lord; such peace as we do that! and He knows, He cares, He loves.

I have been speaking at the Zenana meetings here since October; Thursday is my next day, and I think of Revelation 3:19 to the end,—our dear Lord's own words, straight down from His loving heart to ours. Will you take them as His birthday message, dear? "As many as I love," etc.; and then, "Behold, I stand;"—"if *any* man" must mean *us*. Then let us open the deep-down door in our heart, and welcome in such a guest, "sup *with* Him,"—interchange of closest love; think of His *caring* for our poor foolish company! But, as dear F. said, "the dear Lord wants our poor love to add to His cup of joy." Then the "cup" goes on from time into eternity! when the real bridal feast begins, and never, never ends. Then how strengthening that promise, "To him that overcometh,"—it implies heaps of fights and failures, but certain victory through Him that loved us. "My throne,"—no king takes even his children to share that; but our King promises it—"makes slaves the partners of His throne." That dear old hymn often *sings* to me, "Hark, my soul," with "Partners of my throne *shall* be; Say, poor sinner, lovest thou me?" Yes, yes, dear Lord, we do, we do!

To Mrs. R. B. M.

WINTERDYNE, Oct. 16, 1886.

YOU DEAR FRIEND!—

I can see your winged arms so loving and true! I have not forgotten my missionary promises, but kept hiding away in Wales, and could not trouble dear sister Ellen to hunt. I write to you, not to your husband, because you can write his letters, but not his sermons. Oh! those "fresh oil" sermons, and the dear, plain services "understanded of the people!" I do pray on Saturdays for God's messengers to be filled, and then on Mondays that they may be rested and refreshed. But business—it will give me real pleasure to get my father's music to "From Greenland's Icy Mountains" copied, and my young copyist will be so thankful; or I will get it printed. So no buts and ifs; there will be none "up there." And I don't forget about his music to Abdool Messeeh's "Beloved Saviour;" all in time.

Sister Miriam sent me part of your last letter, so I see how you want some little candlesticks, and He who walketh in the midst of all His lights knows, and in His time will send. So I hope the need will stir up latent sparks in some unlikely ones. Tell me if the two dear aunts are really in glory. I do so think of the dear Miss C——s, my love, please; but I ought not to write, my arm lives in a sling, till disobedient! Now, don't look dismal, you darling. I believe the dear Master's hand has a chloroform touch, and specially exempts me from what I ought to have. My doctor was astonished on my return from Wales (my Patmos) at the retardation. So I said, "Then, doctor, I am not wanted in heaven yet!" He replied, "No; you have a special lease of life; you have marvellous vitality and recuperative powers." It seems to me as if I were snatched back for more special training and purging; all the tin must come off. Oh, to specially glorify my dear Lord! Remember me to good Mrs. B., and tell your mothers, the Lord Jesus never fails those who trust in Him.

"Just to trust Him, that is all."

I cannot write or send to all Sidmouth friends. Don't tell I write, please, or the dear tiresome saints will wonder I do not send to them.

CLOSING SCENES.

MY dear sister Maria's Autobiography and her Diary carry on the history of her life at intervals to the spring of 1887. She joined me at Weston-super-Mare, February 3; but to enable me to receive another relative, she afterwards kindly moved into Wellington Terrace, and, March 21, went to her last earthly home (nearly opposite mine), 3 Paragon Villas, under a most attentive landlady. In the same house I stayed in May and June, our dear niece, Alice S., my maid, and Maria's former trained nurse, all devoting our whole time to her. Alas! we could do little to relieve her terrible suffering, of which the most distressing and obstinate symptom was sickness, almost incessant in the last five weeks; but she bore all with wonderful patience, and with great consideration for her attendants.

For two months after her arrival at Weston-super-Mare she was able to walk and drive out, and though she could no longer visit the sick or poor in their homes, she continued her wayside ministries, speaking of the never-dying soul and the ever-living Saviour to those whom she met when resting on a seat, or standing to view the expanse of sea and sky. Dear Maria also took great interest in the Cabmen's Rest, which was near her apartments, sometimes taking light refreshments and books for the men. One of them (C. Hill), in gratitude, carved on wood with an ornamental border the text, "God is our refuge and strength," and sent it to her when no longer able to leave the house.

As another instance of making use of every opportunity, I may mention that a workman being required to make a little repair in her room, our niece A. E. S. thus writes about it: "Dear aunt asked me to call him back, saying, 'I must speak to him and give him a book.' I only caught some words about 'being washed white in the precious blood bringing such comfort when you come to lie on a dying bed.' He was the last person to whom she really spoke a word for Jesus."

Dear Maria conversed but little in her illness, and could not often bear to be read to, or to receive any messages. Sometimes we repeated texts, but generally her own communings with God seemed sufficient for her soul's peace. Her life had spoken, and so we needed not perpetual assurances from her lips that she was "still looking unto Jesus, the Author and the Finisher of (her) faith."

The Mildmay nurse arrived April 25, and till May 12, when the practice was given up from the patient's exhaustion, she read a Psalm to her every morning, and Maria would then pray aloud, fervently entreating blessings on all her near and dear ones, and embracing also the general subjects of Christian prayer.

From the nurse's memoranda I copy a few items:—

On reading Psalm 15 Miss Havergal said, "I cannot claim the blessing of that Psalm, but I just creep to the Saviour's feet, the lowest of all; I need the continual cleansing of the precious blood." She prayed for all who would be preparing sermons for the morrow, that they might preach Christ in the power of the Holy Ghost.

On Psalm 17 she spoke of the tenderness of God's love, and on "the apple of the eye" shrinking from being touched, and then prayed that all might love Jesus more, and also for Mildmay.

On Psalm 18, "According to my righteousness," said she had none, she had to come down lower and lower; she prayed in her father's words:

"'Just as Thou wilt, O Lord, do Thou!
I to Thy sovereign purpose bow.'

Only let me glorify Thee; O give me patience in suffering."

On Psalm 21 she spoke of the word "strength" being so often used by David; of his trust in God for strength in battle, strength to endure, and that God proved to be his strength.

On Psalm 26:12, said that she could not now bless the Lord in the congregation here, but soon in the great congregation above; but she would want a long time with the Lord Jesus alone first, she had so much to tell Him, and so much to be forgiven; that she had given Him so much trouble, but she came to His feet like Mary Magdalene.

On Psalm 27:2, said she had no earthly enemies to fear; supposed enemies often meant sins. Said she was black, but then thought of the verse, "I am black but comely," and "perfect through my comeliness," which showed it must be all Jesus from first to last. How often she had disobeyed Him by making her own plans; one of her besetting sins was interference. Said "Miss Clay will have a missionary's crown, but only to cast it at Jesus' feet." She prayed for patience to wait God's time, often saying so touchingly, "Only a little longer."

On Psalm 28, "Christ is not only our strength, but our *saving* strength. 'He looked and there was none to help, so His own arm brought salvation.'" Prayed, "Dear Lord, undertake for us; may we learn all Thou wouldst teach us." She gave thanks for sleep, and prayed for all in churches, chapels, and meetings, for Sunday-school teachers, and for sick ones in their rooms, that Jesus would meet with them.

Psalm 30—Said David must have been glad when the sackcloth was taken off, something like a little child with a clean white dress. Expressed a little disappointment about finding herself likely to be here some time, and was pleased with the thought that there might be a loophole somewhere for her, saying, "Loopholes into Glory" would be a pretty title for a book.

Psalm 31 was read to her after a night of severe pain, and she thanked God for a little ease, and just remembered relatives and freinds in prayer; was too weary for more. She said, "Don't tell Mrs. C. how bad the pain has been, it will distress her so. How could I bear for the dear loving hearts at Winterdyne to see my suffering?" When told that Mr. Shaw was coming that evening, she was very pleased, and would get up and make the very best of herself for him. A frame sent by Mrs. H. Shaw with the words, "With His stripes we are healed," being placed where she could see it, she remarked, "He gave His back to the smiters, and did not turn away from one stroke. Both Mr. Shaw and Mr. Hunt talk of God's 'everlasting love,' and that comforts me."

Speaking of Hebrews 12:22–24, Miss Havergal said, "'Ye are come to Mount Zion,' etc. I am so glad it speaks of 'the blood of sprinkling'; no getting to heaven without that!"

May 12.—No more Psalms were read to Miss Havergal after this date.

Mary Farrington.

The last time my dear sister attended divine service was in Trinity Church, April 17, at 3 p.m., for the Litany and Holy Communion specially for invalids. Before going, she said, "Will you forgive me a sin against you years ago? I cannot go to the Lord's Table till I have told you of it." Of course I replied, I would forgive her if it had been seventy-seven times, and she went away quite satisfied, and alone, because I was tired with the morning service, and had no idea she intended going in her increased weakness. Afterwards she said to me, "My peace flows in like a river."

April 22.—Dear Maria called to say good-bye to three sisters, formerly our Astley friends, to whom we are bound by ties of love and grief, and this was her last visit to any one. She then thought she was going to Winterdyne in a few days, as her kind brother-in-law wished that he and his children might minister to her in her remaining days, and that she might be nearer to her favourite doctor. But she was never able to undertake the journey, becoming so rapidly worse.

April 24 was a day of much suffering. She said, "Whatever should I do now, if I had not the promises to rest on! Heathen that I am! I have not read a word of my Bible to-day." It was answered, "Who would expect you to do so? and God is not a hard taskmaster." I think from this time she was never able to read anything. She continued, "But texts pour into my mind, and I like to think the Holy Spirit is teaching me; Jesus is near, I seem to have His very self with me."

Sunday, May 1.—Dear Maria's pulse was 120°, and temperature 102°, and she was so very ill that we telegraphed in the evening for her Birmingham doctor, who arrived the next day, and stayed the night. He said, that so far as the disease was concerned, she might live two or three months, but that the heart was so weak, life might be cut short any day. Dr. Malins' new prescriptions relieved her temporarily, but she did not leave her bed again for some days.

May 4.—She had a good night after taking bromidia, and said, "Do not trouble about me, I am as happy as a queen, and happier. I am very glad it is not my jubilee!" On showing her a flower, she said, "I do so like to think over the wild-flowers, and where I have seen them growing in Wales and Switzerland; it amuses me for hours and hours."

She gave me directions about her funeral at Astley, and for the inscription on a foot-stone, as there is no room for another on her father's tomb. On saying some friends wished to see her, she said, "I can't think why friends can't wait to see one another in heaven." Her feeling of exhaustion and nervousness made her shrink even from the Christian converse she formerly delighted in.

May 6.—Her faithful friend, Miss Elizabeth Clay, came for a ten days' visit, though herself an invalid from the effects of her Indian labours. Dear Maria remarked to her at different times, "I have been thinking so much of—'Fear not, thou worm Jacob;' a worm has no hands, and cannot cling; he is near the gate, and cannot open it. I go as a sinner to my Saviour, His promises have so comforted me, they have all come true; I have felt that He has been leading me all right. Except perhaps in moments of great pain, I have never regretted having this disease."

May 10.—She said, "Dear E, wants to go back to her work in India, and I want to fly away at once; but we would not choose, and she prayed that we might have no will of our own." Another time—"Be Thou their arm every morning! Remember His love is fixed upon you."

"Come and look at me as often as you like, dear Elizabeth; a laugh does me good sometimes."

May 13.—"The pain was so bad this morning, I could have screamed, but I lay still and told the Lord I did not know how to bear it, and after a little while it got better. How nice to think of the glorious bodies! 'We that are in this tabernacle do groan, being burdened.' 'He will not lay upon you more than you are able to bear.' Jesus Himself says to you and to me, 'It is I;' those three words I would not part with, and I believe them. He is now fulfilling to us all the promises, because we are in great tribulation. I have a joyful hope and longing to be with Him, to see Him and never grieve Him more. I abhor the Perfectionist views; in self is no good, and evil thoughts even now trouble me; I only trust His blood and righteousness."

In the following week dear Maria was easier on the whole, but had some heart attacks of great exhaustion. She usually disliked to hear street music, but one day the town band played Handel's "And the glory of the Lord shall be revealed," which she much enjoyed, beating time with her hand; and when sending out some silver commended their playing that style of music, and remarked, "I shall soon have music for nothing in heaven." After May 14 she never left her bed again even for a few minutes.

May 15, Sunday.—Poor Maria had a bad night, and much pain and headache all day. In the evening she revived a little, and asked if I remembered any text in the Bible, or anything in other books, which showed that believers in illness were kept from dying and going to heaven by any sin undiscovered, and therefore unconfessed. I said, "Decidedly not," giving my reasons, to which she agreed, but said, "I have been teasing myself lest there should be some childish sin or something I did not know to be sin." Of course I rejoined that sins of ignorance were atoned for as well as others, and after more talk of the kind, she said, "Well, now you have comforted me a little, you may go, and I will lie quiet." But she returned to the subject the next day, saying, "There are two or three great sins I could scarcely think I was forgiven for, last night." I reminded her that if the Lord Jesus atoned for any of her sins, He did so for all, and that it was the "accuser of the brethren" who took advantage of her weakness to instil these doubts. "Yes," she said; "but now I do think I can lay all my sins on Jesus, I rest on the simple foundation truths of the Bible. Tell your dear J. I often think of his bright face, and pray that, taking Christ for his own in life, he may find the peace in death I have, and tell your dear C. the same."

May 18.—After some "burning pain," she asked me to read a letter from Giles, and said she found his remarks very comforting, and then referred to the Parable of the Prodigal Son, saying that, like herself, he was not only forgiven, but the *best* robe was put upon him. In the morning, thinking herself very near death, she asked me to telegraph for our dear niece, Alice S., who arrived the same evening, and proved a great help and comfort. It was well dear Maria did not know that weary weeks were still before her.

May 19.—I went to dear Maria at 4 A.M., and found her very exhausted after sickness, but whispered that it was Ascension Day, and repeated the Collect. She merely nodded assent; she seldom speaks, only sometimes utters a sentence of faith, humility, or love, or care for others.

May 20.—She rallied wonderfully after the dreadful pain yesterday, and saw her nephew, the Rev. W. H. S., for a few minutes.

May 21.—After a severe attack of sickness, I said, "It is one step nearer home;" not expecting any reply, but she exclaimed aloud, "Thank you." A furious gale was raging, but she has not noticed noises for some time, though formerly so sensitive to them. In the evening, after a long nap, she said, "I have been thinking of that very nice text, 'To depart and be with Christ, which is far better;' I wish we could all go in a lump together." At 10 P.M., after a sudden attack, the heart seemed failing, and the nurse thought life might end in a few minutes. The pulse rallied; but it continued to fluctuate through the night; none of us undressed, as she continued terribly ill. Once she said, as if to herself, "Victory through the blood," and "The gift of God is eternal life." Once again in the night we thought her about to depart, when I quoted a text at intervals, and the verse,

"Lo! He beckons from on high,
Fearless to His presence fly;
Thine the merit of His blood,
Thine the righteousness of God."

But she took no notice of anything. About 7 A.M. she revived, and continued better all day and the two following ones. On the 24th she actually tried to sing Fanny's lost piece, "Behold, God is my salvation, etc. etc., therefore with joy shall ye draw water out of the wells of salvation" (Isaiah 12:2, 3).

The next night she described as "awful;" the following one was not so restless, and in the morning she said to me, "I am not going to heaven yet, but I have quite resigned myself to the will of God; what He appoints must be right. God often gives me beautiful texts and thoughts, but I am too weak to say them out."

May 29, Whit-Sunday.—Notwithstanding continued suffering in many ways, dear M.'s pulse became stronger, and sank to 110°, and Alice read Psalm 145 to her, and she was more inclined to talk.

I saw little of dear Maria from this time, being ill myself till June 7, when she seemed easier and brighter than usual, and, hearing the Rev. W. Hunt's voice, she asked for him, and he came in and prayed with her, which she spoke of afterwards as being very comforting. (She always lay with door and window open night and day, and till the hot weather came our fur cloaks and rugs were in requisition when sitting with her.)

June 8.—As she had rallied sufficiently to be carried by four people into another room, she was placed on a water-bed, and soon recovered from the faintness caused by the motion. Two or three average days and nights followed; after a severe attack she said, "No one knows how fearful this is." I suggested the often-repeated comfort, "Jesus knows," and she referred to it the next day, saying, "You can't think how often little words you say like that come back and soothe me. The word *is* has been a support to me all night! 'There *is* forgiveness with thee.'" I repeated a hymn by the Rev. J. East, which our father set to music in his youth, and as I have not seen it elsewhere in print, and it is the last she ever heard and admired, I transcribe it:—

"Jesus, didst Thou bleed and languish
On the cross in dying anguish,
 For the ills that I have done?
Then, while on this earth I tarry,
Eve and matin gales shall carry
 Grateful praises to Thy throne.

"And when I no more shall number
Days and nights, but sweetly slumber
 In the grave which Thou hast blest,
While my flesh in hope reposes,
Till the day the tomb encloses,
 With Thee, Saviour, I shall rest."

June 12, Sunday.—I was struck with a change in dear Maria's face, it looked so death-like; but she soon opened her eyes, and said, "None but Christ! I could not do without Jesus now, cling to Him." I answered by the lines,—

"Nothing in my hand I bring,
Simply to Thy cross I cling."

June 13.—She told me she had been following A. D. Shaw in the night on his journey through the African deserts, and wishing he could have the nice cool water she has, and she had been praying for him a long time. Afterwards her mind wandered, and it continued to do so frequently till the end came, being often frightened and perplexed, and she talked more than for many days past.

June 18.—Dear Maria's mind seemed clearer, and she asked for different kinds of fruit, which fortunately were at hand or were procured in a few minutes, but she only tasted and then rejected them. For weeks she had refused the delicacies sent by kind friends, and for the last month she had taken nothing in the ordinary way except ice or lemonade. She had become very emaciated, and it was evident the end of the weary journey was at hand, throughout which my diary records many minor miseries, besides the restless feverishness, the pain and sickness, and other distressing symptoms; but our feelings need not be harrowed by dwelling on these, now that perfect rest is given, though we may glorify God for the patience and grace with which He enabled her to endure them.

June 20.—She was evidently sinking, and took no notice when told of a sweet note from her pastor, and of texts from Miss B. at Jaffa. In the evening we helped to prepare adornings for our two houses on the Jubilee Day, sadly wondering whether we should not arise to darkened rooms and quiet weeping.

Tuesday, June 21.—The sun shone gloriously on our good Queen Victoria's Jubilee. We followed in thought the royal procession, the thanksgiving service in Westminster Abbey, and the other arrangements of that ever to be remembered day, when the great heart of the nation throbbed with loyalty and love, and England's distant children joined as one family in praise to the great Ruler and Father of all, and in prayer for the beloved Empress-Queen.

We heard the booming of artillery, the distant sounds of many feet, and the rejoicing voices of our township, in the quiet room where alternately we watched "the footsteps of the end." We felt the mighty presence of a Saviour-God around us, and one of our number even imagined she saw the dim outlines of ministering angels waiting to convey a ransomed soul to celestial regions.

The dear one lay quietly in semi-slumber nearly all that long bright day, and the only words I heard her utter were, "Water—Ice—Pray."

Wednesday, June 22.—Dear Maria always loved the early morning hours, and last summer had written, "If I had a wish, it would be to hear the voice of my Beloved in the very day-dawning, and hear the lark's song as I wing my spirit-flight upwards." And now the wish was to be realized. In the early dawn of that fair summer day we were summoned to her room. She was then muttering incoherently, and continued to do so an hour or more; then we caught at intervals, in an indistinct but loud voice, these last words: "How good the Lord is!—Glory, glory!—My Lord Jesus—He has done it all—The First and the Last—Come—Amen, amen, amen!" Gradually the stillness of death fell, her face changed, her eyes were fixed; the nurse said, "How good God is to let her go so gently!" and in a few minutes, just before six o'clock in the morning, we saw that she slept in Jesus. Blessed sleep! after the long days and longer nights in which we were tempted to say, "Hath the Lord forgotten to be gracious? hath He in anger shut up His tender mercies?" But now He had remembered her in her low estate, and had taken her to be with Himself for ever.

> "O change, O wondrous change!
>   Burst are the prison bars;
>   One moment—there so low,
>   And now—beyond the stars!"
>
> C. B.

> "Her faith is sight,
>   Her hope is full delight,
> The shadowy veil of time is rent in twain;
>   Her untold bliss—
>   What thought can follow this!
> To her to live was Christ, to die indeed is gain."
>
> F. R. H.

On Tuesday, June 28, 1887, the noon-day sun again lighted up the rock-hewn and flower-crowned grave in Astley Churchyard, Worcestershire, in which our father was laid in 1870, his second wife in 1878, and his daughter Frances in 1879. The band of mourners was headed by her brother, the Rev. Francis T. Havergal, and her nephew, John H. Crane. Other relatives and friends, and many cottagers stood around, while our sister Ellen's step-son, the Rev. John Hall Shaw, impressively read the beautiful burial service over all that was mortal of

Maria Vernon Graham Havergal.

> "Death divides, but not for ever,
>   Those whom Christ hath called His own;
> Love's dear bands the grave may sever,
>   Loving hearts meet round His throne!
> Here, the cloud of change is o'er us,
>   Time and earth in courses move;
> Thou art not lost, but gone before us,
>   Soon we meet to live in love!"
>
> W. J.

EXTRACTS FROM LETTERS OF SYMPATHY TO M. V. G. H.'S SISTER, J. M. C.

From Mrs. E. E. A.

July 11, 1887.

WHILE to her loved ones who remain her death will be a great loss, to her it is infinite gain. Apart from the great suffering she has borne so patiently for years, and now laid down for ever, there would be the joy of meeting her dear Saviour and those beloved ones who have gone before, and how great this joy those who have come in contact with her can in some small measure appreciate. With strongly-marked character and the deepest affections, how wonderfully she kept self in the background, content to lose her own individuality in loving and caring for others. Her whole life, it seems to me, might be described in the words *self-sacrifice,* so closely she followed the footsteps of her Lord. I think her place in the New Jerusalem will be close to her Master's side.

Note.—In writing to M. V. G. H. in April 1887, E. E. A. refers to seeing her and her sister Ellen in 1853 thus:—"You were going with Mrs. U. to dine at Mr. M'K.'s, and we girls were naturally interested in seeing you both after you were dressed, but on coming downstairs to our great disappointment you wore only a very plain dress, and when we exclaimed, 'Oh, Miss Havergal, where is your beautiful dress?' you replied that you had been thinking all the afternoon how nice you would look in your prettiest dress, and you had punished yourself by putting on your old one!" In the same letter E. E. A. says, "How few of us are left to recall the meek and gracious character of your dear sister Ellen; she seemed to radiate an atmosphere of holy calm. I well remember my bright visit to Worcester, and the great treat I enjoyed of hearing Mr. Havergal and your sister Frances play so beautifully. It was quite a revelation to me of how much soul could be infused into a sonata."

From Mrs. Charles B.

July 25, 1887.

I can but rejoice that your dear sister is safe home, the shadows over, and all is light now for ever. I came across several of her sweet letters last night, written to me after our loved Fanny's death, and they touched me deeply. How good our God has been to spare her these eight years; she so grandly bore witness to her sister's work in giving it out to the world. Dear F. R. H.'s death thus spoke even more than her life.

From Miss S. A. B.

July 4, 1887.

Sad and lonely as it is to live without our dear ones who are gone home before, it is an untold consolation to look forward to the glorious resurrection, when we shall meet again, never to be parted.

"'Tis sweet, as year by year we lose
Friends out of sight, in faith to muse
How grows in Paradise our store."

I have very loving recollections of your dear sister in those happy peaceful days I spent at Oakhampton. She was always so kind to me, and helped me in my spiritual life by many nice talks, and I gratefully remember with much pleasure the sweet little Bible-readings she had with darling M. and myself. I have many texts marked in my Bible about which she gave us loving, helpful thoughts. Truly, "she being dead yet speaketh;" her loving influence will live on in such numbers of lives, and she must have had the joy of winning so many souls to Jesus. Hers will surely be a very bright crown, and what a joyous welcome hers would be in the heavenly home!

From the Rev. J. C.

July 1, 1887.

It was indeed a sad break to you of the Jubilee gladness. She indeed has entered into that rest of which the jubilee of Israel was a type and a foreshadowing. Perhaps you recollect Pope's lines on a victim of the same disease—

"Heaven, as its purest gold with torture tried,
The saint sustained it, but the woman died."

This really seems true of her, and of others gone before. Her death, however expected, was in one sense desired; all grounds of consolation are indeed present, and you know them all too well to need their suggestion, but accept the fellow-feeling in sorrow, the growth of forty-eight years.

From Miss E. C.

June 23, 1887.

"With Christ, which is far better."

Thank you very much for letting me know so quickly that our beloved one is really there—for ever with the Lord. I have been trying to picture her glory, her joy! It seems the only thing that can lift one out of the crushing sense of desolation to think of that. . . . Wherever she has been in her various wanderings, she was ever to be found ministering to the sick, and carrying to those in darkness the glorious gospel of the grace of God. Not only among such, however, have been her sweet ministries of love. Only the Lord knows to how many of His servants in a different sphere self-denying kindness has been shown for the Master's sake, which He will not forget who has said, "Inasmuch as ye have done it unto one of the least of these my brethren, ye have done it unto me."

From Mrs. R. B. M.

June 26, 1887.

Last night we read the announcement of your dearly loved sister's happy release. Though we have been expecting it, it is difficult to realize that our beloved friend, for whom our prayers have been so constant of late, needs them no more, and that we need never think of her again in connection with weakness and suffering. It is all a light and momentary affliction to her *now,* and there lies before her an endless weight of glory, the first taste of which must be sweet indeed. May God be praised for His grace bestowed upon her, and which truly was not in vain, and you know what reason we have had to love her, and to thank God for ever having had the privilege of knowing her.

From Miss C. D. R.

July 4, 1887.

I see that dear Miss Havergal has been called up higher, even into the blessed presence of her Lord and Master. Happy is she indeed to be safely there, and how great her bliss no heart here below can possibly conceive. But this world is poorer indeed; we cannot but feel the loss when one and another of those who are the salt of the earth and of the Church are removed. How she worked for the Master, and how humble she was! I always specially admire the grace of humility—the first of graces, but I may almost say the last attained to by many.

From the Rev. R. B.

June 1887.

Thank you very much for giving me an account of dear Miss Havergal's last illness. It is comforting when it is light at sunset, and when the last words are peaceful and bright, but they were not needed to assure us of the glory that awaited her.

I cannot tell how deeply I have felt her death, the last link gone, as it were, connecting me with dear Mr. Havergal at Worcester, calling up recollections of St. Nicholas Sunday school, where we so often met and had pleasant intercourse; and since then in connection with Shareshill, and her stay in our house during our first mission will never be forgotten. Her prayerful interest in my boy (her godson) led her to send him an occasional letter, and my thoughts often turn to this with deep thankfulness.

And let me add a word of sympathy on your own behalf in your deep bereavement. You have had to pass through deep waters of trial, but I trust you have found the promise true, "When thou passest through the waters, I will be with thee."

May you have supporting and enabling grace to carry you onwards till called to join the many who have gone before.

From the Rev. E. H.

June 24, 1887.

I hasten to send a line of deep sympathy on hearing of the great loss you and all our family have sustained in the departure of our very dear Aunt Maria for the better life of Paradise. She truly set a Christ-like example here; now she rejoices for evermore in the palace of the "Great King." Death has made during the past twelve years a terrible inroad among the Havergals, and yet we are all united, whether present or absent, in the one Lord, the one faith, and the one love; and may the day be not far distant when we shall all as a family be perfectly united before the great white throne to praise and magnify the one object of universal admiration! At this thought we may well rejoice. God grant you consolation now and always.

Maria was buried in the same family vault with her father William Henry Havergal, her step-mother Caroline Anne (Cooke) Havergal, and F.R.H., in Astley Churchyard. Maria's gravestone is shown on page 94. This is the epitaph of Maria's and Frances' mother, William Henry Havergal's first wife, Jane Head Havergal, in St. Nicholas Church, Worcester.

Jane,
The Beloved Wife of
The Revd W. H. Havergal, M.A.
Rector of This Parish,
And Honorary Canon of the Cathedral
In This City.
Died in Holy Peace July 9th 1848,
Aged 54 Years.
"I give unto them Eternal Life." John x, 28.
(Interred in the Crypt.)

POETRY.

A MEMORY OF A WALK NEAR PEN-Y-BRYN, COLWYN.

Sept. 23, 1858.

We had watched the rainbow o'er the sea
    Tinting the snowy spray;
Then onward sped 'neath rock and tree
    On our pleasant rambling way.

A valley spread beneath our gaze
    With cottage, farm, and wood;
Far distant mountains in the haze
    Of wide horizon stood.

Then stormy wind and drenching rain
    Swept round that bleak hill-side;
We pelted travellers would fain
    From the fierce tempest hide.

We saw a mountain-cottage door,
    And gladly hastened in;
Yet paused, for on that humble floor
    A child lay, pale and thin.

There in a little cradle bed
    A boy, some nine years old,
With infant mind and palsied head
    A tale of sadness told.

And yet poor Willie's face was glad,
    Though speechless, helpless laid;
What smile had chased his sorrow sad
    With joy that may not fade?

Then came a whisper soft and still,
    "Let children come to me,
It is my Heavenly Father's will
    Such should my kingdom see.

"He knows me not, but I know him;
    My blood-red hand unseen
Hath cleansed the stain of Adam's sin,
    And made him snow-white clean.

"Gently I'll wake that tiny mind
    My heights of love to know;
And, folded on my breast, shall find
    He's saved from depths of woe.

"My love, his first and only song;
    My throne his home shall be;
My glory his through ages long,
    My smile his joy shall be."

The glimpse is past, we onward haste
    Through stormy wind and rain,
O'er hilly side and common waste
    Sweet Pen-y-bryn to gain.

Kind friends, may this your shelter be
    In Jesu's covert breast;
Hereafter may we meet and see
    His peaceful, stormless rest!

TO MY SISTER FANNY R. H. ON HER BIRTHDAY, Dec. 14, 1863.

"Let thy garments be always white."—Ecclesiastes 9:8.

"Always white," O echo sweet!
Of Eden chimes long passed away,
When robed in loveliness to greet
The first beloved, Eve shone like day.

"Always white," O mournful knell
Of garments stained, of shame and woe,
Of sin's desert and Satan's spell,
Of Eden lost, of man, God's foe.

"Always white" on Calvary's mount,
Blood hath cleansed the garments' stain;
And now in Jesu's precious blood
A new white robe is found again.

Oh may this garment now be thine!
All fair in Jesu's beauty shine;
Through dusty road, 'midst soiling fight,
Unspotted keep thy garments white.

Remember Jesu's prayer for thee,
"Father, from evil keep them free;
May they behold my glory bright,
And walk with me in raiment white."

O Saviour, keep her undefiled
'Mid tempting scene or thorny wild;
Then dove-winged take her upward flight
To walk with Thee in garments white.

THY FAITHFULNESS.

"Great is Thy faithfulness."—LAMENTATIONS 3:23.

MINE eye upon Thy faithfulness would gaze,
    And pierce "the very heavens," where ever lives
Jesus, my faithful priest; to Him I raise,
    In constant song, my praise for all He gives
        In faithfulness.

Imprinted on His priestly girdle shines
    Royally His faithfulness, unchanging still;
'Mid changeful windings of my paths and times,
    "Yet He abideth faithful;" and His will
        Is faithfulness.

Gently He "called," and drew me to His side,
    In faithfulness, to know His voice and smile;
Then came affliction's dark and surging tide,
    And "fiery trial;" and then I proved, meanwhile,
        His faithfulness.

His still small voice unto my lonely ear
    Said, "Yea, I will betroth thee unto Me
In faithfulness;" Hushed now is every fear,
    For Christ is mine! in life, in death, I sing
        "Thy faithfulness."

HUSH ME![1]

In F. R. H.'s Study, in memory of June 3rd, 1879.

HUSH me, Lord Jesus! I cannot yet be still;
In vain I try to say it is Thy will;
My path is lonely, there is no one nigh
To share my sorrow, or to soothe my sigh,
    Hush me, Lord Jesus!

One voice is hushed; my sister's merry voice,
So sweet, so tuneful, as she sang "rejoice!"
From me my song-bird flew so far away—
Soft echoes leaving when she could not stay.
    Hush me, Lord Jesus!

So strange to miss my darling's footfall light,
Her smile I see not, 'twas my sunshine bright;
No tiny tokens now are brought to me—
Ferns, mosses, flowers, or shells beside the sea.
    Hush me, Lord Jesus!

O bruisèd Saviour! Thou wilt never break
The bruisèd reed, and never wilt Thou take

Thine arm from underneath Thy leaning child,
Who trusts and clings throughout the desert wild—
    Hush me, Lord Jesus!

Yes; I have proved Thy faithful word is true,
"Just as a mother will I comfort you;"
"I know thy sorrow, and thy need of rest"—
Leaning I cry, upon my Saviour's breast,
    Hush me, Lord Jesus!

The hush of Heaven seems stealing over me,
The quiet haven nears in which I long to be;
My Kingly Comforter brings the sweet whisper nigh,
"A little, little while!" no need again to sigh,
    Hush me, Lord Jesus.

AMY'S BIRDIE.[2]

Came into this life, and entered into life eternal, Oct. 3, 1883.

BABY Birdie! why, oh why,
Did you only come to die?
Tell us why your little wing
Swiftly flew where angels sing?

Precious Birdie! such a nest
Waited you on Mother's breast!
Father's strong and loving arm,
Safe would shield you from alarm.

First-born Birdie, precious gift!
With our bleeding hearts we lift,
Lay thee on the Shepherd's breast,
Safely gathered, sweetly rest.

Wondrous Birdie! breath divine,
An immortal spirit thine;
Thine the vesture snowy white,
Thine the mansions fair and bright!

Ransomed Birdie! welcomes ring
From thy dear ones near the King;
Auntie's song will surely greet
Amy's "little thing" so sweet.

Farewell, Birdie! will you wait
Very near the pearly gate?
While we toil 'mid scorching heat,
Sheaves to lay at Jesu's feet.

Birdie's Master, we will bring
Afric's sons to own Thee King;
Jewels dark of heathen gem
Flash in Thy bright diadem!

---

[1] An unknown friend, seeing these lines in *Woman's Work,* sent some pretty verses entitled "Thou shalt be hushed."—July 1882.

[2] Printed at Rabai, East Africa, by the Rev. A. Downes Shaw.

AN INVALID'S PRAYER.

Must I be smitten, Lord;
    Are gentler measures vain?
Must I be smitten, Lord;
    Can nothing save but pain?

Thou trustedst me a while,
    Alas! I was deceived;
I revelled in Thy smile,
    Yet to the dust I cleaved.

Then the fierce tempest broke,
    I knew from whom it came;
I read in that sharp stroke
    A Father's hand and name.

I said, "My God, at length
    This stony heart remove;
Deny all other strength,
    But give me strength to love."

Less wayward may I be,
    More pliable and mild,
In glad simplicity,
    More like a trustful child.

Less, less of self each day,
    And more, my God, of Thee;
Oh keep me in the way,
    However rough it be.

Less of the flesh each day,
    Less of the world and sin;
More of Thy Son I pray,
    More of Thyself within.

June 3, 1885.

ANTICIPATIONS!

"Until the day break, and the shadows flee away."
—Song of Solomon 2:17.

Shadows so darkening,
Dream-like are passing.
Deserts so dreary,
Footfall so weary,
Lonely night weeping,
Vigil watch keeping,
Achings so trying,
Tear-drops and sighing,
Conflicts assailing,
Shadows unveiling,
Mists fleeing away,
Changing to day!
Shadows no longer!
Day-dawning yonder,—
Sweet voices calling,
Seraph-chant falling,
Palm branches waving,
Stormy clouds breaking;
Welcome! sweet morning,
Glory-light dawning.
Haven is nearing,
No breakers fearing,
Gaining the strand,
Safe, safe to land!

Thus I pass yonder,
Lost in sweet wonder,
Praising and soaring,
Always adoring,
Raiment all snow-white,
Blood-washed and sun-bright;
In Christ victorious,
Visions *so* glorious!
Hushed on His breast,
There shall I rest;
Shadows all past,
Daybreak at last!

May 1886.

LIFE'S ORIENT MORN HAS PASSED AWAY.

"At evening time it shall be light."—Zechariah 14:7.

Life's orient morn has passed away,
Hushed all the clamorous cares of day;
Thro' twilight calm, soft steals one chime,
"It shall be light at evening time."

Life's western portal opes for me;
Death's darkening valley near I see;
This promise meets my dimming sight,
At evening time it shall be light.

Jesus, my light of life, draw near;
Shine on my darkness, chase each fear;
Stand by me in life's closing fight,
And cheering say, I am thy light.

Washed in Thy precious blood alone,
Arrayed in righteousness Thine own,
From evening time I pass away
To heaven's eternal, shadeless day.

THE DYING CHRISTIAN'S FAREWELL.

I journey forth rejoicing,
    From this dark vale of tears,
To heavenly joy and freedom.
    From earthly bonds and fears;
Where Christ our Lord shall gather
    All His redeem'd again,
His kingdom to inherit;—
        Good night till then!

Go to thy quiet resting,
    Poor tenement of clay,
From all thy pain and weakness
    I gladly haste away;
But still in faith confiding
    To find Thee yet again,
All glorious and immortal;—
        Good night till then!

Why thus so sadly weeping,
    Belov'd ones of my heart?
The Lord is good and gracious,
    Tho' now He bids us part.
Oft have we met in gladness,
    And we shall meet again.
All sorrow left behind us;—
        Good night till then!

I go to see His glory,
    Whom we have lov'd below;
I go the blessed angels,
    The holy saints to know;
Our lovely ones departed,
    I go to find again,
And wait for you to join us;—
        Good night till then!

I hear the Saviour calling;
    The joyful hour has come;
The angel-guards are ready
    To guide me to our home;
Where Christ our Lord shall gather
    All His redeem'd again,
His kingdom to inherit;—
        Good night till then!

    From *Hymns from the Land of Luther.*

    [Not in the original.]

There's no "good night" in glory!
    No eve to that bright day;
I leave life's finished story,
    Its tears, its thorny way.
The blood-bought robe is o'er me,
    My faith is lost in sight.
Jesus! I <u>see</u> thy glory!
    No more—good night!

                  M.V.G.H.

THE LORD WILL GIVE GRACE AND GLORY.

"Grace"

G race be unto you and peace.		Phil. 1:2.
I commend you to . . . the word of His grace.		Acts 20:32.
L et us come boldly to the throne of grace.		Heb. 4:16.
E ven so might grace reign through righteousness.		Rom. 5:21.
S ee that ye abound in this grace.		2 Cor. 8:7.

"Glory"

S hew me Thy glory.		Ex. 33:18.
H e might present it to Himself a glorious church.		Eph. 5:27.
A fterward receive me to glory.		Ps. 73:24.
W hen the chief Shepherd shall appear, ye shall receive a crown of glory.		1 Pet. 5:4.

            For May 5, 1867.
            M.V.G.H.

"Grace"

G race, peace, and love be thine.
I n words of grace divine,
L et every need by grace supplied,
E ven His righteousness applied:
S ee that thy graces shine.

"Glory"

S hew him Thy glory, even Thine.
H e glorious grant with Thee to shine;
A fter life's journey see Thy face,
W ith glory crown the work of grace!

            For May 5, 1867.
            M.V.G.H.

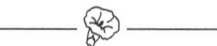

[Note: See also Maria's single verse on page 146 of this book.]

WYRE HILL HOME MISSION,

opened October 10th 1868.

This print was found among Havergal manuscripts and papers. This was apparently the "large new mission room" mentioned on page 135 of this book. The handwritten note looks like Maria's handwriting (when she was not well to write her neatest): opened October 10th 1868.

William Henry Havergal (1793–1870), Maria's father, an undated photograph.

This was the frontispiece of the original book, Records of the Life of the Rev. Wm. H. Havergal, M.A.

Giles Shaw (1813–1903) and his wife Ellen (1823–1886). The photograph of Ellen was also an Elliott & Fry photograph. Both photographs were un-dated.

OUTLINES

OF

A GENTLE LIFE.

𝔄 𝔐𝔢𝔪𝔬𝔯𝔦𝔞𝔩 𝔖𝔨𝔢𝔱𝔠𝔥 𝔬𝔣 𝔈𝔩𝔩𝔢𝔫 𝔓. 𝔖𝔥𝔞𝔴.

EDITED BY HER SISTER,

MARIA V. G. HAVERGAL.

"In Thy presence is fulness of joy."

LONDON:
JAMES NISBET & CO., 21, BERNERS ST.
BEWDLEY: F. R. & T. C. DALLEY; M. E. BRYAN.
1887.

CONTENTS.

CHAP.		PAGE
	Introductory Chapter	189
I.	Holy Memories	191
II.	School Days	192
III.	Home Life	194
IV.	Marriage and a Home in Ireland	196
V.	Return to England—New Home at Winterdyne, Worcestershire	201
VI.	Last Days and Sudden Glory	206

LETTERS TO HER HUSBAND AND CHILDREN 211

BIBLE NOTES 223

A 19th century photograph of Winteredyne, the home of F.R.H.'s sister and her husband, Giles and Ellen Shaw. See also page 237 of this book.

OUTLINES OF A GENTLE LIFE.

INTRODUCTORY CHAPTER.

ONE of God's beautiful mysteries in nature is the varied, invisible, and inseparable perfume of flowers; they may hide beneath their leaves or greenery surrounding, yet cannot conceal their fragrance.

And thus it was with the life of my sister Ellen, whose humility, meekness, and unselfishness adorned her earthly home, till most suddenly gathered and transplanted to the King's fairer garden. It is only possible to give some outlines of that gentle life, and this is done by the express wish of her husband. He desires that God's glory may shine forth to others, as they read her clear testimony to the preciousness of God's Word, and how she adorned the doctrine of God her Saviour in all things.

Not forgetting the interest many friends may feel in this Memorial, her husband wishes to circulate these pages among the large number of excursionists, who in former years have received so many books at her hand. Thousands have been permitted to wander freely in the picturesque and shady walks of Winterdyne. Fervent prayer preceded effort for their good; Mr. and Mrs. Shaw would then take baskets full of books—such as Mr. Stevenson Blackwood's, Rev. George Everard's, and Reid's, with F. R. Havergal's Memoir, "Royal Invitation," etc. etc., offering them with kindly words to the strangers.

In former years, her sister, F. R. Havergal, occasionally and energetically assisted with voice in holy song, as well as hand, in giving away flowers at these gatherings; and they seem to have suggested the following lines in her poem of "The Sowers," as in her own copy she has written "Mr. Shaw" against these lines:—

> "Another watched the sowers longingly:
>   'I cannot sow such seed as they,' he said;
> 'No shining grain of thought is given to me,
>   No fiery words of power bravely sped.
> Will others give me of their bounteous store?
> My hand may scatter that, if I can do no more.'
>
> "So by the wayside he went forth to sow
>   The silent seeds, each wrapped in fruitful prayer,'
> With glad humility; content to know
>   The volume lent, the leaflet culled with care,
> The message placed in stranger hands, were all
> Beneath His guiding eye who notes the sparrow's fall."

A few words from one of Mrs. Shaw's last letters convey the fragrance of her faith and hope. "When I look at the Fifteenth Psalm, in the light of Revelation 7, and I see how that innumerable multitude stand before the throne, I take comfort in seeing that I can claim admission with them, for I have the same right, the same passport—'the blood of the Lamb!' Washed in that all-atoning blood from omissions, commissions, and failures, and clothed in His perfect righteousness instead of my own, I hope and expect to 'abide in His holy hill.'"

MARIA V. G. HAVERGAL.

WINTERDYNE, February 19, 1887.

Two photographs of Ellen Prestage (Havergal) Shaw.

CHAPTER I.

HOLY MEMORIES.

ASTLEY RECTORY, Worcestershire, is no longer an unknown name. Holy memories cluster around its home and adjoining churchyard. And holy footprints may yet be tracked among his people, of the faithful ambassador of Christ, the Rev. W. H. Havergal; while his home influence twines with the bright life of his youngest daughter, Frances.

The church, built on high ground, commands extensive views.

> " . . . . See Woodbury's outline grand,
> Upon whose crest the ancient Briton camped.
> Oh, lovely are the walks that curve between,
> From Yarrow up the Toot
> Back to the meadow in our view, where once
> Lily and Rose, our cows, were often seen,
> And sometimes Gentle, our fine faithful horse;
> And there each other year we made the hay;
> Our pastor father, with well-ordered mind,
> Gave orchard, study, parish, each due care.
> We mimic children, played at church and school,
> And grew up handy, hardy, in our country life."
> —J. MIRIAM CRANE.

The rectory garden then was fair, and it was our mother's delight to train the flowers with skill and care. In its shrubbery nooks, as well as flower-borders, snowdrops grew luxuriantly. When children, we transplanted them from the Astley snowdrop wood, where they grew in thousands; their dark green tufts, crested with snowy bells, springing from under the dead bracken and tangles of moss and ivy.

With February they came, and on February 19, 1823, came our home snowdrop, Ellen, third daughter of the Rev. W. H. Havergal and Jane his wife. Her memory seems always associated with this flower, as appears from her sister Miriam's lines (herself only seven years old) on her second birthday:—

> "Pretty little sister dear,
> See a snowdrop bud appear,
> All beneath the shady tree
> Which, my sweet, resembles thee!"

And in after years her own children delighted in the long drive from Winterdyne to the same Astley snowdrop wood, to gather baskets full of "mother's flower" as a birthday offering.

Even as a little child, Ellen possessed the ornament of a meek and quiet spirit, ever hiding away self and preferring to please others, regardless of her own wishes—

> "So many nice scruples arise in the way,
> Whenever we wish her, her own self to please,
> Or take for herself some comfort and ease!"
> —F. R. H.

Once I questioned our maid about the old nursery days, and she told me that she never knew Miss Ellen naughty but once, and that was to defend sister Maria when corrected! Also, that she was a most good-natured child, dressing up her dolls to give away, and other playthings. Her skill in doll-dressing extended afterwards in making artistic costumes of various nations, and to her delight these dolls were sold for the Church Missionary Society. (It was always a pleasure at Astley Rectory to help *that*.) She learnt knitting from a dear old widow—she was never an idle, listless child—and after learning her little lessons with mother, would quietly work and amuse herself. Some of my earliest and holiest remembrances are of our dear mother's Bible lessons on Sunday. Both Ellen and myself were much impressed one night, rather later than usual, with mother's words about the holy happy heaven, and the great love of Jesus, and they roused me to keen attention, and I thought, "Mamma and Ellen are good, and sure to go to heaven; I wish I was."

We often wondered why our mother always went to her own room some time before tea, and we determined to discover what she did. Opening the door, there she sat reading her large Bible. We thought much more of the Bible from that time, and I believe Ellen early followed that example, and certainly did so in later years, retiring from any other pursuit for those hallowed moments.

"My good little Ellen," or "Papa's harmless dove," was his home call; and his birthday lines must close her childhood's page:—

TO ELLEN, ON HER THIRD BIRTHDAY.

19th February 1826.

Come, my pretty little love,
Sweet and harmless as the dove;
You, my February Queen!
Paper-crowned with pink and green,
Happy, happy may you be,
Often as this day you see.
Onward as through life you go,
May the Bible you well know!
And when days and years are fled,
And you sleep among the dead,
May your spirit happy be,
With the Great and Holy Three,
Clad in robes of holiness,
Crowned with everlasting bliss.

—Rev. W. H. Havergal.

CHAPTER II.

SCHOOL-DAYS.

LIVING in a retired country rectory, my father thought it desirable to give his daughters such school training and education as would fit them for useful and happy lives. Great Campden House was then a well-known school, attended by first-rate professors from London, with other educational advantages; so Ellen's home life and governess were exchanged for school, and the penetrating and persuasive Bible teaching of Mrs. Teed. There was no vacancy on the first application, but the death of one of the pupils made way for her admission in March 1838.

Eagerly did I watch for Ellen's arrival, and very pleasant was it to introduce her to our many companions, and show her the historic tapestried rooms and chapel of Queen Anne, and the quaint wood-carvings in one of the spacious schoolrooms. The garden walks were extensive, and beneath the terrace there was, as supposed in olden times, a subterranean passage to the House of Lords—but our curiosity might never penetrate that.

I did not then know the secret of my sister's anxiety to come to school, and it is only eighteen months ago that I found it out! I was then staying at Hertford, and during a visit from Ellen (Mrs. Shaw) invited some of the deaf girls from Christ's Hospital to breakfast. She then gave them this account of how and when God's Word brought her peace and joy:—

It was in March 1838 that I first went to school at Great Campden House, Kensington. I was so disappointed when, the Christmas previous, Mrs. Teed wrote that she had no room for me; so I was glad when the letter came in March, for I thought I shall surely find out for myself what I could not *then* at all believe. I will tell you the secret why I wished to go to school. It was not that I wanted to get on with lessons and accomplishments only, though I really was very glad of the opportunity of learning more than I could at home, for I was nearly fifteen, and had not been years at school like my sisters. For many reasons I was glad to go and learn; but the secret was, that then I hoped I should really find the Lord Jesus as my own Saviour. I had for long been so miserable. I knew all about Christ, and had had much sweet teaching at home. But I heard that the governess, Mrs. Teed, was so good, and I knew that many of her pupils had really found Christ. It was on a cold morning in March 1838 that papa drove me at 4 A.M. to Worcester to meet the "Star" coach to London, which started at 6 A.M., going through Oxford and High Wycombe, where dear, saintly grandmamma Havergal met me. The coach arrived at Kensington between 7 and 8 P.M. A teacher, Miss Green, met me and took me into the back parlour for tea, and then I had a chair close to the door of the schoolroom, where evening prayers were going on. I heard the organ, and I suppose some one gave me a book for the hymn, which I have never forgotten; it was—

> "How condescending and how kind
>   Was God's eternal Son!
> Our misery reached His heavenly mind,
>   And pity brought Him down.
>
> "When justice, by our sins provoked,
>   Drew forth its dreadful sword,
> He gave His soul up to the stroke
>   Without a murmuring word.
>
> "He sunk beneath our heavy woes,
>   To raise us to His throne;
> There's not a gift His hand bestows,
>   But cost His heart a groan.
>
> "This was compassion like a God,
>   That when the Saviour knew
> The price of pardon was His blood,
>   His pity ne'er withdrew.
>
> "Now though He reigns exalted high,
>   His love is still as great;
> Well He remembers Calvary,
>   Nor let His saints forget.
>
> "Here let our hearts begin to melt,
>   While we His death record,
> And, with our joy for pardoned guilt,
>   Mourn that we pierced the Lord!"
>   —Isaac Watts.

And then sister Maria came to meet me and introduce me to school-life.

And I was not disappointed. God did not disappoint my hope, for before many weeks I found it all true. It was on Good Friday, 5th April 1838, that our chaplain, the Rev. Joseph Parker, preached on Isaiah 53:5; "But He was wounded for our transgressions, He was bruised for our iniquities: the chastisement of our peace was upon Him; and with His stripes we are healed." He spoke so simply and sweetly—did we each for ourselves believe that Jesus, God's dear Son, *was* wounded for our transgressions—bruised for our iniquity? When it came to my usual time for going alone to read my Bible, I looked at the verse, and as I looked at the words they shone into my soul, and I just believed that Jesus was bruised *for me*, and that He had suffered for *my* transgressions, and so all my sin was gone, and there was nothing now but peace between me and my Father. And so that verse became my glorious way mark, and the peace it gave me has lasted on all these years.—(1838–1885).

Many can testify to the reality of this early conversion, and therefore being justified by faith, and having peace with God through our Lord Jesus Christ, good fruit appeared, and henceforth she walked most "justly, holily, and unblameably."

> "It was the rising! the first hour
>   Of the true shining, that should rise and rise
>   From glory unto glory, through God's skies,
> In strengthening brightness and increasing power.
> A rising with no settling, for its height
> Could only culminate in God's eternal light.
>
> . . . . . .
>
> "And so the years flowed on and only cast
>   Light and more light upon the shining way,
>   That more and more shone to the perfect day;
>   Always intenser, clearer than the past;
> Because they only bore *her* on glad wing
> Nearer the Light of Light, the presence of the King."
>   —"Zenith," F. R. H.

I rejoiced in my sister's popularity at school, her winsome gentleness ensuring many friends. In God's providential hand, one of her school friendships was the forging of a golden link, riveted in her happy marriage and home in Ireland, and afterwards at Winterdyne.

On leaving Campden House, Ellen received prizes and a silver medal for drawing from Mons. de Rivière. She excelled in crayon heads and figures, and with further lessons at home attained proficiency, and she eventually sold many pictures, devoting the profit to the Church Missionary Society.

From Mrs. Teed she received a Reference Bible, the special token of her approval, with the words, "The Lord grant that my beloved child may grow in grace and in the knowledge of our Lord and Saviour Jesus Christ."

Mrs. Teed's appreciation of her character is shown by this mention of Ellen after she had left school.

To M. V. G. H., 1841.

Great Campden House.

. . . And how are you prospering? Are you looking into self where no good thing dwells, or looking to Jesus who is all fair, and in whose righteousness we are all fair too? Are you, an unrighteous sinner, living by faith upon the perfect righteousness of the God-man Christ Jesus? The effect of this righteousness is peace and quietness and assurance and holy living; for if our garments have been made white at such a cost, there will be a holy fear of spotting them,—a dove cannot live with a spot on its silver feathers. Keep near to the Lord Jesus; they that wait upon the Lord shall renew their strength.

I hope you pray daily with my sweet dove Ellen. I hope you found her improved in her studies; how I shall miss her I cannot tell. Love to your dear, dear father and sweet mother and Miriam. I love many at Astley Rectory, and have reason to do so.

—Your affectionate friend,

M. A. Teed.

CHAPTER III.

HOME LIFE.

SCHOOL days were followed by the uneventful period of home life at Astley Rectory; taking share with her sisters in the Sunday school. Her collecting-book for the C. M. S. showed loving diligence, many entries being of quarterly pennies and even halfpence from the scattered cottages. During the summer holidays she delighted in assisting sister Miriam in her large sewing and knitting class.

Studies were not neglected, and on our removal from Astley to Henwick House, she had lessons in German from Herr Lorenz, and it was then her little sister Fanny listened and learned precociously, though unobserved. Ellen's translations from Goethe and Schiller are fluent and poetical, or as F. R. H. said, "first-rate."

In 1844 our dear father accepted the rectory of St. Nicholas, Worcester. Her delicate health often prevented her from working in the parish according to her most earnest desires. I know how intensely she longed to work for Christ, how prayerfully and diligently she prepared every lesson for her class, and how deeply the gentle teacher was loved. Some conversations with her sick scholars are given in "Pleasant Fruits."

With her needlework she almost entirely supported a child in an Indian orphanage. Solid useful books were regularly read, and abstracts written. We were thankful that our dear parents' example and wish kept us from wasting time on novels.

Our sweet mother's long and severe illness, from 1845–48, brought our first and darkest shadow. Then it was that Ellen's home ministry shone with unvarying and unceasing brightness. No classes, no pleasures ever kept her from her mother's side. Not satisfied with the night nurse's attendance, Ellen would steal gently down to her mother's room, soothing and alleviating the weary nights, and bringing comfort untold, unseen, save to the Eye that never slumbers or sleeps. Yes, I must bear witness to my sister's self-sacrificing and dutiful love, a true pattern to myself and daughters in general.

Some time after our dear mother's blessed rest and most peaceful departure, on the 5th July 1848, sister Miriam sent her a miniature likeness of her mother. Ellen writes:—

When I first looked at the beautiful and well-known features, I thought, "Oh that those lips had language!" Then again I thought—if it were so, they would only speak our sorrowful words—only a little while, and when I shall meet my loved mother in her glorious home, what new and unimagined tones of love and joy and peace will she then speak! what, oh what will it be to hear her new and tuneful voice. And again I thought—no pain, no passing shadows will then dim that beloved face; and if so lovely when with us, how fairer still will she be then, reflecting the beauty of her Saviour, who ever was to her the "Altogether Lovely."

Our dear father always specially honoured Ellen for her "piety at home," and at her wedding breakfast he emphatically referred to this characteristic trait, and of her mother's special blessing resting upon her. In our father's will he made special bequest to "his most dutiful daughter Ellen," of the elegant silver cake basket which the parishioners of Astley had presented to our dear mother, Jane Havergal, "in remembrance of her uniform kindness, March 1842."

In the autumn of 1853, we both spent some weeks with Mrs. Gross of Ayr, to whom she addressed these lines on her birthday:—

BIRTHDAY THOUGHTS FOR AN AGED FRIEND

> He who has led thee all the way,
> To silvery hairs and life's decay,
> Will not forsake thee now
> When many a care hath aged thy brow.
> Wait patiently—and thou shalt see
> Thy God aye waits for thee.
> Light has He sown, it soon shall rise
> With gladness on thy longing eyes;
> Till then, though evils hedge thy way,
> Thy shield He proves by night or day;
> Leading thee where thou soon shalt see
> Him face to face continually.
> Loving God's law, sweet peace shall roll
> As deepening rivers in thy soul.
> Rejoice then, in the Lord rejoice!
> And listen to His faithful voice,
> "With blessing thou art surely blest,
> Rely on Me for endless rest."
> —E. P. H., 1853.

Eighteen hundred and fifty-three was a sorrowful year. Our dear father's illness and blindness detained him in Germany, and scattered our home circle. Ellen was also recovering from illness, and the sea-breezes of Ayrshire were most beneficial. Her graceful, fragile figure was quite a contrast to the sturdy Scotch lassies. Indeed, visitors called her "the sweet English angel;" and her peaceful smile and simple words about the Lord Jesus, won many new friends. With the close of the year, the clouds brightened, and our home recall came.

THOUGHTS THE NIGHT BEFORE GOING HOME, AFTER LONG ABSENCE.

December 1853.

Another stage of life is drawing to its close—
Strange have its wanderings been, nor few its woes,—
Sickness and sorrow heavy on us lay,
While each one wandered in a solitary way.
Yet sunshine sometimes pierced the clouds, and showed
A wayside flower, or where a streamlet flowed.
Why were we scattered from our much-loved home?
Why did we journey each as pilgrims lone?
E'en as an eagle stirreth up her nest
The Lord did warn us, "this is not your rest."
Did He not often lead His own aside
By burning bush, or pillar'd cloud, and guide
His followers to some lone mountain-side,
That they might learn, "In Me ye must abide"?
So did He lead us; and when storms rose high
Drew nearer, whispering, "It is I."
Oh, let me listen still to that sweet voice,
And in Thy love and guiding grace rejoice.
—The morning dawns—the shadows flee away,
My longings wake—I'm going home to-day!
No sweeter joy my heart shall know
Till ends my pilgrimage below.
And yearning for my Saviour's breast—
He beckons—"Come to Me and rest,
To-day in Paradise with Me be blest!"

—E. P. H.

The St. Nicholas bells were ringing the home-welcome, but we did not know how eagerly one of Ellen's class was listening and longing to see her teacher. Little Sarah had been a rather troublesome child, and yet she would squeeze her teacher's hand even when chiding her. And she would run home to grannie in the almshouse, and tell her, "I was naughty at school to-day, but Miss Ellen told me of it, and I can't bear to vex her, and she does want me to be Jesus' little lamb." The texts learnt at school were found again in grannie's great Bible, and the same great Bible was carried by Sarah to church, tripping by grannie in her ancient satin bonnet and hooded cloak.

We were in Scotland when the child's illness came. Sarah read her Bible much, and consequently found comfort; but her one longing was, "Grannie, can't I live to see Mr. Havergal and dear Miss Ellen? I must tell them Jesus loves me, and saves me; won't they like to see me happy?"

She heard the bells, and the loving little heart was beating her dying welcome, "Grannie, they will come *now.*" She asked for the old Bible, and the 14th chapter of St. John, and then she slept. Just as the chimes ceased, One dearer than pastor or teacher came, and little Sarah was gathered with the Shepherd's arm.

It may encourage some wearied teacher, who *seems* ever sowing and never reaping, to read how surely God's promise comes true, "My word shall not return unto Me void." Let us follow my sister to the bedside of one of her scholars in the first class of St. Nicholas' Sunday school. A reference Bible is open by Susan's side; it is well worn—a good index of its value to the owner. Susan takes it up saying, "My Bible is all my comfort now, it's so sweet to me. I hardly care to go to sleep for thinking of it, and the night never seems long, verse after verse brings me so many sweet thoughts. Yesterday I was so ill, and thought I was dying."

Teacher. "And could you trust yourself in the hands of the Lord Jesus?"

Susan. "Yes, quite so. He is such a Saviour, I could not be afraid. He is very precious to me, and I love to think of Him."

Teacher. "Are you not thankful, Susan, that the Lord Jesus has taught you thus to know and love Him?"

Susan. "Yes, I do thank Him, but I thank Him too for sending *you* to teach me; oh, I do thank you so, Miss Ellen!"

Another visit, Susan remarked, "I am proud of my Sunday school; it's a blessed thing to go to one. I was at St. Nicholas school for eleven years, and do thank God for your teaching. How I listened and tried to remember and ponder over all you said, through the week! You used to beg us to seek the Lord Jesus, and to pray for the Holy Spirit; and if you had not, perhaps I should have gone in wicked ways. How you warned us Sunday after Sunday, and pointed us to Jesus, the living way! And what should I do now, without all the Scripture you encouraged us to learn? When I lie awake at night it all comes back into my mind so sweet, and when I am too weak to hold my Bible, the verses come in my mind like food. I wish all my class would attend to the Bible more; it's *after they will want it.*"

February 12.—A cold wintry day, with snow falling thickly. It was an effort and risk for Ellen to brave the long walk through the storm, but she felt a strong impulse not to delay her visit. She found Susan weary and uncomfortable. Her teacher smoothed the tumbled pillows, and brushed her tangled hair, and sponged her feverish hands, and then she sat down and wiped away the gathering death-drops on her scholar's face, saying, "'God shall wipe away all tears from their eyes; and there shall be no more death, neither sorrow, nor crying, neither shall there be any more pain,' and it will be very soon now, dear Susan."

"Yes, He will, He will. But my Saviour had no kind hand to do for Him what you have been doing for me. I have pure water and nice things to refresh me—the Lord Jesus had none—only that vinegar and gall on the sponge."

And then they talked together of the coming glory. Long had she watched the fruits of grace springing up in her scholar's soul, and now the Holy Spirit had ripened her for glory. She lingered long by the bedside; it was not easy to loose the dying hand that would never again hold hers so lovingly. But they parted, and Susan's last whisper, "Full of hope, dear teacher," gave a glance through the opening door into the bright home she was entering. And when the evening came, Susan passed within the gate,—

"Above the splendours of the sky,
To view Him face to face."

Reference has been made to one of my sister's school friendships. The following letter gives a gleam of that sympathy which she so truly felt for others.

OAKHAMPTON, 19th July 1850.

Can the account sent me from the *Record* be really true, my F.? I can scarcely realize that your much loved treasure is snatched away, how then can you? Oh, my F., how I grieve for you! Yet it is no "strange thing" that has happened. The husbandman and shepherd are wont to remove ripened fruits and loved sheep to the place prepared for them; and now that your heavenly Father has done as seemed Him good, may His grace enable you to say, "Even so, Father; not my will, but Thine, be done."

It must indeed be a bitter cup, a heart-rending wound, yet I *know* as your day, so your strength. May faith be strong and hope bright to enable you to pierce the cloud, and confide in the love that has thus appointed, and to receive the comfort which cometh from God alone. Who comforteth like Him? not by removing the trial, but showing it to be a very proof of His love, and of our fellowship with Him—a means and channel of richest blessing. Surely this one is to wean you from earth and its miserable comforters and "cast" you upon Jesus in His fulness and all-sufficiency as your all in all, and thus enable you to *press* forward to where we shall all be one in Christ Jesus. How often have you prayed for such things,—may this be the means of your obtaining.

I thought of you last night as I read, "I have been cast upon Thee ever since I was born." Is it not sorrow and trial that "casts" us upon our God? Our flesh, our heart, our props all fail; we have nothing left but to rest in Him. What a rock to be "cast" upon! so sure, so sheltering; never failing—all-sufficient, because a smitten rock. May its healing streams abound to you while you find shelter there in this storm of sorrow!...

—Your affectionate friend,
E. P. HAVERGAL.

CHAPTER IV.

MARRIAGE AND A HOME IN IRELAND.

WE are permitted to unveil some letters after Ellen's happy engagement to Giles Shaw, Esq. of Celbridge Lodge, County Kildare, and the wise and prayerful spirit in which she looked forward to this new step in life.

To G. S.

WORCESTER, November 1855.

And of what should my first letter be, but of Him who is our first friend, our first object, our first or "exceeding joy"? His love to us is from everlasting, ours is but just commenced, but was it not from Him? did He not shed His love abroad in our hearts, and then drew us by it to each other? Then may our hearts, being "knit together" by His love, be ever receiving increasing supplies of it that shall bind us closer to Him. I would love you much, but I would love Him most, because He "first loved me, and gave Himself for me." Do you think these two rules would help us to love Him more,—that whenever we think of each other, especially in absence, we should also think of Him who is "with us always," while we are with Him. Also, that whenever we observe anything, either defective or pleasing in each other, we should make it an occasion to admire Him who is "without blemish or spot," and altogether lovely....

E. P. H.

To G. S.

LANSDOWNE CRESCENT,
11th December 1855.

The snow prevented me from going into the parish this morning, so I had the pleasure of going to my room at noon and doing as I hoped you then did. My chapter happened to be Matthew 17. I felt it was indeed "*good*" to "come apart" from the rest and be awhile in the presence of Jesus. It seemed as if you and I might, and did, ascend far higher than *that* happy mount, even to that Mount Zion whither He is gone before us. And if we cannot yet see His brightness with bodily eyes, faith can discern something of His brightness as the "sun of our souls," the "Sun of Righteousness." I could not but pray, "Lord, show *me,* show *us* Thyself." He *has* arisen upon our souls with healing in His beams. May He now shine *more* brightly upon us, not only to cheer with His bright beams of love, but to reflect upon us more of His image. Oh to be changed into His image here, and into His glory hereafter! Surely He did (as you say) "meet us on that occasion"! How gracious of Him to do so! . . .

E. P. H.

December 1855.

I hope our Sunday enjoyment has been mutual,—to me there seemed new need for every prayer, new cause for every praise, and a new light and value in precepts and promises, which it would have been delightful to have enjoyed with you. Never was I so struck before with the figure brought to our notice by our Church, of Christ as the Branch. "I sat under His shadow with great delight," and thought of Him as His Father's "plant of renown," "daily His delight," and yet transplanted by Him to our desert world. Those to whom He was first given saw no beauty in Him, but thanks be to God if He enables us to see that He is "beautiful and glorious," and "altogether lovely." We look unto Him and see Him as a branch drooping and oppressed, with the burden of our sin, laden with the imputation of our guilt and sentences of death. We look again, and see He is the only "righteous Branch" in this "dry ground,"—and more than this, that He is *our* Righteousness. We go and "sit under His shadow," and are "revived," sheltered, and refreshed,—we find His fruit is not only for "healing" to our sin-wounded hearts, but that it is "sweet to our taste," and in full confidence it will "never fail," we may say—"Feed me till I want no more!"

Nor is this enough, we must be "grafted into" this glorious Branch and "abide in Him." And how gracious a command is this; I feel it so very much just now when so much is before me, and yet, that "separate from Him" I can do nothing. Oh that I may so abide as to become neither barren nor unfruitful in holiness. I had many other thoughts about this beauteous Branch which shall "spread through all lands." Only, if it is *pleasant* to be under the shade of what seems now to our blind eyes but as a Branch, what will be the fulness of our joy when we behold Him as the *Tree* of Life in the midst of the Paradise of God!

18th December 1855.

My class chapter, Genesis 42, for to-morrow has been showing me how much of the gospel is laid up for us in the rolls of the Old Testament,—how Jesus is set forth to the spiritual eye. I want to impress my dear class with the thought (ver. 5) that every earthly good must at some time prove barren and disappointing (a lesson for *myself*), that it will be only in the heavenly Canaan that we shall "hunger *no* more." The consequence of neglecting to seek spiritual food (John 3:18, 36, 6:53). To point them to the true Joseph who gives His own body for our food, and is a *full* storehouse for all our wants (Proverbs 8:17, 21; John 6:35; Colossians 1:19; John 1:14, 16). No price to be given by us (Isaiah 55:1). As Joseph spoke "roughly," so God shows "hard things" to His sons—pricks the conscience, convinces of sin, awakens His north wind, or sends trial like His pruning-knife—and why all this?—to convict, search, cleanse, and prune, and so fit them to receive comfort in the revelation of Himself. So would I warn them of sin and danger, and then direct them to Jesus. He will bring sin to remembrance—show us ourselves first and then Himself. Here I may repeat the little book, "Shew me myself."

Is it not thus that He has dealt with you and me? Was not His heart full of tenderness, melting with love when He sent chastening to either? Oh! I hope that in all the pleasant things He is showing *me* now, He will yet reveal *Himself* more clearly, not let me be taken up with the things themselves, nor let me "set my affections" even upon *one object* more than upon Himself, who is *infinitely* lovely, worthy, and precious.

The thought strikes me, too, that as Joseph gave corn and yet reserved the display of his affection and the knowledge of himself for a future time, so the Saviour gradually unfolds to us the riches of His grace, the knowledge of Himself, and of His will, just as He fits us to receive it. He gives, like Joseph, a present supply, and waits for us to come again when we are in want. Then if *we* are hungering now for more of the Bread of Life which we have already tasted, will He not supply us again?—let us "open our mouths wide that He may fill" them. "My soul with all Thy fulness fill." . . .

E. P. H.

December 1855.

I wish I knew the hour for your Saturday Bible class, and of your Sunday readings; it would be so nice to think of you just then, for I hope always to help you in them by *seeking* for you the help that cometh from above. Another thing I should like to know—at what time or hours I may specially meet you in spirit at our Father's footstool?

I am so thankful that you have such praying friends; social prayer seems so little used as it might and ought to be; it is what I have often longed to enjoy more of, and now God seems to be giving me my heart's desire.

I did not know Mr. Bradley's sermon on the Branch,—indeed it was because I could not remember hearing or reading anything upon the subject, that I tried to think for myself, and was surprised, as we often are, to find a single twig of the word of life bearing so much fruit. My subject for my little class next Sunday afternoon is, the Things to which the Word of God is compared. I want to get time to study it, that I may the better estimate its value.

21st December 1855.

To help you to one pleasant, profitable thought seems a sweet privilege, but it makes me feel that in *myself* I am "poor and needy," and need to say, "cleanse the thoughts of my heart," and *teach* me to think "such things as are good." I would be hearing what the Lord doth speak, watching daily at His gates, waiting at His door, that "His thoughts" may become "dearer" to me, and my own be moulded more like His. And if we have even a desire after holy thoughts, is it not because "the Lord thinketh upon us," to keep us from our own naturally earthly ones?

It has been altogether a happy morning. I went down to the vestry, and made it my business to go into the church, where the recipients await their turn, and tried to say a word in season to the different groups, and so, while allaying their impatience, to lead their thoughts to the Giver of all—*the* best gift, etc. Then I had an errand or two to some who could not come to receive,—one, a poor man, who said, "It was twenty years last week, Miss, since I took to my bed. Not a day but those words come to my mind, 'I will not leave you comfortless,' etc., and they make all my sufferings seem but a dream."

Then I went to collect the *last* of my quarterly missionary subscriptions, and was quite refreshed by another nice talk. How good is God to give such! Many a thought passed of this being (so far as we know) my last St. Thomas' Day at home—the new stewardship I am (*D.V.*) to enter upon. And yesterday, at the examination of our National School by the Bishop, as I looked on the dear little faces as they sang their Hosanna, my imagination flew across the Channel to the Irish faces that will be all strange at first, but which I fancy I love already, and long to teach them, too, of "the new song." . . .

E. P. H.

24th December 1855.

A happy Christmas to you!—happy in the possession of thousand blessings from the "upper and nether springs,"—happy in the full enjoyment of that one best gift which is the source and pledge of all others. Oh! is not this Christmas gift from our Heavenly Father a precious one? Let us try to rejoice more in it. I was trying yesterday to teach my little class something of its greatness from Hebrews 1, which tells of His Godhead, His creating and upholding power, His throne of righteousness and majesty,—the worship He receives, and His eternity. Yet He left all this, laid aside His robes of Light and Majesty, took off His crown, left His kingdom, exchanged heaven for earth—His Father's bosom for a hard manger in a poor stable—the love and adoration of angels for the unconscious presence of brute beasts, etc. And why did He thus? Matthew 1:21; Luke 19:10; John 3:16; Acts 3:26; 2 Corinthians 8:9; 1 Timothy 1:15; Titus 2:14, and 3:6, 7; 1 John 4:9, 10, and many other Scriptures tell us. Is it not then a precious gift? As we think of it, may our hearts burn within us, so that they cry out, "Thanks be unto God for His unspeakable gift!" It is all our "salvation and all our desire."

A sermon I was reading suggested to me that God Himself, has in many ways shown the importance of His gift, by representing it beforehand in types and shadows—preached it by prophets and apostles—announced it by angels—proclaimed it by His own voice from heaven. What more could He have done? Yet two thoughts more please me—the holy Church throughout the world feel its importance and exult in its preciousness. We shall join with them to-morrow in giving thanks and "glory to God in the highest" for this His good Will towards us—while we may look forward to joining angels above (for whom He was not slain), but who yet praise Him who "loved *us* and gave Himself for *us*."

I hope your good friends are with you. I am sure you will have Christmas happiness if they are, for He who made Himself "one with us" will be in the midst of you. . . .

E. P. H.

30th December 1855.

It is the eve of the last Sunday in the year—a solemn time, is it not? Has it not a voice of warning of our last Sunday of all, and our last account, as well as a voice to recall the deeds of the one just closing? It reminds me of Sabbath sins—surely the worst of all sins. "If Thou, Lord, shouldest be extreme to mark iniquity, how should *I* stand?"

I am accustomed to spend the two closing hours of the year in self-examination and prayer, and *now* never without a vivid recollection of my dear mamma on her last old year's night. "What thou knowest not *now* thou shalt know hereafter." It is good for us to be humbled by disappointment sometimes in our imperfect endeavours—but look up, "be not weary," at least refresh yourself with the thought that "the counsel of the *Lord* standeth sure." He will surely bring to pass the "counsel of His Will *for us*. His Word *shall* accomplish that which He pleases. . . .

E. P. H.

January 1856.

Once again my fingers would give wings to a few words to you. Thank you for dear ——'s notes: they remind me of the burden of dear papa's sermon—"God is with thee,"—the pillar of the Christian's confidence in the unforeseen events of the New Year. How cheering to find the first Sunday of the year pointing us to the true Light! Oh, how we need it! It has been "the day star" to lead us out of darkness; but *I*, at least, need it to arise with more healing in its beams, for dark films of ignorance and unbelief are around me; and then, in looking forward through the mists of the unknown year, though *hope* would foresee all mists disappearing in bright sunshine, I *know* not "how it will go with me"—how fearfully then should I walk if it were not *promised*—"they shall walk in the light of Thy countenance;" and we are *commanded* to "walk in the light." Then may that Sun shine more and more perfect day into our souls, and guide *our* feet in the way of peace—this is all the light and happiness that we care for. . . .

E. P. H.

I have such increased need of prayer, with such new prospects and duties before me; in *all* of them my desire is to glorify God; to meet them *I* have nothing but utter weakness; help me then to remember to seek for and lean upon Him from whom alone cometh help. How I wished you were at my side yesterday while listening to dear papa's beautiful and striking sermon! It was very specially suitable to *us* in starting anew on life's journey,—it was so *full* that I must reserve description till we meet, and only give the text—1 Samuel 10:7. What can you make of it?

. . . .

It is nearly noon, so I am going to our Father's footstool to ask Him to meet and bless us both. I need so much grace now to prepare me for all God is preparing for me, and only dread becoming forgetful of my constant, momentary need of teaching and strength....

E. P. Havergal.

As in February our home snowdrop came, so in February was she transplanted to a new and happy home in Ireland. Her dear father's "Bridal Thoughts" ("Life Echoes") fitly express the bridegroom's welcome to his daughter on her wedding day, February 5, 1856.

> "Rise up, my love, and come away!
> It is, it is thy bridal day:
>   God's watchers bright
>   Await the sight,
> And joy to chant their sweetest lay.
>
> "'Tis God who hath prepared thy way
> To reach this blest and blessing day;
>   'Twas He who trained
>   When most He pained,
> He meant to chase thy tears away.
>
> "Then rise, my fair one, come away
> To a home of love by night and day;
>   Peace and prayer
>   Await thee there,
> And praise shall tune thy song alway!"

It was a spring-like day with pleasant sunshine. St. Nicholas Church was full of friends, both rich and poor, the benedictions and salutations of the almshouse women culminating at the church porch with—"Bless you, sir; you've picked the right one!"

Her father had prepared a musical surprise for his daughter at the breakfast, handing her these verses printed on bridal paper; and then his voice, with brother Frank and sister Frances, led the assembled guests in singing this—

NUPTIAL GRACE.

G. S. and E. P. H.

> "O Thou whose presence beautified
>   Poor Cana's nuptial board,
> By Thee let ours be sanctified,
>   And Thou shalt be adored.
>
> "Thyself to us, ourselves to Thee,
>   In mystic union join;
> And grant us greater things to see
>   Than water turned to wine.
>
> "Thy glory show, our faith make strong,
>   Like rivers be our peace;
> And seat us where Thy Marriage Song
>   Shall never, never cease.
>
> "To Him who wove the marriage tie
>   In Eden's thornless bower,
> To Him, the Christ of God most High,
>   Be glory, praise, and power!"

—Rev. W. H. Havergal.

Before our travellers left, a chapter was read from the Holy Bible, with a forcible exposition by the Rev. Charles Bradley, Vicar of St. James's, Clapham, and prayer by our dear father, that they who were indeed heirs together of the grace of life might rejoice in the fulness of His blessing here, and hereafter share the fulness of joy in His presence.

We need not give many details of her home-life in Ireland. After only a few weeks' residence, the rector, Rev. R. Pakenham, observed to her husband, "If there is one unselfish woman in the world, it's Mrs. Shaw." To her husband she was ever a "priceless treasure," and to his two elder children both cherishing and wise. How prayerfully she watched over them we gather from the fragment which follows; and when her own four children came, they formed a sixfold cable of happy and united entwining of love.

> The storms are lulled, new scenes appear,
> All passing fair, and sunbeams cheer,
>   And radiate all around.
> My Shepherd's love is now my theme,
> Folded beside the o'erflowing stream
>   Whence life and grace abound;
> 'Mid pastures pleasant, green and fair,
> For me Thy living food prepare
>   Like tender, budding grass.
>
> Not lonely still, as once of old,
> Sweet converse now, I oft can hold
>   Beside my "Shepherd's tent."
> And while we wait to hear His voice,
> May we with thankful hearts rejoice,
>   And praise His love divine.
>
> Nor is this all,—two precious lambs
> As pledges of His love He gave,
>   Whom I for Him should tend—
> And yet again, His bounteous hand
> Bestows a still more tender lamb,
>   To prove His love again.
>
> O Israel's Shepherd! be their God,
> And through their hearts, oh shed abroad
>   The riches of Thy love.
> And grant the elder ones[1] to grow
> In holy fear and simple faith,
>   Like mother safe above.

---

[1] J. H. S. and A. M. S. [John Hall Shaw and Anna M. Shaw, Giles' children by his first wife]

And still, O Lord, Thy grace employ,
That they may lead with sacred joy
  Their sister-lamb to Thee:
That they a threefold cord may be,
A holy, happy trinity,
  United in Thy love.

—E. P. S., 1857.

When visiting at Celbridge Lodge, I was touched to see the warm love gushing up from many an Irish heart for these Protestant friends, who showed their love by their works. I took notes of one literal outpour from a Roman Catholic which represents many more.

Yours can't be a very bad religion if it makes such men as Mr. Shaw, for shure and isn't it to his dure we fly when we're sick or sore in want or distress, isn't his blankets that warm us the length of the long cowld winter, and isn't his hand that's ever stretched with the kindness to us! Didn't he and Master John face the cholera, the crathur's! and run with the hot bottles and the powders and the red flannel everywhere there was a poor sowl sick or sufferin'. Shure the ra-al love of God must be blazin' up in his heart, or he'd never feel for the poor as he does. And it's what I often think in myself that heaven will be a quare place intirely if he warn't there! And the good lady herself, Mrs. Shaw I mane, shure a more tinderer, kinder crathur you couldn't find in the walls of the world. Let a poor body go to her dure when they may, isn't she always ready to see them and spake to them—she doesn't send the cowld message by the mouth of a servant; no, she comes to you her own self (ah, it's asy seen the ra-al true blood of a lady flows in her veins!) and she axes you so kindlike to step into the beautiful, illigant hall and the windy that would dazzle your eyes to look at. And thin she'd listen so quiet and patient-like to all our troubles an' trials, an' spake feelin' words about the holy Saviour of the world, that the sound of her sweet voice, sayin' it so tinder, would bring the comfort into your breast. And she wouldn't stop at the good words either, for she'd have a kind feel for your unfortunate body as well as your sowl, and her hand would be stretched out with the can of sweet milk and the arrowroot and the beautiful fine broth that you might carry home in the tail of your cloak without spillin' a drap of it, it would be so darlint thick! Ah! many an' many's the time the heart might drap out of our bodies wi'd want an' weakness if it warn't for her goodness to us. May it all meet her at the gate of glory, an' may the blessin' an' benediction of our heavenly Father rest about her and Mr. Shaw here an' hereafter. It's a sore day for Celbridge Mr. and Mrs. Shaw laving us warey an' lone.

Turning from cabins to palaces, from peasants to Bishops and Queen's Counsel, we give this tribute of esteem from her Irish friends *after* she had passed away.

To her Husband, G. S.

THE PALACE, KILKENNY,
1st January 1887.

MY VERY DEAR FRIEND AND BROTHER,—

It is a sad New-Year's day to you, and yet I cannot refrain (even at the risk of intruding upon the sacredness of your grief) from writing a few lines to express our joint and sincere sympathy with you and yours in this deep sorrow which has fallen so suddenly upon you. I know full well, from my own experience, how weak and poor all human words of comfort are at such a time, but I know how the one and only Comforter can sustain with His own presence in such an hour. May He be very near to fill, as He alone can do, the blank that is left in your heart and home.

I recall her Christian grace and winning character, all her *gentleness* and faith in Christ, all her love to God's people, and I bless God for the remembrance. It will ever be sweet and instructive and helpful to the many who knew and valued her—for "she being dead yet speaketh"—and all she was, was by the grace of God, which sanctified and ennobled all in her that was "lovely and of good report."

We remember you in our prayers, and bear you on our hearts.—

Yours in best of bonds,

WM. P. OSSORY.

THE PALACE, WATERFORD,
10th January 1887.

MY DEAR MR. SHAW,—

When I saw mentioned the great sorrow which had fallen upon your house, I felt deep sympathy for you; and now that you are so kind as to have a memorial card sent to me, I know that you will not feel it amiss that I should express that sympathy. Yet surely thanksgiving is to be mingled with it, for you are not mourning under the hand of an unknown God, but you know and believe His love to you in the midst of all this. Neither are you sorrowing for her who sleeps in Jesus, as one without hope. Blessed be the Lord for His goodness. She did her work as a wife and mother, and saw its fruits in her children, and now she rests from her labours, until she meets you and them in the presence of the Lord at His coming; and this does not shut out her present conscious happiness "with the Lord," as He beautifully says of those who died hundreds of years before, "all *live* unto Him."

I hope that my dear godson Alfred goes on happily in his ministry. He kindly wrote to me about the time of his ordination; his brother W. is also, I think, in the ministry. Here is blessed fruit of her training and example, which the Lord has crowned with the power of His Spirit. Do not take the trouble of writing to me, but believe me always, your very sincere friend,

M. F. CASHEL.

DUBLIN, 30th December 1886.

MY DEAR MR. SHAW,—

It was with the deepest sympathy for you all in your loss that I read of your bereavement in to-day's paper. What a terrible blank her loss must be to you all! and to come so suddenly, as the paper says it was; and yet what a happy way for her to go to her loved and loving Lord! Truly you sorrow not as those that are without hope when you grieve for the loss of one so kind and *gentle,* so thoughtful for all, so unselfish and so good. Oh, how many will miss her! I know I feel that I have lost one of the friends on earth who are so few, those that one can rest in perfect confidence that their friendship is real and genuine; but what is the loss to you all! May our Father enable you to look more on the gain to her, as she rests in the light and sunshine in the presence of the King, having heard the sweet "Well done, good and faithful servant." After all her kindness to me, and yours—I am sure you will not think this letter an intrusion, but will accept my real sympathy, and believe me, yours ever sincerely,

Thos. P. Law.

CHAPTER V.

RETURN TO ENGLAND—NEW HOME AT WINTERDYNE.

14th December 1866.

OUR next outline brings us to an English railway station, Stourport, and two figures pacing the platform expecting the train with travellers from Ireland. Four little faces recognise dear aunt Fanny and cousin Connie. But all her welcomes to England are quenched by their fervent and faithful adhesion to old Ireland—W. exclaiming, "We won't be John Bulls or little calves; we will be Paddies and pigs!" As the train moves on to Malvern, aunt F. throws into the carriage her "Welcome to Winterdyne," and the verses are eagerly discussed. Poetry is not always convincing, and for them the memory of their sweet Celbridge home and their own clear, shining Liffey, could not be compared to unknown Winterdyne and "silvery Severn," especially as on that wintry day the river certainly looked muddy. After-thoughts are sometimes best! and aunt F.'s verses were found to be true.

WELCOME TO WINTERDYNE.

"Francie and Willie, welcome to you!
Alfred and Alice, welcome too!
To an English home and English love,
Welcome each little Irish dove!
Never again we hope to be
Kept apart by an angry sea;
A thousand welcomes, O darlings mine,
When we see you at Winterdyne.

"Welcome all to a warm new nest,
Just the place for our doves to rest;
Through the oaks and beeches looking down
On the winding valley and quaint old town,
Where ivy green on the red rock grows,
And silvery Severn swiftly flows,
With an extra sparkle and glitter and shine,
Under the woods of Winterdyne.

"On a quiet evening in lovely spring,
In the tall old elms the nightingales sing;
Under the forest, in twilight grey,
I have heard them more than a mile away;
Sweeter and louder and far more dear
Than any thrush you ever did hear;
Perhaps when the evenings grow long and fine
They will sing to you in Winterdyne.

"Little to sadden, and nothing to fear;
Priest and Fenian never come here:
Only the sound of the Protestant bells
Up from the valley pleasantly swells,
And a beautiful arch to church is made,
Under the sycamore avenue's shade;
You pass where the arching boughs entwine
Out of the gates of Winterdyne.

"Welcome to merry old England! And yet
We know that old Ireland you will not forget;
Many a thought and prayer will fly
Over the mountains of Wales so high;
Over the forest and over the sea,
To the home which no longer yours must be.
But farewells are over, O darlings mine,
Now it is Welcome to Winterdyne!"

—Frances Ridley Havergal.

To M. V. G. H.

Osborne House, Great Malvern
16th December 1866.

I feel it is but right to thank and greet *such a father* on reaching again my fatherland. Tell him Giles has just said, "I am sure there is not one happier this morning, at the thought of your being in England, than your father;" it is indeed a large measure of the present sweetness of my cup to be nearer him. So glad to find from your kind greeting this morning that he is so well. What blessings are included to me in such a father!

Tell him the "good management" of my dear husband succeeded well, for when I and the children arrived at Malvern four hours after him, he was waiting at the station with cabs to bring us to *Osborne House,* where I found fires blazing, and the table laid for dinner, so comfortable and cheerful! I knew he would do it with less fatigue, if without "incumbrance," and I trusted, too, that the Angel would go before him, so I had no anxiety. I wish I could express how great I feel the mercies to have been that have thus "led us forth in peace," instead of being driven out from our Irish home by sickness, peril, or any of the thousand things which might have been. D.V., we go to see Winterdyne to-morrow, sleep at Oakhampton, and again to W. Tuesday, to take measures, etc. Mr. Crane kindly met Giles at Stourport, to say we can enter on possession at once. How plain and easy our path!

. . . Your loving sister,
E. P. S.

This passing reference to her sister F. may be of interest.

To M. V. G. H.

. . . Dear Fanny has been making us all so bright and happy, and is so missed. Miss Edwards went violently in love with her, although she did not expect to like her. And then, as she has been such a blessing to Annie—she also is deeply attached to her. I am glad to find she is not spoiled by becoming an authoress,—for certainly it requires much grace to stand all that is said and read about her poems. I like to see her so unaffected as not to disguise the pleasure and thankfulness that it is natural to feel at many of the remarks. I wish we could have been more quiet for her, but could not avoid being rather lively lately, and every one clings to her for sympathy and advice. She is to stay with Mr. and Mrs. Bullock to-morrow, and then goes to brother Frank at Hereford.

We so enjoyed Mr. H.'s visit; he was so thankful to find the change that had taken place in A., and said he could never forget his Sunday here. It is the greatest honour I wish for our house, that it may be said, "this and that one was born there.'

. . . Your loving sister,
Ellen.

Only a faint outline can be traced of twenty years' home-life at Winterdyne, but extracts from letters will supply some details. It was a great pleasure to Mrs. Shaw to be within a drive of her birthplace, Astley Rectory, and her sister's home at Oakhampton in the same parish. The hospitalities of Winterdyne were widely extended, and many friends shared the excursions to the surrounding hills and valleys.

Throughout the summer months, frequent parties of excursionists were admitted to the grounds—sometimes they came with banners and music to the hall door, and were courteously welcomed. Often the evening rendezvous would be around the ancient cedar tree, and holy song and grateful speeches concluded a day of which some poor guest said, "It's just like being in heaven."

During the gale of October 14, 1881, this magnificent cedar suddenly fell; Mrs. Shaw heard the falling crash, and as she saw it lying uprooted and its massive branches prostrate—one thought filled her mind, "Thou remainest." Hence these lines:—

"THEY SHALL PERISH; BUT THOU REMAINEST."

O cedar tree of Winterdyne,
The shading guardian of our peaceful home,
How much we all loved thee!
Thy boughs in summer seemed to cool the air
For those who sat beneath. In wintry frost and snow
A hoary sire thou seem'dst. In stormy winds
We loved to see how bravely thou didst stand,
Nor thought that *thou* couldst fall.

O cedar tree of Winterdyne,
How many a tale thou could'st have told
Of festive pleasant times—
But pass we by the gathering throngs
From far and near with gladsome songs,
The pattering feet with music sweet
And banners bright, and great delight
That thou didst look upon.—

One[1] honoured thee when o'er her thou didst wave
Thine ancient branches. There she oft did sit
Whose presence was as sunshine, gladdening all
She looked upon. She was God's messenger,—
Carolling glad truths like blythsome bird,
Or speaking words in season, softly, lovingly,
And telling forth the honour of her King.—
But her work is done! she has passed away.
And thou *hast* fallen! both leaving us the record sure
Of thy Creator LORD,—that He remains.

—E. P. S.

[1] F. R. H.

Mr. Shaw well remembers the following incident. It was Sunday afternoon, July 16, 1876, when a terrific thunderstorm with vivid lightning had just swept over Winterdyne. He was standing in the dining-room when his wife came in, and instead of referring to the thunder, which usually much affected her, she handed him a hymn just written, "I love, I love my Master." She explained that just before her sister Frances had left for Switzerland, she had been teaching her class about the Hebrew servant's choice, in Exodus 21; and she suggested that Frances should write a hymn with reference to this, and also arranged that at three o'clock on that afternoon she would pray for her help and guidance at "Fins Haut." But while Ellen was thinking how F. would arrange *her* hymn, these lines were suggested amid the crashing storm. The simultaneous verses of both sisters are now given:

"I LOVE MY MASTER."

Exodus 21:5.

I love, I love my Master,
  I will not go out free!
He loves me, O so lovingly,
  He is so good to me!

I love, I love my Master,
  He shed His blood for me,
To ransom me from Satan's power,
  From sin's hard slavery.

I love, I love my Master,
  O how He worked for me!
He worked out God's salvation,
  So great, so full, so free.

My Master, O my Master,
  If I may work for Thee,
And tell out Thy salvation,
  How happy shall I be!

I know not, but my Master
  Will teach me what to do;
Prepare the ground, point out the way,
  And work within me too.

"Take up the cross," He bids me,
  And this for me He bare;
And while I wear His easy yoke,
  He meekly takes a share.

I cannot leave my Master,
  His love has pierced my heart;
He binds me to Himself with love,
  He will not let me part.

I love, I love my Master,
  To Him alone I cling,
For there is none like Jesus,
  My Saviour, Friend, and King.

I love, I love my Master,
  I will not go out free!
He says, His saints shall serve Him,
  And that my heaven shall be.
      —Ellen P. Shaw.

Winterdyne, 16th July 1876.

"MY MASTER."

Exodus 21:5, 6.

"I love, I love my Master,
  I will not go out free;
For He is my Redeemer,
  He paid the price for me.

"I would not leave His service,
  It is so sweet and blest;
And in the weariest moments
  He gives the truest rest.

"I would not halve my service,
  His only it must be,—
His *only*, who so loved me
  And gave Himself for me.

"My Master shed His life-blood
  My vassal life to win,
And save me from the bondage
  Of tyrant self and sin.

"He chose me for his service,
  And gave me power to choose
That blessed 'perfect freedom,'
  Which I shall never lose.

"For He hath met my longing
  With word of golden tone,
That I shall serve for ever
  Himself, Himself alone.

"'Shall serve Him' hour by hour,
  For He will show me how;
My Master is fulfilling
  His promise even now!

"'Shall serve Him,' and 'for ever';
  A hope most sure, most fair!
The perfect love outpouring
  In perfect service there!"
      —F. R. Havergal.
      ("Loyal Responses.")

Fins Haut, 16th July 1876.

WINTERDYNE, 27th February 1882.

DEAR FAITHFUL MARY,—

You never forget or neglect our birthdays. Thank you so much for another pretty memento of the 19th, and also for a beautiful New Year card, which I am sorry to have kept unacknowledged to this day.

Most truly can I say of your birthday text that "His kindness" has not departed from me, but has been "ever more and more toward us." And you too, I am thankful to know, can say the same. How happy is the assurance that this kindness is not only past and present, but "everlasting." We have had such precious tokens of it in our family last year, and in Mr. Shaw's improved health and strength enabling him to abound in the work of the Lord, and made a blessing to many sufferers. One said to me lately, "He *is* the servant of the Lord; how good He is to send him to me, to teach me *how* to trust in Him!"

We had such a pleasant surprise last Tuesday evening. When Mr. Shaw had finished his address in Park School (on Abraham's trial of faith and substitution, as taught in Genesis 22), the church clerk (a bright and active helper in good works) rose and asked those present (the room full) to sit down, as he, George Clarke, was deputed to say that it had long been the wish of those who were there, and at Mr. Shaw's Bible classes at Winterdyne, to make some token of gratitude, etc, for his teaching. And then Thomas Hunt, a shoemaker, member of his class, walked up the room and presented a beautiful inkstand (inlaid Coromandel wood) with silver inscription plate, and an address, signed by seventy-four persons, with a large drawer for holding the notes he makes for his meetings; and said they all felt so much benefit from his teaching, that it was a real pleasure to express some gratitude. I enclose a copy of a note from the same man, which shows the reality of grace in him. But I must amuse you with a sequel. Miss Havergal, seated at the harmonium, rose, saying, "As you are giving Mr. Shaw so much pleasure, I must give you a little. You chose to-day, Shrove Tuesday, for this presentation most fortunately, for I am sure you will like to know that it was on a Shrove Tuesday that Mr. Shaw married my sister, Ellen Havergal (waving her hand toward me), and if he had not married her, he might never have been here!" You may fancy how very effective this little speech was! The warm, grateful feeling of all was so pleasant.

I am sorry to say my sister is not in as good health as we could wish; and letters still come, because she is so kind!

So glad to know you have such bountiful enjoyments. The Lord be with you in them all.

—Affectionately yours,

ELLEN SHAW.

It may seem strange so little reference is made to her dear sister F. R. H., but such extracts have already appeared in her Memoirs and "Miscellaneous Letters," and therefore only this comforting thought is given.

To M. V. G. H.

SANDOWN, 2nd June 1884.

Many will be thinking and praying for you to-morrow, dear sister Maria. May *the* Comforter draw near to hush and calm and cheer you. I have just been putting together "as He is, so are we," with "this same Jesus shall so come in like manner!" And if it was "splendid" to Frances to go, it will be splendid too for her to return, and splendid for *us* to meet them, whether on earth or in air.

Alfred preached such a good, full sermon last night, on "He shall baptize . . . with fire," explaining the Old and New Testament emblems of the Holy Spirit; quite a Bible study, and all so well put. He goes to-morrow to Farnham, preparatory to ordination as priest.

—Your affectionate sister,

"Rejoicing in hope." ELLEN.

The life-lines of any of God's servants cannot be completed by an earthly hand, for the countless and varied details of service for God are known only to Him, but the Master's hand will surely complete in brightness the minutest tracery. In January 1872 Mrs. Shaw began a Sunday morning Bible class for youths, separating them from the large class of senior men, who had for some time previously assembled in the dining-room at Winterdyne for Mr. Shaw's Bible instruction. Her class so increased that it was necessary to form a third class in an adjoining room.

The register books of attendance for fourteen years, and a very wealth of carefully prepared lessons during that long period, are all neatly kept. There are notes critical and practical on Genesis, Exodus, Leviticus, Numbers, Joshua, Samuel, and Kings, also from the Book of Proverbs, with many New Testament chapters and other lessons suitable to our Church festivals. A few specimens of these follow, but they cannot be written out as orally given, so the pith and point of searching appeal must pass unrecorded. Their teacher's value for souls was seen in the light of eternity, and her intense anxiety for her class went far beyond regular attendance and moral behaviour; she longed for their conversion and saving acceptance of Christ's work for them, and that hidden union and life *in* Christ that brings forth holy living and walking *with* Him. She was ever their friend as well as teacher, entering into their individual trials and difficulties, and furnishing them with replies and arguments against scoffers or freethinkers.

In illness Mrs. Shaw visited and comforted them. Only one slight record has been kept of many such visits; often excusing herself from drives and excursions that she might get to their bedsides—and other cottage visits.

July 18.—Read Isaiah 43:1–3 to Henry J. He had repeatedly said he knew he was redeemed and forgiven, and now I asked him if he had believed this long ago? *H.* "It is about two years, since I was taken ill, the work began in me. But it was the teaching in your class, and especially one Sunday when you brought a stranger to speak to us, and I saw then what believing meant." "*What* is it you believe, Henry?" "That Jesus died for me, and that He has forgiven my sins." *Teacher.* "Then you have peace, Henry; for, therefore being justified by faith, we have peace with God, through our

Lord Jesus Christ—the burden all gone—sin put away—nothing between you and God." H. "Yes, that's it—I know it, and I want the class to know it. I have tried to speak of Jesus to others, but some only laughed."

August 23.—I found Henry very suffering and breathless. It soothed him speaking of the Good Shepherd loving and caring for His sheep, and therefore knowing all his sufferings, and that He was watching and tending him. Then I spoke of the Great Shepherd *able* to carry him all the rough way; and then of the Chief Shepherd giving crowns of glory, and that even now His hand held the crown out to him in the weary road, and soon, soon he would have the joy of seing Jesus.

Another day I asked him what text he was leaning on? H. "'My peace I give unto you;' I have it, thank the Lord." *Teacher.* "Yes, He *is* our peace, and Christ made peace for us by the blood of His cross." H. "Yes, that's it, that's it,"—and together they praised God—(and now again, before the throne, they are together saying Alleluia!)

In addition to this Sunday class, Mrs. Shaw had week-day meetings for teetotalism. She herself was a faithful member, and one note-book is filled with the subject in all its bearings. In the long light evenings, pleasant meetings in the summer-house and addresses from strangers helped to rivet the pledge of the abstainers, and she always cordially joined in the rector's Church of England Temperance movements.

When members of her class left for distant towns, magazines and letters followed them. Such patient seed-sowing was ever watered with prayer; and only last autumn, on the Clent hills, she spoke tearfully of her unfulfilled desires for her class, and then and there, hidden by the clumps of gorse and heather, we knelt and commended each member to the Great Teacher, God's Holy Spirit, that He would quicken and awaken them with spiritual life and power. (Very true and deep affection now enshrines her memory, and among the many funeral wreaths, her class sent a beautiful crown of camellias and ferns—" For our own dear Teacher.")

In F.R.H.'s Bible, her sister Ellen's name appears in 1867 as having joined the Young Women's Christian Association about the same time as herself. Mrs. Shaw was secretary for the Bewdley branch, and conducted the monthly meeting of the senior ladies. Her expository thoughts were deeply valued, and we have found many books full of her carefully written notes. Her prayers, even more than her teachings, riveted all who heard them; in choicest language they were the holy, happy communings of one who realized a very near approach to the Holiest—prayers that wafted you into the inner sanctuary, making us ashamed of our own formality and unreality.

Occasionally addresses and tea-meetings were arranged for the junior members. (Beautiful memorial wreaths were sent from the ladies and the junior members.)

Mrs. Shaw also conducted a Young Women's Christian Association class in her servants' hall. We quote the words of one member, Fanny Holloway.

Mrs. Shaw was a splendid teacher; you could take in everything she taught; she explained all about the Tabernacle so nicely. I feel very sad that all her teachings are done and past for us. But if I learnt anything it was to pray. Mrs. Shaw took everything straight to the Lord, and so, of course, it all came right. If anything went wrong among us, she would pray over it with us. To myself she was a dear friend and adviser, as well as mistress, and in all my eighteen years' service here, I never remember *one* cross or hasty word to any of the servants. The Lord Jesus must have been pleased with her gentleness; He knew it all.

From childhood, Mrs. Shaw's warmest sympathy and support was given to the Church Missionary Society, though other societies found place in the longing for Christ's name and kingdom to be exalted. For her dear missionary niece Amy (Mrs. A. D. Shaw), in East Africa, she diligently worked, sending garments suitable for the women and school children. But it was in connection with the Church of England Zenana Society that Mrs. Shaw superintended monthly working parties at Winterdyne. Everything was neatly prepared, and she gave hours and hours in cutting out material, etc. As needlework was not unnoticed in the Tabernacle, so was her equally loyal offering unto the Lord. Our dear and valued friend Elizabeth Clay, whose indomitable perseverance in itinerations in the Punjaub Village Mission are so well known, was a very special subject of interest. And within the last fortnight of her life Mrs. Shaw completed many kurtas or native garments for Ajnala, and though far from well, packed a large parcel for Miss Clay, including work contributed by Bewdley ladies.

And in the last week of her life on earth, her faithful attendant F. H. remembers that when she took her luncheon, her mistress bade her sit down and read the C. M. Gleaner's account of Bishop Hannington, and afterwards she took the book and explained many other pictures and passages.

EDEN. [H. P. 38.]

This is the hymntune composed by William Henry Havergal, sung to the words "Nuptial Grace," sung on the morning of his daughter Ellen's wedding. See page 199 of this book. This score is found in *Havergal's Psalmody and Century of Chants* and also in Hymn No. 68 in *Songs of Grace and Glory*, given on pages 188 and 584 of Volume V of the Havergal editon.

CHAPTER VI.

LAST DAYS AND SUDDEN GLORY.

Mr. AND MRS. SHAW went to their eldest daughter's home in Cheltenham, December 1, visiting Mrs. Maynard and many friends, who remarked her cheerfulness and apparent good health. They much enjoyed some special services held in Canon Bell's church, and Mrs. Shaw took many notes of the sermons by the Rev. Talbot Greaves.

While at Cheltenham she wrote the following letter, a true and remarkable epitome of the foundation on which her faith rested, and her assured and certain hope of the eternal life to which she was unconsciously hastening:—

CHELTENHAM, 5th December 1886.

I have thought many times of what you said about Psalm 15, and it was brought back to my mind in this morning's service by a parallel in Psalm 24:4, and reminds me how beautifully Scripture throws light on Scripture. I find little or no comfort in this Psalm alone, for whatever the general tenor of my life, how could I say that I have always acted up to this standard? I may think much of some occasions of upright walking or truthful speaking, but did my God see no sin, or self, no earthly motive mixing with the seeming good? Ah no! His holy eyes saw it was all sin-stained and imperfect, and all my omissions besides. Conscience tells me there is no hope for me to stand on that Holy Hill for my own doings, and St. Paul tells me "by the deeds of the law no flesh shall be justified in His sight." So far then this Psalm seems rather to mar my comfort than make it; but when I look at it in the light of Revelation 7, and I see how that innumerable multitude stands before the throne, I take comfort in seeing that I can claim admission with them, for I have the same right, the same passport—"the Blood of the Lamb!" Washed in that all-atoning Blood from omissions, commissions, and failures, and clothed in His perfect righteousness instead of my own, I hope and expect to "abide in that Holy Hill."

I wonder if you take this really comfortable view! One is left so without fear when we know that the Lord Jesus is our Substitute and Sin-bearer, taking all our sins and delinquencies, and giving us *Himself* and all His righteousness—taking the place of me the sinner, and letting me stand "accepted in Him the Beloved," "blameless and faultless before His Father's throne." And meanwhile I love, and I *need* to look constantly at the great purchase-price of all this, "the precious Blood of Christ." As my dear sister wrote, "I cannot do without the precious Blood the first thing in the morning as well as the last thing at night." All my safety and peace spring from it. Christ "made peace for me by the Blood of His cross," and "washes me from my sins in His own Blood," and through it "purges me from dead works to serve the living God," I am "made nigh," and "have boldness to enter into the holiest by the Blood of Jesus." Do I want victory? it must be "through the Blood of the Lamb"; if I want to be "perfect in every good work to do His will," it must be "through the Blood of the everlasting covenant."

And then as the Revised Version gives Revelation 22:14, "Blessed are they that *wash their* robes, that they may have the right to come to the Tree of Life, and may *enter* by the gates *into the city*."

Oh, why do we hear so little of this Precious Blood, when so much—nay, *all* depends upon it! Dear ——, may you have increasing comfort by "faith in the Blood of Christ," and so, happy and full assurance of abiding for ever on His "Holy Hill."

E. P. S

December 8.—For a few days after returning from Cheltenham, Mrs. Shaw kept her room with cold and cough. Even then we could not but observe how much she thought about absent friends. Letters were written, and she sent away many copies of *Treasure Trove*. This letter explains her interest in the little book:—

DEAR MRS. GILLMAN,—

I return the MSS. letters of my dear sister Frances, which you so kindly lent. It has been a great interest to me to retrace many incidents in our past lives which they recall, and still more to see the holy thoughts and sanctified feelings with which dear F. viewed them. Some extracts from these and other papers have been selected by my daughter to form a tiny book of fragments called *Treasure Trove*.[1]

—With Christian regard, sincerely yours,

E. P. S.

(How little Ellen thought her own charmingly written Preface would enhance the treasure of her farewell gifts!)

During these last days, Ellen astonished me with her loving anxiety for the souls of others, remembering some of whom we had not even spoken for years; *e.g.* "All day —— has been on my mind; how often we are verily guilty concerning our brother."

The Y. W. C. A. evidently found place in her latest thoughts and intentions, as exemplified in the following letter:—

WINTERDYNE, 18th December 1886.

DEAR MISS C.,—

By way of a little recognition of your Y. W. C. A. class, I send copies of *Christmas Cheer* and a card for each. Will you kindly give them for me for Christmas day?

---

[1] *Treasure Trove*, by F. R. Havergal. Preface by Ellen P. Shaw. James Nisbet & Co.

It grieves me not to have done anything for the Association for so long—I hoped to have had a tea for them at Christmas, but now am unequal to it. May the Lord Himself bind their hearts together with the cords of His love. Will you tell them I hope they will get some real Christmas joy by looking at God's great Gift—"all other gifts in one." A Divine Gift, a Gift for all time and eternity. Oh that they and *we* may study its riches, and so rejoice in Him!

—With kindest wishes for yourself and mother, yours sincerely,

E. P. SHAW.

To her Sister J. M. C.

WINTERDYNE, 21st December 1886.

Many, many thanks, dearest Miriam, for your News Letter, and kind thoughtfulness and peptone present to me, which I will use. I took a little fresh cold going down on Sunday, which irritated the air tubes of my throat, but it passes, thanks to care and nursing. Maria has turned the tables on me wonderfully; instead of anxiously nursing her, as I feared, she waits on me! and is wonderfully active—so brisk in this sharp frost, and talks of going on the ice. On Sunday morning she taught my class, and in the afternoon went to Ribbesford Church as godmother to little Violet Maria Victoria Brooke, and afterwards had prayer at our lodge with the parents and sponsors.

This morning she was off at half-past nine to hear the National School children repeat Isaiah 53 in return for some prize Bibles. . . . I had better thank you now for the sweet scents you kindly sent for us all; they are very acceptable. Oh to enjoy more the fragrance of that Name which is above all others,—that Gift of Gifts, all other gifts in one. May it so refresh you, that you may have indeed a happy Christmas.

—Your affectionate sister,

ELLEN.

One of the last parcels she packed was to her brother Frank, with presents and loving wishes written in pencil for all her nephews and nieces at Upton Bishop Vicarage.

During the last few days Mrs. Shaw was able to come down-stairs, bringing the peculiarly peaceful influence that surrounded her—like some deep quiet lake, reflecting the golden stillness of the sky.

December 24.—The morning was occupied in packing parcels and especially books and rewards for her Sunday morning class. Weariness induced her to allow another hand to complete her Christmas preparations in the afternoon, but she joined us at tea, and spoke cheerfully of many passing events.

For many years Mr. and Mrs. Shaw always retired on Friday evenings for intercessory prayer for their children, their clergy, and the Sunday services and classes; but seeing her weariness, Mr. Shaw went alone. After watching the holly and ivy wreathings, the time for evening prayers came, when Mrs. Shaw left the room—her last words in it showing her unselfish consideration for others—"If I go up-stairs, they can sing a hymn." (It had been omitted when she was very tired.) Following dear Ellen to say good-night, I remarked, "It will be delightful to get rid of this tabernacle with its aches and pains"—the quiet reply came, "The pins of this earthly tabernacle are easily taken out, dear Maria."

Later on her daughter Frances went to her, who writes:—

On Christmas Eve I stayed longer with dear mother than usual, and sat down by the fire for a talk. She spoke of God's goodness to us all these years, and how undeserving we were of it. She quoted, "He drew me out of an horrible pit, and set my feet upon a rock," and then spoke of Christ's great love in giving Himself for us, "such wonderful love! Oh, what a wonder that Jesus loves me!"

Then I read 2 Samuel 7:21, asking her if she thought that verse was applicable to Christmas: "For Thy word's sake, and according to Thine own heart, hast Thou done all these great things, to make Thy servant know them." She said she supposed it might be so applied, but she had not thought of it before in that connection, but that "no doubt it was all according to His heart whose thoughts are so different from our own."

Christmas Day.—She had slept fairly well and enjoyed an early cup of tea; but there were no home birdies to sing as in former years their grandpapa's carol—

"How grand and how bright
That wonderful night,
When angels to Bethlehem came!"

Bagster's *Light on the Daily Path* always lay on the dressing-table, forming their early portion, and was again read at the breakfast-table. To-day Mr. S. read to her the selection for the "Evening Hour"—"Thanks be to God for His unspeakable gift," and Mrs. Shaw requested *this* might be read, instead of the usual chapter, at family prayers, as follows:—

December 25.—"Thanks be unto God for His unspeakable gift."

"Make a joyful noise unto the Lord, all ye lands. Serve the Lord with gladness: come before His presence with singing. Enter into His gates with thanksgiving, *and* into His courts with praise: be thankful unto Him, *and* bless His name. For unto us a Child is born, unto us a Son is given: and the government shall be upon His shoulder: and His name shall be called Wonderful, Counsellor, the mighty God, the everlasting Father, the Prince of Peace."

"He spared not His own Son, but delivered Him up for us all. Having yet one Son, His well-beloved, He sent Him also last unto them."

"Oh that *men* would praise the Lord *for* His goodness, and *for* His wonderful works to the children of men! Bless the Lord, O my soul; and all that is within me, *bless* His holy name."

"My soul doth magnify the Lord, and my spirit hath rejoiced in God my Saviour."

Mr. Shaw took up her breakfast, which she enjoyed more than usual, and said she felt so much better she would rise soon.

Her faithful maid, Holloway, remarking on the sunshine, Mrs. Shaw replied, "Yes, and how nice to think the Sun of Righteousness is shining all over the world—all over the world!" (a true missionary farewell glance). Then some of her presents were taken up, encircling her with love. My offering was a sofa cushion of our dear father's and a couvrette of sister F.'s; and as I stood near her, she admired my lace, and I told her it was our own mother's needlework; thus we spoke of all the dear ones she was just going to join. She looked so happy and even merry, that I said I would go to church; the last word that I heard from her gentle voice was "Emmanuel."

The parcel post did not arrive till after ten o'clock. Mr. Shaw brought up a packet from her daughter-in-law (G. M. S.), and left her admiring its contents. Edward H. S.'s card told of "New gleams of the glory that waits thee!"

About half-past ten Mr. Shaw returned up-stairs, bringing *The Fulness of Joy*, a beautifully-illustrated book of some of her sister Fanny's hymns, as a present from his daughters.

In one of Mrs. Shaw's *first* letters to Mr. S., she had written, "If it is pleasant to be under the shade of what seems now to our blind eyes but as a *Branch*, what will be *the fulness of our joy*, when we behold Him as the Tree of Life in the midst of the Paradise of God?" and now their hands together held this book, thus linking the first and last step of their happy pilgrimage with *The Fulness of Joy*.

Mr. Shaw then read to her the two first hymns, "Accepted, Perfect, and Complete," and "Is it for me, dear Saviour?" and leaving the book in her hand, went to get ready for church.

> "Accepted, Perfect, and Complete,
> For God's inheritance made meet,
> How true, how glorious, and how sweet!
>
> "In the Belovèd—by the King
> Accepted, though not anything
> But forfeit lives had we to bring.
>
> "And Perfect in Christ Jesus made,
> On Him our great transgressions laid,
> We in His righteousness arrayed.
>
> "Complete in Him, our glorious Head,
> With Jesus raisèd from the dead,
> And by His mighty Spirit led!
>
> "O blessed Lord, is this for me?
> Then let my whole life henceforth be
> One Alleluia song to Thee!"
> —F. R. H.

I.

> "Is it for me, dear Saviour,
> Thy glory and Thy rest?
> For me, so weak and sinful,
> Oh shall *I* thus be blessed?
> Is it for me to see Thee
> In all Thy glorious grace,
> And gaze in endless rapture
> On Thy belovèd Face?

II.

> "Is it for me to listen
> To Thy belovèd Voice,
> And hear its sweetest music
> Bid even me rejoice?
> Is it for me, Thy welcome,
> Thy gracious 'Enter in'?
> For me, Thy 'Come, ye blessed!'
> For me, so full of sin?

III.

> "O Saviour, precious Saviour,
> My heart is at Thy feet;
> I bless Thee and I love Thee,
> And Thee I long to meet.
> A thrill of solemn gladness
> Has hushed my very heart,
> To think that I shall really
> Behold Thee as Thou art;

IV.

> "Behold Thee in Thy beauty,
> Behold Thee face to face;
> Behold Thee in Thy glory,
> And reap Thy smile of grace;
> And be with Thee for ever,
> And never grieve Thee more!
> Dear Saviour, I *must* praise Thee,
> And lovingly adore."
> —F. R. H.

Happily her daughter F. went again into the room before leaving for church, and saw her mother looking pale, saying, "Oh, this terrible pain in my head! Give me my tonic." F. went and told her father, who immediately came. She said "tonic," and partly drank it, but was immediately unconscious. Restoratives and warmth were applied, but in a few minutes she ceased to breathe, from syncope of the heart. We found her Bible beneath her left arm, her unfailing pilgrim staff for all the way, and we knew her safe passport in life and death was the blood of the Lamb. For suddenly, as on the first Christmas morning, the glory of the Lord shone round about her, and with glad surprise she entered into the FULNESS OF JOY, sharing with loved ones gone before, His glory and His rest.

None of us thought how soon or how suddenly her remark only the night before would be realized—"The pins of this earthly tabernacle are easily taken out." There was no time for any parting testimony, or even a parting prayer; how precious then to us the following unfinished letter, written the day before the birth of one of her children, and which she gave to her beloved husband twenty-seven years ago, as the testimony of her assured hope, if ever she should unexpectedly be called hence!

CELBRIDGE LODGE, 11th May 1859.

It may be some comfort to you, my precious husband, to have a few words on paper which I may not trust my lips to say, or have opportunity to express, if I should soon be called to go to my Father.

I need not tell *you* in whom I have believed, or that whenever I may be called, I humbly hope it will be to ascend to your Father and my Father, to my God and your God, through Him who loved us and gave Himself for us.

I only want to say, that if I am taken and you are left for "yet a little while," that I go without one restrictive wish concerning you or the dear children, nor will I make one proposal concerning future arrangements for them; for what might now seem to me best, might in the changes of this passing world become in a short time either foolish or impossible. Our Father careth for them, and will guide and counsel you in their temporal well-being, and in training them up for Him. You know that has ever been my only condition with Him for them, "*Only* make them *Thy* children."

I may be unable to give any parting expression of my mind. Long as I have been enabled to set my seal to 1 Timothy 1:15;[1] Psalm 103:3, 8–10;[2] 1 John 2:1, 2.[3] I can only still say of *self*, unclean, unclean, and Job 42:5, 6.[4] How I have lost time in seeking the renewing of the Spirit. . . . (unfinished).

E. P. S.

"I heard a voice from heaven saying unto me, Write, Blessed are the dead which die in the Lord."—Revelation 14:13.

"Hush! blessed are the dead
In Jesus' arms who rest,
And lean their weary head
For ever on His breast.

[1] "This is a faithful saying, and worthy of all acceptation, that Christ Jesus came into the world to save sinners; of whom I am chief."—1 Timothy 1:15.

[2] "Who forgiveth all thine iniquities; who healeth all thy diseases. The Lord is merciful and gracious, slow to anger, and plenteous in mercy. He will not always chide: neither will He keep *His anger* forever. He hath not dealt with us after our sins, nor rewarded us according to our iniquities."—Psalm 103:3, 8–10.

[3] "My little children, these things write I unto you, that ye sin not. And if any man sin, we have an advocate with the Father, Jesus Christ the righteous: and He is the propitiation for our sins: and not for ours only, but also for *the sins of* the whole world."—1 John 2:1, 2.

[4] "I have heard of Thee by the hearing of the ear: but now mine eye seeth Thee. Wherefore I abhor *myself*, and repent in dust and ashes."—Job 42:5, 6.

"O beatific sight!
No darkling veil between,
They see the Light of Light,
Whom here they loved unseen.

"For them the wild is past
With all its toil and care;
Its withering midnight blast,
Its fiery noonday glare.

"Them the Good Shepherd leads,
Where storms are never rife,
In tranquil dewy meads,
Beside the Fount of Life.

"Ours only are the tears,
Who weep around their tomb
The light of bygone years
And shadowing years to come.

"Their voice, their touch, their smile,—
Those love-springs flowing o'er,—
Earth for its little while
Shall never know them more.

"O tender hearts and true,
Our long last vigil kept,
We weep and mourn for you,
Nor blame us: Jesus wept.

"But soon at break of day
His calm Almighty voice,
Stronger than death, shall say,
Awake,—arise,—rejoice."

—BICKERSTETH.

(*Sung in Ribbesford Church, 31st December* 1886.)

In fair and holy memory of

ELLEN PRESTAGE SHAW,

the beloved Wife of

GILES SHAW, ESQ., WINTERDYNE,

who suddenly fell asleep in Jesus

on Christmas Morning, 1886.

Aged 63 years.

"Himself hath done it."—Isaiah 38:15

"Our dear one is with Jesus now!
    Seeing Him face to face,
Gazing upon His own belovèd brow,
    Watching His smile of grace;
Hearing the Master's voice in all its sweetness,
Knowing Him now in all His own completeness;
    With Jesus now, with Him for ever!
    Never to leave Him—grieve Him never!
Could God Himself give more? His will
Is best though we are weeping still."
—Frances R. Havergal.

"It is the Lord, let Him do what seemeth Him good."—1 Samuel 3:18.

"Unto Him that loved us, and washed us from our sins in His own blood, and hath made us kings and priests unto God and His Father; to Him be glory and dominion for ever and ever. Amen."—Revelation 1:5, 6.

More than two hundred letters of sympathy reached the sorrowing family at Winterdyne.

    Vicarage, Rushall, 11th January 1887.

My Dear Mr. Shaw,—

Any words of mine, dear friend, would fail to express my sympathy with you all under this trying mark of the Father's love—and well I know the sad bereavement it must be to you more especially, but I know also where you can find that loving consolation which man can never give, but which *He*—who loves to weep with our suffering humanity—always gives to *His* believing ones. I observe the call was sudden, and that the Master made the river-bed so dry as she went over—that she knew not it was Jordan—suddenly beckoned into the Presence she so long had waited for, and on that precious day—above all, when the Church on earth loves to commemorate *His* first coming to His people. What a blessed Noel it was indeed to her—coming to her, not as the Infant of Bethlehem, but as the Royal Messenger, to usher her into the many mansions, "arrayed in the raiment of needle-work," to present her faultless before the King with exceeding joy. No lingering amid the shadows, nor waiting in the valley, but hearing, amid the daily service she delighted to render to Him and His suffering ones, His voice saying, "Rise up, my fair one, and come away." Long will her sweet memory, and the pleasant days with her at Winterdyne, recur to mind, and the blessed influence she shed on all around come again and again to our thoughts, reminding us how, amid much bodily weakness, she walked with God, and was not, because God took her. What a glorious change, as she awaked up in His likeness and was fully satisfied. What a joyous reunion with the dear ones, gone before, who were waiting her, and how loud and full the anthem as she entered the golden street, and saw His face and worshipped at His feet,—

"So would I die,
Not slain, but caught up as it were
To meet my Saviour in the air—
    So would I die."

God be with you, dear friend; another link unfastened here, another rivet to our Eternal Home. It tells us more and more, this is not our rest; it points us upwards, onwards, bidding us remember our Treasure is above, and speaking to us from her earthly resting-place, that like her we also, if faithful and true, shall, through His perfect righteousness, soon enter within the veil, where the shadows flee away and the everlasting morning will be our portion and our joy.

—Believe me, very sincerely yours,

F. Graeme-Littlecot.

    Dublin, 30th December 1886.

Dear Mr. Shaw,—

I hesitate to write, and yet cannot forbear doing so, for my sister and I were fairly stunned this morning to read that your beloved saint-like companion, our most kind friend, has been taken from the midst of you all—so loving and beloved, was she, so holy in thought, word, and deed. Oh! she is indeed an unutterable loss to her family, and to you more especially. The world is all the poorer, now that her gentle influence is gone from it, except that it must remain an abiding influence in the minds of all who had, like ourselves, the privilege of having known her. She was ripe for glory, that was my first thought, and a sudden death could have no terrors for one whose thoughts were at all times set on Heaven and the Saviour she loved so truly. Great is the trial which God has required of you; may He give you strength to bear it. I cannot think of never seeing her again without blinding tears, she was so good, so affectionately helpful to our unworthy selves, so compassionate to all in need, and her gentle humility so beautiful. I think it would be impossible to imagine a more lovely character. We never can forget the happy peaceful days we have spent with you all at lovely Winterdyne; and very precious is, and will be to the end of one's life, the little book, *Treasure Trove*, which she addressed to us with her own dear handwriting little more than a week ago.

On what a blessed day she is gone *Home*. You would not wish it to be otherwise, for Death was the new Life to her. We do so feel for you, kind friend, in this sudden stroke of sorrow. I will not add more, and you will please excuse me if these few lines seem like an intrusion on your present sorrow. My sister joins with me in true and loving sympathy with you all.

—Yours most sincerely,

C. F. C.

LETTERS TO HER HUSBAND AND CHILDREN.

My Husband.
CELBRIDGE LODGE, May 1856.

FULL many a page of life's eventful tale has passed
Since last a record with my pen I traced,—
Changes and chances, sufferings and joy,
Valleys of sorrow—heavy storms,
When grief, anxiety, and care
Their waves commingled—
Anticipation, too, tossed high its spray
Outstripping far the destined reach of waves
Restrained within a Father's loving hand.
Yes, tempests raged, and night at times prevailed;
Yet, every wave told but of love's unfathomed sea,
Toward which my Captain's hand was guiding me.
Night's darkness only showed how fair
Thou art, my bright, my "morning star"!
    But now—the tale how changed!
    No more prevails the tone of sadness,
    But calm delight and thankful gladness;
    Unwished, unasked, I'm in a peaceful haven—
    Sweet type of *my best* home in heaven.
The tempest oft by its terrific waves
Casts up some jewel fair from ocean caves:
My storm's o'erpast! a jewel, too, is mine!
But not from ocean cave, or earth-wrought mine—
Purchased by Christ from sin's dark land,
Brought to me by my God's good hand;
More precious than earth's brightest gem,
My prize is one in God's own diadem!

—E. P. S.

WINTERDYNE, 15th March,
10.15 A.M.

Now is not this to your mind, my Giles—writing to you the first thing?—not but what I have had bonnet and shawl on before it!

... I was struck this morning when reading Jeremiah 51 (that wonderful typical part about Babylon): "We would have healed Babylon, but she is not healed: forsake her, and let us every one go into his own country,"—what a motto for the Irish Church Missions!

3.40—So glad to get your note, and to find how opportune your visit is after all—exemplifying Psalm 37:23, "The steps of a good man are ordered by the Lord, and He delighteth in his way." Is not the last part of the verse pleasant? "He delights in his way"—delights, I suppose, in guiding the way of His servants, so that it shall result in good,—so it is well to take the way He orders by His providence, or "prepares for us to walk in."

I do pray you may be a blessing to your brother. —— called and stayed an hour; she seems chastened by her deafness, and we had a nice talk about the hearing of faith, Proverbs 22:17, "Bow down thine ear, and hear the words of the wise," etc.

Kind love to any enquiring friends, and very much to you, my *own*.—Your loving

ELLEN.

BUXTON, 1881,

Many thanks, my beloved husband, for yours of yesterday, received as usual this morning. Notes of home-life I might call it; it is so pleasant to know what you are all doing. So glad you have some idea of coming here,—may God bring it to pass,—for it seems so likely to suit and benefit you. I am better, thank God, and I trust it will do Alice good. The temperature must be much lower here than at home. We have taken some drives, and sometimes stroll back pleasantly.

As I knelt down about half-past eight last evening, I thought how blessed to meet at His footstool our Priest upon His throne,—while we look back to see the victim and the altar where we leave our sins. In our reading yesterday we came to Deuteronomy 17:15, "Thou shalt in any wise set him king over thee, whom the Lord thy God shall choose"; and Deuteronomy 18:18, "I will raise them up a Prophet from among their brethren, like unto thee, and will put my words in his mouth; and he shall speak unto them all the words that I command him,"—showing Christ both as king and prophet to be taken from among His brethren.

I hope Mr. Rogers will take your afternoon class, so that you may rest. A happy Sunday to you, my own love.—Your own

ELLEN.

Our Wedding-Day.

A pearl set in golden memories
Stored in my heart's best treasuries,
Oft gazed upon with tender thoughts
And thankful recollections.

A portal fair to paths of truth and peace,
Prepared by our own faithful God,
Where He has led us hitherto,
With many a Hallelujah.

Sweet wedding-day! 'twas crowned so brightly
With sunshine fair in wintry time,
It seemed God's smile descending sweetly
On our heaven-formed union.

His smile! and oh the sweet assurance
Of His own smile, by ours portrayed,
Uniting us to Christ our Head,
For higher sweet communion.

Though six and twenty years have passed away,
Their traces on our foreheads leaving,
I thank my God anew and alway now
For our dear wedding-day.

—E. P. S.

5th February 1882.

Winterdyne, 4th May 1885.

Though my beloved husband has left but a few hours, I must send him a birthday greeting for to-morrow. May you be greeted with rays of heavenly sunshine, grace, mercy and peace, and health. New grace for the new year.

4.30.—Your telegram has just come—thank God for your safe journey.

I was beginning to read of "strangers and pilgrims," and thinking to apply it to birthday thoughts, when Mrs. M. called. We can content ourselves with being strangers here when we realize "heaven is my home," and "whom have I in heaven but *Thee*." Hallelujah, that we are not now aliens from Him, and that He is with us in our pilgrimage. "I am a stranger *with Thee*"—He walking with us, and "holding us by our right hand," how condescending! and how sweet the consciousness that "there no stranger God awaits thee."

May the present little branch of our pilgrimage tend to the realization of the blessed walking with Him. If we knew we, both together, should be caught up to be with Him, we could welcome shortening days and fewer birthdays!

... I suppose you are in your element now—surrounded by good friends and good words—may no ill wind spoil it!

Fondest love and wishes from your ever affectionate

Ellen.

Winterdyne, 4th May 1886.

May best blessings rest richly on you in your birthday, my own beloved husband, and may you enjoy consciously the presence of Him in whose favour is life.

My morning chapter suggests the grand assurance, "Certainly I will be with thee." What a sublime self-consciousness it assumes or indicates of His "all-sufficient sufficiency" for all the great needs of His servant Moses in his great mission, and therefore infinitely enough for you, darling! in pursuing, as I hope, the even tenor of your way through another year. How kind and gracious has He been to you in the past year!—yes, and years!—and so will He continue to be.

... I hope you will enjoy without drawback the pleasant evening you expected. I should like to enjoy it with you; but best as it is.—With fondest love and wishes, your

Ellen.

Fragments.

I can rejoice in the Child born for us, the Alpha and Omega, and oh, may we desire to drink of Him as the fountain of life. My one desire is to abide in Christ; I can do nothing without Him. It seems as if Christ was the *mainspring* which must regulate my heart, thoughts, words, and deeds. If the heart is one with Christ, then of necessity good fruit will spring forth.

What a year of mercies, chastening, yet restoring mercies! What reason to be humbled at its close for oft-repeated sins; how precious His promise, "Thou wilt cast all their sins into the depths of the sea,"—not the shallow sea of time, but the infinite fountain of Jesus' blood.

With the New Year may we cast anchor anew on the Rock, and, safely standing there, take a calm survey, not only of past waves and breakers, but of our security, our possessions here, and our everlasting inheritance. What more can we desire if we can say, as I humbly do, "All things are mine, I am Christ's"—yea, "my beloved is mine, and I am His"—what a portion!

Birthday Thoughts.—Though we cannot help seeing the sins and shortcomings of our lives, yet with the Holy Spirit's help shall we not watch and pray? I think we need positive, definite grace for each service, that it may be unto the Lord. Psalm 84:11. The Lord God, then, will He not shield us from sin and self, and shine more and more of His own image into our hearts?

Winterdyne, Bewdley, 1876.

My dear Boys,—

What may a day bring forth! Thank God it did not bring such news to us as to others. It seems as if God were speaking loudly to Repton—two deaths within a few months! I have often wished some good man could have a mission week at Repton; but this seems God's own mission—and what a solemn one! "Hear ye the rod, and who appointed it"—"Be ye also ready"—"Escape for your lives." But if you, my Willie, my Alfred, know that you are safe because washed in the blood of Jesus, and clothed in His righteousness, rejoice humbly, and be glad in Him who saves you, and "*tell it out* among the sinners that He came to save!" What an opportunity for you to speak of this to others—to break the ice—for I know how hard you find it to speak of this; but many may be longing for a word,—"how can I be saved,"—"how can I *know* I am saved?" Many may be trembling, conscience-stricken; won't you speak a word—lend them a hand? "The Holy Spirit helpeth our infirmities."

Miss Clay has just left to-day for Cheltenham, and stays a day or two with Anna, and then to her sister's in Kensington, to study the Hindoo language. She has had many parting presents, and much sympathy. Many here will feel her loss much. I should like that to be said of you, even on leaving school! May you leave firm, bright footprints on the sand of your time there! Nothing will make them so much so as speaking and shining for Jesus.

I am off to my district, so good-bye—the Lord watch over you.—Your very loving

MOTHER.

WINTERDYNE.

It was pleasant to get your and Alfred's notes on the first morning of our return home, and it is very pleasant to congratulate you on being number one in your class. I hope you will not only retain the place, but do honour to it. Ask for grace to work thoroughly and steadily. Your Report says, "Means well, but is rather noisy at times." Watch against this, remembering "Manners maketh man;" and higher still, "Be perfect, quit you like men, be strong"—"strong in the grace of Christ Jesus." I do pray that you may be directed,—let your heart's prayer be, "Not my way, but Thine;" if you do but sincerely wish for His guidance, He will make your way plain in due time, whether to be a doctor or otherwise. Let it be your ambition (in whatever line) to be "a man of God, thoroughly furnished unto all good works."

Should I not be proud to see you like either of the good clergymen who dined with us lately! One of them told us such interesting stories of his work. One gentleman told him he had been reading and teaching French Infidelity for twenty years. "Oh, my friend, I am not come to talk of that; I am come to talk of Christ." Answer: "Well, I think you have the best of it; you look very happy, and that's more that I am—I'm wretched; and you, if your religion is true, have happiness before you for the future, but I have none."

I hope your papa will tell you the rest of the story, and others when you come home.—Your ever loving

MOTHER.

Thanks for Mr. G.'s paper; there is much that is very nice in it. But what do you understand by "Regeneration"? Article 27th calls it "the new birth;" and Titus 3:5 says, *God saves us by* "the washing of regeneration, and the renewing of the Holy Ghost," which is the new birth of the Spirit—the being born again as in John 3, of which the laver in baptism is merely a sacramental sign. It not only washes the heart from the love and pollution of past sin, but makes way for the renewal of the soul to the Divine Image by the power of the Holy Ghost. So Bible regeneration means much more than ecclesiastical regeneration, or being admitted into the outward Church.

After the "N.B." in your paper, you write "*Baptism* is a sign of what once took place,"—should you not say *Confirmation* is a sign, etc.? To No. II. "desiring them," I would add *earnestly seeking* them, *i.e.* regeneration, repentance, faith, pardon, etc., *so* that it may indeed be an effectual means of grace to you; let it be a time of very earnest prayer for these blessings. Perhaps God *has* begun before this to give them to you, but still pray to be renewed day by day—deeper repentance, clearer, stronger faith.

You say, dear ——, "self is in the way,"—self is every sinner's enemy; "not submitting" to Christ, we like to please ourselves, and have our own way. But, oh! I hope it is the struggling of the new nature within that makes you feel that self hinders you from being or doing what you know would please God. What is to be done? You know you cannot be happy if you follow self against conscience; it is wretched to be ever struggling, kicking against pricks, serving God a little, and self and Satan much. Only one thing can be done,—lay down yourself at the feet of Jesus, and ask Him, your Saviour, to be your Captain, to take possession of you, to rule and reign in you, making His will your will. To put His yoke upon you, so that you may be helped and drawn on by Him, and so made willing to please Him. Make yourself over from the one master to the other—to the One who loves you so, and blesses even you. It will be sweet to please Him who died for you, and He will delight in your making use of Him; talk to Him, tell Him when your will rises up, and ask Him to bring it down, and to make you willing to know and do His will. In coming thus to Him at all times, and for all things, you will find such rest. "We which have believed do enter into *rest.*" Believe in His love and power and willingness to *help,* as well as to save. Lay down your arms, your will, yourself at once, and say, "Yea, let *Him* take all!"

I am sorry any boys should wish "to get it over;" for what they in confirmation take upon themselves will never be over till life is done. A soldier's life is only begun when enlisting "is over." Pleasure and privileges only commence when a deed of adoption into a royal and happy family is signed.

I must go back to *your* "No. III," "at the cost of some self-denial." Only lay down self at Jesus' feet, and all "the cost" will be easy, for He will give the strength and help required. "He *gives power* to them that believe in His name, to become, and then to live, as the sons of God." . . .—Your loving

MOTHER.

I was hearing this morning of what I need, and I thought of you, my dear boys, and that you need it too—the Baptism of the Holy Ghost and of fire—Matthew 3:11, Mr. Everard's text.

He said we may have much natural fire of talent, eloquence, enthusiasm, etc., but yet we need the fire which only Christ Jesus can give. Have you—consider solemnly—a spark of this Divine fire? here is a promise of it for you to claim. Think of the properties of fire. Its *power*—it is one of the most destructive elements,—at a conflagration, how it overpowers all before it! Is not this what we need—a Divine kindling *power* in our religion,—a power to carry all before it? Some have a spark of religion, but scarcely worth calling a fire; we need it divinely increased, so as *to spread* and give heat and light to others—(this is the religion I long for you to have). We want the fire of *zeal* and of *devotion* in our worship; we want the fire of *love,* which prompts *to work* for Him who died for us. Then he said very solemnly, "You *must have fire* from the Lord Jesus some time—this baptism of fire for a happy life now, *or* fire unquenchable at last. Will you ask this gift now? or, by despising, neglecting it, continue dry, useless chaff, and so bring upon yourself justly this unquenchable fire!"

If, then, this baptism of fire is what we need, do, my dear boys, *let us seek it,* plead, claim this promise for ourselves. He said, too, in beginning, that as fire consumes, so we should see that our religion overcomes our sins; if it does not consume, conquer our evil propensities, it is not worth calling religion. Ask yourselves solemnly, have you one spark of this fire in your soul? if you have, stir it up by talking with others; heap on fuel, the fuel of God's Word. You see this is a Divine principle, not one we can raise in ourselves—it is the work, the gift of Jesus; it is to be had for asking, and we are responsible for not asking. Oh, then, do seek it, and may He kindle in you the flame of never dying love!

5th December.

I am often thinking of you, my Willie, and hoping you are better.

I am afraid it is a dreary time for you while you are so lonely up-stairs, and I fancy you were much disappointed at not coming home at once. Your papa and I had talked about it, but Mr. Gould seemed quite to settle the matter; so cheer up and make the best of it—fight it out, and "be a hero in the strife!" There is good to be got from it if you do but seek it. Let it be a time for heart-work—for looking to your ways and your wants—for seeking the gift of the Holy Spirit, His Light and *power,*—is it not this that your soul needs? power to live on Christ and for Christ.

And is it not a time to ask, what have I done here for my Saviour? have I lived for Him, and walked in His steps, so as to help others by my example,—can any one here say, "*you* brought me to Jesus"? Try again, my son, and let your last days at Repton be your best days.

I hope, too, you *study* something, even though you cannot go into school—all study tells some time. You did not say if you wished any more reading books to be sent. . . .—Ever your loving

MOTHER.

For Good Friday.

I am thinking of you, my boys, and hoping that to-morrow may be a "good" day to you,—good in looking at the Lord Jesus as the Lamb of God, bearing away your sin—standing in your place as condemned for sin, and forsaken of God, that you might go free, justified and accounted righteous in Him and for His sake (look at Article XI.). And what then? Why, let your heart sing with joy and thankfulness for what He has done for you. And look for passages that speak of it, such as Isaiah 53, and in Romans 3, Galatians 2, Ephesians 2, and 2 Corinthians 5. And may the Holy Spirit help you to realize and feed on these great things. . . .

To W. and A.

I am pleased, and so is your papa, that you should both go out botanizing, and I hope you will both try to press, place, and keep your specimens in very neat order, for it is time you learned more of that. If you will but take pains in such things now, you will find, as doctors, that habits of neatness, exactness, nicety, and elegance all tell. It will be well to return from such walks in time to arrange the flowers at once for pressing, for that is another important habit for a doctor, to do a thing at once—procrastinate nothing! "Procrastination is the thief of time," says Young; and you would soon find it the thief of money too in your practice.

Thanks for your last note, dear Alfred; remember to pray for the temper of any one who is trying to you, as well as about your own.—Ever your loving

MOTHER.

December 1876.—Beginning life's labours and cares "in the world, yet not of the world," what need I? Surely wisdom from above to lead me in right paths, to show me what I should do.

> "Being in doubt, I say,
>   Lord, make it plain
> Which is the safe, true way,
>   Which would be vain.
>
> "I am not wise to know,
>   Nor sure of foot to go;
> My blind eyes cannot see
>   What is so dear[1] to Thee:
> Lord, make it clear to me;
>   Lord, make it plain!"

---

[1] The word may have been "clear" instead of "dear." The published book had "dear," and the original manuscript letter is not avaible now.

I copied these simple lines yesterday for you, dear Willie, because they made me think of you, and hope that you pray in this sort of way to be guided aright. Do not think that things are not going right, or that prayer is not heard, because they are not going as you wish. We do not always wish what is best, or what would be best. What a comfort to have a *fore*-seeing God—"He knoweth the end from the beginning;" we see only the present, and therefore cannot judge of the future. He loves us, too, more wisely than we love ourselves; so, dear Willie, commit your way, your life, trustingly to Him who doeth all things well.

And if it does seem very disagreeable, tell it all to Him; for He can bring sweetness out of bitter things, darkness out of light, and even turn a curse into a blessing,—believest thou this? "According to your faith, it shall be done." Surely He can smooth or remove, or sweeten, or strengthen in your case, according to your day. Oh yes, "He is able to do exceeding abundantly above all that we ask or think." Only try.—With anxious love, and hoping you are better, your affectionate

MOTHER.

To W. and A.

The thought in my mind just now is that our work, our daily life, depends upon what God is to us, what we realize of His presence and attributes; as some one says, "The believer should remember that Christ is his life, and that Christianity is nothing less than the living exhibition of Christ in his daily walk." Let this be your grand aim, dear Willie, to live in and on Christ, so as not to hinder His dwelling in you; to *let* Him be your life, waiting, "gasping" (as a margin of one of the Psalms puts it) for Him.

Thursday.—Apropos to this is 1 Peter 2:4, "To whom *coming*," as Leonard Bickerstaff read it in the Lesson last night, it shows out to me as a life-long coming, and *as* we come, so shall we be built up in Him. Yes, said Mr. Everard, when I remarked this to him, "Christian life is a continual coming to Christ."

He gave us a capital sermon on Isaiah 53:6—a general confession to be made by all, for all are on the same platform, but each needs to make it *personal* like David: "*I* have gone astray." Going astray is forsaking God and His ways of peace, holiness, and life. *Each* "his *own* way," whether of ungodliness, scepticism, vice, or self-righteousness, etc., but all are included in the one great "broad way." Then he told a story of a lady and her *own* self-righteous religion, continuing, "Look from man's erring to what God has done—not leaving man to destruction, but making known Jehovah's means of recall. Man being powerless to procure his own cure, Jehovah's loving will and work does it all. He provided a Substitute—He bore all the loads, burdens, mountains of sin. The Shepherd became the lamb (1 Peter 2.). He bore sin by *imputation;* the benefit becomes ours by believing." Then he spoke of the many ways by which God leads us back,—of a gay military officer in India, who in tiger-hunting strayed in the jungle towards evening from his companions, lost his way, and then, his ammunition spent, he thought it might be his last night on earth. Horror-stricken, he resolved to climb a tree, but first would pray—a prayer, early taught by his mother, came to his mind; and when he came to the words, "Forgive my sins," he could go no further—his sins rose up before him. That night in the jungle was the turning-point in his life—he was "*found* in the waste, howling wilderness"! . . .—Your affectionate

MOTHER.

WINTERDYNE, 1875.

I should have liked last night to have telegraphed to you, "Be instant in prayer," that the teaching you hear may be blessed to you. Try to take it all as addressed to you, and may the Holy Spirit bring home blessed lessons to your heart. It is so nice to go over one's Confirmation day again, and to be stirred up to renew your resolutions or desires to give full allegiance to your God. I trust you have more loving desires to do so now than on your own Confirmation day, and He is now meeting you (Isaiah 64), and giving you precious opportunities of learning of Him. May He Himself draw near, and draw your heart to Him as the one object of your life here and "up there."

To W. and A.

February 1876.

I have only time to say a little about *doctrine,* and our mission. I wish you were here, all Mr. Peploe's words are so beautiful and profitable—all we could wish for ourselves and others. This day's sermon was from 1 Chronicles 12:38, about "men of war, who could keep rank, *making* David king." David waited at Hebron till "a great host" from each tribe came to make him king. So Christ is waiting for sinners to be gathered out, to own Him and make Him their King. God has given Him right and authority for His kingdom; He *must* reign,—but how few yet have gathered to make Him King! Some for whom He shed His Blood are saying, "We will not have this man to reign over us"—shame, shame! but you do not say that—but that He is, or ought to be, King. But this verse shows what you ought *to do;* you ought to "*make* Him King," and give Him the kingdom—acknowledge, confess, proclaim Him, without fear or shame. Who are they that should do this? Men, "expert in war that can keep rank"—not babes,—you must feed and you must fight; you must grow up in all things into Christ, and "quit you like men," and you must be whole-hearted, perfect, with a single eye towards Him. (Look out texts for these.)

O my boys, this is what I long for you to be—"true-hearted, whole-hearted, faithful and loyal" to Christ as your King. Don't fear to come forward; confessing Him before others would so strengthen you. And then, too, don't fear that confessing Him will hinder your pleasure, or your prospects in life; rather, it will *ensure* both. If people did but know half the blessedness and joy of making Christ their King, and submitting entirely to Him, they would never be so mad as to neglect or refuse doing it. If one offered to a debtor estates and money, and he carelessly refused, men would shrug their shoulders and say, "The poor man is mad!" Oh, be wise! and then you will find what your King can give you—what abundant provision and feasting! and "there is *joy* in Israel" when He is made King.

A fine congregation last night, not many this P.M. Mr. Peploe spoke to our two classes in the dining-room, Sunday A.M., on John 1:12. Christ must be *received*, not merely listened to, etc., but actually and actively received. Take up the gift and use it, receive Him as your righteousness, wisdom, your all, and He will cover you with His righteousness before God. Only open your heart to Him, and He will do all for you—will give you "power" to become and remain His sons—power to keep you from sin. Oh, accept Him!—With so much love from

MOTHER.

To W. and A.

1878.

I have not written to you, my boys, for a week or more, and it seems so long. To me it has been a very solemn week, waking up old memories of loved ones gone before, and especially of my *own* dear mother, and thinking which of us may next fall under the scythe of death. It is well sometimes to try to look straight into eternity, so as to get its solemn light to bear upon our everyday life, that we may live as seeing that which is invisible. And oh, thank God that *ours* is not a dark eternity, no "blackness of darkness" for us, for He has brought us "out of darkness into His marvellous light." "The Lord is my light and my salvation;" "though I walk through the valley and shadow of death, I will fear no evil, for Thou art with me;" "I will walk in the light of the Lord."

I have been feeling very much for your aunts M. and F.; it has been such a trying, wearing time for them; and now our father's last home will be given up, so there is much to remind them of his loss also. I hoped both of them would have come here for a few days' rest, but only aunt Maria is coming this afternoon....

WINTERDYNE, May 11th.

I wish you many happy returns of the 12th, my Alfred; and what does "God the Highest, Mightiest" wish you! look through His Word and see,—it all seems to me to show that His heart yearns for His children's good. "Behold what manner of love the Father hath bestowed upon us" when He says, "Oh that there were such a heart in them . . . that it might be well with them!" and when He says, "This is my Beloved Son, in whom I am well pleased;" and "with Him how shall He not freely give us *all things?*" Look at all the promises and blessedness God "out-poureth for His own,"—so may His birthday message to you be, "Look unto Me," and see what a God I can be to you! what blessings untold to earthly ears and eyes I can give you, if you only open your heart to receive them. Mr. Peploe said, "We often keep the bolts on the back side of our hearts fastened, so that we do not let in God's grace and blessings." Now see that you keep them unfastened, and be seeking to receive them, and "see what 'great things' He can do for you, if you walk in His ways."

Try to get a little time *alone* to-day, dear A., that you may think of and pray for these things.—Your praying

MOTHER.

Short Extracts.

. . . I am often praying you may be strengthened in mind and memory, not only for this examination, but that you may progress in all your studies.

. . . And I suppose you will be watching all the incomers, and taking stock of their appearance and their promise for acquaintanceship. Take your time about that, and may God give you opportunity of forming Christian friendship, such as may be of life-long value. It is well that you are reading Proverbs, now that you particularly need a Pilot for your new course, and it sets up many a warning beacon of dangers you may not yet have encountered, "to which you do well to take heed." Do you notice what a book of contrasts the Proverbs is? And how thankful it should make you that the Holy Spirit has led you to cast in your lot with the wise, the just, and righteous, whose wisdom, wealth, and blessings are so great and so sure. I hope you marked in to-day's chapter 10, "Whoso walketh wisely, walketh surely." . . .

. . . The year is just passing away. Oh what mercies and blessings it brought! What faithfulness, long-suffering forbearance have we experienced in it from our loving Father! May we be more faithful and more loving to Him in the future.

I hope Mr. Townsend's address was worth going for,—a contrast probably to your college sermons on "organic generation," etc., of which Alfred told me; what texts could have been used? You would rather preach on Bible *re*-generation, would you not? and I hope you will some day. How pleasant to be already preparing for such preaching and teaching!—"laying up in store for yourself a good foundation" of knowledge,—you little know how and when you may be permitted to use it in future; and whatever God gives us opportunity to learn, He may find also opportunity for us to use for Him. Oh seek to know and to be whatever will fit you for a calling so high, so Christlike; to know more of Him, your Light, your Life, your Love. And then this will make you seek to *be* like Him, and "a vessel meet for the Master's use, prepared unto every good work."

To W. and A.

RYDE, May 1880.

. . . I have been thinking of you both many times to-day, and that I should write to you from some pleasant glade below Carrisbrook Castle. . . . It was a pleasant walk up to the castle. It is the most extensive castle (English) that we have seen in good preservation. The views from the walls and keep are pleasant,—the towers of Osborne are visible, the hills above Ventnor, and the sea.

I thought of Charles I pacing there in confinement—how different from our light-hearted freedom! We saw the room where his daughter Elizabeth died from grief at her father's death by execution. The Queen has put up a fine monument to the Princess, representing her when dying, leaning over her father's Bible, open at Matthew 11:28. . . . As I sat on the lawn inside the castle, I thought of Psalm 144:2, P. B. V., "My hope, my fortress, my *castle*," and of how much the figure implies— of pleasure, beauty, luxury, and comfort, besides defence, security, and strength,—that may well make us say, "Blessed be the Lord my strength." The more we think of what we possess in Him, the more we wish to *abide* in Him, and go no more out, but only to explore and enjoy Him,—"for how great is His goodness and how great is His beauty"—unsearchable, unspeakable! Oh that your hearts may be occupied with Him, longing after Him, even in the midst of work, etc. May nothing divert your hearts from Him!

. . . I hope your Temperance Meeting went off well, etc. etc.

Short Extracts.

. . . I think you must feel quite relieved at having told us your wish. I was hoping and praying for it, but *could not* believe it, till you told me yourself. So now I am glad and thankful, and know how to pray afresh for you. Before I was up this morning I was thinking you are both God's workmanship and His workman. We may try to trace some of His ways and means of working this wish in you, and we may also trust that He will make you to be a workman that needeth not to be ashamed. And I think this morning's chapter must have inspirited you too, Isaiah 61. Only think of receiving the Spirit as Christ received it, in His sevenfold energy. It was upon Him,

so it will be upon you, for you are His, and all that He has is yours. Oh let your expectation be from Him, your whole dependence upon Him, both for present and future work, for it will be effectual only as you receive out of His fulness.

. . . I am so happy about you. "From this day will I bless you," rings in my mind over you both. How interested you must be in Jeremiah 1. Moses, Samuel, Elijah, and Jeremiah could sympathize with you in fears and sense of unworthiness; but the Omnipotent voice, "I am with thee, I have put my words in thy mouth," that will be enough for you as for them.

I awoke one night lately, from dreaming about you, my Willie, that we had some friends at table, and that you in talking used the expression, "glorious men!" and that I caught it up saying, "Glorious men!" I fear there are few enough of them, but at any rate, Willie, be true to your own expression, and seek to be a "glorious man!" And then I lay awake for some time thinking of you, and that the best recipe for "a glorious man" is that of our Great Exemplar,—"I seek *not mine own* glory, but the glory of Him that sent Me." I do think that in proportion as one seeks humbly and heartily for His glory, so He reflects it back on His creature.

RYDE, 11th May 1880.

Is it really twenty-one years since that cold, rough day when a little delicate babe appeared whom we afterwards named Alfred? For weeks he looked as if a breeze might waft him away, but prayer was offered and answered, and so he has now reached "man's estate." And so, my Alfred, I pray you may also spiritually "grow up unto a perfect man, unto the measure of the stature of the fulness of Christ." That is my heart's wish for you, so that "the name of the Lord Jesus may be glorified in you, and you in Him." No stunted, sin-checked growth, but all in and by and for Him,—growth quickened and hastened by letting in the bright shining of the Sun of Righteousness.

This is a bright sunny morning, and I wish you could be here for a day's holiday!—With fond and prayerful love, your affectionate

MOTHER.

"Grow up *into Him* in *all* things."

DEAREST ALFRED,—

To-morrow is "a day to be much-remembered" in connection with you, and I hope to bear you on my heart before the Lord for new supplies for your new year,—new mercy, grace, and strength, that you may "in all things grow up into Christ."

Did you notice in to-day's chapter, Leviticus 1, how much of spiritual principle is marked out for us in the voluntariness of the *offerings?*—and this is shown in a threefold willingness: for *gifts,* Exodus 35:21, and for work, Exodus 35:29; and, "the offering of a free heart will *I* make, and praise Thy Name." May you do so to-day. Then, all was to be done "before the Lord," and all was to be a "sweet savour to *Him.*" "The *perfect satisfaction* with which a Holy God regards the *perfect work* of His Beloved Son, is the ground of a believing sinner's *perfect peace.*" Just what we need to keep in view in all our doings.

20th June 1881.

"*We* be *not able* to go up."

I was struck with these words yesterday, my Alfred, and thought how easily we can see Israel's folly and faithlessness in stopping short of adding, "but God is able." A parable for you,—you may shrink and see plenty of "lions in the way," but put your cause and your difficulties in His hand, saying, "Undertake for me," "I am Thine, help me to glorify Thee," and your cause becomes His—" the battle is not yours but God's." So take heart and look up! . . . I have invited my class for a Temperance talk on Wednesday evening, for we had two sad warnings last week of the evils of drink,—one man hung himself, and another attempted to cut his own throat, but survives. . . . You have my anxious love and wishes,—but, don't misunderstand, though I do frequently think and feel for you as to the coming examination, I am light-hearted about it, believing that prayer will be answered and faith rewarded.

1882.

Meanwhile, may He keep you leaning upon Him, learning of Him, and so made willing to be, to do, or to suffer as He sees best. Did you notice in this morning's Psalm, "The Lord *trieth* the righteous," and the after reason, "the Lord loveth righteousness," loves to see the fruits ' of righteousness in those who are accounted righteous in His dear Son? So I take it that He, loving you, is thus preparing you to shine in His righteousness the more when He renews (as I trust) your strength like the eagle's. Give auntie that text for me; I shall pray it for you both.

Winterdyne, 3rd January 1883.

Dearest Alfred,—

I must send a line to greet you on the day for entering on your ministerial work. The text on my mind for you is, "I will go in the strength of the Lord, I will make mention of Thy righteousness, even Thine only." That strength and righteousness are yours—you have tried them, and they will never fail you. In that strength may you preach that righteousness and the Lord of it.

A thought on my mind just now is, The *greatness* of the King is the honour of his ambassador. So may you learn more and more of your King, whose greatness is unsearchable, so that you may glory in Him. I am longing to hear of you already. . . .

I was thinking much of you yesterday, and hoping you found some cheering service. The morning Psalm, 93, showed Him the Lord reigning, while the Communion service showed Him as the pierced, thorn-crowned King, asking us to remember Him as such; and I comforted myself in thinking of Him as risen and reigning again, to reign *in* and for you, to subdue all that might oppose itself to you, and *make* all work for your good.

Did you ever put these together?—Job 36:5–7, Nehemiah 9:32, Psalm 24:8, Ephesians 3:16, with Amos 5:12, which shows what there is in us that needs God's might, and makes Isaiah 60:16, 63:1, and Psalm 89:19, to be good news. Over and above that, say Jeremiah 33:3, *e.g.* "J. K.," Psalm 17:7.

Prescription in mighty storm, Psalm 93:4, 107:25–30.

Or when in need of great strength, Judges 14:6, Deuteronomy 7:21; or in other difficulties, Jeremiah 32:19, Revelation 3:18. Christian's daily comfort, Ephesians 1:19, Colossians 1:11.

Contrast all this, and "A Hand Almighty to defend, an ear for every call," etc., with dread of 2 Thessalonians 1:7, 8, Luke 12:5.

Winterdyne, Bewdley, 15th June 1883.

Dearest Alfred,—

The week is going by and I have not yet written to you, though thinking of it day by day.

I was praying last night for rain for our scorched fields and garden, and looming clouds have so often passed over us without rain; and then I thought of "showers of blessing," and prayed for one to come on and around *you.* And some rain did come early, and now again it has been falling steadily for two hours. And so, too, may the Holy Spirit descend on you, fertilizing and refreshing you within and for your work.

I hope you will enjoy your Mildmay visit. By all means call, if you can, at Home Lodge, and I suppose you will see Rev. Joe Rogers too. I hope he has been able to find a house. Mrs. Fuchs, who has been here for two days to give us a drawing-room address, was with her husband, C. M. S. missionary at Benares for many years, and knew Mr. Storrs, and "Ellen Goreh's" parents; her mother was such a sweet woman and used to speak so nicely to the natives. We had a good room full for Mrs. F., and she was very interesting, only her German accent was difficult to understand. One small fact showed the utter ignorance of a heathen man, who said to her, "You no' need to talk so much about sinners and salvation; if a man live sinful life and say wicked words, he has only to look at Ram (idol) and say, Ram, Ram, and all his sin is gone." It brings one back to one of your papa's strong points, the need of right knowledge of God and of sin.

1884.

I must write at this solemn, important time of your ordination, when our thoughts and prayers centre so much on you. Text after text suggests prayers, or raises thought of the high and holy calling to which our God has graciously brought you. "I have made thee a *watchman*"—" the priest's lips should keep knowledge, for he is the *messenger* of Jehovah." "Ye are My *witnesses*." "Now then we are ambassadors"—"Fellow-labourers with GOD." No higher calling could we wish for you! And we know that He who calls you to the work of the ministry provides you the materials and the means for doing it, and will fit and teach you, and be Himself your helper and guide in it. "Fear not," He says, "for I am with thee; be not dismayed, *for I am thy God;* I will help thee, yea, I will uphold thee with the right hand of My righteousness."

And so we may expect (though you may be trembling at your own weakness and unworthiness, and the difficulties that may meet you) that *He* will make you a wise and able minister of Jesus Christ, giving you messages of His grace, and even "fitting them to your lips." Then may we not say "*Bless* ye the Lord, ye ministers of His, that do His pleasure." Delight yourself in Him, and let His glory be seen upon you.

May the Holy Spirit indeed descend on you (and on the other candidates) to-morrow in His sevenfold energy!—Your loving mother,

ELLEN SHAW.

11th May 1885.

Fondest birthday wishes, for you, my Alfie, on the morrow.

This afternoon's subject leads me to give thanks that "the God of peace, the everlasting God," has called you to "the obedience of faith," and "is of power to stablish you according to the Gospel" which He has given you to preach.

And glancing down a "railway" to to-morrow's passage, I shall from that be wishing you to be "*enriched* by Him in all utterance and knowledge, *sanctified* and *confirmed,* that you may be *blameless* now and in the day of the Lord Jesus." How much is comprised in these things! God grant that you may realize them largely.

Sorry I have no birthday present to send, only a few flowers; the greenhouse is well filled, and so gay. Do come quick and see it. The tennis-ground is being mown to-day, and I long to see you on it. Shall be so glad to get you home together.—Your loving, longing

MOTHER.

DEAREST WILLIE,—

I was sorry afterwards that my last was so hurried—that I had made no reference to your recommencement of your work after the sudden and unexpected gap that was made in it. Surely it must lead you to live and work more as by the light of eternity,—to live in and by Christ, so that when called to Him, whether by sudden or tedious causes, you may say, "When I wake up I am *still* with Thee,"—to work as if each day might be the last.

I have just read this: "It is a wholesome process to be taken down occasionally. The grass on every lawn requires to be taken down by a mower; the lawn never looks so well as when the keen-edged cutter has gone over it. Some Christians in my charge have never appeared so attractive in humility and heavenly-mindedness as when God's mowing machine has gone over them." May it be so with you, my Willie!

I feel it was indeed a great mercy that that accident did not mow you down to rise up no more; but that you are yet permitted to be among the "fellow-labourers" with God.

1885.

DEAREST ALFRED,—

The text on my mind to-day, in spite of the sorrowful funeral, is, "The living shall *praise* Thee"—praise for life out of death, praise to eternity, etc.,—and this came after reading yesterday in *your* gift, *Abide in Christ,* about fulness of joy, and its influence on others. "There is nothing so *attractive* as joy, no preaching so attractive as the sight of hearts made glad; it is a mighty element in Christian character,—and for our own welfare joy is indispensable—the joy of the Lord is our strength. With a heart full of joy, no work can weary and no burden depress."

So I am praying for you to-day that *His* joy may be in you—He Himself be your strength and song, so that the joy of your Lord may shine out in your face, *telling* "what a dear Saviour I have found," and make way for the glad tidings of peace. Your cares will be lightened by your vicar's return.

11th May 1886.

Much bright blessedness to you on your birthday, my Alfie, and many blessed birthdays to succeed this one, and in all of them may you still be "increasing in the knowledge of God," so that you may know more of the depth of the ancient promise, "I will be to you a God."

I was pondering after dinner upon Romans 14:9, "To this end Christ both died, and rose, and revived, *that* He might be Lord both of the dead and living." Not *for* His own glory, or even for His Father's joy, but to be Lord to us nothings,—as if, knowing our nothingness, He would give us value, importance, and place, by putting Himself the All-infinite unit before us, that we may be headed up in Him. More and more does His sovereign condescension grow upon me.

Letters to ———

God's blessing rest on your birthday! Begin the day with real, earnest prayer, that as God continues your bodily health, so your soul's life and health may increase. Pray now that you may be more like Jesus—may His Holy Spirit make you so—more like Him in a (1) loving spirit, (2) in cheerful obedience, (3) in self-denying kindness. Remember the Lord Jesus said, "I have left you an example;" so try every day to see how you can follow it in all things. Pray that the Holy Spirit may help you to look at Him so as to see how loving, holy, and lovely He was in all things, and that you may be made like Him in thought and word and deed. If you were like Him you would be a sunbeam to all. Amen!

How I think of you "little travellers" setting out on another term of school-life. I trust all seems seen in a new light—light from above, your faces being set Zionwards. Oh, mind and keep in the light, "walk in the light,"—ever be turning towards it, as often as anything clouds it from you! Above all, when you rise in the morning, look at the Sun of Righteousness—ask Him to shine into your *hearts* with the light of His love—ask Him to shine upon your ways and guide you in everything.

Much birthday blessing and happiness to you! I want you to enjoy the day and its blessings without looking onward vaguely to indefinite "many happy birthdays." If "happy only in His love," you can rise above outer surroundings, and can ask and expect your spiritual life to be invigorated, brightened. But are you "happy in that love?" not as you wish to be? What hinders?—nothing, I should think, but the want of looking at, meditating on it, and letting your heart go out, gush forth without restraint in love to Him;—let your heart sing and make melody upon "He loved me," and *I* am "accepted in the Beloved." "Yes, in spite of my not loving Him, He helped me to come (even if but limping and wavering), and He has not cast me out—no, He accepts me, loves me, blesses me with all spiritual blessings." Cannot you talk and "reason" thus with Him, and try to count over some of His blessings?—such reasoning, communing with Him, will revive you, and help you on, for He will meet with you (Isaiah 64:5), and will revive you (Hosea 14:7).

Give up yourself to the Lord Jesus, and let Him shine into your heart. Don't you want to be His entirely? Was not that your Confirmation wish? "In Thee and all for Thee." You trust Him for putting away your sin—*enjoy* that blessedness, and renew it as often as you have a transgression or an omission to bring to Him. But besides that, open your heart to Him, in everything look up to Him and ask Him to do it for you, or in you.

Weymouth, October 1873.

The coming Sunday makes me think specially of you. Perhaps you feel almost as *unable* as "unworthy to gather up any crumbs under His table;" but ask Him to feed you by bringing to your remembrance the dear Saviour, and what He is, and what He has done for *you*. Think of it not only as a time for feeling your own sins, but for *rejoicing* in the great, complete, God-accepted sacrifice which Christ made for them. I think it will help you much to try to *praise* Him for it, for praise is wing-like, lifting our hearts upwards.

Winterdyne, 31st October 1874.

Another sacrament Sunday is coming to remind you, my child, of "the salvation you have obtained in Christ Jesus with eternal glory,"—try to realize that you *have* obtained it—though perhaps you say with trembling,

"Is it for me, dear Saviour,
Thy glory and Thy rest?"

Yes, it is for you—not your getting, but His *gift*. Well, then, may you "*remember*" Him who bought it for you with His own blood.

Winterdyne, 30th January 1874.

I am thinking of you, and wishing I could help you "sit down with great delight" at our Master's Table on Sunday—yet, though I speak of Him, I feel it is the Holy Spirit's office to draw our souls there, and to give us spiritual appetite, and so to present the Lord Jesus to our remembrance, that we *may feast* upon it. Ask Him then to do this for you now. "He made Him to be sin for us." Try to "remember" all this, and rejoice that you are thus made free from sin's condemnation.

"Payment God cannot twice demand,
First at my bleeding Surety's hand,
And then again at mine."

I am wishing you both well through your "exams;" but I want you to have better comfort under your burdens than merely the world's philosophy, "they will come to an end some time." I want you so determinately to seek help from above, that you may consciously find it, and say, "I am helped," for "the Lord is my helper." The commonest abilities are His gift, and He can help each (knowing our frame), according to their need. Remember, "they looked unto Him, and *were lightened*." He *can do* what a loving, willing mother cannot—or she would.

I want you to share the pleasure of speaking for Jesus. Ask Jesus to help you; live on Him moment by moment, so that you may speak of and for Him when the right moment comes. Ask Him for the right words—ask Him for courage; but oh! let Him reign and rule in you, that they may "take knowledge of you that you have been with Jesus," and learned His mind and ways.... I long for all my children to *be* blessings.

26th June 1875.

I have never written to you all this week! Not that you were forgotten,—you were neither uncared nor unprayed for; and oh, it is a comfort to know that He who "pleads the causes of our souls" will not fail you. I often think Jesus knows just what your little wants are for to-day, and loves to supply them. I hope you ask and expect and watch for His supplies.... The grass is to be mown on Wednesday. His "heart was withered like grass." ...

We read at prayers this morning Isaiah 59 and 63, as showing what *sinners* Christ died for, that we could get no salvation for ourselves, and that He *alone* brought salvation and righteousness to us. What views for our faith to take of Him, as the Lamb of God, bowing His head to receive and bear the sin of the world—the Great High Priest, with our names upon His breast, offering up His one sacrifice for sins for ever; and again, as our Good Shepherd, fighting the foe for us, that He might make us more than conquerors!

So, dear, we are, or have been, "in the same box!"—you with your knee, I with a cold in my throat. I am so sorry about your knee—nothing like entire quiet for it. But it is hindering your work! Nevertheless, get some good out of it. Look *within,* as I am trying to do. Look at your heart machinery and say, "Search me, O God, and show me if there be any evil way in me." Why do I not make more progress? Why am I not more like Jesus? Look thoroughly to see what clogs your wheels, and cast it thoroughly away—and mind you get fresh oil—the right sort to shine. And take special time for your Bible, so that its light may shine into your soul. Did you pray over this morning's lesson? Daniel 6. I noticed how thorough-going was Daniel's religion, for it was "before His God,"—not altered to suit the word of men, even of a king. Oh, try to realize when on your knees that you are "before your God." Aim, too, at Daniel's faultlessness. Both Peter (2 Peter 3:14) and Paul (Philippians 2:15 and 1:10) wished their disciples to be so. Mark these in your Bible with Daniel 6:4.

13th July 1876.

I had a very pleasant holiday yesterday. We drove to the Leasowes—feasted on the pictures, some by old masters. ...
And the grounds are so pretty and interesting; such trees! and a pretty streamlet falling in little cascades, etc., not quite your Swiss waterfalls, but still I enjoyed it all extremely—nevertheless feeling all the while that it would not *satisfy* me without the real, the lasting, the living Friend within! "All this, and Christ beside!" or, should not our hearts say, "*All Christ,* and this beside!" Oh, is it not delightful to enjoy Him deep down in one's heart?

"Him first, Him last, Him midst and without end."

Don't you often say too—

"Thou who hast given me eyes to see
And love these sights so fair,
Grant me the grace to find out Thee,
And *read* Thee everywhere.'

August 1880.

I am sorry ... for your disappointment; "Man proposes," etc. Take it as a bit of life-discipline, one of the ways or paths of your Father's own appointment, remembering "all the paths of the Lord are mercy and truth to such as keep His covenant." "Walk before Him" in it, *i.e.* as in His presence, and He will make His face to shine upon you, and give you peace. Now you can say, "Thy way, O Lord, not mine."

19th February 1881.

... I have had a happy birthday, with many a quiet little pleasure in addition to the deeper sense of the long-suffering and unwearied loving-kindness that have accompanied me *all* these years, and brighten the present; and my very "trivial tasks," too, have been bright with His love. Little Edward said that I had "a very happy birthday in helping him with his ark"! He had made me a marker and an ivy wreath.

BUXTON, 25th July 1881.

As to your future course, I can only say, "Wait on the Lord" for guidance; "as the eyes of servants look unto the hand of their masters, and as the eyes of a maiden unto her mistress," so let your eyes be unto the Lord, until He gives some signal for action. And so in your daily chapter (John 10) for to-day, if you think you have heard His voice calling you to go forth— that is all you know as yet—then keep close to Him, listening, following in His steps, learning of Him, so that you may be ready for whatever He may call you to. Depend on the word, "the way of the righteous is made plain" (Proverbs 15:19). This leads me to conclude that you should not *go before* God in making inquiries, but "wait" for His providence to give you further call or direction. *If* He "has need of" you, can He not send a disciple to you when His time has come?

WINTERDYNE, December 1884.

Best birthday blessings to you, my dear lonely child. I don't like to think of you in the lone distance, only it is, I believe and expect, for your good,—and the sun shines everywhere! So may the Sun of Righteousness arise and shine on you with healing in His beams—healing for body and soul. And may He shine into your heart, and give you more and more of the light of the knowledge of the glory of God, so that you may go on your way rejoicing even if in suffering.

Aunt Maria went yesterday to see her "little Joseph," and found him so happy—such peace and joy flowing in his heart; he said, "It's like gold to our dross, like diamonds to our grits! so good of God to give His Son for me!" May such joy, such music flow on in your heart, my child—it is all for *you*.

November 1885.

. . . This will bring your mother's renewed love and fervent wishes for fresh upsprings in you of the living waters, and continued outflowings of God's bounties to and around you. How good has He been to you, and to me, in sparing you and all our unbroken circle! Oh that life in Him may be more real, so that life for Him may be more earnest! "What a black edge for a birthday note," I thought as I took this sheet of paper; but it is not really very inappropriate, for "in the midst of life we are in death," and there is always much to mourn for in the departed year. How can *He* bear with me! I often say. But look unto Him, the perfect One, delight in His perfections, and live in His fulness.

23rd December 1885.

I must send you my loving Christmas greetings to-day, lest to-morrow's overburdened post should fail. So may the blessedness of the Great Gift be expanded upon you both, my dear ones, in body and in soul. May some fresh enjoyment of the Angel's message come to you, some new realization of the precious Gift delight you. "God's Gift of Gifts, all other gifts in one."

God has showered so many sweet blessings on you all, that there should be the heart's return—still, both the objective and the subjective are of Him, so we may hope that He will work both in you and by you.

WINTERDYNE, December 1885.

Best birthday blessings to you, my child! I hope my basket of somewhat typical things—nourishment and pleasant fruits—are reaching you this afternoon. May the real blessings "prevent" and overtake you day by day throughout your added year. (Deuteronomy 28:2.)

I will specially ask for the help you wish for Sunday and Wednesday. May His words for those times "be fitted to your lips," and they cannot return to Him void!

I have been looking out what the Proverbs say about *friends*—what they should not do, and what they should do, leading to what our best Friend does for us. May He be very near and dear to you as your Counsellor (now you are so much on your own responsibility), your rich Friend who delights to give out of His fulness.

WINTERDYNE, December 1886.

Abundant birthday blessings to you, you dear child, more than I can ask or think! What manifold mercies have been brought you, and it will be "better farther on;" how comfortable to know that! God grant that you may have more enjoyment of the life He gives, and more power to serve Him. And the spiritual life, that is your chief anxiety, is it not? May that too be invigorated—Christ in you be more realized, living in you to energize and quicken to all well-pleasing. Oh to have one's eye always on Him as our life, living for us, to intercede for and bless us, to rule and reign and work in us, and to be consciously always under His control and guidance!

> The PERFECT SATISFACTION with which a HOLY GOD regards the PERFECT WORK of His Beloved SON, is the ground of a believing Sinner's PERFECT PEACE.
>
> Edinburgh: James Taylor, 81 Castle Street.

This small card was found among Havergal manuscripts and papers. Who wrote this is not known. Colossians 2:10 Such cards and leaflets were and are easy and inexpensive to print, a means of God to give rich truths to many people, both friends and strangers. Ellen Prestage Shaw quoted this in a letter to her son Alfred Havergal Shaw (on page 218, left column, lines 5-8).

BIBLE NOTES.

TAKEN FROM MORE THAN FOUR HUNDRED.

(Prepared chiefly for E. P. S.'s Class of Young Men.)

MOSES' CHOICE.

Exodus 2.

MOSES saved, nursed, adopted in the king's house—then we might expect he would remain always there, and share its honours, etc., but ver. 15 shows he left the court, and "went to the land of Midian." Why? Hebrews 11:24–26 explains. "Choosing rather to suffer affliction with the people of God, than to enjoy the pleasures of sin for a season; esteeming the reproach of Christ greater riches than the treasures of Egypt: for he had respect to the recompence of the reward." It was Moses' own doing to leave the court! You would think much of going to the Queen's court, if only as a servant; but Moses gave up real rank and honour.

He refused three things. 1. The rank of a son of the princess. Men like to "rise in the world," to be thought great, but Moses gave it up! 2. Refused "pleasures"—plenty of them in Egypt; learning, art, "*designing,*" and doing grand things; gaiety—just what most people run after, all were given up! 3. Refused the "treasures of Egypt," great wealth there, temples, pyramids, "the mightiest buildings in the world," *still* show it; so Moses might have been very rich. How men toil, travel, etc. for money! Some act as if money could cover all sin and failing—as if money were everything—but Moses gave it up!

Was he *obliged* to give it up? No; he *chose*—considered, and made choice. Was it to get something better? Chose "affliction" and suffering, along with the oppressed, tormented Israelites—to be one of them! Strange! How he would be laughed at, scorned, thought mad! But he was not laughed out of it; he stood to his choice. Nothing like being *sure* we have made a good choice, and then we can keep to it.

What was Moses' reason or principle in choosing? "*Faith*" (Hebrews 11:24) was the mainspring that made him act thus, that made him "refuse" and "choose" as he did. Faith in *what?* In God and His word to Abraham (Genesis 12:3), faith in the promises of blessing—*future* blessing; for faith was as a telescope bringing them to his sight. Hebrews 11:27 tells us *who* he saw—"Him who is invisible." Moses could not see as much of Him as David and Isaiah did, but he saw that some Blessed One of Abraham's seed *would come to bless.* We can see better still. "God, having raised up His Son Jesus, sent Him to bless you, in turning away every one of you from his iniquities" (Acts 3:26). He hath "blessed us with all spiritual blessings in heavenly places in Christ" (Ephesians 1:3). So Moses saw it was better to cast in his lot with God's people, and wait for blessing in the end. Faith helped him to interpret things rightly—that although Israel was oppressed then, there was a glorious future! He saw that glorious future "reward" so plainly that Egyptian pleasures seemed not worth having (as motes in a sunbeam). It was better to belong to the King over all, than to King Pharaoh—and he was right; the name of Pharaoh's city and his daughter are forgotten, the wealth is gone, Egypt became the "basest of kingdoms" *but* there is "an inheritance incorruptible and undefiled, and that fadeth not away, reserved in heaven for you, who are kept by the power of God through faith unto salvation" (1 Peter 1:4, 5). "A kingdom which cannot be moved" (Hebrews 12:28).

Do make Moses' choice and use his telescope. If you don't *choose* God, you remain with the world and Satan. You will never be saved if you don't choose. Decide "this day" (Joshua 24:15). If you used Moses' telescope you *would* choose! *Look up* with it to the everlasting King, the King of glory, and His everlasting love—at what He has in store, "treasure that waxeth not old," "durable riches," and righteousness, grace, and glory—a "kingdom" (Luke 12:32) and a "crown" (James 1:12). Oh, choose these *instead* of Satan's wages!

THE CURTAINS OF THE TABERNACLE.

Exodus 26.

The curtains of the tabernacle were of four sorts. 1st, linen (ver. 1); 2nd, goats' hair (ver. 7); 3rd, rams' skins dyed red (ver. 14); 4th, badger or seal (ver. 14). What supported the curtains? Fifty-four boards (vers. 15, 20). How did they stand? (vers. 11–19). On silver sockets (ch. 27:10, 11), with fillets above. No one was numbered unless he brought redemption money. Silver from whom? (ch. 38:25–27). Given by Israel to God in remembrance of redemption. Exodus 12:13, "And when I see the blood I will pass over you." So the foundation of Israel's and our meeting God is redemption. So He says, "I have found a ransom." How were they held together at the top? By bars and rings (vers. 26–29). So Christ not only raises the spiritual temple, but holds it, binds all together, keeps it. "By Him all things consist" (Colossians 1:17). Ver. 22, Why were there only six boards west? To leave an entrance to the Holiest, which was covered by the veil, or separate curtain (vers. 31–33). This veil (spoken of in Matthew 27:51, Luke 23:45, Hebrews 10:20) was not the only type of Christ. The whole tabernacle was a type of Him. He was *the* meeting-place. He *was* "the true Tabernacle" (Hebrews 8:2) that "tabernacled among us."

Christ became man to become visible to men. "The Word was made flesh" (John 1:14), for we cannot *yet* see God. See what the *curtains* teach of Him. The inner ones were of fine *white* linen. Linen, then the whitest fabric known, denoted Christ's purity. "And to her was granted that she should be arrayed in fine linen, clean and white: for the fine linen is the righteousness of saints" (Revelation 19:8); and He is "able to save them to the uttermost that come unto God by Him, seeing He ever liveth to make intercession for them" (Hebrews 7:25). So it is the emblem of His spotless manhood. "Pure, unspotted, may *we* be."

"*Blue*"—heavenly colour, as for example, the sky. Christ, so heavenly-minded that He could say on earth He was in heaven. "The Son of man which is in heaven" (John 3:13). He never forgot His Father or home in heaven. "If ye then be risen with Christ, seek those things which are above, where Christ sitteth on the right hand of God" (Colossians 3:1, Matthew 6:20).

Purple denotes royalty. He was born King. "Where is He that is born King of the Jews" (Matthew 2:2). He reigns now in heaven (Psalm 24).

Scarlet—sacrificial colour, denotes death (cochineal, chief red, insects made to die to give colour). So Christ was the victim of sacrifice. What do the *goats' hair* curtains teach? They hid (ver. 7), covered the beautiful fine ones—just so Christ's beautiful, spotless, righteous character is not known. "There is no beauty that we should desire Him" (Isaiah 53:2).

The goat was an animal for sacrifice; its blood was sprinkled on the Day of Atonement—(scapegoat). So Christ was numbered with malefactors, that by His death and by His blood your sin might be covered over and blotted out.

Rams' skins dyed red. To show the intense depths of Christ's love; being determined to save, showed the reality of His devotion.

Badger or seal skins were coarse and dark-looking, not attractive to strangers. "He hath no form nor comeliness; and when we shall see Him there is no beauty that we should desire Him" (Isaiah 53:2). What a contrast to the inside! Oh this is like Christ now! *few* come near to see His loveliness, His preciousness. They glance outside, and do not care to look and learn—for the sinful natural heart cannot see His beauty, or its own need. "The natural man receiveth not the things of the Spirit of God: for they are foolishness unto him; neither can he know them, because they are spiritually discerned" (1 Corinthians 2:14). The passer-by might scoff at the black tabernacle, but could he see the inside, which was so different! Only come to Christ. Pray, "Open Thou mine eyes." The beauty of the tabernacle was soon seen, but Christ's beauty will be new through all eternity. Remember this beautiful tabernacle was for a meeting-place with God. Its greatest value was in being a type of Christ as our meeting-place. "Now in Christ Jesus ye who sometime were far off are made nigh by the blood of Christ" (Ephesians 2:13). Like a cypher, its chief value is when a numeral is placed before it—so the great value of the tabernacle is to teach of Christ. It contains a double type of the Church as the dwelling-place of Christ—believers are Christ's tabernacle. As the tabernacle was made to contain the Ark of the Covenant, so the Church is built for Him (Ephesians 2:19–22); dwelt in by Him. "That Christ may dwell in your hearts by faith" (Ephesians 3:15–19). The whole Church is built on redemption—"redeemed . . . with the precious blood of Christ." All that is Christ's is theirs. Best part was within the curtains—unseen by the world (the world cannot know our treasures; our joys are hid in Christ, and enjoyed in secret). The curtains were coupled together from above (Exodus 26:24). "That they all may be one in Us, as Thou, Father, art in Me" (John 17:21).

"*Taches of blue.*" No friendships so firm as Christians. There are many links—Temperance is one—showing the blue tache may couple you with some good friend.

THE SIN-OFFERING FOR IGNORANCE.

Leviticus 4.

See *when* or *for whom* offered. Vers. 2, 3, "If a soul shall sin through ignorance against any of the commandments of the Lord concerning things which ought not to be done, and shall do against any of them: if the priest that is anointed do sin according to the sin of the people." Vers. 13–20, "If the whole congregation of Israel sin through ignorance, . . . and they have done somewhat against any of the commandments of the Lord concerning things which should not be done, and are guilty; when the sin, . . . is known," etc. Leviticus 16:27–30, "And the bullock for the sin-offering, and the goat for the sin-offering, whose blood was brought in to make atonement," etc. For sins of *ignorance,* not so much for a single sin, but for a sinful *nature* that keeps us ignorant, blind, insensible to sin. Do not think because you have not told lies, etc., that you need no offering. You often say, "I didn't think—didn't know—or I did not intend wrong—I did not see or seize opportunity." Think what a holy, prayerful lad you *should* be, shining for Jesus, and how you fall short of it (sin in Hebrew often means "missing the mark"—not coming up to the standard, so "he that sinneth against me wrongeth his own soul," Proverbs 8:36), and then you will be thankful for our sin-offering. "He hath made Him to be sin for us, who knew no sin" (2 Corinthians 5:21). What was the sin-offering? Leviticus 4:14, a bullock, or for any one of the common people, a kid (Numbers 28:22) or a lamb; either being *slain* showed that death was deserved by the sinner who offered it. It was his substitute. No oil or frankincense, no feasting with this, for it taught man was a sinner deserving death—but an animal was slain instead, to be the penalty of sin. The Hebrew for sin-offering is the same as sin, so that the animal *became the sin,* or sin-bearer. The animal was of value, but there is no comparison between it and man's self, or his son. A man would as soon suffer himself as let his son suffer. God did not give an animal or angel for us, but Himself—One, equal with the Father, gave Himself. 1 Peter 2:24, "Who His own self bare our sins in His own body on the tree." 1 Peter 3:18, "Christ also hath once suffered for sins, the just for the unjust." Think how painful to the Holy One, hating, abominating sin, to be "made sin," "reckoned with transgressors." Oh, how He loved!

How did the offerer transfer guilt? Leviticus 4:15, "The elders of the congregation shall lay their hands upon the head of the bullock." Ver. 29, "He shall lay his hand upon the head of the sin-offering." He had to humble himself to do this before the priest and the congregation. Need you do this? No, only come to Christ; there is no hindrance. Have you come? Why not? God is satisfied with Christ's offering—why not with you? Have you "not thought" about it, "not liked to do it," etc.? Then you slight, neglect it. Hebrews 2:3, "How shall we escape, if we neglect so great salvation?" Hebrews 10:29, "Of how much sorer punishment . . . shall he be thought worthy, who hath trodden under foot the Son of God, and hath counted the blood of the covenant, wherewith he was sanctified, an unholy thing." He pleads with you, "Is it nothing to you, all ye that pass by? behold, and see if there be any sorrow like My sorrow" (Lamentations 1:12). How did God show He was satisfied with a sin-offering? Leviticus 4:6, 7, By commanding sprinkling of blood *before* Him, to show that now God would accept the worshipper. This shows that the sin was before God. Do not forget that sin is "against God" (Psalm 51:4), and so the blood must be taken to where sin reached—that the sin might be put away. Where was the blood also put? Ver. 34, on "the horns of the altar," for there God met the sinner. So the precious blood went before us into God's presence, being poured out here below, as an atonement for us. "By His own blood He entered once into the holy place" (Hebrews 9:12).

The fat and inwards were burnt separately (vers. 8–11). These represented the will, thoughts, and affections of Christ. What was done with the rest? All was burnt, consumed (ver. 12). Why? If the animal represented sin, and it was all burnt to ashes, and could not be recovered or made anything of, it showed that sin was brought to nothing—no more to be brought against the sinner. It tells of hell fire which sin deserved. Blessed be God for devising means of escape! The blood and ashes being poured out say all is finished.

Is the blood of Jesus between you and God's awful holiness and justice? Trust *only* to it!

THE BREASTPLATE.
Exodus 28:15.

The breastplate was an ornament, "a span" or 9 or 10 inches square when doubled (ver. 16). It had chains and rings (vers. 22–25). Why? to secure it. How many jewels were in it? (vers. 17–21). Why twelve? As much as to say that each tribe was as precious as a jewel. All were different, *e.g.* carbuncle, fire-red, Zebulon; topaz, golden tinge, for Issachar. But they were all treated alike, all were precious, and all were secure. To put a thing near the heart means to love and value it. Then the breastplate showed Israel the love of the high priest for them all. What more? Ver. 29, It was to remind him of them all when he went in "before the Lord" as *their representative.* How often? Ver. 30, "Continually." What does this teach of *our* High Priest? Do you not wish to know more of Him? or is He nothing to you? But see what He is and feels for His people. Read the Bible to see how He loves and remembers them. A glimpse of how He bears them on His heart to His Father is given in John 17. He knows all their names. John 10:3, "Calleth His own by name." (The Queen cannot.) He *will* not forget. "They may forget, yet will I not forget thee. I have graven thee upon the palms of My hands" (Isaiah 49:15, 16). Pray, as in Song of Solomon 8:6, "Set me as a seal upon Thine heart," and believe He has you there. "My kindness shall not depart from thee" (Isaiah 54:10). "O Israel, thou shalt not be forgotten of Me" (Isaiah 44:21). Put Him in mind of these when tempted and tried. "Having loved His own which were in the world, He loved them unto the end" (John 13:1). "Seeing that we have a great High Priest, that is passed into the heavens . . . let us hold fast our profession" (Hebrews 4:14). Never doubt He is "loving all along." And oh! it is not empty or helpless love. He not only feels for you, but "will with the temptation also make a way of escape, that ye may be able to bear it" (1 Corinthians 10:13). And go back to the onyx stones. Where were they? Exodus 28:12, on the shoulder—place of strength ("put a shoulder to the wheel"). What about our High Priest's strength? Psalm 89:19–21, "I have laid help upon One that is mighty." "Thou hast a mighty arm, strong is Thy hand." "Their Redeemer is strong" (Jeremiah 50:34), and so Isaiah 9:6, "The government shall be upon His shoulder." "Wherefore He is able also to save to the uttermost" (Hebrews 7:25). All this power to help and save is for YOU, whenever you need it, *if* you will ask for it. Who would lose earthly help for lack of asking?

But were the stones safe? The breastplate was fastened firmly to the shoulder, and how were the jewels secured? Each was "*set in gold*" (vers. 11 and 20), gold held them in—*not they held the breastplate*. What makes Christians safe? Being set "*in* Christ." (See 2 Corinthians 1:21.) "The God of all grace . . . make you perfect, stablish, strengthen, settle you" (1 Peter 5:10). "The Lord is faithful, who shall stablish you, and keep you from evil" (2 Thessalonians 3:3). "No man is able to pluck them out of My Father's hand" (John 10:29). Pray then, "keep me, for I cannot keep myself."

But does God reckon sinners as jewels? "Not likely," do you say? "Worthless, unprofitable, of what value am I?" Yet, "they *shall* be Mine, saith the LORD of hosts, in that day when I make up My jewels" (Malachi 3:17). *He says it!* So then, how are sinners like jewels? They are of no intrinsic worth. Originally the sapphire was clay; the opal, sand; the diamond, soot or carbon. Water, crystallized into star-forms, snow-like, becomes crystal. Wonderful changes! So a sinner can be changed too. "He brought me up also out of an horrible pit, out of the miry clay" (Psalm 40:2). "He raiseth up the poor out of the dust, and lifteth up the beggar from the dunghill, to set them among princes, and to make them inherit the throne of glory" (1 Samuel 2:8).

If you want to be one of God's jewels, how can you become so? By being "born again" (John 3:3). By being "changed into the same image, from glory to glory, even as by the Spirit of the Lord" (2 Corinthians 3:18).

THE LAND LOST
NUMBERS 14.

Sad sights and sounds again! Were they caused by God or man? "*Sin* brought death into the world, and *all* our woe." Ver. 1, they "*cried,*" but not to God—*wept,* but not for sin—they *murmured*—our journey is all in vain—our ruler and the spies say we cannot go in. Oh, those giants! better return to Egypt! "They looked *back*" (Luke 9:62). They looked at man—at earthly dangers—at man's words—worse still (see Deuteronomy 1:27), they said—"The Lord hated us!" If ever tempted to think ill of your heavenly Friend, think of this—you can see how wicked and foolish this was, and it is a true picture of other murmurers. The fault was all their own. Moses reminded them of this in Deuteronomy 1:29, 33, "Dread not, neither be afraid of them. Who went in the way before you, to search you out a place . . . in fire by night . . . and in a cloud by day." Contrast Caleb's and Joshua's report (Numbers 14:6–9), "The land . . . is an exceeding good land . . . rebel not, neither fear ye . . . the Lord is with us." God's love, power, was *their* experience *of Him.* When trouble comes to you, fall back on these. "His love in times past," etc., and then instead of fears and murmurs say (Psalm 27:1), "The Lord is my light and my salvation; whom shall I fear?" etc. Who beside Moses reasoned? (see ver. 6). Did the people attend? No (see ver. 10), "the congregation bade stone them." Though the rulers and spies had a right to speak, and stood up for God, all the people raged against them. (So with Christ, John 10:31.) What stopped the stoning? "The glory of the Lord appeared." Think when you do wrong, quarrel, etc., "God is here," He sees and hears—*that* would stop it. God pronounced sentence at once, for He knew all. Ver. 12, He said He would "disinherit them." What hindered the execution of this sentence? Moses' mediation (vers. 13–19). What did he plead? God's mercy (ver. 18). God's honour (ver. 16). With what effect? Ver. 20, "The LORD said, I have pardoned, according to thy word." Ezekiel 20:13, 17, explains how God punished sin, though not disinheriting them, for His "Name's sake." Pestilence fell not on all, but only on ten of the spies (ver. 37). What about people who had wished to die in the wilderness? (ver. 2). They should have their wish (vers. 29, 35), "in this wilderness they shall be consumed"—"your children shall wander in this wilderness forty years." See why, ver. 22, "because all those men . . . have tempted Me now these ten times, and have not hearkened to My voice." Ver. 31, "But your little ones, they shall know the land which ye have despised." Psalm 106:24, "They despised the pleasant land, they believed not His word." God gave respite, the people were not cut off by pestilence, but for forty years (ver. 34) "ye shall bear your iniquities." Now they know their loss, and they "mourned greatly" (ver. 39), they presumed to go up (ver. 44). They had *lost* their land! How? Hebrews 3:18, 19, "So we see they could not enter in because of unbelief." We are reminded, warned, of this on Sundays in the Venite. See Hebrews 3:12, "Take heed, lest there be in any of you an evil heart of unbelief, in departing from the living God,"—for unbelief is eye and heart turned away from God, looking, loving, trusting something else. Israel looked at dangers, weakness. What are *you* looking at that you do not claim the promise and find joy and peace? Do you say "it would not be rest to me to 'come'—not what I want"? Oh, how far you are from God!—you like Egypt, the world, best. *Do not* lose the blessed peace, rest, joy, sunshine of God's love, cheering all life—or you will lose eternal rest.

"Let us labour therefore to enter into that rest, lest any man fall after the same example of unbelief" (Hebrews 4:11).

SAMSON'S WIFE
Judges 14.

What sort of wife might they expect the consecrated Nazarite Samson to choose? What command should he have remembered? "Neither shalt thou make marriages with them" (Deuteronomy 7:3). How did his parents show their surprise? (ver. 3). A good bishop says, "I wish Manoah could speak so loud that all *our* Israelites might hear." Those who wish to be true Christian men had better take no wife than one with "uncircumcised heart." What reason or excuse did Samson give? (margin, "it is right," *i.e.* God wills it?) "Pleases me" is often the worst thing for us, *e.g.* Eve's apple. Ver. 4, It is not *said* that God bade him take this Philistine. I think God left him to follow his own desires to humble him, and to warn others, and to overrule it for good to Israel. He kept sober, etc., yet followed his own foolish imaginations. Don't flatter yourself because you are sober, etc., that *you* are safe. Remember to "keep thy heart with all diligence" (Proverbs 4:23). "Keep thee from the strange woman" (Proverbs 7:5). "Let him that thinketh he standeth take heed lest he fall" (1 Corinthians 10:12).

Yet Samson was right in one thing—who did he speak to about it? His parents.

In going to Timnath he might have made the sluggard's excuse (Proverbs 22:13), "The slothful man saith, There is a lion without, I shall be slain." Samson was in danger, but the strong young lion could not hurt him whom God had said should deliver Israel. "Man is immortal till," etc. "He rent him"—a wonderful feat—it might have taught him that God could strengthen him to overcome Philistines without marrying one, for it was the Spirit's work, an earnest of future victories (see another example of God's power over lions, Daniel 6), and so a preparation for future work. If God gives you lion-like temptations and victory over them, it is to encourage you to fight and overcome. "Thanks be to God who giveth us the victory." The "roaring lion" seeks *you—you* can't overcome him, but God can. Did Samson talk or boast of it? did he forget it? When God delivers us, we should remember it (Psalm 103:1, 2), "forget not all His benefits." What surprised him there? Strange for *clean* bees to build in the carcase and prepare honey for Samson! How God can bring good out of evil, pleasure from terror! What use did Samson make of it? A "riddle," first to entertain his guests, and then an occasion to begin his delivering Israel. A riddle for you! How can this be said of Christ? You can say He is sweet and strong, but how an "eater" and "meat"? See what He is called in Revelation 5:5, "Lion of tribe of Judah," *that* Lion who said (Psalm 50:22) "Consider this, ye that forget God, lest I tear you in pieces." Matthew 10:28, "Him who is able to destroy both soul and body in hell." Is He strong? Psalm 24:8, "The Lord strong and mighty." How does "meat" come forth from Him for us? John 6:51, "I am the living bread," etc. You have often heard and read of Jesus laying down His life for you—to-day He says, "Do this in remembrance of Me."

Samson was angry with his wife for telling his riddle, so he went home. How did he intend to make up the quarrel? Ch. 15:1, "visited his wife with a kid." "Cease from anger, and forsake wrath" (Psalm 37:8). Her father, in giving Samson's wife to his companions, gave Samson an occasion or excuse to attack them; they could not blame him for fighting when they had injured him—this is no rule for Christians.

In ch. 14 we had Samson's riddle, now Samson is a riddle to us. Ch. 16 shows him acting in such worldly and wicked ways—and yet he was a Nazarite,—appointed to deliver Israel—strengthened by the Spirit, and had "good report" (Hebrews 11:32, 39). Think what sort of strength the Spirit gave? only bodily strength. Did that do any good to his heart? that was still corrupt and sinful, and Samson indulged it. See how he gave way to Delilah, allowing her again and again to entice him, as she herself was enticed by Philistines. (1000 pieces or £600.) He amused himself by pretences, deceiving her about his source of strength. At first he would not tell her how it was, the third time he went nearer the truth and made way for ver. 19; but while amusing himself he told untruths, and fell into Satan's snare. (Proverbs 7:21, 22.) Not only was it wicked but foolish of Samson to trust himself with such a woman. If we indulge in one sin, we may soon fall into another. "Trust him in nothing, who makes not conscience of everything." Why did he not go away! The woman's company made him FORGET GOD. We hear of no prayer; we can't walk with God and with wicked persons. Take such a companion, and GOD *goes from us.* If Samson was so foolish and wicked, so you may be. *Your* heart is as wicked, and Satan sows seeds of sin which may spring up at any time. So watch, and pray "keep me, for I cannot keep myself." "Turn away mine *eyes.*" "Set a watch before my mouth."

(*The substance of two lessons.*)

DAVID AND JONATHAN.
1 Samuel 18:1–4, 20.

The FRIENDSHIP of David and Jonathan is a model and a typical one. Jonathan's character and love are sometimes so surpassing that he might be mistaken for the type of Christ; but that is always David's part—his name means beloved.

"Jonathan prefigured the faithful Israel of God, who hailed the advent of the true David, and rejoiced in His triumphs." Saul is typical of the world, the scribe and Pharisee-like enemies.

Two remarkable descriptions of Jonathan's love are recorded. Ver. 1, His soul was "knit with the soul of David." (David's own description of it, 2 Samuel 1:26, intimates communion, not love for one side of character, but for the whole, firmly interwoven. So Jacob and Joseph—"His life is bound up in the lad's life," Genesis 44:30, and David and the men of Judah, 1 Chronicles 12:17, "My heart shall be knit unto you." So Colossians 2:2, "Being knit together in love.") "Loved as his own soul" (vers. 1 and 3). (See the Second Commandment—but how seldom is it fulfilled!) If this be the measure of love to our fellows, how much more to "*the* Beloved of our soul"! Turn aside and see the measure of our David's love to us. "As the Father hath loved Me, so have I loved you." "Greater love hath no man than this, that a man lay down his life for his friends" (John 15:9, 13). "But God commendeth His love toward us, in that, while we were yet sinners, Christ died for us" (Romans 5:8). One proof of Jonathan's love was that he made a covenant with David (ver. 3, and 20:16, 17). What reality it showed, "for better, for worse." Let us not shrink from entering into covenant with God. Away with faithless fears—"I may not be able to keep it," etc., and half-hearted looking back to the world! See what a Friend we have in Jesus! His favour is better than life, and then desire to "present your bodies a living sacrifice," etc. (Romans 12:1). He will keep us. Jonathan's love was *unselfish, self-renouncing;* it led him to strip off his robe, sword, etc., to forego his own right to succeed his father, to endanger his own life (1 Samuel 18:4). *But* his love did not go far enough. Though he gave David his robe, etc., he did not give himself; he still held with his father. ("He that loveth father . . . more than Me is not worthy of Me," Matthew 10:37.) "Natural?" Yes, but "the friendship of the world is enmity with God" (James 4:4). "Could do more for David by staying at court?" But *did* he do any great service there? How far greater if he had declared for David as God's anointed whom He had promised to establish! His underhand, half-hearted conduct led to David's flight and wanderings and persecutions. True he remonstrated with Saul, like Nicodemus (John 7:50), but yet he remained "one with him," on the side of David's enemies; as he took side with them at first, so he continued. Perhaps he waited for "a more convenient season,"—his father's death,—then he would declare for David; but that time never came. Holding to Saul, he perished with Saul. (1 Samuel 31.) Had Jonathan had courage, *faith* to follow David, he would have been in "safe-guard," and have been "next unto him." David remained *faithful,* but Jonathan, refraining to be with him, lost the fulfilment of his covenant. What a picture! How plainly is Jonathan like the "almost persuaded"—loving, respecting, giving something to, doing something for, but not giving self to Christ Jesus,—not ready to "count all things but loss" to win Christ,—not ready to follow "whithersoever"! No cross, no crown; and the end—slain with David's enemies! How Jonathan *might* have supported and helped David's cause! Alas! how many who should be on the Lord's side are with the Sauls of popery, the world, anarchy, infidelity, etc. etc.

Look up from man's faithlessness and failures to *our* David. He does not ask for more than He gave—"Who loved me and gave *Himself* for me" (Galatians 2:20). "Look not every man on his own things, but every man also on the things of others" (Philippians 2:4). Let us not be of the number of them "who draw back unto perdition; but of them that believe to the saving of the soul" (Hebrews 10:39). Yet He "abideth faithful" (2 Timothy 2:13). He says, "Those that Thou gavest Me I have kept" (John 17:12). "Having loved His own which were in the world, He loved them unto the end" (John 13:1). Oh to be "true-hearted, wholehearted, faithful, and loyal!"

THUNDER AND LIGHTNING.
Job 37.

"Hear attentively the noise of His voice . . . He directeth it under the whole heaven, and His lightnings unto the ends of the earth. After it a voice roareth: He thundereth with the voice of His excellency; and He will not stay them when His voice is heard" (Job 37:2–4). *Whose* voice is this? "The voice of the LORD" (Psalm 29:4). *What* is the voice? "God thundereth marvellously with His voice" (Job 37:5). "The voice of the Lord is upon the waters; the God of glory thundereth" (Psalm 29:3). Attend to it (Job 37:2); this is one way of learning of God. What is thunder? The sound made by the air, which has been parted by the lightning flash, when it closes again. Lightning is electricity, when a great force of it has collected and is given out of the clouds. *God* gives it out of the clouds ("He maketh lightnings for the rain," Psalm 135:7), when and where He sees fit. Light and air prove His goodness to man; what do thunder and stormy winds show? "He causeth it to come, whether for CORRECTION, or for His land, or for MERCY" (Job 37:13). For "correction" or *punishment,* for example, the thunderstorm in Egypt upon Pharaoh and his land—the "great wind from the wilderness" which overthrew the house where Job's children feasted (Job 1:19)—the "mighty tempest in the sea," and "great wind" which overtook Jonah (Jonah 1:4); the "rain" of "brimstone and fire from the Lord out of heaven" upon Sodom (Genesis 19:24). But perhaps storms are sent chiefly to *correct* man's thoughts. Man forgets God, and plans, acts, rules without God; he does not own or reverence Him, so it is as if God spoke in majestic thunder, making us tremble, as if He said, "*I* see, though you see not Me. I can kill man, and destroy his cattle and his crops, therefore remember Me, fear Me." Storms are to "correct" man's pride. Clever men get to think they can do everything; this is their greatest danger. The thunderstorm says, "God is over all,— what can you do against the lightning flash, the rain-torrent, or the mighty blast of wind? Ever remember they are God's voice!" the "voice" of "the God of glory." There is no sin or danger greater than pride and forgetfulness of God, so it is in "*mercy*" He "utters His voice" to correct this.

Examples of wind sent in mercy, see Exodus 14:21, "The Lord caused the sea to go back by a strong east wind all that night, and made the sea dry land . . . and the children of Israel went into the midst of the sea upon the dry ground." Numbers 11:31, "A wind from the Lord brought quails from the sea, and let them fall by the camp." A wind in mercy to England destroyed the Spanish Armada.

Storms clear and purify the air, and so destroy many injurious things—for example, blight and disease.

A lightning flash showed an officer that he was urging his horse over the edge of a precipice—was not this in mercy?

Lightning is sometimes a messenger of death; and so are earthquakes and storms. Example is made of one person or place to show what God could do to all—thus warning others. If lightning makes a man think of his soul and eternity, is it not kind of God to send it? Are you ready? What will make you so? You need what will cover you from God's just anger against sin—something to clothe your soul, and fit you to stand before Him. All this is to be found in the Lord Jesus Christ. He is a lightning-conductor for you; a shelter from the storm of God's wrath, and a robe to cover your soul before a holy God. In Him you may be "accepted, perfect, and complete." Are you saved? are you safe in Him? If not, why not? God has provided safety—an ark, a rock of defence, for you in Himself.

> "Beneath the shadow of Thy wing
> Thy saints have dwelt secure."

But are you safe under it? He says "*Come,*"—but you say "not yet," and dare to neglect or refuse His call. Do you not deserve that the next flash should strike you? "To-day, if ye will hear His voice, harden not your hearts" (Hebrews 4:7).

August 19.

THE WORKS OF THE LORD.

Psalm 104:1 and 33–35.

"Bless the Lord, O my soul. O Lord my God, Thou art very great; Thou art clothed with honour and majesty. I will sing unto the Lord as long as I live; I will sing praise to my God while I have my being. My meditation of Him shall be sweet: I will be glad in the Lord. . . . Bless thou the Lord, O my soul. Praise ye the Lord." What praise, gladness, delight in God do these verses express! What was the cause of it? Looking at, and considering His works, led David to admire and adore. He learned God's wisdom and goodness. See ver. 24, "O Lord, how manifold are Thy works! in wisdom hast Thou made them all." "The works of the Lord are great, sought out of all them that have pleasure therein. His work is honourable and glorious" (Psalm 111:2, 3); also look at Psalm 145. So let us be "wise and observe these things" (Psalm 107:43). One way of judging of a man is by his works, *e.g.* in choosing a builder, painter, gardener. We know and judge of ancient poets and painters, etc., by their works.

What is the finest building you have seen? Think of Worcester Cathedral. How came it there? Not like a mushroom! What persons were employed? Masons of course! But how did they know what to build? Some one must have directed—one who planned—the architect. Could *you* plan or design such an edifice? then the architect had a greater mind than you. Such strong, grand arches and pillars, such light, elegant ornament and carving. How clever, how skilful! And what builder and workman did it all? *No doubt* there were such—it could not have been built without them. Why make it? is it of no use? Yes, for a grand and right good purpose.

But there is a far greater Temple for you to explore and admire. Its floor is inlaid with various stones, slate, granite, marble; and carpeted so beautifully, chiefly with green, but variegated,—a carpet never worn out, ever renewing,—a temple full of beauty and good things. Its roof is high as heaven, lighted by God's own lamps. I want to help you to look at it, so that you may judge of its Builder. Suppose you never had any Bible teaching, how might you know the Maker of the world? Look and reason. How came it to be so beautiful, so suited to man's wants and comforts? If I tread on a mole-hill or ant-hill, or see a bird's nest, I know what made them, and I know their purposes. If I pick up a nail, key, pencil, or watch, I know a maker with brains and hands made them for a purpose. When I look at large houses, mills, manufactories, churches, I feel *greater* minds planned them for greater purposes. Then must not the world itself have been planned and made by One *greater* than man! The more wise men examine the world, the more proofs shine out that it was made with *design*, planned and created to suit man's wants—that it is the work of some mastermind. Every journey I take makes me say, "O Lord, how manifold are Thy works! in wisdom hast Thou made them all: the earth is full of Thy riches."

Atheists say, "There is no God" (Psalm 14:1), it is all by chance!! But angels say, "Thou art worthy, O Lord, to receive glory and honour and power; for Thou hast created all things, and for Thy pleasure they are and were created" (Revelation 4:11). "And they sing the song of Moses . . . and the song of the Lamb, saying, Great and marvellous are Thy works, Lord God Almighty; just and true are Thy ways, Thou King of saints" (Revelation 15:3).

24th June 1883.

THE EARTH OR WORLD.

"Who laid the foundations of the earth."—Psalm 104:6.

For what purpose were the light and air, etc. made?—they are God's creation, His workmanship. "The earth is the Lord's, and the fulness thereof" (Psalm 24:1). That thou mayest know how that the earth is the Lord's. Man must remember this. "Where wast thou when I laid the foundations of the earth? declare, if thou hast understanding. Who hath laid the measures thereof, if thou knowest? or who hath stretched the line upon it? Whereupon are the foundations thereof fastened? or who laid the corner-stone thereof?" (Job 38:4–6). What a contrast are the idols of the heathen, "the work of the hands of the workman," "decked with silver and gold," which must needs be borne, because they cannot move, to Jehovah! "*He* hath made the earth by His power, He hath established the world by His wisdom, and hath stretched out the heavens by His discretion" (Jeremiah 10:3–5, 12). *What* is this world which "hangeth upon nothing"? (Job 26:7). Not anything light. Sand, earth, clay are heavy enough, but granite, marble, slate, coal, metals are much heavier—then think of the whole 24,000 miles weight "hanging on nothing"! A bubble rests on the air because it is so very light; but this weighty world, so much heavier than the air, hangs on nothing, for God holds it by His mighty power, like the moon and stars in the sky. How great, how powerful, how wonderful! "For lo, He that formeth the mountains, and createth the wind, and declareth unto man what is his thought, *that* maketh the morning darkness, and treadeth upon the high places of the earth, The Lord, The God of hosts, is His name" (Amos 4:13). "Hast thou not known, hast thou not heard, that the everlasting God, the Lord, the Creator of the ends of the earth, fainteth not, neither is weary? there is no searching of His understanding" (Isaiah 40:28).

Those who *know God* may be sure that the earth is wonderful and beautiful; but men not knowing, but who are wishing to find out what He is from His work, might learn His Power and Wisdom. What are these mountains composed of? Of granite, marble, and basalt, hardest and deepest. Others, of sandstone, slate, lime, not so hard, do not seem to be so old and not all made at the same time. So, although God created all "in the beginning" (God gave no date), long before Adam He was preparing the world for him.

How do men make bricks, china, sugar, lime, etc.? by burning and baking; so these hardest rocks seem to have been formed by intense heat,—even now there are great fires within the earth—volcanoes are witnesses of this. Then the sea and the weather have broken and worn away much from these old rocks, and thus formed gravel, sand, and clay. So for ages God was preparing beautiful marbles, metals, precious stones, coal, for man's use now. What does this show? God's Forethought, Love, and Kindness. Another thing shown is God's Patience. How? Though God can, and does do many things in the twinkling of an eye (such as the late eruptions at Java), yet He does many others by slow degrees, and lets things work round as He sets them (like an alarum). By studying rocks man learns that many thousands of years seem to have been required to heat and melt and press granite, marbles, etc., into their present state,—when one set of rocks were formed, others were formed after. God thus shows His *patience* to *us*— He is forbearing to punish. So often if one man provokes or injures another, it is followed by angry, hasty words, a sudden blow, etc; while God, against whom the sin really is, forbears, waits, and warns, and tries to lead to repentance.

Why did God make the world? "He created it not in vain, He formed it to be inhabited" (Isaiah 45:18). Inhabited by whom? "Let us make man in our image, after our likeness, and let them have dominion over . . . all the earth" (Genesis 1:26). Though rebels, God has *bought back* sinful men, and wills to make them happy and holy (and how patiently He works to make us so!). And He loves His redeemed ones so much that *He* is not content with this world for them, "He hath prepared for them a city" (Hebrews 11:16), and sends His Spirit to prepare them for His own glory. "We, according to His promise, look for new heavens and a new earth, wherein dwelleth righteousness. Wherefore, beloved, seeing that ye look for such things, be diligent, that ye may be found of Him in peace, without spot, and blameless" (2 Peter 3:13, 14).

Psalm 104:6–13.

Let us consider the next thing which David speaks of when glorying in God's great works—it is what you may see from Stagborough and Bewdley Bridge—water! "Thou coveredst it with the deep as with a garment,"—a covering as a "wide" (ver. 25) cloak to the earth. "The waters stood above the mountains"; their traces are left now. How came the lakes and rivers to sink down as they are now? Vers. 7 and 8 answer this, "At Thy rebuke they fled; at the voice of Thy thunder they hasted away. They go up by the mountains; they go down by the valleys unto the place which Thou hast founded for them." *We* say "the river formed its bed," but *God* appointed all. "They go down," that is to the sea. What is "the bound" that is "set"? "Fear ye not Me? saith the LORD, which have placed the sand for the bound of the sea by a perpetual decree, that it cannot pass it; and though the waves thereof toss themselves, yet can they not prevail; though they roar, yet can they not pass over it" (Jeremiah 5:22).

Then David speaks of some of the *uses of water.* Ver. 11, "They *give drink* to every beast of the field." Ver. 12, "By them the fowls of the heaven have their habitation." Ver. 13, "The earth is satisfied." There are many other uses to man—for life, health, refreshment (many other drinks are made from water), cleansing.

Look at the Severn, and *think* and learn. Where does it come from? *God* sends it, not only at first, but He keeps it flowing daily. "He sendeth the spring into the valleys, which run among the hills" (ver. 10). For what reason is it sent? 1. See how it *drains* the lands, carrying off what they do not need. 2. It *nourishes* the ground; for example, floods over our own fields—also you may have read how necessary the Nile floods are for the irrigation of Egypt. "Thou visitest the earth, and waterest it: Thou greatly enrichest it with the river of God. . . . Thou preparest them corn, when Thou hast so provided for it' (Psalm 65:9). 3. It *helps man to work,* by turning his mills, etc. 4. It *carries* his burdens—wood, coal, etc. 5. It *cools* and *purifies* the air. 6. Carries off refuse. 7. It *beautifies*—the river is beautiful in itself—it makes the view, the country beautiful. Man's canals are ugly; God's rivers are beautiful. How good and kind of God to give us so much pleasure by beauty!

Let us notice some Bible lessons from rivers.

"He shall be like a tree planted by the rivers of water, that bringeth forth his fruit in his season: his leaf also shall not wither; and whatsoever he doeth shall prosper" (Psalm 1:3). Who is like a tree? What keeps that tree green and fruitful? So the godly man is refreshed by fresh daily supplies of God's grace, and thus he ever has something fresh to think and speak of: and his soul, being so nourished, refreshed, "delighted," overflows to others—he "prospers." "Blessed is the man that trusteth in the Lord, and whose hope the Lord is. For he shall be as a tree planted by the waters, and that spreadeth out her roots by the river, . . . her leaf shall be green; and shall not be careful in the year of drought, neither shall cease from yielding fruit" (Jeremiah 17:7, 8).

A river is a type of *gladness.* "There is a river, the streams whereof make glad the city of God" (Psalm 46:4). A type of *satisfaction* now, "Whosoever drinketh of the water that I shall give him shall never thirst" (John 4:14); and hereafter, "They shall be abundantly satisfied with the fatness of Thy house; and Thou shalt make them drink of the river of Thy pleasures" (Psalm 36:8). It is an emblem of *peace.* "I will extend peace to her like a river" (Isaiah 66:12). There the glorious Lord will be unto us a place of broad rivers and streams" (Isaiah 33:21). "O that thou hadst hearkened to My commandments! then had thy peace been as a river, and thy righteousness as the waves of the sea" (Isaiah 48:18). It is an emblem of how in times of soul-distress and doubt God can bring *refreshment* and gladness. "I give waters in the wilderness, and rivers in the desert, to give drink to My people" (Isaiah 43:20).

How and where can you find this river of God? Ezekiel shows us, in ch. 47, that when the Word goes forth, accompanied by the Holy Spirit, people will be revived and refreshed, "Everything shall live whither the river cometh" (Ezekiel 47:9).

Rivers are so refreshing and gladdening and beautiful, that a river represents the gladness and overflowing, continuing joy of heaven. "He showed me a pure river of water of life, clear as crystal, proceeding out of the throne of God and of the Lamb" (Revelation 22:1). Is that river for you? Shall *you* walk in holy joy by its side? How can you be fitted to walk there? You must see that your robes are "washed" and made "white in the blood of the Lamb" (Revelation 7:14). "Come now, and let us reason together, saith the LORD: though your sins be as scarlet, they shall be as white as snow; though they be red like crimson, they shall be as wool" (Isaiah 1:18). "In that day there shall be a fountain opened . . . for sin and for uncleanness" (Zechariah 13:1). Choose this, or see the terrible alternative in Luke 16:24, "And he cried and said, . . . have mercy on me, and send Lazarus, that he may dip the tip of his finger in water, and cool my tongue; for I am tormented in this flame."

30th September 1883.

DANIEL'S PRAYER.

DANIEL 9.

This prayer was uttered in Daniel's old age. Try to remember some things we have learned of him. 1st, He feared God from his youth. 2nd, He was self-denying. 3rd, When God gave him wisdom and revealed dreams, he gave God praise. 4th, He was faithful to the king (though new and strange). 5th, He was blameless in conduct. 6th, He prayed regularly. 7th, Served God continually. 8th, He believed, trusted in God. Now in his old age Daniel continues in prayer; so look at Luke 18:1, "Men ought always to pray, and not to faint." "Continue in prayer, and watch in the same with thanksgiving" (Colossians 4:2).

Why did he pray this? Because he "understood by books . . . that God would accomplish seventy years in the desolations of Jerusalem" (ver. 2). Books showed him that the seventy years were nearly ended, so, hoping and expecting that God would fulfil His word, Daniel asked Him to do so. There is nothing like getting a promise to pray upon! "Remember the word unto Thy servant, upon which Thou hast caused me to hope." For example, this Whitsunday take John 14:26, "The Comforter, which is the Holy Ghost, whom the Father will send in My name, He shall teach you all things, and bring all things to your remembrance, whatsoever I have said unto you."

Now see the first subject of Daniel's prayer. "I made my confession, and said, . . . we have sinned, and have committed iniquity, and have done wickedly, and have rebelled, even by departing from Thy precepts, and from Thy judgments." Our Church teaches thus—first confession TO GOD. Why? Sins come between us and God, and so must be put away before we can ask new gifts. If you want a heartful of mercies, and joy, and peace, turn out the sins! Learn from Daniel to call sins by their right names. Ver. 5, "rebelling;" "not hearkening;" ver. 10, "not obeying;" ver. 11, "departing;" ver. 13, "not making prayer." Say not, "it is only a little sin," "I am not so bad as ——," etc., but "against Thee, Thee only, have I sinned" (Psalm 51:4).

What comforting came while he was confessing? He remembers that "To the Lord our God belong mercies and forgivenesses" (ver. 9). But if God was righteous in fulfilling threatened punishment ("If thou wilt not hearken to the voice of the Lord thy God, to observe to do all His commandments . . . that all these curses shall come upon thee; and overtake thee," Deuteronomy 28:15), how could He be "righteous" in "turning away anger"? Because Jesus "made peace through the blood of His cross" (Colossians 1:20). "Reconciling the world unto Himself, not imputing their trespasses unto them; . . . for He hath made Him to be sin for us, who knew no sin; that we might be made the righteousness of God in Him" (2 Corinthians 5:19–21); and so He is "faithful and just to forgive us our sins" (1 John 1:9). After these encouraging thoughts see how Daniel continued to plead. Do not be content with one cry of "God have mercy."

But who was all this prayer for? Not for himself. Do you pray for your country? Take the lesson. When you hear of swearing, Sabbath-breaking, dishonesty, etc. etc., pray over it.

Now for the answer. *When* came it? Vers. 20–23, "*Whiles* I was speaking in prayer, even the man Gabriel, . . . being caused to fly swiftly, touched me, and said, . . . I am come to show thee." Also see Jeremiah 29:12, "Then shall ye call upon Me, and ye shall go and pray unto Me, and I will hearken unto you;" and Isaiah 65:24, "Before they call, I will answer; and while they are yet speaking, I will hear." Our Lord, when on earth, gave immediate answers; and so He does now. "Where two or three are gathered together in My name, there am I in the midst of them" (Matthew 18:20).

Who brought the answer? The angel Gabriel; but our Great High Priest takes our prayers up in His own incense censer, and says, "*I give*." He is "able to do exceeding abundantly above all we ask or think." Now see this fulfilled here. Daniel had asked for pardon and return. What more was given? He was shown things to come, and that Christ should come! He is called here "Messiah (see John 1:41, "We have found the Messias") the Prince;" so Isaiah 9:6, "the Prince of Peace;" "a Prince and Saviour" (Acts 5:31); "the Prince of life" (Acts 3:15). *When* should He come? When seventy weeks of years from the going out of the commandment were fulfilled. So the Jews might know when He was coming. What was then to be done? "finish" (or restrain) sin—(the great sin of the Jews in rejecting and crucifying the Messiah). He should "make an end of sins," or sin-offerings. How? By Messiah being "cut off" in the midst of His days, "but not for Himself"—the one perfect offering—the Lamb of God, of whom all others were types. When He offered Himself without spot to God, God rent the Temple vail to show it was no longer needed. Messiah's offering made reconciliation. If you feel you have sinned, and wish that you could do something to please God, etc. etc., what is best to do? "Behold the Lamb of God." But *will* God be reconciled? "When we were enemies we were reconciled to God by the death of His Son" (Romans 5:10); "God, who hath reconciled us to Himself by Jesus Christ" (2 Corinthians 5:18). What wonderful willingness and desire to reconcile us!—an example to us with others. Thus sin is taken away. What is to be brought in its place? "Everlasting righteousness." If "everlasting," whose must it be? "My righteousness" (Isaiah 51:6). "My righteous servant" shall "justify many" (Isaiah 53:12). "The righteousness of God" (Romans 3:21). For whom is it? "For us" (2 Corinthians 5:21), "That I may . . . be found in Him, not having mine own righteousness, . . . but that which is through the faith of Christ, the righteousness which is of God by faith" (Philippians 3:8, 9).

WHITSUNDAY, 1881.

THE LORD'S PEOPLE.

ROMANS 14:8.

"For whether we live, we live unto the Lord; and whether we die, we die unto the Lord: whether we live therefore, or die, we are the Lord's."

"We are the Lord's"—by creation. Does that give peace? "Remember now thy Creator" (Ecclesiastes 12:1). "Thus saith the LORD that made thee, and formed thee" (Isaiah 44:2). If your conscience says, "I have not remembered, I have not answered the purpose of my creation," there can be no peace, but "a fearful looking for of judgment" (Hebrews 10:27).

Some call themselves God's, but He does not own them. "Many will say to Me in that day, Lord, Lord . . . and then will I profess unto them, I never knew you" (Matthew 7:22, 23). Then there is *danger* lest we should only seem, not really be, the Lord's. People in heaven must be God's, so look up there, and ask how they came there. "They sung a new song, saying, Thou art worthy . . . for Thou wast slain, and hast redeemed us to God by Thy blood out of every kindred, tongue, and people, and nation" (Revelation 5:9). "Who gave Himself for our sins, that He might deliver us from this present evil world" (Galatians 1:4). See also Isaiah 43:1, "Thus saith the LORD that created thee, O Jacob, and He that formed thee, O Israel, Fear not: for I have redeemed thee, I have called thee by thy name; thou art Mine." "Ye are not your own, for ye are bought with a price: therefore glorify God in your body and in your spirit, which are God's" (1 Corinthians 6:19, 20). "The flock . . . the church of God, which He purchased with His own blood" (Acts 20:28).

Belonging to God makes us safe, for—

He knows us. 2 Timothy 2:19, "The Lord knoweth them that are His."

I know Him. 2 Timothy 1:12, "I know in whom I have believed."

He loves us. John 13:1, "Having loved His own which were in the world, He loved them unto the end." "He loved me" (Galatians 2:20).

"My Beloved is mine, and I am His" (Song of Solomon 2:16).

He values us. Malachi 3:17, "They shall be Mine, saith the Lord of hosts, in that day when I make up My jewels."

"Unto you which believe He is precious" (1 Peter 2:7).

He wants us to be with Him. John 17:24, "Father, I will that they also, whom Thou hast given Me, be with Me where I am."

He is with me. Matthew 28:20, "Lo, I am with you alway," Psalm 23:3, "Thou art with me."

And so He will not let us be lost. John 10:28, "They shall never perish, neither shall any man pluck them out of My hand."

He sought me wandering and brought me back. "The Lord is my Shepherd" (Psalm 23:1).

So secure, so safe, so certain of being ever with the Lord. "If I am found in Jesus' hands." It is worth everything to know this! So then come to the point. Are you His? If so, enjoy it, live like His children, "unspotted from the world," pure, "departing from iniquity" (2 Timothy 2:19). "Whatsoever is born of God doth not commit sin. In this the children of God are manifest, and the children of the devil" (1 John 3:9, 10). "Herein is our love made perfect, that we may have boldness in the day of judgment; because as He is, so are we in this world" (1 John 4:17). If you are not His, say, "This is the last year I shall belong to Satan." Say, "*I will* arise and go to my Father" (Luke 15:18).

"Now to be Thine, yea, Thine alone,
O Lamb of God, I come!"

"Here's my heart, O take and seal it,
Seal it for Thy courts above."

31st December 1882.

THE EPISTLE TO THE EPHESIANS.

This is supposed by some to be the Epistle from Laodicea mentioned in Colossians 4:16. It was unanimously received by the early Church as St. Paul's, and is quoted as such by Polycarp and Irenaeus and by Valentinus (about 120 A.D.). Though containing various doctrines, as election, the Trinity, much teaching about the Holy Spirit's work, the headship of Christ, and many practical duties, we are to select for this month—"Unity—Christians are one in Christ."

Consider I. *God's Purpose.* "That He might gather together in one all things in Christ" (Ephesians 1:10 to 20–23). St. Paul speaks of *two* who are to be united—Gentiles and Jews (ch. 2:11–16)—and so we may distinguish these two in ch. 1:12, "That we should be to the praise of His glory, who first trusted in Christ." We first believed (who had long looked for Messiah), and ver. 13, Ye Gentiles also trusted (who knew not of Him till after He came).

II. This was the mystery which was not known but is now revealed, "That the Gentiles should be fellow-heirs, and of the same body, and partakers of His promise in Christ by the gospel" (ch. 3:3–6). "The middle wall of partition" (ch. 2:14) (*i.e.* fence, thorn hedge, and often a wall also) is now taken away, and Christians from both sides are united in one. "According to the eternal purpose which He purposed in Christ Jesus our Lord" (Ephesians 3:11). "*Mystery*," *i.e.* "something into which one must be initiated, a knowledge of things unknowable without a special communication of it." "Because it is given unto *you* to know the mysteries of the kingdom of heaven, but to them it is not given" (Matthew 13:11).

III. See how this union is brought about. "And having made peace through the blood of His cross, by Him to reconcile all things unto Himself" (Colossians 1:20, 2:14–17). Mark the price of it, the price that purchased our peace and so makes us one with Him. *But* are *we* "very members incorporate in this mystical body" (Communion Service) united to Christ? "Abide in Me; and I in you. As the branch cannot bear fruit of itself, except it abide in the vine; no more can ye, except ye abide in Me" (John 15:4). "That they all may be one; as Thou, Father, art in Me, and I in Thee" (John 17:21). Union with Him is more close than with any other. There is no true union with other branches, unless we are grafted in. Faith is the means of union with Him. (Galatians 2:20.) We must touch the centre of unity. The more we enjoy *this union* and its blessings, its peace ("He is our peace," ch. 2:14 and ch. 1:4, 5, 6, 7, 11), the more shall we burn with desire to draw others into it. It was our Lord's desire (John 17:11, 21), and as His life and love flow into us, so will ours flow out towards others. But think how *safe* we are if united to Christ—it was when He thought of His disciples' safety that He prayed this. But union with God is not only our safety but our *highest happiness*. Then we long for all to be united with us, not in mere outward things, but in union with God and with us.

IV. But how are we to bring this beautiful theory into practice? Look and see, "There is one body and one Spirit, even as ye are called in one hope of your calling" (Ephesians 4:4, 5, 16), this with 1 Corinthians 12:4–13 leads us to look to the Holy Spirit's work. His influence is the "bond of peace" and unity between us. Then seek His teaching, revealing, and drawing of those with whom we desire union. There is much in this epistle about the Holy Spirit; perhaps a reason for it is given in Acts 19:1, 2, "Have ye received the Holy Ghost since ye believed? And they say unto him, We have not so much as heard whether there be any Holy Ghost."

Let us see what is said of His work.

1. We are "sealed by the Holy Spirit" (Ephesians 1:13).
2. He "reveals" the "mystery of Christ" (ch. 3:3–5).
3. We "have access by one Spirit" (ch. 2:18).
4. The "household of God" is "builded together through the Spirit" (ch. 2:22).
5. The Spirit strengthens us (ch. 3:16).
6. He brings forth fruit in us (ch. 5:9).

He is the Spirit of unity (ch. 4:3). There is but "one" Holy Spirit (ch. 4:4). "The sword of the Spirit is the Word of God" (ch. 6:17).

The Spirit must not be grieved (ch. 4:30).

We should be "filled with the Spirit" (ch. 5:18).

We should "pray in the Spirit" (ch. 6:18).

How much then we owe to Him!

In ch. 4:1–6 we have a seven-fold oneness. There are many types of this beautiful union, one of which, the marriage union, is given in ch. 5:24–27. Oh the depth and height of Christ's love, coming down to us in our sin, that He might wash and save us, then raising us up to sanctification and then to share His own glory. There are other types of this union.—1. The *body*, composed of many members. 2. *The Church* with its sections and members world wide. 3. *Israel*, though twelve tribes, and now all scattered, yet shall all be one, for God promises "I will make them one nation; they shall be no more two nations" (Ezekiel 37:22). 4. *The Universe* with its vast numbers of systems, suns, planets, moons, is all one, all created, governed, and upheld by One mind.

Seek to promote and enjoy this unity by prayer and converse, by mutual kindness and Bible study.

(For Y. W. C. A.)

THE CONSTITUTION OF ISRAEL—THE SUPREMACY OF GOD'S LAW.

Deuteronomy 17, 18.

The constitution of the nation of Israel was a theocracy. God was its former, possessor, and king. The land and the people were His special choice and possession, and therefore were governed only by His law. That law was given to Moses, and by him to priests and Levites (Deuteronomy 31:9), that they might *keep it,* and *read it* to the people ("Thou shalt read this law before all Israel in their hearing"); and *teach* it, "They shall teach Jacob Thy judgments, and Israel Thy law" (Deuteronomy 33:10). "The priest's lips should keep knowledge, and they should seek the law at his mouth: for he is the messenger of the Lord of hosts" (Malachi 2:7); *e.g.* "All the people gathered themselves together as one man into the street ... and they spake unto Ezra the scribe to bring the book of the law of Moses, which the Lord had commanded to Israel. And Ezra the priest brought the law before the congregation, and he read therein" (Nehemiah 8:1–3). They were to *judge* and give sentence by it: "If there arise a matter too hard for thee in judgment ... thou shalt come unto the priests the Levites ... according to the sentence of the law which they shall teach thee, shalt thou do" (Deuteronomy 17:8–11). Men could make no appeal against it: "The man that will do presumptuously, and will not hearken unto the priest ... even that man shall die" (ver. 12). There were afterwards to be judges, then kings, and the priests were to help and counsel them; they were to "show," "teach," "inform," "tell" the sentence of judgment.

The king was to transcribe the law, and rule by it: "It shall be, when he sitteth upon the throne of his kingdom, that he shall write him a copy of this law in a book, out of that which is before the priests the Levites: and it shall be with him, and he shall read therein all the days of his life: that he may learn to fear the Lord his God, to keep all the words of this law, and these statutes, and do them" (Deuteronomy 17:18, 19).

Deuteronomy is especially precious to us, as its authority is specially verified in the New Testament; also it is endeared by our Lord's use of it in His temptation. (Matthew 4.) He drew His arrows from it.

Thus from Deuteronomy we see the origin of the first five books of the Bible. God spake the words to Moses, and Moses wrote them in a book. (So with the prophets, *e.g.* Jeremiah and Baruch.) Moses was inspired while writing; "Holy men of God spake as they were moved by the Holy Ghost" (2 Peter 1:21). This writing was kept; "When Moses had made an end of writing the words of this law in a book . . . Moses commanded the Levites . . . saying, Take this book of the law, and put it in the side of the ark of the covenant of the Lord your God, that it may be there for a witness against thee" (Deuteronomy 31:24–26). Thus their *authority* was patent to the Jews. In Deuteronomy 4:2 is a strict prohibition to add to or alter the law: "Ye shall not add to the word which I command you, neither shall ye diminish ought from it." Just so with *all* the "lively oracles" committed to the Jews, and kept for us. The Bible was given *to*, not by the Church. See Article xx.[1]

> "What are they but the dowry
>   God to His Church has given,
> In giving her as heir-loom
>   The oracles of heaven?"

As it was the duty of the priests of old to read, teach, and decide by it, so is it now. St. Paul bids bishops and deacons to "meditate," "take heed to the doctrine, continue in it," teach, exhort (1 Timothy 4:13–16), and "consent" to "the words of the Lord Jesus" (1 Timothy 6:3); also to "keep the commandment," to continue in, to *instruct*, and *preach* the Word. See Article vi.[1]

The same authority is given to the New Testament, and the same prohibition in Revelation 22:18, 19, as in Deuteronomy 4:2: "If any man shall add unto these things, God shall add unto him the plagues that are written in this book: and if any man shall take away from the words of the book of this prophecy, God shall take away his part out of the book of life, and out of the holy city, and from the things which are written in this book." Clergy should still give "the sentence of the *written* law," and not take up new religious or false doctrines. Remember, the Bible being the work of the Holy Spirit during more than fifteen centuries (and He still working by it), we need Him to reveal it to us and to our clergy. Let us see that we make it *the rule* of our faith—"to the law and to the testimony," etc. Pray, "Show me Thy ways." If we depart from the words or spirit of the Bible, it is *because we depart from our God*. Be like Bunyan's Christian, ever taking the roll from his bosom. The Bible is such a precious means of communication between us and our God,—by it the Spirit shines truth into our hearts, and reveals our God, ourselves, our past, present, and future; our only hope, our one Way, and one Saviour. Let us think of the hymn,

> "I cannot do without Thee,
> O Saviour of the lost."

For every care, circumstance, fear, want, wish, the Bible gives our Father's direction, sympathy, and comfort. "The Bible is God's *all-sufficient* answer to all the needs of human souls." If God is our God, our King, His word must be supreme to us; it must have supremacy in our hearts and lives,—supreme, not only to guide and teach, but also to counsel and comfort us. "In God's word will I rejoice: in the Lord's word will I comfort me" (Psalm 56:10, P.B.V.[2]). "Whatsoever things were written aforetime were written for our learning; that we, through patience and comfort of the Scriptures, might have hope" (Romans 15:4). (See next Sunday's Collect, second in Advent.) God gave its "great and precious promises" to raise hope and expectation. "Remember the word unto Thy servant, upon which Thou hast caused me to hope." "My soul fainteth for Thy salvation; but I hope in Thy word" (Psalm 119:49, 81). In *every* need we may find a suitable promise—read it, and take it back to the *Great Promiser*, and ask Him to fulfil it. Spurgeon says, "Banquet your faith upon God's Word, and whatever your fears or wants, repair to the Bank of Faith with your Father's note of hand, saying, 'Remember the word unto Thy servant, upon which Thou hast caused me to hope.'"

One proof of the intrinsic worth of Scripture is,—the more it is searched, the more its value and beauty appears. Again, the darker the night of trial, the brighter and more precious does it prove.

(*The last Y.W.C.A. Notes for November* 29, 1886.)

CHRIST'S LAST PASSOVER.
Matthew 26.

The last evening with His disciples had come, and for the last time Christ partook of the Passover with them. With desire He had heartily desired so to do (Luke 22:15, marg.); not for Himself, for all His desires had reference to His Father's glory, or His people's good. Was it not for *us*, for He knew how much it would teach and cheer us. Let us look back to the first Passover, and how God appointed that should be kept in mind. Exodus 12 shows it was the time of Israel's greatest danger, not from the plagues of flies or fire or locusts, but the angel, the God-sent angel of death. The Israelites were exempted, not by any claim or merit, but by using a God-appointed token (Exodus 12:7, 13.) On the simple use of that token, the sprinkled blood, did it alone depend, whether the destroying

---

[1] This refers to the Thirty-nine Articles, the doctrinal statement of faith of the Church of England.   [2] Prayer Book Version (Book of Common Prayer).

angel came in to smite them like the Egyptians, or whether He passed over to defend them. Notice the blood was sprinkled *first,* the feast came afterwards. We know how the guiltless, perfect, uncomplaining lamb was slain, that its blood might procure safety for Israel; so Christ, our Passover, was sacrificed for us.

Christ kept the Passover on the right day, Thursday, which was the Jewish eve of Friday, though John 19:14 says, "preparation of the Passover," according to Jewish authority it means Passover Friday.

If God desired His passing over the Israelites should be remembered, which was but a type, how much more probable He would have us remember the Antitype; and this is just what Christ taught by the institution of His Supper. Oh to sit at that Supper, as *with* Christ, and to hear Him saying to us, "Do this in remembrance of Me."

Three Gospels tell us of the last Supper. John supplements it with our Lord's discourses and other last words. Our Church reminds us how He took bread (not like our loaves, but large flat cakes), and blessed it, and brake it, and gave thanks. We, too, may give thanks at the consecrating or setting apart bread to remind us of Him. We know Christ did not change that bread into His body, but bid us see that it represents it. Rejoice that our Church cast away that "dangerous deceit," and beware of returning to it. (Christ's words could not mean this bread is *now* My body, this wine My blood, for the one had not then been offered, the other not then shed; it meant *then* what it still means and represents.) Besides, our Lord says, "This cup is the new testament in My blood," which means a covenant. (Jeremiah 31:33; Hebrews 8:6.) The Old Testament was signed with blood. (Exodus 24:3–8.) Heathens in covenanting "offered sacrifices, and prayed that they themselves might so be slain, if they did not perform their part." God taught Abraham how to make a covenant. (Genesis 15; Hebrews 7:22, 9:16, 17.) So then Christ would remind us of His new covenant for us, which He confirmed by His death—thus His blood is the evidence of the covenant. (Hebrews 13:20.) "The *life* that was made sin for us is gone, so the blood is exhibited apart from the body to show that it has been slain, bereft of the blood which was its life."

Christ's work of redemption is a finished work—hence we have not to repeat it, but remember it, "Do this in remembrance of Me." Let us then remember the exceeding great love of our Lord and Master, and think of all His sufferings as our Substitute—the finishing of the ceremonial law. Christ has wound up and fulfilled every type, every sacrifice is finished. Christ completed the great work of His Father's love in redeeming man, so may we remember, and rest on His finished work. Our Saviour is the Lord of life, who, by laying down that life, paid all, accomplished and performed all that God requires for our salvation. "Who is he that condemneth? it is Christ that died, yea rather, that is risen again, who is even at the right hand of God, who also maketh intercession for us" (Romans 8:34). "Ye are complete in Him" (Colossians 2:10).

This is the epitaph on the gravestone of Giles and Ellen Shaw:

To / the fair and / Holy memory of / ELLEN PRESTAGE SHAW / the beloved Wife of / GILES SHAW ESQ. / Winterdyne / who suddenly fell asleep in Jesus / on Christmas morning 1886 / Aged 63 Years / "Blessed are they that do / his commandments, that they may / have right to the / Tree of Life and may enter / in through the gates into the City" / Revelation XXII. XIV / I love, I love my Master / I will not go out free / He says His saints shall serve Him / And that my heaven shall be / E.P.S. / Also / in Loving memory / of the above named / GILES SHAW / Born May 5 1813 / Fell asleep January 24 1903 / "God so loved the world that/He gave his only begotten / Son that whosoever believeth / in him should not perish, but / have everlasting life" / St. John III.16

Note: The / indicates the end of one line and the start of the next line. Please excuse any small inaccuracies: much of this gravestone was very hard to read or illegible in the spring of 2009. Sincere thanks to David Marlow of Worcestershire, who cleared away much brush and brambles from the gravesite of Giles and Ellen Shaw, and who provided this epitaph on their gravestone.

CEDAR TREE, WINTERDYNE.

(See pages 6 and 49.)

This print of the cedar tree at Winterdyne was the frontispiece facing the title page of the original book Outlines of a Gentle Life. *See pages 187, 188, and 202.*

Frances Ridley Havergal

This is the most famous photograph of Frances Ridley Havergal, one of eight of her taken by the prestigious portrait photographers Elliott and Fry in London on February 1, 1879. In a letter dated February 7, 1879, F.R.H. wrote this: "I have been photographed! Mr. Elliott himself came for me, Saturday, and they tried eight times, and hope one will do! Elliott and Fry both superintended in person; such a fuss! And I forgot to put on tidy frill and cuffs!" (See page 234 of Volume IV of the Havergal edition, and also page v of this book.) This would have been Saturday, February 1, 1879, only seven weeks after her forty-second birthday and four months before her unexpected early death on June 3. No one thought that she would die so young. She glowed Jesus Christ and His truth.

Maria wrote (on page 297), "With the utmost skill, no artist or photograph gives a *real* idea of her lighted up expression. Is it because soul cannot be represented any more than a sunbeam?" In her *Autobiography* (see page 117) Maria wrote of the session when eight photographs of F.R.H. were taken on February 1, 1879, "Messrs. Elliott & Fry were most painstaking, but no ray could transfer her radiant expression." At the end of a letter on June 23, 1879 (see the photograph below this) Maria wrote, "Elliot & Fry have her photo but <u>not</u> her smile – not that <u>flash</u> of joy – I <u>saw</u> often."

Elliot & Fry have her photo but
<u>not</u> her smile – not that <u>flash</u> of
joy – I <u>saw</u> often. If you [? unclear, possibly c^d for "could"] get to
an artiste .J. Hughes
    2. Elm row
        Hampstead
he took a <u>crayon</u> in Jany far more
life speaking .It is the same artist who
took [Mr. ? William] Pennefather ['] s. [She likely
meant William Pennefather's portrait.] You will excuse real
haste - just <u>keep</u> the articles & I will write directions for
        transit. Yours ever M. V. G. Havergal

This is the end of a letter that F.R.H.'s sister Maria wrote to Mr. Wright (very likely a member of the Church Missionary Society in London) on June 23, 1879, twenty days after Frances died. T. J. Hughes' protrait that Maria describes is given on page 373 of this book. Here and in other places Maria indicated that no portrait really conveyed the brightness and life in F.R.H.'s countenance and eyes.

Engraved by E. Evans.

S.E. VIEW OF ASTLEY CHURCH AND RECTORY.
From a Sketch by Mrs. Crane in 1839.

At this time, F.R.H.'s oldest sister, Jane Miriam Crane, lived here in the rectory home, and tutored Frances. In 1842 she married Henry Crane, when Frances was 5. Miriam was a fine artist, as this and other drawings clearly show.

Frances Ridley Havergal, Aged 8, Portrait by Solomon Cole in 1845

An oil portrait of Frances Ridley Havergal, painted by Solomon Cole in 1845. Her ninth birthday was December 14, 1845.

CHAPTER I.

THAT which was from the *a* beginning, which we have heard, which we have seen *c* with our eyes, which we have looked upon, and our hands have *d* handled, of the Word of life;

2 (For the life was manifested, and we have seen *it*, and bear witness, and shew unto you that eternal life, *f* which was with the Father, and was manifested unto us;)

3 That which we have seen and heard declare we unto you, that ye also may have fellowship with us: and truly our fellowship *l* is with the Father, and with his Son Jesus Christ.

4 And these things write we unto you, that *n* your joy may be full.

5 This then is the message which we have heard of him, and declare unto you, that God is light, *r* and in him is no darkness at all.

6 If we say that we have fellowship with him, and walk in darkness, we lie, and do not the truth:

7 But if we walk *t* in the light, as he is in the light, we have fellowship one with another, and the blood *x* of Jesus Christ his Son cleanseth us from all sin.

8 If we say that we have no sin, *y* we deceive ourselves, and the truth is not in us.

9 If we confess *z* our sins, he is faithful and just to forgive us *our* sins, and to cleanse *b* us from all unrighteousness.

10 If we say that we have not sinned, we make him a liar, and his word is not in us.

This is a magnification of part of I John 1 in F.R.H.'s Bagster Bible that she read and studied at the end of her life.

MEMORIALS

OF

FRANCES RIDLEY HAVERGAL.

BY HER SISTER,

M. V. G. H.

―――

EIGHTEENTH THOUSAND.

―――

London:

JAMES NISBET & CO.,
21, BERNERS STREET.

PREFACE.

IT is with a reverent hand that these "hidden leaves" of my dear sister's life are now laid at the Master's feet, for His acceptance and blessing.

> "Leaves which grave Experience ponders,
>   Soundings for her pilot-charts;
> Leaves which God Himself is storing,
> Records which we read, adoring
>   Him, who writes on human hearts.
>
> Leaflets long unpaged and scattered
>   Time's great library receives;
> When eternity shall bind them,
> Golden volumes we shall find them,
>   God's light falling on the leaves."

No attempt has been made to write a Biography, but rather to allow her to relate her own life-story—a sister's loving touch uniting the several links. Her letters, so kindly lent to me by many friends, have furnished abundant materials for this purpose.

These pages will reveal, to some extent, her "true-hearted, whole-hearted" loyalty in the service of God. Often was it as unseen as the lonely watchfulness of the sentinel on some distant outpost; although in later years she seemed as one pacing the ramparts in the very presence of the King. And so—

> "The joy of loyal service to the King
>   Shone through her days, and lit up other lives
>   With the new fire of faith, that ever strives,
>   Like a swift-kindling beacon, far to fling
> The tidings of His victory, and claim
> New subjects for His realm, new honour for His Name."

May Christ be magnified by this record of her life and death! To her, Christ was indeed "all and in all"; and she did but describe her own experience in the words:

> "There were strange soul depths, restless, vast, and broad,
>   Unfathomed as the sea;
> An infinite craving for some infinite stilling:
> But now Thy perfect love is perfect filling,
> Lord Jesus Christ, my Lord, my God,
>   Thou, Thou art enough for me!"

Yes, she was satisfied with Him, and knew what it was to "rest *in* the Lord," whilst she worked *for* Him. May I not add that an equally joyous and blessed experience may be ours; and that His grace, which was sufficient for her, is sufficient for all who, possessing "like precious faith," "follow His steps."

MARIA V. G. HAVERGAL.

CASWELL BAY ROAD, THE MUMBLES,
   SOUTH WALES.
      April, 1880.

CONTENTS.

	page
Preface	244

Chapter I.
(1836–1844.)

Introduction — Birth — Brothers and sisters — Name — Birthday wreaths — Astley Rectory (illustration) — Her father's music — New home at Henwick — Flora's epitaph — Reading under the table — First rhyme . . 247

Chapter II.
(1843–1848.)

Autobiography from six years old — Wanting to be happy — Sunday chapters and prayer — Golden light — Waving boughs — "The caged lark" — No hypocrisy — Mother's last words — Death — No trance — The cry of the motherless — Wales — Oakhampton. 249

page

Chapter III.
(1848–1852.)

The new decade — Meteor flashes — "Oh for faith" — School at last — Showers, but *no* blessing — Breaking the ice — The climax — The school sunbeam — A gleam of hope — Trusting Jesus — School again — Illness and patience — Wales — Singing and responding at "Taffy services" 253

Chapter IV.
(1852–1855.)

School at Düsseldorf — Journey to Westphalia — Leaving school — Numero I. — Autobiography resumed — Life in the pastor's family — The Countess von Lippe — Letter from Pastor Schulze-Berge — The day of confirmation — In Worcester cathedral — "Thine for ever" — Home life — Oakhampton enjoyment — "Welcome home to my father" 257

Chapter V.
(1856–1860.)

Ireland — F. R. H. and the Irish girls — Hebrew studies — Grateful memory of Bible class teachings — "Nearer heaven!" — Chapters learnt — "Touching the hem" — Leaving St. Nicholas' — The loving teacher — Last page in Sunday Scholar's Register — Welcome to Shareshill. 261

Chapter VI.
(1861–1869.)

Oakhampton — A new power — Musical gifts — Deep borings — Subjects for prayer — Hiller's commendation — Remarkable power of harmonizing — Welcome to Winterdyne — Stormy petrelism — Sent empty away — Calmer waters — Joining Young Women's Christian Association — London — "Guess my birthday treat!" — Signor Randegger — Epitome of his first singing lesson — New home at Leamington — How poems came — My Evelyn! — "The Two Rings" — Weary and sad — First sight of Alpine mountains 264

Chapter VII.
(1870–1871.)

A father's holy teachings — Peaceful death — "Yet speaketh" — "Songs of Grace and Glory" — How harmony was learnt — Letter on tunes in "Havergal's Psalmody" — The "hush of praise" — Sympathy — The great transition — The most enjoyable trip to Switzerland — A real Alpine dawn — The Vaudois chaplain — Vivas on the Col de la Seigne — Christmas Day — Waiting, not working. 271

page

Chapter VIII.
(1872–1874.)

"The Right Way" — Snowdon — Evenings at Harlech — Jesus our Reality — Switzerland once more — Ascent to the Grands Mulets — Glissade peril and escape — Active service — Winterdyne — Bright sunshine — Full surrender — 1 John 1:7 — Definitive standpoint — Chimes in the night of "Ever, only, all for Thee" — No cheque — Songs, not sighs — How "Golden harps," "Tell it out," etc., came — Wayside enjoyments. 275

Chapter IX.
(1874.)

Circular letters — Sunset on the Faulhorn — Ormont Dessus — Interruptions to poems — Other work done — "Little Pillows," etc. — Swiss singing — That great transfer — A musical reverie — Return to England — Bright work and results. 282

Chapter X.
(1874–1875.)

A dark enigma — Typhoid fever — "Waiting at the golden gates" — Coming back from them — Winterdyne — Relapse — Oakhampton — The ministry of kind servants — Return to work — Letters — Gleams — Whitby — "Reality" — The old friend's letter — Kindness of friends. . . . 285

Chapter XI.
(1876.)

"The Turned Lesson" — Patient work — Sympathy with E. C., going to India — Upton Bishop Vicarage — The brother's organ and last singing — The last visit to Switzerland — "*Seulement pour Toi*" — Bible reading to peasants — The Great St. Bernard — Champéry Baroness Helga von Cramm — Alpine cards — Illness at Pension Wengen — Return home — "My King" — Pruning. . 293

Chapter XII.
(1877.)

Letters — The mystery of pain — The Lord's graving tool — Loyal letters — "Won't you decide to-night?" — Manhood for Christ's service — Splendid promises — "My silver and my gold" — Mildmay: its intercessions, greetings, hushing power — A crumb from the King's table — The Christian Progress Union. 303

Chapter XIII.
(1878.)

Sympathy with sorrowful suffering — "Just as Thou wilt" — The mother's last smile — Called to rest — The home

	page		page
nest stirred up — Clear guidance — "Another little step" — Last days in Leamington — Nieces and nephews — Devonshire visits — The Welsh nest — "My study" — The harp-piano — More work — The sweep of Jehovah's pencil — Bible readings — "Take my love" — Songs in a weary Christmas night 308

Chapter XIV.
(1879.)

New Year's sunshine — Journal of mercies — (*Facsimiles of Bible pages*) — Prayer and intercessions — Work, "if the Lord will" — London — The law of the Lord a delight — Prospering — "Loving all Along" — "Bruey" success — Irish plans — Temperance work — The oldest friend's visit — "Can I go to India?" — Last Y.W.C.A. address — "Little Nony" — Last letters — Costly stones — The last "Sunday crumb" card. 314

Chapter XV.
The Last Week.

The donkey-boy — My Temperance regiment — Work on the village bank — Sailor friends — Helga's pictures — "God's will delicious" — Good Mary and kind nurse — "How good and kind to come" — The last Sunday — The last hymns — Last messages — "Do speak bright words for Jesus" — The last song at the Golden Gate — With the King — Astley Churchyard. 324

Appendix 330

This print by Miriam Crane was published in Chapter I of Memorials of Frances Ridley Haveral. *See another print by Miriam in 1839 of this same place, from a different position, on page 240 of this book.*

MEMORIALS OF F.R.H.

CHAPTER I.

(1836–1844.)

Introduction — Birth — Brothers and sisters — Name — Birthday wreaths — Astley Rectory (*illustration*) — Her father's music — New home at Henwick — Flora's epitaph — Reading under the table — First rhyme.

WE do not often see the risings of our rivers, the tiny spring lies hidden in some mountain home. Even when the stream gathers strength in its downward course, it meets with many an obstructing boulder, passes through many an unfrequented valley, and traverses here and there a sunless ravine. But the river deepens and widens, and is most known, most navigable, just as it passes away for ever from our gaze, lost in the ocean depths.

And thus it was with the early life of that dear sister whose course I would now attempt to trace. Those who only knew her when her words were flowing deeply and widely, around, little guess the dark shadows on her early course. It is most difficult to know what to give, and what to withhold, in these pages. In simple dependence on God's overruling guidance, a selection is now made from what she little thought would ever be published. Remembering one of her latest whispers, "I did so want to glorify Him in every step of my way," it is thought right to unfold these life-records. May her desire be fulfilled!

"Come nearer, Sun of Righteousness, that we,
  Whose dim, short hours of day so swiftly run,
So overflowed with love and light may be,
  So lost in glory of the nearing Sun,
That not *our* light, but *Thine*, the world may see,
New praise to Thee through our poor lives be won!"

FRANCES RIDLEY HAVERGAL was born on the 14th of December, 1836, and was the youngest child of William Henry Havergal and Jane his wife. Her father was then Rector of Astley, Worcestershire. The names of her brothers and sisters, in the order of their birth, were:—

1. Jane Miriam, who married Henry Crane, Esq., of Oakhampton, near Stourport.
2. Henry East; vicar of Cople, Bedfordshire, who died 1875. Married Frances Mary, daughter of George J. A. Walker, Esq., Norton, near Worcester.
3. Maria Vernon Graham.
4. Ellen Prestage, who married Giles Shaw, Esq., of Celbridge Lodge, county Kildare, now of Winterdyne, Bewdley.
5. Francis Tebbs, vicar of Upton Bishop, near Ross. Married Isabel Susan, daughter of Colonel W. Martin.

On the 25th of January, 1837, Frances was baptized in Astley Church by the Rev. John Cawood, incumbent of St. Ann's, Bewdley. Her godmothers were Miss Lucy Emra, of St. George's Vicarage, near Bristol, authoress of "Lawrence the Martyr," "Heavenly Themes," and other poems; and Miss Elizabeth Cawood, whose clever and attractive brightness had ever great influence over her little goddaughter. Her godfather was the Rev. W. H. Ridley, Rector of Hambleden.

In the "Ministry of Song" we read how Frances loved her name of Ridley, and that she bore it from one descended from the godly and learned Bishop Ridley, of the noble army of martyrs.

"But 'what the R. doth represent'
  I value and revere,
A diamond clasp it seems to be,
  On golden chains, enlinking me
In loyal love to England's hope,
  The Church I hold so dear."

"Our sweet baby," her father wrote, "grows nicely. She was baptized last Wednesday, 'Frances Ridley.' All are eager for her to be called Fanny, but I do not like it." However, as a child we called her Fanny, but from the time of the publication of her first book, "The Ministry of Song," Frances was her usual signature, and she much preferred her baptismal name. Her unique surname was spelt Heavergill in 1694, afterwards Havergill, or Havergall; but always Havergal since orthography in general ceased to vary. The derivation of the name is thought to be "*Heaver-gill,* the heaving or rising of the brook or gill."

My sister Miriam supplies the next link.

"My recollection of Frances begins with the first day of her life; a pretty little babe even then, and by the time she reached two years of age, with her fair complexion, light curling hair, and bright expression, a prettier child was seldom seen. At that age she spoke with perfect distinctness, and with greater fluency and variety of language than is usual in so young a child. She comprehended and enjoyed any little stories that were told her. I remember her animated look of attention when the Rev. J. East told her about a little Mary who loved the Lord Jesus. We were all taught to read early, and to repeat, by our dear mother; but as I had now left school I undertook this charming little pupil: teaching her reading, spelling, and a rhyme (generally one of Jane Taylor's), for half an hour every morning, and in the afternoon twenty or thirty stitches of patchwork, with a very short text to repeat next morning at breakfast. When three years old, she could read easy books, and her brother Frank remembers how often she was found hiding under a table with some engrossing story."

The Rev. F. Jeffery, afterwards Vicar of Sway, was at this time our father's curate at Astley. The following is an extract from his letter, September 29th, 1879.

"I well recollect Astley Rectory more than forty years ago. At that time your sister Frances was rather more than two years old, a very fairy-like creature. Her chief companion was then a white and tan spaniel, such as Landseer might have loved, and this little favourite she called Flora or Flo. At morning prayers she always sat on her father's knee while he read the Scriptures. It is likely that she learned to read as a mere pastime. I well remember her sweet infant voice singing little hymns in imitation of her father. Her nursemaid was recommended by Miss Cawood, from the Bewdley Sunday School. The day she was four years old her little maid brought her down after dinner to dessert, crowned with a wreath of bay-leaves. I shall never forget the picture! She was her dear mother in miniature, especially in the brightness of her expression and the sparkle of her eye. A line from a classic poet was quoted exactly expressing this. I mention as well remembering the great beauty of your dear mother.... To-day it is exactly fourteen years since I saw the sun for the last time, but it would need many more years than that, to blot out my recollection of Astley Rectory.

"Ah! how each dear domestic scene I knew

. . . . . .

Charms with the magic of a moonlight view,
Its colours mellowed not impaired by time!"

Her sister Miriam continues:

"At four years old, Frances could read the Bible and any ordinary book correctly, and had learned to write in round hand. French and music were gradually added; but great care was always taken not to tire her or excite the precocity of her mind, and she never had a regular governess.

"Mr. Jeffery has referred to her wreath of bay on her fourth birthday, and I remember making a wreath of the pink china roses which grew among the ivy on the rectory on her third birthday. Alas! the rose and the prophetic bay reappeared among her funeral wreaths."

The surroundings of dear Frances' early days in our Astley home may as well be given in the descriptive lines of my sister Miriam, written in 1863, accompanying her sketch of the church and rectory.

"Behold thy birthplace, Frances! The old house
Entwined with ivy, roses, and the vine;
Beneath the shadow of the ancient shrine
Where ministered our father twenty years.
He built the northern aisle, and gave the clock,
A musical memento of his love
For time and tune and punctuality!
Fair is the garden ground, and there the flowers
Were trained with care and skill by *one* who now
Rests from her labours in the heavenly land.
Here life and death together meet; the tombs
Stand close beside the mossy bank, where once
Sisters and brothers met in frolic play.
Around, the wooded hills in beauty rise!
Earth has not many scenes more fair than this,
And none more dear to those who called it Home!"

Our Sunday evening hymn-singing is vividly recalled, in which little Fanny soon took part. At this time our dear father was an invalid; music was his solace, and he composed cathedral services, also many hundreds of chants and tunes, and several sacred songs, the profits of which were always devoted to various Societies, home and foreign, and the restoration of churches.[1]

Beside the rich chords and tuneful song in our home, there were wise and holy influences. Our parents' prayers and example in searching the Scriptures, and their loving cheery ways, activity and punctuality, were the keynotes of our child-life.

---

[1] My father's first published musical composition was a setting of Bishop Heber's hymn, "From Greenland's icy mountains." The proceeds amounted to £180, and were devoted to the Church Missionary Society. In 1836 the Gresham prize medal was awarded to him for a cathedral service in A. In 1841 a second gold medal was adjudged for his anthem, "Give Thanks."

One of our mother's letters is given, written when Fanny was away on her first visit (1840).

I am so glad to hear how happy you are at Wycombe. Try and be very obedient to dear grandmamma and your sister Ellen, and I hope you will do all you can to please dear grandpapa. I miss you very much, and often think I hear you call "mamma," or expect you are coming to me. You remember the three little babies at Dunley. Jane, the one that you nursed, is gone to heaven. May my Fanny know and love Jesus Christ! then she will be sure to go to heaven whether she dies young or old. Some of the seeds are come up in your garden; I love to watch them, because you helped me to sow them. Dear papa sends his love. Good bye, dear Fanny.

From dear Mamma.

In 1842 the living of Astley was resigned, and Henwick House, in the parish of Hallow, was our temporary home till our dear father's appointment by Bishop Pepys to the Rectory of St. Nicholas, Worcester, in 1845. The only distinct remembrance of this time is of Frances' delight in the gardens and long terrace walk at Henwick, with sundry agile tree climbings. Perhaps her first grief was the death of her little dog Flo, which was buried under the snowy Mespilus tree in the back lawn. The sheet of paper is preserved on which she wrote:

"Here lies little Flora. Died April 16th, 1844.
Aged 7. Reverence her remains."

Frances always took care to be in the drawing-room while a professor was giving German lessons. Without any one knowing it, she was listening and acquiring the language. When discovered, she had made such progress that Mr. Lorentz begged he might instruct her.

The treasured little book in which she wrote her childish hymns and rhymes begins with the following verses written at the age of seven.

> Sunday is a pleasant day,
>   When we to church do go;
> For there we sing and read and pray,
>   And hear the sermon too.
>
> On Sunday hear the village bells;
>   It seems as if they said,
> Go to the church where the pastor tells
>   How Christ for man has bled.
>
> And if we love to pray and read
>   While we are in our youth,
> The Lord will help us in our need
>   And keep us in His truth.

All her rhymes are dated, and also some simple tales, written in a copybook for the benefit of her little niece Miriam. From nine years old and upwards she wrote long and amusingly descriptive letters, in perfect rhyme and rhythm, to her brother Frank and her young friends.

There would have been a long blank now but for the Autobiography of her inner child-life. It was written for her sister Maria, and unsealed only a few weeks ago. As the shadows on her morning pathway contrast with the light that shone more and more unto the perfect day, it is thought right to give these pages in all their truthful simplicity.

CHAPTER II.

(1843–1848.)

Autobiography from six years old — Wanting to be happy — Sunday chapters and prayer — Golden light — Waving boughs — "The caged lark" — No hypocrisy — Mother's last words — Death — No trance — The cry of the motherless — Wales — Oakhampton.

Autobiography. (*Written in* 1859.)

I have often already planned and half intended to write for my own amusement in coming years a sort of little autobiography of those which are past; but *this* idea, although my life would furnish plenty of small adventures and incidents, I have now for several reasons laid aside; I scarcely think it would repay the necessary outlay of many precious hours. For, more and more, do I feel what valuable capital Time is, capital which must not be put out at merely *any* interest, but as far as possible at the best and highest. In lieu however of a history of my *outer* life, I do think that a little account of my own *inner* life would be a not unprofitable investment of an evening hour. And may He who has led me these twenty-two "years through the wilderness" send His blessing upon me while I "remember all the way" by which He, I trust, has brought me hitherto.

My reasons for undertaking this little task are these. 1st. I have found it so very pleasant and profitable to look back frequently upon what have been God's dealings with me, that a written retrospect is likely, with His blessing, to prove still more useful and delightful, as being less cursory and more definite. 2nd. I have always avoided keeping a diary, feeling certain that it never would or could be a strictly faithful picture of passing soul-life; yet I think an account of the *past,* in a bird's-eye view, would be far easier to give in a true and uncoloured light than any memoranda of a *present,* which would be tinged with the prevailing hues of the moment, morning, noon, or twilight. Therefore, as I feel sure that I shall not retain such a clear recollection of each year's history when memory is more burdened, and as I believe that even our own "experience" is a thing given to be used and improved, it seems almost a duty to endeavour to preserve it as clear and ready for reference and use (at times when "His love in times past" may be an anchor for the storm-beset spirit) as may be. 3rd. A diary no eye but mine should ever see. But, for one reason, one eye shall read these pages, if it should be God's will that the volume of my life should soon close. It is this. While I do humbly trust, though tremblingly, that I am a child of God, I know, and knowing bewail it, that much in my life and conversation has not been, and is not, "as becometh the gospel of Christ"; and there must be some, if not many, among my own beloved ones, who have no direct evidence concerning me, and whom I must have often grieved by my inconsistency. And it might be that no opportunity of any "death-bed evidence" may be given me, or that my remaining time may be so short that I may never be able to show, by a closer walk with God, that I am truly His. And as He has in His wonderful, most wonderful, mercy given me hope, I would not that any dear to me should sorrow for me as without hope. So I shall give this to my dear sister Maria, to be opened only in case of my death; that she may have the comfort of hoping, that even in my darkest and most careless days I was not utterly forsaken of that Spirit, who I pray may never cease to strive with me.

"Call to remembrance the days of old."
"Thou shalt remember all the way which the Lord thy God
hath led thee."

1843–1845.

Up to the time that I was six years old I have no remembrance of any religious ideas whatever. Even, when taken once to see the corpse of a little boy of my own age (four years), lying in a coffin strewn with flowers, in dear papa's parish of Astley, I did not think about it as otherwise than a very sad and very curious thing that that little child should lie so still and cold. I do not think I could ever have said any of those "pretty things" that little children often do, though there were sweet and beloved and holy ones round me who must have often tried to put good thoughts into my little mind. But from six to eight I recall a different state of things. The beginning of it was a sermon preached one Sunday morning, at Hallow Church, by Mr. (now Archdeacon) Phillpotts. Of this I even now retain a distinct impression. It was to me a very terrible one, dwelling much on hell and judgment, and what a fearful thing it is to fall into the hands of the living God. No one ever knew it, but this sermon haunted me, and day and night it crossed me. I began to pray a good deal, though only night and morning, with a sort of fidget and impatience, almost angry at feeling so unhappy, and wanting and expecting to get a new heart, and have everything put straight and be made happy, all at once.

This sort of thing went on at intervals, not at all continuously, for often a month or two would pass without a serious thought or anything like true prayer. At such times I utterly abominated being "talked to," would do anything on earth to escape the kindly meant admonitions of dear M——; or the prayers which she would offer for me. Any cut or bruise (and such were more the rule than exception in those wild days of tree-climbing, wall-scaling, etc.) was instantly adduced as a reason why I could not possibly kneel down. A chapter in the Bible was often a terrible bore. Then, after, a time of this sort, some mere trifle, very often the influence of a calm beautiful evening, or perhaps a "Sunday book" of some affecting kind, would rouse me up to uncomfortableness again. One sort of habit I got into in a steady way, which was persevered in with more or less fervour according to the particular fit in which I might be. Every Sunday afternoon I went alone into a little front room (at Henwick) over the hall, and there used to read a chapter in the Testament, and then knelt down and prayed for a few minutes, after which I usually felt soothed and less naughty. Once, when Marian P. was spending a few days with me, she being my only little visitor at Henwick, I did not like any omission, and so took her with me, saying a few words of prayer "out of my head" without any embarrassment at her presence.

I think I had a far more vivid sense of the beauty of nature as a little child than I have even now; and its power over me was greater than any one would imagine. I have hardly felt anything so intensely since, in the way of a sort of unbearable enjoyment. Especially, and I think more than anything else, the golden quiet of a bright summer's day used to enter into me and do me good. What only some great and rare musical enjoyment is to me now, the shade of a tree under a clear blue sky, with a sunbeam glancing through the boughs, was to me then. But I did not feel happy in my very enjoyment; I wanted *more.* I do not think I was eight when I hit upon Cowper's lines, ending

"My Father made them all!"

That was what I wanted to be able to say; and, after once seeing the words, I never saw a lovely scene again without being *teased* by them. One spring (I think 1845) I kept thinking of them, and a dozen times a day said to myself, "Oh if God would but make me a Christian before the summer comes!" because I longed so to enjoy His works as I felt they could be enjoyed. And I could not bear to think of *another* summer coming and going, and finding and leaving me still "not a Christian." I shall know some day *why* my Father left me to walk thus alone in my early childhood, why such long years of dissatisfaction and restlessness were apportioned me, while others fancied me a happy thoughtless child. But He must have been teaching me, and "who teacheth like Him?" Another soothing influence to me was the presence of any one whom I believed to be more than commonly holy: not among those nearest and dearest to me at home; how perversely I overlooked *them!* but any very pious clergyman, or other manifest and shining Christian. The Rev. John Davies, of St. Clement's, I particularly reverenced; and his or any similar presence did me a sort of indefinite good. I used to want such to speak a word about good things to me, much as I hated it from those who would willingly have given it me.

All this while I don't think any one could have given the remotest guess at what passed in my mind, or have given me credit for a single serious thought. I *knew* I was "a naughty child," never entertained any doubts on the subject; in fact, I almost enjoyed my naughtiness in a savage desperate kind of way, because I utterly despaired of getting any better, except by being "made a Christian," which, as months passed on, leaving me rather worse than better, was a less and less *hoped* for, though more and more *longed* for, change. Towards the end of these two years I think (though I do not distinctly remember) that I must have become a shade quieter and happier, because of what is the first memory in my next little soul era.

July, 1845–Spring, 1850.

We went to St. Nicholas' Rectory in 1845, and it was in very great bitterness that I bade adieu to my pleasant country life, and became, as I remember dear papa calling me, "a caged lark." This made a *great* difference to me, for I do think that the quiet every day beauty of trees and sunshine was *the* chief external influence upon my early childhood. Waving boughs and golden light always touched and quieted me, and spoke to me, and told me about God. Being a "youngest" by so many years, and not knowing many children, I very rarely had a companion except my little Flora, in that large Henwick garden, where I first learned to *think*; and that may have been the reason why trees and grass were so much to me. They were the first pleasant leaf in God's great lesson book with me. But at St. Nicholas' Rectory I had a little tiny room all my own, and that was quite the next best thing; its little window was my "country" (for a "walk" with another was never the same thing as those lonely loiterings in the garden), and soon the sky and the clouds were the same sort of relations to my spirit that trees and flowers had been.

Soon after coming, a sermon by the curate on "Fear not, little flock," etc., struck me very much, and woke me up again from a longer slumber to a more restless unhappiness than usual. I did so want to be happy and be "a Christian," which term embraced everything I could possibly think of in the way of happiness. And I didn't at all see how I was to be, except by praying very hard; and that I had done so often that I got quite disheartened at its resultlessness. At this time I don't think I had any clear ideas about believing on the Lord Jesus, and so getting rid of the burden which had pressed so long upon my little soul. My general notion was that I didn't love God at all, and was very bad and wicked altogether; that if I went on praying very much, something would come to me and change me all at once, and make me like many whom I read about and a few whom I saw. As for *trying* to be good, that seemed of next to no use; it was like struggling in a quicksand, the more you struggle the deeper you sink. To come back to the sermon. I had never yet spoken a word to any mortal about religion; but now I was so uneasy that, after nearly a fortnight's hesitation, taking the emboldening opportunity of being alone with the curate one evening when almost dark, I told him my trouble; saying especially that I thought I was getting worse, because since I had come to St. Nicholas' I had not cared at all for Sunday afternoon reading and prayer. His advice did not satisfy me. He said the excitement of moving and coming into new scenes was the cause most likely of my feeling worse, and that would soon go off; then I was to try and be a good child, and pray, etc., etc. So, after that, my lips were utterly sealed to all but God for another five years or rather more. Even when feeling most, I fancied I could as soon speak Sanscrit, or die, as utter a word to a human being on what was only between me and God. This intense reserve must have grieved those who loved me. Consequently too, anything like hypocrisy was the sin of all others which I could least understand, and imagined the most *impossible* to commit. How *could* any one say or seem *more* than they felt, when it was so impossible to say as much as one felt!

My dear mamma's illness and death (July 5th, 1848) did not make the impression on me which might have been expected; I mean as regards my spiritual state, for my intense sorrow, childish though it was, seems even now, after the lapse of eleven years, a thing of which I do not like to speak or think. A mother's death must be childhood's greatest grief. But I am trying now to write only of my soul's life. I did not at all expect her departure, and shut my ears in a very hardened way to those who tried to prepare me for it; so when it came I was not ready, and there was nothing but bitterness in it to me. I did not, *would* not, see God's hand in it, and the stroke left me worse than it found me.

One subject *often* occupied my mind in these years, which would seem unusual for a child—the Lord's Supper. After coming to St. Nicholas', almost every monthly sacrament made me thoughtful. I begged to be allowed to stay in the church and see it administered "only once," but this apparently mere curiosity was not gratified, so I used to go round to the vestry and listen to the service through the door. One Sunday the hymn "My God, and is Thy table spread," was sung before sermon; it quite upset me, and I cried violently, though being in a corner of the pew I managed to conceal it. I used to reckon the years to the time when the invitation would extend to me too, not by any means happily, for I wondered what I should ever do; I could not stay away, but how could I dare to go? "Well, I hope I shall be a Christian by then!" was my only comfort.

Turning from the Autobiography, some of her mother's words are given.

"You are my youngest little girl, and I feel more anxious about you than the rest. I do pray for the Holy Spirit to lead you and guide you. And remember, nothing but the precious blood of Christ can make you clean and lovely in God's sight."

Frances. "Oh, mamma, I am sure you will get better and go to church again!"

"No, dear child; the church mamma is going to is the general assembly and church of the firstborn in heaven. How glorious to know I shall soon see my Saviour face to face! Now go and play and sing some of your little hymns for me; there is one verse I should like you to sing twice over:

> "And when her path is darkened
> She lifts her trusting eye,
> And says 'my Father calls me
> To mansions in the sky!'"

Before her mother's death (when she was eleven years old) her wish was gratified to see the Lord's Supper administered. We remember her grave, flushed face, when kneeling at her mother's bed during the "Communion of the Sick."

The whole story of her child life at this time is told in her "Four Happy Days," in which, under the name of "Annie," she reveals the bitterness of this first grief. We can almost see her in her tiny bedroom, "kneeling on the chair, leaning her little arms on the window-seat, and feeling as if she wished she had something to lean her little heart on too. The clouds had been her great friends since she had had no trees to sit in and make up fancies about. Sometimes she watched the clouds and wondered all sorts of things about them, and especially wished she could reach the splendid white ones which looked like snow mountains that could be climbed and rested upon. But she found in a book that they were only vapour like the others, and that there would be nothing to rest upon and look down upon, only dismal thick mist and rain. Poor child! there are other bright things besides shining clouds, which when reached are only mist and tears. . . . She was musing over some words which had just been spoken in her mother's room. 'Fanny dear, pray to God to prepare you for all that He is preparing for you.' Her mamma said them very feebly and solemnly when she said good-night, and now they seemed to sound over and over again, so that they never should or could be forgotten. 'I wonder what He is preparing for me,' she thought. 'Oh I do hope He is preparing one of the many mansions for me! how I wish I knew whether He is! But I don't think He is preparing me for it, else I should not feel naughty so often.' But her mamma meant something sadder and nearer, which she knew God was surely preparing day by day for her little girl; she knew it could not be very long before she would be singing the 'new song' in perfect joy, while all her child's little songs would be hushed in great sorrow, the greatest that a child can know. Her mamma saw how strangely she was unprepared for all this, and she never would stay to listen to anything her sisters said about their dear mamma being worse."

Only a few weeks before her own death, Frances referred to this: "The words mamma taught me in 1848 have been a *life prayer with me*. This 'preparing' goes on; it is as when gaining one horizon, another and another spreads before you. So every event prepares us for the next that is prepared for us. Mamma's words I also remember, 'Dear child, you have your own little bedroom now, it ought to be a little Bethel.' I could not *then* make head or tail of what she meant, and often wondered, till some months after, when reading in Genesis I came to the chapter; and then I understood it. Having that small room to myself developed me much as a child; it was *mine,* and to me it was the cosiest little nest in the world."

We must take one more look (from the "Four Happy Days") at St. Nicholas' Rectory on the 11th of July, 1848. "Annie [Frances] was standing by the window in a front room, looking through a little space between the window and blind. All the shops were shut up, though it was not Sunday. She knew it would be dreadful to look out of that window, and yet she felt she *must* look. She did not cry, she only stood and shivered in the warm air.

"Very slowly and quietly a funeral passed out of the front [Rectory] gate, and in another minute was out of sight, turning into the church. Then she stood no longer, but rushed away to her own little room, and flung herself on her little bed, and cried 'oh, mamma! mamma! mamma!' It seemed as if there was nothing else in her little heart but that one word. The strange hope which had lasted all that week was gone. She had found curious things in books, and one was that people had sometimes been supposed to be dead and yet it was only a trance, and they had revived and even recovered. And so, when no one was near, she had gone again and again into that room, and drawn the curtain aside, half expecting to see the dear eyes unclose, and to feel the cold cheek warm again to her kiss. But it was no trance. The dear suffering mother was at rest, seeing Jesus face to face. Only the smile of holy peace was left on that lovely face, and that remained to the last, telling of life beyond death; she had never seen the solemn beauty of that smile before. But now all hope was gone, and she knew that she was motherless."

In her little book of poems she wrote:

> Eye hath not seen, nor ear hath heard,
> Neither can man's heart conceive,
> The blessed things God hath prepared
> For those who love Him and believe.
> July 5th, 1848.

And again:

> Oh! had I the wings of a dove,
> Soon, soon would I be at my rest;

> I would fly to the Saviour I love,
> And there would I lie on His breast.
>   July 9th.

On a marble tablet in St. Nicholas' Church, Worcester, is this inscription.

JANE,
The beloved Wife of Rev. W. H. HAVERGAL, M.A.,
Rector of this Parish, and Hon. Canon of Worcester Cathedral,
Died in holy peace, July 5th, 1848,
AGED 54 YEARS.
"*I give unto them eternal life.*"

After this sorrowful time our dear father took us all away to North Wales. On our return Frances often visited her sister Miriam's home, Oakhampton, where she is remembered as a clever amusing child, sometimes a little wilful and troublesome from mere excess of animal spirits, but always affectionate and grateful for any little treat; reading a good deal of poetry, and leaving traces of her studies in volumes found in hayloft and manger and garden nooks.

When at St. Nicholas' Rectory, she threw herself into the work of her society for providing warm clothing; and her chief coadjutor (whom she calls "Maria" in "Four Happy Days") was the youngest daughter of Michael Thomas Sadler, M.P.

Though her grief for her dear mother's death was very deep, she ever tried to conceal it. Not that it was always heavy upon her, for as she writes: "If anything else occupied my attention I had a happy faculty of forgetting everything else for the moment. And thus it happened that a merry laugh or a sudden light-heeled scamper upstairs and downstairs led others to think I had not many sad thoughts, whereas not a minute before my little heart was heavy and sad."

CHAPTER III.

(1848–1852.)

The new decade — Meteor flashes — "Oh for faith" — School at last — Showers, but *no* blessing — Breaking the ice — The climax — The school sunbeam — A gleam of hope — Trusting Jesus — School again — Illness and patience — Wales — Singing and responding at "Taffy services."

AUTOBIOGRAPHY RESUMED.

I KNOW I did not love God at this time, the very thought of Him frightened me; but sometimes a feeling not unlike love would make me go to sleep with a wet pillow. It would often be thus. Going to bed, I would determine I would try to think about God, hard as it was; and after I lay down, as my thoughts did not flow at all naturally heavenward, any more than water flows upward, I forced them into a definite channel by a half whisper. "How good it was of God to send Jesus to die!" was my usual beginning, while I by no means felt or believed that wonderful goodness. Nevertheless it usually ended in my crying most heartily because I was so bad and He was so good, and because I didn't and couldn't love Him when He even died for sinners.

Here I ought to say that, for preservation from one deadly error, I ought especially to be thankful to my ever watchful Keeper. Never for one moment, even from my earliest childhood, have I ever been tempted to think otherwise of myself than as a great and miserable and helpless sinner. Never have I dared to think myself "as good as others," for even as a little child I knew and felt the sinfulness of my own heart. Never has the shadow of a hope in my own righteousness, or of any trust in myself, crossed my mind. Yet even this I say with the reservation that it is and has been so, as far as my own consciousness goes, for every year shows me more and more the utter deceitfulness of the heart: "who can know it!" Oh the comfort of thinking that there is One who *knows* it, and can therefore cleanse its most hidden chambers from their dark pollution. "O God, unto whom all hearts be open," etc., is one of the sweetest things in our sweet Liturgy, to me, and it is wonderful what confidence it has often given me.

So passed the five years till the spring of 1850, a time full of many recollections which I should like to retrace, had I not determined to abide by my intention of recalling only the history of what I would now dare to hope, though for many years I doubted it, is God's own work in me, which He, according to His promise, will perfect in His own time.

1850 (Spring) to 1851 (February).

The bells were ringing in the new year, and not *year* only but *decade*, when Maria woke me and said, "It is 1850 now, Fanny!" It was quite dark, and I lay listening to the new year's birth-song in silence. A dim looking onward through a fresh "ten years" all the way till 1860 came before me; I should be grown up if I lived; I a woman, how curious it seemed! Perhaps I should be dead, and where? If I lived, should I be a Christian? That was the great thing in all my anticipations of coming years; but in a solemn hour, like a new year's midnight, it grew greater and more important than ever. The sound of the bells died away, and all was quiet again. I did not muse long, but fell asleep to wake up in the first grey twilight of 1850.

Now the decade has nearly glided by (the first entire one in my recollection); the new year's bells of 1860 will soon be sounding forth; God has preserved my life hitherto; and how shall I answer the great question then, not "shall I be" but "am I, a Christian?" May I, trusting and believing in the Lord Jesus as I do hope He has taught me to do, answer this great question of my life with a humble yet confident "yes"? And, in entering upon another ten years, may I not hope that "to him that hath shall be given," that He will give me more faith, hope, and love, more knowledge of Himself, more meetness for His presence? *Amen!*

I don't so much remember particular incidents in the early part of this year as general feelings and impressions, which were then rather altered in character, so much so as to form the beginning of a new division in my heart story. This much I know, that a soberizing thoughtful time seemed to fall on me like a mantle, and my strivings were no longer the passionate spasmodic meteor flashes which they had been, but something deeper, more settled, more sorrowful. All this was secret and only within my own breast, for not only at this time but all through my early life there were but a very few who knew me to be anything but a careless merry girl, light hearted in the extreme. This spring a strange new sense of the vanity of life and earth and everything but the *one* thing came over me, and when alone I sat and mused till I often cried. I began to look onward more, and feel that I should not be a child much longer (I was thirteen); and then years would go by so quickly, people said they did, they went faster even then to me; and what would they bring? vanity and sameness and vexation? And life began to seem such a little thing to me, such "a handbreadth," and what was there in it to care for? I couldn't expect a happier lot than I had, and yet all I had was unsatisfactory; and I should always be *myself* too, and I hated *myself*, so what was to be done?

Two or three things happened (though I do not at all remember what), which tended very strongly to confirm these sad thoughts; death seemed around me; "passing away" earth's motto; "vanity" life's keynote. As the beautiful spring came on there was a mist of melancholy over the very flowers: they had opened, well, what matter? they would fade again, and so would everything! I did not enjoy that spring as I had others, its charm was gone. In the end of May I joined Ellen in London, and we spent six weeks of gorgeous summer weather together at Wycombe with grandpapa. What brought it before me I don't know, but now came a more definite and earnest prayer, for *faith*. Oh to believe in Jesus, to believe that He had pardoned me! I used to go to bed rather early, and lie awake in the long summer twilight till Ellen came up, praying for this precious gift. Oh for faith! That was my cry; but it was not given, at least not *as* and *when* I asked. I read a great deal of the Bible at this time in a "straight on" sort of way, expecting to come to something which would set me free and bring the great gift of faith within my grasp. How I got it I can't in the least tell; but certainly about this time I had a clearer idea of salvation than ever before, though I fancied myself farther than ever from its blessedness.

This reminds me that as a child I read a good deal of the Bible, Isaiah being nearly my favourite book from the time I was ten or eleven. I never succeeded in reading for any length of time on any regular plan, because if I missed at all in one I got disheartened and *ennuyée*[1], and after giving up altogether for a little while began something else. Once I determined, if eternal life were in the Scriptures, find it *I would*, and resolved to begin giving an hour a day to very careful and prayerful reading of the New Testament.

Then came the great break in the current of my outer life, and with it a development of the inner. August 15th, 1850, to my great delight I went to school. And that single half-year with dear Mrs. Teed, formerly of Great Campden House, at Belmont now, was perhaps the most important to me of any in my life. The night before I went, Ellen,—dear, gentle, heavenly sister that she was, stood by me, brushing my hair, and taking the last opportunity of loving counsel. She told me that I was going to begin a new chapter in my life: stay, her words were, "One of the great events of your life, Fanny!" and then she was silent. I was captiously disposed, and rather wanted to avoid a serious conversation, so I answered carelessly, for I knew by the tone of her voice what she wanted to lead on to. But it would not do, she went on till I was softened,—a most unusual thing under the process of being talked to, which generally had the most opposite effect. She spoke of God's love, and of how pleasant and sweet a thing it was to love Him who first loved us. I could not stand it, and for the first time for five years I spoke out: "I can't love God yet, Nellie!" was all I said, but I felt a great deal more.

Next day I went. Maria took me, and we reached Belmont quite in the evening. It was nearly prayer-time, and Maria and I were left to have some tea alone in the great drawing-room. We had just finished when voices reached us, and we tried to find our way in their direction. They came from the schoolroom, where the girls were singing their evening hymn prior to the weekly address of their chaplain. It sounded very sweet and soothing, as we stood behind the door in the last glow of sunset, and somewhat subdued the spirits and the curiosity which were exciting me considerably. Then Miss Teed came out and brought us in, just as Mr. Parker was beginning his sermon. It was from some text in Samuel which I forget; but the two leading ideas were, that we should begin the new half-year with the Saviour who loved us and gave Himself for us, and in a spirit of helpful love one toward another. It was a rather long address, and I was very tired and excited, so I know I did not listen to it nearly all; but this much I have retained until now, and it was the keynote of my prayer that evening as I knelt for the first time beside my little school bed, so white and curtainless.

How I should like to run on with many reminiscences of school life! But I *will* not! It was not long before I felt that Mrs. Teed's teaching was something more than common, but, till towards the end of the half-year, things went on much as usual with me.

[1] *ennuyée*: wearied or exhausted, annoyed, bothered, worried

After the middle of the half-year there was a difference. It was Mrs. Teed's *finale* to her long course of school work, and she longed and prayed that it might indeed be finished with joy through the outpouring of God's blessing upon her labours. That none might leave her roof unimpressed was her desire, and it was to a great extent fulfilled. She prayed and spoke with us, together and individually, with a fervour which I have never since seen equalled, and seemed a very St. Paul in the intensity of her yearning over us. The result was what might be really called a *revival* among her young charge. There may have been, and probably was, some excitement; but that the Holy Spirit was, even then and there, sent down into many a young heart, and that many dated from that time their real conversion to God, and went home that Christmas rejoicing in a newly and truly found Saviour, I have no doubt whatever. My own two dearest friends were among these.

But, before the full tide of all this blessing set in, I was much in earnest. To begin with; it must indeed have been a heart of stone, that could resist dear Mrs. Teed's sweet and holy power. Besides, we had pious teachers who often spoke on the best things to us, and had little meetings for prayer weekly in their own rooms. And there were many Christian girls too, easily recognised by their general "walk and conversation," almost by their very countenances; these I knew "took sweet counsel together," and I envied them and longed to *dare* to share it. Mary —— was one of these; we were naturally a great deal together, and I longed to be able to speak and tell her how unhappy I often was; but it was long before I summoned courage. At last I did. "Mary, dites-moi, est-ce que vous aimez Dieu?"[1] (We always had to speak French.) She looked almost surprised, there was no doubt about the matter with her. "Oui, certainement," she said, "je L'aime plus que je ne pourrais vous dire." Then I burst into tears and sobbed out "Eh bien, c'est cela que je désire tant, et moi je ne le puis pas!" The ice was broken, and dear Mary spoke very sweetly to me: I did not regret my confidence this time. "Pouvez vous ou voulez vous dire que vous êtes encore un petit enfant?" "Oh, oui, je sais que je ne suis qu'un enfant." "Alors, écoutez! Jésus disait, 'Suffer the little children,' etc. C'est chaque petit enfant qui doit venir à Lui, chaque petit enfant qu'll appelle, qu'll veut embrasser." She begged me to go to Jesus and tell Him I wanted to love Him and could not, and then He would teach me to. The words of wise and even eminent men have since then fallen on my ear, but few have brought the dewy refreshment to my soul which the simple loving words of my little Heaven-taught schoolfellow did. But as yet they were only as a "very lovely song," etc., though I loved to listen to them, and acted upon them in darkness and trembling. After this I had many talks with Mary, but with no one else. Even with Diana, the goddess almost among my school friendships, and whom I believed to be like Mary, not a syllable could I utter on the subject; though I longed to hear her speak to me as Mary did.

---

[1] English translation: "Mary, tell me, do you love God?" "Yes, certainly, I love Him more than I could tell you." "Ah well, it is that that I desire so much, and I cannot do it!" "Can you or do you want to say that you are still a little child?" "Oh, yes, I know that I am only a child." "Then, listen! Jesus said, 'Suffer the little children,' etc. That is each little child who ought to come to Him, each little child whom He calls, whom He wants to embrace."

November came, and with it a marked increase of anxiety among undecided, and earnestness among decided ones. I remember a feeling of awe stealing over me sometimes, at the consciousness that the "power of the Lord was present" among us. For so indeed it was. As day after day passed on, one after another might be observed (even though little or nothing were said) to be going through the great sorrow which seemed to prelude the after-sent peace; and day after day one after another, hitherto silent, spoke out and told what peace and joy in believing they had found, and blessed God that they ever came to Belmont. Religious topics became the common subjects of conversation among the girls; for even those as yet untouched could not but be struck with what passed around them. In very general conversation I occasionally joined, but more reservedly than any almost, and never alluding to my own feelings, though I knew what it was for my heart to feel as if it must burst. I am not quite sure, but I think, when Elizabeth —— told me that she too had found peace, I told her enough of my heart to establish confidence between us.

As I heard of one and another speaking in such terms of confidence and gladness, my heart used to sink within me, it seemed so utterly unattainable. I prayed despairingly, as a drowning man cries for help who sees no help near. I had prayed and sought so long, and yet I was farther off than these girls, many of whom had only begun to think of religion a few weeks before. It was so very dark around me; I could not see Jesus in the storm nor hear His voice. They spoke of His power and willingness to save, but I could find nothing to prove that He was willing to save *me*, and I wanted some special personal evidence about it. To *know,* surely, that *my* sins were forgiven, and to have all my doubts taken away, was what I prayed and waited for. Every day as it passed, while more were added to the rejoicing ones around me, only left me more hopeless, more heartsick at the hope deferred and often almost lost.

Yet I drank in every word (and they were many) that I heard about Jesus and His salvation. I came to see that it was Christ *alone* that could satisfy me. I longed *intensely* to come to Him, I wept and prayed day and night; but "there was no voice nor any that answered."

The climax came about the first or second week in December. I shall never, never forget the evening of Sunday, December 8th. Either the sermon at church or Mrs. Teed's subject, or both, had been Mark 2:1–12. Anyhow, I know we had heard much of that palsied one in his lonely helplessness, and of Christ's words of forgiveness, bringing joy and power and healing. Diana had hardly seen me all day, which was an unusual thing. (She was the sunbeam of the school, and a most particular friend of mine, and I loved her with a perfectly idolatrous affection,—such as, until that time, I had never given to any one. I, and most others, always supposed that her charming disposition and general sweetness arose from a purer and deeper fount than could dwell in her own nature; yet she never spoke on sacred things, though she seemed as faultless as a child could be.)

For some days previously she had mixed as little as possible with others, though apparently unintentionally, and there had been a slight depression about her which, though probably unnoticed by others, struck me, from being accustomed to watch every changing light on her face with something approaching adoration. That evening, as I sat nearly opposite to her at tea, I could not help seeing—nobody could—a new and remarkable radiance about her countenance. It seemed literally lighted up from within, while her voice (I wonder whether it was as musical to others as to me!) even in the commonest necessary remarks sounded like a song of gladness. Something was coming I was sure. Diana was not the same. I looked at her almost with awe, as one would on some spirit visitant. As soon as tea was over she came round to my side of the table, sat down by me on the form, threw her arm round me, and said: "Oh, Fanny, dearest Fanny, the blessing has come to me at last. Jesus has forgiven me, I know. He is my Saviour, and I am so happy! He is such a Saviour as I never imagined, so good, so loving! He has not cast me out, He said so, and He says so to you. Only come to Him and He will receive you. Even now He loves you though you don't know it." Much more she said which I do not remember, but the tone of her voice is as clearly sounding in my ear as if she still spoke. Yes, she had found peace, and more than peace,—overflowing unspeakable joy; yet, even in the first gush of its shining waters, she thought of those around, and almost her first impulse was to desire that her friends should possess what had been given to her to find. Then she told me how, while every one had supposed her to be a Christian, she had not been so, though she had been seeking and praying for a long time; and how, that day, the words "thy sins be forgiven thee" had struck her suddenly, and she had thought them over all day till the time came when she could be alone with Him who spoke them; and then came the joyful power of believing in the love and might of that gracious Saviour, and His death-bought pardon.

Afterwards, she told me how new and strange many things seemed to her. The way in which she spoke of motives particularly impressed me. It was a new light to me. Actions, words, and intentions had been enough for me before, but from that evening I felt that my standard was raised, and that henceforth my strivings after a holy life must include more than I had dreamt of. A consciousness of the purity of heart required by God came over me; and, though more disheartened than ever, I had learnt a great lesson.

The few remaining days, till the holidays, passed much as before, except that the last two or three unsettled me, and made me very much indisposed for a continuance of the earnest steady toil of the foregoing weeks; for the *first* coming home from school, at the end of an unbroken half-year, is not *a little thing* to a child.

From that time till the spring of the present year I date a course of weary seeking, inconstant and variable; often departed from, but as often renewed, and by God's grace never entirely given up; brightened from time to time with a gleam of hope; sweetened from time to time with a drop, though but a drop, of the still fountain of heavenly peace; yet, as a rule, passed in the cold mists of doubt, and the chilly storms of temptation and inward strife, and the dim twilight of miserable and even disappointed longing.

Oh, how gladly I would have exchanged my best things of earth, my happiest months and years, as far as outward things were concerned, with any one's lot, however wretched, who possessed that joy in the Lord which I could not find. At any time I would willingly have lost or suffered *anything*, might it but have brought me to the attainment of "full assurance." And I am quite sure that *nothing*, in the way of earthly and external trials, could have been to me what the inner darkness and strife and utter weariness of spirit, through the greater part of these years, has been. Many may have thought mine a comparatively thornless path; but often when the path was smoothest there were hidden thorns within, and wounds bleeding and rankling.

February, 1851.

I feel that the beginning of this year ought to be marked as the commencement of a new life-chapter, because it was then that, for the *first* time, I ever knew what it was to have one gleam of hope or trust in Christ, or one spark of conscious faith. Not that I would date conversion exactly from this time; that I cannot fix. The *time* I know not, the *fact* I would desire to "make sure" more and more.

Having broken the ice by speaking on sacred things with a few at Belmont, it was the less difficult to do so again, and before long I had made a confidante of Miss Cooke (who afterwards became my loved mother). I think it must have been February when she was visiting at Oakhampton at the same time with me and had several conversations with me, each of which made me more earnest and hopeful. At last, one evening, (I remember it was twilight,) I sat on the drawing-room sofa alone with her, and told her again how I longed to know that I was forgiven. She asked me a question which led to the hearty answer that I was sure I desired it above everything on earth, that even my precious papa was nothing in comparison,—brothers and sisters, and all I loved, I could lose everything were it but to attain this. She paused, and then said slowly: "Then Fanny, I think, *I am sure,* it will not be very long before your desire is granted, your hope fulfilled." After a few more words she said: "Why cannot you trust yourself to your Saviour at once? Supposing that now, at this moment, Christ were to come in the clouds of heaven, and take up His redeemed, could you not trust Him? Would not His call, His promise, be enough for you? Could you not commit your soul to Him, to your Saviour, Jesus?" Then came a flash of hope across me, which made me feel literally breathless. I remember how my heart beat. "I *could,* surely," was my response; and I left her suddenly and ran away upstairs to think it out. I flung myself on my knees in my room, and strove to realize the sudden hope. I was very happy at last. I could commit my soul to Jesus. I did not, and need not, fear His coming. I could trust Him with my all for eternity. It was so utterly new to have any bright thoughts about religion that I could hardly believe it could be so, that I had really gained such a step. Then and there, I committed my soul to the Saviour, I do not mean to say without *any* trembling or fear, but I did—and earth and heaven seemed bright from that moment—*I did trust the Lord Jesus.*

For the next few days my happiness continued. Over and over again, I renewed that giving up my soul to the Saviour which had made entrance for the joy. For the *first* time my Bible was *sweet* to me, and the first passage which I distinctly remember reading, in a new and glad light, was the fourteenth and following chapters of St. John's Gospel. We went to Bewdley in the large carriage, and I rode outside, so had no conversation to disturb me. In coming home I took out a little Testament from my pocket, and read those beautiful chapters, feeling how wondrously loving and tender they were, and that now I too might share in their beauty and comfort.

We must again leave the Autobiography, to supply some needed links.

In July 1851 our father married Caroline Ann, daughter of John Cooke, Esq., of Gloucester. One of Frances' poetical letters lovingly describes her satisfaction at this event.

Her great desire to go to school was again gratified, and on the 5th of August, 1851, she went to Powick Court, near Worcester. Being one of the first arrivals, Frances was invited to tea in the drawing-room, and exceedingly astonished Miss Haynes by throwing her arms around her, exclaiming "I am *so* delighted to come to school!" Towards December, however, when enjoying her studies, the intensity of her application was checked by severe erysipelas[1] in her face and head. She was soon removed home, and both school and home studies were prohibited by medical order. I well remember her patience even then, when almost blind, and passing many weeks of precaution, wearisome to her naturally active mind and body. She was so extremely agile in every movement, a very fairy with her golden curls and light step, her dear father calling her his "Little Quicksilver," that to "lie still" was no light trial.

Extracts from letters to Elizabeth Clay, her schoolfellow and life-long correspondent, will here and elsewhere supply an otherwise lost link; they extend over a period of twenty-eight years, and are those referred to in future pages as letters "to E. C."

COLWYN, NORTH WALES, August 1852.

We came here on the 2nd. The change is doing us all good, and we think dear papa's eyes are a little better. Colwyn suits me much better than Llandudno, and I am as well as possible. We find pretty walks *ad infinitum*. The donkey-girl teaches me Welsh. I think I learn it very fast, and I have a Welsh Testament and Prayer Book. At what Mary calls the "Taffy service" I can sing and chant and respond as fully as the natives themselves. . . .

Now for a little quiet bit, to tell you how I am getting on. I wish I were not so impatient as I am, at hearing the (to me) dreadful news that I must on no account go to school again till after Christmas, and perhaps not at all! Oh I am so disappointed! I cannot bear to be ignorant and behind others in learning, so this check is just what I most needed. Still, I am sure it will be all right; and if I receive good things at the hand of such a Father, shall I murmur at such a drawback, which is only to teach me a lesson I must learn after all. . . . How bright everything seems with you! I fear I shall never have such joy, still I do not give up seeking; but there seem so many things in the way. I have been thinking a great deal about my confirmation, though it will not be for two years. It seems such a solemn vow. I fear I should never have strength to keep it; but it is one of my most constant prayers that, if I am spared to be confirmed, I may never act as if I had not been.

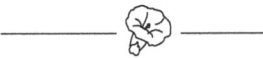

CHAPTER IV.

(1852–1855.)

School at Düsseldorf — Journey to Westphalia — Leaving school — Numero 1. — Autobiography resumed — Life in the pastor's family — The Countess von Lippe — Letter from Pastor Schulze-Berge — The day of confirmation — In Worcester cathedral — "Thine for ever" — Home life — Oakhampton enjoyment — "Welcome home to my father."

IN November she accompanied her parents to Germany.

(*To* E. C.)

GRÄFRATH, November 1852.

. . . We arrived here, that papa might consult the great oculist, Dr. De Leuw. The Hofrath is very good to his poor patients, and attends to them most carefully, and never charges them anything; the village is full of them. The country round Gräfrath must be pretty in summer, and I have found some nice walks. The master of our hotel has a partiality for cats and dogs, and, as they follow him up to bed every night, the gentle patter of fifty-two feet is extremely amusing.

The Hofrath says papa has incipient cataract, which he hopes to be able to disperse. As we need remain here only three weeks, we shall winter in Düsseldorf. I will tell you about my school there, to which I am longing to return. The "Louisenschule" is so called from the Queen of Prussia. There are no private schools here, and all the young ladies seem to attend this school, which numbers one hundred and ten scholars. . . .

---

[1] erysipelas: an acute disease of the skin, streptococcal infection causing red inflammation of the skin and mucous membranes

(To E. C.)

KÖNIGSWINTER, May 13, 1853.

... Having had a month's holiday here, I am going back to the Louisenschule. Fraulein Quincke is a very excellent schoolmistress, and the masters are undoubtedly very good. My music master is extremely particular. I find some harmonic scales by Mendelssohn good practice, but all my pretty English splashy pieces are interdicted. I have joined the drawing class and am so fond of it. The school is under the direction of that good man, Pastor Krafft, so altogether papa has decided to let me have my way and return to school, while he and mamma travel about. I can chatter pretty fast in German, and am so well *in* with all their lesson plans, that I should be sorry not to return. I had an excellent testimony at the Easter examination.

Papa has taken us an excursion into Westphalia, partly in the hope of finding some interesting cousins there, inasmuch as Dr. De Leuw and others assure us our name is Westphalian. But so far we have not succeeded. We were delighted with Münster, the capital, a curious old German town. The market place is surrounded with beautiful arcades of massive stone (instead of wood as at Chester), the light figurate pillars and open stonework are extremely elegant. While mamma rested at the hotel, papa took me to the cathedral. The bells were chiming confusedly. It was a lovely evening after sunset. We went in, and I never saw anything so enchanting. The light, soft and faint, streamed in through the western window, casting upon the pavement, beneath, the shadows of the marble pillars which supported the organ, in a peculiar way. Scattered about were a few solitary worshippers, some before a cross or image, and some with books and tapers. We listened to what seemed to be the sound of very sweet chanting in the choir, but on going nearer it had ceased, and was echoing in another part. It was in fact the sound of the bells, their extremely beautiful tones floating softly through the long aisles of the cathedral. Altogether I cannot describe the impressions made upon one, but I can well imagine how the worshippers, kneeling about the cathedral, might mistake the quiet soothing feeling, which such a scene easily induces, for holy devotion. Popery knows well how to lull and deceive, knows well how to entrap the senses and feelings; and nothing can be better suited to the natural heart than such a religion. Next morning a confirmation was held in one of the churches we happened to visit, and there, for the first time, I saw the elevation of the host. Have you ever seen it? You should for once. It is so saddening, so dreadful, at the tinkling of a bell to see a whole congregation kneel and worship a wafer! Afterwards there was a procession round the church twenty times, with the host, acolytes, and incense, which same incense gives everything the most heathenish look; and, while banners and crosses and pictures of saints passed round, a litany to the saints was chanted, with "*Ora pro nobis*" coming over and over again.

We have made other excursions, etc. How much pleasure I have had, all I wish and all I want; but am I having my good things here? I wish I knew which Master I am serving. Should I let go my hold on Christ so often and so readily, if mine were a true hold on Him? I began so well at school, and thought that earthly learning would not for this time tempt me to forget heavenly things; but day after day I grew more eager for my lessons, and less earnest in seeking Jesus. ... It is pleasant to get good news from England. I am so proud and pleased about my brother Frank. He was ordained at Christmas, and accepted a curacy at Hereford with good Mr. Hanbury. Six months afterwards he was appointed to a minor canonry at Hereford Cathedral; so he is the youngest Minor Canon ever elected in England. My dear brother. Henry has another little daughter; how I love my brothers!

(To E. C.)

OBERCASSEL, September 17, 1853.

... I have left school for ever I suppose, and came here from Düsseldorf. What a suffocating feeling it is, leaving school *for ever*—a period, an era, completely passed and left behind! One feels that childhood is over now, and a sense of tenfold increased responsibility and independence, so to speak, is a weight upon the spirit. The strings seem loosed which have hitherto bound and yet protected one,—a child's obedience and diligence. One's future education and formation of character, whether for good or evil, depends now upon oneself; indeed in a measure one's whole life, one's happiness or misery through the whole pilgrimage, must be very, *very* greatly influenced by, and dependent on, that important time, the first year after leaving school. Many a power of mind must be exercised which, as yet, has had little opportunity to try its flight; judgment and discretion in a thousand things are needful; one must think and act far more for oneself; self-denial must be learnt; oh so much has to be done! As a child, the education of the mind was more in other hands, but now the education of mind and heart is confided to one's own care, and there will be an account to give of how this has been performed. One's spirit is a precious diamond; the rougher cutting work has been done by other hands, now one must undertake its further beautifying oneself, the polishing and grinding needs care and diligence and attention, and if neglected how shall we find an excuse with the great Master Jeweller, who had given the costly stone into our care? Now a different place in life, in society, and in one's own family must be occupied; more is expected from one, many a little burden from which the child is exempt must now be taken up voluntarily. Then the past years, as memory brings the long panorama slowly, one picture after another, before one's view, how spotted, how defiled are even the fairest of these scenes; every year having brought new guilt to be mourned over! But thankfulness must not be forgotten amid the whirl of conflicting feelings and thoughts; not *drops* but rich full measure of happiness filled *my* cup, at least through the greater part of this time; and many blessings, which till now I have scarcely been aware of, ought to make me very grateful to Him, who does indeed let His sun shine on the most unthankful and evil. You experienced all this a year ago, and so will understand it. ...

You will like to know the result of my last examination. Only fancy, when the testimonies were given out at the Louisenschule, amidst heart beating and cheek flushing (especially mine), "Frances Havergal, *Numero Eins!*" broke the still silence of the awed assemblage. You understand German enough to know that *eins* means one. Proud I was, partly on account of being a daughter of Britain. I did not go to sleep till nearly midnight, for pure delight and satisfaction. I can't be satisfied without telling my friend the whole of the history. In the Louisenschule, when a girl has not learnt everything (as you know I did not), she receives merely her testimony but *no number*. This half-year, however, it seems that all the masters, in council assembled, were so very well pleased with the *Engländerin's* (English girl's) papers and conduct that they agreed to break their rule for once, and honour me with *Numero I.*, a thing which they had never done before!

Autobiography Resumed.

The year 1853 was unique in some things. I was at school at Düsseldorf part of it; and stood alone (as far as I know) among the 110 girls. I do not think there was one besides myself who cared for religion. This was very bracing. I felt I must try to walk worthy of my calling, for Christ's sake; and it brought a new and very strong desire to bear witness for my Master, to adorn His doctrine, and to win others for Him. It made me more watchful and earnest than perhaps ever before, for I knew that any slip, in word or deed, would bring discredit on my profession. There was very much enmity to any profession, and I came in for more unkindness than would have been possible in an average English school, where I believe the tone is infinitely higher in every way and the supervision far more strict. Results were: as to my schoolfellows *none*, I do not *know* that I did *any* good among them; though, towards the end of the time, several were certainly disarmed, and left off the small persecutions in which they had delighted, and were even affectionate to me. As to teachers, I had the reward of leaving with the best *zeugniss* in the whole school, and with the highest praise and regret from every one. As to myself, it was a sort of nailing my colours to the mast. I had taken a higher standard than ever before, and had come out more boldly and decidedly on the Lord's side than I might have done for years under ordinary circumstances. Yet the tide ebbed again before many months had passed, and I remember longing to be able to say "O God, my heart is fixed,"—in bitter mourning over its weakness and wavering.

(*Letter to E. C.*)

Obercassel, 1853.

You will want to know, dear Elizabeth, what brings me here. Dear papa's eyes have been lately quite at a standstill as to improvement. He is now with mamma at Heidelberg, leaving me under the care of a good pastor and his wife. Obercassel is a pleasant village on the Rhine. We see the Drachenfels, with a peep into a narrow rock-shut-in valley, through which the Rhine flows from Coblenz. That you may glance into my room, I send herewith a Raphaelistic sketch thereof! Busts of Goethe and Schiller, shelves and table covered with German and French books, etc., etc. It will soon be dusk, and then I go down and take my place by the Pastor Schulze-Berge, who will read aloud, while the pleasant frau pastorin and Lottchen work or knit. Conversational interruptions, serious or amusing, will take their turn; and Goethe, whose life is the subject, will be criticised in every light. Now, is not this very pleasant? I like my quarters amazingly, and am very happy. I get up at five o'clock, breakfast at seven; then I study for four hours. Of course my books are nearly all German, and I write abstracts; I also give one hour to French literature. How I do enjoy myself when I get to the German poets and Universal History, which I dive into with avidity. If anything strikes me, I can always refer to the good pastor. . . .

. . . I have opportunities here of seeing a little of German high life. Close by is the "court" of the Count von Lippe, a family worthy of their rank and title. They live very simply, because they give more than half their income away. The dowager countess is a perfect pattern of a Christian noble lady, also her gentle suffering daughter, Mathilde. The count and his wife are now travelling in Italy. Then there is an adopted daughter, Fraulein von Clondt, whom I like very much. To her I go now regularly from 9 to 10 a.m., to read some German author, which is very nice for me and very kind of her. Besides that, I am constantly invited there to tea or for some excursions, so that I see many of the German aristocracy who are often there. One of the countess's daughters is a princess; I should like her to come while I am here, as I have never spoken to a princess in my life! I am often on the Rhine, and I always row a little, it's such fun! . . . The German language is very easy to me, for except on Sundays, which I spend with the English clergyman of Düsseldorf, I never hear or speak English. It is most absurd now when I begin to speak English; I cannot get to think in it, and keep translating German expressions which seem so much more natural to me to use. I must go to Düsseldorf to visit Fraulein Quincke, whose especially beloved pupil I was. One of her friends, Herr Niessen, an artist, was to paint a portrait of me for her; but he was ill and could not do it till the last day, and so he only sketched one.[1] Not many weeks more till I see you,—hurrah!

(*Pastor Schulze-Berge to M. V. G. H.*)

September 24, 1879.

It is a joy to myself to give you some information about your beloved sister Frances' progress in those studies in which I had the privilege of being her instructor. I had the greatest esteem for her while she was in our house, which only deepened each time I saw her again or heard of her work. She was committed to my care for her studies in 1853, at Obercassel. I instructed her in German composition, literature, and history; I learned to appreciate her rich talents and mental powers, so that the lessons were more pleasure than work. She showed from the first such application, such rare talent, such depth of comprehension, that I can only speak of her progress as extraordinary. She acquired such a knowledge of our most celebrated authors in a short time as even German ladies attain only after much longer study. They were precious moments when I unfolded to her the character of one of our noblest poets and thinkers, and let her have a glimpse into the splendour of his works. Stirred to the depths of her soul, she burst out enthusiastically, "Oh what mental giants, what gifted men, these Germans are!" What imprinted the stamp of nobility upon her whole being, and influenced all her opinions, was her true piety, and the deep reverence she had for her Lord and Saviour, whose example penetrated her young life through and through.

---

[1] This fact about the artist's sketch led to recent search for it. After many failures, Messrs. Elliott and Fry traced it by some artist friends. The portrait was first heard of at Cologne, then at Bonn, and finally found in Fraulein Quincke's possession there, and sent to London.

Seldom have I been more touched than by the news of her early "going home," but she is with Him to whom her soul belonged, her Lord. With the united remembrance of Adelheid (her goddaughter) and all my family,

Yours very sincerely,

PASTOR SCHULZE-BERGE.

In December 1853 Fanny returned with her parents to England. Passing over many months, we come to the solemn and long anticipated time of her confirmation in Worcester Cathedral, by Dr. Henry Pepys, Bishop of Worcester.

[FROM HER SEALED PAPERS.]

July 17, 1854.

Now, on the evening of my confirmation day, I will look back upon it, and briefly endeavour to write some little record of it, for my own interest and profit in coming years.

Satan has been busy with me all this day. I rose early; he then tried to persuade me to put off, little by little, my reading of the Bible and prayer, and to some extent succeeded in making me do other minor things first, and in preoccupying my mind. At length I knelt. I looked back on all my past life, and tried to thank God for all; but the praise was not so fervent as it should have been, nor the prayer so earnest, for a blessing not only on this day but on my future life; and my soul was grieved at this coldness. But, ere I rose, my heart did seem a little warmer and Jesus a little nearer. . . .

In the procession to Worcester Cathedral Ellen Wakeman was my companion. On reaching our seat very near the rails, I sunk on my knees, and for the first time to-day the thought of "whose I am" burst upon me, and I prayed "my God, oh, my *own* Father, Thou blessed Jesus my *own* Saviour, Thou Holy Spirit my *own* Comforter," and I stopped. It scarcely seemed right for me to use the language of such strong assurance as this, but yet I did not retract. The Litany only was chanted; and, though my thoughts would fain have flown with each petition heavenward, yet every little thing seemed *trebly* a distraction, and the chanting was too often the subject of my thoughts. My heart beat very fast, and my breath almost seemed to stop, while the solemn question was being put by the bishop. Never I think did I feel my own weakness and utter helplessness so much. I hardly dared answer; but "the Lord is my strength" was graciously suggested to me, and then the words quickly came from (I trust) my very heart; "Lord, I cannot without Thee, but oh, with Thy almighty help,—I DO."

I believe that the solemnity of what had just been uttered, with its exceeding comprehensiveness, was realized by me as far as my mind could grasp it. I thought a good deal of the words "now unto Him that is able to keep you from falling"; and that was my chief comfort. We were the first to go up, and I was the fourth or fifth on whom the bishop laid his hands. At first, the thought came as to who was kneeling next to me, but then the next moment I felt alone, unconscious of my fellow candidates, of the many eyes fixed upon us, and the many thoughts of and prayers for me, alone with God and His chief minister. My feelings when his hands were placed on my head (and there was solemnity and earnestness in the very touch and manner) I cannot describe, they were too confused; but when the words "Defend, O Lord, this Thy child with Thy heavenly grace, that she may continue Thine for ever, and daily increase in Thy Holy Spirit more and more, until she come unto Thy everlasting kingdom," were solemnly pronounced, if ever my heart followed a prayer it did then, if ever it thrilled with earnest longing not unmixed with joy, it did at the words "Thine for ever." But, as if in *no* feeling I might or could rest satisfied, there was still a longing " oh that I desired this *yet* more earnestly, that I believed it *yet* more fully." We returned to our seats, and for some time I wept, why I hardly know, it was not grief, nor anxiety, nor exactly joy. About an hour and a quarter elapsed before all the candidates had been up to the rails; part of the time being spent in meditation on the double transaction which was now sealed, and in thinking that I was now more than ever His; but I still rather sadly wished that I could *feel* more. Many portions of Scripture passed through my mind, particularly part of Romans 8. . . . Each time that the "Amen" was chanted in a more distant part of the cathedral, after the "Defend" had been pronounced, it seemed as though a choir of angels had come down to witness, and pour out from their pure spirits a deep and felt "Amen."

The bishop pronounced the closing blessing so very impressively that it was like soothing balm to me, and the thought came "why should I doubt that my soul will indeed receive the blessing which God's minister is thus giving? why did God appoint him thus to bless if it were to be a mere idle form? May not His blessing accompany them, and . . ."

The paper was not finished, nor can any account of her first communion be found. In her manuscript book of poems she wrote:

"THINE FOR EVER."

Oh! "Thine for ever," what a blessed thing
To be for ever His who died for me!
My Saviour, all my life Thy praise I'll sing,
Nor cease my song throughout eternity.

In the Cathedral, July 17, 1854.

She always kept the anniversary of her confirmation day. When at Celbridge (1856), her juvenile instructor in Hebrew (John H. Shaw) remembers on one of these occasions missing her at their hour for study, and that she spent most of the day in holy retirement. So lately as 1876 and 1877 she seems to have renewed her confirmation vow, in the following verses.

A COVENANT.

Now, Lord, I give myself to Thee,
I would be wholly Thine;
As Thou hast given Thyself to me,
And Thou art wholly mine;
Oh take me, seal me as Thine own,
Thine altogether—Thine alone.

(July 1876.)

Only for Jesus! Lord, keep it for ever,
  Sealed on the heart and engraved on the life!
Pulse of all gladness, and nerve of endeavour,
  Secret of rest, and the strength of our strife!

(July, 1877.)

We now return to her home life after her confirmation in 1854.

She carefully kept up all her studies, her abstracts in German, French, and English showing the rapidity and variety of her reading. With her father's help she acquired sufficient knowledge of Greek to enjoy studying the New Testament. Her manuscript book contains twenty-five original German and English poems, beside poetical enigmas and charades, which she contributed to various pocket books under the name of "Sabrina" and "Zoide," and for which she often obtained prizes, the money thus gained being sent to the Church Missionary Society.

Oakhampton, May 14, 1855.

Here I am in the height of enjoyment with my brother Frank. Little Miriam's absence is a drawback. My Evelyn is ill; but she is very gentle and patient, indeed I never saw a sick child so utterly without fretfulness. She is lovely, a perfect sunbeam, with golden wavy hair. . . .

How rife everything in spring seems with beautiful emblems. I don't mean such as are already down in poetry books, but those wildly, lovely, intangible similes which flit across the mind, like the shadows of a flying bird!

Our dear father had again been to Gräfrath in 1855, and returned with his eyesight much better. Frances writes:

Is not this glorious? Such sudden improvement we hardly dared to hope for. We shall see papa in the reading desk on Sunday, where he has not been for nearly four years! Oh, we are so happy. Papa and mamma came home on Saturday. We welcomed them in style. I made a triumphal arch over the hall-door with flowers and greenery, over the study door papa's crest in flowers, and over the dining-room a banner with the words in rosebuds and leaves, 'Welcome Home.' Oh it was so nice that dear papa was able to *see* it; directly he came in he knelt down with us all, and offered such beautiful prayer or rather praise!

CHAPTER V.

(1856–1860.)

Ireland — F. R. H. and the Irish girls — Hebrew studies — Grateful memory of Bible class teachings — "Nearer heaven!" — Chapters learnt — "Touching the hem" — Leaving St. Nicholas' — The loving teacher — Last page in Sunday Scholar's Register — Welcome to Shareshill.

An Irish school-girl pens the following recollections of meeting F. R. H. on her first visit to Celbridge Lodge, Ireland, May 1856.

Five o'clock p.m. was the hour appointed for the elder girls from the school to arrive at the Lodge. Mrs. Shaw met us at the hall door with gentle words to each, and then brought us into the drawing-room, we being in a great state of delight at the thought of seeing "the little English lady." In a few seconds Miss Frances, carolling like a bird, flashed into the room! Flashed! yes, I say the word advisedly, flashed in like a burst of sunshine, like a hillside breeze, and stood before us, her fair sunny curls falling round her shoulders, her bright eyes dancing, and her fresh sweet voice ringing through the room. I shall never forget that afternoon, never! I sat perfectly spellbound as she sang chant and hymn with marvellous sweetness, and then played two or three pieces of Handel, which thrilled me through and through. She finished with singing her father's tune (Hobah) to "The Church of our fathers." She shook hands with each, and said with a merry laugh: "the next time I come to Ireland I think we must get up a little singing class, and then you know you must all sing with me!"

As we walked home down the shady avenue one and another said: "Oh, isn't she lovely? and doesn't she sing like a born angel!" "I love her, I do; and I'd follow her every step of the way back to England if I could." "Oh, she's a real Colleen Bawn!"

Another of the class felt, all the time, that there must be the music of God's own love in that fair singer's heart, and that so there was joy in her face, joy in her words, joy in her ways. And the secret cry went up from that young Irish heart: "Lord, teach me, even me, to know and love Thee too."

On her next visit to Ireland the singing class was formed. An invalid remembers at this time her "tender lovingkindness in lonely days of sorrow and suffering. It was Miss Frances who first taught me Greek, which was *such* an interest and help to me, and afterwards she gave me Hebrew lessons too. Truly can I say, 'I thank my God on every remembrance of thee!'"

Frances much enjoyed the study of Hebrew this summer with J. H. S. During a pleasant expedition through county Wicklow one of our party was a learned Hebrew scholar. It rather discomfited our good brother-in-law that Frances' attention seemed deeper in investigating his knowledge of Hebrew psalms and grammar than in the surrounding geography of glens and passes. One other incident of her Irish visits was her attendance at a Bible class, conducted by the Rev. M. J. Bickerstaffe (now Vicar of Cookley). Side by side with the tiniest children Frances took her seat, and long afterwards referred to the pleasure and benefit of his instructions.

September 20, 1869.

Dear Mr. Bickerstaffe,—

.... I am so sorry not to be well enough to hear you preach this morning. Your sermons and Bible classes in 1865 were more real help to me than any I ever heard. I always look gratefully back to them as having done more to open my eyes to the "wondrous things" in God's word than any other human instrumentality.

Yours affectionately and gratefully.

The year 1858 had not much incident. She mentions her pleasure in listening to her father's Lent lectures on the Queen of Sheba, and tells her friend E——: "the lectures are beautiful; you could not form an idea of their fulness and freshness without hearing them. These typical sermons are what papa specially excels in!" She writes of

—gleams and glimpses, but oh to be filled with joy and the Holy Ghost! Oh, why cannot I trust Him fully? How very sweet those words are, "I write unto you, little children, because your sins are forgiven you for His name's sake." They have comforted me, for I am but a little child, only a babe in the spiritual life, and this seems so tenderly addressed to *such*. But oh that I could grow up in Him! Sometimes I have felt almost happy in trying to realize what you write to me about, and at times I have gone on praying and pouring out all to Him, till time seemed forgotten, and I could scarcely rise and come back to earthly things. Once I had a strange thrill of joy at a passing, and may-be foolish, thought. You know how suffering I have been. Well, one evening, passing the looking-glass in the twilight, I caught sight of myself rather flushed, and I thought it looked like the hectic spot that foretells mortal disease. I know I am not in the remotest degree consumptive, but for an instant I thought it might be so. Oh the extraordinary thrill of delight the idea brought, that possibly I might be nearer heaven than I thought! It was almost ecstatic gladness; and then a chill of disappointment came when my common sense told me it could not be so! But, in whatever way or time death comes to either of us, may our lamps be trimmed and burning....

From this time her letters tell of

"The tremulous gleams of early days,
The first faint thrills of love and praise,
Vibrating fitfully."

She seems to have read and learned the Scriptures systematically with her friend E. C. In this I had joined them, and remember that in our country walks Frances repeated alternate verses with me. She knew the whole of the Gospels, Epistles, Revelation, the Psalms, and Isaiah, and the Minor Prophets she learnt in later years. At this time she was taking the titles of Christ for her daily searchings and remarks. "Yesterday I took Christ our Advocate, it is one of the sweet titles. Alpha and Omega will be a very suitable one for Sunday. I like to think about the Lord Jesus as He is in Himself, not *only* in relation to myself."

Incidental traces of holy walking as well as holy writing come out naturally; *e.g.*, "I said something yesterday, dear Elizabeth, which I much regret, though thoughtlessly and not intentionally uttered. I thought, after, it seemed an imputation upon —; the faintest impression of which I would remove at once from your mind. Perhaps you did not notice it; but I did, and grieved that I said it." Her home life was beautiful, though often only One knew the self-restraint and the self-denial of actions, trivial in themselves, but springing from the desire to please God. I remember her refusing to go with me for a pleasant visit to Oakhampton, because she would not leave our dear mother alone, adding "if I can only go errands it will be of some use."

(*To* E. C.)

August.

As time passes on, dear Elizabeth, so does my hope strengthen that I really took a step onward when with you in the spring. It was then that (like the woman in the press) I was enabled to come and touch the hem of His garment. It was then that the truth made me free. I have lost that weary bondage of doubt, and almost despair, which chained me for so many years. I have the same sins and temptations as before, and I do not strive against them more than before, and it is often just as hard work. But, whereas I could not see why *I should* be saved, I now cannot see why I should not be saved if Christ died for all. On that word I take my stand and *rest there*. I still wait for the hour when I believe He will reveal Himself to me more directly; but it is the quiet waiting of present trust, not the restless waiting of anxiety and danger. *His death* is really my confidence, and I have tasted the sweetness of one new thing, *praise*!

In 1860 our father resigned the living of St. Nicholas, but not before the bishop had kindly promised that his successor should be his much esteemed curate and friend, the Rev. Charles Bullock.

Many parting gifts from the parishioners flowed in, both for the Rector and his wife, whose organizing powers and activity had much endeared her to the parish. A most troublesome class of adult boys was quite a trophy of what loving words and gentle rule could effect, and their parting address and present to her came with more costly gifts. One of her class became a Scripture reader, another an ordained minister of our Church, and all brought forth good fruit in after years.

Frances writes to E. C.:

What could be more conducive to spiritual improvement than what God has sent me lately, besides innumerable mercies, extra gratifications in many ways; all these beautiful testimonials to my precious papa, and lovely ones to dear mamma, and my own undeserved share in them, and my success in writing (for I have just received a formal application from the Editor of *Good Words* for poetical contributions).[1] On the other hand I have just enough bodily infirmity to keep me mindful and humble. Gold watches for dear Maria and myself came yesterday. The inscriptions are both the same inside the cases: "From the parishioners of St. Nicholas, Worcester, March 1860." The teachers and children of the Sunday School have also sent us books, nicely chosen by Mr. Bullock. One special little token from my own children I shall ever treasure.

Her Sunday School work was a loved employment. In the neatly kept register, entitled "My Sunday Scholars, from 1846 to 1860," each child's birthday, entrance date, occurrences in their home, general impressions of their character, and subsequent events in their life, are all carefully noted. While absent for a few weeks, Frances writes to them, and says: "My dear children have kept up quite a correspondence with me, and printing all my answers is quite a work of time and patience, but one I do not grudge. Some of their letters are very sweet and encouraging, and all are at least affectionate and interesting. At one time I had desperately uphill work, for mine was then the worst class in the school, and, out of fourteen, only a small minority were even hopeful. Sunday after Sunday I absolutely cry about them! Still, for some I thank God and take courage."

---

[1] See "A Line Left Out," in Appendix, page 343. Her well known hymn, "I gave My life for thee," first appeared in *Good Words*. It was written in Germany, 1858. She had come in weary, and sat down opposite a picture with this motto. At once the lines flashed upon her, and she wrote them in pencil on a scrap of paper. Reading them over, they did not satisfy her. She tossed them into the fire, but they fell out untouched! Showing them some months after to her father, he encouraged her to preserve them, and wrote the tune "Baca" specially for them. [See page 343 of this book.]

"MY SUNDAY SCHOLAR'S REGISTER."

[*The last page.*]

I did not think when I ruled this page that it would be unfilled. Yet so it is, and the last of my dear second class fills its first space. He who appointeth the bounds of our habitation has, in manifest providence, removed our own after fifteen years' sojourn. And it will probably be some time ere I again have a regular class to care for, as other claims will fill my Sunday hours.

Among all my St. Nicholas memories, none will be fonder or deeper than my class. I cannot tell any one how I loved them, I should hardly be believed; no one in the parish, either rich or poor, called forth the same love that they did. Neither could I tell how bitter and grievous any misbehaviour among them was to me, no one knows the tears they have cost me; and because no one guessed at the depth of either the love or the sorrow, I had but little sympathy under disappointments with them. I am wrong in one thing I know, but cannot help it; the feeling that, though I may have a very sincere love and interest in other children, yet I should never be able to give any future class the same intensity of affection which these have won and some of them have reciprocated.

It has been to my own soul a means of grace. Often, when cold and lifeless in prayer, my nightly intercession for them has unsealed the frozen fountain, and the blessings sought for them seemed to fall on myself.

Often and often have my own words to them been as a message to myself of warning or peace. My only regret is that I did not spend more time in preparing my lessons for them, not more on their account than my own, for seldom have Bible truths seemed to reach and touch me more than when seeking to arrange and simplify them for my children. Therefore, I thank God that these children have been entrusted to me!

For some time past several of them have come to me, once a week, for separate reading and prayer. These times I have enjoyed very much. I rather dissuaded than otherwise, unless any real desire after salvation was manifested; and I do think that this was so far effectual that nearly all of those who did come were, at least at the time, truly in earnest on the great question. I mark * the regular, × the occasional comers. Nearly two years have already passed since they were "my children," and I cannot say that my love and interest have yet diminished. I went to Oakhampton at Midsummer 1859, and on my return relinquished them with great secret regret for another class. I have one token of their love; given me, not by the then existing "2nd class," but by those of both 1st and 2nd who were "my children." This I treasure for their sakes, yet the remembrance of their love is more than its outward sign.

I trust it has been *true* bread which I have cast upon these waters; my Saviour knows, and He only, my earnest longings that these little ones should be His own. I think I am quite content now that others should see the fruit, so that it be but truly borne, that others should enter into my feeble and wanting labours. But, in dear papa's words, I do most fervently pray,

"May all whose names are written here
In the Lamb's Book of Life appear!"

F. R. H., March 1860.

Leaving St. Nicholas was to Frances a strange mixture of sorrow and thankfulness, "because I do care more for papa and his health than for anything else in all the whole world! But it is not a trifle to leave the many, rich and poor, with whom one has necessarily become more or less entwined in a way which none but a clergyman's family can. Yet I hope dear papa will find comparative rest and strength in consequence, by going to the little country parish of Shareshill. Papa is so very much to me, so much more than all besides! He has been very ill again, and this puts an end to all ideas of farewell sermons or visits. It is wonderfully thrilling to see him in illness, such utter peacefulness, such grand conceptions of God's absolute sovereignty in everything, such quiet rejoicing in His will, be it what it may; such shining trust in Him, in and for everything, personal or parochial."

The removal to Shareshill proved beneficial, and the welcome of the parishioners was pleasing and encouraging. Frances writes: "The first step, in the way of improvement at Shareshill, has been to abolish the Sunday post; to obtain this, the inhabitants were, as required, unanimous." This subject was deeply felt by her, ever sympathising, as she did, with the men deprived of their Sunday rest; and she often grieved that some of her Christian friends did not take it up. Among the subjects upon which she intended writing, when called home in 1879, was "Sunday Postal Burdens." And, in a letter the same year, she writes: "I do think we Church of England are more conscientious about Sunday post than some others. I was delighted when visiting 'B. M.' to see with the notice of post times (in the hall) 'no delivery or despatch on Sunday.' 'No manner of work' must include postal delivery, and it is not right to ignore it; it grieves me when some double-first-class Christians do not consider the subject."

CHAPTER VI.

(1861–1869.)

Oakhampton — A new power — Musical gifts — Deep borings — Subjects for prayer — Hiller's commendation — Remarkable power of harmonizing — Welcome to Winterdyne — Stormy petrelism — Sent empty away — Calmer waters — Joining Young Women's Christian Association — London — "Guess my birthday treat!" — Signor Randegger — Epitome of his first singing lesson — New home at Leamington — How poems came — My Evelyn! — "The Two Rings" — Weary and sad — First sight of Alpine mountains.

IN February 1861, by the wish of her sister and her brother-in-law Henry Crane, Frances undertook the instruction of her two youngest nieces, and made Oakhampton her second home. Her father approved of this plan, because he thought it would prevent her from pursuing the severe studies so prejudicial to her health. The lesson hours were very short, owing to the temperament of both teacher and pupils, and she had many and long changes of scene, at the seaside, at home and abroad. She entered with zest into the recreations of her young companions, riding and scrambling, swimming and skating, croquet and chess, each in its turn, and excelled in them all. Her needlework was exquisite, from the often despised darning to the most delicate lace work and embroidery. How she redeemed her time these few lines will prove: "Stirring you up, dearie, to mental improvement is no new subject to me. I know, by my own teaching days, how very much might be learnt in all the odds and ends of time, how (*e.g.*) I learnt all the Italian verbs while my nieces were washing their hands for dinner after our walk, because I could be ready in five minutes less time than they could." The faithful old nurse well remembers "vexing over Miss Frances's hard studying, and that she found her at those Latin books long before breakfast."

Her one great object was the education of her nieces for eternity, not for time only; and not merely religious knowledge, but the realities of faith and holy living, were dwelt upon.

From the close of her Autobiography, darkness seems often to have clouded her path. From time to time she writes:

I had hoped that a kind of table-land had been reached in my journey, where I might walk awhile in the light, without the weary succession of rock and hollow, crag and morass, stumbling and striving; but I seem borne back into all the old difficulties of the way, with many sin-made aggravations. I think the great root of all my trouble and alienation, is that I do not now make an unreserved surrender of myself to God; and until this is done I shall know no peace. I am sure of it. I have so much to regret: a greater dread of the opinion of worldly friends, a loving of the world, and proportionate cooling in heavenly desire and love. A power utterly new and unexpected was given me (singing and composition of music), and rejoicing in this I forgot the Giver, and found such delight in this that other things paled before it. It need not have been so; and, in better moments, I prayed that if it were indeed hindering me the gift of song might be withdrawn. And now that through my ill health it is so, and that the pleasure of public applause when singing in the Philharmonic concerts is not again to exercise its delicious delusion, I do thank Him who heard my prayer. But I often pray in the dark, as it were, and feel no response from above. Is this to test me? Oh that I may be preserved from giving up in despair, and yielding, as I so often do, to the floodtide enemy.

I want to make the most of my life and to do the best with it, but here I feel my desires and motives need much purifying; for, even where all would sound fair enough in words, an element of self, of lurking pride, may be detected. Oh, that He would indeed purify me and make me white at any cost! No one professing to be a Christian at all could possibly have had a more cloudy, fearing, doubting, sinning, and wandering heart history than mine has been through many years.

The first part of this year (1865) I was very poorly, and on the old régime of having to give up everything, Sunday school and Saturday evening class, visiting, music, etc. It was very trying to me, specially so because I had rather built upon being stronger, and several points of interest had arisen which made me feel the more being shut off from all. But it was very good for me; I was able to feel thankful for it, and to be glad that God had taken me in hand as it were. I do not think I would have chosen otherwise than as He ordered it for me; but it seems as if my spiritual life would never go without weights, and I dread needing more discipline.

Deep borings, even down into darksome depths, often precede the supply of unfailing springs of refreshing water. Thus my dear sister knew much of doubt and gloom, so that she might be able to comfort others and reveal to them God's deep teachings in the darkness. Then, when she afterwards found such joy in the wells of salvation, she drew forth these teachings, refreshing other weary and thirsty ones with her words of sympathy both in poetry and prose.

It may be useful to copy the paper kept in her Bible, showing how she arranged the subjects of her prayers.

For daily Morning Prayer.

Watchfulness. Guard over temper. Consistency. Faithfulness to opportunities. For the Holy Spirit. For a vivid love to Christ.

Mid-day Prayer.

Earnestness of spirit in desire, in prayer, and in all work. Faith, hope, love.

Evening Prayer.

Forgiveness. To see my sinfulness in its true light. Growth in grace. Against morning sleepiness as hindrance to time for prayer.

The initials of all her relatives and friends are distributed to each day, and various items of intercession added, such as:

That my life may be laid out to the best advantage as to God's glory and others' good. For the Church Missionary Society and Zenana work. For success and usefulness with my subscribers. For the poor whom I visit. For the Irish Society. Guidance and (if it is God's will) success as to music. For my Sunday school class. For the servants.

In the winter of 1865–6 Frances revisited her German friends, and also resided some time with her parents at Bonn.

Having composed many songs, she was anxious for some verdict on their merit. The following letter describes her interview with Hiller, the German musician.

CLAPTON SQUARE, February 1, 1866.
DEAR MIRIAM,—

I must take up my history where I left off, and give you the Cologne story at last. To begin at the beginning, Elizabeth C. told the Schulzeberges of my composing, and so they were curious about it and wanted me to go to the Musical Academy of Cologne. As I declared that out of the question, they hoped I would go to Ferdinand Hiller, whom they consider the greatest living composer and authority, and show him my songs. I shrunk from this because I expected nothing but utter quenching from such a man; still I thought that after all I might as well know the worst, and if he thought scorn of all I had done, that would decide me to waste no more time over it; while, if I got a favourable verdict, if ever opportunity should arise of prosecuting the *study* of composition, I should do so with a clearer conscience and better hopes. To my utter amazement, papa quite urged me to go, and a pleasant mirage of a possible musical term at Cologne screwed my courage up to writing to Hiller, who replied kindly, and made an appointment with me. I went with mamma, such a queer way among the Rhine wharfs, and through narrow streets scarcely wide enough for the droschky to pass, till we emerged in a more open part, and found Hiller's abode. He is a small elderly man, quiet in manner, of handsome and peculiar Jewish physiognomy (he is a Jew), with a forehead remarkably like papa's, and terribly clever looking eyes; I think one would single him out as a genius among any number. He was in a double room full of musical litter, with a handsome grand piano in the middle. He received us very politely, and asked me a few questions (he is a man of few words), and then took my book of songs and sat down to *read* it through, giving me a volume of poetry to amuse myself with meanwhile. You may imagine I didn't read much! He made no remark till he was about three quarters through, when he turned and said: "What instruction have you had?" I told him of Haterley's having corrected my first six songs, and that I had a musical father to whom I occasionally referred difficult points, and with whom I had musical talk in general. "I do not care anything about that," said he, "I mean what regular musical course have you gone through, and under what professor?" I told him I had done nothing of the sort. He looked very hard at me, as if to see if I was telling the truth, and then turned back to my music, saying, "In that case I find this very remarkable!" When he had finished he delivered his verdict, the worst part first. He said my melodies bore the stamp of talent, not of genius. "In the early works of great composers," he said, "one comes across things that startle and strike you; ideas so utterly fresh and novel that you feel there is great creative power. I do not find this in your melodies; they are not bad; on the contrary I find them very pleasing and many really very good, but they are thoroughly English in character and type; I do not consider that English melodies rank highest. But as for your harmonies, I must say I am astonished. It is something singular to find such grasp of the subject, such power of harmonization, except where there has been long and thorough study and instruction; here I can give almost unlimited praise." I told him my question was (for I thought I would take a high standard at once) not, had I talent enough to make music a mere pleasure to myself and my friends? but had I enough to make it worth while to devote myself to music as a serious thing, as a life work? Was there promise enough to make it an advisable investment of my life, in case I wished to do so? He said: "Sincerely and unhesitatingly I can say that you *have*." I remarked how much I should like to study at Cologne, and under himself. He said he should like to have the training of me; but, if distance were a difficulty, there were reliable men in London, and he would recommend his friend Macfarren. But I was to go to no second-rate man, that would be simply no use to me; I could only gain the polish and "form" which my work wanted, from some one really first-rate. He recommended me a book on harmony (which I procured in Cologne), and then wrote a few lines to papa, saying he had found a good deal of musical talent in my compositions, and that "but a short time would be sufficient to place me in a state to give a good form to the musical ideas with which I was gifted." I did not expect all this; and though I shall not do anything at present, it is pleasant to know I have a talent, which I may some day develop to some purpose, for I never quite believed what Dr. Marshall said about it, and I thought, if I had the talent he said I had, I should *feel* cleverer, somehow, than I do. Papa is vexed because when Hiller asked "Spielen sie gut?" (do you play well?) I replied simply "No, not well," because I thought he would judge by a professional standard. Papa says I ought to have then offered to play one of my things, but I had not the pluck or the presence of mind. . . . I supposed you would like to hear *all* about Hiller, else it seems conceited to have written so much.

Now for the home journey to Lille and a pleasant visit to Mons. and Madame V——'s. Their country house is about a mile out of the town. . . . It was pleasant to meet old friends, and it is quite fascinating to get, also, a spice of fresh characters and life. Next morning Mons. V. took me about the lower rooms, and gave me an amusing description of Lille life. He is a sort of chieftain of the clan, which consists of about 270 nephews and nieces, and their children. He keeps them all in order. "On a grand peur de mon oncle Emile," says he; "if I see what I do not like I lecture them de manière qu'on s'en souviendra." But, on the other hand, "mon oncle Emile" is rich, and can be very gracious, and is worth keeping on good terms with. Every Sunday there are thirty-eight who "have the right" to dine with him, and every Wednesday evening he receives a wider circle in a large *galerie,* glass above and all round, like an immense enclosed verandah, so pretty with creepers and fancy plants all about. It overlooks his orangery and greenhouses, ornamental water with two bridges, pretty trees, a most charming view altogether. . . .

Such a good crossing from Calais; the sea quite glassy! I leaned over the side and watched the foam and curl of the water behind the paddles, and wrote verses ("Travelling Thoughts") in my account book. I was able to *see* the white cliffs of Dover for the first time, and was almost sorry to leave the boat. . . .

Your loving sister.

It may not be out of place here to mention that such was the strength of her musical memory, that she would play through Handel, much of Beethoven and Mendelssohn, without any notes. A pupil of Beethoven thought her rendering of the Moonlight Sonata perfect; her touch was instinct with soul, as also was her singing.

During her stay at Oakhampton her brother-in-law engaged Dr. Wm. Marshall to give her singing lessons; and she attended the meetings of the Philharmonic Society at Kidderminster, of which he was the conductor. The practice of sacred music was an extreme gratification to her, and she soon became a valued solo singer. Her rendering of Mendelssohn's "Woe unto them," "But the Lord is mindful of His own," are remembered as peculiarly effective, though it was in Handel's music that she more particularly delighted.

The ease with which Frances constantly versified family events is shown in the following lines, written when Mr. and Mrs. Shaw left Ireland, for their English home at Winterdyne.

WELCOME TO WINTERDYNE.

(For December 14th, 1866.)

Francie and Willie, welcome to you!
   Alfred and Alice, welcome too!
To an English home and English love
Welcome each little Irish dove:
Never again we hope to be
Kept apart by an angry sea.
A thousand welcomes, O darlings mine,
   When we see you at Winterdyne.
Welcome all to a warm new nest,
   Just the place for our doves to rest,

Through the oaks and beeches looking down
On the winding valley and quaint old town,
Where ivy green on the red rock grows,
And silvery Severn swiftly flows,
With an extra sparkle and glitter and shine
    Under the woods of Winterdyne.
On a quiet evening in lovely spring,
    In the tall old elms the nightingales sing;
Under the forest in twilight grey
I have heard them more than a mile away,
Sweeter and louder and far more clear
Than any thrush you ever did hear;
Perhaps when the evenings grow long and fine
    They will sing to you in Winterdyne.
Little to sadden, and nothing to fear;
    Priest, and Fenian, never come here;
Only the sound of the Protestant bells
Up from the valley pleasantly swells,
And a beautiful arch, to church, is made
Under the sycamore avenue's shade;
You pass where its arching boughs entwine,
    Out of the gates of Winterdyne.
Welcome to merry old England! And yet
    We know that old Ireland you will not forget;
Many a thought and prayer will fly
Over the mountains of Wales, so high,
Over the forest and over the sea,
To the home which no longer yours must be.
But farewells are over, O darlings mine,
    Now it is Welcome to Winterdyne!

Her own words will continue the record of her inner life in the year 1866.

Few things have a more salutary effect upon me than reading secular biographies. For, successful or unsuccessful alike, "vanity of vanities" seems the truest characteristic of every life not devoted to the very highest aim. "Queens of Society," "Autobiography of Louis Spohr," and others, have left this feeling strongly upon me, and have been auxiliary in making me wish that my life may be laid out for Him, whose it is by right. Oh, that He may make me a vessel sanctified and meet for the Master's use! I look at trial and training of every kind in this light, not its effect upon oneself *for* oneself, but in its gradual *fitting* of me to do the Master's work. So, in very painful spiritual darkness or conflict, it has already comforted me to think that God might be leading me through strange dark ways, so that I might afterward be His messenger to some of His children in similar distress. My ill health this summer has been very trying to me. I am held back from much I wanted to do in every way, and have had to lay poetizing aside. And yet such open doors seemed set before me. Perhaps this check is sent that I may consecrate what I do more entirely. I have a curious vivid sense, not merely of my verse faculty in general being given me, but also of every separate poem or hymn, nay every line, being given. It is peculiarly pleasant thus to take it as a direct gift, not a matter of effort, but purely involuntarily. . . .

I suppose that God's crosses are often made of most unexpected and strange material. Perhaps trial must be felt keenly, or it would not be powerful enough as a medicine in the hands of our beloved Healer; and I think it has been a medicine to me latterly. You may wonder that I write thus, when I was so merry at L——; but, among the best gifts of God to me, I count a certain stormy petrelism of nature, which seems to enable me to skim any waves when I am not under them. I have an elasticity which often makes me wonder at myself, a power of throwing myself into any present interest or enjoyment, though the sorrow is only suspended not removed.

But once I seemed permitted to suffer mentally in an unmitigated sort of way, which I never knew before. Perhaps to teach me how to feel for others who have not that stormy petrelism which bears me through most things. For that forsook me utterly, and I felt crushed and forsaken of all or any help or cheer, to an extent I never felt before.

I wish I rejoiced more, not only on my own account, "but if I may so say, on *His,* for surely I should praise Him more by both lip and life. Mine has been such a shady Christian life, yet "He led them forth by the right way" must somehow be true here, though I don't see how. I ought to make one exception; I have learned a real sympathy with others walking in darkness, and sometimes it has seemed to help me to help them.

I send you this text, Matthew 25:40, and I want to let it brighten all your work; but one can never come to the end of the graciousness of it. Some months ago, I called on one of my dear old women in Worcester. She talked of the King; and, coming away, I felt impelled to give her something which I had not intended for her, and knew I could not afford without a trifling self-denial. She took it silently, paused, and then said, with a simple sweet solemnity, "Inasmuch!" Well, ever since I have revelled in that wonderful "Inasmuch." Only think of His really considering all our poor little services as done unto Him! And this is quite apart from what we consider success or results. It is not only spiritual ministrations, but all other little kindnesses. How one would have liked to have been one of the women who ministered unto Him, but it is so marvellously gracious of Him to give you and me, to wit, opportunities of doing what He considers the same thing. . . . You may think it strange, but I have long almost shrunk from going to the sacrament, dreading the being sent empty away. Oh, if He would but grant me my request just once—that I might "taste and see!" Communion Sundays are so often my saddest days; great tension of feeling, longing unsatisfied desire, and sorrowful pleading, followed by the reaction of miserable apathy. It is only one or two who know about my clouds, though many know what I *believe* about sunshine. . . . Sunday is over. "Sent empty away." Just *empty*, no other word seems to express it; not full of anything. I would rather even have been full of distress than thus empty. Not one sweet verse or comforting thought seemed given me. All the beautiful service seemed to pass through the ear and never reach my heart. Oh, if He would only show me "wherefore He contendeth with me." It has brought me to the terrible old feeling, "how can I be one of His sheep if I never hear the Shepherd's voice, if He never meets me where He meets others?"

Her nieces Evelyn and Constance went to school in 1866–7; and, in consequence, Frances then left Oakhampton, and always afterwards resided at home.

(*From F. R. H.'s manuscript papers, May* 1867.)

It seems as if the Lord had led me into a calmer and more equable frame of mind; not joy, but peace. And texts light up to me very pleasantly sometimes. Why should I not take for granted all I find in the Bible? why should I hesitate and tremble over it, as I have been doing for years? I have been appropriating all the promises with a calm sort of twilight happiness, waiting for a clearer light to show me their full beauty and value.

It does seem to me that "free grace" does not mean there is *nothing* on our side. We may phrase it "coming," "accepting," "believing," "touching the hem"; but there is something which these words represent, which is necessary to salvation; and then comes the question, have *I* this condition? Yet as soon as *I* in any form comes in, there is shadow upon the light. Still, this shadow need not fall when the eye is fixed upon Christ as the Substitute, the Lamb slain; then all is clear. But it is in reading, when one's heart leaps at some precious promise made to the children of God, that a cold check comes, "am *I* one of them? what is my title?" Answer, "Ye are all the children of God by faith in Jesus Christ." Have I faith? Once introduce that *I*, and you get bewildered between faith and feeling. When I go on and grapple with the difficulty, it comes to this. As far as I know, I have come to Jesus, not once but many times. I have knelt, and literally prostrated myself before Him, and told Him all, that I have no other hope but what His *written* word *says* He did and said, that I know it is true, that the salvation it tells of is just *what* I want and *all* I want, and that my heart goes out to it, and that I do accept it; that I do not fully grasp it, but I *cling* to it; that I want to be His only and entirely, now and for ever.

(*The last entry.*)

I have been so happy lately, and the words "Thou hast put gladness in my heart" I can use, as true of my own case; especially as to one point, I am *sure* now (and I never was before) that I do love God. I love Him distinctly, positively; and I think I have loved Him more and longer than I thought, only I dared not own it to myself. Oh that I loved Him more and more! How I abhor myself for having loved, for loving, so little.

In the autumn of 1867 she enjoyed a visit to the lakes with her former schoolfellow, J. H. E., and J. T., a charming poetess. Frances writes: "I had every possible variety of effects, from grey lake mists and rain to silver and gold, and rosy transparent purple and soft dreamy hazes, and marvellous clearness and veilings and unveilings, and everything that is lovely except snow."

(*F. R. H. to Miss Clara Gedge, September* 1867.)

... I thank you very specially for having asked me to join the Young Women's Christian Association. On my side it will be an extra strong link; because, whatever help and blessing for myself and others I may find through it, I shall not forget that I owe my membership to you. I have written the date of my joining in the cover of my Bible, as a continual reminder (if any could be needed) of such a privilege; and under it the names of all whom I know to be members, yours of course standing first. How little we know each other's need! How often the text we want to send must be a bow drawn at a venture! Yet again, how alike are our needs, and how pleasant to know that we may ask Him, to whom each heart is open, to guide us to choose the right gem from the precious mine of His word! I do not feel inclined to send you anything out of the way to-day, dear Clara, but just one of the dear old rock-texts, which are always something to stand upon, and this one especially so for your birthday: "He hath said, I will never leave thee nor forsake thee." For this embraces all our years; if true at all, it has been so all along, even when we felt far off. He was near when we felt alone; He was surely, though hidden, beside us. . . .

The date on the Y. W. C. A. card of membership is September 23, 1867; No. 2181. This Association proved a lifelong rivet; and manifold were her efforts, to link others in its helpful fellowship.

It is impossible to give even an idea of her efforts for many societies. Just at this time, she was wishful to give lessons in singing, for the Church Missionary Society; and her steady work in collecting for it never ceased. The Jews', the Church Pastoral-Aid, and the Bible Society were alike valued. Skilfully did she induce others to take an interest in them; and in the February of her last winter (1879), one bitter night, she headed a number of Welsh neighbours and lads to go, for the first time in their lives, to a Bible Society meeting at the Mumbles.

We again give some extracts from her letters.

Pembridge Crescent, November 1867.
... Among other pleasures in London, I have made acquaintance with the authoress of "Doing and Suffering." She gave me a good deal of practical advice about my schemes for milliners' classes. I want very much to give singing lessons for the Church Missionary Society, and German lessons for the Irish Society; this would be clear gain, and also give me opportunities for influence among the class which interest me so much.

... I must tell you about the east window in Mr. Bickersteth's church at Hampstead. Nothing in the window line ever made such an impression upon me. It is all filled in with simple arabesque and diaper work, merely quiet harmonious colour, nothing to arrest the eye, except the centre light, and in that is a white scroll on a blue ground, with just the words in crimson and gold letters, "Till He come." It sent quite a thrill through me. It is so exactly what one would like to look up to from the holy table. . . . I must send you "In whom we have the forgiveness of sins," because I have just had a glimpse of the beauty and power of it, and I like best to send you what has been given me. Of course I lost it again; but, in praying for forgiveness, and sorrowfully enough, as usual, I remembered your quotation from Adelaide Newton, and *then* this flashed upon me, "*in whom—we have*," and was so satisfactory. Perhaps you don't feel the utter need of it that I do but still I know it *is* precious truth for every one.

GODSTONE, December 1867.

Guess my birthday treat? To the Zoological Gardens. I don't know anything I would rather see in London. I am a perfect baby as to animals! I managed to get three more singing lessons, though I was never in voice, and had a bad cold. Signor Randegger says I have many mechanical difficulties to overcome, but gives me credit for "talent, taste, feeling, and brains." I might improve if under him for a year, and he consoled me by saying "I might always calculate on expressive singing." His first lesson was a lecture on the formation of the throat and production of sound, which he told me to write out as an abstract. I was very poorly in bed the next day; so, having nothing to do, it occurred to me to rhyme it. Afterwards I was afraid lest he might be touchy and think I was making game of it. However it was quite the other way, and he asked for a copy to show his pupils.

MY SINGING LESSON. (*Abstract.*)

HERE beginneth,—Chapter the first of a series,
To be followed by manifold notes and queries;
So novel the queries, so trying the notes,
I think I must have the queerest of throats,
And most notable dulness, or else long ago
The Signor had given up teaching, I trow.
I wonder if ever before he has taught
A pupil who can't do a thing as she ought!

The voice has machinery (now to be serious),
Invisible, delicate, strange, and mysterious.
A wonderful organ-pipe firstly we trace,
Which is small in a tenor and wide in a bass;
Below an Æolian harp is provided,
Through whose fairy-like fibres the air will be guided.
Above is an orifice, larger or small,
As the singer desires to rise or to fall;
Expand and depress it, to deepen your roar,
But raise and contract it, when high you would soar.
Alas for the player, the pipes, and the keys,
If the bellows give out an inadequate breeze!
So this is the method of getting up steam,
The one motive power for song or for scream.
Slowly and deeply, and just like a sigh,
Fill the whole chest with a mighty supply;
Through the mouth only, and not through the nose;
And the lungs must condense it ere farther it goes.
(*How* to condense it I really don't know,
And very much hope the next lesson will show.)
Then, forced from each side, through the larynx it comes,
And reaches the region of molars and gums,
And half of the sound will be ruined or lost
If by any impediment here it is crossed.
On the soft of the palate beware lest it strike,
The effect would be such as your ear would not like.
And arch not the tongue, or the terrified note
Will straightway be driven back into the throat.
Look well to your trigger, nor hasten to pull it,
Once hear the report and you've done with your bullet.

In the feminine voice there are registers three,
Which upper, and middle, and lower must be;
And each has a sounding-board all of its own,
The chest, lips, and head, to reverberate tone.
But in cavities nasal it never must ring,
Or no one is likely to wish you to sing.
And if on this subject you waver in doubt,
By listening and feeling the truth will come out.
The lips, by-the-bye, will have plenty to do
In forming the vowels Italian and true;
Eschewing the English, uncertain and hideous,
With an *o* and a *u* that are simply amphibious.
In flexible freedom let both work together,
And the under one must not be stiffened like leather.

Here endeth the substance of what I remember,
Indited this twenty-sixth day of November.

The following extracts will illustrate my dear sister's life at this time.

PYRMONT VILLA, LEAMINGTON, December 27, 1867.

... My first note in my new room in our new home must be to you. It is solemn to think of what I may go through in this room: probably many happy hours, certainly many sorrowful ones. In all human probability it will be my room until the great sorrow falls which has already often seemed imminent, unless I die before my precious father. I have just been praying words from my own mamma's lips, when I was a little girl, "Prepare me for all that Thou art preparing for me." Yet, spite of these thoughts, I have not been at all in a good frame of mind; oh, how often hidden evil is brought to light by some unexpected Ithuriel touch. Every one calls me sweet tempered; but oh, I have been so ruffled two or three times, that I wonder and grieve at myself. I always suffer for being naughty; I lose all enjoyment in prayer directly. "Oh, for a heart that never sins!"

January 18th, 1868, after describing her room:

Can you fancy me there? The only drawback is that, being at the top of the house, it will not be available for classes. I do wish all good carpets and furniture were at the bottom of the sea! They are among the devices to hinder usefulness. I have done nothing about a class yet, and do hope I shall not be wilful in choosing for myself!... I never saw such a place as Leamington, every hole and corner seems dusted out! Such a number of earnest loving workers; some are wonderful, I am not worthy to sit at their feet.

(*To E. C.*)

LEAMINGTON, February 22, 1868.

"Grace unto you and peace from God our Father and the Lord Jesus Christ." I send for your birthday the result of a year's daily and loving thought for you [a Bible marked]. It is the worse for wear, having been with me in boxes, bags, and pockets. I have marked what struck me as containing food, light, and teaching of some sort. I do hope you will find my markings a help and pleasure, because not one chapter has been read without prayer for the Holy Spirit's teaching.

... Can you not take Psalm 23:6 as a birthday text? only, the goodness and mercy *are* following all the days, even when their bright outline is lost in the shadow of closely pressing trials, and sometimes in our own shadow.... I am getting on with my book, and might finish it in a week or two by putting on steam; but I am resolutely not hurrying it....

February, 1868.

... I have not had a single poem come to me for some time, till last night, when one shot into my mind. All my best have come in that way, Minerva fashion, full grown. It is so curious, one minute I have not an idea of writing anything, the next I *have* a poem; it is *mine*, I see it all, except laying out rhymes and metre, which is then easy work! I rarely write anything which has not come thus. "Hidden Leaves" is the title; I wonder how you would work it out after this beginning:

"Oh the hidden leaves of life,
Closely folded in the breast!"

The illness and death of her niece, Evelyn Emily Crane, was deeply felt. We may not give full details; but it was her Aunt Frances who had led her to Christ some three years before, and her dying message confirmed the reality of her joyful trust in the Lord Jesus.

April 14, 1868.

Dearest Maria,—

That is indeed a precious message. The tension of this last week has been terrible. I think it so excessively kind of you to tell me all you do. I hunger for it; *you* will understand how. My Evelyn's ring![1] This is kind! I shall always wear it. Once she wanted to wear mine. I have had most beautiful and comforting notes from J. H. E. and many others. The Hebrew word J. H. S. sent me pleased me much. I have had such sympathy from my new friends here. Oh, Marie dear, it *is* answer to prayer indeed. Don't think me selfish in letting out a little to you, or that I do not intensely feel for *them* because I feel so much myself. I wrote some verses Saturday evening (which I intended no one to see), "Dying? Evelyn, darling! Dying? can it be?"[2] but will send them you; and, if you think they would be more pleasure than pain, show them poor ——. The memorial card made me realize it at last. Last night I sat long with it before me, with such an utter flood of love for that child in my heart. It rose and rose, and the sorrow and sense of loss with it, and how I last saw her, in all her graceful beauty. Then, at last, came a sudden glimpse, almost a vision, of seeing her again and having *such* a full and loving welcome from her above!...

Your loving sister.

Leamington, May 1868.

... I am not ill, but overdone and tired. A nice letter even to you is an impossibility. This has been trial, but as yet I see no "nevertheless afterwards." I have been falling back on "O Lord, Thou knowest."... I only send you two words; but they are, and will be seen to be, the true "theme" or "subject," speaking musically, carried through all the majors and minors of life: "MARVELLOUS LOVINGKINDNESS."...

(*To E. C.*)

Leamington, February.

Another birthday! so I send you another note of birthday love; "Surely my judgment is with the Lord, and my work with my God." That word "work" seems to include and imply "*reward* of work," so the whole thing is with your God; it is as if you carry home your daily portion of work to Him, and He lays it up safe with what preceded it; and some day He will bring it out all in one beautiful completed piece, with many finishings and beautifyings beyond what your hand wrought; and His "Well done!" will be your reward, whether it be delayed till He adds "Enter thou" or not. At last I *have* had my longed for "pause in life," but as yet I am not well enough to enjoy it. Maria will tell you how wretchedly ill I have been....

May 8th.

I only heard of your accident last night. My dear old text flashed upon me the instant I heard of it, "Meet for the Master's use"; surely it is for that He has taken His vessel away from active use, that it may be made more meet. I feel so disposed to look out for much marked blessing upon you and your work when He permits you to resume it. Let me give you another, "He will be very gracious unto thee at the voice of thy cry." That has comforted me often, more than any promise of answer; it includes answers and a great deal more besides; it tells us what He is towards us, and that is more than what He will *do*. And the "cry" is not long, connected, thoughtful prayers; a cry is just an *unworried dart upwards* of the heart, and at *that* "voice" He will be very gracious. What a *smile* there is in these words!...

In May 1869 our brother-in-law, Mr. Crane, took Frances, with his wife and eldest daughter Miriam, to Switzerland, by the Rhine route to Heidelberg, Frieburg, Basle and Schaffhausen. Her neatly kept journal has photographs of the several places visited, and the Alpine flowers she dried for its pages.

The Rhine Falls, June 9th.

It was fascinating to look down at the wild rapids, sheets of glass-like transparency, flowing swiftly over rock tables, then a sudden precipice below water, which might go down to any depth, only that you are not looking down into darkness, but into emerald and snow mingled and transfused marvellously. The rocks beneath are not a smooth ledge; thus the water is thrown out into a chaos of magnificent curves and leaps, infinitely more beautiful than any single chute could be. You look up, and see masses of bright water hurled everlastingly irresistibly down, down, down with a sort of exuberance of the joy of utter strength; you look across, and see shattered diamonds by millions leaping and glittering in the sunshine; you look down, and it is a tremendous wrestling and overcoming of flood upon flood, all the more weirdly grand that it is half hidden in the clouds of spray. Every drop is so full of light that the eye is soon dazzled and weary:

---

[1] See "The Two Rings," in "Under the Surface," page 221. [See pages 467–470 of Volume I of the Havergal edition.]

[2] See "Under His Shadow," page 167. [Volume I, pages 332–336.]

oh if one were only all spirit! The next day it was great luxury to sit on the terrace overlooking the falls. I jotted some verses ("He hath spoken in the darkness"),[1] which have been haunting me for two or three days. The text was sent me lately, "What I tell you in darkness that speak ye in light." I never noticed it before; how strange it is what treasures we miss every time we read His word!

Berne, June 12th.

At last! Miriam crept quietly to the window about 5 a.m., and I woke as she passed. "Anything to see?" "Oh yes, I really do believe I see them!" Of course I was up in a second. The sun had risen above the thick mist, and away in the south east were the weird giant outlines of the Bernese Oberland mountains bending towards the sun, as if they had been our mighty guardian spirits all night, and were resigning their charge ere they flew away into farther light. The very mist was a folding of wings about their feet, and a veiling of what might be angel brows, quiet and serene. It is no use laughing at "fancies"; wait till you have seen what we did from the roof of the Berner Hof!

[1] See "Under the Surface," page 161.[Volume I, pages 431–432.]

So now the dream of all my life is realized, and I have seen snow mountains! When I was quite a little child of eight years old I used to reverie about them, and when I heard the name of the snow-covered Sierra de la Summa Paz (perfect peace) the idea was completed; and I thenceforth always thought of eternal snow and perfect peace together, and longed to see the one and drink in the other. And I am not disappointed. They are just as pure, and bright, and peace-suggestive as ever I dreamt them. It may be rather in the style of the old women who invariably say "It's just like heaven," when they get a tolerably comfortable tea-meeting; but really I never saw anything material and earthly which so suggested the ethereal and heavenly, which so seemed to lead up to the unseen, to be the very steps of the Throne; and one could better fancy them to be the visible foundations of the invisible celestial city, bearing some wonderful relation to its transparent gold and crystal sea, than only snow and granite, rising out of this same every-day earth we are treading, dusty and stony! . . .

In the autumn of this year Frances went to Scotland, and extremely enjoyed the Highland scenery; at the same time visiting various friends.

CHAPTER VII.

(1870–1871.)

A father's holy teachings — Peaceful death — "Yet speaketh" — "Songs of Grace and Glory!" — How harmony was learnt — Letter on tunes in "Havergal's Psalmody" — The "hush of praise" — Sympathy — The great transition — The most enjoyable trip to Switzerland — A real Alpine dawn — The Vaudois chaplain — Vivas on the Col de la Seigne — Christmas Day — Waiting, not working.

MANY pictures could be drawn of Frances' home life at Leamington. Especially did she value the sympathy of her dear father in all her studies. With him she delighted to talk out hard questions; and his classical knowledge, his poetic and musical skill, settled many a point. She would rush down with her new poems or thoughts, awaiting his criticisms. And very charming was it to hear her lively coaxing that he would "just sing," as she accompanied his sacred songs; while at other times I have seen her absorbed with his improvised melodies, fugues and intricate progressions, thrilling yet passing. His holy and consistent example, ever holding forth the word of life and sound doctrine, had been as a guiding light on his child's path; of this Frances writes in "Yet Speaketh."

"Deep teachings from the Word he held so dear,
    Things new and old in that great treasure found,
A valiant cry, a witness strong and clear,
    A trumpet with no dull uncertain sound;
These shall not die, but live; his rich bequest
    To that beloved Church whose servant is at rest."

Another daughter describes him very truthfully; and her lines are also given.

A Tribute to my Father, on his Birthday, 1866.

> While we reckon up thy years,
> Balancing our hopes and fears,
> Praise we our Redeemer's grace
> Shining on thy pilgrim race.

He hath given thee work to do,
And the task to suffer too.
He hath given thee art to twine
Music-chords with song sublime,
Holy chant and choral hymn,
Praise-notes fit for seraphim;
Tuneful voice and ready pen
Charm and teach the souls of men;
And thy God hath given thee skill,
Guiding youth to do His will;
And, as pastor in His fold,
Christ's salvation to uphold.
Now a time for rest is thine
In the land of Beulah's shine,
Where the angels come and go,
Bringing help and hope, and low
Sweet echoes of the heavenly chime,
Cheering on the flight of time.
Oh may health and peace be given,
Till the ties of earth be riven,
And this birthday happy be
With the light of heaven on Thee!

J. Miriam Crane.

The shadow of death fell swiftly and stealthily on our dear father's path. The care of his devoted wife had, doubtless, warded off many an attack of serious illness. On Easter Even, 1870, he was unusually well and had walked out during the day. Later on he sat down to his harmonium, playing and singing the tune composed by him in the morning.[1] He rose early, as usual, on Easter Day; but apoplexy ensued; and, after forty-eight hours of unconsciousness, he passed away.

"Yet speaketh!" there was no last word of love,
　So suddenly on us the sorrow fell;
His bright translation to the home above
　Was clouded with no shadow of farewell;
His last Lent evening closed with praise and prayer,
And then began the songs of endless Easter there."

In Astley churchyard, under the fir tree (the place which he had chosen years before), he rests "till that day." The epitaph on the white marble tomb is as follows:

The Rev. WILLIAM HENRY HAVERGAL, M.A., Vicar of Shareshill and Hon. Canon of Worcester Cathedral. Died at Leamington, 19th April, 1870, aged 77. Curate 7, and Rector 13 years, of this parish, 1822 to 1843. "A faithful minister in the Lord" (Ephesians 6:21).

Memorial tablets were also placed in Worcester Cathedral, St. Nicholas and Shareshill Churches.

Some weeks after, Frances wrote to Elizabeth Clay:

[1] No. 163 in "Havergal's Psalmody."

I was terribly upset last night, and yet not all sadness; one of papa's chants was gloriously sung at the Westminster Abbey evening service; such a scene and such music!... "I know their sorrows" (Exodus 3:7) is full of intensest comfort when it *is* needed; it is the climax in it which has so much struck me as corresponding to three degrees of sorrow which I suppose all know; anyhow, you do and I do. That sorrow which can be *seen* is the lightest form really, however apparently heavy; then there is that which is *not* seen, secret sorrows which yet can be put into words, and can be told to near friends as well as be poured out to God; but there are sorrows beyond these, such as are *never* told, and cannot be put into words, and may only be wordlessly laid before God: these are the deepest. Now comes the supply for each: "I have *seen*" that which is patent and external; "I have heard their *cry*," which is the expression of this, and of as much of the external as is expressible; but this would not go deep enough, so God adds, "I *know* their sorrows," down to very depths of all, those which no eye sees or ear ever heard. Is it not a beautiful climax?

It was soon after her father's death that my sister undertook the preparation for the press of "Havergal's Psalmody," which afterwards was largely used in connection with the Rev. C. B. Snepp's Hymnal, "Songs of Grace and Glory," of which full details will be found in the Appendix.

The preparation for the work of harmonizing she alludes to in a letter to her friend Mary C. in 1866.

How I should like to teach you harmony! I do believe I could make it lucid; you can't think what exquisite symmetry there is in chords and intervals, so that I always feel, as well as believe, that man by no means invented harmony, but only found out God's beautiful arrangements in it. As for my own compositions, I am (at some cost of resolution) abstaining entirely. Hiller, of Cologne, recommended me an excellent book, which I got, and determined to write no more till I had gone through it; this I am steadily doing, and enjoy writing the exercises. I suppose, after Hiller's professional opinion, it would be affectation to say I had no talent, and I certainly do feel I have at least a sort of inherited instinct for seeing into harmonies. The way I studied harmony was rather unique; some years ago (at home) I kept a treatise on harmony in my bedroom, read as much as I could conveniently grasp the last thing, and then worked out the exercises in my head before going to sleep. This I did for several weeks, and suppose I must have taken it in very comfortably under this system, inasmuch as I had some work to persuade Hiller that I had gone through no "academical course!"

Frances writes (1870) of difficulties in the work:

I was so struck this morning with "Thou art the Helper of the fatherless,"—the very first time one of those special orphan promises has come home to me. I had been puzzling over a tune which papa would have decided about in a minute, and missed him so much, when suddenly this verse flashed upon me brightly. I think that even in music the Lord is my helper now; much more in other things.

When composing some tunes at this time, I selected six about which I felt doubtful, and sent them to Sir Frederic Ouseley, asking him to say if they were all right. This he most kindly did; to my great delight he endorsed them every one, and praised them too.

Very prayerfully did she write several hymns for "Songs of Grace and Glory"; and, when she heard from time to time of their being blessed, she wrote in answer to a friend's communication:

It does seem wonderful that God should so use and bless my hymns; and yet it really does seem as if the seal of His own blessing were set upon them, for so many testimonies have reached me. Writing is *praying,* with me, for I never seem to write even a verse by myself, and feel like a little child writing; you know a child would look up at every sentence and say "And what shall I say next?" That is just what I do; I ask that at every line He would give me, not merely thoughts and power, but also every *word,* even the very *rhymes.* Very often I have a most distinct and happy consciousness of direct answers. As you use "Havergal's Psalmody" I thought you might be interested to know a little more about my dear father, so will you accept a "Memorial" of him.

Literal "singing for Jesus" is to me, somehow, the most personal and direct commission I hold from my beloved Master; and my opportunities for it are often most curious, and have been greatly blessed; every line in my little poem "Singing for Jesus" is from personal experience. . . .

I was so overwhelmed on Sunday at hearing three of my hymns touchingly sung at Perry Church. I never before realized the high privilege of writing for "the great congregation"; especially 633, "I gave My life for thee" to papa's tune "Baca"; the others were 120 and 921 in "S. G. G."

(*To Margaret W———.*)

. . . Last night they sang "To Him who for our sins was slain," to my little tune "Tryphosa"; it went so deliciously, and choir and congregation really rang out the Alleluias so brightly that it suddenly came over me, as it never did before, what a privilege it is even to have contributed a bit of music for His direct praise. It was a sort of *hush* of praise, all alone with Jesus, for His great goodness. I had no idea "Tryphosa" was such a pretty tune before! . . .

About coming to hear ———, I see that I shall glorify Him most by staying away. *Fruits* of my profession are looked for, and what will be looked for in this case is *submission* to known wishes and the yielding up of my own. It is sure to be all right. I don't think *He* will let me lose the blessing and the help I had looked for in coming. . . .

One result of her own trials was sympathy with others, beautifully expressed in the following letter.

LEAMINGTON, December 10, 1870.

DEAR, DEAR MRS. SNEPP,—

What can one do but just weep with you! *I* can only *guess* what this sorrow is. Only, I know it must be the greatest, except *one,* which could come to you. That dear little beautiful thing! He looked so sweet and happy when I saw him at the station: no baby face ever haunted me as, somehow, his did. If you could only see him now, how beautiful he must be now that he has seen Jesus and shines in the light of God. It is even more wonderful to think of that great transition for a baby than for a grown person; one cannot imagine the sudden expansion into such knowledge and conscious joy. I was looking back, early this morning, upon long memories of soul trials, years of groping and stumbling and longing, sinning and sorrowing, of heart weariness and faintness, temptation and failure; all these things which I suppose *every* Christian must pass through, more or less, at some stage or other on the way home; and the first distinct thought which came through the surprise and sorrow at the sad news was, "that dear little redeemed one is spared all *this,* taken home without any of these roughest roughnesses of the way; he will never fear or doubt or sin, *never grieve the Saviour.*" Is it not the very best and kindest thing that tender Saviour could do for him? Only it is not what you meant when you prayed that he might be His own. But *better,* for he is *with Him* at once and for ever, and waiting for you to come home too. I am only writing all this because my heart is full, and must pour out a little. I know we can't comfort, only Jesus can; and I shall go and plead long and intensely for this as soon as I have closed my letter. He must be specially "touched" in such a sorrow, for He knows by actual experience what human love is. Three such great sorrows in one year! how specially He must be watching you in such a furnace! . . . Yours, with deepest sympathy and love.

In June of 1871 Frances and her friend Elizabeth Clay spent some weeks in Switzerland; with no encumbering luggage, just carpet bags and knapsacks, they often diverged from beaten routes. Frances always spoke of *this* as the most enjoyable of all her Swiss tours. Walking up the Reuss valley she writes from Geschenen:

Hurrah! we are in a most exhilarated state of mind, just like children; and, except a little undercurrent of general thanksgiving we don't feel solemn at all, and have been in the wildest spirits.

From Andermatt we took the diligence to the Furca pass. It is so early that, in some places, the road lay between walls of snow. We were obliged to take a guide up the Furca horn, as there is no vestige of a track; the snow slopes were most entertaining to cross, and I enjoyed the scramble excessively.

Going up the Aeggischhorn (she continues), an Alpine Clubist with the guide Fischer was before us, and he afterwards told our guide, Alexander, that he watched us from above, and that I "went up like a chamois!" and he was quite astonished how quickly I got up a difficult climb; but I always had an instinct I should find myself a rather extra good climber. The glissades down are simply delicious.

BEL ALP, July 8. To-day has been the best of all. We secured Anton Walden for the Sparrenhorn, which is nearly 10,000 feet. Another lady, Miss Anstey, joined. Coffee at 3.30, started before 4 a.m.

Now I have seen it at last, a real Alpine dawn and sunrise to perfection! When we came out we saw the "daffodil sky," which Tyndall describes, in the east a calm glory of expectant light as if something positively celestial must come next, instead of merely the usual sun. In the south west the grand mountains stood, white and perfectly clear, as if they might be waiting for the resurrection, with the moon shining pale and radiant over them, the deep Rhone valley dark and grave-like in contrast below. As we got higher, the first rose flush struck the Mischabel and Weisshorn, and Monte Leon came to life too; it was *real* rose-fire, delicate yet intense. The Weisshorn was in its full glory, looking more perfectly lovely than any earthly thing I ever saw. When the tip of the Matterhorn caught the red light on its evil-looking rocky peak, it was just like a volcano and looked rather awful than lovely, giving one the idea of an evil angel, impotently wrathful, shrinking away from the serene glory and utter purity of a holy angel, which that Weisshorn at dawn might represent if anything earthly could. The eastern ridges were almost jet, in front of the great golden glow into which the daffodil sky heightened. By 4.30 a.m. it was all over, and thenceforth we devoted ourselves to getting up the Sparrenhorn.

After many other excursions they went down into the Italian valleys.

July 28th. COURMAYEUR. . . . I have been writing in a delicious den, under a rock, cool and shady, a discovery of Elizabeth's. It commands a grand front of Mont Blanc. We had a stiff climb to the shoulder of a mountain whose Courmayeur face is a striking precipice. There is a tolerable path up a gorge, leading to a ride just below the cone of Mont Chétif. From this point we had a face-to-face view of the most precipitous side of Mont Blanc, with the ice fall of the Glacier de Brenva. The summit of Mont Blanc was veiled, but I think that added to the weird sublimity of the view.

One evening the English chaplain and Mrs. Phinn asked us to come to tea, to meet Costabel, the Vaudois missionary pastor stationed here. This was very interesting; he is a nice, simple, good man, and told us a great deal about Vaudois work. Costabel is very isolated here (but Mr. Phinn has quite taken him up), for he has only a few poor Christian friends, and never any superior society unless the English find him out. He told us that the fear of death among the people here is awful, and that he is frequently present at the most painful death scenes. During life and health they leave everything to the priest, and believe that he will make it all right for them; and, except complying with certain forms, do not think or trouble themselves about religion at all. Then, when they are dying they get alarmed, and see that this natural shifting of their religion upon another (the priest) will not do; they lose confidence in him, and have no other; they want peace and have none; they would like to feel assured, but they have no assurance; and they die in agonies of terror. It was terrible to hear Costabel's description of what he says is the rule as to Romish death beds. "Unto the poor the gospel is preached," and he says it is so here. Only the poor will listen to him, and those in the outlying villages where no priest resides. We find the people there quite different from the Swiss, and not at all so ready to accept Gospels. It is the first place where, on offering any, we have been asked "whether it was a Protestant book"; however they always end by taking them.

Mont Blanc is more than ever supreme to me; it is quite strange what a difference in effect there is between him and Monte Rosa, though this is second in height and only 500 feet lower. Monte Rosa is quite disappointing and unimposing; and, as there are four other mountains round Zermatt very nearly as high, and seven or eight more not much lower, there is nothing of this imperial supremacy which makes Mont Blanc so unmistakable from *anywhere*.

I think that, either for strong or weak folk, Courmayeur is the very best place I know of for making a long stay at; the walks and excursions are inexhaustible, there are any amount of grand things to do for mountaineers, and lovely little easy walks, as short as you like, for mere invalids. Valleys and gorges fork and re-fork in all directions. Another advantage is that it lies on a gentle slope some little height above the noisy, foaming Dora, and so one has not the perpetual roar which I always think the greatest drawback to Swiss enjoyment. If the rivers would but go to sleep at night, what a relief it would be! I certainly have not been so well for years, and except for some wakeful nights I should have done the whole tour without flagging at all.

Saturday, 5.30 p.m. CHAPIU. We have got off at last; it was not at all hopeful yesterday, and I began the day rather anxiously (as I should really have been in a fix if we could not have left till Monday), and there was the clearest, most transparent, dawn sky imaginable; not a cloud; and a delicious north wind, which is an infallible sign of first-rate weather. We got off exactly at five, in great spirits, as the views must be first-rate on such a morning, and the cool wind would make walking very easy. As we passed our old hotel, we found a caravan of about eighteen mules and nearly as many guides, as all the Italians pensioning there were going up the Col de la Seigne for the day. We hastened on, as we of course did not want to be mixed up, and succeeded in keeping ahead the whole way, five hours, though we were alternately on foot and they all riding, and got to the top just before them. We chose our spot to lunch, and they camped at a little distance with many bows and "Bon appetits!" and other small foreign civilities, as they passed us. When we had finished and were moving off, they shouted to us to stay, and all rose and came to us offering us wine and fruit, and saying they wished to propose a toast and drink with us before we left. It was far too gracefully done to refuse; so red wine was poured, and all raised a most cordial "Vive l'Angleterre!" with great enthusiasm and clinking of glasses, to which we responded with a "Viva l' Italia!" which seemed to please them. Then an old priest said, "Mesdemoiselles, êtes vous catholiques? Viva Roma!" to which I replied in Italian, "We can at least say, *Viva Roma capitale d' Italia!*" which response he quite understood and said, "Ah well, ah well, viva Christianity," to which we of course responded *con amore*. Then two or three more (probably freethinkers, I'm afraid) said, "Oui bien, but no more Popery", and two or three similar exclamations, at which we were very much astonished, as at least three priests were in the party. Then we were allowed to depart, with no end of hat wavings and good wishes. We were so taken by surprise with the whole thing, and all passed so quickly, and so many rapid exclamations and vivas firing off in French and Italian, that I was quite sorry afterwards that I had not recollected all quite distinctly. It was such a curious little episode, and occurring too at such a superb spot, and close to the cross which marks the boundary and bears on one side "France" and on the other "Italia." We reached Chapiu at two, having only been eight hours in actual progress, as we stayed nearly an hour on the col, as we hoped it might be possible to put on steam and get over the Col de Bonhomme this afternoon, and thereby be yet able to do

Chamounix. But we found that, owing to the great snow, it would take five hours from Chapiu, and that *all* on foot, as a mule could not go at all; so we were obliged to give it up, (though feeling quite equal to it,) as the guide said we could not do it before dark, and it would not do to risk that. So we have put up here for Sunday, at a funny little inn, many miles from any village.

It has been a glorious day, as clear as crystal, almost too clear, as it rather takes from the sublimity, the summits look so near. We passed the Lac de Combat, an exquisitely soft-tinted lake, pearly blue (but less intense than Geneva), reflecting a grand and lovely group of snow summits and ridges, more like a fairy fancy than a reality in its unique loveliness. That lake was red in Napoleon's days, and a wretched garrison was kept freezing there four whole winters, guarding the pass at the boundary. The ruins of their rough fortifications are reflected in one corner, a melancholy contrast. The col is 8450 feet high, but the ascent was unusually gradual, and we were as fresh when we got to the top as when we started. But then we had ignominiously descended to having a mule between us: so it was only two hours and a half walking for each. There is no post at all here, but any chance guide or traveller takes letters on to Bourg St. Maurice!

We pass on to Christmas Day of this year, 1871; which was spent at Leamington, and in connection with which she writes to her old friend as follows.

(*To E. C.*)

… Christmas has as much of pain as of joy in it now, *more* perhaps, and yet one would not blot out the memories which cause the pain. I have found this second return home after my dear father's death fully as trying as the first. … One or two pet schemes are defeated; but let me rather dwell on Christmas mercies, and much that can infinitely satisfy one's cravings.

Subsequent ill health obliged Frances to give up much pleasant work, and especially the training of the St. Paul's voluntary choir, which had been committed to her. But (she writes) "when a disappointment comes in that way it must be His appointment!"

(*To M. W.*)

… I am stopped in every attempt at consecutive work. It has for years been special discipline to me, because I am naturally fond of going through with a thing, and have always had a strong yearning for definite settled work. Yet I have never been permitted anything but desultory work; either ailments or something beyond my own control has always interfered ever since I was about twenty. … Margaret, is it that He cannot trust me with any work for Him, even after all these years? I have been feeling very down, and I hope really humbled; it seemed rather marked, His not letting me write at all this year; and, now, taking away all work from me seems another sentence of the same lesson. I feel such a "cumberer," every one doing more and better than myself. Pray for me, that I may really learn *all* He is teaching me. …

(*To the same.*)

I am always getting surprises at my own stupidity! Why could not I have seen that lovely trio of texts? This only confirms my strong belief that if I am to write to any good, a great deal of *living* must go to a very little *writing*, and that this is why I have always been held back from writing a tithe of what I wanted to write; and I see the wisdom of it.

CHAPTER VIII.

(1872–1874.)

"The Right Way" — Snowdon — Evenings at Harlech — Jesus our Reality — Switzerland once more — Ascent to the Grands Mulets — Glissade peril and escape — Active service — Winterdyne — Bright sunshine — Full surrender — 1 John 1:7 — Definitive standpoint — Chimes in the night of "Ever, only, all for Thee" — No cheque — Songs, not sighs — How "Golden harps," "Tell it out," etc., came — Wayside enjoyments.

IN the summer of 1872 we enjoyed a few weeks' tour together in North Wales, the change being desirable for my dear sister, who immediately recovered her health and buoyancy. She writes from Barmouth, July 6, 1872:

Dear G——,

Surely "The Right Way" will be the shining inscription on every Christian's home path at last; all will be alike in this one thing, however diverse in all else. … We have been two nights at Dolgelly;

it is lovely, and so *different* in character, that it no more suffers after Switzerland than a forget-me-not beside a rose.... My sister has the scent of a Red Indian for good old widow women and people needing consolation....

P.S.—Isaiah 48:17: do suck all the honey out of this full and sweet text.

(*To* E. C.)

Pen-y-guryd, July 16.

... It seems very natural to scribble to you, after our Swiss experiences last summer. I leave circulars and generalities to Maria. I see by my little register that I have received above 600 letters between January and July 1st. It would be impossible, unless you were with me day by day, to give you a notion of the unaccountable variety of things that people will persist in writing to me about....

I think Wales will put me out of conceit of Switzerland! One gets so very much beauty and enjoyment with so much less expense or fatigue. This year, too, I had such a craving for rest rather than for exertion, that our plan suits me far better. I intensely enjoyed the feeling of rest and leisure at Harlech, without having to "do" any places next day *or* next! I am glad you were at the Mildmay Conference. I did so want to go, but dear mother so strongly advised me *not* that I thought it clear duty to refrain. I think the very thing which would be pleasure and help to you would be a serious spiritual drawback to me, meeting those you know or could speak to. The human element, however delightful, would distract and hinder me from meeting "Jesus only." How all these differences of need and desire will be overflowed in the glorious assembly above! I do like to think of *that*. I prayed that Wales might be *my* conference, and that I might not miss a blessing; and in some degree it has been answered, for I have been rather specially happy. I seemed to have arrears of prayer, things I wanted as it were to talk over and talk out with God, and especially the three last evenings at Harlech, when I went out alone for the purpose; I found two or three hours none too long for uninterrupted communion of this kind.

I am finishing this at the top of Snowdon; the ascents are all so easy; no need of ponies or guides when we can walk twelve to fifteen miles. We shall run down from this the Llanberis side, and camp for a week, half way down, with one of my sister's charming old women.

I have had such interesting openings for work the last few weeks, some only beginnings, others I trust real conversions; I tell my sister what I could not write. So He gives us different work to do, but all His work.... We must return from Wales to be present at the wedding of my dear niece, Miriam Crane, the end of July.

. . . . . .

From Moel Siabod we had series of glimpses of the sunny world below, and magnificent veilings and unveilings of Snowdon, soft white wreaths folding and unfolding among the massive heights. In Llyn Dinas I saw an effect quite new to me. The slanting sunlight took the ripples at just such an angle that an exquisite gold network, waving and gleaming upon the dark brown stones, was produced, in some places concentrating like a golden web, in others like open trellis work. The harmony of colour, the rich warm brown of the stones with the intense gold, was not a combination *we* should have struck out. My favourite mountain verse is: "Unto Thee, O Lord, do we give thanks, for that Thy name is near Thy wondrous works declare."

Thoughts from various Letters, 1873.

"How I should like to be with you now! it would be so nice to throw one little flower among your thorns. However, I think He *would* send me, impossible as it seems, if really best; so, as I am not sent, I know it is better so."

"So your fiery trial is still unextinguished. But what if it be but His beacon light on your upward path!"

"This is bitter desolation for you, so I send you 'I will not leave you comfortless.' It was a greater loss than any, which the disciples were to endure, His own personal presence withdrawn. Can He have changed since He spoke those loving words? What a test of the disciples' faith! What could make up for this greatest loss of all? How could He go away, and yet not leave them comfortless? You are called now to the same sort of trial of faith; can you not trust the truth and love of the Master who sends it? And then 'I will come to you.' You know something of *how* He can 'come,' but do you think you have reached the end of His gracious comings?"

"It is a question whether a really thoughtful mind *could possibly* yield the homage of its entire being to a God whom it could understand and fathom. The instinct of such a mind would revolt from it."

"'As for thee, the Lord thy God has not suffered thee to do so.' What a stepping stone! We give thanks, often with a tearful doubtful voice, for our spiritual mercies *positive*; but what an almost infinite field there is for mercies negative! We cannot even imagine all that God has suffered us *not* to do, *not* to be."

"... Did you ever hear of any one being very much used for Christ who did not have some *special* waiting time, some complete *upset* of all his or her plans first; from St. Paul's being sent off into the desert of Arabia for three years, when he must have been boiling over with the glad tidings, down to the present day? You were looking forward to tell about trusting Jesus in Syria; now He says, 'I want you to *show* what it is to trust Me, without waiting for Syria.' Even if you never say one word, it will be seen your trust is a reality, because Jesus is a Reality.

"My own case is far less severe, but the same in principle, that when I thought the door was flung open for me to go with a bound into literary work, it is opposed, and doctor steps in and says simply 'Never! She must choose between writing and living, she can't do both.' That was in 1860. Then I came out of the shell with 'Ministry of Song,' in 1869, and saw the evident wisdom of having been kept nine years waiting in the shade.

"God's love being unchangeable, He is just as loving when we do not see or feel His love. Also His sovereignty and His love are coequal and universal; so He withholds the enjoyment and conscious progress, because He knows best what will really ripen and further His work in us."

"'Ye shall be gathered one by one, O ye children of Israel.' (Isaiah 27:12.) Hence, individual love and care, personal calling and guidance. Yet this is only for the wilderness journey, for the 'one by one' will blossom at last into a grand answer to His prayer, 'that they all may be *one*,' no longer 'one *by* one.'"

"Tired, disappointed, and depressed, I thought of Matthew 11:28, 'Come unto Me all ye that labour,' but felt quite tantalized at it because 'labour' did not apply to me. I took up my Greek Testament and Lexicon, and to my delight saw that the very same word is used in John 4:6, 'Jesus therefore being *wearied*.' Just human, natural, physical fatigue! So I didn't see why I should not take the comfort of it, and I did not trouble to think, but He let the words rest me altogether."

In the summer of 1873 Frances accompanied her friends Mr. and Mrs. Snepp and their daughter Emily to Switzerland.

She describes her ascent to the Grands Mulets on Mont Blanc, arriving at its desolate rocks in the midst of an ocean of snow.

We had some lovely effects, such as I had never seen before, in passing the colossal ice blocks on the shady side, the sun behind them touching the edges with a sort of transparent aureole, and shining through a glittering drip from the overhanging ones.

On their descent from Mont Blanc, Frances' delight in glissading led to most perilous and imminent danger, from which Mr. Snepp's instantaneous presence of mind saved her life and also the life of one of the guides. She writes:

They would not unrope me; when we got to Pierre à l'Echelle, I was so enjoying my glissades, and presently thought we were come to a sufficiently easy part to go carelessly, whereupon I slipped, and Payot the guide, who was next to me, totally lost himself too. Below us was a dark abyss; we both started a decidedly too rapid spin down a very steep incline to sheer precipice below; when, instantaneously, Mr. S. did the only possible thing which could have saved all four of us, flung himself right on his back with his heels in the snow, the orthodox thing to do if only any one has the presence of mind to do it. Thus he was enabled to bear the immense strain on the rope, and check our impetus; thank God, we soon recovered our footing. After this I was unroped, which I greatly prefer, it is so hampering, and had some splendid glissades alone, and we returned to Chamounix in two hours less than the regulation time.

Returning from Switzerland to Oakhampton, our dear mother being at the seaside, Frances at once began most diligent work. Her active service had no intervals of dreamy enjoyment; but cottage visitations, and four Bible classes weekly, attended with unwearied exertions, at last culminated in crowded attendances in the servants' hall. Soon after this, she assisted in preparatory work for a Mission at Bewdley. With the late Vicar's consent, the Rev. G. Everard had promised to come; but the fever in his family and the death of his dear children frustrated this arrangement, and the Rev. C. B. Snepp undertook all the services. My sister, though very fragile, gave much help in the choir and other opportunities for work.

The family at Winterdyne will ever have reason to thank God for Frances' visit, though no words here may tell of its lasting influence and blessed results.

During a Mission Week at Liverpool she was again at work.

(*To Margaret W.*)

ECCLESTON HALL, October 23, 1873.

To think of my actually being here! J—— is so good to me, nursing me after my Liverpool work, which rather used me up. I had a young women's meeting on Wednesday, was at work all Thursday morning, and intended to make sure of an hour's very needful rest, and preparation for my hymn meeting, when some callers came who had, I trust, really got a blessing the night before. I am hardly as much used up as I feared, after five days' incessant work, but it is long since I had any real rest. . . .

I have just been writing my request for praise. What can I do? I can't curtail it! Oh, how I wish I could have come over to your praise meeting, and just tried to tell you all how gracious, and faithful, and *near*, God has been all this summer! If I kept a diary it would be just a record of answers to prayer, and such great ones too! I wish you would tell the members of the Y. W. C. A., because they would be encouraged to hear how wonderfully God has answered one of their members, and He is the same God, rich to all that call upon Him. . . .

We now reach a period in the life of dear Frances that was characterized by surpassing blessing to her soul. The year 1873 was drawing to a close, and she was again visiting at Winterdyne. One day she received in a letter from N—— a tiny book with the title "All for Jesus."[1] She read it carefully. Its contents arrested her attention. It set forth a fulness of Christian experience and blessing exceeding that to which she had as yet attained. She was gratefully conscious of having for many years loved the Lord and delighted in His service; but her experience was not up to the standard of full consecration and spiritual power, or of uniform brightness and continuous enjoyment in the Divine life. "All for Jesus" she found went straight to this point of the need and longing of her soul. Writing in reply to the author of the little book, she said: "I do so long for deeper and fuller teaching in my own heart. 'All for Jesus' has touched me very much. . . . I know I love Jesus, and there are times when I feel such intensity of love to Him that I have not words to describe it. I rejoice, too, in Him as my 'Master' and 'Sovereign,' but I want to come nearer still, to have the full realization of John 14:21, and to know 'the power of His resurrection,' even if it be with the fellowship of His sufferings. And

---

[1] "All for Jesus!" S. W. Partridge & Co. [See pages 388–391 of Volume IV of the Havergal edition.]

all this, not exactly for my own joy alone, but for others.... So I want Jesus to speak to me, to say 'many things' to me, that I may speak for Him to others with real power. It is not knowing doctrine, but *being with* Him, which will give this."

God did not leave her long in this state of mind. He Himself had shown her that there were "regions beyond" of blessed experience and service; had kindled in her very soul the intense desire to go forward and possess them; and now, in His own grace and love, He took her by the hand, and led her into the goodly land. A few words from her correspondent on the power of Jesus to *keep* those who abide in Him from falling, and on the continually present power of His blood ("*the blood of Jesus Christ His Son* cleanseth *us from all sin*"[1]) were used by the Master in effecting this. Very joyously she replied: "*I see it all, and I* HAVE *the blessing.*"

The "sunless ravines" were now for ever passed, and henceforth her peace and joy flowed onwards, deepening and widening under the teaching of God the Holy Ghost. The blessing she had received had (to use her own words) "lifted her whole life into sunshine, of which all she had previously experienced was but as pale and passing April gleams, compared with the fulness of summer glory."

The practical effect of this was most evident in her daily, true-hearted, whole-hearted, service for her King, and also in the increased joyousness of the unswerving obedience of her home life, the surest test of all.

To the reality of this, I do most willingly and fully testify. Some time afterwards, in answer to my question, when we were talking quietly together, Frances said: "Yes, it was on Advent Sunday, December 2nd, 1873, I first saw clearly the blessedness of true consecration. I saw it as a flash of electric light, and what you *see* you can never *unsee*. There must be full surrender before there can be full blessedness. God admits you by the one into the other. He Himself showed me all this most clearly. You know how singularly I have been withheld from attending all conventions and conferences; man's teaching has, consequently, had but little to do with it. First, I was shown that 'the blood of Jesus Christ His Son cleanseth us from all sin,' and then it was made plain to me that He who had thus cleansed me had power to keep me clean; so I just utterly yielded myself to Him, and utterly trusted Him to keep me."

I replied that "it seemed to me, if we did thus yield ourselves to the Lord, we could not take ourselves back again, any more than the Levitical sacrifices, once accepted by the priest, were returned by him to the offerer."

"Yes," she rejoined, "just so. Still, I see there can be the *renewal* of the surrender, as in our Communion Service, where we say: 'And here we offer and present unto Thee, O Lord, ourselves, our souls and bodies.' And there may also be a *fuller* surrender, even long after a surrender has once, or many times before, been made. And then as to sanctification: that it is the work of the Holy Spirit, and progressive, is the very thing I see and rejoice in. He has brought me into the 'highway of holiness,' up which I trust every day to progress, continually pressing forward, led by the Spirit of God. And I do indeed find that with it comes a happy trusting, not only in all great matters, but in all the little things also, so that I cannot say 'so and so worries me.'"

Some months afterwards I received the following letter on the same subject:

DEAREST MARIA,—

... Certainly your letters have filled me with gladness and thanksgiving. Loving thanks to Mr. Shaw for his message....

I have long wanted to explain to you and others in writing (which is easier to me to be *clear* in, than in conversation, with its natural interruptions) what I see as to the subject which to me was undoubtedly the portal into a happy life. As to "perfectionism" or "sinlessness," I have all along, and over and over again, said I never did, and do not, hold either. "Sinlessness" belongs *only* to Christ now, and to our glorified state in heaven. I believe it to be not merely an impossibility on earth, but an actual contradiction of our very being, which cannot be "sinless" till the resurrection change has passed upon us. But being kept from falling, kept from sins, is quite another thing, and the Bible seems to teem with commands and promises about it. First, however, I would distinctly state, that it is *only* as and while a soul is under the full power of the blood of Christ that it can be cleansed from all sin; that one moment's withdrawal from that power, and it is again actively because really sinning; and that it is *only* as, and while, kept by the power of God Himself that we are not sinning against Him; one instant of standing alone is certain fall! But, (premising that,) have we not been limiting the cleansing power of the precious blood when applied by the Holy Spirit, and also the keeping power of our God? Have we not been limiting 1 John 1:7, by practically making it refer only to "the remission of sins that are past," instead of taking the grand simplicity of "cleanseth us from *all* sin"? "All" is *all*; and as we may trust Him to cleanse from the stain of past sins, so we may trust Him to cleanse from all present defilement; yes, *all!* If not, we take away from this most precious promise, and, by refusing to take it in its fulness, lose the fulness of its application and power. Then we limit God's power to "keep"; we look at our frailty more than at His omnipotence. Where is the line to be drawn, beyond which He is *not* "able"? The very *keeping* implies total helplessness without it, and the very cleansing most distinctly implies defilement without it. It was that one word "*cleanseth*" which opened the door of a very glory of hope and joy to me. I had never seen the force of the tense before, a continual present, always a present tense, not a present which the next moment becomes a past. It *goes on* cleansing, and I have no words to tell how my heart rejoices in it. Not a coming to be cleansed in the fountain only, but a *remaining* in the fountain, so that it may and can go on cleansing.

---
[1] 1 John 1:7.

Why should we pare down the commands and promises of God to the level of what we have hitherto experienced of what God is "able to do," or even of what we have thought He might be able to do for us? Why not receive God's promises, nothing doubting, just as they stand? "Take the shield of faith, whereby ye shall be able to quench *all* the fiery darts of the wicked"; "He is able to make *all* grace abound toward you, that ye, always having all sufficiency in all things"; and so on, through whole constellations of promises, which surely mean really and fully what they say.

One arrives at the same thing, starting almost from anywhere. Take Philippians 4:19, "your need"; well, what is my great need and craving of soul? Surely it is now, (having been justified by faith, and having assurance of salvation,) to be made holy by the continual sanctifying power of God's Spirit; to be kept from grieving the Lord Jesus; to be kept from thinking or doing whatever is not accordant with His holy will. Oh *what* a need is this! And it is said "He *shall* supply all need"; now, shall we turn round and say "all" does not mean quite all? Both as to the commands and the promises, it seems to me that anything short of believing them *as they stand* is but another form of "yea, hath God said?"

Thus accepting, in simple and unquestioning faith, God's commands and promises, one seems to be at once brought into intensified views of everything. Never, oh never before, did sin seem so hateful, so really "intolerable," nor watchfulness so necessary, and a keenness and uninterruptedness of watchfulness too, beyond what one ever thought of, only somehow different, not a distressed sort but a happy sort. It is the watchfulness of a sentinel when *his captain is standing by him* on the ramparts, when his eye is more than ever on the alert for any sign of the approaching enemy, because he knows they can only approach to be defeated. Then, too, the "*all* for Jesus" comes in; one sees there is no halfway, it must be absolutely *all* yielded up, because the least unyielded or doubtful point is sin, let alone the great fact of owing all to Him. And one cannot, dare not, temporize with sin. I know, and have found, that even a momentary hesitation about yielding, or obeying, or trusting and believing, vitiates all, the communion is broken, the joy vanished; only, thank God, this never need continue even five minutes, faith may plunge instantly into "the fountain open for sin and uncleanness," and again find its power to cleanse and restore. Then one wants to have more and more light; one does not shrink from painful discoveries of evil, because one so wants to have the unknown depths of it cleansed as well as what comes to the surface. "Cleanse me *throughly* from my sin"; and one prays to be shown this. But so far as one does see, one *must* "put away sin" and obey entirely; and here again His power is our resource, enabling us to do what without it we could not do.

One of the intensest moments of my life was when I saw the force of that word "*cleanseth*." The utterly unexpected and altogether unimagined sense of its fulfilment to me, on simply believing it in its fulness, was just indescribable. I expected nothing like it short of heaven. I am so thankful that, in the whole matter, there was as little human instrumentality as well could be, for certainly two sentences in letters from a total stranger, *were* little. I say only two sentences, for nothing else seemed to make much difference to me; all the rest was, I am sure, God's own direct teaching. And you know I had read no books and attended no meetings or conferences! I am so conscious of His direct teaching and guidance, through His word and Spirit, in the matter that I cannot think I can ever unsee it again. I have waited many months before writing this, so it is no new and untested theory to me; in fact, experience came before theory and is more to me than any theory. But, understand me, it is "not as though *I* had already attained, either were already perfect; but I follow after, I press *toward* the mark, for the prize of the high calling of God in Christ Jesus."

Frances wrote to her friend J—— K——:

I send you my own New Year's motto and message. It is a wonderful word, "from glory unto glory." May we more and more claim and realize all that is folded up in it. I know you have prayed for me, so I must tell you that your prayers are answered. 1873 has been a year of unprecedented blessing to me. I think you will see this in "From Glory unto Glory." So now will you join me in praise. . . . .

This hymn was written at Winterdyne, and Mr. Shaw well remembers Frances bringing it and reading it to him, saying, 'There! I could not have written this before." And as she stood, even in the twilight, the sunny radiance of her countenance was sealing her words:

"The fulness of His blessing encompasseth our way;
The fulness of His promises crowns every brightening day;
The fulness of His glory is beaming from above;
While more and more we realize the fulness of His love."

Every visit seemed now to open doors for her loving words, and she longed for whole households to taste with her of the goodness of the Lord. One extract must be as it were a glimpse of many others.

Perhaps you will be interested to know the origin of the consecration hymn, "Take my life." I went for a little visit of five days. There were ten persons in the house, some unconverted and long prayed for, some converted but not rejoicing Christians. He gave me the prayer, "Lord, give me *all* in this house!" And He just *did!* Before I left the house every one had got a blessing. The last night of my visit I was too happy to sleep, and passed most of the night in praise and renewal of my own consecration, and these little couplets formed themselves and chimed in my heart one after another, till they finished with, "*Ever,* ONLY, ALL for Thee!"

The beautiful couplet in the same hymn,

"Take my voice, and let me sing,
Always, only, for my King,"

was thenceforth (from December 1873) really carried out. She writes:

Let us sing words which we feel and love, sacrificing everything to clearness of enunciation, and looking up to meet His smile all the while we are singing; our songs will reach more hearts than those of finer voices and more brilliant execution, unaccompanied by His power. A sacred song thus sung often gives a higher tone to the evening, and affords, both to singer and listeners, some opportunity of speaking a word for Jesus.

. . . . I was at a large regular London party lately, and I was so happy. He seemed to give me "the secret of His presence," and of course I sang "for Jesus," and did not I have dead silence? Afterwards I had two really important conversations with strangers; one seemed extremely surprised at finding himself *quite easily* drifted from the badinage with which he started into a right-down personal talk about *his* personal danger and *his* only hope for safety; he took it very well, and thanked me. Perhaps that seed may bear fruit. Somehow it is wonderful how the Master manages for me in such cases. I don't think any one can say I force the subject; it just all develops one thing out of another, quite naturally, till very soon they find themselves face to face with eternal things, and the Lord Jesus can be freely "lifted up" before them. I could not *contrive* a conversation thus.

And the following letter gives another reference to the reality of her experience.

January 26, 1874.

Dear Mr. S——,

I have just had such a blessing in the shape of what would have been only two months ago a really bitter blow to me; and now it is actual accession of joy, because I find that it does not even *touch* me! I was expecting a letter from America, enclosing £35 now due to me, and possibly news that "Bruey" was going on like steam, and "Under the Surface" pressingly wanted. The letter has come, and, instead of all this, my publisher has failed in the universal crash. He holds my written promise to publish *only* with him as the condition of his launching me; so this is not simply a little loss, but an end of all my American prospects of either cash, influence, or fame, at any rate for a long time to come. I really had not expected that He would do for me so much above all I asked, as not merely to help me to acquiesce in this, but positively not to feel it at all, and only to rejoice in it as a clear test of the reality of victorious faith which I do find brightening almost daily. Two months ago this would have been a real trial to me, for I had built a good deal on my American prospects; now "Thy will be done" is not a sigh but only a *song!* I think if it had been all my English footing, present and prospective, as well as the American, that I thus found suddenly gone, it would have been worth it, for the joy it has been to find my Lord so faithful and true to all His promises. With regard to many of the promises, there seems no room for even the exercise of faith. It is not that I believe or grasp them, but that I find them all come true as I never did before. The sense of His unutterable lovingkindness to me is simply overwhelming. . . . . Several times lately I have felt literally overwhelmed and overpowered with the realization of God's unspeakable goodness to me. I say it deliberately, and with thankfulness and joy for which I have no words. I have not a fear, or a doubt, or a care, or a shadow upon the sunshine of my heart. Every day brings some quite new cause for thankfulness; only to-day He has given me such a victory as I never had before, in a very strong temptation; He lifted me above it in a way I never experienced yet. . . . .

Two months afterwards she writes:

March 19, 1874.

Dear Mr. W——,

. . . I can never set myself to write verse. I believe my King suggests a thought and whispers me a musical line or two, and then I look up and thank Him delightedly, and go on with it. That is how the hymns and poems come. Just now there is silence. I have not had the least stir of music in my mind since I wrote that tiny consecration hymn, a most unusually long interval; and till He sends it there will be none. I am always ready to welcome it and work it when it comes, but I never press for it. . . .

And the following letter confirms this statement.

Dear Mr. W——,

I can't make you quite understand me! You say "F. R. H. could do 'Satisfied' grandly"! *No,* she couldn't! Not unless He gave it me line by line! That is how verses come. The Master has not put a chest of poetic gold into my possession and said "Now use it as you like!" But He keeps the gold, and gives it me piece by piece just when He will and as much as He will, and no more. Some day perhaps He will send me a bright *line* of verse on "Satisfied" ringing through my mind, and then I shall look up and thank Him, and say, "Now, dear Master, give me another to rhyme with it, and then another"; and then perhaps He will send it all in one flow of musical thoughts, but more likely one at a time, that I may be kept asking Him for every line. There, that is the process, and you see there is no "I can do it" at all. That isn't His way with me. I often smile to myself when people talk about "gifted pen" or "clever verses," etc.; because they don't know that it is neither, but something really much nicer than being "talented" or "clever."

Nearly every poem would verify the above. Some instances are given. When visiting at Perry Barr she walked to the boys' schoolroom, and being very tired she leaned against the playground wall while Mr. Snepp went in. Returning in ten minutes, he found her scribbling on an old envelope, and at his request she handed him the hymn just pencilled, "Golden harps are sounding."

In my dear sister's copy of the "Ministry of Song" she has written particulars, which may be interesting, in connection with others of her well known hymns.

"This Same Jesus" is founded on a recollection of one sentence in a sermon of my father's, at St. Nicholas, which struck me most vividly and happily. I shall not forget the thrill which went through me when he said, "it will be 'this same Jesus.'" It also developed a much earlier impression of the same kind in 1851. "This same Jesus" is one of the chief watchwords of my faith. I constantly recur to it, and I think it will be my comfort in the dark valley. I wrote the lines at Oakhampton, one Sunday, when detained from church by a slight accident, and gave them to my niece Miriam.

"Daily Strength." The New Year's bells were ringing (1859), when Maria awoke me to hear them, and quoted to me the text, "As thy days, so shall thy strength be," as a New Year's motto. I did not answer, but presently returned it to her in rhyme. She was pleased; so the next day I wrote it in her album.[1]

"Making Poetry" was suggested by a nice little girl, Charlotte Kirke, who was spending her holidays in Wales, when I was there in 1863. She made some really pretty little quatrains, and repeated one, about a daisy, to me sitting on the window seat. She called it "making poetry," as children always do.

"Adoration" ("O Master, at Thy feet I bow in rapture sweet") was written on December 31st, 1866. I felt that I had not written anything specially in praise to Christ; a strong longing to do so possessed me. I wanted to show forth *His* praise, to *Him,* not to others; even if no mortal ever saw it, He would see every line, would know the unwritten longing to praise Him, even if words failed utterly. It describes, as most of my poems do, rather reminiscence than present feeling.

"O Master!" It is perhaps my favourite title, because it implies rule and submission; and this is what love craves. Men may feel differently, but a true woman's submission is inseparable from deep love. I wrote it in the cold and twilight in a little back room at Shareshill Parsonage.

As I began my book ("Ministry of Song") with the expression of its devotion to God's glory, I wished to close it with a distinctive ascription of praise to the Lord Jesus, and therefore at once decided to place "Adoration" at the close.

Her missionary hymn "Tell it out among the heathen" was written at Winterdyne, when unable to go to church one snowy Sunday morning. She asked for her Prayer-Book (in bed), always liking to follow the services for the day. On Mr. Shaw's return from church, he heard her touch on the piano. "Why, Frances, I thought you were upstairs!" "Yes; but I had my Prayer-Book, and in the psalms for to-day I read 'Tell it out among the heathen that the Lord is King. I thought, what a splendid first line! and then words and music came rushing in to me. There it's all written out." With copperplate neatness she had rapidly written out the words, music and harmonies complete.

Only those who heard her could imagine the brisk ringing time with which she sang this tune. It distressed her when told how slowly and drowsily it was sometimes given.

Further extracts from the correspondence of the period will close the present chapter.

---

[1] The facsimile of the last verse, "When thy days on earth are passed," will be found beneath the engraved portrait of my dear sister. It shows her handwriting when copying. [See page xxxii of Volume IV of the Havergal edition.]

My dearest G——,

I am waiting for the carriage to take me back to Oakhampton, having been spending a few hours in Worcester, and seeing some old parishioners of years ago, who recollect me as "little Miss Fanny." . . . The last two days I have been very busy, having spent the whole day before at Winterdyne, and even a *day* always throws me behind in letters, etc. I meant to *rest* here, but somehow there always seems to be too much to do. Such a very nice "open door" is set before me that I cannot but enter in, and so I have four different Bible classes a week! besides which, as many cottagers as I can possibly visit are grateful for reading. Yesterday evening I had a "farmers' daughters" class; twelve came, but I think a few more will join. I enjoyed it extremely, was frightened and nervous beforehand, and unavoidable visitors detained and distracted me up to the last minute, which seemed most unfortunate, but probably cast me all the more upon Jesus and His strength. . . . Dear G——, will you pray for my little work here. I do think that in each of my classes here there is something going on, and a most earnest spirit of attention among the servants. And will you ask that I may be kept near to Jesus.

I have brought you a crystal and amethyst locket from Geneva. . . They told me it was a quite new device, but somehow the novelty did not weigh with me in choosing for you, so much as the suggestiveness of the stones; the very words "crystal and amethyst" are like a far gleam from the heavenly city.

. . . . . .

I have been thinking much lately of the Lord's loving-kindness in giving us so much wayside enjoyment, and so much present reward in all our work for Him. In spite of dark life enigmas, and real and heavy trials, and often keen inner conflict, not to mention daily burdens of weariness or anxiety or worry, we can set to our seal that His "ways are ways of pleasantness." For, over and above the great gifts, the "blessed hope" set before us, and the quiet "peace with God through our Lord Jesus Christ," what numbers of bits and drops of pleasure and delight one gets, which simply would not exist for us if we were not His children. Just look at Christian intercourse, the meetings without any cloud of suspicion or doubt of each other, the consciousness of true sweet sympathy, the thrill that one does feel when His beloved name is named; all this, even with Christian *acquaintances,* is a great deal more than all the pleasure or good to be got out of any worldly intimacy or friendship so called. I want to hand over to you what I have been enjoying very much this week, a simple thought enough, but so nice. Dr. Candlish gives (in his beautiful book on the First Epistle of St. John) as one of the proofs of "fellowship with the Father," etc., our *sympathy of aim,* His cause being our cause, His kingdom and its advancement our interest, what interests Him interests us, and so on. This seemed at once to transfigure all one's daily life, and poor little small efforts to speak or write or work for God, and to exalt it into "fellowship." I cannot convey to you how much I enjoyed it, and what a bright reality and force it gave to the words "Truly our fellowship is with the Father and with His Son Jesus Christ." I like to think how impossible it would be to untwine Christ and the things of Christ from our life, inner and outer; when one comes to think about it He is so really and truly interwoven with our life that one seems to feel the "no separation" not merely as a grand promise, but an actuality which *cannot* be otherwise.

CHAPTER IX.

(1874.)

Circular letters — Sunset on the Faulhorn — Ormont Dessus — Interruptions to poems — Other work done — "Little Pillows," etc. — Swiss singing — That great transfer — A musical reverie — Return to England — Bright work and results.

WE give extracts from F. R. H.'s circular letters on her journey to Switzerland in 1874, with her niece Constance Crane, other friends (Elizabeth, Margaret, and Bessie) joining in their mountain excursions.

"Sunset on the Faulhorn!" All day there had been strange rifts in the clouds, and sudden pictures of peaks or of abysses framed in white and grey; but towards seven o'clock the wind rose, and there was a grand outpour of colour upon everything, sky, clouds, and mountains.

Imagine yourself midway between heaven and earth, the sharp point of rock on which we stood hardly seeming more of earth than if we had been in a balloon, the whole space around, above, and below filled with wild, weird, spectral clouds, driving and whirling in incessant change and with tremendous rapidity; horizon *none,* but every part of where horizon should be, crowded with unimaginable shapes of unimagined colours, with rifts of every shade of blue, from indigo to pearl, and burning with every tint of fire, from gold to intensest red; shafts of keen light shot down into abysses of purple thousands of feet below, enormous surging masses of grey hurled up from beneath, and changing in an instant to glorified brightness of fire as they seemed on the point of swallowing up the shining masses above them; then, all in an instant, a wild grey shroud flung over us, as swiftly passing and leaving us in a blaze of sunshine; then a bursting open of the very heavens, and a vision of what might be celestial heights, pure and still and shining, high above it all; then, an instantaneous cleft in another wild cloud, and a revelation of a perfect paradise of golden and rosy slopes and summits; then, quick gleams of white peaks through veilings and unveilings of flying semi-transparent clouds; then, as quickly as the eye could follow, a rim of dazzling light running round the edges of a black castle of cloud, and flaming windows suddenly pierced in it; oh, mother dear, I might go on for sheets, for it was never twice the same, nor any single minute the same, in any one direction. At one juncture a cloud stood still, apparently about 200 yards off, and we each saw our own shadows gigantically reflected on it, surrounded by a complete rainbow arch, but a full circle of bright prismatic colours, a transfiguration of our shadows almost startling, each moreover seeing only their own glorification! When the whole pageant, lasting nearly an hour, was past, we sang "Abide with me," and then the dear old joyous "Glory to Thee, my God."

ORMONT DESSUS, September.

This second month of my Swiss journey is altogether different from the first, for now I am making *writing* the first thing instead of idleness. I am doing it quite in moderation, and taking plenty of fresh air as well; one can be out half the day and yet get four or five good hours writing as well, under these circumstances, when there are no other calls upon time or strength whatever; and this combination of work and leisure is very delightful. Besides, I feel as if I had got quite a fresh start with that month's rest; it seems as if nature had then walked into my brain and taken possession (turning *me* out meanwhile), and given it a kind of spring cleaning! rubbing up the furniture, and fresh papering some of the rooms, and cleaning the windows! That perpetual "moving on," which some so delight in, does not suit me nearly so well as staying in a place and taking it easy. The weather has been so much colder and more variable, since I changed my tactics, that the two things coincided beautifully; for, except two days, it has been too cold the last fortnight for any sitting out of doors.

I don't know why I always seem to shrink from writing much, or even anything, of the "under the surface" life, (which is so much more than the "on the surface" and the mere surroundings,) in my circulars. They would be much fuller if I told one tithe of the hourly bits of gentle guidance and clear lovingkindness which make the real enjoyment, or of the perpetual little opportunities of a "word for Jesus" which He seems to give me, and often of real work for Him, which yet seems to come so unsought, so easily and naturally, so altogether without any effort, as to be not felt to be any working at all. Now I will give you an instance of how He took me at my word the other day. It was one of the few warm days, and I established myself with pen and ink in a shady nook by a little, steep, down-hill torrent. I had suddenly got that sort of strong impulse to write on a certain theme, without which I never do my best, but with which I always do my best poems. The theme was a grand one ("The Thoughts of God"); I had thought of it for months, and never before had this impulse to begin upon it; though, once begun, I expected it to be one of my best poems. I spent a little time in prayer first, and then the warning and the promise in Jeremiah 15:19 came strongly to my mind:

"if thou take forth the precious from the vile, thou shalt be as My mouth." I felt that wanted looking into; I wanted Him to take forth the precious from the vile for me, and to reveal and purge away, then and there, all the self and mingled motive which would utterly mar the work that I wanted to be for His glory. After that the question came, was I—had He made me—just as willing to do any little bit of work for Him, something for little children or poor people, simple and unseen, as this other piece of work, which might win something of man's praise? Then, I was intensely happy in feeling that I could tell HIM that I had no choice at all about it; but would really rather do just what He chose for me to do, whatever it might be. However, there seemed nothing else to do, so I began my poem. I don't think I had written four lines when a labourer with a scythe came along a tiny path to drink at the stream a few yards below me. He did not see me, and started when I hailed him and offered him a little book. He climbed up to receive it, and then, instead of departing as I expected, deliberately sat down on a big stone at my feet, and commenced turning over the leaves, and evidently laying himself out to be talked to. So here was clearly a little call; and I talked to him for some time, he being very interested and responsive. Just as he was going to move off, two lads, of about fifteen and eighteen, his sons, came crashing through the bushes; I don't recollect whether the father beckoned them or not, anyhow up they came, and he quietly sat down again, and they sat down too, and seemed quite as willing to listen to the "old, old story" as he had been, only I could not get so much out of them. At last the whole crew departed, and I was just collecting my thoughts and reviving the aforesaid "impulse," when in about ten minutes the younger lad reappeared, with his sister, a girl of about seventeen. They did not say a word, but scrambled straight up to me, and, seating themselves at my feet, looked up into my face, saying by their look as plain as any words, "Please talk to us!" What could one do but accede! and they stayed at least another half hour, so quiet and interested that one could not but hope the seed was falling on "good ground." The girl, Félicie was more communicative than the lads, very simple, but intelligent. By the time they departed a good part of the morning was gone, and the "impulse" too! but I enjoyed the morning probably twice as much as if I had done a good piece of my poem; and it seemed so clear that the Master had taken me at my word, and come and given me this to do for Him among His "little ones," and that He was there hearing and answering and accepting me, that it was worth any amount of poem-power.

However, *next* day the "impulse" came again, which is by no means always the case when once interrupted; and once fairly started, I have worked out what I *think* is perhaps the best poem I ever wrote, so far as I can judge.

But this is only one of constant instances which I could tell. I do so feel that every hour is distinctly and definitely guided by Him. I have taken Him at His word *in everything,* and He takes me at my word in *everything*. Oh, I *can* say now that Jesus *is* "to me a living bright Reality," and that He really and truly *is* "more dear, more intimately nigh, than e'en the sweetest earthly tie." No friendship could be what I find His to be. I have more now than a few months ago, even though I was so happy then; for the joy of giving *myself,* and my will, and my all to Him seems as if it were succeeded, and even superseded, by the deeper joy of a conscious certainty that He has tak- en all that He led me to give; and "I am persuaded that He is able to keep that which I have committed unto Him": so, having entrusted my very trust to Him, I look forward ever so happily to the future (if there be yet much of earthly future for me) as "one vista of brightness and blessedness." Only I do so want everybody to "taste and see." Yesterday I somehow came to a good full stop in my writing much earlier than I expected, and asked what He would have me do next, go on, or go out at once? Just then a young lady came in; "Had I just a few minutes to spare?" So I went out with her at once. She had overheard a short chat I had had some days ago with another, didn't know *what,* but it had set her longing for something more than she had got. She had started out for a walk alone, thinking and praying, and the thought came to her to come straight to me, which she seemed to think an unaccountably bold step. Well, God seemed to give me exactly the right message for her, just as with Miss M— last week, the two cases starting from a very different level but the result the same, a real turning point. Don't conclude, however, from these that I am always seeing results, because I am not; but that I am entirely content about, just as He chooses it to be.

It has occurred to me that, as I profess to be "writing," you will expect a new book as the result, and will be disappointed; so I tell you simply what I *have* written, and what I am going to write.

"Our Swiss Guide." Article for *Sunday Magazine,* on the spiritual analogies in all sorts of little details of mountaineering.

"For Charity." Song for Hutchings and Romer.

"Enough." Short sacred poem.

"How much for Jesus?" A sort of little true story for children; for an American edition.[1]

"True Hearted." New Year's Address (in verse) for Y.W.C.A., for January 1875.

"Tiny Tokens." A small poem for *Good Words*.

"Precious Things." A poem.

"A Suggestion." Short paper for *Home Words*.

"The Precious Blood of Jesus." A hymn.

"The Thoughts of God." The aforesaid poem.

"Shining for Jesus." Verses addressed to my nieces and nephews at Winterdyne.

"New Year's Wishes," by Caswell's request, for a very pretty card.

These are all written, and copied, and done with. Next week, D.V.*, I set about what I have long wanted to do: "Little Pillows," thirty-one short papers as a little book for children of, say, twelve years old; a short, easily recollected text, to go to sleep upon for each night of the month, with a page or two of simple practical thoughts about it, such as a little girl might read every night while having her hair brushed. I think this will take me about a fortnight to write and arrange for press; adding probably a verse or two of a hymn at the end of each of the little papers. There are lots of little monthly morning and evening books for grown up people, but I don't know of one for children except those containing *only* texts. I dare say I shall get in

---

[1] This manuscript we have no clue to; any information concerning it would be acceptable. [Found, see page 367 of Volume IV of the Havergal edition.]

*D.V., Deo volente (Latin), meaning "God willing"

somehow three other little poems that want writing (being on the simmer): "The Splendour of God's Will," "The Good Master," and (don't be startled at the transition) "Playthings"; also "Johann von Allmen," a little article for the *Dayspring*. I can clear off things easily here, especially through not having so many letters. If I could manage three months every year in a Swiss or Welsh valley, I should keep my printer going.

Ormont Dessus, September 29, 1874.

Dearest Mother,—

I don't know whether there is enough of interest for a final circular. Not being sure of your address, the last went to Maria. . . . The last week at the Ormont Dessus the weather was perfect, and, without being unpleasantly hot, was warm enough for sitting out not merely in the sunshine but in the moonlight too. Sunday was one of the most exquisite days imaginable, brilliantly clear, the autumn tints throwing in touches of crimson and gold in splendid contrast to the pine woods, and (what is so rare in Switzerland) the noon and afternoon as glowing as the morning, everything vivid all day. At the little French service I soon saw we had "somebody" in the pulpit, and it was M. de Pressensé, who is, I have been told, one of the first French orators. His sermon was both eloquent and good. The people sing beautifully, a downright treat, in German choral style as to music, slow rich harmonies that bear dwelling on; one tune was Cassel, No. 190 in "Havergal's Psalmody." It was such sweet singing, every one keeping to *cres* and *dim.*, neither instrument nor apparently any stated choir, but all the parts correctly sung by the congregation of peasants. . . . I have finished not only "*Little Pillows,*" but a little companion to it for morning use, "Morning Bells"; both manuscripts are ready for press. I do not think it is nearly so easy to write for children as for adults; constantly I refrained from what I would most like to say about the texts, because it would not be simple enough for the little ones. I have purposely avoided any stories or anecdotes, lest children should skim the book through in search of them, instead of reading them night and morning steadily. At least I know that is what I should have done! I do so hope these books will be really helpful to some of His little ones. . . . I am so sorry that I shall not see Miss Whately at Montreux; I have a nice letter from her; she has been delayed in England. You ask me how I am, dearest mother. Very well indeed; those pleasant mountain ascents with Constance were delightful. She is a first rate Alpinist, and we both enjoyed getting over crevasses and glissading. Since then I have done nothing to tire myself, and in every way have set health first; I do wish to be very prudent, only by prudence I don't mean idleness. I sought to gain health and strength, that I might use it on my return. . . .

I had a short conversation with two respectable men from West Bromwich, who had been for a Swiss holiday with Cook's tickets. They applied to me to interpret something for them, and this led to a little talk which drifted as usual into better things, and I found a decided response. I had alluded to Christ's finished work for us, when one of them answered quietly, "Yes, it's a *transfer*, that's the word. The last three days I have had that word always in my mind; that's just what it is, a transfer, He takes our sins and makes over to us His righteousness." Then he told me that he had met on the Rigi an invalid Irish clergyman, who seemed full of that one thing; that he began telling him of Christ's finished work and he ended with it. "And I never saw it so clearly before, though I've been, so to say, looking about for it this long time; it was worth all my journey to get hold of this truth. It seemed curious that such an excellent clergyman should be obliged to give up his living from ill health and ordered abroad; but he was sowing the seed in fifty places instead of one. Yes, that great transfer! It's blessed!"

Was it not a nice instance of the real use of such seed sowing? . . .

. . . In the train I had one of those curious musical visions, which only very rarely visit me. I hear strange and very beautiful chords, generally full, slow and grand, succeeding each other in most interesting sequences. I do not invent them, I could not; they pass before my mind, and I only listen. Now and then my will seems aroused when I see ahead how some fine resolution might follow, and I seem to *will* that certain chords should come, and then they do come; but then my will seems suspended again, and they go on quite independently. It is so interesting, the chords seem to *fold over each other* and die away down into music of infinite softness, and then they *un*fold and open out, as if great curtains were being withdrawn one after another, widening the view, till, with a gathering power and intensity and fulness, it seems as if the very skies were being opened out before one, and a sort of great blaze and glory of music, such as my outward ears never heard, gradually swells out in perfectly sublime splendour. This time there was an added feature: I seemed to hear depths and heights of sound beyond the scale which human ears can receive, keen, far-up octaves, like vividly twinkling *starlight* of music, and mighty, slow vibrations of gigantic strings going down into grand thunders of depths, octaves below anything otherwise appreciable as musical notes. Then, all at once, it seemed as if my soul had got a new sense, and I could *see* this inner music as well as hear it; and then it was like gazing down into marvellous *abysses of sound,* and up into dazzling regions of what, to the eye, would have been light and colour, but to this new sense was *sound*. Wasn't it odd! It lasted perhaps half an hour, but I don't know exactly, and it is very difficult to describe in words.

The long letter ends with:

I wish you had seen and heard the welcome my cousins gave me! It was so nice, and altogether I am so well and happy! It was curious, dearest mother, that you should send me Psalm 103:1–3, for my mind was specially full of it, only adding verses 4 and 5. I have so very much to thank Him for, and the beautiful sequence of five blessings seemed to sum it all up: "forgiveth," "healeth," "redeemeth," "crowneth thee with lovingkindness and tender mercies," and "satisfieth thy mouth with good things." And, really, I may add "so that thy youth is renewed like the eagle's," for I feel so *mentally* fresh and unweary, and my cousins say they never saw me looking so well. Hoping soon to reach home, herewith ends the circular series of 1874!

Your very loving child.

Returning from Switzerland in perfect health, much could be told of her active work. We are glad to be permitted to give one result of a visit, before returning home to Leamington, as a representative of many others.

Dear Maria,—

This is *not* a circular. Just pray for all here. —— is first-fruits! full and joyous decision for Christ, singularly tested and acted on at once. I knew she was not happy. When alone, I asked why she should let days and weeks go by, drifting away in the cold. I told her I should leave her room after praying, and begged her to remain praying alone, and surrender her whole self to the Lord Jesus. By and by, the time came for her music practising. There was a ringingness in her touch, playing with such joyance. Presently, I went in and just put my arm round her: "Is it for Jesus?" "Yes, I've made up my mind, it is *all for Jesus!*" Every action spoke it, the smile and bright determination of her voice. Without any suggestion from me she told her mamma, the next day, that she could no longer act in a French play at school. Here was a test at once. We told her to "pray about it and trust." The governess was astonished at her decision, and the girls still more so. So the good confession was made, and she took her stand on the Lord's side at once, in a way which is a real crossing of the Rubicon at school. I never talk to girls about "giving up." . . .

I sent my sister the address of a young stranger, thinking that a visit would comfort her, and knowing how loyally she accepted work, but not knowing how inconvenient and pressing it would be.

Dearest Marie,—

I felt tempted to the old sense of pressure with your request, and cannot really possibly manage either of the calls you suggest, without getting totally overdone; that I can't feel would be right. I know you will approve, for you and I always understand each other.

Then follows the characteristic postscript:

I have thought it over, and decide to telegraph to your friend to meet me at Willesden Station on my journey home, and I could stay an hour at the station with her. It will be well worth *any* fatigue if I can comfort her. . . .

CHAPTER X.

(1874–1875.)

A dark enigma — Typhoid fever — "Waiting at the golden gates" — Coming back from them — Winterdyne — Relapse — Oakhampton — The ministry of kind servants — Return to work — Letters — Gleams — Whitby — "Reality!" — The old friend's letter — Kindness of friends.

"What though to-day
Thou canst not trace at all the hidden reason
For His strange dealings through the trial season,
    Trust and obey!
Though God's cloud-mystery enfold thee here,
In after life and light *all* shall be plain and clear."

In the latter part of this year (1874) came one of the strange enigmas of her life, stranger to our weaker faith than to her own implicit trust.

Somehow or somewhere she caught fever, and commenced her homeward journey with dull headache and sickness. But she did not fail in that loving care for the stranger to whom reference was made on the preceding page; and, through some mistake on her not arriving at Willesden, Frances waited an hour and a half, and then took her in the train some miles on her journey, that she might not forego the promised interview. This testimony was received after the conversation: "Oh, if I could only feel as she looked; your sister Frances was so young and lovely, and I am glad I saw for once that God-satisfied face. A ray of hope came as she talked to me in the train. . . ."

Home was reached, shiverings and feverish symptoms rapidly set in, and she was soon utterly prostrate with typhoid fever. All that motherly watchfulness, medical skill, and trained nursing could do failed to arrest the attack. About the middle of November the balancings of our hopes and fears were just between life and death. Prayer was made unceasingly for the life so dear to us, and even special prayer meetings were held to plead for one known so widely, though principally by her writings. Our prayers and cries and tears were answered, and our beloved one was restored.

Some weeks after she told me many things which may be profitable to others.

"All through my long illness I was very happy; the first part was the most painful, I think it must have been neuralgia[1] with the fever.

---
[1] neuralgia: nerve pain; sharp, paroxysmal pain along a nerve or group of nerves

I don't really think I was impatient deep down in my heart, and yet the pain and agony I was in made me anxious for the poultices, and to try anything. I do think I am sensitive to pain, and what was agony to me would be slight to others. My one wish was to glorify God and to let my doctor and nurse see it; so at the very first I determined to ask for nothing and just *obey*. Nothing could exceed dear mother's kindness and tenderness to me day and night, and getting everything I wished for. For some time, even in those bright days in the Ormont Dessus, I had a presentiment that, may be, my faith would be tried, and that my Father would not leave me without chastisement. Not that I think illness such a trial as many others I have gone through; oh, it's nothing to *unseen* trials! Besides, you get such sympathy in illness, and I knew many would pray for me. Only, I did *not* want them to pray that I might get well at all. Sometimes I could not *quite* see His Face, yet there was His promise 'I will never leave thee.' I knew He said it and that He was there."

M. "Had you any fear at all to die?"

F. "Oh no, not a shadow. It was on the first day of this illness I dictated to Constance, 'Just when Thou wilt, O Master, call!'"

M. "Then, was it delightful to think you were going home, dear Fan?"

F. "No, it was not the idea of going home, but that *He* was coming for me and that I should *see my King*. I never thought of death as going through the dark valley or down to the river; it often seemed to me a going up to the golden gates and lying there in the brightness, just waiting for the gate to open for me. . . . I never before was, so to speak, face to face with death. It was like a look into heaven; and yet, when my Father sent me back again, I felt it was His will, and so I could not be *disappointed*."

About the middle of January (1875) change of air was recommended, and I brought her to Winterdyne. I remember that, just as we were assisting her into the carriage at our Leamington home, the telegram came with the almost sudden news of our dear brother Henry's death, but it was thought right not to tell her till the journey was over.

Only a few days passed of comparative recovery, when a relapse set in, and she was again ill for many weeks. It was really delightful work to nurse one so patient, so thankful, so considerate; and, when it seemed needful to relieve the servants, and send for a nurse, they pleaded to be let sit up in turn with "dear Miss Frances."

Turning to my notebook I find some recollections which may be given.

January 29, 1875. Sitting by dear Frances she said to me, "Isn't He gracious not to send me so severe an attack as in November? I felt sure the night I was shivering that illness was coming again; and, as I lay down, the sweet consciousness that I was just lying down in His dear hand was so stilling."

"Marie, do you think this simile holds good, that when we cast our burden on the Lord, at our *first* prayer He cuts the strings that bind it on us; then, if we give a leap, the burden will slide off, and we shall not go on toiling with it up the hill! I mean, if we just thanked and praised Him, at *once* the burden would be clean gone!"

M. "Were you thinking of the burden of sin, dear?"

F. "Yes, and other burdens; specially aggravations of things that you have no strength to bear."

M. "I suppose if He is carrying *us*, then He carries our burdens too."

F. "Yes, that was our text last night, 'I will carry'; if carried, no weight on us at all."

M. "I think carrying is His first and last act; when He finds the lost sheep He lays it on His shoulder and just carries it *all* the way, even *into* His fold above. It will be nice to see Him, Fan!"

F. "'*Nice*,' I like that; but I never heard any one but you say it just like that, except Mary ———. She once told me of a missionary and his wife who had reached the end of their voyage to India, and were to have landed that night but were prevented; a sudden cyclone arose, and the ship and all in it went down instantaneously. Mary added, 'Was it not nice?'"[1]

My dear sister always enjoyed the early morning air for a few minutes, and often we had sweet talks before the break of day, and then she would get a little sleep.

Sunday, February 1, I found her very exhausted, and moaning with pain. She said: "No sleep last night, Marie. The Master wants me to bring forth more fruit, more patience." I said: "The Husbandman must be very *near* when He is pruning the branch, and He is the God of patience."

F. "That's nice."

Another morning I said: "I will give you your Morning Bell, 'Thou hast given me the shield of Thy salvation.'"

F. "*His* shield is the biggest, and brightest! I want you to ask some of His praying people to pray for me; it's not I suppose a question of recovery, but that it may be blessed and sanctified to me. But I know the Lord Jesus is praying for me."

M. "Yes, and He prays even *before* the trial or temptation comes to us, as He said to Peter, 'But I *have* prayed for thee.'"

F. "And He must have presented all those intercessions *for* Peter before they heard him knocking at the door."

After some days Frances was so extremely ill, that we telegraphed for our mother to come to Winterdyne. Remarking to Frances that dear mother was so wise, and that I could always trust her judgment in illness, she added, "Yes, and such watchfulness and handiness too."

When our dear mother arrived Frances said, "I am trusting Him for every bit of the way."

Mother. "Yes, dear, and He will not bring us by the right way and then leave us in the midst."

---

[1] "*Nice*, nice, nice indeed!" were the last words of Fanny Bickersteth. See "Doing and Suffering." [See page 360 of this book.]

F. "But perhaps the vessel won't get in *just* the tack she expects to."

After the feverish attack had passed, she suffered very much from supervening results; but even when in acute pain would say lively things, to divert our thoughts from herself. The servants were indeed astonished at her cheerful patience; and I well remember a remark she made to me: "Oh, Marie, if I might but have five minutes ease from pain! I don't want ever to moan when gentle sister Ellen comes in. How I am troubling you all!"

M. "But, Fan! we should not think it trouble to minister to the Lord Jesus!"

F. "Well no, I only hope relationship won't preclude a big 'inasmuch' for you all."

"... It's no mistake, Marie, about the blessing God sent me December 2, 1873; it is far more distinct than my conversion, I can't date that. I am always happy, and it is *such* peace; I could not help smiling when my kind doctor said, 'I dare say you feel rather depressed.' I said: 'No indeed! quite happy, only tired and want to be quiet.' Of course I should like to be at work, and it seems strange how often I am hindered from it. You are always pegging away; but I like to think I *shall* serve Him up there, and I would rather serve than rest. . . . The work I should so like to take up is drawing-room Bible readings; I so enjoyed one I took down at Bocking, but was rather startled to see the good folks taking notes! You see, I had just overcome the nervousness I used to feel, and I could so trust about this also."

Another day Frances said: "I think my special anticipation of heaven is seeing the Lord Jesus exalted, glorified, vindicated, reigning King of kings, and all His enemies owning Him."

M. "Have you thought that as, in the Gospels, Christ's special manifestations were to people when *alone,* so when we first see Him in heaven it will be *alone?*"

F. "Yes, and that is most beautifully brought out in Mr. Bickersteth's 'Yesterday, To-day, and For ever,' it's the very gem of the book. When I read it, and came to where the angel leaves him waiting for the King to come, I almost trembled as I turned the page; for, if Mr. B. had treated it with a light hand, it would have been profane; but it's lovely."

"I have been thinking, Marie, how much more God gives me than I need. Look at this illness! Well, except the bearing it, there is no other sting in it. I feel illness is the least trial, and it comes so directly from the hand of God. And how kind they all are to me! Winterdyne always seems to me a sort of millennial household!"

Her recovery was extremely slow, but her room was the brightest in the house. At last she was carried downstairs, but for some time used crutches. Needlework for the Zenana Missions was a great enjoyment to her. Sitting by her one day she told me her reasons for giving up singing at the Philharmonic.

It is a long time ago that I made the choice of singing sacred music *only.* I did so some months before I wrote:

"Take my lips, and let me sing,
Always, only, for my King."

I was visiting at Perry Villa when Dr. Marshall sent me the programme of the next Kidderminster concert, and strongly urged me to sing the part of Jezebel in the "Elijah," saying that he could not depend on any one else for it. I knew I *could* do it; for once, at the practice, the doctor said I threw such life into it. Mentioning it to Mr. Snepp, he expressed surprise, and his words struck me: "How can a Christian girl personate Jezebel?" So I thought about it, saw the inconsistency, and gave it up. I think the last thing I sang in the hall was "Come unto Him!" Then at Leamington, the first large party I went to, they asked me to sing, and I sang "Whom having not seen ye love." Every one seemed astonished, and especially some Christian girls who had begun to think music could not be for the King's service, and were rather rebelling at their daily practice. They had never thought of consecrating their voices and fingers, but began from thenceforth. I would advise any one thoroughly to master one song, make it part of yourself, throw your whole self into it, then pray it may be His message, and it will be all right. For myself, I have more confidence in singing Scripture words than any other, because they are *His*. And, Marie dear, as I sing I am praying, too, that it may soothe or reach some one, though I may never know whom.

I have been resting lately on "The Lord is my portion." All else is so unsatisfying, and even the best earthly gifts fail to reach the true depths of the heart. I do so love that hymn:

"To Thee, O dear, dear Saviour,
My spirit turns for rest."

What could we do without Him in this lonely world of shadows? And He will not let us do without Him! And may we not reverently and wonderingly say, "Neither can He do without us!" His people are so entwined around His heart that it must be so.

I have also been thinking that only the Holy Spirit can teach any one the mystery of "the blood which cleanseth from all sin." For years I believed it, without seeing as I do now into the mystery, and there are depths yet unseen, which God's Spirit reveals as His work of sanctification goes on.

We are kindly allowed to insert two or three letters of this period.

WINTERDYNE, February 22, 1875.

DEAR MR. ——,

I want to thank you for all your prayers for me. Only, only, have the prayers of my dear friends held me back from going to be with the Beloved One? Or is it that He has some more little work for me to do, and so has only been richly answering all your prayers in the "perfect peace" in which He has kept me? Oh, He has been so tenderly gracious to me; it has been such gentle, faithful lovingkindness all through. It seems worth even coming back from the very golden gates if I may but in some way "tell of His faithfulness." I do wish people would but trust Jesus *out and out,* and give themselves up utterly to Him; and then wouldn't they find rest to their souls! But it will be a long waiting time yet, "at least six months" says my doctor, before I may write or do anything. But now just see how wonderfully kind He is to me. He has taken my will as I gave it to Him, and now I really am not conscious of even a wish crossing His will concerning me. I seem to be enabled to be PERFECTLY satisfied with whatever He chooses, and it is so nice. This is all of Him, otherwise I should fidget and kick! Somehow, of late, I mean for many months, He seems not to have allowed the enemy to come near me. From the hour my illness began I have only had one dark hour, and that was when I thought my special prayer, "that this sickness might be for the glory of God," had been denied, for I felt I had not "glorified Him in the fires," because, after I had lost all my strength, I could not bear the pain without moaning and crying out, and showing eagerness for remedies. But He so tenderly assured me of pardon, and gave me "He knoweth our frame," that even that cloud soon passed. In this second illness He has mercifully spared me any recurrence of such pain, only laying upon me discomfort enough to exercise the patience which has perhaps been His chief lesson for me. Perhaps you and other dear friends will be disappointed. I know you expect that the Master will give me new and fuller messages for others after all this. But I really do not know what He has been teaching me; I do not seem conscious (at present) of having gained anything for others; it has been just lying fallow. For myself I feel as if it had intensified my trust; I *do* trust Him utterly, and feel as if I could not help trusting Him; it seems to "come natural" now! And "I will fear *no* evil" seems a natural sequence; what should I fear? There is no terror in anything when "safe in the arms of Jesus," and nothing can take me out of them. The marvellous way in which God has inclined you especially, and others too, to pray for me does seem such a token of His incomprehensible love to me, that I see I need an eternity to praise Him to my heart's content! Now, dear friend, I am asking Him that, somehow, and in His own time, He would graciously let me, even me, be the means of some new sweet blessing to you, perhaps to your people too, as a tiny return for all your loving prayers for me.

Do you think that the Lord does show unto His servants things which must shortly come to pass? It was so strange that, while perfectly well and strong in Switzerland, I had a constant presentiment that some form of physical suffering would be the next step in His dealings with me, that His loving wisdom would see it needful for me. But I had not a vestige of fear or shrinking; I rather felt I could welcome it, if it might but make me more "meet for the Master's use." So I was not a bit surprised when the illness came.

How infinitely blessed it is to be *entirely* Christ's! To think that you and I are never to have another care or another fear, but that Jesus has undertaken simply everything for us! And isn't it *grand* to have the privilege of being His instruments? It does seem such loving condescension that He should use us.

I don't know when I shall get downstairs; much too weak as yet. But I am in no hurry, He will give me strength at the right time.
Yours, etc., etc.

WINTERDYNE, February 1875.

DEAR MR.———,

Your letter came on the evening of a day of more than usual languor, after a bad night, and it was spiritual salvolatile to me! I am so glad to hear of your ten.

Many thanks for your remembrance of me on Wednesday evening, and for letting me have the pleasure of joining you. Will you tell your "band" that God seemed to put it into my heart, in a very special way, to pray that they all might be soul-winners, and *at once!* No waiting for further orders, they have got their commission *now*: "let him that heareth say, Come!" And I prayed long at Acts 4:29, 30, for them; "grant unto Thy servants," etc. But there must be power from on high, or they are helpless; and I asked that this might be given. Then, I think the Master gave me a special text for them, will you ask them to take it *each one* as from Him: "Behold I give you power over all the power of the enemy, and nothing shall by any means hurt you." Why, it is *grand*; "power over *all* the *power* of the enemy!" Just where he is strongest, there they shall prevail; not over his weak points and places, but over the very focus of his power; not over his power here and there, or now and then, but over *all* his power. And Jesus said it! Isn't it enough to go into any battle with! And it is not future; not "I *will* give," but present, now: "I *give* unto you," "unto *you*," to every one whom He sends out, to every one of your dear "ten" if they will but put out the hand of faith to take it. One hardly seems to need any addition to this, and yet His tender love adds the personal assurance, "nothing shall by any means hurt you." Nothing, really and absolutely nothing! So there is not the least loophole left for the shadow of a fear to steal in. No end to the promise, it won't leave off good for every day and moment all along, "till glory." Now, with such a clear commission and such an inspiring promise, which of your "ten," will be content to let another day pass without an attack upon "the power of the enemy"? When shall I hear of the victories that must follow? You will tell me of them, won't you? I want each one of your "ten" to begin at once to work out with God the fulfilment of Isaiah 49:25, so that numbers of captives may be delivered from the enemy, and led as blessed, willing, rejoicing captives in the triumph of Jesus Christ. I should like also to send to your "loving F———" "more than conquerors through Him that loved us," and to your "little S———" Jeremiah 1:7. Why, only think if he begins winning souls at fourteen, and goes straight on, (God sparing him,) what splendid sheaves he will have to lay at the Master's feet! Will you ask them to send me a text for myself.

In what I have said I need hardly say I do not forget the other side, that "no man can come to Me except," etc. and so on; but then is not the seeking and obtaining His power a proof that we are on the track of His purposes? "Thy people shall be willing in the day of Thy power," and it is *only in* "Thy power" that we hope to succeed. I rejoice in your joy in Him. How good He is to us!

I never find that He fails to respond to trust; it is indeed "*whatsoever*" in its fulness. And now I see that "able" means *able,* and "all" means *all.* Do you not find that, even in proportion as we realize this marvellous power upon us and in us, we realize as never before our utter dependence upon it, and utter weakness without it, AND our utter vileness and sinfulness were the cleansing power of His precious blood withdrawn for one moment! But why should we ever refuse to believe in its glorious fulness? (1 John 1:7.)

I keep wondering every day what new lovingkindness is coming next! It is such a glorious life! And the really leaving EVERYTHING to Him is so inexpressibly sweet, and surely He does arrange so much better than we could for ourselves, when we leave it all to Him.

(To J. E. J.)

DEAR J——,

I realize, "Lord, I have given my life to Thee, and every day and hour is Thine." For, literally, every hour seems in His hand, and filled with His work in some form or other, either preparation, actual service, or, as now, weakness and pain. It is quite marvellous how He really seems answering my prayer that He would accept my whole life, down to its very moments.

. . . It always seems to me the worst compliment possible to our dear Church of England, when a certain class of minds regard anything which has a little extra life, and love, and warmth, and glow, as being, well—*suspicious!* As if WE are never to ask, and never to expect, and never to *have* any such extra blessing as He is pouring out in our very midst!

In April, 1875, it was thought desirable that my sister should try change of air; and on the 3rd the Winterdyne servants gathered round for farewell words, and she thanked them warmly for all their kindness, adding: "It was a great comfort, in my illness, the way in which you waited upon me; I saw you never grudged the trouble I gave you; *that* would have distressed me. Remember, God's promises are for each of you; faith is just holding out your hand, and taking them. It is what I am learning every day; it makes me happy, and I want all of you to be always happy, trusting in the Lord Jesus."

One inscription written in the books she gave them is: "Fanny Holloway, with the writer's warm thanks for her great kindness and attention during her illness at Winterdyne, January to April, 1875. 'INASMUCH.' (Matthew 25:40.)"

A short drive to Oakhampton, and there all the comforts of her eldest sister's pleasant home awaited her.

Frances' constant consideration for the servants, wherever she visited, secured the most loving service. Bible readings in the servants' halls, kind talks alone, and helpful prayers are all remembered. The large reference Bibles she gave them are treasured remembrances of this visit. She was delighted when every servant at Oakhampton joined the Christian Progress Union.

(To J. T. W.)

OAKHAMPTON, April 1875.

DEAR MR. W——,

I see now! And the whole thing is brightened up splendidly! I both meant myself, and took your remarks to apply, to "fallow" as to service and preparation for service; and so, while I read them with great interest and pleasure, I did not get the full benefit of them, because I said, "Oh yes, but I *am* all right on this point!" But I was all wrong on the point you aimed at, and by your second letter *hit.* I see that "lamenting" and "trusting" are not compatible; and that, while I fancied I was trusting for everything, I was not trusting as to His *spiritual* dealings with me, and that I might rest as satisfied about this as about all else.

Yes, I "could not read His prescription," but I can now take it without trying to spell it. I see that my growth in grace is *His* affair, and that He is certainly taking care of it, even though I don't see it. Only, I am so sorry I did not trust Him perfectly; it makes me feel that I shall henceforth mistrust myself more than ever, and yet trust Him more than ever.

I am beginning to taste a little bit of the real blessedness of waiting. One does not wait *alone,* for He waits too. Our waiting times are His also. I have been so delighted with the two "*waits*" in Isaiah 30:18, surely it implies a fellowship of waiting.

(To the same.)

April, 1875.

I must just begin a letter to you. Intercourse, even by letter, with real and dear Christian friends, is one of the pleasures which one only *sips* here, but don't you think it will be a great delight above? I have been thinking how nice it will be to have a long talk with you in heaven, in the grand leisure of eternity, and interchange the blessed things which the Master will (I suppose) be showing and saying to each, with just as much individuality of revelation as here. Perhaps I look forward to this peculiarly, because I have so very many congenial Christian friends whom I rarely see, and correspondents, known and unknown, with whom I cannot have the intercourse I would; and, owing to my delicate health, there have always been so many interruptions to communications, and of late so much entire isolation. But I think you probably have the same keen anticipation, for you can't have time on earth for much "sweet counsel"! And how well we can afford to wait for *some* of our "good things"!

Nearly nine months, since I was last at morning family worship! I was in almost *too* great spirits about it, which is not good for me, and of course I had to subside, and go and lie down for a considerable part of the morning; still it was quite an epoch! After four months' illness and weakness, I am told that I must not expect to be able for any sort of work for at least six months longer; but I do not feel one regret. Somebody wrote to me about resignation the other day; but I don't feel as if the word suited at all; there is an *undertone* of "feeling it rather hard nevertheless" in it, of submitting to a will which is different from one's own. He has granted me fully to *rejoice* in His will, I am not conscious of even a wish crossing it; I do really and altogether desire that His will may be done, *whatever* it is. It was so sweet, when my second illness began, to lie down under His dear hand, not knowing how long or how much I might have to suffer, but perfectly happy and trustful about it, and *quite* satisfied that He should do with me just as He would. Oh, isn't it good of Him to have wrought this for me! This terrible pain,—I cannot feel that I *wish* it taken away a day sooner than His far-sighted faithful love appoints. . . . .

This morning I opened on Deuteronomy 32:2, "My speech shall distil *as the dew*." It seemed a direct answer from Him, for one does not see the dew fall, one never sees it at all till morning, and then! So perhaps He is speaking to me more than I think for, and, when the "afterward" comes, it may be that I shall find He has said a good deal to me after all!

Yours ever.

(*To the same.*)

I find (having fairly tried) that the whole gift of verse is taken from me. I think it will some day be restored (as once before after five years' suspension); but at present I could not write a hymn or poem. Thus God proves to me it is directly from Him, not a power to be used at my will, but only when He will; and I would rather have it so. But, even if I were in full vein, I only consciously write up to my own experience; so, though I might write what you would like to see on "Rest and Brightness," I should have to leave out praise for "power," because I do not feel that, as yet, God has ever endued me with *that*. It is not "come, see, and conquer," as to souls, with me as it is with you. I know some of my words do not fall to the ground, but most of them do; and the blessing which He does seem to send with my printed writings, and sometimes with my letters, does not seem to me quite the same thing as the blessed "power" which some have. That reminds me, this morning I read 2 Corinthians 4 in the Greek, and was so wonderingly happy over that "far more exceeding weight of glory." I had not specially noticed the Greek before, how magnificently far reaching and strong it is! I suppose "*from* glory *to* glory" is even here and now, and *then* to go beyond this to an eternal weight of glory, and *then* for *this* to be καθ' ὑπερβολὴν εἰς ὑπερβολὴν, is such a marvellous leading on of finite thought into *infinite* glory! It is like those flights that one now and then takes from planets to suns, and suns to star systems and cycles, and then away to the farthest nebulae, and then one sees no end, for imagination and analogy go on till they get lost in infinity. But to think that we are actually going right *into* all this glory, and have actually begun with it; having the earnest of the purchased possession *now*, and absolute certainty of all of it before long! What are flights among stars and nebulæ compared to this! I have not thought it out, but I *feel* a connection between this and the Greek in Ephesians 3:19.

(*To J. G. M. Kirckhoffer.*)

May 9.

DEAR JULIA,—

Thank you very much for your very pretty little ballad, and for the leaflets. I shall watch your pen, if we live, with much interest, and pray that you may be enabled to consecrate it, always and entirely, to our beloved Master. You will need to be very watchful, for Satan will try to sow tares among your wheat, and to introduce *self* into what we want to be *only* for Christ.

But His grace is sufficient, and if He keeps you, by that grace, humble and looking unto Him, the gift He entrusts to you will be help to yourself, and I hope to many others, and the enemy will not be able to turn it into a hindrance. I am so glad you have been at work already for the dear old Irish Society, and with such thorough good will. Will you make it a matter of prayer? It is often wonderful what unexpected opportunities God gives us when we ask. I have so often found it so in collecting for this very thing. Your taking the card was an answer to myself, for I was feeling rather disheartened that day in the work, and prayed that I might have some extra bit of success at last, as a token for good. And then you consented to *collect*, where I only looked for a single subscription. I am afraid it will be, still, a long time before I come home, but I hope to see you and your kind friends when I do. I send you one of my favourite texts, "He *is* precious." Think of the absolute "is," always and unspeakably precious, whether we realize it or not. How little we know of His preciousness yet, but how much there is to know, and how much we shall know! Press on then to find more of His preciousness.

Yours affectionately.

(*Extracts from Letters to Miss E. J. Whately.*)

June 1875.

.... Though I have had plenty of invalided times, and of short sharp suffering, this has been my very first experience of really severe and prolonged illness (since October); and I do not merely think I *ought* to feel, but I DO feel, that it was the crowning blessing of a year of unprecedented blessing and yet of many trials. "Great is Thy faithfulness" shines on every day of it; and "I will fear no evil" is more than ever a very *song* to me. It was as if, while laying His own dear hand ever so heavily upon me, He kept the enemy completely at a distance, and did not let him even approach me, encompassing me with a wall of fire.... For three or four weeks I was too prostrate for any consecutive prayer, or for even a text to be given me; and this was the time for realizing what "silent in love" meant (Zephaniah 3:17). And then it seemed doubly sweet when I was again able to "hold converse" with Him. He seemed, too, so often to send answers from His own word with wonderful power. One evening, (after a relapse,) I longed so much to be able to pray, but found I was too weak for the least effort of thought, and I only looked up and said, "Lord Jesus, I am *so* tired!" And then He brought to my mind "rest in the Lord," with its lovely marginal reading, "*be silent* to the Lord," and so I just was silent to Him, and He seemed to overflow me with perfect peace, in the sense of His own perfect love. It was worth anything to lie and think that it might be really "the Master's home call"; but I do think it was worth almost more to find, when the tide turned, that He had really *taken* the will I had laid at His feet, and could and did take away all the disappointment which I had fancied must be so keen at being turned back from the golden gates. I was more astonished at finding that He could make me quite as glad and willing to live and suffer, as to go straight away to heaven, than at anything, I think. And it is just the same now. I have no idea how long I may have to wait, for (though not now ill, but only invalided), what with relapses and results, I am making very slow progress, and not likely to be able for any sort of work for months yet: but I do so feel the truth of "blessed are they that *wait* for Him." It seems a necessary sequence of the first part of the verse, "therefore will the Lord wait," for waiting *for* Him is waiting WITH Him. I am breaking rules in writing so much, but I could not help wanting to tell you how very kind He has been to me, and I don't think any Christian could be more utterly unworthy than I of such gentle, gracious dealing. I doubted and mistrusted Him for so many years, and what I used to call "terrible conflict" I now see to have been simple unbelief.

.... It is so nice to meet those with whom one is in full sympathy. One meets so many who only go such a little way; I mean really Christians, yet taking such faint interest in Christ's cause and kingdom, all alive as to art, or music, or general on-goings, yet not seeming to feel the music of His name. One does so long for all who are looking to Him for salvation to be "true-hearted, whole-hearted." And I have been thinking how inevitably such half-hearted Christians will be at a disadvantage when "He cometh," as compared with those whose whole gladness is from Him only, and whose whole interests are centred in His kingdom and that which advances it.

With the return of health came a return to work. Her quick sympathy and loving help, by word and by letter, can hardly be represented. "Aunt Fanny always understands me" indicates the source of her influence. Pencil notes of hers, which are really treasures, lie before me, but only glimpses may be given.

(*In the train*) September 29, 1875.

My own dear "Little Thing",—

... I have been thinking so much and so sadly of the hint you gave me.... We must be much in prayer about it. For yourself, dear little thing, whatever the *near* bothers or the *far* griefs may be, you and all your "matters" are in the dear Saviour's hand, and He says, "My grace is sufficient for thee," and I like to take a still simpler Saxon word and say, "My grace is *quite enough* for thee." Yes, "quite enough," dear, for all the sorrows and all the trials, little ones as well as great, and all the weakness and all the insufficiency and all the coldness and hardness of heart, *quite* enough for you in spite of all!

(*To the same.*)

Dearest "Little Thing",—

Let the Lord lead you, *let* Him have you *altogether*. And, dear pet, blessing hardly ever comes alone; if He has the joy of winning you altogether for Himself, He won't stop there, He will do more, He is doing so here. I do trust two of the servants are resting and trusting, and I quite hope the gardener has laid hold on eternal life; and I am expecting more for the angels to rejoice over.... I feel most deeply for you. Keep very close to Jesus, my darling, and ask Him never to let you take back what you have now given Him. Be His entirely, without any reserve, and He will be yours entirely....

My own "Little Thing",—

If you knew how glad we all are! But, better still, I know Jesus is glad. He wanted you, or He would not have drawn you. And now, dearie, just *rest* in Him. Listen to all He has to say, and you will find He has "somewhat to say to thee" every time you open His word. Listen, and obey whatever He says (John 2:5). Mr. Mountain said, "our souls should be like aspen leaves, responsive to the least breath of the Spirit." Dear little thing, be one of the Lord's aspen leaves; don't wait for great strong blasts, but yield to the least whisper from Him of "this is the way, walk ye in it." And, now, expect great things! You don't know what He is going to astonish you with. "Open thy mouth wide, and I will fill it." Go to work for Him at once, put your little sickle in, and see if the Lord does not make the sheaves fall before it! *Don't hold back from letting Him use you.* Your blessing will probably, if you are quite faithful with it, result in fresh blessing all around you to those who have been blessed already, and who knows what to those who do not yet know the fulness of the blessing! Keep trusting the Lord Jesus, or rather let Him keep you trusting, and draw every word from Him; ask Him always, all day long, what to do, what to say. Pray Mr. Aitken's prayer: "Lord, take my lips and speak through them; take my mind and think through it; take my heart and set it on fire!"

Your loving aunt.

P.S.—Yes, sing for Jesus! do *all* in the name of the Lord Jesus Christ.

(*To C. H.*)

Dear Clement,—

You are all alone, so I must send you a line. However, you will not find it very dismal in this lovely weather and the bright look out of seeing your dear ones. Last evening I was at a young women's meeting, and asked to sing, so I prayed the dear Master would let me bring them a message of song from Himself. There are so many "all for Jesus" Christians here. Seriously, dear Clement, if that is indeed our heart's motto, we find that Jesus *is* all for us, and all in all to us. I hit upon two little texts yesterday which fitted together beautifully. First, a prayer, "Do Thou for me, O Lord," did you ever notice it? "*do* Thou," just whatever wants doing for us or in us, just whatever we cannot do at all for ourselves. Then, if we really pray this, we shall follow it up with "God that performeth all things for me!" Think of *His* simply *doing every thing* for you and me. What can we wish more?

Your loving aunt.

"Don't hold back from letting Him use you!" Loyal words, often repeated. A friend in Leamington remembers showing F. R. H. a letter she had received from Miss Weston, asking her to write "Monthly Letters for Seamen." Frances read the letter and said to Mrs. B., "What are you going to do? Accept it of course!"

Mrs. B. "I am not fit for such a work. I know nothing of ships and sailors."

F. "If you reject it, God does not want for instruments to do His work; don't shrink from the honour He puts upon you."

Such was her faithful encouragement.

(To ——.)

Ashley Moor, September, 1875.

I can hardly say I am sorry for you, dear friend, although you tell me of suffering and trial, and although I feel very much for you in it; because I am so *sure* the Master is leading you by the right way, and only means it to issue in all the more blessing. What mistakes we should make if we had the choosing, and marked out nice smooth paths for our friends! It has struck me too, very much lately, that the Lord's most used and blessed workers are always almost *weighted* in some way or other. I don't know one who, to our limited view, is not working under weights and hindrances of some sort, contrasting with mere professors who seem so much more favourably placed for what they *don't* do....

I am so very glad that He did not answer prayer for my recovery all those eight months of illness; why I should have missed all sorts of blessing and precious teaching if He had! But when one feels that He Himself gives " the prayer of faith," then I would pray it " nothing doubting."

After the 14th, my address will be Post Office, Whitby, Yorkshire. I am so thankful and rejoiced at what you tell me about the two ladies; it is so gracious of Him to use my hymns.

Yours, in His grace and love.

In the autumn of 1875 Frances went to Whitby with Mr. and Mrs. Shaw; *en route* she visited Miss Sadler and her sister, the friends of early days. She also enjoyed a visit to York Minster, and a pleasant interview with Dr. Dykes.

It was at Whitby she heard, in the noon prayer meeting, the petition of a working man, " *Father, we know the reality of Jesus Christ.*" The same evening she wrote the poem: " Reality, Reality, Lord Jesus Christ, Thou art to me."

(*To E. C.*)

WHITBY, September.

... So singular! you know I have not been able to write verses at all for a long time, but reading a naughty article in —— —— set me going, and I wrote "Without Carefulness." Curiously enough, it was written just in time for the International Women's Christian Association Conference at New York. I was invited to this, and if I could not come, to write a poem to be read at it. I was going to answer " I can't write a line," when this came to me, and it will reach the committee just in time, though I did not write it with that intention. Then Mr. Shaw lent a copy to a friend, and reply came asking permission by telegraph to use it at another Conference. Had the article reached me a day later, it would have been too late for both!

Does not this look like God's hand? It seemed like coming back into the stream again, out of the shadowy pool of silent waiting. Somehow, I don't feel enough physical strength to be at all eager to get into the current at present....

WHITBY, October, 1875.

DEAREST G——,

... I hope to be at home the end of next week (but don't publish it, as I can't see everybody immediately on arriving).

Mamma is better, but has been so ill that it was a question whether she could reach England. I am so thankful for her.

For myself, I have not been ill, though often poorly, since my last relapse in June; but I decidedly do not get strong, and am not nearly so strong as before my illness, even under these most favourable circumstances of bracing air, and nobody that *must* be seen, and nothing that *must* be done; so I am hardly likely to get any stronger at Leamington. I can do a little, write an hour or two, see one or two people, sing one song, go to church once on Sunday and subside all the rest of the day; but that is the length of my tether. I came upon some verses which seem just to express it.

" I am not eager, bold, or strong,
    All that is past;
I'm ready *not* to do,
    At last, at last.

My half-day's work is almost done,
    'Tis all my part;
I bring my patient God
    A patient heart."

For I am quite satisfied to do *half-day's* work henceforth, if He pleases; and well I may be when I have plenty of proof that He can make a *half-hour's* work worth a whole day's if He will: yes, or half-a-minute's either!

... So curious your praise meeting (Young Women's Christian Association) being November 19th, for it will be the anniversary of my very worst day last year. You can't think how much I am looking forward to being at a meeting again, and to seeing you, and a few other special Y. W. C. A.'s. But I shall always have an idea that I was *prayed back* from the golden gates! I can't think why God always so graciously lets me see such heaps of reasons for every trial He sends me. Why, as to this year of calling apart, I wouldn't have done without it if I could, and I couldn't have done without it if I would; it seems to me a consummately wisely sent and wisely timed trial (only that I hardly like to use that word for it, except perhaps as regards the physical pain). I want to tell everybody, now, that they need " fear *no* evil."

On page 5 [page 248 of this book] we have already referred to our dear father's curate, Rev. F. Jeffery, and his recollection of the early birthday crown of bay-leaves. That reference will make clear the allusions in the following letter.

December, 1875.

DEAR MR. JEFFERY,—

If you only knew the gush of early recollections your beautiful little verses[1] brought up! my birthday wreaths, and dear papa's and

---

[1] The following are the verses referred to:

To F. R. H., *on Her Birthday*, December 14th, 1875.

"Non sine Diis animosus infans."—*Horace.*

FANNY, canst thou still remember
    How, of old, they kept this day?
How they marked thy fourth December,
    Crowning thee with wreath of bay?

" Child belov'd, these leaves poetic
    Hence shall aye to thee belong,
Wear them as a wreath prophetic
    Of the Ministry of Song."

Say not now thy task is ended;
    Sing the lovely, pure, and true
Sing until thy verse is blended
    With the Song for ever new.

F. J.

mamma's birthday kisses and wishes, which I always felt meant a great deal more than I could possibly understand. And now the Lord hath led me, not quite, but pretty nearly, the "forty years," though only the very old friends give me credit for much beyond thirty.

How kind of you to recollect the little chit! And how I should like to thank you personally for the pleasant remembrance! But I must tell you how refreshing it is, quite apart from the sentiment, to come across such *trochaics*. It is rarely that I light on such, among the thousands of hymns I have gone over in my work of "Songs of Grace and Glory"; yours have such a perfect ringing rhythm as very few seem to hit upon now-a-day.

I have just begun to work a little, as a sort of "half-timer" (to use the factory expression), after twelve months of "calling apart": typhoid fever, which, with relapses and results, kept me ill for eight months, and part of the time very suffering; and then four months of very slow convalescence. But it has been the most precious year of my life to me. It is worth any suffering to prove for oneself the truth of "when thou passest through the waters I will be with thee," and worth being turned back (as it seemed) from the very golden gates, if one may but "tell of His faithfulness." It is so *real*.

Your own signature, dear Mr. Jeffery, makes the verses doubly valuable, written "in the shadow" (your darkness is the shadow of His hand). I do feel so much for you in your blindness! How I should like to come and sing to you! My dear mother is very bright in spirits but very suffering in body.

Yours affectionately.

Pyrmont Villa, December 13, 1875.

My dear E——,

Nothing surprised me so much as, and nothing pleased me more than, your beautiful flowers and card. I have had a battle with mamma as to where they are to go; she thinks them too good for her room, where I wanted to have the pleasure of putting them. However, I think I have won! Thank you *so* much for them. I must tell you why they are such special pleasure: because I don't think you would have sent them if you had just simply hated all I said the other day. Dear ——, I never told you, but you can't think how I have longed for you ever since I first saw you. I have prayed for you again and again. I want you for Jesus! It is not only that I want you to be safe in Him, I do want that; but I want you to be altogether His own, knowing all the sweet peace of being His very own, and using all your bright days for Him. I want you to be "all for Jesus." I do so long for you to give Him your heart and life now, so that you might never have the terrible sorrow of having only a death-bed to give Him! And I am sure He wants you; really and truly now, at this very moment, is waiting for you, and wanting you to come to Him and let Him show you His "exceeding great love." There are so few comparatively that are on His side: won't you be one? If you could see Him now, this minute, *waiting for you,* you wouldn't like to keep Him waiting I am sure; and you wouldn't and *couldn't* think about anything else till you had heard what He, Jesus, your real Saviour, wanted to say to you. Dear child, I have asked my own dear Master to give me some token of His love on my birthday: shall it be this, that He will call you, *so* call you that you shall come to Him and "find rest"?

Your loving friend.

Mention should be made of the kindness of many Leamington friends constantly shown to both our dear mother and Frances. But it is impossible even to give outline of any such, or the names of most valued friends, whose ceaseless ministry threw flowers of sympathy on paths of weariness and suffering.

CHAPTER XI.

(1876.)

"The Turned Lesson" — Patient work — Sympathy with E. C., going to India — Upton Bishop Vicarage — The brother's organ and last singing — The last visit to Switzerland — "*Seulement pour Toi*" — Bible reading to peasants — The Great St. Bernard — Champéry — Baroness Helga von Cramm — Alpine cards — Illness at Pension Wengen — Return home — "My King" — Pruning.

"Was it not kinder the task to turn,
  Than to let it pass,
As a lost, lost leaf that she did not learn?

Is it not often so,
  That we only learn in part,
And the Master's testing-time may show
  That it was not quite "by heart"?

Then He gives, in His wise and patient grace,
    That lesson again
With the mark still set in the self-same place." [1]

THERE were many "turned lessons" in my dear sister's life to which no clue can be given in these Memorials; but we may here refer to one testing-time. Very patiently had she prepared for press many sheets of manuscript music in connection with the Appendix to "Songs of Grace and Glory." Well do I remember the day it was completed. We were at home, and she came down from her study with a large roll for post, and with holiday glee exclaimed, "There it is all done! and now I am free to write a book!" Only a week passed, when the post brought her the news: "Messrs. Henderson's premises were burned down this morning about four o'clock. We fear the whole of the stereotypes of your musical edition are destroyed, as they were busy printing it. It will be many days before the *débris* will be sufficiently cooled to ascertain how the stereotype plates stand."

Further news confirmed the loss: "Your musical edition, together with the paper sent for printing it, has been totally destroyed." On the same sheet Frances wrote to her sisters in Worcestershire:

The signification hereof to me is that, instead of having finished my whole work, I have to begin again *de novo,* and I shall probably have at least six months of it. The greater part of the manuscript of my Appendix is simply *gone,* for I had kept no copy whatever, and have not even a list of the tunes! Every chord of my own will have to be reproduced; every chord of any one else re-examined and revised. All through my previous "Songs of Grace and Glory" work, and my own books, I had always taken the trouble to copy off every correction on to a duplicate proof; but, finding I never gained any practical benefit, I did not (as I considered) waste time in this case! Of most of the new work, which has cost me the winter's labour, I have not even a memorandum left, having sent everything to the printers. However it is so clearly "Himself hath done it," that I can only say "*Thy way not mine, O Lord.*" I only tell you how the case stands, not as complaining of it, only because I want you to ask that I may do what seems drudgery quite patiently, and that I may have health enough for it, and that He may overrule it for good. It may be that He has more to teach me, before He sets me free to write the two books to which N —— alludes, and which I hoped to have begun directly. Perhaps they will be all the better because I cannot now write them for next season. Thus I am suddenly shut off from the bright stream of successful writing, and stopped in all my own plans for this spring, and bid work a few months longer in the shade at what is to me special exercise of quiet patience. . . . I have thanked Him for it more than I have prayed about it. It is just what He did with me last year, it is another *turned lesson.* I had mourned over not bearing pain in my first illness, and so He gave me another opportunity of learning the lesson by sending me another painful illness, at Winterdyne, instead of giving me up as a hopeless pupil; and now I have been eager to get done with "Songs of Grace and Glory" that I might hurry on to begin work of my own choosing and planning, and so He is giving me the opportunity *over again* of doing it more patiently, and of making it the "willing service" which I don't think it was before. If I could not rejoice in letting Him do what He will with me, when He thus sends me such very marked and individual dealing, I should feel that my desire for sanctification, for His will to be done in me, had been merely nominal, or fancied and not real.

(*To Miss E. J. Whately.*)

One must be an infidel not to see God's hand upon one, most distinctly, in such a matter as this. But it was very good of Him to give me the opportunity of learning the unlearnt lesson, and of offering, as more willing service, what had been *un*willing. I must tell you, however, how overwhelmingly gracious He has been to me the last few days, quite startling me. I thought it had been such a useless spring, that I had not been allowed to be any service to any one. Then all at once, during three days, a number of notes poured in upon me, quite astonishing me with telling that I had been made such real use and blessing, in some cases quite unconsciously, in others where I thought my efforts had produced little or no effect. . . . Now, is not this enough to make one's heart overflow with praise? It has been a most sweet lesson of trust, and of more simple and absolute dependence on Him.

(*To J. T. W.*)

Pyrmont Villa, March 21, 1876.

Dear Friend,—

Your letter, which I was providentially prevented from reading before breakfast, sent me straight away to my knees. I have been putting it all into my Saviour's hands, pouring out to Him. I don't *feel* cured, but I believe He has taken me into His hands afresh. No, it has not been all for Him of late; I don't mean anything definite, but breaches in the enclosure, made not by any outward foe or even "the religious world," but by self, which I wanted to be crushed out of me, that He might take its place wholly. I think that has been the "something between," and it has dimmed not only the inner brightness, but the free-hearted testimony. It is so utterly horrid not to have been *all* for Him. I do feel ready to say "sinners, of whom *I* am *chief,*" and no expressions of self bemoaning are too strong for me. He has been so much to me, so very, *very* gracious; and yet I have wandered, without knowing it except by finding that He withdrew the brightness of His shining, graciously so, because I felt the chill; and yet, at times, off and on, it has even of late been very bright, very happy, only it has not been the steady and growing brightness. Thank you very much for telling me how it is with you; that helps, because I have to do with the "*same* Jesus." I want Him to prove me to the very depths, to "search and try" and cleanse entirely. I am glad He did not set me free to write. I distinctly believe it to be His holding me back from teaching before I am taught! I am so grateful for your letter, it is so good of Him to put it into your heart to watch over

---

[1] The Turned Lesson, in "Under His Shadow," page 113. [See pages 176–178 of Volume I of the Havergal edition.]

me. Will you pray for me? I imagined I had thought much of the "keep," as well as of the "take," but I have not *lived* it somehow. I know you must feel disappointed with me; I have not "run well" as you hoped, but don't give me up and throw me overboard altogether, pray for me, and "watch over me" still for the dear Master's sake, for I know He has not thrown me overboard, and oh *I do* love Him. Thanks for the card; I thought it *was* "*none* of self and *all* of Thee." I have immense temptations. I don't mean that as any excuse, only it is so; temptations to self seeking and self complacency, etc.; and I am made too much of, looked up to by plenty who should rather look down on me, both here and by strangers; and I thought I was on my guard against it all; and yet I see it has insensibly undermined the "enclosure," even though I have been having exceptionally great outward privileges. I wonder whether one thing has been wrong! I have been, for some time, nearly every day giving half an hour to careful reading of Shakespeare; I felt as if I rather wanted a little intellectual bracing, as if something of contact with *intellect* were necessary to prevent my getting into a weak and wishy-washy kind of thought and language. I like intellects to rub against, and have no present access to books which would do it; so I bethought myself of seeing what Shakespeare would do for me, and I think my motive was really that I might polish my own instruments for the Master's use. But there is so much that is entirely of the earth earthy, amid all the marvellous genius and even the sparkles of the highest truth which flash here and there, so much that jars upon one's spirit, so much that is downward instead of upward; that it has crossed me whether I am not trusting an arm of flesh in seeking intellectual benefit, thus. Yet, on the other hand, if one admits the principle, one would throw over all means as to study and mental culture, and it does really seem as a rule as if God endorsed those means, and uses cultivated powers, and only very exceptionally uses the uncultured ones.

Yours gratefully.

(*To F. A. S.*)

Leamington, February 16, 1876.

I hope you have had a happy week, dear F———. Only you must not let the temptation come, to fancy that He cannot, or will not, be as much to you afterwards as He perhaps was to you during the special week; for, to begin with, "He faileth not," "I change not." He will be every day "*this same Jesus*"; and, to go on with, your whole Bible does not contain one word about His giving less grace, but always and only "more grace." If He gave you blessing last week, it is only an earnest of MORE, if you "open your mouth," etc. "*Always* more to follow."

Your loving aunt.

(*To J. T. W.*)

The Leasowes, April 9, 1876.

It seems to come natural to send you whatever odds and ends come out, so I enclose this last leaflet, "I could not do without Him." I very seldom write at the suggestion of another, but a London worker said she so wanted an appeal to the outsiders based on my hymn "I could not do without Thee." So I told her she must pray if she wanted it, and I forthwith forgot all about it. Three months after, a most strong and sudden sense came over me of "what *can* they, what *will* they, do without Jesus?" that I *must* write it; and it was not until afterwards I recollected that this was the very thing that had been asked. And, on sending it, I found it was *just at the right time* for her special wish to distribute it before one of Mr. Aitken's mission weeks! It will be in *Home Words* for June, which means going straight to 300,000 homes, let alone leaflets and American copies. Somehow, I have felt able to ask great blessings on this leaflet, though it is such a poor little simple thing, without a spark of poetry about it.

Yours ever gratefully.

I got just a glimpse of the marvellous indwelling of *Father, Son, and Holy Ghost* last week; it was so sweet and glorious; I want to realize it *always*.

(*To J. G. Kirchhoffer.*)

April 9.

Dearest Julia,—

You deserve an immense long letter, and I have really only time for a few lines, as I am giving up my whole available time to work at the new edition of "Songs of Grace and Glory." Though your letter-case looks too pretty to use, yet I immediately adopted it for unanswered letters, putting in yours to begin with. Yours must be indeed a pretty home. It is not just words, but both wish and prayer, that it may be a happy one to you, and that you may make many around you happy and happier. Of course I mean this in the very fullest and deepest sense. Ever since I knew you, I have specially wished and prayed that you might entirely live for Jesus, and shine very brightly for Him. And you have immense responsibilities.

Why not work out your "plan of education" as a little ballad? I think it would be a capital subject, and might be really useful. Send it to the Editor of *The Children's Friend*. (S. W. Partridge & Co.)

As to imperfect scanning, I must try to answer seriously, for it is rather important to you. Never leave imperfect scanning, to save the trouble of making it perfect, *never!* Discipline yourself for the next few years most sternly in this, and you will be thankful, later on, for the habit and facility which it will give you. But irregular scanning may be used with great artistic effect, where you purposely wish to suggest abrupt, broken, startling, rugged, spasmodic, etc., effects. A good critic will easily detect the difference between the devices of an artist and the negligence or clumsiness of a tyro[1] in this matter.

I have an idea that metre answers to key in music, and that one may introduce modulation of metre exactly as one introduces modulation of key, and with similar mental effect. I have tried it in several recent longish poems, using different metres for different parts, and modulating from one into the other instead of passing directly. You will see what I mean in "The Sowers," where, instead of jumping direct into the rather jubilant metre of the last part, I work up to it through "One by one no longer," etc.

I must not scribble more.

Yours lovingly.

(*To the same.*)[2]

Pyrmont Villa, Monday.

Dear Julia,—

How I *do* wish I had known! It would have been the most

---

[1] tyro (also spelled tiro): a novice or beginner   [2] See page 347 of this book.

exquisite pleasure to have come to sing to you. I know that longing for music *so* well, though I do not think many know what it is. Sometimes I have thought that this very "music-thirst" is part of God's gentle discipline, leaving us with that thirst instilled, just that we may turn afresh to that which stills all longings, the music of His name. I have had plenty of verses headed "F. R. H.," but I am telling the truth when I say that I never had any which touched me more, or gave me such a thrill of loving fellow-feeling towards the writer. Thank you very much for sending them to me.

Now I have a request. Will you give me a copy of your extremely good verses on the recovery of the Prince of Wales. . . .

(*To the same.*)

Many thanks, not only for the enclosure, but for your most amusing note.

N.B.—It is only fair to tell you that you and Ellen Lakshmi Goreh are the solitary ones, out of any number of dozen possible geniuses, whose "efforts" I have seen or had to do with, in whom I *do* believe. I have come across no others who, I honestly believe, may have a "future" in the literary part of the vineyard. This may show you I am not quite indiscriminate! and perhaps add weight to the encouragement which I want to give you, and the seriousness of the hope and aim before you.

My sister's expectations were correct; but Miss Kirchhoffer's early death left, as it were, only a prelude to what might have been a life of song.[1] (See Appendix I, original page 354.)

The following shows how faithfully she pointed out the inconsistency of some conversation.

Tuesday, 7 a.m.

My dear ——,

As I have already had one bad night, and several troubled wakings, all about *you*, I had better get it off my mind. I write to you as one who is really wanting to follow Jesus altogether, really wanting to live and speak EXACTLY according to His commands and His beautiful example; and when this is the standard, what seems a little thing, or nothing at all, to others, is seen to be *sin*, because it is disobeying His dear word and not "following *fully*." "Whatsoever ye would that men should do unto you, do ye *even so* to them."

Now, darling, be true to yourself, and to Him, as to these His own words. Would you like any one to retail, and dwell upon, little incidents which made you appear weak, tiresome, capricious, foolish? Yet, dear, everything which we say of another which we would not like them to say of us, (unless said with some right and pure object which Jesus Himself would approve,) is transgression of this distinct command of our dear Lord's, and therefore *sin*,—sin which needs nothing less than His blood to cleanse, sin in which we indulge at our peril and to the certain detriment of our spiritual life. And Jesus hears every word, and sees, to the depth, the want of real conformity to His own loving spirit, from which they spring. Do not think I am condemning you without seeing my own failures. It is just because it is a *special* battle-field of my own that I am the more pained and quick to feel it, when others, who love Jesus, yield to the temptation or do not see it to be temptation. I know the temptation it is to allow oneself to say things which one would not say if the person were present, yes, and if Jesus were visibly present. And I have seen and felt how even a momentary indulgence in the mildest forms of "speaking evil," which is so absolutely forbidden, injures one's own soul, and totally prevents clear, unclouded communion with Jesus. So I want you to recognise and shun and resolutely and totally "put away" this thing.

I should not write all this but that I long for your eyes to be opened to the *principle,* for others' sakes, for your own soul's sake, and for Christ's sake. I want you to pray over it, to search bravely to the bottom, and to put it all into the hands of Jesus, that He may not only forgive but cleanse, and so fill you with His love that it (and nothing else) may overflow into all your words, that He may "make you to increase and abound in love . . . . to the end He may establish your heart *unblameable in holiness.*" Oh, if you knew how I pray for this for myself, you would not wonder at my anxiety about it for you and for others! So don't be vexed with,

Yours ever lovingly

(*To E. C.*)

1876.

. . . This seems a great and solemn step. I could never lift up my finger against what looks so like a call from God, though you would seem a long way off from us, and would be much mourned and missed from your Bewdley work. You know how I have always desired, with you, to lay out one's life at *the best interest* for God; and, of course, if you can do ten per cent. of work at Rome, and only five per cent. among the Severn fogs, that is to my mind a strong argument. . . . I send you "I will direct their work in truth," and He *will* direct. Have you thought of work in Syria?

(*To the same.*)

Although dear Miss Nott told me she thought you were thinking of Zenana work in India, I did not expect this! Whether Rome or India, I quite think you are one of those so situated that you are "free to serve," and that the question may be wholly between you and God. . . . I am specially glad it is that Society; it is decidedly my favourite, and I have been interested in it for fifteen years. Dear Elizabeth, I feel so solemnly glad about all this; I myself seem, more and more, a "cumberer," so I am the more glad when others are able for more service than

Yours lovingly.

(*To the same.*)

. . . It often strikes me as one of the wonderful wheels of God's providence that He lays different parts of His work on different hearts, brings one nearer to the focus of one worker's vision and another to another, and thus all the different things get taken up. . . . I

---

[1] "Poems and Essays." By Julia G. M. Kirchhoffer. Paisley: J. and R. Parlane. [See page 347 of this book.]

had only thought of the disappointment it would be, if you were prevented going to India! I suppose, partly, because I do not feel separation so keenly as you would, and partly because *all my life* it has been a sort of "castle in the air" *to be a missionary,* only that the door for me seemed always closed by the state of my health; and, even with my many ties, it would be nothing like the sacrifice to me that it will be to you. I shall long to hear that the Lord has made the way quite clear, and set before you an open door.

June 1876. During a visit to her brother Frank, at Upton Bishop Vicarage, she was much interested in his schools and cottages. Every day she went about from house to house, reading the Bible and telling in simple words of God's love in sending Jesus Christ to save sinners.

In one instance, at a garden party, my sister's happy face attracted a young stranger, so that she sought conversation with her. Often have I been told: " F. R. H. looks so really happy, she must have something we have not." (With the utmost skill, no artist or photograph gives a *real* idea of her lighted up expression. Is it because soul cannot be represented any more than a sunbeam?) And my *pen* fails, too, in giving an idea to strangers of her sunny ways, merrily playing with children, and heartily enjoying all things. But her deep sympathy with others' joys and sorrows, and her loyal longings that all should know the "joy unspeakable and full of glory," were the secret of her influence with others.

I may mention that her singing from Handel's "Messiah," accompanying herself on her brother's organ, after service on her last Sunday evening at Upton Bishop, will long be remembered by all who heard. The old parish clerk remarked, " I never heard the like of that before." Frances then became the first contributor to a fund for erecting a vestry. (Since her death it has been determined that this vestry shall be specially " in memory of F. R. H." Her brother has also had her name cast in a new treble bell, thus completing the peal of six.)

Her own words seem to describe passing events and visits better than others can, and therefore we again copy from them.

(*To Margaret W.*)

. . . I came to Newport with the idea of not being responsible for any one's soul at all! I enjoyed the first three days in a general sort of way, but no real gain to myself. I declined addressing the Y. W. C. A. meeting, but was present and was asked to sing. I sang my arrangement of Isaiah 12. After a few more words, and prayer from Mr. W——, I sang for them "When thou passest."[1] After that I had to shake hands with many. It was all very nice, but not real work. I felt dissatisfied, notwithstanding the affectionate greetings and thanks for singing. Saturday I said I should like to go to work, and went with Mr. W—— to the Infirmary. In the women's ward I read and prayed and sang, and then spoke to each alone. I saw there was sowing and reaping work wanted, and many entreated me to come again. When I went again God sent much blessing. One, very suffering, and who had a most distressed expression the day before, had found peace soon after I left her. She lay looking so happy, saying, " I've left it all with Him now, and oh it's so beautiful!" Another, a moping groping Christian, told me that the words God helped me to say to her lifted her straight up into the sunlight. Before I left the ward, I do think another was enabled by God's Spirit to trust in the Lord Jesus. From that time, it pleased God to send such continuous blessing. But (I hardly know how it began, I think from my own couplet ". . . let me sing, Always, *only,* for my King," in connection with that Thursday evening) somehow I felt that on both sides, singer and listeners, it was not really " only for Him," but too much of F. R. H. That word "*only*" seemed to be pressed on my own heart. I saw it as I never saw it before, and that the "*all* for Jesus" must be supplemented and sealed with "*only* for Jesus." It was a great and humbling revelation to me of failure in full consecration, where I really did not see it before; and of course I dare not and would not hold back from accepting and following, at any cost, what I felt God's Holy Spirit was teaching me. I felt I could not, and would not, sing again the next Thursday as before, and that I must pass on this "*only*" to the Y. W. C. A. Then I had copies printed of the Consecration Hymn, and had my name left out, and a blank line instead for the signature, which each might fill up alone and prayerfully.

At the meeting, Mr. W—— opened it and then went away. Then I told them I had meant to sing them beautiful songs of Handel, but I *could* not and *dare* not; that I could not, after what my King had shown me last week, sing even partly to please them, it must be "only for my King." Then I told them about this "only," not merely totality of surrender but exclusiveness of allegiance, and how I wanted every one there to take *this* step with me that night, and to accept with me " ONLY for Jesus," as our life motto, henceforth. To keep my word as to singing, I just sang " Precious Saviour, may I live only for Thee"[2] (to "Onesimus"). After prayer, I resumed the subject and then distributed the Consecration Hymns (very systematically done in one minute without disturbance); and, after running through it, asked those and those only to sign their names who meant it. Oh, M——, it was *such* singing, one felt it was so real!

Then I gave an interval of silent prayer which I felt was a time of real consecration. I was sure of His presence, so sure that He was bowing the hearts before Him by the Holy Spirit's power. Was it not strange that the first "consecration meeting" I ever came in for should have been in my own hands?

After, I gave each at the door " Enough." I hardly liked giving my own leaflets, but I really couldn't think of anything else just suitable for what I wanted. One, whom I had spoken to after church on Sunday evening, stayed to tell me how bright her hope continued; but she needn't have *spoken,* the change of expression was quite enough to tell. Well, dear M——, I felt there had been real blessing.

---

[1] "When thou Passest through the Waters." Music by F. R. H. London: Hutchings and Romer.

[2] Hymn 695 in " Songs of Grace and Glory."

As days went on, Mr. and Mrs. W—— saw numbers of those who were there, and who testified that they had really been helped and had gained a step onward by God's grace.

Then, I could tell you much of some dear boys who had never unfurled their banners, or done any work for their King (I always thought I had no notion how to go to work with boys, and this has often hindered me from trying; that idea is overboard now). With these young soldiers it was a sort of leap into "life more abundantly," a going just headlong into life and love and work for Jesus. After a week of prayer, one has decided to give his whole life, instead of the chips and shavings of it, and become a medical missionary. Now they are praying for others; they have pitched upon the worst boy in the school, and asked me to join in special prayer for him. The most remarkable feature is the way they took to their Bibles, and, though holiday time, spent four or five hours a day with intensest enjoyment over them. . . . I never thought of asking a tenth part of all the blessing I received there since then. I shall have to lump my requests for praise at your next Y.W.C.A. meeting.

I must pass on to you what I have been rejoicing in all this week, Exodus 21:5, "I love my Master, I will not go out free"; and then connect the end of verse 6 with Revelation 22:3, "shall serve Him" for ever. I can't imagine why I never exulted in that declaration before, "I love my Master!"

———

A few weeks after, Frances wrote the hymn "I love, I love my Master"; and, coincidentally, her sister Ellen (Mrs. Shaw) also wrote a very similar one (published by Caswell).

Then came a visit to Ashley Moor, always so refreshing to herself; and, while enjoying breezy rides and drives and delightful friendships, she did not forget work for her King. She has left a sunbeam track in many cottages in that neighbourhood.

Year after year, my dear sister had pressed me to take a long rest in Switzerland; and so, on July 6th, 1876, we left England, *viâ* Dieppe, for Lausanne. That delightful journey! her sisterly care and unselfishness in revisiting well known places just to give *me* the pleasure! It was with difficulty I persuaded her to go to any new scenes for herself. From Montreux she went up to "Les Avants" to visit her "delightful friend," Miss E. J. Whately. From Vernayaz we went to a quiet pension at Fins Haut, *en route* to Argentière. Sunday came, and the sight of crowds of peasants passing by our door to early mass suggested the desire to try a Bible address for them in the afternoon. Valerie, the daughter of our host, had been so fascinated by my sister's singing that, with the promise that Mdlle. would sing to the meeting, she threw herself heartily into the arrangement. Three o'clock was the time fixed, but an hour before several maidens assembled, so we set them to copy out a French hymn Frances had just written, thereby fixing its truths on their memory; and they then practised it as a choir. Frances shall tell the rest.

(*To J. T. W.*)

. . . . . .

About thirty or forty came; some remained in a room behind our folding doors, these came from curiosity and would not come inside, and there was laughing and talking, evidently led by the priest's servant who was there for no good! First I sang to them, and then got the girls to join in the hymn they had copied out. Then I read some passages from Romans, and Maria spoke to them beautifully (in French) on Romans 6:23, and afterwards prayed.

A few went away as soon as I began to read, there was evidently *some* opposition. Even those who seemed really to wish to hear were evidently hindered by the total novelty of the whole thing: an intensified form of the hindrance which I told you I felt existed when I first sang at N——. You will wonder what I sang! Well, I had been singing snatches of hymns to myself, and especially "Only for Thee," and found this gave immense gratification in our little pension; so I thought God could as well give me French as English, if He would, and I set to and wrote "*Seulement pour Toi!*" (as they had liked the tune so much.) Only it is quite a different hymn, making prominent the other side, He and He ONLY is and does all for us. We come to the Father "*only* by Thee," place our trust "*only* in Thee"; retaining merely a few lines of the "only *for* Thee," as it is useless to teach "only for Thee" till one has seen "only *by* Thee." I also wrote a free imitation of "Will ye not come?" and part of another. I could write quite easily in French verse! so it may be I shall have to do some more in this direction, a totally new opening!

Maria had had the priest himself strongly on her mind all the week; and, not having the smallest fear of man, actually went and called on him! with the excuse of borrowing a French Bible, and asking him to see if my verses were correct. Just imagine going to "M. le Curé" for a Bible, and for revision of Protestant hymns! He was very courteous, and Maria relieved her mind entirely; told him how happy she was in Christ, and what was the secret of peace and joy. He did not attempt controversy, and seemed interested, but only assented to all she said, so that she could not get him to open out.

As for taking readings myself, the prospect seems to recede. Even taking part in this little meeting seemed to throw me back. For years, I have always suffered from any work of the kind, and then been made unable for my own more special work, as I never produce a line when overdone. And I find more distinctly, here, that I have not anything like my former strength, and even three weeks (by which time other years I have got into tip-top training) have not brought me up to where I used to start from. All the old elasticity and physical strength are gone. I don't feel the "atmospheric salvolatile," and go out on the freshest of Swiss mornings feeling up *to nothing* instead of equal to *anything*! Yet it is thirteen months since I was really cured from my illness.

Leaving the Chamounix valley for the Great St. Bernard Hospice, we took diligence from Orsière. The passengers sang some French songs remarkably well. We listened and commended, and then asked if they would join us in a new tune, "*Seulement pour Toi.*" Finding the driver took up the chorus in bass, Frances went outside that he might see the words, and most heartily was it sung by all. Sunday we rested at the hospice. The weather was fine, and the crowds of peasants who partook of that wonderful hospitality were sitting on the rocks in all directions, and of course many a seed was cast among them. My sister's brilliant touch on the piano in the saloon attracted the good fathers, and they requested that, after dinner, she would sing for the assembled strangers. She asked me to pray that she might give the King's message in song, and that it might reach some hearts. As there were different nationalities present, she very simply but gracefully said she was going to sing from the Holy Scriptures, repeating the words in German and Italian, and then sang Handel's "Comfort ye," "He shall feed His flock," and afterwards "Rest in the Lord." An Italian professor of music with many others thanked her, and were expressing their admiration to me when Frances bade them "Good night," saying to me, "You see, Marie, I gave my message, and so it is better to come away." Returning from the hospice we diverged to Lac de Champé, thence to Martigny and Champéry. There we met her Leamington friends, Mr. and Mrs. Rogers (of St. Paul's); Mr. Rogers was, then, summer chaplain at Champéry.

I could testify of much happy work here, in leading others to rejoice in God her Saviour: strangers, invalids, tourists, to all she was a shining light. And she was never satisfied with any one's profession, without a corresponding *life* for Christ and *work* for Christ. I may give the testimony of one, as representing that of many others.

I feel sure that God led us to Champéry that we might meet your dear sister Frances. Oh, I cannot tell what a blessing she was to me there. I always looked for those fair curls; and the saloon seemed desolate if I could not hear her voice and often merry laugh. She was so happy and whole-hearted, and she spoke to me of the Lord Jesus, and the joy of being altogether and *only* His. Yes, it was on the balcony at Champéry that a new life and love seemed lighted up in my soul. Even as she was speaking to me I felt that, with God's grace, I must take the same step she had, and henceforth live "only for Jesus." That was indeed turning over a perfectly new and bright page in my life.

Another Champéry friendship was with the Baroness Helga von Cramm. We were staying in the same pension; and a few words the first time we met her resulted in many pleasant entwinings of work. I give my sister's reference to the fact, in a letter to Mr. W——.

One of my Champéry gains was the Baroness Helga v. Cramm; such an artiste, every picture is a poem, such a soul in all she paints; her two specialities are Alpine scenery with the weirdest effects of snow and clouds, and the marvellous beauty of the tiny Alpine flowers. Well now, of course, she wants to paint for Jesus somehow! So I suggested that we might do something together, and we would first ask Him to give *me* half-a-dozen nice little Easter verses (new ground to me!), and then that He would hold *her* hand, and make her do some exquisite flowers. So the verses all came tumbling in that evening!

Such was the origin of the varied series of lovely "Alpine cards," subsequently published by Caswell.

Leaving Champéry, we went to the Bernese Oberland. Our longest sojourn was in the Pension Wengen, above Lauterbrunnen, just opposite Mürren, with the full range of the Jungfrau and Silberhorn in view. Getting wet through in a thunderstorm was followed by a chill, and my dear sister was seriously ill for a month. The Lauerners were most kind, and we were happy in having the pension to ourselves and being favoured with brilliant weather.

Two or three pages from my notebook recall our often pleasant talks, and the two following letters are about the same date.

September 30th, a.m. I found Frances with her Bible after a wakeful night: "O Marie, I've just had such a find! I hope you've not stumbled on it." You remember I was speaking of that delightful verse in 2 Chronicles 32:8, "the people rested themselves upon the words of the King'; now I have found 'the word of my Lord the King shall now be for rest' (margin 2 Samuel 14:17): is it not lovely? it will do for one of my night pillows; it's a down pillow, and no rucks in it! Of course it's a woman who said it; all the women in Scripture do say excessively pretty things."

Then she went on telling me that she thought her next volume of poetry would be her "Nunc Dimittis" (see Preface to "Under His Shadow"). On October 8 she had many weary hours of pain. She was so patient in all her suffering, and very thankful for some remedies a lady kindly brought us from Interlaken. One afternoon, after trying a new remedy, I begged her to shut her eyes and try to sleep. When I returned she gave me the lines, "I take this pain, Lord Jesus." "You see, Marie, I know something of the sweetness of taking pain direct from His hand. I had just been saying all this to the Lord, and then it came to me in this hymn; it wants no correction; I always think God gives me verse when it comes so, and it is worth any suffering if what I write will comfort some one at some time!" The next day she told me: "While I was in such pain, the very lines I've been waiting for came to me. Three years ago I began some on the Queen of Sheba, and brought the unfinished sheet here. Very often, strangers write and tell me that my lines comfort or help them, even when I know there is not a spark of poetry in them. Now *I* cannot tell what will comfort others, so I ask God to let me write what will do so."

Another day she told me she hoped to write a paper on "Men see not the bright light that is in the clouds." "Dear Anne M—— suggested it to me long ago. Many bright young Christians have never been down in the depths of the waves (as I have), and they wait for some *great* cloud to come, instead of seeing His light in the *little*, daily, home clouds! Marie dear, some may think it is presumptuous, my writing

'For Thee my heart has never
A trustless Nay!'

But it really is so, I could not look up in His face and say, 'Nay, my Lord, I do not trust Thee in everything.'"

(*To Miss E. J. Whately.*)

Pension Wengen, October 1876.

... I am just waiting for strength to go home; I have been ill again, and am only arrived at the stage of a few minutes' walk, on my sister's arm. I was splendidly better till the end of August, and meant to have settled down to a delicious month or so of leisurely writing out here, and then gone home to dear mamma, and begun almost a new era of life. However, God has chosen otherwise for me; I am just where I was this time last year, and any book writing is indefinitely postponed.... How glad I am that our work is not measured by quantity, and that its results depend neither on quantity nor quality, but only on the sovereignty of His blessing.... It was just a bit tantalizing to see you and yet to see so little of you, there were so many things I wanted to talk to you about....

One never does have anything but sips and glimpses here! No fear of satiety anyhow; we don't have a chance of that misfortune! Yet the sips and glimpses are so pleasant and so varied that, perhaps, each has just that proportion which makes our lives the most really enjoyable. Over and above the intense delight of the coming perfect and leisurely intercourse above, I think we shall almost revel in perfect power of *expression*. Do we ever feel that we have, either by word or pen, expressed our *whole thought,* still less *our whole feeling?* And is there not a peculiar pleasure in finding oneself able to make even the partial expression of it a little more complete than usual? Why is it that such pleasure seems attached to our finding power of proportionate expression (of any kind) of what is surging within? Is it a hint of the wonderful delight it will be to have the totally new power of clothing, unerringly and invariably, the infinitely expanded thoughts and intensified feelings in absolutely perfect expression, *perfect* vehicle of word and song? And, then, this delight will be met and completed by perfect understanding and reciprocation. There must be this last, because the One Spirit will dwell so fully and so equally in both speaker and hearer....

Talking of sips, what unexpected delicious little sips one gets, sometimes, when one is really too tired for a whole draught from His word! Yesterday I was *so* tired, just on the edge of fainting more than once from mere weakness. I turned over the leaves for a sip, and came upon "the word of my Lord the King shall now be for rest" (margin). I need not tell you how it rested me! I am extremely fond of the typical scraps in the history of David, but I never saw this one before....

(*To Mrs. R.*)

I must send you the last texts I have been dwelling on; the force, beauty, and sweetness of the combination of the King and yet the Father, the kingdom and yet the home, have struck me so much. And it is, in almost every case, first the Father and home, then the kingdom (Matthew 13:43; Luke 12:32). And this royal home of this kingly Father is yours and mine! I suppose you and I are fully half way to it, and the view is clearer and nearer, and will be clearer and nearer yet!

As soon as strength was given we returned to England, in October.

I well remember when Frances first thought of writing "My King." We were returning from Switzerland. Her illness there had quite hindered any writing, and she seemed to regret having no book ready for Christmas. It was October 21st, we had passed Oxford station, on our way to Winterdyne, and I thought she was dozing, when she exclaimed, with that herald flash in her eye, "Marie! I see it all, I can write a little book, 'My King'" and rapidly went through divisions for thirty-one chapters. The setting sun shone on her face; and, even then, it seemed to me she could not be far distant from the land of the King. Illness came on again, accompanied by severe suffering, yet the book was quickly written and published. We may regard the pages in "My King" as the fruit of her patiently taking back "the turned lesson," which prevented her writing for so many months. The following letters of this period speak for themselves.

(*To* ———)

Leamington.

I send you a prayer which I heard yesterday, and which has been arising from my heart ever since. "Lord, take my lips and speak through them, *take my mind and think through it,* take my heart and set it on fire!" Quite possible for Him to do, though it seems so much to ask. I am asking it; you ask it too. Christ's words, Christ's thoughts, Christ's love, not our own any more! How He does love you, how His very chastening proves it! He has not let you alone, and "blessed is the man whom Thou chastenest." So, the very sense of the reality of chastening proves the reality that you are "blessed," and "I wot that he whom Thou blessest *is* blessed." Only think that you are to "come forth as *gold*." I wonder what He will do with His gold when He does bring it forth! We shall see. He never would thus deal with you, if He had not some very special ends to reach. Trust on; He is worthy of all trust, isn't He?

Leamington.

I was rejoicingly thankful that you have tasted the delight of real spiritual work for Jesus. Perhaps He is training you, by all this stopping of your own wishes and aims, for something much better, for very much and very happy work for Himself. I have no doubt about it; it seemed such very marked individual dealing with you, that, as He also so graciously made you willing to let Him teach you in His own way, I had not a shadow of a doubt that He meant it to work out real and great blessings to you. Every other aim has to be thwarted and crossed; our soul's health needs it. Even if seemingly right and reasonable, He will not LET one whom He really takes in hand, to make "a vessel unto honour and meet for the Master's use," rest in any aim short of Himself and His glory. He knows that our real happiness lies here, and He loves us so much that He sees to it that we shall not go on "feeding on ashes," if we are feeding on them instead of on Himself.... You know He must be right, and most certainly has something better to give instead of whatever He takes away. But I am so glad you see it, and can trust Him. It would be too bad not to trust Him, wouldn't it? He will not, cannot change, even if your trust should be weak and flickering (2 Timothy 2:13; James 1:3, 4).

(*To J. T. W.*)

November 1876.

This has been a slight edition of my previous illness, but it will be some weeks before I am really as strong as usual. That long illness in 1874 has so weakened me, besides seeming to have left a curious liability to fever, which has returned so many times. But I am not troubled about the "fallow," and your words, "The Lord is right, you can trust Him I know," have not done chiming yet! Just before this last attack I was in my sister's conservatory watching the gardener cut off every bunch he could find upon a splendid vine. He has been training it for twelve years, never let it bear even one bunch of fruit for two years, and now it is 200 feet long in the main stem alone, and 400 feet with the principal branches. He has pruned off a thousand bunches this spring. "And what do you expect it to bear, by and by?" "Four hundredweight of grapes! and, please God I live to manage it, it will be the finest vine in the county." He was having long patience for *fourteen years* with this choice vine, and I suppose my Husbandman's waiting with me won't be as many months, so that is not a very long trial of trust. "My *faithful* Saviour!" That seemed my one thought while awake last night. I was delighted one day on noticing the Greek of Jude 24, ἀπταίστους "without stumbling," let alone without falling!...

No, I am not "basking in the sunshine"; it is not bright and vivid. I seem too tired, somehow, for brightness; but it is not dark either. I know He is faithful, and I am learning and resting. I think I miss outward helps and privileges, and having no direct work for Christ; I know this is all right too, so I am not fidgeting about it. I was able before this attack to go twice to church, a short afternoon service; but the preacher's chief lesson, from Luke 24, was that Jesus couldn't be always with us, and that we must *expect* Him to speedily vanish out of our sight whenever we did get one of the rare glimpses of His presence! So it wasn't very enlivening, but I was glad indeed that I knew better! Oh, I am so glad that "alway" (Matthew 28:20) means *always,* and that "never" (Hebrew 13:5) means *not ever* and not "only sometimes," which is really about as much as I used practically to take the words for! But the "alway" and the "never" are always *now* for us, and I believe them now just as they stand. And so, whether the day is dull or bright, and whether my eyes are heavy or clear, I know Jesus is with me. What a difference it does make, doesn't it?... I think "The Thoughts of God," printed in *The Sunday Magazine,* is the very best poem I ever wrote; but I have not heard one word about its doing anybody any real good. It's generally something that I don't think worth copying out or getting printed (like "I did this for thee," and "Take my life"), that God sees fit to use.

Do you remember my telling you my difficulty about saving any of my literary earnings for a rainy day? Well, after a deal of puzzle and prayer, I gave it *all* up to the Lord in Switzerland (1874), and intended to give *all* I ever earned straight away to Him. While in London I had an unexpected cheque from Hutchings and Romer, and was arranging how to give it, when down came this fever upon me, and mere doctors and nurses made a clean sweep of this cheque and all my available resources. Was this an indication the other way? and should I be acting rightly towards my relatives, if, when next I receive a cheque, I should give all away without making some provision for future illness? Of course some one must pay doctors, and if I had nothing in hand it would fall on them. So it seems robbing Peter to pay Paul! And yet *He* knows I would LIKE to give *all* into His treasury, direct and at once.

You spoke in a former letter of rejoicing over good news of your converts. I have been thinking over verse 4 of St. John's Third Epistle, and it seems to me that we too have "*no* greater joy." One is very glad when souls come to Christ, but I do think it is a "greater" joy when the work has been tested, and one finds them growing and working and *shining* for Jesus. On the other hand, it does so pain and depress me when I see that those who do profess to be His, often Christians of long standing, are cool and lukewarm, and taking little or no interest in His cause. Is it wrong that what I feel on such matters often amounts to real suffering, and brings more tears than I ever shed for any personal trouble? Yours ever in Him.

(*To the same.*)

November 1876.

Isn't it odd I should be *hors de combat* just now? And yet it is stranger still not to feel even the least temptation to say "how excessively provoking!" as I should have been saying three years ago; so everything only proves how real the peace of God is. I have not a fear or a flutter, not a care or anxiety, for time or eternity; and I know this is not nature, for the *natural* thing to me would be to fidget as to both present and prospective health, neither being very cheering! But the Lord is right, as you wrote me; only, I have not the vivid joy of December 1873, and I am very much inclined to say "Where is the blessedness I knew?" But then I have deeper experience in several respects, and anyhow I have made trial of His love.

(*To F. A. S.*)

November 17.

Just a loving line for your birthday, dear F——, and fondest wishes for every blessing; yes, "*all* spiritual blessings" (see Ephesians 1:3).

I feel so inclined to send you, instead of a proper "birthday text," a word which I never noticed till lately, and which has struck me very much in connection with your saying you had not thought before of "do ye *even so* to them" as an absolute command. It is I Chronicles 28:8, "Keep, *and seek for,* all the commandments," etc. (*look* at it!) You see we are not merely to keep what we know of, and what lie on the surface of His law, but to "*seek for all.*" And verily this is no hard lines, for more and more I see that "in keeping of them there is great reward" even in this life. 'Don't you think this would be a good and helpful aim for the year? I mean, God helping me, to take it as such for myself; and as it was new to me, it may be so for you too. Don't shrink from finding hitherto unrecognised commands; He only "commands *for our good*"; let us shrink rather from living in unknown disobedience to any. "Blessed are they that *do* His commandments"; may that blessedness be really yours and mine.

(*To J. T. W.*)

I see clearly now about the "satisfaction," *i.e.*, that I am so satisfied with the Lord Jesus that it is "Yea, let any Ziba take all, forasmuch as my Lord the King has come to His own house in peace" ("whose house are we," Hebrews 3:6). Ziba is entirely welcome to all my other property, so that I may but be "with the King." If that isn't being satisfied with my King I don't exactly see what is! So I have said and sung the last verse of my hymn "Enough" again and again.

"But now Thy perfect love is perfect filling!
Lord Jesus Christ, my Lord, my God;
Thou, Thou art enough for me!"

All the same, I see I can't be satisfied till I get to heaven, in the other sense; I shall always be wanting "more and more" of His gifts, and His gracious words and manifestations of *Himself*. I got perfectly clear about it in writing "Full Satisfaction" ("My King," page 30); only, I am anything but satisfied with that same chapter, and I am afraid you are expecting a great deal too much from my poor little book. But, it is *for* "my King." I am so happy. That's all!

(*To* ———.)

MY DEAR LITTLE K———,

The sad, sad news has reached me, and I know a little bit of what you are bearing now, for I lost my dear mamma when I was about as old as you, and my dear papa died, almost suddenly, not so very long ago. And Jesus knows: knows exactly all you feel, has watched every tear, and listened, oh so lovingly, to every little cry. I think you must be in His very special care now, and He will give you, and *is* giving you, even *more* than all the care and love that your dear papa could give you. Now this very minute, K——— dear, He does so love you and feel for you; and I think your dear papa knows how much Jesus loves you, better than he ever knew before; and so he can be quite, quite happy, even though you are left behind. He is in Christ's safe keeping, and only think that, this very minute, he is seeing the King in His beauty, really seeing Jesus! Can you not be almost glad that he is seeing Him now? And he has really heard Jesus say to him, "Well done, good and faithful servant; thou hast been faithful over a few things, I will make thee ruler over many things; enter thou into the joy of thy Lord." Think how wonderfully happy it must have made him to hear his own dear Master's voice saying that to him!

I have two little texts for you, which must come true now, because the very time is come: "He shall *gather* the lambs with His arm" (Isaiah 40:11); and you perhaps think "Yes, I should like Jesus to keep that promise, but *when* will He do it?" Look at the margin of Psalm 27:10, and you will see, "When my father and my mother forsake me, then the Lord will *gather* me." So it is *now* that He will gather you in His arms. But He has left you your dear mamma. Will you give her my deepest sympathy! You need not think that you must answer this, it was only I felt so sorry for you and your dear mamma that I could not help writing.

Yours very lovingly.

A few gleanings from letters to her friend Mary F——— embody some miscellaneous thoughts, and may fitly close this chapter.

Psalm 60:4: "Thou hast given a banner to them that fear Thee." Then He has given it to you. Don't keep it furled. What is its device? what is its motto?

See if you come to the same conclusion I have. And may we not take "the Truth" personally? (John 14:6.) It must be the breeze of the Spirit which waves its often drooping folds. Pray that it may be displayed faithfully and bravely by yourself and your friend.

Jeremiah 31:14: "My people shall be satisfied with My goodness." Do this and similar promises refer to this life? do they not group themselves with "I shall be satisfied when I *awake* with Thy likeness?" Look at John 4:14 in Greek: "shall never thirst"; does not that rather imply futurity? Yet I should like to know whether any, except such as are already in the land of Beulah, can say that. Still, present or future, there it stands and cannot pass away, being His word, His *own* word, "My people shall be satisfied."

"Thy will be done." In applying this to sorrow, trial, and disappointment, do we not forget the brighter pendants to this teardropped jewel? "*This* is the will of God, even your sanctification." "Father, I *will* that they, whom Thou hast given Me, be with Me where I am." Also Ephesians 1:5, Galatians 1:4, and many other instances.

"When thou passest through the waters I will be with thee." Really and truly *with* you, even if the rushing of the waters seems to deafen and blind you for the moment, so that you cannot see or hear Him.

Hebrews 12:11: "Afterward *it* yieldeth," singular not plural, and therefore definite and applying to each separate trial; "it yieldeth." So one need only wonder *what* afterward, not wonder *whether!*

"Hitherto," "henceforth." The Christian's whole course, in two words.

CHAPTER XII.

(1877.)

Letters — The mystery of pain — The Lord's graving tool — Loyal letters — "Won't you decide to-night?" — Manhood for Christ's service — Splendid promises — "My silver and my gold" — Mildmay: its intercessions, greetings, hushing power — A crumb from the King's table — The Christian Progress Union.

OUR only available sources, for a record of many months in 1877, are my dear sister's letters.

(*To Elizabeth Clay.*)

... Shall we not find that all parts of our lives will prove to have been training for whatever is our truest work even on earth, and also for the heavenly service to which one, more and more, looks forward? But the bits of wayside work are very sweet. Perhaps the *odd* bits, when all is done, will really come to more than the seemingly greater pieces! the chance conversations with rich or poor, the seed sown in odd five minutes, even the tables-d'-hôte for me, and the rides and friends' tables for you. It is nice to know that the King's servants are always really on duty, even while some can only stand and wait. Your going to India seems a very special "boring of the ear." How curiously your path and mine have diverged; your going to do great things for God, and I able for less and less. My hope that, at last this winter, I might be allowed one Bible class at home is uncertain; ditto my choir practice, as I am to avoid cold and fatigue. Everybody is so sorry for me except myself! For the same peace which will be yours in work will be mine in waiting; and the very fact of having a busy and active nature, with no proclivity for *dolce far niente*,[1] seems to make the rest under God's felt *restraints* so much the more really His doing.

(*To the same.*) 1877.

Best wishes for your first birthday in India, and 1 Chronicles 4:23, "*there* they dwelt with the King for His work," "*there*" is Amritsur for you. How specially it is for His work that you are there! I send you a lovely little book by Miss Elliott.... I feel how very precious your time will be in acquiring the language; and, if you spent an hour writing to me, I should feel like David did about the water of the well at Bethlehem. I have but little physical strength; perhaps He withholds the active service; and also I see His wisdom in, all along, having held me back from any chance of Conferences, or hearing any speakers of any sort for several years past (with the sole exception of the Mildmay Conference in 1874). For, if I had, I should have learnt from man, and should almost necessarily have echoed what I heard from others, in what I write.

(To ———.)

I think that, during certain stages of Christian life and experience, pain is always a mystery. And *so long* it is a grand trial of trust in God's *perfect* wisdom and love and *rightness*. "*His* work is perfect": Deuteronomy 32:4. (But wait patiently till you have had, first, some years of *pastoral* work, and, second, some personal experience of great pain; and then you will *see*.) To myself the whole thing is clear as sunshine, but tenfold clearer since the *intense* pain through which He has led me of late. I would not have foregone *that* teaching for anything!

I. Pain, as to outsiders, is no mystery when looked at in the light of God's holiness, and in the light of *Calvary*. The deeper our views of and hatred of sin (as the Holy Spirit's teaching in our hearts progresses), the more clear will all that is connected with sin become; and as had there been no sin there would have been no pain, it is all, and more than all, deserved. I can say for myself that I feel I have deserved the very suffering of hell for my transgression of the first great commandment of the law, ("thou shalt love the Lord thy God," etc.,) and for my sin of unbelief.

It is, further, a real proof of God's love. He cannot (being Love) *enjoy* the sight of suffering, IT MUST be as much worse to Him than to you, as He is infinitely greater and more loving than you! And yet He inflicts or permits it, that He may rouse, and warn, and check, and *save*. What thousands have blessed Him for the pain that came like a rough hand catching them as they fell over a precipice, hurting and pinching their very flesh, but *saving* their lives! In how many ways a skilful doctor gives pain, that he may prevent much greater and worse suffering! At the same time, I am *quite sure* that with very, very rare exceptions bodily pain, though far more trying to witness, is not anything to compare with mental pain, and it leaves no sting or scar, as almost every other form of real trial must do. (I am perhaps in a specially good position to judge of this point, because all my doctors agree in saying that, from my unusually finely strung nerves, I am and always shall be peculiarly sensitive to physical pain, and feel it far more keenly than ordinary people.)

II. Pain, as to God's own children, is, truly and really, only blessing in disguise. It is but His chiselling, one of His graving tools, producing the likeness to Jesus for which we long. I never yet came across a suffering (*real*) Christian who could not *thank* Him for pain! Is not "this a strong and comforting fact? I do not say that they always do so during the very moments of keenest pain, though much more often than not I think they are able to do this; but, certainly, they do deliberately praise Him for it afterwards. I think one must pass through it for oneself before one can fully realize the actual *blessedness* of suffering; meanwhile, you may well take the testimony of those who have. Its conscious effects are to give one deeper feeling of one's entire weakness and helplessness, (a lesson which we are all slow to learn in health,) and of the real *nothingness* of earthly aims

---

[1] *dolce far niente*: pleasant idleness

and comforts, and the fleetingness and unsatisfactoriness of everything except Christ. Then, it drives one to Him each moment, one cannot bear it even one minute alone, one *must* lean and cling (and *anything* is blessed which does this!). And then, one finds that He *is* tender and gracious, that His promises *are* precious, that His presence IS A REALITY *even if unrealized!* (a true paradox!) Then, one has opportunities which one could not otherwise have of learning trust, and patience, and meekness; it is a time of growing up into Him in these things. Then, one realizes more what it must have been to Jesus to endure real, actual, bodily pain *for us*. I never saw such tremendous force in 1 Peter 2:24 ("in His own *body*") as when suffering great pain myself; it seemed a new page of His love unfolded to me. I could write sheets more on the blessed teachings of pain, but if I did I should perhaps bring it on! So far, the whole question of pain is rather one of sight than of faith to me now; it has become so clear to me, as a part of God's great plan which could not be done without. But I find yet scope for faith beyond. I believe there is a mysterious connection between suffering here and actual capabilities of enjoyment hereafter, and that suffering here is training (I cannot tell how) for that glorious service above, to which I delight to look forward. But now look for yourself at what God's word says about it, and dwell on *that* instead of on your own thoughts about it, for His thoughts are not as your thoughts; see Isaiah 55:8, 9. Look at 2 Corinthians 4:17, 18; and then see how much more you can find in His word which bears on the subject. . . .

Trust Jesus in and for everything. When a trial is past, one does so bitterly regret not having trusted Him entirely in it; and one sees that we might as well have had all the joy and rest of perfect trust all along.

(*To* ———.)

. . . I know that nothing short of the Holy Spirit's power can enable any one to accept God's way of salvation as a little child. . . . I will tell you the two passages which have been the greatest help to me, two great anchors which have stood many a strain of personal conflict and doubt: John 5:24 and 1 John 5:10, 11. It does not matter what we suppose God *might* propose or declare; it all hangs upon what *has* God said about it? And can words be plainer than these two passages? "He that believeth *hath everlasting life*." Only think deliberately out that those words must mean *everlasting* life, for it would be a mockery and a lie to call it so if it might last only a day or a year. If the life which Jesus imparts (His own life by His Spirit) *can* come to an end to-morrow, *it is not, cannot be, and never was, everlasting life at all!* Our natural life is even as a vapour, but *this* would be a poorer thing still, if it might be lost even sooner. "Everlasting" either means that which shall really last for ever, or it is a meaningless delusion and not worth the paper it is printed on. "*Hath:*" it is never said *shall* have, but always the *actual present possession* by every one who believes, not always consciously but certainly. If you believe in Jesus as your only and all-sufficient Saviour, either you have at this moment everlasting life, a life which shall and can never perish; *or* God is a liar. Don't you see the inevitable force of "*everlasting*"? It *must* be everything or nothing. How can it be everlasting life, if it can be quenched in eternal death? The two passages you mention present no difficulty at all. Philippians 2:12, 13 seems to me clearly to imply that those to whom St. Paul wrote had got salvation as an actual possession, "*your own*"; and, having got it, they are now to "work it out," *i.e.*, to carry out all the details and consequences of it, act up to it. Give a man a great gold mine; it *is* his, he has not got to work *for* it (it is all there, his very own), but only to work it out, draw upon it, and enjoy it. I think the figure holds good, for enjoyment seems to hold an almost invariable proportion to work for Christ. I never knew any idle Christian really a rejoicing one (I do not of course speak of invalids); and, conversely, if you see a man or woman, whatever their position, doing all they can for the cause of Christ, giving up time to work for Him, and trying hard to win others, either rich or poor, for Him, you may be almost certain that they are happy in Christ. (Mark, I do not say those who merely ride religious or benevolent hobbies, or who work for *externals* of religion, these are often as miserable as any; but those who are working *for Christ*.) Further, just look at the "for" in verse 13, and take the two verses together and you will see that it is all of God and not of us. As to 1 Corinthians 9:27, why did you not see that the Greek ἀδόκιμος, is literally and clearly "not approved," being simply the negative of δόκιμος. You cannot read the Greek word otherwise; and how it came to be translated "castaway" I can't imagine. I can wish you no greater blessing than that salvation may be no longer a "theory" but a glorious *reality* to you, constraining you henceforth to live unto Him entirely and joyfully. If you once get hold of this, everything will seem different; the false lights of the world will no longer throw their flickering, deceiving lights around you, but you will view and estimate all in the true light, the glorious light which makes the earthly delusions altogether unattractive, and the grand eternal realities appear what they are, just *realities*. But, whatever you do, don't delay; go fully and most earnestly into the question at once; a magnificent treasure is within your reach, don't drift away from it. If any other passage, or set of passages present any difficulty to your mind, I wish you would let me know. Just one thing: this matter is not merely the intellectual acceptance of a theory, but also the acceptance, by the *heart*, of God's loving and free offer and plan. It is a personal transaction between Christ and the soul, to be carried out alone with Him.

(*To a young friend.*)

You will not mind my writing to you; you needn't feel obliged to answer. I hear you go back to school on Thursday; are you to go back doubtful, uneasy, fearful, dissatisfied, *alone*? or, is it to be going back *with Jesus, safe* in Him, *happy* in Him? When the Holy Spirit stirs up a heart to feel uneasy, it is very solemn, because it is His doing; Satan will do his best to say "peace, peace, when there is no peace." It is very solemn, because it results either in grieving that loving Spirit by stifling His secret call, *or* in passing from death unto life: the one or the other, I know of no other alternative. Which shall it be? Don't linger just outside the gate of the city of refuge; *just* outside is danger, perhaps destruction; you are not safe for one instant till you are inside. And oh, have you ever thought that it is not merely negative, not merely *not safe*, but that unless your sins now are on Jesus they are *now on you*, and God's wrath is upon them and so upon you? It is a tremendous question, "where are your sins?" I do not stay to prove that they are somewhere, you have learnt that; but now where are they? On you, or on Jesus? Oh, that He may now send His own faithful word about it with power to your soul, "the Lord hath laid *on Him* the iniquity of us all!" Accept that, believe His word, venture your soul upon it, and "he that believeth *hath* everlasting life." I won't write more to-day; all hinges on this question, "*where* are your sins?" If on *you*, you are not safe one instant, there is but a step between you and hell, "the wrath of God abideth on him"; it is awfully true, don't dare to sleep another night with condemnation upon you. But if *on Jesus* (and He only asks you to believe that He has borne them, in His own body, on the tree, and that Jehovah hath laid them *on Him,*) then you are free, gloriously free! They can't be on *both*! If *on Jesus*, you are saved and *have* everlasting life, and you will prove it by "henceforth" being His entirely and living to Him. I desire and pray that the great question of your life, of *your whole eternity*, may be decided before you go back. It will be easier now than it ever can be again, *if* He ever gives you another call.

(*To the same.*)

... Let me say just this; when one is really and utterly "all for Jesus," then and not till then we find Jesus is *all for us,* and all in all *to* us. Now I want you to be "*all* for Jesus." I can't describe the happiness He puts into any heart that will only give itself up altogether to Him, not wishing to keep one single bit back. And I want you to have this, and to have it *now*; not to wait till illness or great trouble come, and you feel driven at last to Him. No! that is simply "too bad!" Jesus says, "Come *now!*" not, "come when everything else has turned bitter." And if you come now, and surrender to Him now, you will have the peace now and the gladness now; and I can tell you it is worth having, because I *have* it, and so I *know* it is. It is a grand thing to start out early, and be on the Lord's side all along. Oh, what an amount of sorrow it will save you if He gives you grace to do it! But come *now*, for Jesus of Nazareth is passing by, and many are getting His blessing. Don't wait, either to get better *or to feel worse!*

(*To the same.*)

I know you must have thought me very hard upon you on Friday morning: but what could I do? I see you, a young, fresh life, redeemed by the precious blood of Christ, believing and owning what He has done for you, with grand possibilities of power in *His* cause, and I think endowed with special gifts of influence and attraction, one who might be, and do so much, for Jesus; and, yet, Jesus does not come first! And you know it might be otherwise and ought to be otherwise. You are "entangled" when you might be "free" in His "glorious liberty"; you are unsatisfied, yes, and dissatisfied, and you might be "abundantly satisfied." He has dealt bountifully with you, and now what shall you render to Him? Has not the practical answer been: "Just as much as I can conveniently spare, after I have rendered all that society asks, and that self or personal enjoyment claims! just as much as I can spare Him with risk of the least awkwardness, or remark, or self denial? Of course, one must give up the bulk of one's time, and talents, and influence, and thoughts, and desires, and efforts, to other things; but He shall have just the chips and shavings, the odds and ends, of whatever I don't particularly want for myself or for anybody else!" Does it not, practically, amount to this? And shall it continue to do so? Oh, be "true-hearted, *whole*-hearted." Be really His faithful soldier and servant. Throw overboard for ever the divided allegiance, which is valueless. Be "*only* for Jesus," and you will start out on a new life of blessedness, beyond anything you can imagine; and you will never, *never,* NEVER have a regret that you listened to, and obeyed, His own "*Follow* Me," even if it involves (as it will) taking up a cross, for there is no true following exempt from it, only the very cross will be *gilded* with *glory*. Do not be surprised if *I* never say another word again about it. I feel that I have said my say to you, and that I can say no more. The Master will send me to others, but I think not again to you. I can now only leave you, with one more *cry* for blessing, at *His* feet. Oh that He would say to you "Arise and shine!"

(*To* ———.)

To-morrow your manhood begins. Whose shall it be? How much of it shall be for Him? Shall it be, still, "some for self, and some for Thee"? What if *He* had not made a whole offering? what if *He* had not given His *whole* self for you? Answer the question, face it tonight, "How much owest *thou* unto my Lord?" Think of that, and you will be glad that there is anything to give up for Him. And, as for "giving up," there is not a true servant of Christ who does not know that the Master's words come true, "he shall receive an hundred-fold *now in this time.*" I know it for myself. Can't you take your Lord's own word for it, and trustfully say, "Yea, let Him take *all*"? CAN you deliberately say, "Well, Jesus shall have *part*; I'll see what I can spare for Him AFTER my boating friends, and all the things that 'a man *must* do, you know,' have had their due share." That is what it comes to. But you cannot serve two, much less several, masters. For, if you are serving self, and pleasure, and the world, even a little, you are serving Christ's enemy, and not serving Him really at all, because He accepts no divided service. It is very solemn; but won't you, on this solemn, great, dividing time of your life, look steadily at the *reality* of the case, and decide, once for all, whose your real service shall be? Oh, if it might but be that the great, joyful transaction might be done this very night, before the clock strikes twelve, so that not even one hour of your manhood should be "for another," but only and *all* for Jesus! Oh, don't be afraid of taking the plunge; give yourself over into His hands, and then it will be His part to *keep* you, and you may trust Him for the keeping; you will not find Him fail you. Yield yourself unto God (Romans 6:13) altogether, body, soul, and spirit, all your powers and all your members. And then see if He won't use you! He always does! Dear ———, I wish I had an angel's tongue to persuade you to believe what blessedness you are on the edge of, if you would only give yourself "in FULL and glad surrender" to Jesus, and be "true-hearted, *whole*-hearted." But I want you for my Master's sake, far more than for your own! I can't bear those who might be even officers, let alone recruits, in His army to be contented to stay at home as it were, and only fight their own little private battles for their own ends, and the cause of the Redeemer left to take its chance! Oh, if we might be able to say to-morrow the verses I have stuck on this letter! I am so happy whenever there is "another voice to tell it out"; won't you be "another"? I must not stay up writing, but I don't think I shall soon sleep. God helping me, I will not let Him go except He bless *you.*

Once more, *How much* for Jesus?

(To ———.)

I am so glad and thankful you have been to the Mildmay Conference. People don't go, because they don't know, till they have been, what it really is. Your description is one of the best I ever heard. "To him that hath shall be given" is always coming true; it is the folks who already have grace enough, who make the effort to put themselves in the way of having more.

I could not, do what I would, manage to get up any very strong emotion at hearing of your being laid up again! It did seem so very like as if the Lord were determined you should not drift away, at once, into a different atmosphere, where all the "other things entering in" should choke the word you have heard. And, suppose you have to stay and get mixed up with the tent work, it will be worth more to you as a sworn soldier of Jesus Christ than all the honours Cambridge has to bestow.

. . . I am most anxious that you should be a true Christian friend to ——— ———. Don't, oh don't help to introduce him to any men, or anything, which would be hindrance and *not help* either in seeking or following Jesus. Don't, merely because it might be pleasant to him, have the responsibility of bringing him into any path which *you* have found does not lead nearer to Jesus. And do take him to hear Mr. Aitken when he comes to ———. Forgive me, but *souls are souls,* and it does not do to play with them, and seniors have serious responsibilities.

I think you would find it very useful to take in *The Clergyman's Magazine* for yourself now, without waiting till you are ordained. I sent you a prospectus of it. There were capital articles all last year.

(*To Miss Shekleton.*)

LEAMINGTON.

. . . My experience is, that it is nearly always just in proportion to my sense of personal insufficiency in writing anything, that God sends His blessing and power with it; so I don't wonder that your papers are so sweet and helpful! I think He must give us that total dependence on Him for every word, which can only come by feeling one's own helplessness and incapacity, before He can very much use us. And so I think this very sense of not having gifts is the best and most useful gift of them all. It is so much sweeter to have to look up to Him for every word one writes. I often smile when people call me "gifted," and think how little they know the real state of the case, which is that I not only feel that I can't, but *really can't,* write a single verse unless I go to Him for it and get it from Him.

But, in this sweet access and supply, you and I have a "better thing" than the grandest natural gifts; and as for being slow or quick in production, it may be some tiny sentence written in five seconds, and never thought of before, which may do the widest and truest work for Jesus.

Yours, in our dear Master.

(To ———.)

. . . I suppose it was the "silver and gold" line that was objected to; and I do think that couplet, "Take my silver and my gold, Not a mite would I withhold," is peculiarly liable to be objected to by those who do not really understand the *spirit* of it, don't you? So I am not a bit surprised! Yes, "not a mite would I withhold"; but that does not mean that, because we have ten shillings in our purse, we are pledged to put it *all* into the next collecting plate, else we should have none for the next call! But it does mean that every shilling is to be, and I think I may say *is,* held at my Lord's disposal, and is distinctly not my own; but, as He has entrusted to me a body for my special charge, I am bound to clothe that body with His silver and gold, so that it shall neither suffer from cold, nor bring discredit upon His cause! I still forget sometimes, but as a rule I never spend a sixpence without the distinct feeling that it is His, and must be spent for Him only, even if indirectly.

With the same common sense, she explains her reasons for dressing very nicely.

The outer should be the expression of the inner, not an ugly mask or disguise. If the King's daughter is to be "all glorious within," she must not be outwardly a fright! I must dress both as a lady and a Christian. The question of cost I see very strongly, and do not consider myself at liberty to spend on dress that which might be spared for God's work; but it costs no more to have a thing well and prettily made, and I should only feel justified in getting a costly dress if it would last proportionately longer. When working among strangers, if I dressed below par, it would attract attention and might excite opposition; by dressing unremarkably, and yet with a generally pleasing effect, no attention is distracted. Also, what is suitable in one house is not so in another, and it would be almost an insult to appear at dinner among some of my relatives and friends in what I could wear without apology at home; it would be an actual breach of the rule "Be courteous"; also, I should not think it right to appear among wedding guests in a dress which would be perfectly suitable for wearing to the Infirmary. But I shall always ask for guidance in all things!

The year 1877 was passed uneventfully at her home, or in visits to her brother or sisters, to Ashley Moor, and to London. The distressing illness of our dear mother was a source of deep anxiety; Frances writes to her:

More pain, dearest mother? May it be more support, more grace, more tenderness, from the God of all comfort, more and more! May we not expect the "mores" always to be in tender proportion to each other?

Your loving child.

A few characteristic extracts from some of her letters at this time may here be given.

Instead of printing E. L. Goreh's verses to me ("Sweet Singer"), which can do no good at all, persuade her to print and sell her splendid little appeal, "Listen, Christian sisters"; there would be some use in that, and I would much rather *not* those to myself.

Do get *instantly* "Our Coffee Room," by Miss Cotton. It is so racily graphic and natural, so telling, and so hard to put down, that you had better not begin it late at night!

I have been immensely struck with the passages in which our

Master, our *Example,* uses the word "*must,*" and the great contrast with our use of it. Only compare when any one says "but I *must* do so and so," with Christ's "I *must's.*" It is a really helpful bit of Bible search, for we must follow Him in this or we are "not worthy of Him."

Do not hesitate to smite me. I dread nothing so much as smooth things. I would rather have "faithful wounds." I do not see how I can like doing . . . and yet I am in honour bound to carry it through. I was absolutely content and happy in it as being His doing, but subsequent delays and mistakes seemed altogether human and not His doing at all.

God has been leading me for some time by a way which I knew not, both outwardly and inwardly. I want closer contact with Jesus, more constant communion, more patience, more everything; sometimes I seem to have *nothing,* only that I know Jesus will not fail, will not loose me. He is very wisely giving me a much longer learning time, before letting me do any more teaching. . . .

I do indeed need grace and tact and patience and comfort very much just now. It's just a case of "Nobody knows but Jesus"; and I feel it is good for me. I am thrown the more on His own strength and sympathy, in what is to me "under the surface" trial; but I know the Lord is right. . . .

I am to be godmother to dear little H——; will it not be a peculiarly solemn trust! Do pray that he may be Christ's faithful soldier and servant, not only unto the *end,* but from the *beginning!* I do so want him to be a *boy*-witness for Christ. I long, more and more, for people to be not just "saved so as by fire," but to be right-down thorough-going witnesses for Christ.

(*To D. S.*)

What shall I do? Your letter would take two hours to answer, and I have not ten minutes; fifteen to twenty letters to write every morning, proofs to correct, editors waiting for articles, poems and music I cannot touch, American publishers clamouring for poems or *any* manuscripts, four Bible readings or classes weekly, many anxious ones waiting for help, a mission week coming, and other work after that. And my doctor says my physique is too weak to balance the nerves and brain, and that I ought not to touch a pen. If you could see the pressure on me, you would not think me wet-blanketing if I do not answer *all* your queries. "Mission Week!" if that sort of thing won't do in ——, it is the very reason why it is wanted; no agency seems to me more blessed than that.

"Bride of Christ?" *Study* (I don't mean read through) the Canticles, and look at the practical sweetness, comfort, and beauty of the type; also look at Ezekiel 16 and Hosea 2. Your own Bible will be your best answerer.

Work out this glorious subject: 1 Samuel 12:24, "Consider," Psalm 126:3 "hath done," Joel 2:21 "will do"; and then (practical) Luke 8:39, "*show,*" not merely "*tell,*" what great things He has done. *What* "great things" does your Bible tell He *hath* done and *will* do? You will find it inexhaustible!

Yours in affectionate haste.

(*To* ——.)

Don't you see He *has* broken the yoke (Isaiah 10:27), only you keep rubbing the place where it pressed, and are feeling *stiff!* When splints are taken off a broken leg, you feel as if they were still on. "Believe, and ye shall be free indeed." Will you set yourself to search out what He says about it? Put all the texts down, and be prepared to write under them either, "I believe what God says," or "I believe what I *feel,* and not what He says." Try it! Now I must dash off to another topic, because I must hand to you what flashed out splendidly to me last night: "Beloved of God, called to be saints!" *That* for you and me. Only think! It seems to include everything. Will you let *that* be your pillow tomorrow night?

(*To Miss Williams.*)

Thanks for your sweet benediction. If you remember me in prayer, will you ask that I may be kept always and only at Jesus' feet, never anywhere else. It is the only place safe from vain glory. Thank you for your valuable gift of the "History of Wales." I do so like your book, "Literary Women." The sad sketch of L. E. L.'s life and character struck me very much. What a contrast to Hannah More!

It seems as if more waiting than working were to be my lot; but it is such rest to be quite satisfied with *His* choice for me.

(*To Mrs. R*——.)

68, Mildmay Park, October 1877.

Would Lizzie like to send her baby-house with its twenty dolls to the Mildmay Orphanage? I see it would be most gratefully received as a gift to the Mildmay work. Mrs. Pennefather invited me here. I was going away on Saturday, but caught cold at the quarterly meeting of the Association of Female Workers. I sat in a draught. I knew I was in for a proper cold, so implored them to let me go across to their Home for Invalids (which I had taken a great fancy to), and lie there a few days. But they would *not* let me get into a cold cab as a specimen of Mildmay nursing, so thereupon I resigned myself to an extra week here. And, verily, they *do* know how to nurse, *and,* what's more (!), how to keep you quiet. Also they do know how to pray! I have learnt a little, I hope, on *that* subject this last week. What I hear and see here is quite a new light on intercessory prayer. I thought I knew something of its power and reality, but I see I did not know much.

Mrs. Pennefather took me (before my cold) to Clapton House. I only wish every girl I care for was there; such a beautiful, Christian school. I got any amount of bright looks (as it seems they knew my books), and I wanted exceedingly to go among them. Hearing the Principal say she would be prevented taking their Bible class, I ventured the proposal to take it. Afterwards, I had about a dozen all to myself in the drawing-room, for a talk with any that wanted special help. They were told to get chairs. "Oh," I said, "don't sit all in a row a long way off; come up close and cosy; we can talk ever so much better then, can't we?" You should have seen how charmed they were, and clustered niece-fashion all round me. We did have such a sweet hour; it was rather after the "question-drawer" manner; but all their little questions or difficulties seemed summed up by one of them, "We do *so* want to come closer to Jesus."

I was very sorry not to hear one of Mrs. Pennefather's beautiful addresses, but she could not move her head from the pillow. Mrs. Charlesworth took the subject. I was so cosily out of the way in the back seat, revelling in being quite incog., when it was announced, "Miss F. R. H. is here, and we hope she will say a few words." I sat quiet. "She is here," said Miss S——, so that I was obliged to startle my neighbours by rising, but I simply said I came there to learn, not to teach. Then Annie Macpherson made a bright little speech on encouragements to prayer. Then followed such greetings from her and from Misses De Broen and Blundell, Mrs. Hudson Taylor, just come from China, and Miss Maclean, who has been working twelve years all alone, and both the latter told me how the Lord had sent them the same blessing He had to us. Mrs. Bayly, of "Ragged Homes," Miss Bayly, just back from Australia, and many more spoke to me. It *is* such a privilege to be one of such an Association. And you don't see a dismal face among them! And they are so affectionate, the Sun is so bright that there's no ice left to be broken. But oh, Mrs. R——, what shall *I* render to the Lord for His immense mercies to me? for there was not one that spoke to me but wanted to tell me of some blessing through my books or leaflets.

Everything is so well ordered at Mildmay, and Mrs. P. is so very calm and calming; she comes and gives me a text at night with a sort of hushing power.

(*To S. B. P.*)

I want to hand over to you my own last crumb from the King's table,—only it is more than a crumb. "Beloved of God, called to be saints." All that for you and me! "Greatly beloved," for of course God *cannot* love just a little! And what a calling! "high," "holy," heavenly! Does not this seem a little lovely epitome of our position?

The following lines were written impromptu in S. B. P.'s album.

"Enoch Walked with God.'

(Genesis 5:22)

So may'st thou walk! from hour to hour
   Of every brightening year;
   Keeping so very near
To Him, whose power is love, whose love is power.

So may'st thou walk! in His clear light,
   Leaning on Him alone,
   Thy life His very own,
Until He takes thee up to walk with Him in white.

FRANCES RIDLEY HAVERGAL.
March, 31st, 1877.

Though no reference has been made to the "Christian Progress Scripture Reading Union," my dear sister was a most active member, and the means of enrolling hundreds of others. The number on her card of membership is 1667. She often wrote for the magazine, and at one time (to relieve her friend, Mr. Boys) undertook his work as editor for three months. One sentence from a letter, and her explanatory paper on the object of the Union, will suffice to show her practical interest.

(*To S. G. P.*)

Do you know the "Christian Progress Union"? I find it is the most valuable adjunct to work, *i.e.* work with souls, that I have ever had. It puts people on the rails of regular reading, and a double line is worth more than twice as much as a single one. Hence I value its arrangement for two chapters to be read daily. I enjoy it immensely for myself, but value it for others. Do join!

For further explanation as to the Union and its benefits, the reader is referred to the Appendix, where F. R. H.'s paper on the subject is given in full.

CHAPTER XIII.

(1878.)

Sympathy with sorrowful suffering. — "Just as Thou wilt" — The mother's last smile — Called to rest — The home nest stirred up — Clear guidance — "Another little step" — Last days in Leamington — Nieces and nephews — Devonshire visits — The Welsh nest — "My study" — The harp piano — More work — The sweep of Jehovah's pencil — Bible readings — "Take my love" — Songs in a weary Christmas night.

"IF one member suffer, all the members suffer with it." During the winter and spring of 1877–8 our dear second mother was passing through intense suffering. Though most patiently borne, it was very sorrowful to witness. The sympathy of many friends in Leamington, and the devotion of our dear old friend, Miss Nott, gave untold comfort both to the sufferer and to Frances. But with marvellous energy our mother still carried on her Zenana meetings and those of the A. F. W. Society, until at last the diligent worker, the bright and loving friend, the counsellor of many, was called away. Some lines, by our dear father, exactly describe the patience and the desire of his beloved wife:

> Just as Thou wilt! Be all to me,
> E'en when Thy hand smites heavily!
> On brightest day or darkest night,
> Whate'er is Thine is right.
>
> Just as Thou wilt! Should anguish fierce
> With scorpion stings my body pierce,
> I'll praise Thee if on me Thou'lt shine,
> And whisper "I am thine!"

On her last day, and after long unconsciousness, she suddenly recognised Frances, who was kneeling by her. Her smile was startlingly sweet; it was the last.

On Sunday, May 26th, 1878, the end came; for weariness, rest; for suffering, glory; for the loneliness of widowhood, the reunion for ever. In Astley Churchyard she

> "Rests where her loved ones rest,
>   And joins the throng
> Of them who see the Lamb
>   And sing that endless song."
>   (W. H. H.)

(*To Hon. F. Dillon.*)

If ever a cup of cold water came at the right moment, it was your overwhelmingly kind letter. It came on the seventh day of poor suffering mother's dying. The painful tension to me has been excessive; your note was a singular relief, if only for a few minutes, in those days of grief. To witness that strangely distressing illness has been by "terrible things" answering my eager prayer for more teaching and closer drawing at any cost. So now I expect the "afterwards," which, as yet, I certainly don't feel. But it is something to set to one's own personal seal that God is true to a whole set of promises, with which one could have nothing to do except in very real trial of some sort, and one may as well let Him choose *what* sort.

Many arrangements and perplexities now devolved upon us, in the breaking up of our Leamington home. Dear Frances' unfailing trust, and her assurance that God would guide our steps aright, was to me most calming and sustaining. She was just a daily illustration of "Without Carefulness." We both needed quiet; and as we remembered our pleasant rambles many years ago on the cliffs beyond the Mumbles, we went there, and our brother joined us. Frances at once wished us to secure united lodgings for our winter home; and in this I entirely agreed. Returning from Wales I went with my dear sister into Herefordshire, staying with some worthy people at the "Highlands" farm, near Titley. The good man was quite deaf, and my sister's dexterity, in talking on her fingers to him and rapidly transferring on them the sermons at church, was another of her ceaseless ministries. From the high ground of the rabbit warren the view is panoramic. And there stands the fir tree, beneath which my sister had written her poem "Zenith." It was there she sketched the earthly zeniths, and compared them with the broad sunlight of the true zenith, the true shining—

> "... That should rise and rise,
> From glory unto glory, through God's skies,
> In strengthening brightness and increasing power;
> A rising with no setting, for its height
> Could only culminate in God's eternal light."

Those quiet lodgings were restful to us both, and we received such kind attentions from Mr. and Mrs. Mainwaring as ensured our comfort, until we returned to Leamington to break up our home. The following letters belong to that period.

LEAMINGTON, August 1878.

The Lord has shown me another little step, and of course I have taken it with extreme delight. "Take my silver and my gold" now means shipping off all my ornaments (including a jewel cabinet which is really fit for a countess) to the Church Missionary House, where they will be accepted and disposed of for me. I retain only a brooch or two for daily wear, which are memorials of my dear parents; also a locket with the only portrait I have of my niece in heaven, my Evelyn; and her "two rings," mentioned in "Under the Surface." But these I redeem, so that the whole value goes to the Church Missionary Society. I had no idea I had such a jeweller's shop, nearly fifty articles are being packed off. I don't think I need tell you I never packed a box with such pleasure.

(*To Hon. F. Dillon.*)

... Don't I recollect you, and the wonderful sermon we had just heard on Revelation 3:12? I always read your articles first in *Woman's Work,* for oh, I do like writing which is both ♭ and #, and yours is exceedingly both. I don't think there has been a day these three weeks that your name has not been in my mind, so that I was quite startled to see your name at the end of the letter! "Reason why": the editor of *Christian Progress* has broken down ill; and, though some of my friends thought it almost sinful of me, I could not refuse his request that I would relieve him for three months as editor. Never, except as an act of sheer mercy and pity, will I be an editor. Letter after letter to various "lights," whom I entreated to illuminate their 14,000 readers on various topics, brought hardly anything but regretful refusals.

Everybody is too busy. (I wish people would believe I was; if they did I should get a little more breathing time to do my own work.) May I ask you to contribute a paper on a Bible subject, as Miss Whately and I are both writing a series on practical points, she on the negatives, I on the positives, of Christian life. Otherwise some of your "Dead Flies" or "Polished Corners" series would have done splendidly. I am so glad you touch the seniors in your paper this month; you are generally hardest on the juniors. I longed for a second paper on unpunctuality, for the seniors. My experiences have been chiefly more of the hindrance their unpunctuality is! for if the mistress is late at meals, and does not see the value of punctuality in general, everybody has to suffer far more than for any juvenile delinquent. I can't let your letter pass without loving thanks (and I have thanked Him), and just a word of wonder that you should find help from *my* words. There are few things one feels so unworthy of as even to bear His messages, let alone see His seal set upon them. I can understand others being used, but not my being used. I can only say I am not worthy of the least of His mercies. What you said about His "telling," and the love revealed in it, was so real and sweet to hear. Is it not one of the many secrets of the Lord, this "telling"? . . . Last, but not least, my sister and I are both so struck with your thought on "The Lord shall be thy rereward." Some special circumstances make it just the right word for me. Then of course this sent me to the whole chapter, and that has been food and strength. Yesterday was my last Sunday evening in [what had been] my father's home. I don't suppose I shall ever, exactly, have a home again.. But I am very *happy* in the "stirring up" of the nest; every new experience of the "changes and chances" takes one into a new province of the land of promise. And I have my sister, and we are going to live together for the winter in South Wales. She is almost everything to me. I wish I could entirely "tell it out" how good God is to me! Don't you find there are some things one can say better than write! I can't write at all, as I would, how good He is, the ink would boil in my pen! Oh for a seraph's tongue to tell! Well, we shall be able some day. Till then, *and* then, I am and shall be

Yours lovingly.

On our last Sunday evening in Leamington we went to Trinity Church; and the concluding hymn was my sister's, "Thou art coming, O my Saviour." The farewell kindness of many clergy and friends is well remembered. Characteristically, on our last home evening, Frances sent for a number of night-school boys, giving them baskets of books and magazines, maps for their library, a magic lantern, etc. And I don't think they have forgotten how she gathered them round her piano, singing with them "Tell it out"; and then followed her bright farewell words. For these boys she wrote some simple verses and chorus "Jesus delivers me now" (unpublished).

Frances spent a great part of the month of August with our dear brother Henry's widow and family, in Somersetshire. They had bright loving intercourse; deep searchings together with their Bibles; and music, in which all could take a skilful part, solos and choruses resounding the praises of Him they loved, and whom one of them was so soon to see.

May I say that the love of every one of her numerous nieces and nephews was ever accounted by their aunt as one of God's good gifts, casting refreshing fragrance on her path. What *she* was to them, no words of mine can tell!

Then came a journey into Devonshire; she writes from Looseleigh, near Plymouth: "I am indeed in clover with these kind friends, and it is very pleasant meeting so many who prayed for me in my illness, though quite a stranger." My sister addressed a large gathering of ladies in Plymouth, in connection with the Y.W.C.A. Some time after this she wrote out her notes on the subject of her address, "All Things." (See Appendix.)

One happy Sunday was spent with other new friends, in a very Eden of trees, and flowers, and birds, and holy fellowship. A brief visit was also paid to her friends at Newport, of which she said it was "like breathing the air of the land of Beulah."

Early in October my sister joined me in our Welsh retreat. How I remember her first words to me: "I wanted so to get to you, Marie dear!" She was so very tired, that even the sea air and perfect rest failed to refresh her for some time. Afterwards, she thoroughly enjoyed the walks and scrambles on the cliffs; at low tide springing lightly over boulders to beds of seaweeds, and rocky pools bright with sea anemones, and then calling to me to watch the white-crested waves, "the wind dashing them back like confirmation veils." Or, watching the vessels with all sails up entering the harbour, she would speak of the "abundant entrance into the everlasting kingdom." Delighting in all knowledge, she studied the "Nautical Almanac," and at the top of the Mumbles lighthouse learnt all that the keeper could tell her. Her tastes were so simple, delighting in wild flowers, and in animals, from the great St. Bernard dogs to her pet kittens.

We made her study cosy with home comforts, and she called it her "workshop." She arranged her pictures: by the door was her motto "For Jesus' sake only," and her Temperance pledge card; besides, were her father's portrait, and below it "Sunset on the Lake of Geneva," "The martyrs in prison," "Astley Church and Rectory," also "The Snow Peaks of the Dent du Midi," and the "Alpine Geum," (choice gifts from her friend Helga v. Cramm,) with many home portraits and busts.

Her small but choice library showed the variety of her taste, classical, foreign, poetical, with many works on science, geology, etc.; Humboldt's and Professor Ritchie's works (his last gift) she much enjoyed, *when* the scant leisure came. (The last books she had in reading were: "The Earth's Formation on Dynamical Principles," by A. T. Ritchie; Goodwin's Works; "The Life and Letters of the Rev. W. Pennefather," of which she said, "I find such food in that book"; and "The Upward Gaze," by her friend Agnes Giberne, with which she was delighted.)

May I sketch her at her study table, in her favourite chair from Astley Rectory, older than herself? Her American typewriter was close by, so that she could turn to it from her desk; it was a great relief to her eyes, but its rapid working often told me she was busy when she should have rested. Her desk and table drawers were all methodically arranged for letters from editors, friends, relatives, strangers, matters of business, multitudinous requests, Irish Society work, manuscripts; paper and string in their allotted corners, no litter ever allowed. It was at her study table that she read her Bible by seven o'clock in the summer and eight o'clock in winter; her Hebrew Bible, Greek Testament, and lexicons being at hand. Sometimes, on bitterly cold mornings, I begged that she would read with her feet comfortably to the fire, and received the reply: "But then, Marie, I can't rule my lines neatly; just see what a find I've got! If one only searches, there are such extraordinary things in the Bible!"

Her harp-piano was placed on a stand she contrived by dexterous carpentering. It was at this instrument she composed her last sacred song, "Loving all Along," and many other melodies to her hymns in "Loyal Responses."[1] Often I heard flashes of melody thereon, that came unbidden amid severer work.

In the south window, its sea view stretching over to Ilfracombe, stood her little table, flowers, and easy chair. Her sofa faced the west window, with the view of Caswell Bay and its rocks, and there the sunsets came, which we so often watched together.

It may be useful to younger readers to mention how resolutely she refrained from late hours, and frittering talks at night, instead of Bible searching and holy communings. Early rising and early studying were her rule through life, while punctuality, and bright, quick, cheeriness characterized all she did. She writes: "'*In order*' (1 Corinthians 14:40) is something *more* than being *tidy*! something analogous to 'keeping rank.'"

To a friend, Frances wrote at this time:

I don't think I ever felt more thankful and glad for anything than on reaching this quiet little nest. God has so graciously and perfectly met our special need. I must pass on to you the last text I have been enjoying, Exodus 15:13; what can we want more! and it is Thy mercy and strength all along. And then the "holy habitation" of the present, and the future one, from which we shall "go no more out."

But the "lull in life" never came, even in Wales.

"*Rest!*" There is none for me apparently. Every post brings more letters from strangers alone than I and my sister can answer. It is nine months since I have had a chance of doing a stroke of new work! But letters were a trouble to Nehemiah as well as to me (Nehemiah 6:4), and I must try to make it always work for my King.

It may seem strange that she should have had so to wear her strength away; and the following requests, which came by one post, will show what labour was required in answering them all.

Request for contribution to *Irish Church Advocate*. Hymns for special New Year services wanted. To write cards suitable for mourners. For set of six more "Marching Orders." Request for poems to illustrate six pictures. For prayer, sympathy and counsel (two sheets crossed). Two sheets from a septuagenarian, requiring thought. Request to write a book suitable for Unitarians. Sundry inquiries and apologies from one who had been printing her verses with another author's name. Request to reprint an article, with four explanatory enclosures. Also to revise a proof and add my opinion. To revise many sheets of musical manuscripts. Three requests to supply cards for bazaars. Advice wanted how to get articles inserted in magazines. To recommend pupils. To promote a new magazine. To give opinion on an oratorio. Some long poems in manuscript to revise and advise thereon. Besides packets of leaflets and cards wanted.

In addition to all this, musical proofs reached her almost daily, which often required many hours of careful revision and thought; and those accustomed to the sight of the *Fireside Almanack* will remember how "the sayings of the Lord Jesus" had there been arranged by her for the year which was her last. All this absorbed an amount of time which can scarcely now be realized; and yet she always wrote pleasantly and cheerily, and many a word of refreshment came from that wearied hand. Unasked, she undertook to chapterize the manuscript of "Never Say Die,"[2] and to add the required headings. Writing to S. G. P., she says:

Time spent on it is overpaid; it brings to me all the sweetness and freshness of the old, old story. I keep reading it for myself. My sister agrees with me that the book is exceptional, and in fact unique; and I do trust that you may have, or rather that the Master may have, a very harvest of souls from its circulation.

To its author, when working among the mourners at the Nant-y-glo colliery, she writes:

I enclose you a wee bit more, it has been quite a weight on my mind that I could not do more to help such terrible need. I was pledged to other collections, and my own purse is not unfathomable. So I was driven to do at last what I had much better have done at first, viz. pray that the Lord would show me some way of sending a *little*, and of course two or three ways flashed into my mind. May the good Lord give you many souls for your hire, for this service.

---

[1] These were published by Hutchings and Romer.

[2] "Never Say Die." By S. G. Prout. Nisbet & Co.

(*To Cecilia.*)

The Mumbles, October 1878.

Dear Ceci,—

.... I have often found that the greater the difficulties, the greater the "very present help"; and of course Jesus will be "the same" to you, dear Ceci.... If ever one had *gracious* guidance in one's life it is now; the place is so precisely what we wanted, a regular case of Philippians 4:19. I was terribly tired and used up when I got here, but am ever so much better already, though the "rest "has at present been only as to no "interviews."... Must hand on to you and Edith the text which more than any other has struck me in our readings lately; I have *lived* on it.

Exodus 15:13 { Led forth / Guided } { *In Thy mercy.* / *In Thy strength*. }

What would one have more! And then:

{ Redemption / Holy habitation / Holy habitation } { past. / present: Psalm 91: 9 / future. }

"*Sweet* is Thy mercy," and "*great* is Thy mercy toward *me*." On Sunday look at Exodus 32:29, and connect with John 6:53–55. Think of "*those* things" and "*eat*" them: living *on*, and satisfied *with*, Christ's precious body and blood. "Eat, O friends!"

Your loving Aunt.

(*To an American Friend.*)

October 28, 1878.

My dear Mrs. Brunot,—

I have not forgotten that I have owed you a letter for a long time. And I owe one to —— and Mrs. McCready. Now would you be so very kind as to forward this letter to them, and will they be so very kind as to accept it instead of separate letters. . . .

Most graciously God strengthened my health wonderfully, as the need deepened during the long and terrible suffering of my poor dear mother, a marked instance of "as thy day." Still, of course, the strain on mind and body has been very great, both for my dear elder sister Maria and myself.

Next followed all that is involved in a final break up of home, and overlooking the "accumulations of half a century—all my precious father's books, papers, etc. The beginning of this month my dear sister and I came here, and settled into snug lodgings on the ridge of the western horn of Swansea Bay (six miles from Swansea).

I simply could not live, I think, anywhere within hail of London, nor much longer in any such lively place as Leamington. So I have got away, now, well out of everybody's reach! I am trying, trying, trying, in a sort of Tantalian hopelessness, to overtake the letters that pour in on me, and to fulfil such requests as I have already promised. But, very seriously, I feel that unless I draw a line hard and fast, and refuse everybody all round all that is asked me to do, until I have cleared up the said promises and secured a little rest, I shall get mentally as well as bodily exhausted. So, dear friend, I *must* decline to write what you ask for; it is always pain to me to say "no," and I might keep a secretary only to write these refusals. That is all the outside. As for *under* the surface, of course it is the old story of marvels of love and faithfulness, from microscopically minute to grandly magnificent, and sometimes the minutest seem the most magnificent. I don't think all the previous years, put together, equal this last twelve months for these daily miracles of love. Only, most of them, and the most wonderful, are from special circumstances, such as have to remain among the secrets between one's own soul and the ever dearer Master. . . . . It seems to me that God has done for me more than He promised, not only supplying all my need, but all my notions. . . . Our present abode suits us so perfectly in all manner of little ways, that I tell our gracious Father I really don't know how to thank Him enough for it. . . . How I should like to meet my American friends! But I dare not come over. I should be sick all the way, and only be a trouble to you; but, "*there* shall be no more sea!"

(*To S. G. P.*)

"Blessed is he that considereth the poor, the Lord shall deliver him in the time of trouble." So, dear friend, "thou art, now, the blessed of the Lord." *Now,* while I am writing and when you are reading the words, "now" the "blessed" of Jehovah. That word "blessed" seems to me like a grand outline, traced with one sweep of Jehovah's mighty pencil; and who shall say what the filling up shall be? Because, you see, it is not *our* idea of "blessed," but *God's own idea* of it that will fill it up. I think, sometimes, Christian workers do not take the great comfort for themselves that the good Lord means and has provided for them; there is a sort of shrinking from presuming to appropriate the conditional character connected with a promise, even when it is quite distinctly applicable; and I regard this as a device of the enemy to contrive to withhold from them the whole glorious comfort which belongs to them. He puts it as a sort of humility; and I think it must grieve our dear Master to have His kindness thus frustrated. So, somehow, I am exceedingly anxious today that you should just revel in the grand definiteness, and the still grander *in*definiteness, of this word, which is yours at this moment. If words mean anything, you have been considering the poor; and so, if words mean anything, you are "blessed." I have been praying that the Lord would water your own soul very abundantly in the midst of your watering, that you may find more and more "fresh springs" in Himself, and may receive every day His own anointing with "fresh oil" for your service. You are treading peculiarly closely in the plain footsteps of the Master, your "own Master"; and you have not even to wait for His sure "Come, ye blessed," you have the fore-echo of it now. May He Himself whisper it into your heart in the midst of your work, which "He is not unrighteous to forget." May I give you another thought? He is sending you into the places whither He Himself will come: Luke 10:1. You go into one of these places of suffering, because Jesus Himself will come there, come with His saving power or His pitying love.

The cottagers around us soon won my sister's interest and regard, and she invited them to a Bible reading in our house (I may say that she never began any work of this kind without the Vicar's consent).[1] She wrote to ask "for a real great blessing on an open Bible class which I am starting this evening. I don't know who will come, few or many; but I want God's real converting grace poured out, and I want to be enabled so to speak of Jesus that souls may be won to Him. There is the centre; how it just *goes through* one, when one touches upon His own beloved name. And how we do want Him to be understood and loved."

(*To* ———.)

I have just been preparing for my next Bible reading. You thought I used a great many texts in my Bible notes, but it is my way of work. I very seldom run on a dozen lines in any book without embodying a text. I don't see how one can put too large a proportion of God's own words among our own. He never said *our* words should not return void. Besides, I have got into the way of it. I don't want to be a spider spinning out of myself! I am so interested in my Bible class. I have just been telling one of them I don't wish to lead them a nice interesting walk all round the walls of the city of refuge, and get them to think what a charming place it is; I want to give them a good hard push inside.

The room in which the class was held was always full. She began at once with a subject selected from the *Christian Progress* chapter for the day, asking all who came to read the intervening chapters by the next meeting, and thus ensuring that study of God's word she so eagerly sought to encourage. She told me that illustrations seemed to overflow upon her when speaking, and the reality of her words certainly thrilled her hearers. The last evening, she was so exhausted that I persuaded her to give up her class, and not to attempt larger meetings in the Newton schoolroom, which had been thought of.

On the fourth anniversary of December 2nd, 1873[2], my dear sister had written:

It was a peculiarly trying day as to other things; but, as I was remembering that blessed day, and all the blessedness of the way ever since, and the words in Jeremiah 2:2, I cannot tell you the sweetness of it and the assurance that He was indeed remembering me. "The love of thine espousals." Do look at the verse, for it applies just as much to you, dear H———, as to me. Only, it is but very rarely He gives me such a vividly felt message of love. I think it was that He saw I was in special need of it; it was just like Him to send it.

The hymn in "Loyal Responses," "My Lord, dost Thou remember me?" bears the same date.

[1] I may also add (to remove misapprehension) that this work was not in or connected with the town of Swansea, where she only once took the Y. W. C. A. meeting, but in the village of Newton, six miles from that town.

[2] [That is, on Dec. 2, 1877.] See page 385 of Volume IV of the Havergal editon.

On the fifth and last anniversary, December 2nd, 1878, Frances writes.

(*To J. T. W.*)

I had a great time early this morning, renewing the never regretted consecration. I seemed led to run over the "Take my life," and could bless Him verse by verse for having led me on to much more definite consecration than even when I wrote it, voice, gold, intellect, etc. But the eleventh couplet, "love,"—that has been unconsciously *not filled up*. Somehow, I felt mystified and out of my depth here: it was a simple and definite thing to be *done*, to settle the voice, or silver and gold! but "*love*"? I have to love others, and I do; and I've not a small treasure of it, and even loving *in Him* does not quite meet the inner difficulty. Of course, I told Him all that was in my heart as far down as ever I knew it myself, and that He knew the rest, and so I could only hand over the whole concern to Him, and implore Him to make it clear and definite. I don't see much clearer, or feel much different; but I have said intensely this morning, "Take my love," and He knows I have. So I did not fidget any more, or worry the Master any more about it. I shall just go forward and expect Him to fill it up and let my life from this day answer really to that couplet. The worst part to me is that I don't in practice prove my love to Him, by delight in much and long communion with Him; hands and head seem so full of "other things," (which yet are His given work,) that "heart" seems not "free to serve" in fresh and vivid love.

Swiftly were her words to be realized:

"For He hath met my longing
 With word of golden tone,
That I shall serve for ever
 Himself, Himself alone.
Shall serve Him, and for ever;
 O hope most sure, most fair!
The *perfect* love outpouring
 In perfect service there!"

From my notebook:

December 17, 1878. The sun was shining in our breakfast room, when Frances said: "It is a great mercy the sunshine of heaven is veiled from our sight, or we should be just unfit for earthly duties. I think there is a gravitation of the soul to life, as there is in bodies to the earth. It's delightful being here; it was curious the strong impression I had to come, I think God gave me the wish, and it has turned out all right. It is like what poor Howells said to me on the cliffs yesterday. I met him in his threadbare coat, and he told me how good the Lord was to him, and then, as if talking to Him not to me, he said, 'He's been *particularly* good to me!'"

"That splendid sovereign will of our God, made up of infinite love and infinite wisdom, nothing seems out of perspective when this is our standpoint; all His words and all His ways then stand out, harmonized and beautiful."

"Perhaps in heaven we shall be permitted to remember all the way the Lord led us, and to recall distinctly all the puzzling parts of His guidance and providence, so to see glory reflected *back* from them, as it were, upon His wonderful wisdom."

(*To* ———.)

December 16, 1878.

Dearest H———,

You regularly overwhelm me with such kindness. Tell Mr. Bullock I don't deserve the *Fireside* annuals and Tablets, one bit. The beautiful shawl will be such a comfort.... Tell the dear juniors I shall imagine there is a little packet of love in the top of each finger of the delightful gloves.... The Memoir of Mr. Pennefather will always be a treasure to me. Do you see that he was a pledged supporter of the Irish Society? I was charmed when I saw that! I know people wonder why I am so warm about it, but you see I am in first-rate company!

Very early on her last Christmas morning she awoke in severe pain, and was very ill for some days. But she said cheerily: "I really have had such songs given me in the night, and some Christmas verses for next year came so easily." An hour after: "Oh, Marie; I've done a half-day's work already, a whole set of mottoes; it seemed poured into me." These she named "Christmas Sunshine," and "Love and Light for the New Year." "You can't think the enjoyment it is to me to produce anything new. What books I should write if I had time! I wonder if I shall always be so pressed with other things; but never mind, it is all 'service.'" And then she spoke of her own mother and the little prayer she taught her: "'O Lord, prepare me for all Thou art preparing for me'; that has been my life prayer." Many days of pain and weakness followed, and the doctor wished her to have perfect rest. I was most thankful to write all the letters I could for her now, and at other times. Dear wearied sister! once she said: "I do hope the angels will have orders to let me alone a bit, when I first get to heaven!"

CHAPTER XIV.

(1879.)

New Year's sunshine — Journal of mercies — (*Facsimiles of Bible pages*) — Prayer and intercessions — "Work, if the Lord will" — London — His law a delight — Prospering — "Loving all Along" — "Bruey" success — Irish plans — Temperance work — The oldest friend's visit — "Can I go to India?" — Last Y. W. C. A. address — "Little Nony" — Last letters — Costly stones — The last "Sunday crumb" card.

"And so the years flowed on, and only cast
   Light, and more light, upon the shining way,
   That more and more shone to the perfect day;
  Always intenser, clearer than the past;
  Because they only bore *her*, on glad wing,
  Nearer the Light of Light, the Presence of *her* King."

("*Zenith*")

I REMEMBER her New Year's greeting, (*i.e.* January 1, 1879) "'He crowneth the year with His goodness,' and He crowneth me 'with loving-kindness and tender mercies.' You, dear Marie, are one of my mercies; and I do hope He will let me do something for you up in heaven!"

A diary she never kept; but Mrs. Charles Bullock sent her a little "Journal of Mercies for 1879." The entries in this are a mirror of her very self, "in every thing giving thanks." Frances wrote in acknowledgment:

"Thanks for the charming Journal you sent me, I like it greatly. I put down whichever 'mercy' seems uppermost in my mind for each day; not one in a thousand though!"

We believe the entries for the first three months will interest our readers.

F. R. H.'s "Journal of Mercies" for 1879.

Jan. 1st. Able to come downstairs first time.
" 2nd. Sleep.
" 3rd. Maria, and all her care of me.
" 4th. Opportunities of speaking of Christ.
" 5th. Rest and leisure to-day.
" 6th. Warmth and comfort.

"	7th.	Spirit of prayer in answer to prayer.	" 24th.	Able to walk about.

"   7th.   Spirit of prayer in answer to prayer.
"   8th.   Relief from mental pressure.
"   9th.   Maria's health and strength renewed.
"   10th. Being enabled to cast care on God.
"   11th. Having money to give away.
"   12th. Finding great spoil in the Word.
"   13th. Deliverance out of many trials and difficulties.
"   14th. Being withheld from resuming work, and sense of God's wise hand in it.
"   15th. For His hand upon me in *weakness*.
"   16th. Finding something of the *habit of trust*.
"   17th. A little respite from letter writing.
"   18th. Milder and beautiful weather.
"   19th. Opportunity of help to Mrs. M———.
"   20th. That blessing may reach the Princess Beatrice.
"   21st. Clearance of my path.
"   22nd. My study!
"   23rd. More strength.
"   24th. Help in writing for C. S. S. M.
"   25th. The promise in Deuteronomy 30:6.
"   26th. Head and eyes decidedly better.
"   27th. Being evidently sent to the Mumbles.
"   28th. Travelling mercies.
"   29th. Travelling opportunities (to London).
"   30th. Kindness from Mr. and Mrs. W———.
"   31st. Being allowed to give a word of real comfort.
Feb. 1st. Being in Nisbet and Co.'s hands.
"   2nd. A happy Sunday.
"   3rd. Acceptance by Hutchings and Romer of "Loving all Along."
"   4th. Immediate answer to prayer.
"   5th. Strength for extra pulls.
"   6th. Shielding from cold and rain.
"   7th. Need supplied.
"   8th. Pleasant guidance.
"   9th. Dr. D———'s sermons.
"   10th. Safe transit to Rev. C. Bullock's.
"   11th. Quiet day.
"   12th. Hettie B.'s friendship.
"   13th. Portrait finished.
"   14th. Pleasant interviews with good men.
"   15th. Finishing "Echoes," and seeing Amy and Clement.
"   16th. Frustration of plans, and solemn lessons.
"   17th. Such a comfortable nest to come back to.
"   18th. Our good maid, Mary Farrington.
"   19th. Fresh air.
"   20th. Immediate answer to prayer for a token for good.
"   21st. Help in need.
"   22nd. *Done* with some musical work.
"   23rd. Freedom from pain.

"   24th. Able to walk about.
"   25th. Opportunities of usefulness.
"   26th. Finding the *Lord's* poor.
"   27th. Maria returned all right.
"   28th. Fulfilment of Psalm 37:5, 6.
Mar. 1st. Spring sunshine!
"   2nd. Strange experience.
"   3rd. Freedom.
"   4th. Maria's writing letters for me.
"   5th. Preservation from cold.
"   6th. Finding myself freed from what was temptation.
"   7th. Answer to prayer that the Lord's call might not be wasted.
"   8th. Beautiful spring sunset.
"   9th. Irresponsibility to any but my Master.
"   10th. Finishing my "Kept."
"   11th. Donkeys!
"   12th. Special application of I Peter 4:14.
"   13th. For God's *withholdings* all my life.
"   14th. A good day's work done.
"   15th. Contentment in walking by faith, *not* by sight.
"   16th. Having been guided here.
"   17th. Succeeded in starting Mary F——— with a Sunday school class.
"   18th. Clearer views of Jesus.
"   19th. Acceptance among poor.
"   20th. H——— converted, and O——— P——— consecrated.
"   21st. Irish Society success *far* beyond my asking.
"   22nd. Study comforts.
"   23rd. Grace not dependent on means.
"   24th. Preservation from fire.
"   25th. Pardon and victory.
"   26th. Permitted to speak *out* to ———, and setting Board School *Bible reading* afloat.
"   27th. Instant guidance in sudden emergency.
"   28th. Preservation from a serious fall.
"   29th. Faculties.
"   30th. A gospel sermon at church.
"   31st. Musical gifts.

It is at our brother Frank's suggestion that the accompanying facsimiles have been taken from my sister's Bible. She had thus referenced two of Bagster's Bibles, the Old Testament, as well as the New, showing her diligent searchings. Truly, her delight was in the law of the Lord, it was always her standard of appeal; and, by comparing Scripture with Scripture, she grasped its all-sided truth, rejoicing therein as one that findeth great spoil. To her niece Cecilia she wrote:

In reading the Scripture it is best to combine plans. Once a day read straight on, with prayer and careful referencing. But always try to give a half hour to Bible study; work out Bible subjects, and

JOURNAL OF MERCIES

FOR

1879.

COUNT YOUR MERCIES.

LONDON: JARROLD AND SONS,
3, PATERNOSTER BUILDINGS.

CHRISTIANS do not think enough of the duty and privilege of praise. They often receive their mercies as matters of course, and lose much by not counting them. It is hoped this little Journal of Mercies, if faithfully kept during the coming year, will be found a help to understanding and realizing the daily loving-kindnesses of the Lord.

M. S.

Northrepps Rectory,
January 1st, 1879.

Inscribed "With H B's love", this was the Journal of Mercies for 1879 that Mrs. Charles Bullock gave F.R.H. These are facsimiles of the original pages with Frances' entries into this Journal, for all the days of January, February, and March. The pages for the remaining nine months are completely blank. She died June 3, 1879.

"Whoso is wise, and will *observe* these things, even *they* shall understand the loving-kindness of the Lord."—Ps. cvii. 43.

JANUARY.

1. Able to come downstairs, 1st time
2. Sleep
3. Maria & all her care
4. Opportunities of speaking of Xt
5. Rest & leisure
6. Warmth & comfort
7. Spirit of prayer in answer to prayer
8. Relief from mental pressure
9. M's health & strength
10. Being enabled to rest care on God about M.B.
11. Having money to give away
12. Finding "great spoil" in the Word
13. Deliverance out of many trials & difficulties
14. Being withheld from resuming work & sense of God's wise hand in it

JANUARY.

15. For His hand upon me in weakness
16. Finding something of the "habit of trust"
17. Quiet, & respite from letter-writing
18. Milder & very beautiful weather
19. Opportunity of help to S.M.
20. Reading Ms Beatrice
21. Clearing up as to B. & clearance of matter
22. My study
23. More strength
24. Help in writing for C.S.S.M.
25. The promise in Deut. 30. 6.
26. Head & eyes decidedly better
27. Being evidently sent to the M's
28. Travelling mercies
29. Travelling opportunities
30. Kindness from the M's
31. Being allowed to give a word of real comfort

"Bless the Lord, O my soul; and *forget* not all His benefits."—Ps. ciii. 2.

FEBRUARY.

1. Being in Nisbet & Co's hands
2. A happy Sunday
3. Immediate answer about portrait
4. Acceptance of L.L.L.
5. Strength for extra pulls
6. Shielding from cold & rain while out
7. Cheque from Nisbet & Co
8. Pleasant guidance
9. Dr D's sermons
10. Safe transit to B.
11. Quiet day in bed
12. Bettie B's friendship
13. Portraits finished
14. Pleasant interviews with good men

FEBRUARY.

15. Finishing "Echoes" & seeing Amy & Ellen
16. Frustration of plans & solemn lessons
17. Such a comfortable rest to come back to
18. Mr. Farrington
19. Fresh air
20. Immediate answer to prayer for a token for good
21. Help in work
22. Done with Amens & Monday's times!
23. Freedom from pain
24. Able to walk about
25. Opportunities of helping poor
26. Finding the Lord's poor
27. M. brought back all right
28. Fulfilment of Psa. 37. 5, 6.

Thanks be to God for His indescribable gift to us in Christ.

"I beseech you therefore, brethren, by the *mercies* of God, that ye present your bodies a living sacrifice, holy, acceptable unto God, which is your reasonable service."—*Rom.* xii. 1.

MARCH.

1. Spring sunshine
2. Strange experience
3. Freedom
4. C's writing letters for me
5. Preservation from cold
6. Finding myself freed from what was a temptation
7. Answer to prayer that the L's call might not be wasted
8. Beautiful spring music
9. Irresponsibility to any but my Master
10. Finishing my "Kept"
11. Donkeys!
12. Special application of I Pet. 4. 14.
13. For God's withholding all my life
14. A good day's work done

MARCH.

15. Contentment in walking by faith
16. Having been guided here
17. Succeeded in starting M. F. with class
18. Clearer view of Jesus
19. Acceptance among poor
20. Henson converted & Owen M. consecrated
21. Irish success far beyond my asking
22. Study fires
23. Grace not dependent on means
24. Preservation from fire
25. Pardon & victory
× 26. Permitted to speak out to M. F. also to set Board school Bible reading afloat
27. Instant guidance in sudden emergency
28. Preservation from a fall
29. Faculties
× 30. M. F's first joyful decision
31. Musical gifts

"Let my mouth be filled with Thy praise and with Thy honour all the day long."—*Ps.* lxxi. 8.

APRIL.

1.
2.
3.
4.
5.
6.
7.
8.
9.
10.
11.
12.
13.
14.

APRIL.

15.
16.
17.
18.
19.
20.
21.
22.
23.
24.
25.
26.
27.
28.
29.
30.

Work for 1879
"If the Lord will."

"Starlight through the Shadows." Daily book for Caswell.

Six more C.M.S. papers – "Abiding Orders".

Set "Loyal Responses" to music.

Prepare "Kept for Jesus" for press, rewriting earlier chapters.

Tales from the Wilds of Auvergne: Poem

About Bible-washing. Magazine article

"All Things": Work up notes into Magazine article

Whitsuntide food to me; verses or short article

The Stray Kitten. Juvenile magazine paper

Work up C.S.S.M. anecdotes into papers or book.

X Complete 12 "Wayside Chimes" for Home Words.

[over]

———

X Select or write "Echoes from the Word" for "Day of Days"

X Lots of New Year's Mottoes &c. to enroll — Large lots of M.S.S.

Bright Thoughts for Dull Days. (not for Caswell.)

Series of Irish Sketches for D.I.B.

Sunday Picture Alphabet — mag. paper

Our Brother; or Daily Thoughts for those who love Him

X Morning Stars, or Daily Thoughts about Jesus for the little ones.
Evening Stars; or Minutes for the little ones.

Complete the series of Sunday evening Crumbs.

Six poems for Sunday Magazine

make notes of them. I will give you two or three which I have found profitable.

What does the Bible say God *is* { in Himself?
to us?

"*Everlasting.*" Search out and *classify* the places where it is used. (This is very comforting, "everlasting covenant," "everlasting joy," etc.)

"*Called.*" How is our "calling" described? Unto what are we "called"?

"*Keep.*" Who will keep? Whom does He keep? From what does He keep?

"*Able.*" See how applied to Christ; arrange in order.

Keep a fine steel pen on purpose at hand, and mark the references you thus find in your own Bible, this will greatly enrich it. . . . This plan is *very* helpful, both for intellectual and spiritual knowledge of His word.

The other facsimile is taken from one of the fly leaves of my sister's Bible, and shows the way in which she constantly arranged Bible teachings.

SUBJECTS FOR PRAYER. (*Found in F. R. H.'s Bible.*)

(1878–9.)

"I have greatly enjoyed the regular praying of the Lord's Prayer, and take a petition each morning in the week. Intercession for others I generally make at evening. I take the fruits of the Holy Spirit in the same way, and find this helpful."

GENERAL.

Morning
For the Holy Spirit.
Perfect trust all day.
Watchfulness.
To be kept from sin.
That I may please Him.
Guidance, growth in grace.
That I may do His will.
That He would use my mind, lips, pen, *all*.
Blessing and guidance in each engagement and interview of the day.

Evening
For forgiveness and cleansing.
Mistakes overruled.
Blessing on all said, written, and done.
For conformity to His will and Christ's likeness.
That His will may be done *in* me.
For a *holy* night.
Confession.
For every one for whom I have been specially asked to pray.

SPECIAL SUBJECTS.—SUNDAY.

That I may make the most of Sabbath hours, and gain much from the word.
Deliverance from wandering thoughts.
Pure praise.
Blessing on services and choir.
"Hallowed be Thy Name."
Intercessions. (Initials of many clergymen, of her brother, her godchildren, and "our servants.")

MONDAY. "*For Joy and Peace.*"

That the life of Jesus may be manifest in me.
"Thy kingdom come."
Intercession for Church Missionary Society and Irish Society. (Initials of her eldest sister, *all* her family, and "Oakhampton servants.")

TUESDAY. "*For Longsuffering.*"

That my unconscious influence may be all for Him.
"Thy will be done."
Intercession for Mildmay (and initials of her brother Henry's children and many Leamington friends).

WEDNESDAY. "*Gentleness.*"

For spirit of prayer and shadowless communion.
"Give us this day our daily bread."
Intercession for the universities and public schools, for many friends, for M. V. G. H., and E. C.

THURSDAY. "*Goodness.*"

For much fruit to His praise. Soul winning. Spirit of praise.
"Forgive us our trespasses."
Local work. Swansea, and Mrs. M——. For my sister Ellen, all at Winterdyne, and "the servants."

FRIDAY. "*Faith.*"

Wisdom to be shown more of His will and commands.
"Lead us not into temptation."
For my brother and all at U. B.[1]

SATURDAY. "*Meekness and Temperance.*"

That the word of Christ may dwell in me richly, open treasures of Thy word to me, fill my seed basket.
"Deliver us from evil."
For the Church of England and the Queen.
Initials of many friends.

WORK FOR 1879: "If the Lord will."

(*In F. R. H.'s Desk.*)

To write "Starlight through the Shadows," daily book for invalids. Six more Church Missionary Society papers. "Marching Orders." Set "Loyal Responses" to music. * Prepare "Kept" for press. To write "Lilies from the Waters of Quietness" (poem). "About Bible Reading and Bible Marking," magazine article. * "All Things;" work up my notes. "*Particularly* good to me," verses or short article. "The Stray Kitten," juvenile paper. Work up C. S. S. M. anecdotes into papers or book." * Complete twelve "Wayside Chimes" for *Home Words*. * Select or write "Echoes from the Word" for *Day of Days*. * Double sets of New Year's mottoes (Caswell). "Bright

---

[1] Francis Tebbs Havergal, and his family and church at Upton Bishop, Herefordshire.

Thoughts for Dark Days." Series of Irish Sketches for *Day of Days*. On "Sunday Postal Burdens"; how to relieve the postmen. "Our Brother"; or daily thoughts for those who love Him. * "Morning Stars," daily thoughts about Jesus for little ones. "Evening Stars," or promises for the little ones. Complete the series of "Sunday Morning Crumbs." Six poems for *Sunday Magazine*.

[The daily pressure of letters prevented many of these being attempted; * denotes those completed.]

January 28th she went to London, visiting Mr. and Mrs. Watson and the Rev. C. Bullock. Other visits were purposed, but singularly frustrated by the appearance of infectious illness in her dear friend's (Mrs. Bullock's) family, and she thought it right to return speedily to Wales. The day she went to town I read (at prayers) the *Christian Progress* chapter for the day, Deuteronomy 33:1–17. Afterwards Frances said: "I wondered if you would read the eighteenth verse. It is a fresh promise for me. You say I belong to the tribe of Zebulun, 'them that handle the pen,' and early this morning I read 'rejoice Zebulun in thy going out,' and so I do in going to London. I never went a journey I feel so delighted about. I gave up the thought of going last week, for I wanted to make the most of my time and money for my King, and didn't want to please myself a bit. Then, after prayer about it, that promise seemed to direct my going, 'Certainly I will be with thee,' and I have had no misgiving since."

On her return from London her work seemed to increase; letters poured in; many came for advice or instruction, and she gave up every available moment. I distinctly remember the gladness of her service, delighting to do whatever seemed the will of the Lord. One morning she said to me: "Marie, it is really very remarkable how everything I do seems to prosper and flourish. There is my 'Bruey Branch' growing and increasing, and now the Temperance work. And so many letters tell me that God is blessing my little books. I thought this morning *why* it was so; in the first Psalm we have the condition and the promise: 'his delight is in the law of the Lord; . . . and whatsoever he doeth shall prosper.' You know how I do love my Bible, more and more; and so, of course, the promise comes true to me."

To our Vicar and other friends she sent this simple request for prayer, asking them to sign their own names and secure others to join:

"I agree to pray every evening for three months from this date, (God helping me,) for the outpouring of His Holy Spirit upon this parish and neighbourhood."—F. R. H., March 7, 1879.

It was as answer to this prayer that my sister attributed the awakening interest which much encouraged her in daily conversations in the cottages around us.

In the village school her frequent visits and bright words won the deepest love. To encourage them to learn God's word perfectly, she offered a new Bible to every child who would repeat the 53rd chapter of Isaiah. Good Friday was the day fixed, but she was ill then. A few days after, she was delighted with the perfect repetition by many of the children; and, though she would not excuse a single mistake, she gave some another trial. I was often struck with the pains she took with very little children, so really making the gospel story glad news to them.

Once she went rather unwillingly to return a stranger's call. She afterwards told me she was quite ashamed of her reluctance (though it arose from weariness), for she had "found such direct work," adding: "I must screw up to a notch higher, and improve all conversations. Certainly my King is very good, to give me such nice little bits of work for Him."

In the early part of March, Frances re-wrote and completed her last book, "Kept." She told me she could work but slowly and with some difficulty, owing to pressure of other things. Again and again, she said how strongly she felt that her pen was to be used *only* for the Master, and how she had found His blessing in that course hitherto. My sister had also begun a series of papers for invalids; but it seemed strongly impressed on her that the children should have a turn, and so she rapidly wrote "Morning Stars."

She was interested in looking over some musical settings to her words by Mr. Purday, an old correspondent of our father's. She approved of the title, "Songs of Peace and Joy"; and against some of his tunes wrote "very sweet," "very good," "fair, third strain interesting," etc.

My dear sister was delighted that Messrs. Hutchings and Romer accepted for publication her music to Mr. Prout's words "Loving all Along."

(*To S. G. P.*)

. . . About your "Loving all Along." I wrote the music to suit myself, and I never yet found words which were so exactly what I wanted. I hope to sing it in many drawing-rooms, it is delightful to do the King's business there, and singing often opens the door for quiet conversations. I do so pray the words may touch some weary hearts under silks and satins, and dress-coats too, may-be. . . .

All the same, I do not think the song will ever be popular, because it is just one of those which are utterly ruined if stumbled over, or even if well played by one who does not *dash* off the recitative-like style with real *spirit,* and bring out the sharp contrasts which give effect.

. . . Seriously, dear friend, the points have been carried one after another; Hutchings and Romer accepting it, Sankey saying it haunts him, and taking it to America; now two prayers, that God will make it acceptable, and most of all that He will let it do real work and send the great power of His Spirit with it.

P.S.—The *best* last! —— converted by "N.S.D." He was slightly ill; I called, talked, and prayed twice or three times, and gave him "Never Say Die." And *that* was blessed! Now give thanks!

THE MUMBLES, March 25, 1879.

DEAREST G——,

... I am being answered about my "Bruey Branch" to an extent that literally alarms me! I don't know how I can keep pace with the influx of young collectors, and the Dublin secretaries are "astonished." I sent up £108 a few days ago, and that is only what comes to *me*; Mr. Roe tells me hundreds of "Bruey" cards are being taken all over the kingdom, and I see the whole thing will want complete organizing; I myself have sent up, including Miss E. Titterton's, no less than seventy-nine collectors' lists and amounts, and I begun two years ago with a list of *eight* collectors, consequently I am believing in prayer a little more than ever!

THE MUMBLES, March 28.

DEAR WILLIE AND ALFRED [SHAW].

Is the Green Isle big enough to hold you and me at the same time, do you think? Because, if it is, I am thinking, please God, of coming over about the beginning of June. The real reason why I have made up my mind to brave the terrors of the deep, *i.e.* of the ladies' cabin, is that things are growing so marvellously fast in my department of the Irish Society work, that I must go and see for myself what *is* being done in the fields of work, and also have a regular consultation at head quarters about organizing the "Bruey Branch," which is sprouting like anything in all directions. And now the thing is, I want one of you to come with me, (of course at my expense,) on a sort of tour round some of the Irish stations. I think it will be delightful. The fun would be to have you both; but that might complicate matters as to accommodation in some of these "backwoods," so how would it be if one of you came, for the first week or two, and then change over? I thought it would be such a very nice opportunity for you to see something of the land of your birth beyond the civilization of college and the metropolis! Think it over and pray over it, and let me know what conclusion you come to. If one of you could come, you would probably be a great comfort, as you would see to such matters as hiring cars for me and other small services. It is not only that I really want to see the work for myself, as I am getting more and more deeply pledged to it, but we have got Mr. Bullock to make the *Day of Days* a sort of *quasi* Irish Society organ, he having put two pages of the magazine at our disposal every month, instead of our going to the expense of setting up a separate magazine for the Society's information. This was my scheme, and we are starting pretty well; but they want me extremely to write some papers for it, and I tell them I can't make brick without straw, and therefore if I am to write I must go to Ireland. Let me know as soon as you can when your term ends, and you would be at liberty. Mr. Fitzpatrick is very anxious to make part of his inspecting tour fit in with mine, so as to show me that part of the work, which of course would be a great advantage to my papers; but I tell him that I wish, also, to see some of the undress as well as the full parade, so he is to be with us part of the time, and I am to visit some stations by myself. I have stipulated that I only go to observe and take notes, *not* to take classes or give addresses, as I have not strength for that; and, to keep myself fresh for the writing, which I want to do as much as possible on the spot, is far more important.

Your loving Aunt.

The following letter refers to the action taken by her on the Total Abstinence question.

(*To Eustace Havergal*)

April 12, 1879.

DEAR EUSTACE,—

... As to actual signing I only deferred that, that I might use the act at good interest, which I did by getting six persons to sign with me. ... I have found by experience, as thousands of other Christian workers are finding, that this "outward and visible sign" is just the needed means to prevent the beginnings of that terrible evil. See now, I have here eight growing lads, besides several others, all in surroundings of more or less temptation, who have signed my book and are thus helped to say *no*; and, instead of swimming with the stream, not one has been into a public house since, trying their best to get others to abstain also. ... I could not feel impatient at your not seeing it yet, because four or five years ago I felt exactly as you do; but, hearing so much of the great work done by this means, I set myself to pray for clear light and guidance about it, asking that I might be able to lay aside prejudice on the one hand, and that I might be kept from going without God's leading on the other. From that time, conviction gradually dawned and deepened in my mind that I could not hold aloof from a movement on which God has set so very evident a seal of blessing. ...

Endorsed on a pamphlet dealing with the Total Abstinence question, enclosed in the same letter, is the following.

I have gone in altogether for it now, and find it gives me opportunities at once which I had not before.

May 1, 1879.

... I haven't taken up teetotal work, but teetotal work has taken up me! Morgan and Scott made me accept a big, handsome, pledge book in February, and somehow the thing has fairly *caught fire* here. One led to another, and yesterday boys were coming all day to sign! I had twenty-five recruits yesterday alone, and a whole squad more are coming this evening! and we are going in for getting EVERY boy in the whole village! And now, "Please, miss, mayn't the girls sign?" So I've got to open a girls' branch as well! So work grows!

I adopt the title of "The Newton Temperance Regiment," to please my boys, who are a strong majority in it, and very hearty about it. I do love these little lads.

Our dear and faithful friend, Elizabeth Clay, was with us at Easter. Frances was deeply interested in the details of her Indian journeys and Zenana work, and consulted with her as to the possibility of eventually going to India herself, that she might be able to write for her King in Oriental languages. Frances was not at all well, and a feverish cold prevented her from singing when Mr. and Mrs. Sankey paid us a pleasant visit. To them she spoke much of the bright City, and that music which alone could satisfy her intense craving.

Almost the last time we walked to church together, she turned round to me and said: "Marie, I've come to the conclusion it will be *very nice* to go to heaven! The perfect harmony, the perfect praise, no jarring tunes. You don't know the intense enjoyment it is to me to sing in part music. I don't think I could hear the Hallelujah Chorus and not sing it; but *there*—!"

Another Sunday evening, not being able to go to church, she called Mary to read with her. Searching into the meaning of those words (John 8:51), "If a man keep My saying, he shall never see death," her conclusion was, "so, when we come to die, our eyes will so really see Jesus *Himself* that we shall not see death." Thus it was to her:

> "Death is a hushed and glorious tryst,
> With *Thee*, my King, my Saviour Christ!"

Truly, her loyal life shone brightly, day by day. Her appeals stirred many a one to choose the King's service. I think it was in April she took (once only) the Young Women's Christian Association meeting in Swansea for her friend, Mrs. Morgan. They well remember how she played and sang with them, "Precious Saviour, may I live, only for Thee!" (to her tune "Onesimus.") At the close of her address she took round to each a copy of

> "Take my life, and let it be
> Consecrated, Lord, to Thee,"

with a blank space, where each might sign her name who could do so, in true and loyal allegiance. My dear sister *always* went to such meetings, in the truest humility of spirit. She often said, "I can only ask the Lord to give me words; I am only learning, myself, day by day"; but a real power seemed to rest on all her words, and especially during the last years.

Our friend the Baroness Helga von Cramm joined us in May. She thought dear Frances looking well and young and bright. We had some pleasant seaside walks; and Frances sat by her friend, on the sands, when she sketched the "Mumbles Lighthouse." Many kind friends near us, and their children and servants, wondered at the sweetness and power with which my sister spoke to them for and of her Lord and King.

(*To Mrs. H.*)

May 5, 1879.

Thank God for her! and thank God that you are able to thank Him. I never read anything sweeter than Nony's welcome to her Lord's coming for her. I have ventured to keep a copy of your beautiful letter to ——. Would you let me make some extract from it in my next circulars? I should so like to tell my dear little collectors about Nony, whose name will be highest on the list in the next report. I feel it such a privilege to have been permitted to number this little saint of God among my little band of collectors. One from the seniors (E. R. N.)[1] and one from the juniors are "safe home" now, and both such abundant entrances. How beautiful Nony must be now!

Yours, in most loving sympathy.

(*To the same.*)

May 20.

... On further consideration and prayer, I see that I cannot write Nony's memoir, at least not unless the autumn shapes itself quite differently from what God is at present indicating. After Christmas, I *may* be free to decide on fresh work, and then I might try and do my best. But I think you would not like to postpone the memoir so long. ...[2]

EXTRACTS FROM LAST LETTERS.

May 17, 1879.

DEAR MR. SNEPP,—

I cannot forbear just a line of affectionate sympathy in reply to your note. And I do so rejoice with you in the brighter parts of it.

I begin my Irish campaign, please God, on June 4th; I stay first with the good Bishop of Cashel. Really a wonderful little Temperance work here; all the rising generation have joined the pledge except about twelve, and now the men want to speak to me, and I am to meet them to-night at the corner of the village (open air, having no place else) with my pledge book. I have got 118 pledged, and each with prayer over it, and personal talk about better things. In haste, etc., etc.

(*To Mrs. Charles Bullock.*)

... I do not want to work out a text this morning because I want to give the same time to working a few, in the chapter for to-day, with the Baroness. But I choose for next Sunday (May 18) 1 Kings 5:17: "*The King*" "*commanded*" "*great stones*," "*costly stones*," "*hewed stones*," "*foundation of the house.*" Those six points will bear a lot of referencing; *the* point that struck me being that all these great, costly, and hewed stones were to be laid *out of sight,* yet making the strong and needed foundation for a beautiful superstructure. Do you see my thought?

This letter leads to the remark that for many months my dear sister had selected texts on some verse in the *Christian Progress* chapter for Sunday mornings. She sent them on postcards to her friend Mrs. Bullock on the previous Fridays, calling

---

[1] E.R. Nicholas, Esq., long revered in Bewdley, who died April 30, 1879, the day before little Nony.

[2] This memoir of her little friend is now published by Messrs. Nisbet & Co., "The Memorials of Little Nony." [See pages 899–925 of Volume IV of the Havergal edition.]

them "Sunday Morning Crumbs." We give only two others, for her friend will publish them with the title of "My Bible Study."

Zechariah 6:11: "Make crowns, and set them on the head of Joshua the high priest." Revelation 19:12: "Many crowns." Is it not our privilege to have something to do with preparing the crowns, and the jewels in them? You see it is "make," not merely "take." Meanwhile "we see" Him already "crowned with glory and honour" (Hebrews 2:9). Outsiders don't see it at all, and many of us don't "see" because we don't steadily "look." I suppose it is the coronation day of Jesus in our hearts when we "take" all that is most precious to us, typified by the silver and gold, and "make crowns" with it for Him in the double aspect of High Priest, *i.e.* Atoner and Mediator, and Joshua our accepted and recognised "Leader and Commander."

May 23, 1879.

For May 25: 1 Kings 12:24, "This thing is from Me" (railway to ver. 15). If anything wasn't from the Lord, one would have thought Rehoboam's infatuation was that thing! So, it seems a lesson of acquiescence in those most difficult things to acquiesce in, *i.e.* what seem to arise from man's (or lad's) foolishness and tryingness. See 2 Corinthians 5:18, "all things"; and 2 Corinthians 4:15. Compare Genesis 45:8, and 50:20. . . . So thankful for the good news in your note, as to both your sister and your friend. Thanks for your dear husband's. Very kind to register it!

CHAPTER XV.

The Last Week.

The donkey-boy — My Temperance regiment — Work on the village bank — Sailor friends — Helga's pictures — "God's will delicious" — Good Mary and kind nurse — "How good and kind to come!" — The last Sunday — The last hymns — Last messages — "Do speak bright words for Jesus" — The last song at the Golden Gate — With the King — Astley Churchyard.

MY dear sister Frances had promised to meet some men and boys on the village bank on May 21st. Though the day was very damp, she went, taking her Bible and her Temperance book with her. While standing a long time on this cold spot, heavy clouds came up from the Channel, and she returned, wet and chilly with the rain and mist; even then some were waiting for her to speak to them.

May 22nd, being Ascension Day, she wished to go to church with our friend, but looked so poorly that I urged her to come for the Communion only. She was very tired, and took a donkey home. As she passed through our village of Newton, quite a procession gathered round her, her regiment of boys eagerly listening. Her donkey boy, Fred Rosser, remembers that Miss Frances told him, "I had better leave the devil's side and get on the safe side; that Jesus Christ's was the winning side; that He loved us and was calling us, and wouldn't I choose Him for my Captain?" Arriving at home, Frances ran in for her book, and on the saddle Fred signed the pledge. A young sailor, W. Llewellyn, was going to sea the next day. Frances was anxious to speak to him, and in the evening went to the cottage. He signed the book and heard one of her closing messages;[1] and this was the last time her feet were

"Swift and beautiful for Thee."

That evening she spoke to several; her intense earnestness, her pleading words in the kitchen, are not forgotten. To our worthy landlord, his wife and boys, she spoke loving words. David and Johnnie Tucker will not forget how often she had them in her study.

May 23rd. The chilliness increased; and though she was in her study as usual, I requested the doctor to see my dear sister, and desired him to come again. The Temperance meeting was to be held in the evening, and my sister arranged 150 large Temperance cards, then to be given. Very cheerfully she gave up the wish to go, saying (*so like her!*) "You will do all so much better than I can; will you give them two messages from me: to those who have signed, 'Behold God Himself is . . . our Captain' (2 Chronicles 13:12); to those who have not signed,

---

[1] His last letter, from Brazil, states that he has faithfully kept the pledge.

'Come thou with us, and we will do thee good' (Numbers 10:29)." Our Vicar and Mr. Bishop, from Swansea, were to be present; and to them she sent her good wishes and request for bright short addresses. While we were at the meeting, she was stitching strong paper tract-bags for sailors at sea, till she felt ill and Mary assisted her into her room. A feverish night ensued.

Saturday, 24th. Our friend, the Baroness, left us; but she was not uneasy about Frances. In the afternoon my sister asked me to rearrange her pictures near her bed. "Put Mary Fay's text next to me, 'Jesus Christ, the same yesterday, today, and for ever"; above that, 'Sunrise from the Bel Alp,' and 'The Glacier of La Tour.'" I read to her the text painted by Helga, on the rock: "I saw a sea of glass, clear as crystal." Frances said, "Strangely sweet! tell Helga her pictures take my thoughts away from the pain,—up there." Then Frances asked me to place "my own text," "the blood of Jesus Christ, His Son, cleanseth from all sin"; and beyond it Emily Coombe's illumination, "I reckon that the sufferings," etc.

The following are her last notes, in pencil.

(*To Miss E. Titterton.*)

May 28, 1879.

Dearest Emily,—

I am laid up again with a return of these feverish attacks, which the doctor says are really from debility; so must only send love, and assure you that whatever is the reason of no answer, it can't possibly be that Mrs. P. is "offended"—that's not the last possibility, but an *im*possibility! It may be that she does not see her way and is in a fix what to say; this is highly probable, as the Mildmay institutions are, financially, at a low ebb, and of course she must throw all available strength into this. I have got the *whole* rising generation of the village to sign the pledge (all between eight and sixteen), except two boys who won't sign, three who broke, and one girl "going to sign"! Also about fifty grown-ups. My little lads are splendid: such hearty enthusiasm about it! Temperance meeting to-night, at which I was popularly supposed to be going to speak! but I have to entrust it all to others under God. I dare not let the fact transpire that I can't go. "They are such affectionate people, these poor Welsh."

If I am able to go to Ireland (June 4), I will explain to Mr. Fitzpatrick about pence cards for you and the Bruey Branch. . . .

The Mumbles, May 24.

Dear Mr. Watson,—

I am in bed again with another of these tryingly frequent feverish attacks, and am writing on the back of your own letter, not having other paper within reach!

The fact is, I have knocked myself up with this Temperance work; but having got the whole rising generation of the village into my Temperance regiment, except four naughty little black sheep, seems to me quite worth being knocked up for!

I am *sorry* I demurred to Dr. B.'s book appearing in my special livery; it was rather small of me, and I feel small accordingly. I forgot to say that the subject is one of my unfinished "invalid book" papers, but I don't think I need sacrifice it, need I? I could put a footnote, something of this sort—For fuller and far better thoughts on this passage, my readers are referred to the 'Brook Besor,' by Andrew A. Bonar, D.D.," etc.

I have had such a kind letter from Dr. Macduff, sending me "Palms of Elim." I like it best of his, since the "Faithful Promiser."

Maria says I must not write any more.

Yours ever,

F. R. H.

Of Sunday I have kept no account.

May 26th. She could not attend to her letters, but corrected the proof of "Morning Stars," on the text "I am the bright and morning Star"; and then the pen so long used in the service of her King was laid down. She was not suffering very much, lying quietly in bed, her pet kittens Trot and Dot on her duvet. She rather astonished her doctor by saying, "Do you think I've a chance of going?" He told her that she was not seriously ill; and asked if she really liked lying there, and in pain.

Frances. "Yes, I do; it is as if an errand-boy were told to take a message, and afterwards the master bids him *not* to go. I was going to Ireland next week, hoping to write for the Irish Society, but God has upset all my plans, and it's all right."

The last passage she looked at in her Bible was the *Christian Progress* chapter for May 28th (Revelation 2:1–10). She asked Mary to read it for her, dwelling on "Be thou faithful unto death, and I will give thee a crown of life," bidding her turn to the reference in James 1:12.

(It is remarkable that the same promise of "the crown of life" was the last passage our dear father ever read.)

May 29th. Fever and internal inflammation rapidly came on, and all the symptoms and agony of peritonitis. God seemed to permit severest suffering, and all remedies failed. But her peace and joy shone through it all, while her patience and unselfish consideration for others were most striking, arranging that all who nursed her should rest also. When we were distressed for her, she whispered, "It's home the faster!" She told Mary she was quite sure now she should never go to Ireland, adding, "God's will is *delicious*; He makes no mistakes." Our good Mary was a great comfort at all times.

May 30th. She was speaking of justification by faith: "Not for our own works or deservings; oh, what vanity it seems now to rest on our own obedience for salvation, any merit of our own takes away the glory of the atoning blood. 'Unto Him that loved us, and washed us from our sins in His own blood,' *that's it.*"

M. "Have you any fear?"

F. "Why should I? Jesus said 'It is finished,' and what was His precious blood shed for? *I trust that.*"

Another time: "I am sure 'I am not worthy to be called His son,' or His servant, but Jesus covers all; I am unworthy, but in Him complete."

The last letter she could listen to was from my brother Frank's twin sons, and her message was: "Thank Willie for that nice text, 'Sorrow may endure for a night, but joy cometh in the morning'; and I do hope that Willie and Ethelbert will be ambassadors for Christ; even if they are not clergymen, may they win souls."

To her sister Ellen: "I have not strength to send messages *to yours*. I should have liked my death to be like Samson's, doing more for God's glory than by my life; but He wills it otherwise."

Ellen. "St. Paul said 'The will of the Lord be done,' and 'let Christ be magnified, whether by my life or by my death.'"

I think it was then my beloved sister whispered: "Let my own text, 'the blood of Jesus Christ, His Son, cleanseth us from all sin' be on my tomb; *all* the verse, if there is room."

I must mention the skilful and tender care of the nurse, Sarah Carveley (from the Derby Institute). A year before, when in perfect health, Frances had playfully said, "You must come and nurse me."

The constant sickness was very distressing, and nothing alleviated the agonizing pain; but my sister's patient endurance was most lovely, trying to comfort *us,* and thanking us so sweetly for all we did.

Another time she said: "Marie dear, God is dealing differently with me in this illness; I don't know what He means by it; no new thoughts for books or poems come now."

Then, "Will you ask the Lord Jesus it may not be long before He speaks to me Himself some little love token." I knelt and asked that He would speak "peace" to her, even as He did to His disciples.

F. "I have peace, but it's *Himself* I am longing for."

M. "The little boats on the stormy sea had not to row back to Jesus; He drew nigh to them, and said, 'It is I, be not afraid.'"

Saturday afternoon she was very ill and feverish, saying, "I know now what it means, 'my tongue cleaveth to my gums.'" When fanning her she said, "Marie, you have made this last year of my life the brightest."

M. "Do you at all regret coming here?"

F. "I should think not; the pleasantest time I ever had, *delicious!*"

Whit Sunday she felt better and was able to talk a little to her brother and sisters, saying: "How good and kind to come! Frank, do you remember when we knelt together at dear papa's dying bed, what you said to me? It so comforted me. Ever since I trusted Jesus *altogether*, I have been so happy. I cannot tell how lovely, how precious, He is to me."

Her doctors were most watchful, and Frances expressed her confidence in them and declined further advice. She asked them, "What is the element of danger?"

"You are seriously ill, and the inflammation is increasing."

F. "I thought so, but if I am going it is too good to be true!"

In the early dawn of Whit Monday Frances said to me: "'Spite of the breakers, Marie, I am so happy; God's promises are so true. Not a fear."

About 8 a.m. we thought she was departing, and asked for her brother. He knelt by her, inquiring if he should pray. "Yes; let it be a sacramental service." She softly but emphatically joined in the words, "Therefore with angels," etc. Reverently, she asked her brother to say the (administration) words "once for all."

After some peaceful rest, she whispered: "Frank dear, it is not the performance of the rite, *no safety in that*; but it is obedience to His command and as a *remembrance* of His dying love"; to which he assented.

When one of her doctors was leaving he said, "Good-bye, I shall not see you again."

F. "Then do you really think I am going?"

Dr. "Yes."

F. "To-day?"

Dr. "Probably."

F. "Beautiful, too good to be true!"

Soon after she looked up smiling. "Splendid to be so near the gates of heaven!" (Again and again we heard this, and "So beautiful to go!" through the last hours.)

To Frank: "Will you sing 'Jerusalem, my happy home,' to papa's tune 'St. Chrysostom,'[1] and play it on my harp-piano. Sing from the copy that has

'Jesus my Saviour dwells therein,
  In glorious majesty;
And Him through every stormy scene
  I onward press to see!'

Oh, it is the Lord Jesus that is so dear to me, I can't tell how precious! how much He has been to me!"

Afterwards she asked for "How sweet the name of Jesus sounds," to the same tune.

The Vicar of Swansea came for a few minutes. He said: "You have talked and written a great deal about the King; and you will soon see Him in His beauty. Is Jesus with you now?"

F. "*Of course!* It's splendid! I thought He would have left me here a long while; but He is *so* good to take me now. Give my love to dear Mrs. Morgan, and tell all the Association

---

[1] No. 53, "Havergal's Psalmody."

(Y. W. C. A.) that what she and I have told them is all right, God's promises are all true, and the Lord Jesus is a good big foundation to rest upon. Ask Mr. A—— to speak *plainly* about Jesus. I want all young clergymen to be faithful ambassadors, and win souls. Tell Mr. W—— I can never thank him enough for his help. Oh, I want all of you to speak *bright*, BRIGHT, words about Jesus, oh, do, *do!* It is all perfect peace, I am only waiting for Jesus to take me in."

Soon after her friend Mrs. Morgan came, and Frances whispered: "There is no bottom to God's mercy and love; all His promises are true, not one thing hath failed."

In the afternoon, she asked us if it was wrong to groan when in such pain. We told her how very, very patient she had been; that even her doctors had noticed it, and her calmness.

F. "Oh, I am so glad you tell me this. I did want to glorify Him, *every step* of the way, and especially in this suffering. I hope none of you will have five minutes of this pain."

Her brother sang "Christ for me"; and Ellen repeated

"On Christ the solid Rock I stand,
All other ground is sinking sand";

adding "I want to rejoice more *for* you, dear Frances; you are on the Rock, and we want no other."

F. "It is the *one* God has laid for us."

Many times she whispered: "Come, Lord Jesus, come and fetch me; oh, run, run." Then, "Do you think I shall be disappointed?"

"No, dearest, we are quite sure you are going to Him now."

F., smiling, "I think Jesus will be glad."

On Tuesday, June 3rd, Whit Tuesday, at dawn the change came. One of her sisters repeated, "When thou passest through the waters I will be with thee."

F. "He *must* keep His word."

Isaiah 41:10 was repeated *incorrectly*; she whispered it correctly for us. After a short doze, she exclaimed: "I am lost in amazement! There hath not failed one word of all His good promise!"

She just spoke of Miss Leigh's work in Paris, and her friend Margaret C. there, adding "Strange I think of it now."

Whispering the names of many dear ones, she added "I love them all." Then, as it were with her last look on them from the opening golden gates, she said yearningly "I want *all* to come to me in heaven; oh, don't, *don't* disappoint me, tell them 'Trust Jesus.'"

Ellen repeated: (altering the word "canst")

"Jesus, I will trust Thee,
Trust Thee with my soul;
Guilty, lost, and helpless,
Thou *hast made* me whole:

There is none in heaven,
Or on earth, like Thee;
Thou hast died for sinners,
Therefore Lord for *me*."

Clearly, though faintly, she sang the whole verse, to her own tune "Hermas."

Then came a terrible rush of convulsive sickness. It ceased; the nurse gently assisting her, she nestled down in the pillows, folded her hands on her breast, saying, "There, now it is all over! Blessed rest!"

And now she looked up steadfastly as if she saw the Lord; and, surely, nothing less heavenly could have reflected such a glorious radiance upon her face. For ten minutes, we watched that almost visible meeting with her King, and her countenance was so glad, as if she were already talking to Him. Then she tried to sing; but after one sweet high note, "HE ——," her voice failed; and, as her brother commended her soul into her Redeemer's hand, she passed away. Our precious sister was gone,—satisfied,—glorified,—within the palace of her King!

. . . "So *she* took . . .
The one grand step, beyond the stars of God,
Into the splendour, shadowless and broad,
Into the everlasting joy and light.
The zenith of the earthly life was come.

.   .   .   .   .

What then? Eye hath not seen, ear hath not heard!
  Wait till thou too hast fought the noble strife,
  And won, through Jesus Christ, the crown of life!
Then shalt thou know the glory of the word,
Then as the stars for ever, ever shine,
Beneath the King's own smile, perpetual zenith thine!"

On Monday, June 9th, at 6 a.m., the villagers and others assembled on the lawn while her flower-crowned coffin passed out. The Rev. S. C. Morgan, Vicar of Swansea, addressed them after we had left for Worcestershire.

Many relatives and friends joined us at Stourport, following our beloved sister to her father's tomb in Astley churchyard. A golden *star,* of Banksia roses, a poet's wreath of laurel and bay, and, many white crowns, were laid upon her. There, within sight of her birth-room in the rectory, and under the branches of the fir-tree her father planted, (and, away beyond, the hills and valleys of her childhood's haunts encircling us,) we laid our dear sister in sure and certain hope of her "resurrection to eternal life."

The following is the inscription, on the north side of our dear father's tomb, in Astley churchyard:

FRANCES RIDLEY HAVERGAL,

Youngest Daughter of the Rev. W. H. Havergal,
and Jane his Wife.

Born at Astley Rectory, 14th December, 1836. Died at Caswell Bay, Swansea, 3rd June, 1879. Aged 42.

By her writings in prose and verse, she, "being dead yet speaketh."

"*The blood of Jesus Christ, His Son, cleanseth us from all sin.*"
1 John 1:7.

There had been heavy storms all day, even as she had passed through many (and our own storm-grief had been bitter and desolating). But the sunshine came, just as the service was ending, and the birds suddenly sang sweetly all around. Very hushing was the thought that our dear sister's life had been the prelude of the everlasting song; and that she was then looking upon the face of her King, and praising Him "evermore, and evermore."

"Worthy of all adoration
　Is the Lamb that once was slain,"
Cry, in raptured exultation,
His redeemed from every nation;
　Angel myriads join the strain;
　　Sounding from their sinless strings
　　Glory to the King of kings;
　　Harping, with their harps of gold,
　　Praise which never can be told.

Hallelujahs full and swelling
　Rise around His throne of might.
All our highest laud excelling,
Holy and Immortal, dwelling
　In the unapproachèd light,
　　He is worthy to receive
　　All that heaven and earth can give.
　　Blessing, honour, glory, might,
　　All are His by glorious right.

As the sound of many waters
　Let the full Amen arise!
Hallelujah! Ceasing never,
Sounding through the great For Ever,
　Linking all its harmonies;
　　Through eternities of bliss,
　　Lord, our rapture shall be this;
　　And our endless life shall be
　　One Amen of praise to Thee!

(F. R. H.)

"Unto Him that loved us and washed us from our sins in His own blood, and hath made us kings and priests unto God and His Father; to Him be glory and dominion, for ever and ever. Amen."

Tune, Hermas; No. 105, in "Havergal's Psalmody."

Jesus, I Will Trust Thee.

"I will trust in Thee."—Psalm 55:23.

Jesus, I will trust Thee, trust Thee with my soul;
Guilty, lost, and helpless, Thou canst make me whole.
There is none in heaven or on earth like Thee:
Thou hast died for sinners—therefore, Lord, for me.

Jesus, I may trust Thee, name of matchless worth,
Spoken by the angel at Thy wondrous birth;
Written, and for ever, on Thy cross of shame,
Sinners read and worship, trusting in that name.

Jesus, I must trust Thee, pondering Thy ways,
Full of love and mercy, all Thy earthly days:
Sinners gathered round Thee, lepers sought Thy face;
None too vile or loathsome for a Saviour's grace.

Jesus, I can trust Thee, trust Thy written word,
Though Thy voice of pity I have never heard.
When Thy Spirit teacheth, to my taste how sweet—
Only may I hearken, sitting at Thy feet.

Jesus, I do trust Thee, trust without a doubt:
"Whosoever cometh, Thou wilt not cast out."
Faithful is Thy promise, precious is Thy blood—
These my soul's salvation, Thou my Saviour God!

MARY JANE WALKER, 1864

APPENDIX.

	page
FRAGMENTS. By F. R. H.:—	
The Dream Cathedral	331
Christmas Decorations	332
United Bible Reading	333
"All Things."	335
Words about Work.	339
Motto Verses, for Open Air Mission Workers.	341
Excerpts: on Music, etc.	341
A "Line Left Out".	343
LETTERS, ETC.	
By Rev. C. B. Snepp, Miss Clay, Miss Ada Leigh, "B. M.," Miss Kirchhoffer, Bishop Alexander, etc.	343
F. R. H. CHURCH MISSIONARY MEMORIAL FUND	349
F. R. H. AND CHURCH PASTORAL-AID SOCIETY	352
F. R. H. AND IRISH SOCIETY WORK	353
IN MEMORIAM	
By various Authors.	355

This was F.R.H.'s card designed by her Irish friend Mary Fay. In her final illness, Frances asked her sister Maria, "Fetch me Mary Fay's card, 'Jesus Christ the same yesterday, to-day, and forever,' and bring a nail. I can see those nice large letters, and put it quite straight under Helga's [von Cramm's painting of] 'Glacier.' " (See page 379 of this book.) Maria placed this in the Photograph Album that she donated to the Church Missionary Society in June, 1886 (see pages 162–163), and Maria wrote the comments at the top and the right end:

    F.R.H.'s life motto! The original designed & painted by Mary Fay, F.R.H.'s Irish friend.

FRAGMENTS. By F.R.H.

THE DREAM CATHEDRAL.

[*The outline of this early composition* (1857) *was a real dream.*]

I STOOD in the nave of a strangely magnificent cathedral. Such a cathedral it was as seemed to be the very embodiment of the highest ideal of beauty and grandeur. Around me were fluted columns of snowy marble, enriched with carvings of foliage, such as the artist might have seen in a vision of Eden, meeting above in pointed arches, whose upward curve seemed to beckon heavenwards and to speak of celestial aspirings; the floor was marble too, and as unsullied in its whiteness as the dewy petal of a lily, ere the dusty breath of day has passed upon it, and telling me of purity and innocence; then the vaulted roof, the union of those arching columns, with its dim twilight of undefined yet beautiful interlacings, spoke of holy mysteries. There were long shadowy aisles stretching far away, and their whispering echoes suggested sacred solitude and retirement. There were marble steps leading up to a screen of such cunning work that the very stone seemed to breathe forth beauty, and, if possible, to shadow forth the loveliness of religion. And beyond this were glimpses of such a choir, so wonderful in its transcendent beauty, as seemed scarcely fitted for mortal worshippers to kneel within. All this was seen, as it were, through the veil of a softened, shadowy radiance, poured through windows whose Gothic tracery enclosed, not stained glass, but a mosaic of the most gorgeous gems, casting the glow of their rich deep colouring on portions of the fair whiteness of pillar and arch and pavement, bathing all in a light, splendid even in the solemnity of its dimness.

Scarcely had admiration and wonder time to unfold, when the tones of cathedral music swelled through the marvellous temple. Soft and sweet as a symphony of angel harps, the sound seemed to enwreathe itself around the marble shafts, and to melt into the dark vaultings of the lofty roof, as though there were some strange affinity between them; and then, at every pause, it hovered away far down the lessening aisles, till the whole building was like one great living instrument. Then voices came floating down that glorious nave: sweet and melodious, shall I call them? words do not express what those voices were; and the anthem which they chanted was such as Handel might dream, perhaps, but never wrote.

Do you not know what it is to see something very beautiful, and yet feel unsatisfied? to hear the sweetest sounds, and yet feel they might be sweeter? to enjoy the greatest apparent delight, and yet feel that it is not the perfection of happiness? I cannot think that the human spirit is ever positively and absolutely *satisfied*; it is too great, too vast, (though we scarcely know it,) to be filled with anything on earth; its real ideal is never found; it is ever striving and yearning after something greater, higher, lovelier; and its Maker is its only satisfaction.

But I was satisfied. It was the perfection of beauty, the perfection of enjoyment; my longings realized, and more still. All this *seemed* to carry my heart upwards, I felt filled with joyful devotion, and adoration was the keynote of the silent anthem of my spirit. Then the thought came across me: "Can it be that such a temple is unfavourable to true devotion? can it be that a spirit could remain earthbound here, and not soar far, far upwards: in the holiest, happiest, adoration?"

Suddenly I heard a voice, clear, calm, and very grave, though I saw not the speaker. It spoke to me: "*Your Saviour is here*, you have long sought Him, He is about to manifest Himself to you. See! He is standing there in His own glorious Person!" In an instant all else had lost its interest. Oh! it was so strange, that sudden revulsion of feeling. Fancied devotion gave way to the reality of the intensest earnestness; the temple in all its fascinating grandeur was nothing, absolutely nothing; His Presence there was the *only* thing I longed for. I gazed intently where the voice indicated; I saw One standing alone, and knew and *felt* that it was Himself. But the many-lined shadow of one of the gem-filled windows fell upon His Form, and I could not discern its outline, much less His countenance.

"Listen!" said the voice again; "He is speaking to you. Are not His words sweet and gracious!" But a fresh burst of music pealed from the organ, the voices of the invisible choristers rose higher and louder, and the tide of melody carried away the sound of that heavenly Voice, whose words would have been more than life to me. Oh, how each note grated upon me! how I hated the music, which drowned the gentle tones of that Voice!

I determined to approach, and at least be gladdened by His look, though His words might not reach my ear. I hastened on, but the marble steps grew in height under my feet, and I could not ascend them as quickly as I thought to do, each one seemed a mountain. But He was turning to look on me, and something seemed to tell me certainly that He was going to rejoice me with one of His own sweet smiles, another instant, and His eye would have met mine, when one of the fluted pillars suddenly rose in front of me, the blessed moment was gone, and He passed away down one of the dim shadowy aisles.

In desperation I rushed on, as if every hope, every desire, of a lifetime were concentrated in that one passing instant; I gained the entrance of the aisle, when the exquisite screen, which a moment before had so charmed me, stretched itself in defiance across it, barring the only way by which I could reach the departing Saviour.

He was gone! and all seemed changed to darkness and discord. In the very agonies of regret and despair I sank on the pavement, and *awoke*!

The moral, so to speak, of this dream will be apparent to every one. What is earthly beauty to a soul longing for its Saviour, and thirsting for His grace? What are externals compared to internals? But I would not be misunderstood, there is no reason why the other extreme should be advocated. I am, and always have been, a warm admirer of those time-honoured ornaments of our land, the crown jewels, as it were, of our outward and visible Church, our English cathedrals. He who giveth us *all* things richly to enjoy must have awakened, or rather created, those thoughts of beauty which expressed themselves in these glorious temples, notwithstanding the tainted atmosphere of superstition which then darkened our land; and if their original purpose, the setting forth of Jehovah's praise and glory, is sometimes far from being attained, the fault is not in the temples, but in any who do not within them worship God in spirit and truth. It is not the grace and grandeur of their architecture which frustrate their noble object, but the earthliness of men's hearts, which rises not above pillar and roof and spire, but lies like the cold pavement itself, resting in things seen and temporal. If it be true that "unto the pure all things are pure," just as true is it that, to the unrenewed mind and unwatchful heart, the holiest things may and do become snares and stumbling blocks; satisfied with the beauty of earthly sanctuaries, and the solemnity of mere earthly forms, they yearn not for the "beauty of the Lord our God," who "dwelleth not in temples made with hands." But the soul of one who knows Him who is "altogether lovely," and longs for the day when he shall "see the King in His beauty," while rejoicing in, and loving, our old cathedrals in their ancient hoariness, will yet esteem them as nothing in comparison with the higher things on which his heart is set. And it will probably be found that, after all, he who thus gives such things their right and subordinate place has the purest enjoyment in, and the truest appreciation of, those ancient fanes which have stood for centuries, the silent witnesses of the beauty of religion.

May each one who reads this dream find, and know, and rejoice in that Saviour, whose whisper of pardoning love is sweeter than earth's sweetest music, whose smile of acceptance is lovelier than earth's loveliest scene! May he himself become a " temple of the Holy Ghost," bright with the beauty of holiness, and shining in the light of the countenance of our God!

F. R. H.

CHRISTMAS DECORATIONS.

WHEN our young friends use their taste, and skill, in what seems, on the surface of things, a sacred work,—the beautifying of God's sanctuary for a holy festival, do they ever consider that, whatever the theoretical aim may be, the practical result is, necessarily and distinctly, temptation? Temptation, moreover, in exact proportion to the taste and skill displayed! The experience of every honest conscience shows that when we, who naturally love all that is beautiful, enter a church beautifully decorated, the temptation to wandering eyes and thoughts is just in proportion to the exquisiteness and elaborateness of the decorations. We have come to seek Jesus, to find the Shepherd "by the footsteps of the flock"; we want to commune with Him, and we want Him to speak to our hearts; we want to be freshly and specially "looking unto Jesus" in all the meaning of that word, looking away from all else, looking unto Him. And at once our eye is caught by an elegant festoon, and a singularly effective twining of a pillar or picking out of a moulding, and a most charming device on the reading desk, and a novel arrangement of the panels of the pulpit. It is all lovely, much prettier than last year, the general effect is so good, and so on. And suddenly we remember what we came for, and we make a great effort to turn away our eyes and fix them on "Jesus only"; but somehow the electric chain has been severed, the other things have entered in; and when we again look up, to meet the smile of the "Prince of Peace," we find there has been "something between"; our eyes have involuntarily turned away from the "King in His beauty" to the passing prettiness of garland and wreath. What have we not lost? But simple texts of Scripture I see no objection to.

The dilemma for the decorators is, do they wish their work to be looked at and admired, or do they not? If not, why put it where it must attract the eye? But if they do, let them remember that the mind cannot be equally occupied with two things at the same time; and that the moments spent in admiring gaze on their graceful work cannot be spent in adoring gaze on the Lord of Christmas, the Altogether Lovely One.

But there is something to be said for "Christmas decorations," where they will lead to no wandering thoughts in worship. If our bright young decorators could but see the gleam, on suffering or aged faces, when "a bit of Christmas" reaches the lonely lives in a hospital or workhouse ward; if they would but listen to the echo from the Mount of Olives, "Inasmuch as ye have done it unto one of the least of these My brethren, ye have done it unto Me"; surely they would gladly try to use their taste and energies for them, instead of the mere delectation, or even spiritual hindrance, of a fashionable congregation. It would be so easy; just a little bouquet of evergreens, for each poor bedside; just a little festoonery, for the bare walls; just a Christmas motto or two; they cannot tell, till they have seen for themselves, what an amount of pleasure they would give to those who have so little to cheer them! Will not some of our young friends do this little service for the Master's sake this next Christmas, each in his or her own locality? For London, they might communicate with the Hon. Secretary of the Flower Mission, 3, Clyde Street, S.W., or with the Secretary of the Mildmay Flower Mission, Deaconess House, Mildmay Park, N.; or the work might be done in the country workhouses and infirmaries, for, as a rule, far less is done to brighten them than the larger ones.

Where there is a will there is a way, and, as an old poet says, "love will find out the way." May the love of Christ constrain many, even in this, not to please themselves, but Him who came to seek and to save that which was lost.

F. R. H. (1875)

"CHRISTIAN PROGRESS" SCRIPTURE READING AND PRAYER UNION. UNITED BIBLE READING.

"WELL, Miss, as long as I *was* reading regular, I thought I might as well read what the others were reading," said a young man-servant, as his reason for joining the "Christian Progress Union."

"As well!" Yes, and much better. To begin with, we ought, every one of us, to be "reading regular." There is no doubt about that. How is any soul to "grow" on one meal a day, or on uncertain and occasional draughts of the "sincere milk of the word"? Regularly, not only as to constancy, but *as to system.* How much time is wasted in indecision, and wondering what to read next! How many are familiar only with their favourite parts of God's word, neglecting others almost entirely; thus overlooking many a royal commandment, and losing much of the royal bounty, and gaining no wide and balanced views, of the great field of His truth! How can we be "throughly furnished unto *all* good works," if we do not use God's means thereto, "all Scripture"?

And if we are, as every Christian ought to be, reading *both* parts of His word regularly every day, why not "read what others are reading"? Why should you read Galatians while others are reading Ephesians; Ephesians while they are in Philippians? Why not "keep rank" with all one's Christian friends, and thousands of fellow members, praying for the same light, the same teaching, day by day, for them and for ourselves? Why not lie down *together* in the green pastures, instead of scattering all about?

There are several arrangements for united reading, and membership of any will be more or less profitable. But some features of the "*Christian Progress Scripture Reading and Prayer Union*" seem to me to render it not only profitable, in a special degree, for ourselves, but peculiarly valuable, as an adjunct to our work among others.

Our members read one chapter every day in the Old Testament, going straight through; and a short evening reading in the New Testament, in consecutive portions, averaging about fifteen verses.

Personally, I believe each will find it a real help, and *not* a fetter or limit, to have these assigned portions. There is, or should be, plenty of time for any further Bible study, which may attract us. But this is a reminder to the young or unestablished Christian. It is a guard against desultoriness. It is a counteractive to one-sidedness, and a gentle guide into "the whole counsel of God." It forms a pleasant bond alike for the near and the distant. It is a connecting link for scattered families and severed friends. It is also an immense help to profitable intercourse. The mere fact of knowing that those around have certainly been reading the same chapters opens the way for questions or remarks, or mention of striking verses, which might not otherwise have been ventured on, and thus raises the tone of our household conversation. How few of us realize that we have to give account for our empty table-talk! Constantly, too, it will give easier opportunity for improvement of even a passing greeting, or enrichment of a quickly written note with a living gem of truth.

I would plead for the servants to be "partakers of the benefit." With a little kindly explanation, they are almost invariably pleased to join, and the practical benefit is perhaps even greater in the servants' hall than in the drawing-room. Children, too, if old enough to read for themselves, are important accessions. "It is so nice for our little boy and girl to join with us," said a Christian mother; "it may be the means of making them steady Bible-readers for life!" I am convinced that it would be a great blessing in schools. Many have already joined. In one young ladies' school about sixty of the pupils are members.

Most especially would I commend it to Christian workers. Those who have a settled charge will find that no amount of general exhortations, to read the Bible, will be so effectual as "Come, join with me!" This is immediate and definite, and will bring persons to a point. One lady, after joining herself, obtained some fifty members in about a week, from her two Bible-classes. Just try it! Join yourself, first; and then see if it is not a new power and blessing among those for whose souls you are labouring. Do not train them into bad ways by getting them to read only once a day. If you do that, you encourage the comfortable idea that they have done their duty very sufficiently by a chapter at night, while the whole day has been Scriptureless. Aim higher at once, and you will strike higher. There is no power in half measures. It is one of the great benefits of this Union, that it is lifting such numbers out of their easy-going, once-a-day, reading, into a more excellent way.

I believe it will be found to be a most valuable parochial agent, and that members of any congregation will be strengthening the hands of their ministers, by bringing it before them in this light. *Very* much might be said on this aspect of the Union, which it would be stepping out of my province to enlarge upon. Perhaps no item of parochial machinery would be so fraught with real spiritual blessing as this noiselessly powerful one, wherever heartily and *thoroughly* introduced.

For those who have temporary opportunities of special work with souls, this Union is simply invaluable. It is just what we want to consolidate our work. It is our best legacy when leaving those to whom we have been privileged to be God's messengers of blessing. It is putting them on the rails; putting them in the way of further blessing; making the surest provision for their nourishment; giving them something which will be definite and perpetual help in the new path. It will be a delightful link, and a reminder to mutual prayer. It will help them to help each other, and give them something to do in trying to get others to join. Work for our young converts is often a difficulty, but this will give immediate opportunity both for confession of Christ and direct usefulness, and often lead to more.

Now, who will join us? You may do so by sending your full name and address (stating whether Rev., Mr., Esq., Mrs., or Miss, and inclosing a penny stamp) to the Rev. Ernest Boys, Bengeo, Hertford. You will receive in return a card of membership, a copy of the *Christian Progress Magazine*, and other papers containing full information respecting it. If you are not *quite* sure whether you would like it, send for the papers only, and try it for a month.

There need be no hesitation about joining, on the idea of its being a sort of irrevocable promise. You can cease to be a member any day, by *returning your card of membership*. If you forget a reading, you have not broken a vow, but missed a privilege. Those who cannot read for themselves can have the portions read to them; one of our heartiest members is "no scholar," but his little daughter reads to him.

If you shrink a little from laying aside some favourite plan, or *want* of plan, of your own, will you not remember that "none of us liveth to himself"? If you join for the sake of being in a better position to lead and lift others into the benefits of regular reading, you surely will not feel it any sacrifice! Rather you will find, as many of us thankfully, that it is a decided personal benefit to ourselves..

"*Christian Progress*," the Organ of the Union, is well described as a "Magazine of help and encouragement in Christian life, testimony, and work." "Its aim," says the Editor, "is to encourage believers in the Lord Jesus Christ in their daily walk amidst the realities of life." Members can send questions relating to practical Christian life and work, or to the interpretation of Holy Scriptures; also special requests for prayer, which are inserted monthly. The Magazine contains tables of the readings and special notices to members.

In conclusion, let me say to every one of my friends, known and unknown, "Come *thou* with us, and we will do thee good!"

F. R. H.

ADDRESS TO YOUNG WOMEN'S CHRISTIAN ASSOCIATION, AT PLYMOUTH, September 1878.

"ALL THINGS."

EVERY year, I might almost say every day that I live, I seem to see more clearly how all the rest and gladness and power of our Christian life hinges on one thing; and that is,—taking God at His word, believing that He really means exactly what He says, and accepting the very words in which He reveals His goodness and grace, without substituting others or altering the precise moods and tenses which He has seen fit to use. Now scarcely any word is so often altered by His dear children, (let alone outsiders,) as the word "all." Satan can't bear it. He always meets it with a "Yea, hath God said *all?*" It is surprising what a number of substitutionary words he has ready to suggest—"some," "a few," "certain things," and perhaps his favourite is "all—except." Now to whom shall we listen to-day, as we think over a few of the passages where God says "All things"? Will you listen to His word, or will you accept the devil's "all—except"? This is what I want this afternoon,—that we should every one of us simply take God's words about "all things," and my prayer is that the Holy Spirit may apply at least some *one* of the passages to *every* heart, and let it ring on a powerful chime of encouragement or comfort as may be needed, through many days to come. I don't think it very much matters what I say about the texts, they themselves are the message.

In seeking out what God has said about "all things," the texts found seem to group themselves into four sets.

I. All things are of God.
II. All things are by Jesus Christ.
III. All things are for your sakes.
IV. All things are yours.

I. "All things are *of God*." (2 Corinthians 5:18.) Here we seem to have a grand foundation laid in the past, and a most beautiful and perfect daily building upon it in the present.

1. Look back for a moment at the foundation, it is very strengthening to do so. Recollect how the great plan of our salvation, yours and mine, was "of God." The great promise of eternal life was "of God," given by Him before the world began, when we were not there to receive it, and therefore given to Jesus to hold for us. Search out, (from memory, or with concordance,) what God did for us before the foundation of the world, how He chose us in Christ, wrote our names in the Lamb's book of life, provided our redemption, and prepared the kingdom for us—think of all this being "of God," and seal it with the words "I know that whatsoever God doeth, it shall be for ever: nothing can be put to it, nor anything taken from it" (Ecclesiastes 3:14). What He hath done cannot be reversed, what is of Him cannot come to naught. Now just let us take the strong consolation of this. For this is the foundation of Christ's promise, "My sheep shall never perish,"—for "salvation is of the Lord" (Jonah 2:9).

2. But many of us have learnt the blessedness of seeing that all this is "of God," who do not quite take the comfort of the daily building upon it.

Now here comes in the splendid fact of the literality of "all things," with no added "except." For see Romans 11:36, John 17:7, 1 Chronicles 29:14. Just look at it! Positively "all things!" All that surrounds our lives and position, all that affects our work, our health, all that moulds our characters, *all* that is, and all that comes to His children, is "of God" and cometh "of God" to us. Of course the objection arises,—But what of things which really don't seem to be "of God" at all? Some one has beautifully said that though a wrong or injurious word or action may not be God's will for the person who says or does it, by the time it reaches me it is God's will for *me*, and is "of God" to me. Take as instances I Kings 12; it seemed a sad and distressing thing that Rehoboam should so act as to divide the kingdom, but God says "this thing is from Me." He had His own purposes to fulfil by it. Then Genesis 45:8, and 1:20. Don't you think it would have been terribly hard for you, if you had been Joseph's sister, to believe beforehand that his being sold was "of God"? Yet, when God has once for all told us that "all things are of Him," why should we not believe at once, instead of feeling all the misery of first doubting and then being ever so sorry that we did doubt, when after a while we see that it was of God! Now to be practical: just use this thought. The very next time something turns up which seems all wrong and disappointing, say "all things are of God," therefore this thing is "of God." Of Whom? God, the *Father*,—of whom are all things (1 Corinthians 8:6). Some of us know the force of that word by possession, and some by loss. The Father that pitieth, knoweth, careth for you, loveth you—the God whom Jesus called "My Father and your Father!" He knows the sorrows, the way that you take, the works (for He hath prepared them for us, and has wrought them in us); He knows *all things*, and all these things are "of Him." Now if there were no more, is it not enough that "all things are *of God!*"

II. But *how* are all things of God? We can't grasp a mere passive being, we crave a personal agent. Here it is. "One Lord Jesus Christ, *by whom* are all things" (1 Corinthians 8:6, Hebrews 2:10). The Father has appointed and exalted Him to this. Did you ever think of the immense comfort it is to know that God has given Him to be (1) Head over all things to His church, that it is to you and me,—the things that we can't manage, can't bring about, can't control,—the persons or circumstances, which seem altogether beyond our reach to bend, Jesus is over them all, *given* to us to be not only *our* Head, but Head over all things! What rest it is to know this! Then all things are put under His (2) *feet*. No matter that we *see* not yet "Thou *hast* put," the two can't be separated: Satan is under His feet with a bruised head; the world is under His feet (wonderful footstool that!); and we, if in Christ, joined to Him, must have all these things under our feet too. Then God has given all things into His (3) *hand* (John 3:35). Jesus knows it, He knew it even before He went forth to the great conflict (John 13:3). All His *saints* are in Thy hand (Deuteronomy 33:3), our *work's* (Ecclesiastes 9:1), and our *times* (Psalm 31:15).

Now with *our* Lord Jesus Christ given to be Head over all things, having all things put under His feet, and all things given into His hand, what in the world have we to fear! Somebody met this the other day with "nothing, except myself!" And God meets this "except" with another "all things." He tells us of the Saviour, the Lord Jesus Christ, being able to subdue *all things* unto Himself. Then He must be able to subdue myself unto Himself. "But I don't find that He has done so!" And why not? "Because of your unbelief." As God has appointed faith as the means and the measure of our reception of His promises, is it any wonder that, when we don't, and won't, and don't even *want* to, believe a given promise, we don't find it fulfilled? Of course not! Here we have come to a most practical and closely touching test of taking God at His word. I put it to you, dear friends, *solemnly*. God says Jesus is able to subdue *all things* unto Himself. At this moment the devil is whispering at the hearts of some of you,—"Yes, hath God said *all* things? it only means able to subdue all things *except*." And some of you are adding to the word, and saying,—Yes, except my will, or except my wandering thoughts, or except my sinful nature, or except my forgetfulness, or something! Face it! Which is it to be? God says "all things." Satan says "*all things except*." Believing God's bare word, no matter how unlikely it seems, you shall find strength, freedom, yes, such a blessing as only He can give. Believing Satan, you shall just go on without all this, you shall go on doubting His power, and calling your doubt humility; and more than this, you shall go on sinning against God, the great monster sin of unbelief. It is no light thing to come face to face with any one of God's promises, and to turn away from it with a devil-breathed "Except."

Shall I go on now to think of what Jesus actually is doing? The great covenant is ordered in all things by God, but the agent of that covenant is Jesus Christ. As He has already fulfilled its conditions, so He is now carrying out its provisions. God is supplying all our need by Jesus Christ, just as much as He created all things by Him. And as Jesus is now upholding all by the word of His power, so He is upholding us from moment to moment. Must be! for unless we were annihilated we must be among the "all things." But still He loves to be inquired of, and so we pray. (Psalm 119:116) "Uphold me according to Thy word," and "hold Thou me up," and how do you sometimes finish it up? "Hold Thou me up, and I know I shall fall to-day, notwithstanding!" Have you not had *that* ending pretty often in your hearts? Only you did not put it in so many words. Now trust that glorious Arm, trust that mighty Hand, that *pierced* Hand, and say, looking up to Jesus, "and I *shall* be safe!" Leaning on that Arm, letting ourselves rest in the hollow of that Hand, we shall be at leisure, so to speak, to look around, and watch the goings of our King, and to see the wonderful things He is doing in the world, in His church, in our lives, and I am not afraid to add, even in our hearts. Then, inevitably, we shall burst out into praise, and say "He hath done all things well," (Mark 7:37), while we wonder every one at *all things* which Jesus does (Luke 9:43).

This leads us to what seems to me the central thought and greatest passage of all, Colossians 1:16–18. Here we see God's great object in doing all things by Jesus Christ, "that in all things He might have the preeminence." Now it is very easy to concede this as a grand general truth, and to see how it applies to creation, providence, and redemption. But remember that "all things" includes every little detail of our lives and service. Has Jesus Christ really and truly the preeminence in all things here? The word implies coming first and being first. Does He really come first in our plans? I don't mean ultimately and nominally; but, oh, you know the difference! is Jesus just really the first thought, the first consideration?. Especially in routine work, things that come round every week, has He this *real* coming *first*? In our homes has *He* the preeminence? are they really ordered not merely as if Jesus were the chief guest, but ordered so because He *is* the chief and always abiding Guest? Has He the preeminence always? Has He now, at this very moment? Is Jesus, our own dear Lord, really preeminent? Did you come to meet Him? Are you looking for *His* message only? That in all things *He! Himself!* Who else is worthy? It is His right. Once touch on His name, and one has no words. One wants so very much that He should have it. He whom we *do* love, He who so loves us. Well, *has* He? Some, thing or some one must have it, must come first. If He doesn't come first, something else does, and that won't do! No matter how dear a cause may be, that must not have it. There is wrong done to our Master if any cause, any denominational interest, any personal feeling, any prejudice, has for even one single five minutes the preeminence in our consideration or motive. Go deeper still, what if self has the preeminence! One almost writhes with shame that it should ever be so; yet probably many hearts go with mine in bitter self accusation that it has been so. Just to think that whenever either self or anything else comes first, Jesus does *not*, and we are at that moment in actual, even if unconscious or rather unrecognised, rebellion against God's great purpose that His dear Son should have the preeminence! Why, it is actually the sin of the fallen angels! And perhaps we have never seen it to be sin at all! Now let us bring it to the fountain opened, and now let us entreat Him so entirely to reign over us and in us, that henceforth in *all* things He may really have the preeminence!

III. "All things are for your sakes" (2 Corinthians 4:15). Connect this with Proverbs 16:4, "the Lord hath made all things for Himself," and we get a wonderful view of the love of God and unity of interest with Him. Another parallel pair is Romans 8:28 with Ephesians 1:11. No wonder that all things work together for good when He worketh all things after the counsel of His will! For the will is the very centre point of conscious being; and as the nature is, so is the will. How if God's nature is revealed to be Love, His will must be all love too. So When we are told that He worketh all things after the counsel of His will, that is the same as saying He worketh according to His love,—"the great love wherewith He loveth us."

Can love work willingly anything but good to its object? So, too, if He has made all things for Himself, love is the link which leads to the more wonderful declaration, "all things are for your sakes." Look out on creation,—stars by night, all that light reveals by day,—not only that your Father made them all, but all for your sakes. Look at wonders of natural history, and science, some of us have keen enjoyment in these. Recollect not only that they are the wonderful works and laws and embodied thoughts of your Father, but all for your sakes. Look at the strange entangled mazes (as they seem to us, being the wrong side of the tapestry,) of His government of the world, His ways with man in history, His singular present overrulings and developings of things,—all for your sakes. Look nearer at the surroundings of our own lives, things great and small affecting us, all for your sakes. Again, are you prepared actually to believe this? Perhaps you can accept the great facts that God made the world and governs the world all for His children's sakes, and yet do not practically believe that the things quite close to you every day, *this* day, are all for your sakes. You don't like some of these things, yet they are for your sakes. They are so arranged as to turn out for the very *best* for you. We talk of killing two birds with one stone, and think it clever to manage it. Think of the incomprehensible wisdom which fits all things into your single life so that all shall work together for good, and then that these "all things" are also and at the same time fitted all round into the lives of all His children with which they come in contact. "Ordered in all things." Do you think you could improve upon this ordering? Would you like to have a try at it, just for yourself only, and just for one day? Ah, would you dare it? What a terrible mess we should make if He left us to it, or if He entrusted us to order a little bit of the lives of those dear ones about whom we are so trustless!

Well then, if you would not dare to take the reins, why not leave them where they are, in His own hand? Is it not *senseless*, when one comes to think of it, let alone wrong, to fidget and worry about any one thing at all, when He says His covenant is ordered in *all* things and sure, and that all things are for your sakes? We do specially want to remember here that all things means all things, because when the things present are sorrowful, and faith-testing, and painful, and perplexing, we begin again with that dreadful word "except." Are some of us face to face with some of these things now? What shall we then say to these things? What have others said? *Take* three instances. Genesis 42:36: Jacob said, "All these things are against me." *Were* they? How tremendously he was mistaken! But he had not the clear promises we have. Hezekiah (Isaiah 38:16) got a great deal farther. He said: "By these things men live, and in all these things is the life of my spirit." "These things" meant for him going down to the gates of the grave, and being well-nigh cut off with pining sickness. Yet that which was almost death to the body was life to the spirit. Have not some of us found it so? I have, and many others. I won't ask others to take our word about it, but I do ask them to take this inspired word about it, and to trust and not be afraid if such things come to you. It is worth suffering to prove it. But St. Paul got farther still (Romans 8:37): "In all these things we are more than conquerors," etc. *What* things? We can't write out quite such a serious list as he did of things which seem to be against us.

He not only makes all things work together for good, but does more: "performeth all things for me." And if we did but open our eyes and *notice*, we should see Him at work for us. Every day is full of miracles when the Holy Spirit really opens our eyes to see God working them, and I often think it is the very little things which most magnify His lovingkindness. We talk about the telescope of faith, but I think we want even more the microscope of watchful and grateful love. Apply this to the little bits of our daily lives, in the light of the Spirit, and how wonderfully they come out! We see these little things in their true greatness, and in the beauty of their fitness as parts of His own perfect plan of our lives, which He is working out for us hour by hour. Don't wait for to-morrow; take this day, the morning hours past, the evening ones to come; and apply this microscope, and see if you don't find you are walking in the midst of miracles of love, and that all things are for your sakes.

IV. But there is a step beyond even this: "All things are yours." Here it seems as if we want increase of faith, not only as to willingness and energy, but as to actual capacity to take it in. It seems more than we can *grasp*, we are narrow-necked bottles set under a very Niagara of grace and blessing. One really can only look at what He says about it, and bow one's head and say, "what *shall* I render?" And the only true answer is, "I will take the cup of salvation, and call upon the name of the Lord" (Psalm 116:13). What does He say? (Proverbs 28:10) "The upright shall have good things *in possession*," not in possibility or even in promise. Then we find one bearing witness to it and saying 2 Corinthians 6:10; then we have it in parable (Luke 15:31); then explicitly and in detail (2 Peter 1:3); then we hear of some one who had claimed and received it (1 Corinthians 1:5); then we find the splendid proof that God means what He says about it (Romans 8:32); then we have it set forth so positively that there is no room left, it would seem, for any Satanic "except" (2 Corinthians 9:8); and then it is summed up in these grand words which we are now looking at (1 Corinthians 3:21). *Can* you take that in? See what God has given you! Have you ever *really* said "thank you" for it? Oh give unto God the glory *due* unto His name, and may He give us "that due sense of all His mercies, that our hearts may be unfeignedly thankful." If life has given us all things, have we any business to live as spiritual paupers? Half the reason why we don't praise Him as we ought is because we don't really believe what great things He has given us. Oh "*consider* what great things He hath done for you" (1 Samuel 12:24). Let us ask Him for much more of His Holy Spirit, that we may know the things that are freely given to us of God (1 Corinthians 2:12). And then, in proportion as we know these things, and most of all, in proportion as we know God's greatest gift, Jesus Himself, we shall say, "Yea, doubtless, and I count all things but loss for the excellency of the knowledge of Christ Jesus my Lord" (Philippians 3:8).

"All things are yours." "Perhaps so," says Satan, "but that means only spiritual things, and has nothing to do with these temporal things which are pressing you!" Is *this* the special trouble of any here? Money matters do come awkward sometimes!

Again we are met with an "all things": "seek ye first the kingdom of God, and His righteousness; and all these things shall be added unto you" (Matthew 6:33). All *these* things, food and clothing, etc. No doubt some of us could bear witness to how really *curiously* God has fulfilled this, adding to the first sought grace of His kingdom just the thing that we didn't quite see our way to, as to some needed supply of dress, change of air, or other of "these things." Why should one ever have an anxious thought in this direction, when He has downright forbidden it on the one hand, "take no thought," etc., and when He so tenderly says "your Father knoweth," on the other!

Great gifts and privileges are always linked with duties and precepts, so we will just glance at a few. Here are our marching orders.

All things are of God; therefore, "let all your things be done with charity" (1 Corinthians 16:14); and also, "all things without murmurings," etc. (Philippians 2:14.) "All things are by Jesus Christ"; therefore, let us seek to "adorn the doctrine of God our Saviour in all things" (Titus 2:10); "in all things showing thyself a pattern of good works" (ver. 7). All things are for your sakes, and all things are yours; therefore, let us be "giving thanks always for all things" (Ephesians 5:20). Thus we shall "grow up into Him in all things, which is the Head, even Christ" (Ephesians 4:15); "being obedient in all things" (2 Corinthians 2:9). Then we may tell Him all things (Mark 6:30), and rest in His omniscience and omnipotence, for "all things are naked and opened unto the eyes of Him with whom we have to do" (Hebrews 4:13), and with Him "all things are possible" (Matthew 19:26).

My wish for you is that in your hearts and homes, service and rest, God "in all things" may be glorified through Jesus Christ.

F. R. H.

WORDS ABOUT WORK.

For New Year's Day, 1879.

From *Word and Work* Magazine.

AMONG the multitude of our thoughts within us, at the solemn passing from the year for ever closed into the veiled and trackless paths of the New Year, our work, past and future, is, most likely, very prominent. Perhaps the very first thing all the true workers will be telling the patient Master, about their work, is what one of the most Christ-like workers I ever heard of said to me the other day: "It all wants forgiving." For conscience responds to the truth of His declaration, "Neither shall they cover themselves with their own works." One flash of the Spirit's light is enough to show us how true that is, and how really and truly we have been unprofitable servants. Yes, forgiveness for all our sins comes *first*, failures and successes alike all needing the sprinkled blood.

What does the next flash, or even the same flash, show? Not a promise merely, but a declaration of one of God's grand facts: "Thou hast forgiven Thy people from Egypt even until now." All along, ever since He brought us out of the house of bondage, that we might be His own happy servants, even until now, this very New Year's day, He *has* forgiven; yes, "even until now," this very minute. And so we start out upon the New Year, forgiven; our work begins again, "*forgiven*."

What about all this forgiven work? What has become of it? Where is it? "Surely my judgment is with the Lord, and my *work with my God*." That is where it is, yours and mine: poor, feeble, failing, forgiveness-needing, passing and past, though it be; not done with, and on the way to being forgotten; not even stored away in the archives of eternity; safer, more honoured than that, it is with our God, and "surely" so. Do not you think that what is with Him is in sufficiently safe keeping? Is it not enough that the glory of the Lord is thus our reward in our work? Well may Paul say that "God is not unrighteous to forget your work and labour of love," when it is all, just where we ourselves are, in the safe keeping of His own hand. For "the righteous, and the wise, and their works, are in the hand of God." Works past, as well as works present and future, are *there*.

Then as to the work before us. There really is nothing but encouragement in His word for His workers: not a precept without a corresponding promise; not an allusion to difficulties without ten times as many clear corresponding notes of hope and help. And, of course, what He promises He not only means, but actually does fulfil to His faithful ones.

Let us just think for a few minutes, for our comfort, what He *does* say. "Work; for I am with you, saith the Lord of hosts." That alone is the grandest, sweetest, richest "guerdon" here that any loving heart can ask. "*With* you"; not merely looking down out of the sky at you struggling in your work, but by your very side, closer than the nearest colleague, holding you by the hand, whispering words of strange power for you to use, and words of still stranger power for your own heart only, calming, and strengthening, and gladdening it; so that if you are "men wondered at" by others, you are a great deal more wondered at by yourself. You are so "marvellously helped," that you "never would have thought it!" No, of course not; but, you see, His thoughts towards you in your work were much better than yours, and you can say:

> "And now I find Thy promise true,
> Of perfect peace and rest;
> I cannot sigh—I can but sing
> While leaning on Thy breast,
> And leaving everything to Thee
> Whose ways are always best."

Some of us know what it is to be miserably afraid of making mistakes in our work. How graciously He meets this with "I will direct their work in truth." If we could see under the surface, surely we should see that no mistakes are made when we are *really* trusting this word. Asking without trusting, *i.e.* not "in faith," or asking as a sort of experiment upon the promise, or taking it for granted in a general way that God is directing us, or going ahead in our particular line without constant uplooking, with the unacknowledged idea that, because we were directed yesterday, things will come all right to-day: all this is not the simple, implicit, and continual waiting of our eyes upon the Lord our God, which meets the constant guidance of His eye. But watching daily, and trusting simply, this promise will no more fail than any other. And this, too, is ordained in the hand of a Mediator. He who appeared to Saul and said, "It shall be told thee what thou must do," but delegated to none the showing how great things he must suffer, seems to be foreshadowed by Moses, who was not only to bring the causes of the people to God, but to "show them the work that they must do." So will our Lord Jesus Christ Himself show us the work that we must do day by day. And when we look onward, perhaps a little wearily, down the long vista of a busy year, and say, "Neither is this a work of one day or two," He answers, with quick understanding of our thoughts, "Lo, I am with you *all the days*." So, like Asaph and his brethren, we may go on "ministering *before the Ark* (*i.e.*, in the special and immediate presence of our Lord) continually, as every day's work required."

Again, in the interests of the bright side and true side of "His guerdon here," glance at the typical contrast between the labour in the house of bondage, making bricks in full tale without any straw given or provided, and the splendid supply of materials for "the work of the service of the sanctuary." "For the stuff they had was sufficient for all the work to make it, and too much!" Was not this written for our learning, dear fellow workers? We may have no "stuff" at all, to our thinking; we may be saying, "Have I now any power at all to say *anything?*" But just as these costly and fitting materials were brought to Bezaleel and Aholiab "every morning," so regularly and abundantly shall the "stuff" be supplied to "every one whose heart stirred him up to come unto the work to do it." For it is written, "My God shall supply all your need, according to His riches in glory by Jesus Christ." Surely that measure of pledged supply is "sufficient and too much." And, again, we see the hand of the Mediator, for this magnificent supply is given "by Christ Jesus," God's great Almoner.[1]

Now for another promise, which certainly does not look like that wretched linking of "labour" with "many a sorrow," and "many a tear," of which so many seem to have a dread. But God says, "Mine elect shall long *enjoy* the work of their hands." Quite fearlessly I appeal to you to bear witness if God is not true to His word! And I would challenge the world to produce a band of men and women who "enjoy" their work as we enjoy ours! Just let the faces of the workers at any gathering bear unconscious witness whether they enjoy their work, or not. Look at them as they come away, tired, but happy and thankful! I don't think the fagged home goers from any ballroom would witness in the same way to real, downright enjoyment of *their* work, "pleasure" though they choose to call it. Or compare the faces that leave the Stock Exchange, or a political meeting, or any place where they have been simply doing their own work. Yes, there are plenty of troubles, and delays, and failures, and headaches, and much weariness, too, I know all about that; but nevertheless, when His elect are truly doing His work, sowing His seed, and reaping His precious sheaves, they enjoy that work, as He says they *shall*. And they shall *long* enjoy it, too; other enjoyments pass away in passing, but this only passes on to eternal fruition of enjoyment. No wonder if work that *abides* shall be *long enjoyed*.

When the Lord says to us, "Prepare thy work," we have the comfort of recollecting that He has prepared our works for us (Ephesians 2:10, marg.). Why not take the comfort of this as to any untried work which we may be "called unto"? That sphere did not make itself, neither did man form it into just what it is at his own will; it was God who prepared it for the worker whom He intended for it; and if there is sufficient evidence that you are called to it, then you may rest assured that He "prepared" it and "ordained" it for you. Do not let us dwell *only* on our side of the preparation; but let us recollect that He who prepares the workers prepares the works too, and prepares them for us to walk in, *i.e.*, just to go on *step by step*; for that is "walking." Then, for our own side, let us recollect, "Thou also hast wrought all our works in us"; or, as the very striking margin has it, "for us." So we see that He has wrought in us, and for us, every bit of work we have ever succeeded in doing as yet; therefore to Him be all the glory! And, no less evidently, it will be He Himself who will work in us and for us every single bit that we shall yet do; therefore in Him be all our trust! And yet (oh, wonderful condescension!), though it is all His own doing from beginning to end, "your work shall be rewarded." "Every man"; (just think; every one of us poor workers!) "shall receive his own reward," not a general premium all round. And this, too, by the hand of our Mediator. Knowing that *of the Lord* ye shall receive the reward of the inheritance, for ye serve the "Lord Christ."

May we, for, and in, and all through, the coming year, be so many individual illustrations of St. Paul's sevenfold desire for his converts as to "every good work."

May we—
1. Be "*prepared* unto every good work."
2. "Be *ready to* every good work."
3. Be "*thoroughly furnished* unto all good works."
4. "*Abound* in every good work."
5. "Being *fruitful* in every good work."
6. Be *stablished* " in every good word and work."
7. Be made "*perfect* in every good work."

F. R. H.

---

[1] Almoner: one who distributes alms on behalf of another

This is a continuation of the footnote at the bottom of the facing page 341: F.R.H. had a special love for Handel's and Mendelssohn's music, and extensively studied their scores. Mendelssohn wrote on the front of his manuscript of this *Symphony No. 2* a quotation of Martin Luther: "*Sandern ich walt all Kunste, sanderlich die Musica, gern sehen im Dienst des der sie geben un geschaffen hat.*" "But I would that all the arts, and especially music, glorify Him Who created them and gave them life."

MOTTOES FOR OPEN AIR MISSION WORKERS.

The *Open-Air Mission Magazine* introduces the verses written by my dear sister with the following words.

MEMBERS' MOTTOES.

For the past six years the members of the Mission have had fellowship with each other by a printed motto, selected by the Committee. Miss Frances Ridley Havergal has woven these texts into verse. In sending them, with 6000 of her leaflets, for distribution by the Mission, she says: "I do think yours is such *brave* work for Jesus. May I pass on to you a text I never noticed till this morning? 'My glory was fresh in me, and my bow was renewed in my hand' (Job 29:20), taken with 'Christ in you, the hope of glory' (Colossians 1:27), and 'His bow abode in strength' (Genesis 49:24). May your glory thus be fresh in you, and your bow renewed in your hand." This gifted Christian sister went to her rest with God on June 3rd, 1879, aged 42.

1874. "Occupy till I Come." *Luke* 19:13.

> "Occupy till I return!"
> Let us, Lord, this lesson learn;
> May our every moment be
> Faithfully filled up for Thee.

1875. "Be not Far from Me." *Psalm* 22:11.

> "Be not far from me," we pray;
> "I am with thee all the day";
> This Thy answer, strong and clear,
> Master, Thou art always near.

1876. "He is Faithful that Promised." *Hebrews* 10:23.

> Thou art faithful! Praise Thy name,
> Thou art evermore the same;
> Thou hast promised! Oh how blest
> On Thy royal word to rest.

1877. "He that Winneth Souls is Wise." *Proverbs* 11:30.

> "He that winneth souls is wise"
> In the Master's gracious eyes;
> Well may we contented be
> To be counted fools for Thee.

1878. "Redeeming the Time." *Colossians* 4:5.

> So may we redeem the time,
> That with every evening chime
> Our rejoicing hearts may see
> Blood-bought souls brought back to Thee.

1879. "Lay up His Words in thine Heart." *Job* 22: 22.

> Let us, by Thy Spirit stirred,
> In our hearts lay up Thy word.
> Daily, Lord, increase our store,
> Fill our treasures more and more.

Frances Ridley Havergal.

EXCERPTS: ON MUSIC, ETC.

To me the overture to the Lobgesang[1] is a *vision of Christian life* with its own peculiar struggles and sorrows as well as joys. It is the sixth, seventh, and eighth chapters of the Epistle to the Romans in essence. The mingling of twilight yearnings, ever pressing *onward*, with calm and trustful praise, ever pressing *upward*, is an almost unbearably true echo of the heart, especially in the 6/8 Allegretto agitato; then the Andante religioso is the still, mellow glow of "light at eventide," to which one looks forward; then I go just one step farther, and find a fore-echo of the eternal song in the burst of *vocal* praise, after the long tension of the voiceless overture.

On no form of "The Beautiful" is "passing away" *so engraven* as on music; I have felt this with painful vividness. In "passing away" lies its very *essence*, not merely its *accidents*. The most exquisite passage, if lingered on, loses its very existence as well as beauty; the time, the motion, is the life, the actual notes only a dead letter without it; while to *hold* it is simply an

---

[1] This is the Symphony No. 2 in B-flat major by Felix Mendelssohn, Op. 52, for soloists, chorus, and orchestra, named *Lobgesang* (meaning *Song of Praise*). See Mendelssohn's quotation in the bottom right corner of the facing page 340.

inherent impossibility.

Is not the tendency of the human voice to fall from the true pitch, one of the results of "the Fall"? Adam and Eve must have sung in tune, like the birds. How wonderful it is, that the birds not only sing their own songs in tune, but all the songs always seem in tune with each other, except the cuckoo, when passing from his major third in May to his minor third (or even second) in June!

May not one apply this to the dissonances within, that stun and bewilder and weary us, and believe that if we are indeed God's chosen praise-harps, all that is not as yet *tune* [1] is but the *tuning*, which is *not* in itself beautiful.

Next after prayer, nothing is so healing and calming as pouring out oneself in music. Not in singing; there, one is limited by words, but playing, it restores the balance marvellously. Conventionality would forbid this "antidote of medicated music" in *some* sorrows, but in *such* one can have the outlet of words and the balm of human sympathy; music seems an especial medicine, for all things in which this is not to be had, or could not be sought.

Gregorians are to me only curious and interesting, like dried plants or fossils, not living and lovely.

Of the chorus "And the glory of the Lord" (Handel's "Messiah") I shall never forget the impression of its first bars at the Birmingham Festival, 1867; it gave such a sense of clear *sunny* grandeur, massive open-browed stateliness, and fearless, glorious, overwhelmingness; a musical expression of one's ideal personification of TRUTH, majestically going forth conquering and to conquer.

Beethoven's 95th Psalm is a grandly jubilant thing, with contrasts of sternness and melancholy.

I believe that everything earthly contains analogies of the heavenly, but that we have not yet the key to *all* the golden ciphers; and it may be that our yet "unpurgèd vision" is not capable of reading them, beyond a certain point. This too, all *designedly*, is the material fitted and planned to reflect the spiritual.

Rubens' sacred paintings impress one with his wonderful *art*, Vandyke's with the reverent love he betrays for the subject itself.

Poetry is a *second translation* of the soul's feeling; it must be rendered into thought, and thought must change its nebulous robe of semi-wording into definite language, before it reaches another heart. *Music* is a *first* translation of feeling, needing no second, but entering the heart direct.

Music seems the only universal language understood by men of every tongue and age, and by the angels too. It is an alphabet of the language of heaven, not any more equal to it than an A B C book is to Milton. Why should such a mysteriously subtle and unaccountable gratification have been provided for us? Verily He is Love!

The magnificent massive choruses in the "Israel in Egypt" need a gigantic orchestra to give scope for their great swing of grandeur. The mighty flinging of sound from side to side, in some of the double choruses, is what might be carried out if Handel had Salisbury Plain for his concert room, cannon for his basses, an army for his tenors, and angelic legions for his sopranos.

As to the "infinite suggestiveness" of music, the "Israel in Egypt" choruses exemplify this to a marvellous degree; so does "Let their celestial concerts" with its *blaze* of light; so does Beethoven's Pastoral Symphony.

A hush comes over one at the very thought of one so loved being on the very threshold of eternal rest and joy, so near Christ's own immediate presence. It is as if the veil were growing half transparent, which hangs between life and its dreams, eternal life and its realities.

The shadow of orphanhood has now fallen upon you; and therefore His blessed name of Father acquires depth and reality; "doubtless Thou art our Father." Some day, when we are where they reckon not by days and years, He will tell you *why* He has tried you, and let you look back on your life story and see the golden thread of His fatherly love and care shining over and around it all,—not as it is now, winding in and out, and only seen by glimpses.

"Faithful and True." What a keystone to the grand bridge which His promises have made for us, over the abyss of despair and misery! Faithful as regards us; True, essentially and inherently.

Experience of life is a great commentary on the Bible, and a sort of realization of it. At first, the Bible is a detailed map, which we study and admire; but on the road we find the very same things noticed, but not realized, in one's map. Many of the hills and valleys I read of (and *only* read of), in the Psalms, seem to have come across my own journey of late. It has been so to-day with Isaiah 26:3, which is rather like sitting under the shadow of a great rock, which was marked in one's map, but was not in sight a few days ago.

"I have given them Thy word": John 17. To me this has been a golden key to many other texts, or a sort of seal upon

---

[1] She said and meant "*tune*," not "*in tune*," meaning not just technical perfection of pitch (in tune), but the very music itself (tune). F.R.H. very likely meant here that what is not yet true music ("tune," praise of Him) is but the preparation for the music, preparing His own for the true music. See pages 537–538 of Volume II of the Havergal edition.

them; the Father's and the Saviour's gift. Apply this first to *the* "word of reconciliation," the Father's message of salvation through Christ. Then to the whole Bible; it makes it ten times dearer, and it seems our claim to appropriate every sweet promise.

F. R. H.

A "LINE LEFT OUT."

SINCE compiling the Memorials of my dear sister, I have discovered this little note among our dear father's papers. It is a "line left out," showing the generosity of my sister's character, her delight in giving away most unselfishly, long before the true impulse of "full and glad surrender" balanced all her gifts.

Frances had just received her first cheque from Messrs. Strahan for contributions to *Good Words*, and she writes to her mother in 1863:

The cheque is so much larger than I expected, £10 17s. 6d. Now will you please give £10 of this to my precious papa for anything he would like to employ it on; either keep it for church alterations, or if any more immediate and pressing object, I would rather he used it for that; I should be so delighted to be able for once to further any little object which he may desire. I should be glad if you would send 10s. to J.H.E. for the Scripture Readers' collection, and the 7s. 6d. to keep for any similar emergency.

We add the following, found among Frances' papers.

My dear little Fan can hardly think how much her poor papa loves her, thinks about her, and prays for her. Yes, he does.

Thank you, dear child, for remembering me; I will keep all your love, but not the cheque. Our God send you His sweetest and choicest blessings.

W. H. H.

LETTERS, ETC.

(*To M. V. G. Havergal.*)

PERRY VILLA, January 5, 1880.

MY DEAR FRIEND,—

I cannot refuse your natural desire for a few particulars concerning your beloved sister's work in connection with the Hymnal, "Songs of Grace and Glory."[1] "In June, 1870, she came to reside with us at Perry Villa, and to render her valuable assistance in the joint editing of "Songs of Grace and Glory," sometimes composing hymns and sometimes tunes, and taking the warmest interest in the perfecting of that work, which forms the most comprehensive hymnal in the Church of England. It was a real happiness to be working together for Christ, and to have seen and known much of the hidden history of her life, and traced those deep springs from whence welled forth her glorious productions in poetry, prose, and music. It pleased God to bless our friendship, and to make use of the preaching of the full gospel to instruct and refresh her soul. New light dawned in upon her; until, at length, a full and blessed assurance of her present and everlasting salvation in Christ Jesus irradiated her whole being. The former intense longings—"Oh that I could enjoy that sweet sense of pardon and the happiness you have in Christ," were, at length, most fully realized! She had passed through deep waters, and the fiery ordeal had purged the dross and purified the gold. Great and lasting changes now took place; richer and fuller views of Christ, clearer discernment in the deep mysteries of the covenant of grace, doctrinal truths more accurately learned and more firmly grasped. "Full assurance of faith" was reached, Christ became daily more precious, joy in the Lord abounded, faith and hope and love grew exceedingly.

---

[1] Referred to on [original] page 103 and elsewhere. [See page 272 of this book.]

Your late beloved father, Canon Havergal, had previously shown a warm and genial interest in arranging for the supply of tunes to meet the requirements of "Songs of Grace and Glory." Indeed, the last of his own beautiful compositions was written expressly for this volume, only a few days before his sudden removal. It is a fine tune, and I have since, by permission, named it "Havergal."

Visiting his late residence, "Pyrmont Villa," after his death, a curious kind of instinct seemed to impress my mind with the firm persuasion that his youngest daughter could supply his place, and carry on the work as musical editor. After events fully verified all this, and showed the father's mantle had fallen with double blessing upon his child. It was at this period she came over to reside with us, and from time to time, as required, she was guided and enabled to write her most beautiful tunes and hymns. She would frequently remark: "It is only *as*, and *when*, God sees fit to give me a hymn, that I can ever write one." In and through all, the Divine Spirit was sought, and most gratefully acknowledged, in answer to prayer.

We were now engaged upon one of the largest hymnals in the Church of England; restoring the hymns to their originals; discovering authors' names and dates; selecting texts and tunes; and arranging more than a thousand hymns under their proper themes and subjects. Some of this material I had been collecting during thirty years, desiring to represent every doctrine of Holy Scripture, every varying phase of the Christian life, and all the sacred seasons of the year.

In assisting me to carry out, through the press, this great work, we had many difficulties, but also many answers to prayer. On more occasions than one, when the proof sheets were waiting, and the next hymn, upon some important and difficult subject, had scarcely reached the high standard desired, we paused for prayer, and, spreading the matter before the Lord, asked for His Divine Spirit to guide her pen; and, ere a brief hour or so had passed away, the much needed guidance was vouchsafed, and a beautiful hymn produced, in well balanced rhyme and rhythm, and sweetly flowing verse.

The history connected with many of our hymns would form an instructive volume, indicating the tidal wave in the Christian church, and depicting the ebb and flow of ripening experience and doctrine. So, with your sister, her exquisite compositions have their *special* history, while at the same time they mark the wondrous growth in faith and love and Scripture doctrine.

After many years' experience in the study of hymnology, I do not hesitate to affirm that the hymnal compositions of Frances Ridley Havergal must ever rank among the finest in the English language, and portray the fullest and ripest fruits of the Christian character. Further, upon the most difficult of all themes, "The Attributes of Deity," those written by her upon "The Infinity of God," and upon "The Eternity of God," have seldom been surpassed, if ever equalled.

Her Birthday and New Year hymns; her Consecration hymns; the popular Missionary hymn; the Second Advent hymn; the Sacramental hymns; the hymn of praise, "Worthy of all Adoration"; and such hymns as "O Saviour, precious Saviour," and "Our Saviour, our King," "Is it for me, dear Saviour?" and "From glory unto glory," and others of this same character, have laid the whole church of Christ under great obligations, by this volume. And we have been much cheered with many testimonies, from all parts, of the Divine blessing upon our work. "She being dead yet speaketh," and we thank God the last nine years of her eventful life manifested such ripening in knowledge and in grace, in extended usefulness, in entire consecration, in holy, happy, and honoured service for her Saviour and her King. So that, in all my ministerial experience of thirty years, I have never witnessed such growth and such marvellous progress, still less such talents, laid so humbly at the Master's feet, and so entirely consecrated to His glory!

I have just been looking over a number of interesting documents, comprising letters and manuscript originals of her beautiful tunes, as well as hymns, written about this time, all of which bear the same impress as that stated above.

Doubtless the joint editing of so many beautiful hymns and tunes exerted their happy influence, and brought a reflex blessing upon her own soul. The hymns themselves, expressive of the brightest hopes of the church of Christ, would naturally lift the mind from the regions of uncertainty and doubt to the higher atmosphere of communion and fellowship with God.

I remain, my dear Friend, yours faithfully in Christ Jesus,

CHARLES B. SNEPP.

(From her friend ELIZABETH CLAY.*)*

AMONG the most distinct recollections of my childhood is my first sight of dear F. R. H. On my return to school at Belmont, after the summer holidays, in 1850, I was taken into the large room, where all the teachers and pupils had just assembled for tea. Seated amongst a group of little ones, at the bottom of a long table, was a new pupil, with long golden curls falling around her head. Her appearance at once attracted me, for I remember that as I joined the party my thought was, "I should like her for my friend." Little did I imagine that before the close of that half-year a friendship would have commenced between us which resulted in the closest intimacy, uninterrupted until her entrance into glory twenty-eight and a half years afterwards. It was from the beginning based on an earnest desire to know and to follow the Saviour. During the first holidays we visited one another's homes, and had Bible reading and prayer together. For some years she had not the settled peace and joy in the Lord which were so characteristic of her after life; she seemed to seek in vain for any assurance of salvation. In later years her impression was that her trying and painful early experience was permitted, partly, that it might be evident that her after joy had nothing to do with her naturally happy buoyant temperament.

One night in March, 1859, when we were sharing the same room, after rising from prayer, she told me that the words we had read together earlier in the evening about the woman in Mark 5:27, who "came in the press behind" and touched Jesus, had brought comfort to her heart, and that she could now trust that He would not turn her away either. This bright gleam of light never passed away, but gradually increased and brightened, shining "more and more unto the perfect day." She always seemed fully to act up to the light given her, and thus, doubtless, it was that some who started with her, or before her, found themselves left behind as she pressed on in the upward path. Her poetical power impressed me even in childhood. I well remember one summer evening walk we took together when she was visiting us in the summer of 1851, and her rapidly composing some sweet lines on the lovely sunset and surrounding scene.

Letter from Miss Ada Leigh.

77, Avenue Wagram, Paris, June 1879.

It is five years ago since I met F. R. H. at the Mildmay Conference: our first and last meeting face to face, yet not in spirit, for the words she wrote were treasured, falling with the dew of loving sympathy, pure and fresh, because God-given after the toil and heat of a weary day. . . . Just after the first meeting at Mildmay for our Paris Homes, when I was feeling the chill which creeps over one after a great effort, and in my weakness fearing that it had all been a failure, F. R. H. came, threw her arms round my neck, her eyes filled with tears, and offered me a handful of her jewellery for my work; as she expressed it, "such as I have to give."

The next day, after partaking of the Holy Communion in St. Jude's Church, the last day of the Conference, 1874, we met again. The rain was descending in torrents, making one yearn for showers of blessings on souls. I said I could cry aloud, in the burden and loneliness of my heart, for showers such as these. "Could you," she answered, stopping in the rain, and looking lovingly in my face, "could you? then be comforted, God will do great things for you." The solemn power and sympathy of her words have never been forgotten; and often, when the burden of souls has lain heavy, the path narrow, lonely, and rugged, the spirit weak and sore with fightings within and fears without, comes back the echo of those gentle words of one who well knew what heart dealing with the Master was, and His way of dealing with the hearts He would make all His own. *"Be comforted, God will do great things for you."*

Letter to M. V. G. H. *from* "B. M.,"[1] *authoress of* "Ezekiel," "Elijah," *and other poems.*

September 24, 1879.

My dear Madam,—

It is indeed a pleasure to recall the few simple incidents of my intercourse with your beloved one, and to record them now for you. Our friendship was so sweet, so perfect, and, alas for me, so short, that it seems almost now like a very lovely dream when one awaketh. But no dream, however bright, could have left such a light behind it.

The first communication which passed between us was her note, two years ago, asking permission to publish part of "One by One" with her own music. This note lies before me now, and is very characteristic of the writer. It begins formally, as to a total stranger, but her own loving spirit looks out in the closing words, "My heart is indeed with thy heart. Yours most cordially, Frances Ridley Havergal"; and the little postscript runs, "With the voice together shall they sing, for they shall see eye to eye."

My first sight of her was, as you know, last year, when she passed near our home by rail. I went to our station to meet a friend, who had travelled accidentally in the same carriage, and pointed me out to her as they drew up. There was a bustle that day at our little station, and the train was a long one; as it moved off I saw a bright face

[1] This was Barbara Miller McAndrew.

leaning out a good way down, and an eager hand kissed to me again and again, but I did not quite know till afterwards that it really was to me, for the bright face was that of a stranger, and there were many people standing about. It gives me a little pang still, to think that the sweet impulsive greeting was unreturned..

Soon after this we met, as you know; and then came the two happy days she spent with us. None of the time was lost in "making acquaintance"; we knew each the heart of the other, though only till then in cold print, and commenced on the level of that knowledge. We asked each other countless questions and compared many notes, as to how "things" occurred to us, how they changed and began to live and grow and take possession of us, and how finally they "got written." She said once or twice," I have never had exactly this kind of intercourse with any one, how deliciously interesting it is." She told me that she almost always completed each "thing" that occurred to her, and was not haunted by hints and dreams of possible poems which never shaped themselves. Also, that she seldom felt a chill of disappointment with what she had written, but hoped for the best, knew she had done what she could with the material given her, and went on content to another bit of work. In this I felt that she took indeed at once, the lowliest and the highest view of her vocation. She said, in one of these happy talks, "I am so glad you call Him the Master,' it was one of the first things that made me love what you wrote. Is it not a *dear* name?" We spoke of death, and she said, "I can't say I am exactly in a *hurry* to go, are you? We need not wish to be taken away in the midst of our days, for there is so much delightful work to do here, and in any case we shall have time,—eternity,—for the glory and the rest."

On one of her two evenings with us, she offered to have a Bible reading for our maid servants and a few others, which was much appreciated. The other evening she played and sang to us in the drawing-room, moving our hearts. In all she did one could see that the Master was always with her and her eyes unto Him, the "secret of His presence" had been revealed to her, and was the joy and rejoicing of her heart. An instance of this continual sense of His real presence rises before me. We had been talking of strange and dark events in the world, and I expressed an unguarded wonder that such things were permitted. Instantly I felt her hand on my arm, and she said quickly, "Dear, dear B. M., *don't!* He does not like to hear us say these things." It was just the hurried movement and word, with which one might recall to a friend the forgotten presence of a Third, yet done with solemnity as "touching the King."

In reference to the above, I should tell you that she *begged* to call me by my initials, which she said had been so long dear to her. She persuaded me at once to call her by her own sweet Christian name, and was so glad that I preferred Frances to Fanny.

Observing the little pillar post which stands in our hall, and on which the hour of despatch is printed, with "No delivery or despatch on Sunday," she said in her bright way, "Capital! that's as it should be." To our coachman's wife, touching her baby's cheek with a gentle hand, she said softly, "Is it not nice to think that He took up young children in His arms, laid His hands on them, and blessed them?" He was in all her thoughts.

Her words when we parted lingered in my heart: "Oh, is it not sweet of the Master to give us such days as these? It is not merely 'all our *need*,' but delicious extra things too, such treats as this has been, He planned it all for us."

To us both, this had seemed the beginning of a long friendship. We spoke of future visits in the years to come, and of publishing songs together, and of other plans. But her time was at hand. Our brief friendship held only that one parting, which was to lead to no earthly meeting. One birthday (her's), one exchange of Christmas greetings, a few of her bright loving letters, and she was gone,—gone to the land that is gathering to itself, day by day, our best and loveliest.

Two days after her birthday she wrote:

"How kind of you, darling friend, to recollect my day, and send me such a charming book.[1] I do like it so much. I want a long chat with you most sorely, but can't make time just now without confirming a growling headache. I have just been relieving my mind by writing a little poem 'The Key Found.'[2] I have been wishing for a long time to have a very direct shot at this dreary, misty, semi-unbelief, that some people pride themselves on. Oh, if they would but 'come and see' our Lord Jesus!

Your ever loving Frances."

Her last letter, written so shortly before her death, is also before me now.

"Dearest B.M.

Thanks many for your dear note. . . . I have no respite, I *must* make a little lull in life. Whilst most thankful for success, I am almost alarmedly wondering whereunto this work will grow. Yet oh, how one wants Him to make the very most of all we have and are. Remember me warmly to Mr. M——. I am going to send you 'Kept' as soon as published.

Your loving friend, F. R. H."

Before I had time to reply to this letter, she was gone to Him whom her soul so fervently loved. I was struck by an expression you used in your first note to me, that "surely she must enjoy heaven more than most." I know exactly what you mean, and I find it singularly easy to realize her there, to picture her bright spirit at home in the Father's house, and to imagine the sacred ecstasy with which she serves Him day and night in the temple. Is it not sweet also, and comforting, to think of her tender greeting by and by; of the joyful grace with which she will welcome her dear ones to share the blessed rest? And it is an inspiring thought that even such as she, gifted with noble imaginations, and fervent hearts, and unutterable longing after God, have found the place prepared for them, and, above all, the open vision of the King Himself transcends without measure their most glorious hope.

With true sympathy in your grief and in your gratitude,

Believe me, Dear Madam,

Affectionately yours,

B. M.

---

[1] "The Romance of Astronomy." By Professor Kalley Miller, M.A., F.R.A.S. Macmillan and Co.

[2] See "Under His Shadow," page 186. [See pages 633–635 of Volume I of the Havergal edition.]

"NEARER NOW THAN WE THINK."

"I have no respite, I must make a little lull in life."
(*Last letter, received May 16th, 1879.*)

She stood in the glorious shadow
   Of the Father's house of love,
But she saw not the shining threshold
   Where the Angel-Watchmen move;
She heard not their garments faintly stir
As they opened the golden gates for her.

She had toiled in the blessed Vineyard,
   And as she toiled she sang,
Till far through the sunny distance
   That sweetest music rang;
And her fellow-workers, far and near,
Gave thanks to God for her words of cheer.

We heard her sing in the dawning,
   When the mists hung low and chill;
In the heavy heat of the noontide
   Her clear voice cheered us still;
And when evening shadows were closing round,
We folded our hands to that tender sound.

And those who were watching at midnight,
   Watching in pain or fear,—
Heard oft in that sorrowful stillness
   One sweet voice ringing clear,
For God her Maker, her God and King,
Had given her songs in the night to sing.

And the souls that were passing in silence
   To the River dreary and dim,
Heard, down by its desolate margin,
   A sweet voice sing of Him,
Who will welcome His children "one by one"
To the smiling city beyond the sun.

Far off on the desert mountains
   To wandering souls it came,
That sound of a tender message,
   That pleading in Christ's dear name;
It followed the sorrowful path they trod,
Till the wandering spirits were turned to God.

And she sang to the little children,
   Of the children's God and King;
When heart and voice were weary
   She sang, unfaltering;
And her fervent spirit leapt to see
The little ones gather, sweet Lord, to Thee.

But at length she longed for a "respite,"
   To gather in silence, alone,

New strength for her mighty harvest,
    For the great work yet to be done;
She prayed for a "lull" in the labour of life,
    A breathing space in the glorious strife,—

For only a little shadow
    From the red sun's fiery glow,
One hour's brief rest by the fountains
    Where the waters of comfort flow,
Where the flowers are blowing, so pale and sweet,
In the tender gloom by the Master's feet.

Yet,—could she have rested ever
    Where the cool soft shadows lie,
Whilst weary and faint in the noontide
    One soul went wandering by?—
Nay; one sad step on the dreary road
Would have troubled her heart as it leant on God:

So willing to toil and travel,
    To suffer and watch for all,
So near in heart to the Master,
    So eager to follow His call,—
She spent her soul in the service sweet,
And only in Death could rest at His feet.

So *this* is the needed respite,
    Her shadow from noonday sun
Falls dark, from the wing of the Angel,
    Who comes when our work is done,
To bring no "lull" in the hurry of life,
But the Conqueror's Rest after toil and strife.

And now, in the King's own Palace,
    She sings to her harp of gold,
With the seal of God on her forehead,
    In her spirit His peace untold,
Where never a sorrowful step nor cry
Shall break on the lull of Eternity.

B. M.

(Lines by the late Miss Julia Kirchhoffer, *and explanatory Letter, to F. R. H. See page* 197.[1])

Ask her to come and sing to me,
    For day by day I long,
With a craving never known before,
    For the magic of a song—
'Twere like a sweet, stray wanderer
    From heaven's choral throng.

"You hardly ever spoke to her,
    So little of her know!"
But read her verses once:
    "Sing to them sweet and low,
And the pain-dimmed eye will brighten,
    As the soothing verses flow."

You see she feels the gift of song
    A holy, high bequest,
Then how could she refuse to grant
    A poor sick child's request!
Methinks 'twould soothe this constant pain,
    And lull me into rest.

I want "The old, old story,"
    How Jesus set us free;
Or the riven "Rock of Ages,"
    Or else "Abide with Me";
Or what we used to sing at night,
    "Nearer, my God, to Thee."

Then tell her how I'm lying here,
    In weariness and pain,
And how I long to feel the charm
    Of music's voice again!
I know she'll come and sing for me
    Some old familiar strain.

Nov., 1870.

"The time these verses refer to was before my confirmation. I was very ill, and no one thought I could get through such an exertion. I used to lie all day long, feeling pretty wretched. Then came a passionate longing for music, which no one here could gratify. You were the only person I knew of, but none of us had ever spoken to you.... That is the story of these verses; perhaps it may encourage you sometimes in the ministry of song. It would be hard to tell all that your book has been for me.... When in the holidays at home I was in great pain and suffering, my sister used to sit on the bed, and read out your poems to soothe me.—Julia Kirchhoffer."

Letter of Dr. Alexander, *Bishop of Derry.*

The Committee of preparation for the Church Congress at Swansea had invited my dear sister to write a paper on hymnology. At their meeting in October, 1879, touching allusion was made to the beauty of her hymns and her lamented removal from the church below.

Dr. Alexander, Bishop of Derry, wrote to me:

"I am to speak briefly at the Swansea Congress upon the use and abuse of hymnology. The exquisitely pathetic hymns of your sister, F. R. H., the subtle and loving music of their versification, I shall esteem it a privilege and a duty to mention to my auditors. The beautiful circumstance of her dying song will afford me the most affecting and most touching of illustrations. I shall certainly quote from her hymns. Whether fifteen minutes will give me time to read a whole hymn, I very much doubt; but I wish to quote some of her noble Advent hymn: 'Thou art coming, O my Saviour.'"

---

[1] See pages 295–296 of this book.

Letter from the SECRETARY OF WOMAN'S FOREIGN MISSIONARY SOCIETY.

1334, CHESTNUT ST., PHILADELPHIA, July 15, 1879.

MY DEAR MISS HAVERGAL,—

I feel a delicacy in intruding upon the sacredness of your grief at this time; and yet I cannot forbear sending a few words of sympathy to the sister of F. R. H. In thinking of her here, she was not a far off writer to us, but a woman of the highest type, and a friend whom we had learned to love. Every word she wrote me came as from a dear friend, and I had hoped some day to see her face to face; I hope so still, but in a far more glorious meeting. We have always appreciated her writing for our little magazine, in the midst of her many cares and of her physical weakness and pain; and we *know* that it has done a work for the Master here which He will own and bless; how much good we cannot know until the hereafter. I have part of her "Marching Orders" still to publish, and feel that they are a sacred legacy to the readers of our magazine, and pray that their sweet, forcible, scriptural words may go to the hearts of the thousands they will reach. How many, many words of your dear one will go on and on, in their mission of love, while there are mortals to need their stimulus and comfort! She is well known and loved by a large circle of friends in America, whom she has helped by her writings and by the knowledge of her devoted life. How blessed is her rest, and how truly do her works follow her! In reading of her last triumphant moments, one longs for the time for meeting on the other shore, and of leaving for ever this sin-stained, tempest-tossed world. While we rejoice with her over the victory won, the dear ones left must bear the pain, and still press on in the conflict of life. This is such a hard part of life; but oh, the Master's strength and love are sufficient for even this, and how tenderly does He ever lead us through the deep waters. May He place round about you His everlasting arms in this your time of sorrow!

Yours in true sympathy, and in the love and service of the one Master,

(Miss) JULIA C. THOMPSON,
Editor "Woman's Work for Woman."

[*From* "FAITH AND WORKS" *Magazine.*]

THE DEATH OF FRANCES RIDLEY HAVERGAL.

WHAT a flood of sorrow swept over many hearts in America, when the news flashed over the wires that Frances Ridley Havergal was dead! We had so long loved the sweet outgushings of her poetic nature; always ringing to the one beloved theme—a Saviour's love. And now the voice is hushed, the lyre unstrung, ere it had lost any of its early force; taken from her family and from the world in the prime of her life, just when she seemed about to gather fresh strength in rest from her labours of love; known to many in this western world only by the sweet interchanges of correspondence, and the writings so highly valued, she leaves a void not soon to be filled. And yet who can read the accounts of her last illness, and its triumphant close, without echoing her own words, "So glorious to go home."

Her little books, "My King," "Royal Commandments and Royal Bounty," with "Daily Thoughts on Coming to Christ," are the constant companions of a very large number of Christians here, whilst "Little Pillows" and "Morning Bells" are dear to many a child's heart. Even on the Christmas and birthday cards the ever loved "F. R. H." is always eagerly sought, as sure to be appended to the sweetest sentiments. It has long been the writer's privilege to number Miss Havergal amongst her friends; during a period of six years, the hope had been growing in both our hearts, that we might meet; but God has ordered it otherwise. To the one for whom many years of loving work seemed in store, He has said, "Friend, come up higher"; whilst to the other, nearing the allotted space, it is His pleasure to say, "Tarry awhile." Oh, may all who sorrow, "yet not as others," over this most unexpected stroke, so read the lessons drawn from her beautiful life that her heart's wish may be theirs;

"Take my life, and let it be,
Ever, only, all for Thee."

JANE M'CREADY.

PHILADELPHIA, July 1879.

Lines by the REV. F. JEFFERY.

TO F. R. H., AFTER READING "UNDER THE SURFACE."

How restless seems man's outward life,
   Like billows of the sea,
With every jarring wind at strife,
   From dangers never free!

Yet, safe beneath its storm-lashed face,
   See ocean's treasures lie;
So rests the heart secured by grace
   In deep tranquillity.

. . . . .

The summer sun lit up the bay,
   No breath its bosom curled,
When youth and pleasure launched away
   Upon their ocean world.

Foul slimy monsters lurk within,
   Below those waters fair;
And so the smiling life of sin
   Hides death and fell despair.

F. J.

December 13, 1875.

REPLIED TO BY F. R. H. ON A POST CARD.

RIGHTLY you have read my song!
   Who in Jesus liveth,
'Neath life's turmoil strange and strong
   Knows the peace He giveth.

Peace that overflows our days,
 Silently victorious;
Peace that blossoms into praise,
 Hidden, yet most glorious.

December 16, 1875.

Of course many pages might be filled with reviews and eulogies from English and American sources; far more grateful to my dear sister was the record, which often greeted her, how God had blessed her word and work. Whilst it is quite unnecessary here to extract or repeat any of these appreciative notices (quite a hundred might be given from America alone), it may be interesting to some to read the following extracts from letters of the late Rev. Charles Tennyson Turner, of Grasby Vicarage (the poet), 1870.

Since I looked critically at "The Ministry of Song," I have been surprised and delighted with the great beauty and power of a good proportion of the poems, and the sweetness of the residue. I particularly like "On the Last Leaf," "How should they Know Me?" and "Making Poetry." I have not often met with such vital truth illustrated by an imagination so subtle and so true as the two last evince.

Nor is the metre apart from this estimate, being very charming and spirited. . . . "Wounded" is very charming, and so is "Faith and Reason." I cannot say these are the very best in the book, for there are equals; but the "How should they Know Me?" and "Making Poetry" are before all others.

Extract from another letter from the same, 1870.

I quite agree with you that "Life Crystals" is very thoughtful and beautiful, but I continue to like those I mentioned best of all.

Miss Havergal, Sappho, and Mrs. Browning constitute my present female trio. There may be others lying *perdues* to me in foreign languages, but I know at present of none equal to these.

THE CHURCH MISSIONARY SOCIETY MEMORIAL FUND.

The following letter appeared in *The Record*, in July, 1879, suggesting the "Frances Ridley Havergal Church Missionary Memorial Fund."

To the Editor of The Record.

Sir,—I am but giving expression to the thoughts of others when I venture to suggest an "In Memoriam Thank Offering" from the tens of thousands of readers whose hearts have so often been gladdened and stimulated to labour for the Master by the "sweet singer, and yet strong," who is now

"Among the choir of Paradise,
 A singer evermore."

Many objects dear to her in life, to which these offerings could be devoted, might easily be named; but perhaps the most fitting and appropriate, and one that will assuredly commend itself to all who sympathise with her in her loyal devotion to the "King's Marching Orders," would be a special Church Missionary Memorial Fund.

Those who knew her best can best testify to the deep interest ever taken by our beloved friend in the God-commanded work of missions. Early associations led her to identify herself specially with the work of the Church Missionary Society. When only a child, "the golden-haired fairy of the home circle," as the youngest member of the family, it was her Sunday morning delight to carry the missionary plate round to all assembled for prayers, for the willingly offered pence. When six or seven years old she had her first missionary-box, and for years, especially at St. Nicholas', Worcester, energetically and systematically she obtained weekly and monthly contributions. It was one of her special treats to hear her father tell of his pioneering deputation visits to the far end of Cornwall and Devonshire, where, as early as 1822–24, he was the very first to preach and speak for the Church Missionary Society. In 1850 she writes: "Our Church Missionary Association has increased to over £40. For myself, I have nearly thirty subscribers, half quarterly and half monthly; and though the sum in some cases is small, I think that is a pretty tolerable list. But I want to have more internal missionary spirit, it is more natural to me to work than to feel. I do more collecting than praying! Oh, to be like *Him* in this as in all other things. I have at last hit upon a new device, and earned something by my brains for my pet Church Missionary Society. Some half-crown pocket books advertised so many copies gratis as prizes for the best poetical enigmas. So I wrote sixteen of all sorts, signed Zoide and Sabrina, and have just received six copies. I reserved one copy, and have sold all the rest for the Society."

Her self denying life, pleasing others, and so pleasing herself, found her ever "ready to give" to missionary work. And truly she gave that which "cost her something." In a letter from her sister I read the following: "Just this time last year, in July, she came to me with that light in her eye which always told of some bright thought. 'Marie! It has come over me this morning that I shall send all my jewellery to the Church Missionary Society. I wrote long ago:

> "Take my silver and my gold;
> Not a mite would I withhold."

And I really have given every shilling I could to God's service, but I never thought of my jewels.' I pleaded in vain the pleasure of leaving them to others. 'No,' she said, 'my King wants them, and they must go; delightful to have anything to give Him. I can't go to India, but I can help to send some one.' The massive gold chain she had worn for four years, the gift for some literary toil, she took off her neck, substituting a very old one. A friend at once gave her a handsome price for her chain, and she brought the gold to me, rattling the sovereigns merrily in her hands. 'There, this goes at once to the Church Missionary Society, and I shall make it up to £50, which I long wanted to give.' Though we were very busy, she had all her jewellery cleaned and packed, fifty-three articles (even her useful gold pencils), in a beautiful casket, and sent up to London to the care of the Rev. H. Wright."

It may be the offering of "jewellery" is not the sacrifice required from many for the King; but some offering of a grateful heart will, we think, be prompted in the case of thousands who will feel it a high privilege thus far to be associated in spirit with one of the noblest and truest hearted and most loyal of His servants.

I refrain from doing more than suggest. I must leave to others the details of any plan that may be adopted; only I think it would be well from the first to have a definite plan. The translation and circulation of selected portions of her works in the mission field would be a distinct object of great interest to many. Doubtless the Rev. H. Wright would be able to give information which would guide action here. Palestine has been named as a special field, but perhaps India or South Africa might awaken more general interest. Some will remember her thrillingly earnest appeal for " Our Hindoo Sisters "

"Oh! for a fiery scroll, and a trumpet of thunder might,
   To startle the silken dreams of English women at ease,
Circled with peace and joy, and dwelling where truth and light
   Are shining fair as the stars, and free as the western breeze!

Oh! for a clarion voice to reach and stir their nest
   With the story of sisters' woes, gathering day by day,
Over the Indian homes (sepulchres rather than rest),
   Till they rouse in the strength of the Lord, and roll the stone away.

Is it too great a thing? Will not *one* rise and go,
   Laying her joys aside, as the Master laid them down?
Seeking His lone and lost in the veiled abodes of woe,
   Winning His Indian gems to shine in His glorious crown!"

It will be interesting to mention that one item of Miss Havergal's "List of Work for 1879" is given thus: "To complete my set of 'Marching Orders' for the *Church Missionary Gleaner*." The last paper, in the June number of the *Gleaner*, contained the following passage.

"What an honour to be one of the 'few' forerunners of the King, the herald of a silent yet real and mighty advent of 'the very God of very God.' Because the harvest is great and the labourers few, the Lord Jesus said, 'Pray ye therefore the Lord of the harvest, that He would send forth labourers into His harvest.' If the fact remains, the command remains. And the fact does indeed remain, and we have no excuse in not knowing it. We know how few the labourers are. We cannot say, 'Behold! we knew it not.' The need is recognised, and the Lord has put the supply within the reach of the voice of prayer and the hand of faith. He has told us what to do, and so now the responsibility rests upon us. Perhaps we read these pages, and we sorrow a little for the burden of the King of princes, and wish the accounts were more glowing. But we do not turn the passing emotion into obedient and faithful and purposeful prayer, and so our sluggard soul desireth and hath nothing. 'He shall not fail nor be discouraged'; but if we fail as His 'helpers' in this easiest and most graciously appointed share of His glorious work, how shall we hope to share in our Master's harvest joy, and what claim shall we have to join in the great harvest Hallelujah?"

I am, Sir, yours faithfully,
Blackheath.   CHARLES BULLOCK.

The response to the suggestions thus made was immediate and most generous. The Rev. Prebendary Wright, the Hon. Secretary of the Church Missionary Society, at once took a deep interest in the proposal, and the Committee of the Society passed the following minute, inserted in the *Church Missionary Gleaner* for September, 1879.

GENERAL COMMITTEE, July 22.

The Secretaries stated that it had been determined by the friends of the late Miss Frances Ridley Havergal to raise a memorial fund, to be called "The Frances Ridley Havergal Missionary Fund," with the intentions of handing it, when raised, to the Committee of the Society, to be expended in the training of Native Bible women, and in the translation and circulation in India, (and, should the fund allow, other mission fields,) of suitable and selected portions of Miss Havergal's books. The Committee expressed the pleasure it would give them to administer the Fund if entrusted to them, and their satisfaction that the name of Miss Frances Ridley Havergal, whose devoted interest in the Society's work was so marked in her lifetime, should be permanently inscribed on the records of the Society, and her loving loyal spirit be thus by God's blessing perpetuated in its Missions.

The *Day of Days* for February 1880 contained the following acknowledgment of contributions received towards the Fund.

THE FRANCES RIDLEY HAVERGAL "CHURCH MISSIONARY MEMORIAL FUND."

WE wish it were possible to convey to others the feeling produced in our own mind by the widespread and generous response accorded to the proposed Church Missionary Fund in memory of Frances

Ridley Havergal.

The amount received now exceeds £1,900. But even this noble sum cannot be rightly estimated, unless it is borne in mind that it represents the distinct offerings, as nearly as we can calculate, of *some twelve thousand contributors*. Many also of the letters accompanying the contributions indicate that even the smallest offerings "have cost" the givers "something," and are literally expressions of heart-gratitude to "the sweet singer," who stimulated so many to the consecrated life, and whose voice, happily, in her Royal books, still—

"Rings on with holy influence deep and strong."

We venture to express the hope that others will yet "cast in their mite." It should be borne in mind that the twofold object of the Fund affords scope for the expenditure of almost any amount that could be raised. The openings for the employment of native Bible women in India might indeed almost engross the funds of a Society; and the circulation of translated and selected portions of F. R. H.'s writings, in India and other mission fields, would well employ the amount already raised.

As one indication only of the need of Christian literature in our mission fields, and the special fitness of selections from F. R. H.'s books for circulation, the Rev. Prebendary Wright says: "The following extract from a letter just received from one of our missionaries in Ceylon shows that there need be no fear of our being able to put the F. R. H. Memorial Fund to good account:—'I have begun to translate Miss Havergal's "My King" into Singhalese, and ask for a grant to print and bind the same. I intend to translate her other works.'"

The Christian Vernacular Education Society for India has also just issued a circular, stating that "for lack of Christian literature in the mother tongues (the sixteen native languages spoken by the 240,000,000 of our fellow subjects in India) the work of the missionary and Zenana teacher is greatly crippled, and parents have been known to object to their daughters acquiring the art of reading, from the non-existence of a pure vernacular literature to interest and instruct them, which induces them to exercise their new power in perusing the polluting publications of the native press."

We hope "other mission fields" (European, African, and American, as well as Asiatic) will also be reached by F. R. H.'s translated books; but even confining ourselves to India, it is sufficiently clear that further offerings to the Memorial Fund may well and wisely be made by those who have not already contributed.

Contributions can be sent to the Rev. Charles Bullock, Hon. Sec. of the Fund, 7, The Paragon, Blackheath, S.E. Cheques and P.O. Orders payable to C. Douglas Fox, Esq.; Hon. Treasurer. All sums received are acknowledged weekly in *Hand and Heart*.

The family of Frances Ridley Havergal must express their gratitude for the love to their sister which these offerings so fully testify. They also wish to thank the Rev. Charles and Mrs. Bullock for their energy and personal labour in widely scattering appeals, and then answering thousands of letters. This is indeed a tribute of love from the friends of both our beloved father and sister.

From the deeply touching letters received we copy the following,

(*To* Rev. C. Bullock.)

I humbly write enclosing one shilling for the F. R. H. Memorial Fund; it is a poor invalid's humble mite. I will, with your permission, relate the circumstances under which it is sent. I have been afflicted more than nine years. A friend sent me "Royal Commandments"; this book is indeed a joy and comfort to my soul, and I read my daily commandment with a pure happiness, and each day gain a renewal of strength from my King. The portions for the tenth and eighteenth days have been an especial blessing to me. The book is very dear to me. I most willingly deny myself some little necessity that I may contribute to the Fund.

Joseph Harrison.

(*To* Rev. C. Bullock, *enclosing a post office order for ten shillings.*)

Wolverhampton, February 23, 1880.

It is my privilege to be able to add my humble testimony to the work of that devoted servant of Christ, Miss F. R. Havergal, so lately called away to receive her reward, and not only so, but I am also glad as a railway working man to be able to send you a little help towards swelling the Memorial Fund of one so truly blessed. I have latterly obtained some of her writings, which I find to be of the greatest value, and I trust, with God's help and blessing, will be so esteemed by us as to rank next in value to the word of God itself. My own spiritual experiences I find so clearly marked out in what she has written in that beautiful book, "Kept for the Master's Use," that I am sure God will give great success to the extension of such a dissemination of precious truths, which (with the aid of His Spirit) not only show the erring child the besetting sin which keeps back the entire consecration to His service, but must also stand as a "lamp" to guide the feet of many a poor sinner grovelling amidst the darkness of this world, and lead them up to that light and liberty wherewith Christ doth make His children free.

Yours respectfully,

William Butler.

Very many letters have been received, from all parts, acknowledging blessings received through the books which it is proposed by this Fund to translate and circulate; and as specimens, and incentives, we may reprint the following.

(*Extract from a letter of the* Baroness Wrewsky, *Golubowo, Russia, November 1879, to* J. E. J.)

Thank you for your kindness in sending those two lovely little books of Miss Havergal's, which reached me quite safely, and have come to rejoice both me and my little girl, who with her brother studies every morning the chapters quoted in "Morning Stars," and finds out the verses.

I am just delighting in "Kept for the Master's Use," and thank you so much for sending it. It is so full of earnest, realizing faith and love in Jesus, that it quite stirs one's heart to the very depths.

Oh for such entire consecration, for such a life of faith and close communion! Oh, how I long for it, how I pray for it!

(*From* Mrs. Keightley, *Mynora, Sydney, December 1879, to* J. M. C.)

I received' "The Last Week" which you were so kind as to send me. Our clergyman, Mr. Taylor, was so impressed with the account, that he took the liberty of writing an article on it in *The Australian Churchman*, which I now send. I also saw a very nice article in *The Christian Herald*; and there have been several sermons preached on the life and death of your dear sister in various parts of the colony.

She was indeed a shining light. There is a gentleman in this district, now officiating as catechist to Mr. Taylor, a Mr. Frazer, who entirely ascribes his conversion, under God's blessing, to F. R. H.'s writings.

Very handsome contributions to the Memorial Fund have come from this colony.

Many similar testimonies have been received from all parts of the world; and thus, though not permitted to carry out her lifelong wish to be a missionary, yet the Lord has used my dear sister's books, in far distant missionary stations.

It has been suggested that it would be very desirable if yearly subscriptions were paid to the F. R. H. Fund, thus continuously to carry on the support of trained Bible women, who, with the living voice in the Zenanas, may long echo her words, as well as the translation of her works.

FROM THE CHURCH PASTORAL-AID SOCIETY'S QUARTERLY PAPER.

THE death of Miss Frances Ridley Havergal, which took place at Caswell Bay, near Swansea, on the 3rd of June last, has been deeply deplored by the Christian church at large. The many volumes of hymns and meditations from her pen on the "things touching the King" are so vividly impressed on the minds of most of our readers that it is sometimes difficult to feel that she could possibly have written of anything else. Her illness was of short duration, and the circumstances of her early removal, almost by a sudden stroke, invest with a peculiar interest the following extract from correspondence with reference to the offer which she made of devoting the proceeds of the sale of her piano, the gift of her talented father, to the funds of the Society.

In a letter to the Secretary, from which he is privileged to quote, her sister wrote:

"It may be of use to you, in writing about the gift, to recall the exact circumstances. Towards the end of last year, my dear sister read the statement of the failing funds of the Church Pastoral-Aid Society, whose noble work she always admired and sympathised with. She expressed to me her desire and intention of sending a cheque for £50, but just then the claims of some other Societies were so urgently laid before her that she gave to them instead. But the longing also to help the noble and half-paid workers in the Church vineyard still weighed on her and I remember her saying, 'How I wish I *could* send off a cheque at once! but I fear I must wait a year.' But, as with other generous gifts, she waited not, but with much delight told me that she would give her much-valued piano, left to her by her beloved father. It originally cost 110 guineas, and as it had been so little used she would not let it go under the half price. It was too large for our rooms in Wales, hence she resolved to give it to your Society."

Little did the Committee think, in the course of their correspondence with Miss F. R. Havergal on the subject of her offer, that she who had so often sung in sweetest strains of expectation of future and endless joy in Christ was so near the border of the land of promised rest. Since her death, the gift, £50, has been received.

IRISH SOCIETY,

For Promoting the Scriptural Education and Religious Instruction of the Irish-speaking Population, chiefly through the medium of their own language.

17, Upper Sackville Street, Dublin,
10th June, 1879.

Resolved—

That this Committee has learned with very deep regret of the death of Miss Frances Ridley Havergal, to her a blessed change, for her removal from the work for Christ on earth was to be with Christ, which is far better; but a loss to the church of Christ throughout the world, and a serious loss to the Irish Society, for which she had been an indefatigable collector and advocate, for which she had written her popular little book "Bruey," and established the Juvenile Branch called the "Bruey" Branch, and for which she was about to undertake a tour of visits to its mission stations in Ireland, with the intention of writing sketches of her tour, when it pleased God to take her to Himself. The Committee desires to convey to her family the expression of deep and heartfelt sympathy; copies of this resolution to be sent, in sorrowing remembrance, to her sister, Miss Havergal, of the Mumbles, Swansea, and to Giles Shaw, Esq., her brother-in-law.

Moved by Rev. Henry Carleton, Hon. Sec.
Seconded by Denis Crofton, Esq.
Frederick Homan, Esq., Chairman.

Unanimously.

HOW F. R. H.'S WORK FOR THE IRISH SOCIETY BEGAN, IN 1856.

IT was her brother-in-law's custom to drive into Dublin every Tuesday morning, at seven, to attend the committees of the Hibernian Bible and the Irish Society. Frances often accompanied him. While Mr. Shaw was preparing the financial report she got into conversation with Mr. Robert Wyon, the accountant of the Irish Society. He interested her so much in its work, and gave her such stirring details, that she at once took her first collecting card. From collecting £1 in 1856, she had in March, 1879, sent in more than £900 to this Society.

In 1859, with her dear father's full consent, she organized a branch society in Worcester. Its meeting was addressed by the Rev. Thomas Moriarty, and we give her own bright words at this time.

June 6, 1859.

Our Irish "go" went off tip top. I determined to leave no stone unturned within my power. I wrote a sketch of Mr. Moriarty's conversion from Romanism, and papa let me send it to the *Worcester Journal*. The room was full, and the platform too. Mr. Moriarty's speech was glorious, not faultless, but effective and telling. The hardships he has gone through are incredible, but in his beautiful seagirt Ventry he has now two hundred confirmants around him. He is still sowing and watering, and may a yet richer ingathering be vouchsafed to him! That man fascinated me to the last degree. After the meeting he and papa were deep in "signs of the times," and all that style of thing, so interesting! When Mr. Moriarty went away, he laid his hand on my head and said in a way I shall never forget, so gently, solemnly, and holily, "God be very gracious to you, my child." It was like dew, as if a tangible blessing came in it.

In connection with the progress of her Irish Society's work, the following particulars will be interesting. Frances' first collector in Worcester was a little girl named "Bruey." The book so called was written after her death. The outline of her simple story is true. One of her names was Bruce, hence her pet name of Bruey; the sketch of her character is founded on recollections and incidents. Bruey's Sunday-school work, the Irish meeting, the Irish card, and the forty-one names, her illness and peaceful death, are all facts. "Bruey" has been translated into most lively and idiomatic French by Mdlle. Tabarié, changing the name to "Lilla."[1]

My dear sister's collectors so increased, that she thought it would be well to make them a branch of the Irish Society's tree. Because Bruey was her first collector, she called it the "Bruey Branch." The first who collected in this branch was a lovely child, "Little Nony." Hearing of her illness some months after, Frances sent her this sweet little note.

My dear Nony,—

I had no idea you were suffering so much all this time. I think Jesus must have been carrying you in His arms all the while, because, you see, when anybody can't even walk they *must* be carried. And I am quite sure He must be loving you ever so much, I mean with a very special and tender love, because it says, 'Whom the Lord loveth He chasteneth.' I thank you so much for the violets. I have such a number of Bruey collectors that I hardly know how I shall manage them all. We shall have a famous Report next year I hope. . . .

Very much love from your loving friend, F. R. H.

---

[1] "Lilla, traduit librement par Mdlle. Marie Tabarié." Paris: J. Bonheure, 48 Rue de Lille.

Dear little Nony's work for Jesus, and patient suffering, ended on the evening of May 1st, 1879, only a month before the founder of the Bruey Branch of the Irish Society was herself called away to rest from her labours.

Possibly my sister's circular letters to her young friends may hereafter be printed; but the two following epistles will show how thankfully she wrote to those who helped in the work, and how she did not scruple to ask, for the Society, an introduction which she would never think of working out for herself.

(*To Emmeline Parkinson.*)

My dear little Fellow Worker,—

I have had a good many pleasant surprises in the course of my Irish collecting, but I don't recollect that I ever had a pleasanter one than yours. You have actually beaten Bruey herself, for she had forty-one and you have forty-four names! I wonder if this is your first attempt at working for Christ! I think, dear Emmeline, the Lord Jesus knows all about it, knows that you have been trying to be a little worker for Him; is not that very nice? Now, I will ask Him to send you a great blessing on what you have collected, so that those who are taught by means of your money may not only learn to read of Jesus in His word, but may learn to love Him and tell others about Him. Perhaps you have done more for the Irish Society than you suppose! because you have put an idea in my head. Three little girls lately wrote me a letter, something like your first one, having liked "Bruey" so much. I was not well enough to write to them at the time, but now I shall write and send them each a book, and make the same request I did to you, and then possibly they too may go to work; and it will really be your doing if they also collect.

I will tell you about one of my collectors, an invalid. When going to visit her one day, I prayed that the Lord Jesus would help me to say something to comfort her. And then He seemed to put into my mind that if I could only think of some work for Christ for her to do, it would do her more good than anything. So I put a collecting card in my pocket. When I got there she had been particularly wanting to see me that day, for she had been so sad, thinking she could do nothing for Jesus, and for a whole week had prayed He would let her do just something for Him. So I took out my green card, and told her I thought He had guided me to bring her a bit of work to do, and would she try and collect just a little for these poor Irish, who cannot be reached by people who can only speak English? So she was delighted, and took it as God's own answer, and has ever considered it as the work He had given her to do. May I send my special thanks to your mamma, both for allowing you to collect and for so kindly helping you.

Your loving Friend,
F. R. H.

(*To* ——.)

Pyrmont Villa, Leamington, November 20, 1872.

Dear Sir,—

I must send a few lines of grateful thanks for your prayer for me. I do indeed thank you most earnestly, and may our great and beloved Intercessor not only present those petitions with His own sweet incense for me, but return the blessing sevenfold upon yourself and your work. . . .

I wonder if I may ask a little favour! Will you hand the enclosed little notices of a new book of mine to any members of your congregation who may be on the look out for Christmas presents for children of ten to fourteen years of age. I particularly want to reach by it those of Christ's *little* ones who are beginning to wish to love Him and to work for Him. It is "a story book," but founded on fact. "Bruey" was the real name of a dear little girl in my beloved father's parish at Worcester.

Your work is immense indeed. How glad you will be of the "rest that remaineth"; but it is nicer still to think that "His servants *shall* serve Him," without fatigue, or fear, or imperfection, or any failure.

With very best wishes I am, dear sir, yours in Him whom having not seen we love,

Frances R. Havergal.

By F. R. H.'s wish her work is still carried on, by two Secretaries appointed for the Bruey Branch: Miss Emily Titterton, The Lindens, Leamington, and Miss Mary Fay, Ivy Cottage, Celbridge. And a letter lately received from Mr. Fitzpatrick says: "I find that on the completion of our 'Bruey' accounts there appears an amount far larger than I mentioned. . . . It now proves to be £789 18s. How wonderful! We thank God."

IN MEMORIAM.

[From the many loving tributes to my sister's memory, the following are selected for reproduction here.]

IN LOVING MEMORY OF MY DEAR AUNT, F. R. H.

June 3rd, 1879.

The King's "all glorious" daughter
    Hath reached her home to-day;
She was so true and loyal
    Along her heavenward way!
Her faith was ever gazing
    Towards that peaceful shore,
Her eyes were ever watching
    The Everlasting "Door."

As on the "wheels of fire,"
    The chariot bore her home,
The King hath called her higher
    Into His royal dome.
The trumpet tone hath sounded,
    Her willing voice replied;
Now, with encircled glory,
    She sitteth at His side.

Christ's perfect "blood that cleanseth"
    Was all her entrance plea;
That crimson stream which floweth
    Hath set her spirit free;
And, "I am trusting Jesus"
    Was the keynote of her life,
She realized His power
    Throughout her earthly strife.

She gloried in His Presence,
    Exulted in His Love!
Thus making earth a foretaste
    Of richer joys above!
She gave up human favour
    To win a soul for Him,
Nor did her own life's shadows
    Ever her ardour dim.

Like Him, her blessèd Master,
    She ever sought to cheer
Those weary ones in darkness,
    Along this desert drear.
Her soul-inspiring music
    Enchained the listening throng;
And countless hearts were lightened
    By her "Ministry of Song."

That gentle, holy streamlet,
    Which "Under the Surface" lay,
Hath reached the mighty ocean
    Where all is perfect day!
Her "Life Mosaic" glittered
    With many a sparkling gem;
Her King's hand now hath set it
    In His royal diadem.

Now, sisters, ye who mourn her,
    Let this your tribute be;
E'en as this sainted minstrel,
    "Tell out" Christ's love so free!
Lay at His feet your song-gift,
    Ask Him your voice to fill
With holy, heavenly music,
    Echo of His sweet will.

Cecilia Havergal.

OUR "SWEET SINGER."

Was there silence over yonder?
    Did the angels cease to sing,
As they waited on in wonder
    For the mandate of their King?
When the royal word was given,
    By which all our hopes were crushed,
Was there silence up in heaven?
    Were the Hallelujahs hushed?

When the shining golden sceptre
    Touched the form we loved so well,
As we wished we could have kept her,
    That she still with us might dwell;
While the messenger descended,
    Calling her from us away,
While our knees in prayer were bended,
    Pleading hard for her to stay;

Was there restless earnest longing
    Mid the white-robed choral band,
As with eager footsteps thronging
    At the gate they took their stand?
Was there overflowing gladness,
    On each bright expectant face,
While *our* hearts were bowed with sadness,
    And we mourned her vacant place?

Ah! methinks that when she entered
    Those celestial courts above,
Every thought and eye was centred
    On the object of their love,
That the silence then was broken
    By triumphant bursts of song,
For the word the King had spoken,
    Which had bid her join their throng.

But she passed them all unheeded,
    With a quick impatient spring;
As she onward, onward speeded,
    Till she stood before her King.
How her raptured eyes would glisten,
    With a lustre, oh, so bright!
And she still would stand to listen,
    And to revel in that sight!

Then methinks she struck the chorus,
    And her rich melodious voice
Was above their tones sonorous,
    Even sweeter and more choice.
But to us the echo, stealing,
    Of the beautiful refrain,
Bringeth life, and light, and healing,
    Bidding us look up again.

Now we need not, cannot sorrow,
    We must wipe our tears away;
And from her example borrow
    Courage in the darkest day.
We must think of her as dwelling
    In the presence of her King,
Where the angel-voices swelling
    Make the palace walls to ring.

If we daily do our duty
    With her singleness of aim,
We shall see His wondrous beauty,
    And shall magnify His name.
We may not be highly gifted,
    We may fill a little space;
But the meek shall be uplifted,
    And the pure ones see His face.

Ellen Lakshmi Goreh.

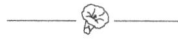

"THE GATES OF HEAVEN."

In the forefront of God's embattled host,
    Long in her Master's service had she striven,
So she could raise the evangelic boast—
    "Splendid to be so near the Gates of Heaven."

Amid the sacred choir who praise the King
    A harp of sweetest strings to her was given;
And now she felt what she was wont to sing—
    "Splendid to be so near the Gates of Heaven."

With self-consuming labour she had cast
    In the world's careless mass the gospel leaven,
And now could say, her tired hand stayed at last,—
    "Splendid to be so near the Gates of Heaven."

Much had she loved Him whom she had not seen;
    The veil which hid His face was almost riven;
Deep was the outburst of her joy serene—
    "Splendid to be so near the Gates of Heaven."

And now she stands before the Father's throne,
    The Lamb who once was slain, the Spirits seven;
Ah, who can tell the bliss which thrills her tone—
    "Splendid to be *within* the Gates of Heaven!"

Richard Wilton, M.A.
Londesborough Rectory.

In Memoriam.
FRANCES RIDLEY HAVERGAL.

F arewell, fond spirit, bright before the throne,
R adiant thy robe, transfigured like the sun;
A ngel of song, with harp and heart and voice,
N ear the bright Seraphim of God rejoice;
C ould we but see thee in thy "palace" fair,
E ver with God, His glory now to share,
S hould we not sing our loudest chorus there?

R est thee, dear soul, thy toils and trials o'er,
I n Heaven is rest, for pilgrims evermore;
D eath takes the body out of mortal sight,
L ife lifts the spirit into Heaven's own light;
E ver with God, thy fathers' God, to be,
Y outh without age, a bright Eternity.

H ark! 'tis a song, as never sung before;
A nthem more sweet, from yon bright happy shore;
V oice ever thrilling, singing now above,
E ndless its praises of the Father's love.
R est, aching head! for after toil is rest;
G od takes thee home—home to thy Father's breast,
A ll weary pain and travel of the road
L ost in the light and glory of thy God!

Robert Maguire, D.D.

"SO BEAUTIFUL TO GO."

"So beautiful to go!" The joys of time are waning;
   The friends I loved so well have hastened on before;
And, as they passed away,—my longing heart restraining,
   I've asked when *I* should join them on the blessèd shore?

"So beautiful to go!" for heaven is wondrous dearer,
   Since cherished human links have bound me to the Throne!
Oft hath the veil seemed rent, and heaven itself been nearer,
   As hope by hope hath faded,—some but newly blown!

"So beautiful to go!" to leave earth's many sorrows,
   To enter on the fulness of eternal joy!
But I had fondly dreamt of many bright to-morrows,—
   Of harder labour still in my dear Lord's employ!

"So beautiful to go!" for now my spirit boundeth
   At mention of that name,—that Name I love the best!
Behold a shoreless sea faith's plummet never soundeth,—
   The name of Jesus,—telling me of peace and rest!

"So beautiful to go," then!—I shall be with Jesus;
   Yea, with that glorious Father He made known to me;
Whose love that "passeth knowledge" did from sin release us,
   And who now calls me with Him evermore to be!

"So beautiful to go!" my life of trusting ended,—
   For I have trusted Thee, Lord Jesus, day by day;
And I have sung to others how Thy love transcended
   Earth's noblest joys, in many a brief, but heartfelt lay!

"So beautiful to go!" yet I had hoped to linger
   Among Thy chosen ones, to sing yet blither songs;
For my supremest joy hath been, a humble singer,
   To win fresh trophies to the blood-washed throngs!

"So beautiful to go!" yea, it will be "far better"!
   'Twas always better far to bow to Thy sweet will;
And I have *trusted*, Saviour, to the very letter,
   Thy well-tried promises,—am *dying*, trusting still!

  . . . . . .

And thus she passed away;—so beautiful in dying,
   As she had been in living,—grand in simple faith:
Her watchword, "*Trust Him*," tells the secret underlying
   Her fragrant life of beauty, her victorious death!

So beautiful! And now she, being dead, yet speaketh!
   Her songs of faith and hope shall never, never die!
And even by her last, sweet, lifelike words she seeketh
   To prove that *simple trust* will our last foe defy!

Then be it ours to garner, as a peerless treasure,
   Those living words that such a vital courage show;
Ever to trust in Jesus,—love Him without measure;
   Then, too, *our* song shall be "How beautiful to go!"

                    Edwin Chas. Wrenford.

Millbank House, Nairn, June 5th, 1879.

JUNE 3rd, 1879.

"Such sad, sad news." We say;
   And the heart bids forth weak tears.
Our foolish eyes, through their own mists dim,
Cannot see the resting joy of Him
   Who treads with her the golden way,
Where the star-lamps pale in the passing ray,
   And the throne uplifted nears.

It came with such high urgency—
   The summons from her King!
   He might not be denied to stay
Through the weary night, and faint hope of day,
   In that quiet home beside the sea;
   Who would not charge an angel's wing
   His message to His own to bring.

And we held our dear one lovingly:—
Ah, the strong, scarred Hand we could not see,
When one tender touch on her wrist had lain,
   Stayed its faint pulse with ecstasy,
   And made our claspings vain.
   Was there not a whispered name?
"Thou art Mine—My wanted one!
In Our palace that stands by the crystal sea,
   Thy place is ready—up near to Me;
   The seas of earth ever chafe and moan,
On her sweetest homes are her shadows thrown,
   And her night must fall the same;—
No murmur is heard, no dimness known,
   In My land beyond the sun."

   It is sweet to prepare our home
     With Love's close-searching thought,
All through a long, glad day, for one
Who for us true, loving work has done:
To arrange the seat where the warm rays come—
   Where the fairest view is caught,
   And a little picture shall meet the eye
That the dear hand painted in years gone by:
   To gather and place our guarded flowers,
   And set out all our choicest things,—
   Chiding slow Time through the counted hours
     That *will* fold so close their wings;—
Coming pausingly back, ere the step we meet,
To make sure of all we have planned, to greet
     With voiceless welcomings.

   And the joy—in our home made fair,
     Yet again to clasp a hand;
To meet the full light of dear, trustful eyes,
And watch for the smile of glad surprise
   At Love's simple triumphs there;

While the day is fading off the land,
As the sun shuts slowly his opal gate,
    And in the tremulous, fragrant air,
All through the hush of the hours we wait
For the sentinel stars that come forth late,
    In their gleaming watch to stand.

Ah! we dare not grudge to the Master His joy
    In her gaze of speechful love
At the unpriced treasures His Love has bought,
    The gathered bliss of Eternal Thought;
    In the hidden face raised wonderingly
At a memory of fervent words inwrought,
An echo of her own music caught
    In the melodies above:
    As the dim earth sinks wearily
    Beneath the verge of a waveless sea,
    And so near her Saviour's breast,
From the white-robed ones who round her press
    With offered stars her crown to gem,
    She learns the accent of the hymn
    That may not be sung by Seraphim;
    Its rapture of bliss is sealed to them—
That is filling the endless silences
    Where unsetting glories rest.

    In this little life's chill twilight
We shall miss her sweet words and strong;
    Yet for us the stars shall come with night,
And through all the pitiless heat of the day
Our hearts must wrestle, and throb, and pray,
    And trust for Evensong.
    Would we take from His heart one joyous thrill
    Who for us bore all the shame?
In the still, lifted light of the Sapphire Throne
That no child of earth may behold alone,
    She hears a voice:—"I will,
Father, that Mine whom Thou gavest Me
    Be with Me where I am."—
And while the heavens are swept and bowed
    By the might of the angel-song,
And veiling their hills as a golden cloud,
    Float by the ransomed throng;
She lifts to His an untroubled face,
That caught of Heaven's light a wondrous grace,
    When It lit earth's frontier dim.
        Home, in the palace of her King!
    Yet in her loyal heart a prayer
    That only may be spoken now,
    With the promised glory on her brow,
That in fullest service, and sweetest hymn,
    Her love may *still* its tribute bring
        To His—that led her there.

    S. G. Prout, author of "Never Say Die."

IN MEMORIAM.—F. R. H.

Where are the well-remembered lays,
    Whose lingering echoes memory still
Prolongs, with fond regretful gaze,
    Bent heavenward, toward the holy hill?
Where the sweet voice whose tones are mute,
    The magic music of the lute?
Whither have wended the unearthly strains,
Too pure, too full of heaven to die on earth's dark plains?

They die not! As the opening flower,
    That drooped at night with closèd eye,
Awakes with morn's reviving power,
    In beauty, when the sun is nigh;
E'en so the notes of praise expand,
    Diviner, in the spirit land,
Breathing immortal incense of the skies,
Blended in sweet accord with heavenly harmonies.

Instinct e'en here with life Divine,
    Attuned to heaven e'en here on earth,
With brighter beauty now they shine,
    What men call death is their new birth;
In sweeter melody they rise,
    Fragrant as flowers of paradise;
Like the angelic choir, they cannot die,
Preludes of triumph-songs of immortality!

E'en while they spring to life and light,
    Wafted on seraph-wings to heaven,
Their beauty lingers round our night,
    Their sweetness to our earth is given;
Upon our darkling path below
    Their glory, streaming, gilds our woe,
Their heaven-born tone, earth's voices in refrain,
Mingling responsive music, echo back again.

    W. J. Vernon, B.A.

Sydling Vicarage, Dorset.

"SWEET SINGER AND YET STRONG."

    Sweet singer! singing long
Songs that have found an echo in the heart
Of thousands, in life's conflict bearing part—
    Sweet singer, and yet strong!

    The strength and sweetness meet
In thee, as day-dawn on some mountain's head,
Or summer sunset on the ocean shed—
    Strong singer, and yet sweet!

Wise singer! To the sad
Giving the comfort that thy God gave thee,
Even to "all" thy "living," it may be—
    Wise singer, making glad!

Glad singer! upon eyes
Opened to see the light that shone for thine,
A brighter light, thy singing brought, would shine—
    Glad singer, making wise!

God's singer! In a land
Of alien thought and language thou didst sing
The songs of Zion; now before thy King,
    Blest singer, thou dost stand!

Thine earthly singing o'er—
Thy singing sweet, and strong, and glad, and wise—
Thou art, among the choir of paradise,
    A singer evermore!

Swaffield, North Walsham,   G. R. Taylor, M.A.
   June 10th, 1879.

IN MEMORY OF F. R. H.,
WHO ENTERED INTO REST JUNE 3RD, 1879.

Aged 42 Years.

Forty-two stations, and then fair Canaan's rest,
God's Israel journeyed, and in full time were blest;
The number of the waymarks their Guide could tell,
The route of all the wanderings He ordered well.
                                    (*Numbers* 33)

Forty-two portions according to God's will,
Varied the labours, and diverse too the skill;
Forty-two portions, then Salem's wall was raised,
The work was finished—Jehovah God was praised.
                                    (*Nehemiah* 3)

Forty-two descents, and then the Christ was born,
Crown and sceptre His, and ours the eternal morn;
The hour of Advent all wisely fixed above,
"Forty-two," counted by rich Almighty Love.
                                    (*Matthew* 1:17)

Forty-two brief years, and then the rest of heaven,
God's pure home was hers, the welcome sweet was given;
Journeys and buildings, all now for ever o'er,
'Neath Love's own banner, "with Christ" for evermore.
                                    (*Philippians* 1:23)
                                    A. C. Thiselton.

Parsonage, Upper Bagot St., Dublin.

JUNE 3rd, 1879.

The Church's sweetest minstrel
    Has left her ranks to-day;
The Master sent His summons
    To call her hence away:
A summons to His presence,
    To see Him face to face,
To share with Him His glory,
    In her appointed place.

She sees Him in His beauty,
    "The King" she served so well,
Of whose perfections daily
    She loved so much to tell.
His least command she followed,
    His slightest wish obeyed;
So when His herald met her,
    She could not be afraid.

But oh! our sweet, sweet singer,
    Gone from our midst for aye!
Who now shall lead our choirs
    Since thou hast passed away?
No hand can tune the lyre
    So tenderly as thine;
No other voice can reach us,
    With strains almost Divine.

Thousands on earth have loved thee,
    Who never saw thy face;
In countless hearts thy teachings
    Have found abiding place.
The truths which thou hast uttered,
    In purest melody,
Have reached the souls of numbers,
    Though all unknown to thee.

Through England's wide dominions
    We mourn from shore to shore,
That Frances Ridley Havergal
    Is in our midst no more.
That name so dear, so precious,
    Loved as a "household word,"
Henceforth to us is sacred,
    For she is "with the Lord!"

We mourn in silent sadness
    The loss we have sustained;
The tears still flow unbidden,
    Our hearts within are pained.
And yet we dare not murmur,
    Nor ask why this must be,
Since God's own hand has silenced
    That sweetest minstrelsy.
                          Alice Forrest.

FRANCES RIDLEY HAVERGAL.

F ruitful in every good work, and increasing in the knowledge of God.—*Colossians* 1:10.

R ooted and built up in *Him*.—*Colossians* 2:7.

A chosen vessel unto Me, to bear My name.—*Acts* 9:15.

N ow lettest Thou Thy servant depart in peace.—*Luke* 2:29.

C hrist shall be magnified in my body, whether by life or by death.—*Philippians* 1:20.

E verlasting joy shall be upon their head.—*Isaiah* 51:11.

S atisfied with favour, and full with the blessing of the Lord.—*Deuteronomy* 33:23.

R ise up, My love, My fair one, and come away!—*Song of Solomon* 2:10.

I f ye loved Me, ye would rejoice.—*John* 14:28.

D elight thyself also in the Lord.—*Psalm* 37:4.

L et the beauty of the Lord our God be upon us.—*Psalm* 90:17.

E nter thou into the joy of thy Lord!—*Matthew* 25:21.

Y e know that your labour is not in vain in the Lord.—1 *Corinthians* 15:58.

H aving the glory of God, her light was like unto a stone most precious.—*Revelation* 21:11.

A s the lily among thorns, so is My love among the daughters.—*Song of Solomon* 2:2.

V erily, verily, I say unto you … your sorrow shall be turned into joy.—*John* 16:20.

E xcept a corn of wheat fall into the ground and die, it abideth alone.—*John* 12:24.

R ejoice in the Lord alway, and again I say, rejoice.—*Philippians* 4:4.

G od Himself shall be with them, and be their God.—*Revelation* 21:3.

A nd they shall see His face, and His name shall be in their foreheads.—*Revelation* 22: 4.

L et Me go, for the day breaketh.—*Genesis* 32:26.

"I trust I shall shortly see thee, and we shall speak face to face."—3 *John* 14.

Emily M. Coombe.

The acrostic by Emily M. Coombe was the last item in Maria's volume *Memorials of Frances Ridley Havergal*. In a later printing of *Memorials*, at the very end of the book, after this acrostic, there was a note added about the section (on page 286 of this book, page 159 of the original book) about the death of the family on the ship, and a poem, which are given next.

Note to Page 159.

The melancholy story of the running down of a vessel a few years ago in Dunedin harbour, shortly after her arrival from England, will be remembered. The family alluded to (a clergyman, his wife, young children—the youngest an infant, and faithful servant) were the only persons remaining on board, and were drowned. The crew were all on deck, and just escaped. F. R. H. and her friend were speaking of death and what constituted its sadness to the Christian; and they agreed there were only two *sad* ingredients, previous sickness and pain, and *separation*. Thus, in this singular instance of a whole family's entrance together into glory, for *them* it was indeed "nice"!

DEATH AND LIFE.

It was a day of Death,
  But not a day of tears;—
A day of wondrous change,
  But not of hopes and fears.
No parting look was given,
  No farewell word was spoken,
As the link that kept eight souls from heaven
  By a single touch was broken.

No heart-ache and no pain,—
  No weary breath, no sighing,—
No speechless look of love,—
  No death-watch and no dying:
No eyes were softly closed,
  No hands were gently folded,
No living face hung in anguish wild
  O'er the statue Death had moulded.

It was a day of Life,
  A day of wondrous bliss;—
What entrance through the gates of pearl
  Could ever equal this?
How rapturous then the greeting,
  What looks of love outspoken,
As the union of those souls in heaven
  Was sealed, ne'er to be broken!

M. C., 1867.

The acrostic of Scriptures by Emily M. Coombe is the last thing in Maria's volume *Memorials of Frances Ridley Havergal*. Maria wrote this poem, which she did not include in her *Memorials* but which her sister Miriam included in the posthumously compiled and edited *The Autobiography of Maria Vernon Graham Havergal* (on page 180 of this book). Thanks be to God.

Hush Me!

In F. R. H.'s Study, in memory of June 3rd, 1879.

Hush me, Lord Jesus! I cannot yet be still;
In vain I try to say it is Thy will;
My path is lonely, there is no one nigh
To share my sorrow, or to soothe my sigh,
  Hush me, Lord Jesus!

One voice is hushed; my sister's merry voice,
So sweet, so tuneful, as she sang "rejoice!"
From me my song-bird flew so far away—
Soft echoes leaving when she could not stay.
  Hush me, Lord Jesus!

So strange to miss my darling's footfall light,
Her smile I see not, 'twas my sunshine bright;
No tiny tokens now are brought to me—
Ferns, mosses, flowers, or shells beside the sea.
  Hush me, Lord Jesus!

O bruisèd Saviour! Thou wilt never break
The bruisèd reed, and never wilt Thou take
Thine arm from underneath Thy leaning child,
Who trusts and clings throughout the desert wild—
  Hush me, Lord Jesus!

Yes; I have proved Thy faithful word is true,
"Just as a mother will I comfort you";
"I know thy sorrow, and thy need of rest"—
Leaning I cry, upon my Saviour's breast,
  Hush me, Lord Jesus!

The hush of Heaven seems stealing over me,
The quiet haven nears in which I long to be;
My Kingly Comforter brings the sweet whisper nigh,
"A little, little while!" no need again to sigh,
  Hush me, Lord Jesus.

      MARIA V. G. HAVERGAL (1821–1887).

The Epistle of PAUL the Apostle to the HEBREWS.
"Better."

CHAPTER I. Son of God.

GOD, who at sundry times and in divers manners, spake in time past unto the fathers by the prophets,

2 Hath in these last days spoken unto us by his Son, whom he hath appointed heir of all things, by whom also he made the worlds;

3 Who being the brightness of his glory, and the express image of his person, and upholding all things by the word of his power, when he had by himself purged our sins, sat down on the right hand of the Majesty on high;

4 Being made so much better than the angels, as he hath by inheritance obtained a more excellent name than they.

5 For unto which of the angels said he at any time, Thou art my Son, this day have I begotten thee? And again, I will be to him a Father, and he shall be to me a Son?

6 And again, when he bringeth in the firstbegotten into the world, he saith, And let all the angels of God worship him.

7 And of the angels he saith, Who maketh his angels spirits, and his ministers a flame of fire.

8 But unto the Son he saith, Thy throne, O God, is for ever and ever: a sceptre of righteousness is the sceptre of thy kingdom:

9 Thou hast loved righteousness, and hated iniquity; therefore God, even thy God, hath anointed thee with the oil of gladness above thy fellows.

10 And, Thou, Lord, in the beginning hast laid the foundation of the earth; and the heavens are the works of thine hands:

11 They shall perish, but thou remainest: and they all shall wax old as doth a garment;

12 And as a vesture shalt thou fold them up, and they shall be changed: but thou art the same, and thy years shall not fail.

13 But to which of the angels said he at any time, Sit on my right hand, until I make thine enemies thy footstool?

14 Are they not all ministering spirits, sent forth to minister for them who shall be heirs of salvation?

CHAPTER II. Son of Man.

THEREFORE we ought to give the more earnest heed to the things which we have heard, lest at any time we should let them slip.

2 For if the word spoken by angels was stedfast, and every transgression and disobedience received a just recompence of reward;

3 How shall we escape, if we neglect so great salvation; which at the first began to be spoken by the Lord, and was confirmed unto us by them that heard him;

4 God also bearing them witness, both with signs and wonders, and with divers miracles, and gifts of the Holy Ghost, according to his own will?

5 For unto the angels hath he not put in subjection the world to come, whereof we speak.

6 But one in a certain place testified, saying, What is man, that thou art mindful of him? or the son of man, that thou visitest him?

7 Thou madest him a little lower than the angels; thou crownedst him with glory and honour, and didst set him over the works of thy hands:

8 Thou hast put all things in subjection under his feet. For in that he put all in subjection under him, he left nothing that is not put under him. But now we see not yet all things put under him.

9 But we see Jesus, who was made a little lower than the angels, for the suffering of death, crowned with glory and honour; that he by the grace of God should taste death for every man.

10 For it became him, for whom are all things, and by whom are all things, in bringing many sons unto glory, to make the captain of their salvation perfect through sufferings.

11 For both he that sanctifieth and they who are sanctified, are all of one: for which cause he is not ashamed to call them brethren,

12 Saying, I will declare thy name unto my brethren, in the midst of the church will I sing praise unto thee.

13 And again, I will put my trust in him. And again, Behold I and the children which God hath given me.

14 Forasmuch then as the children are partakers of flesh and blood, he also himself likewise took part of the same; that through death he might destroy him that had the power of death, that is, the devil;

15 And deliver them who through fear of death were all their lifetime subject to bondage.

16 For verily he took not on him the nature of angels; but he took on him the seed of Abraham.

17 Wherefore in all things it behoved him to be made like unto his brethren, that he might be a merciful and faithful high priest in things pertaining to God, to make reconciliation for the sins of the people.

18 For in that he himself hath suffered being tempted, he is able to succour them that are tempted.

CHAPTER III.

WHEREFORE, holy brethren, partakers of the heavenly calling, consider the Apostle and High Priest of our profession, Christ Jesus;

2 Who was faithful to him that appointed him, as also Moses was faithful in all his house.

3 For this man was counted worthy of more glory than Moses, inasmuch as he who hath builded the house hath more honour than the house.

These two pages from F.R.H.'s personal Bagster study Bible were published in facsimile in the original edition of Memorials of Frances Ridley Havergal.

"HAVE YOU NOT A WORD FOR JESUS?"

A Question For all who love Him.

You can make use of this if you like.

I.
Have you not a word for Jesus? not a word to say for Him?
He is listening through the chorus of the burning seraphim!
HE IS LISTENING; does He hear you speaking of the things of earth,
Only of its passing pleasure, selfish sorrow, empty mirth?
He has spoken words of blessing, pardon, peace, and love to you,
Glorious hopes and gracious comfort, strong and tender, sweet and true;
Does He hear you telling others something of His love untold,
Overflowings of thanksgiving for His mercies manifold?

II.
Have you not a word for Jesus? Will the world His praise proclaim?
Who shall speak if ye are silent? ye who know and love His name.
You, whom He hath called and chosen His own witnesses to be,
Will you tell your gracious Master, "Lord, we cannot speak for Thee!"
"Cannot!" though He suffered for you, died because He loved you so!
"Cannot!" though He has forgiven, making scarlet white as snow!
"Cannot!" though His grace abounding is your freely promised aid!
"Cannot!" though HE stands beside you, though He says, "Be not afraid!"

III.
Have you not a word for Jesus? Some, perchance, while ye are dumb,
Wait and weary for your message, hoping you will bid them "come";
Never telling hidden sorrows, lingering just outside the door,
Longing for your hand to lead them into rest for evermore.
Yours may be the joy and honour His redeemed ones to bring,
Jewels for the coronation of your coming Lord and King.
Will you cast away the gladness thus your Master's joy to share,
All because a word for Jesus seems too much for you to dare?

IV.
What shall be our word for Jesus? Master, give it day by day;
Ever as the need arises, teach Thy children what to say.
Give us holy love and patience; grant us deep humility,
That of self we may be emptied, and our hearts be full of Thee;
Give us zeal and faith and fervour, make us winning, make us wise,
Single-hearted, strong and fearless,—Thou hast called us, we will rise!
Let the might of Thy good Spirit go with every loving word;
And by hearts prepared and opened be our message always heard!

V.
Yes, we have a word for Jesus! Living echoes we will be
Of Thine own sweet words of blessing, of Thy gracious "Come to Me."
Jesus, Master! yes, we love Thee, and to prove our love, would lay
Fruit of lips which Thou wilt open, at Thy blessed feet to-day.
Many an effort it may cost us, many a heart-beat, many a fear,
But Thou knowest, and wilt strengthen, and Thy help is always near.
Give us grace to follow fully, vanquishing our faithless shame,
Feebly it may be, but truly, witnessing for Thy dear Name.

VI.
Yes, we have a word for Jesus! we will bravely speak for Thee,
And Thy bold and faithful soldiers, Saviour, we would henceforth be:
In Thy name set up our banners, while Thine own shall wave above,
With Thy crimson Name of Mercy, and Thy golden Name of Love.
Help us lovingly to labour, looking for Thy present smile,
Looking for Thy promised blessing, through the brightening "little while."
Words for Thee in weakness spoken, Thou wilt here accept and own,
And confess them in Thy glory, when we see Thee on Thy throne.

Frances Ridley Havergal.

"O LORD, OPEN THOU MY LIPS; AND MY MOUTH SHALL SHEW FORTH THY PRAISE."
Psalm li. 15.

PAISLEY: J. AND R. PARLANE. 1s. 6d. per 100

The sentence at the top of the first page was written by F.R.H. Such published leaflets were an inexpensive, readily available way to reach many with the truth.

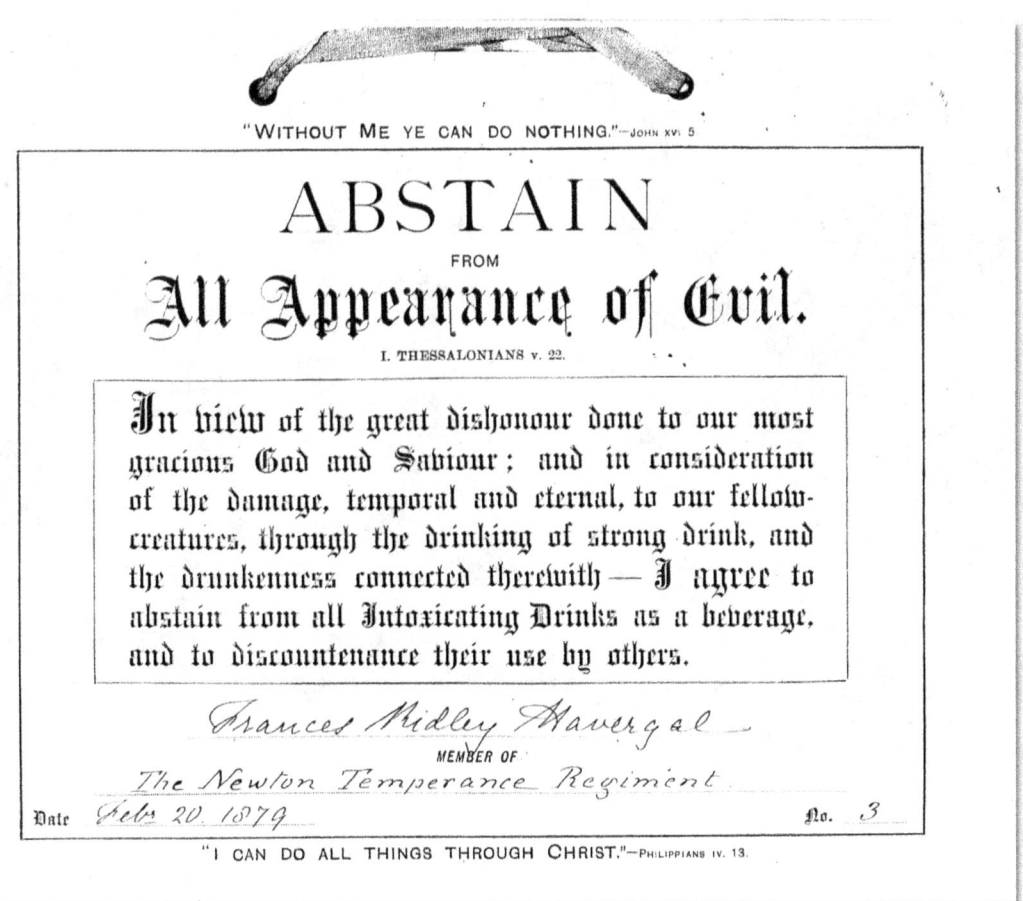

"WITHOUT ME YE CAN DO NOTHING."—JOHN XV. 5

ABSTAIN
FROM
All Appearance of Evil.
I. THESSALONIANS v. 22.

In view of the great dishonour done to our most gracious God and Saviour; and in consideration of the damage, temporal and eternal, to our fellow-creatures, through the drinking of strong drink, and the drunkenness connected therewith — I agree to abstain from all Intoxicating Drinks as a beverage, and to discountenance their use by others.

Frances Ridley Havergal

MEMBER OF *The Newton Temperance Regiment*

Date *Feb. 20, 1879*   No. *3*

"I CAN DO ALL THINGS THROUGH CHRIST."—PHILIPPIANS IV. 13.

This was a heavy card stock placard with two holes and ribbon to be hung on a wall. See pages 322 and 377–378 of this book.

Great Campden House.

Great Campden House was the London school that Miriam, Maria, Ellen, and Frances attended. This article on the school was written by Maria and published in the December 19, 1863 issue of the *Sunday at Home* magazine. Further comments on Great Campden House are found at the beginning of Chapter II of the *Autobiography of Maria Vernon Graham Havergal*, on pages 102–107 of this book, and in Chapter II of *Outlines of a Gentle Life* on pages 192–193 of this book.

GREAT CAMPDEN HOUSE.

"Campden House is burnt down; dear old Campden!" was the thought of one who knew it many many years ago. It was then a well-known and first-rate ladies' school. Half a century ago, some of the noblest of the land spent their early days beneath its well-ordered disciplinary arrangements. Royalty had dwelt there. It was built in the reign of James I about the year 1612. It was a fine specimen of old English architecture, and the great school-room, and what was called the long-room, seemed to us girls immensely large rooms. There were relics of the past, in the crimson tapestry still hanging on the wall of Queen Anne's room. Another room was called Queen Anne's Chapel, and from that a stone staircase from the glass door led to a terrace-walk. Beyond this terrace there was the remains of a subterraneous passage, leading as the legend said, and as we innocently believed, to the House of Lords. Much we puzzled as to what it had been used for, and visions of mysterious knights bearing important messages, flitted before us. Queen Anne herself, with her courtly ladies, might have used it for some midnight visit, to listen to her lords in Parliament assembled. At all events, we often wished for hammers and torches, to explore for ourselves the long shut-up passages. The little schoolroom was remarkable for its quaint carvings. The ceiling was very beautiful, and the panelling too.

On Sundays, it was a comely sight to see all arranged in this room for Divine service. On a gallery-recess the younger girls sat, one above the other; and grouped about the room long rows of older pupils. There was an organ to lead our hymns and chants. Our beloved and revered governess, Madame T———,[1] sat facing us with her piercing eye, and often some wearied little sleeping darling would be taken up in those truly motherly arms.

Our chaplain, of venerated memory, well instructed us, in addresses rich with Scriptural truth, and so methodically divided, as greatly to aid the young listeners, who afterwards wrote very fair notes of the sermon. It was well for us they were sermons that could be remembered, or else we could not have answered (even up till Friday morning sometimes), questions on the previous Sunday morning discourse. Some of these sermons have recently been published. It is interesting to add, that in response to the proposal for publication, the names of above eight hundred old pupils were sent in as subscribers for this memorial of their school life at Campden House.[2] After service came a pleasant walk in the grounds.

At four o'clock a large Bible-class gathered round our beloved Mrs. T———. Would that memory could give back her very words of burning love and earnest pleadings with us, to give our youthful hearts to the Saviour. Hers was the genius of teaching. Clear, concise explanations and varied illustrations were followed by searching questions; she made us think, and kept us in constant attention. She seemed ever to lead us to explore the richest veins of Scripture, and whether it were Levitical types, the words of the wise and their dark sayings, the roll of the prophets, or the parables and narratives of the New Testament, in all she led us to the hidden treasure—Jesus Christ himself.

Then comes a pleasant memory, of half an hour spent in walking up and down the long school-room, talking or singing sweet hymns, till the tea bell summoned us to the next

---

[1] There is no need for our correspondent's reserve in withholding a name that can only be mentioned with praise and honour. Mrs. Teed was principal of the school at Campden House from about 1825 till, on the expiry of the lease, it was occupied by Colonel Waugh, and turned to other uses. At an earlier period of the century Campden House was a "fashionable finishing school," in high repute especially for its elegant dancers, the professor of the art receiving a salary of £600 a year. Mrs. Teed, from conscientious feeling, gave up the dancing, probably that she might not be responsible in preparing her pupils for scenes of worldly gaiety and dissipation. At first this was a severe shock to the school, and many of the pupils were withdrawn. It then became the resort of the children of Christian parents. Mrs. Teed removed to Barnet, and finally retired from school life in 1850. She died Jan. 5, 1858, at Bath. Her memory is cherished with the utmost respect and affection by her surviving pupils. Would that there were many such principals of schools!

[2] Sermons by the late Rev. Joseph Parker, M.A., formerly Chaplain of Great Campden House, Kensington. Nisbet & Co. 1863. An extract is given in the "Pulpit in the Family" in this number.

room. Evening service followed, and the holy, happy Sunday at Campden closed.

The detail of school life would only interest those who shared its wise and salutary discipline. Not a word of English was to be spoken the whole half year, and French became our school tongue. The rule was rigidly enforced, the only relaxation being when some of the elder ones took exercise beyond the high walls, in Kensington Gardens. Very marvellous was the silence learnt and practised by those girlish tongues. Often at tea-time, did the edict for silence go forth, "Mesdemoiselles, not a word is to be spoken till we meet at breakfast." And when after fourteen hours silence, we were asked, "Who has spoken?" any delinquent would honourably rise immediately. It was not the fault of Campden House if ever we became chatterboxes in after life. It really prevented one of the great evils of school life, gossiping and foolish talking.

We were great admirers of beauty, and every new comer was ranked among the beautiful, the pretty, the elegant, or the awkward, or the nice girls. And really, among eighty or ninety, with Spanish, Swiss, and West Indians, we had variety of beauty at least. The arrival of five fair sisters, in their Swiss hats, was a great addition to our rival queens. The love of the beautiful led me to risk many a scrape by adventuring within our dear governess's private room, to gaze on the lovely portraits of former scholars. There was one of Lady J——, that seemed to me of angelic beauty, and with childish admiration I would look and look till I felt quite sure she must have been almost an angel when that picture was drawn. Very naughty was that stolen picture worship; and few would have braved the risk of being caught on the staircase, without the mark of permission.

Especial care was taken of our exercise, and admirable was the rule so rarely found in any school—that the first hour and a half after breakfast was secured for walking. In cold, frosty weather, we had fine races up and down the Terrace and Broad Walk.

Among the pleasant memories of Campden days, the 11th of October stands out in sunshine. It was the birthday of our beloved Madame T——, and our only holiday in the half year. Who does not remember waking early because we might talk English, and in our bedrooms too? A pretty basket ornamented with flowers, and crowded with ninety notes of "felicitations," all written in our best French, and with our best pens, was placed on her breakfast-table. Pleasantly the morning passed among the chosen groups of friends, busy with trim work of pincushion, mats, and marker makings. Then came the cutting up of home cakes, with pleasantries which were relished in those young times. Before the dinner bell rang, all were dressed in Sunday silks. What would have been said of crinolines in those days, when even the first inroad of hanging sleeves was met with the remark—"My dear child, what do you wear dusters for?" Silently did we stand round the long tables, the centre one being reserved for our beloved madame and her sister, our kind and dearly loved chaplain, with many Campdenites of former days, now invited guests. Do we not remember now, as the bell rang and the door opened, the almost queenlike entrance, and stately step of Madame T——, in her rich black satin dress, Elizabethan lace cap and neck-ruffles, and scarlet Indian scarf on her arm? That eagle-piercing eye glanced lovingly round on her dear children, as she bid us enjoy her birthday feast. What an eye she had! How the good ones admired it, how the naughty ones shrank from its detective scan!

But the crowning of the day was the birthday games after tea. The trusty manservant cleared away forms, and merrily did the old English games fare in those spacious rooms—"Blind Man's Buff," "Oranges and Lemons," "Hunt the Slipper"; and when rosy and tired, our kind teacher, Miss A——, gave us "Magic Music." How quickly and happily that evening passed; our innocent pleasures not preventing our being ready to join with the organ's solemn chords to our evening hymn of praise and thankfulness as our holiday closed.

The incident of one half year may now be recalled with interest, if perchance this meets the eye of old school friends, and I trust with profit to any other fair young reader. One of our new schoolfellows about the middle of the half year sickened with measles. She was at once removed through the mysterious green baize doors which separated the nursing rooms from the rest of the house. She was one of the quiet, good girls, whom we all loved, and I think being an only child, had never left her parents before. We were not generally told if there was illness, but we had seen two physicians' carriages driving up for consultation. And then the doorbell at midnight awoke us, and we were told Mary's papa was come to see his darling child.

Very earnest were the prayers offered for the life of the child, but above all that her soul might have the life that never dies. Often, often had our dear governess said, "I must educate you for heaven, my children." And now that death was withering one fair flower, of what account were accomplishments? Oh, what was skill in music, if she had not learnt the first strain of heaven's new song—"Worthy is the Lamb that was slain?" And where was the use of languages, if she had not learnt one soul-word—"salvation"? And what was amiability and docility of character, without the heart-renewing, life-giving influence of the Holy Spirit. No wonder that our dear governess tremblingly pleaded that some ray of sure and certain hope might shine around that dying one's bed. The unconsciousness of subsequent inflammation prevented much conversation, and the numbered hours of life were swiftly passing by. But there was one lamp that could light that darkening path, there was His word which yet could make wise unto salvation. On a large cardboard these words of love were written in distinct hand, "The Father sent the Son to be the Saviour of the world" (1 John 4:14). With prayerful faith, this was fastened where the eye could rest on the life-giving words. Often did dear Mary look at them. Then it pleased the Holy Spirit to open her inner eye, and through those words she looked at Jesus the Saviour, sent to save her. It was the look of faith, the same look which the bitten, poisoned Israelites raised to the serpent on the pole, and lived. And so did dear Mary look and live, and with few but simple words told what He had done for her soul, and that she had found the Saviour.

There was deep silence in the school, for we knew that the spirit of one of our number was even then passing away into the eternal world. Mademoiselle the French governess was alone called into that dying room, that she might see the reality of a soul calmly at peace, while the breath was ebbing away into the great ocean of eternity. Many tears were flowing, and we looked at the clouds and far blue sky, and thought how near the ministering angels were, hovering round to bear away the ransomed spirit of our schoolfellow. We seemed to see the golden gates open, and wished we could go in too; but there was a rougher and longer journey for us to take. And then we were told, "Dear Mary is dead!" and though we cried bitterly, yet even then, many of us felt for the first time in our young lives, "how blessed to die in the Lord: oh, how precious is the blood of Jesus, which has washed dear Mary, so now she is in robes of white for ever."

Our dear governess thus wrote of her death—

You have heard of our late very heavy affliction, and that we have gone through deep waters of anxiety, fatigue and watchings, which two days before the beloved child's death, were all forgotten in the wonderful, but not unprayed for testimony of this little one's simple but strong faith in God, as her God in Christ—the God that loved her and "sent his Son to be the Saviour of the world." It was joy to her death bed, and to our aching hearts. It is our prayer that God may bless this voice to the dear children here, that his triumphant grace and goodness may be seen. Death and salvation, mercy and judgment, have come very near us; may many hear his voice and live!

And now one word to Campden friends of other days, who perchance may glance at this page. Since last we met in Campden walks and rooms, how various have been our pathways, through sunshine and shade, through joy and sorrow! Hardly should we recognize each other now, as mothers or grey-haired matrons. And we are going onwards and upwards in the bright pathway we were so early invited to follow? Is the Lord Jesus our life, our fulness, our all? Do we know, to our soul's safety and comfort, that for *us* "the Father sent the Son to be the Saviour of the world?" We have seen many changes, but is the Unchanging One ours? We have seen our roses wither and only thorns remain; earthly cisterns broken; but do we know Jesus as the same yesterday, today and forever? And are we drinking of that living water which he offered us in our early days, and once again stoops to bid us drink freely?

In Campden we shall never meet again. We know how it passed into very different hands. The rooms where our youthful hosannas ascended, heard the hollow sound of gaiety and folly. The holy voices that bid us choose the paths of peace and pleasantness, were exchanged for the glare and noise of worldly pleasure. The fire on that sabbath morning (March 23, 1863) recalled, to some minds at least, such recollections and contrasts.

Let me quote one sentence of that revered one, who will live in our memories, though Campden is passed away.

My dear child, see that you live Jesus. Live by what he did for you on Calvary, live by what he is now doing for you at God's right hand in heaven. Live for Jesus in a life devoted to his sweet service. A dove does not like her silvery wings to be fluttering in the dust; oh, see that you keep yourself unspotted from the world.

And now her own dying words shall be the last echo from burnt Campden ruins, "I am fast going home, but I find the blood of Jesus my all-sufficient sufficiency!"

Here also are precious words of affectionate counsel. They are taken from a letter, yellow with lying by, and bearing the old franked signature of "Carnarvon."

Great Campden House, 183_.

..... Your letter, dear child, has been long unanswered: are you thinking of me, as we so often dare to think of our Best Friend—"Oh, I am forgotten"? And how is my dear child prospering? are you looking into self, where no good thing dwells, or looking unto Jesus who is all fair, and in whose righteousness we are all fair too?. Are you an unrighteous sinner, living by faith upon the perfect righteousness of the God-man Christ Jesus? This is very hard, born as we are under a covenant of works, but we are born again under a covenant of grace; and as an old woman said to one who was reading the law to her, "Oh, sir, I have been taught that my lawgiver is my law-fulfiller." The effect of this righteousness is peace and quietness and assurance. And holy living, too, will follow; for if our garments have been made white at such a cost, there will be a holy fear of spotting them. Keep near to Jesus, my beloved child—near in prayer, near in reading his word, near in hearing, and "they that wait upon the Lord shall renew their strength." May God the Holy Ghost show you the fulness of Jesus! We must know our need to draw out of that fulness—grace for grace. The Lord bless you more and more. May our meeting at dear Campden, which has been blessed to you in time, be only the beginning of a happy eternity. Ever yours, most affectionately—M. A. T.

I conclude my recollections by quoting some lines, which if not of much literary merit, truly express the grateful feelings with which many remember the spiritual as well as outward advantages enjoyed at Madame Teed's school.

FAREWELL TO CAMPDEN.

Lines written on leaving school.

"Farewell to Campden!" Yes, we've learn'd to spell
That sad, that melancholy word, farewell!
Each day and hour of this quick passing year
Has had its knell to strike upon our ear,
And every flower a voice that seem'd to say,
"We bloom no more to cheer you on your way."
Perhaps we loved too well thy pleasant nest,
And needed to be taught 'twas not our rest;
Perhaps we loved too well thy trees and flowers,
Thy terraced walk, thy shady wood and bowers;
We loved them for themselves; yet far beyond
We loved them as the gift of His dear hand
Who gave himself; and gave us here to know
Himself, the best of all his gifts below.
Farewell to Campden, birthplace of our soul!
How shall we e'er the tide of love control
That binds us to thee! Dearest Saviour, say,
Thou wilt go with us, thou wilt with us stay;
And we will follow where thou lead'st—most blest,
Our home thy presence, and thy will our rest.

Campden, 1847.

Great Campden House. The Little School-Room. 1820.

This school at Great Campden House in Kensington was later moved to Belmont, near Campden Hill, and thus was later called "Belmont." Elizabeth Clay was also a student there, and years later she wrote this about the first time she met Frances:[1]

"On my return to school at Belmont, after the summer holidays, in 1850, I was taken into the large room where all the teachers and pupils had just assembled for tea. Seated among a group of little ones, at the bottom of a long table, was a new pupil, with long golden curls falling round her head. Her appearance at once attracted me, for I remember that as I joined the party my thought was, "I should like her for my friend." Little did I imagine that before the close of that half-year a friendship would have commenced between us which resulted in the closest intimacy, uninterrupted until her entrance into glory twenty-eight and a half years afterwards."

---

[1] This is part of a letter Elizabeth Clay wrote after F.R.H.'s death, quoted in the Appendix of *Memorials of Frances Ridley Havergal* (see page 344 of this book).

MONTHLY REGISTER
AND ANNUAL REPORT.

	No. on Roll.	Average attendance	Scholars Visited.	Scholars Admitted.	Left.	REMARKS.
Jan.						
Feb.						
Mar.						
April			X	X	X	Hannah Palmer
May			X	X	X	Emma Loynes
June			—	—	X	Mary Shepherd
July			X	X	X	Eliza Littler
Aug.			X	X	X	Emma White
Sept.			X	—	—	Susan Groves
Oct.			X	X	X	Hannah Bay
Nov.			X	X	X	Ellen Lippitt
Dec.			X	X	X	Sarah Stokes
Annual Report			—	X	X	Jane Bruce
Last year's Report			X	X	X	Alice Toombs
Increase on last year			X	X	X	Ellen Goodall
Decrease		13 20 27 3 10 17 24 31	July	August		

MARKS.
Present, - - - blank
Absent, - - -
Absent through Sickness, S
Absent with satisfactory excuse, E
From home, - - - f

In the case of non-attendance, when the Teacher has during the week ascertained the cause, the absent mark . can be easily displaced by the S, E, or f. If no sufficient reason can be given the mark . remains, which will indicate "absent without excuse."

There being no marks for the present members, the regularity or irregularity of attendance will be seen at a glance.

RULE FOR AVERAGE ATTENDANCE.

To find out the Average number of members in the class during the month—Divide the number of "blanks" in the month by the number of weeks in the month: Thus, in a class of 10 scholars, the full attendance of a month of five Sabbaths would be 50; but if the number of "blanks" be only 40, according to the rule given, the weekly average is reduced from 10 to 8.

Teachers will find it considerably to their advantage, and to the prosperity of their work, to enter regularly, at the end of each month, in the "Monthly Register" on the opposite page, the No. on Roll, Average Attendance, Members Visited, Admitted, and Left.

Frances R. Havergal Present.

	July			August					
	13	20	27	3	10	17	24	31	
Ellen Goodall	X	X	X	X	X	X	X		
Alice Toombs	X	X	X	X	X	X	X		
Jane Bruce	X	—	X	X	X	—			
Sarah Stokes	X	X	X	X	X	X			
Ellen Lippitt	X	X	X	X	X	X			
Hannah Bay	X	X	—	X	X	X			
Susan Groves	X	X	X	—	X	—			
Emma White	X	X	X	X	X	X			
Eliza Littler	X	X	X	X	—	X			
Mary Shepherd	—	—	—	X	X	—			
Emma Loynes	—	—	X	X	X	gone to service			
Hannah Palmer	—	—	—	X	X	X			

This was part of F.R.H.'s Sunday School Register, the names written by her.

Elizabeth Clay was a very dear, close friend of F.R.H. from their teenage years until Frances' death. She wrote, "On my return to school at Belmont, after the summer holidays, in 1850, I was taken into the large room where all the teachers and pupils had just assembled for tea. Seated among a group of little ones, at the bottom of a long table, was a new pupil, with long golden curls falling round her head. Her appearance at once attracted me, for I remember that as I joined the party my thought was, 'I should like her for my friend.' Little did I imagine that before the close of that half-year a friendship would have commenced between us which resulted in the closest intimacy, uninterrupted until her entrance into glory twenty-eight and a half years afterwards."[1] We read of her in several places in this edition as a close friend of Frances and also of Maria. Elizabeth, after years of ministry in England, went to India as a missionary with the Church of England Zenana Missionary Society. Frances would have gladly been a foreign missionary if her fragile health had not prevented her. Elizabeth visited Frances and Maria at Easter, 1879, on a return trip from India, and she remained close to Maria the rest of Maria's life. This "In Memoriam" article was found in *India's Women*, 1934, provided by Ken Osborne, Archivist, Church Missionary Society, London. See her portrait on page 70 of this book.

[1] Elizabeth Clay's letter after F.R.H.'s death. See page 344 of this book.

In Memoriam.

MISS ELIZABETH CLAY.

The Home Call of Miss Elizabeth Clay has removed from our midst the devoted pioneer missionary who was privileged to lay the foundation of the Panjab Village Mission forty-two years ago. She records in her diary that it was in 1879–80 that the Lord laid the need of the villages upon her heart. Up to that time—although 90 per cent of the Panjabis live in villages—nothing beyond opening a little school in one or two of them near Amritsar had been attempted to take the Gospel to the people.

There were many difficulties in the way. It was considered unsafe for English women to live alone, away from other Europeans, and in those days it was impossible to find any sort of accommodation for Christians in a Hindu or Mohammedan village; but, like most pioneers, Miss Clay possessed strong faith and courage, and a determined will, so that a difficulty was only something to be overcome.

She began work by itinerating with a faithful Biblewoman, living in tents, or taking advantage of small Government Rest-houses, until at last she was able to secure and enlarge a small C.M.S. Bungalow at Jandiala, twelve miles from Amritsar, and the first Village Mission Station was opened.

The district in which these first attempts at evangelisation were made contained no less than 1,550 villages. Finding that the doors were widely open, and that the people as a rule gave her a warm welcome, Miss Clay realised the urgent need of more workers, and from time to time paid short visits to England, and by her eloquent addresses and burning enthusiasm stirred the hearts of her hearers, and gained several recruits for the Mission Field.

Returning from one of these short furloughs, she built another station at Ajnala, which eventually became her headquarters, and in time not only a Bungalow for the missionaries but a Church and Pastor's house, a Zenana Hospital, and rooms for the Biblewomen were erected there. Small schools were opened in some of the villages, and steady and systematic work was carried on for many years.

Even this did not satisfy the ardent zeal of this devoted missionary and, leaving Ajnala in charge of some of her fellow-workers, she went forward and opened another station at Khutrain, where she hoped to settle down and die "in harness." But it was not to be. The early trials and hardships of pioneer work and her strenuous labours for the cause she had so much at heart had undermined her health. She suffered much from malarial fever, and from a form of nerve deafness which was so great a handicap in her intercourse with the people that she was eventually obliged to retire from active work in the exhausting climate of the Panjab, and from thenceforth by her quiet influence and constant prayer, do what she could in the Home Land to strengthen the hands of those who were seeking to build upon the foundation which she had laid.

It was a great grief to her in her last years that both Ajnala and Rhutrain—stations for which she had sacrificed her health and strength and money—were closed for lack of workers and funds. Will not her death sound as a trumpet-call to some younger Christian women to offer themselves willingly for the Lord's service in these needy districts?

Frances' oldest sister Miriam Crane drew these two homes. Henwick House, in a suburb of Worcester, was Frances' home from 1842 to 1845 (after Astley Rectory and before St. Nicholas Rectory). See pages 109 and 251 of this book. Shareshill Parsonage near Wolverhampton was her home from 1860 to 1867 (after St. Nicholas Rectory, Worcester, and before Leamington). These were richly blessed homes to F.R.H. and her family, mentioned many times.

Confidence — "And if to fate." Handel.

I

In Thee I trust, on Thee I rest,
O Saviour dear, Redeemer blest.
No earthly friend, no brother knows
My weariness, my wants, my woes;
   On Thee I call
   Who knowest all,
O Saviour dear, Redeemer blest,
In Thee I trust, on Thee I rest.

II

Thy power, Thy love, Thy faithfulness
With lip & life I long to bless.
Thy faithfulness shall be my tower,
My sun Thy love, my shield Thy power,
   In darkest night,
   In fiercest fight,
With lip & life I long to bless
Thy power, Thy love, Thy faithfulness.

F. R. H.
Sept. 26.

"Confidence" was written on September 26, 1870, and was later given the sub-title "Impromptu on the road to Warwick." In this manuscript in F.R.H.'s handwriting, she assigned this to be set to Handel's score, an Air sung by Susanna in Act Two, Scene 4, of Handel's Oratorio Susanna. Frances was likely the one who made this arrangement published by Hutchings & Romer. This manuscript, a fair copy autograph, was provided by Dorothy Havergal Shaw, a great granddaughter of F.R.H.'s sister Ellen Prestage Shaw. The published score of this is given on pages 2197–2203 of Volume V of the Havergal edition. The poem was published in Under the Surface, on pages 374–375 of Volume I.

This portrait was made in Frances' last year, when she was visiting friends in London, in February 1879 (after her 42nd birthday on December 14). There are strong reasons to think that this portrait is in no way flattering but gives an accurate copy of how she looked at that time. Ira Sankey, D. L. Moody's song leader, visited her weeks before her very unexpected early death, and he later commented on how young she looked; others also commented on how she looked younger than her age in years. Both Frances and her family would have accepted only an accurate, realistic, truthful portrait, never a flattering one. The brooch was a gift to her from her father, having Frances' personal emblem, a harp; this was one of very few pieces of jewelry she kept, clearly special to her, and she had months earlier sold nearly all her other jewelry, to give the proceeds to the support of foreign missions. She was full of life and love, glowing Christ, and those who knew her or saw and heard her realized what can scarcely be conveyed on paper. In this way her sister Miriam wrote of how she sang "in quick tune, and with the spirit which only those who heard her can imagine" (from the small book *Footprints and Living Songs*, the essay on Frances' hymns by Miriam Crane). Her sister Maria was quoted in the following notice printed in the newspaper *The Christian* for July 3, 1879: "THE LATE MISS F. RIDLEY HAVERGAL.—Mr. T. J. Hughes, of 2 Elm Row, Hampstead [London], has shown us a portrait in chalk for which Miss Havergal sat to him several times. This likeness is recommended by her sister, Miss M. V. G. Havergal, as being so life-like. Orders for photographic copies, at a guinea each, may be sent to Mr. Hughes."

    See also pages 74 and 239 of this book.
    David Chalkley

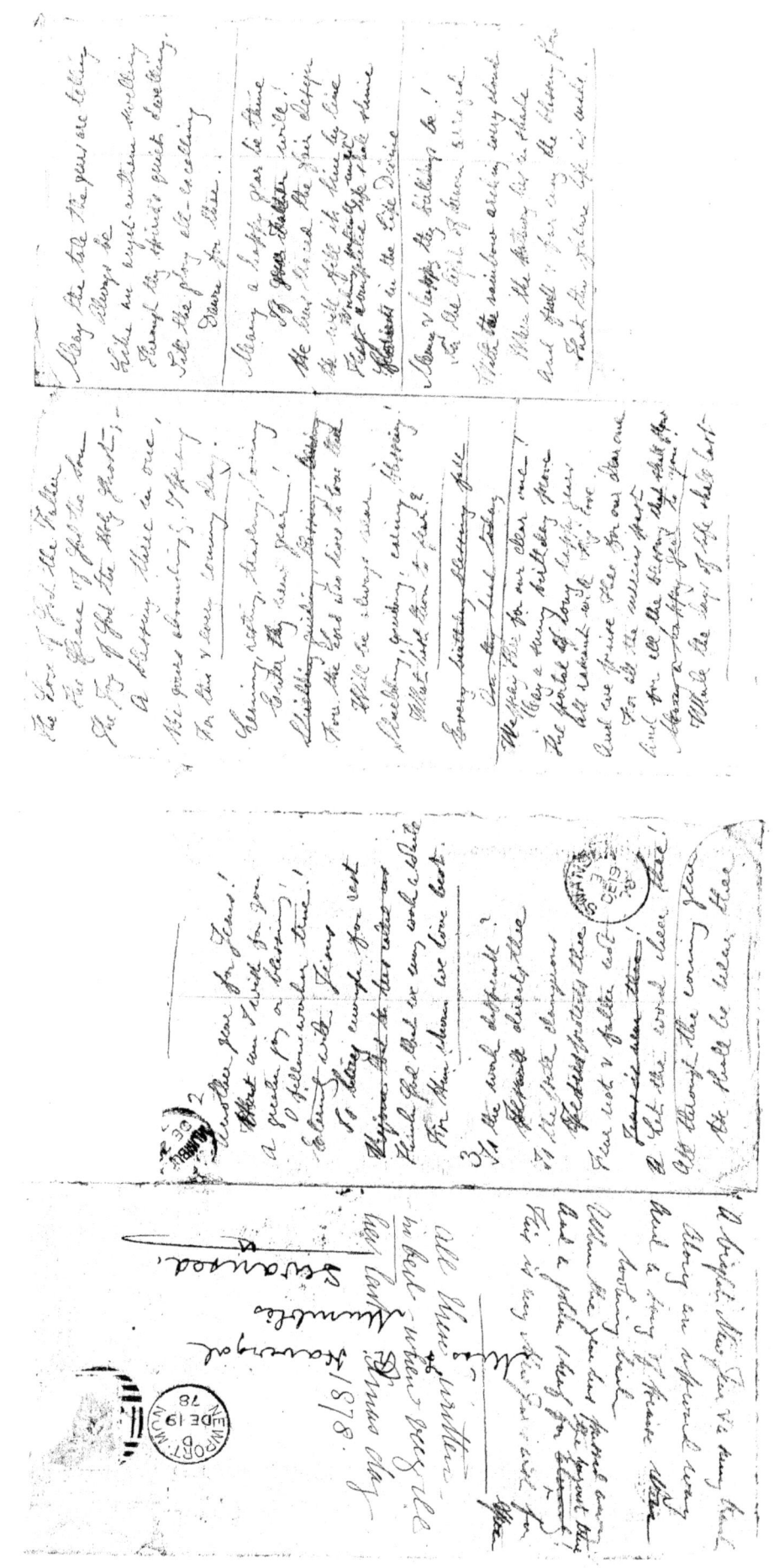

This is an example of F.R.H.'s starting a poem on the back of an envelope or any piece of paper readily available. When she thought that she had finalized the poem, she would copy it in a fair copy autograph in the Manuscript Book of poems that she was using at the time. She was writing in her Manuscript Book Nº IX at the end of her life.

Manuscript of Poem in F.R.H.'s Handwriting on an Envelope, and Memorial Card

This is a manuscript in F.R.H.'s hand, written on the front and back of an envelope. Maria V. G. Havergal wrote on the envelope, "All these written in bed when very ill her last Christmas day 1878."

These verses are found on pages 306 and 312–314 of Volume I of the Havergal edition. Frances seldom made significant changes to her poems, and major revisions were very rare. Even small changes of words were very uncommon. See pages 743–766 of Volume I of the Havergal edition for details on the comparatively very few changes that she made in her poems.

A bright New Year, and a sunny track
    Along an upward way,
And a song of praise on looking back,
    When the year has passed away,
And golden sheaves nor small nor few!
    This is my New Year's wish for you!

Another year for Jesus!
    How can I wish for you
A greater joy or blessing,
    O fellow-worker true?
Eternity with Jesus
    Is long enough for rest,
Thank God that we may work a while
    For Him whom we love best.

Is the work difficult?
    Jesus directs thee.
Is the path dangerous?
    Jesus protects thee,
Fear not, and falter not,—
    Let the word cheer thee!—
All through the coming year
    He will be with thee!

The Love of God the Father,
    The Grace of God the Son,
The joy of God the Holy Ghost,—
    A blessing three in one,
Be yours aboundingly, I pray,
    For this and every coming day!

Leaning, resting, trusting, loving,
    Enter thy new year!
For the Lord who lives to love thee
    Will be always near,
Shielding, guiding, caring, blessing!—
    What hast thou to fear?

We pray Thee for our dear one!
    May a sunny birthday prove
The portal of long happy years,
    All radiant with Thy love.
And we praise Thee for our dear one!
    For all the mercies past,
And for all the blessing that shall flow
    While life itself shall last.

May the tale the years are telling,
    Always be
Like an angel-anthem swelling
Through thy spirit's quiet dwelling,
Till the glory all-excelling
    Dawn for thee!

Many a happy year be thine,
    If our Father will!
He has traced the fair design,
He will fill it, line by line,
    Working patiently, until
Thy completed life shall shine,
Glorious in the life divine.

Many and happy thy birthdays be!
    In the light of heaven arrayed;
With the rainbow arching every cloud
    When the pathway lies in shade;
And full and far may the blessing flow,
    That thy future life is made.

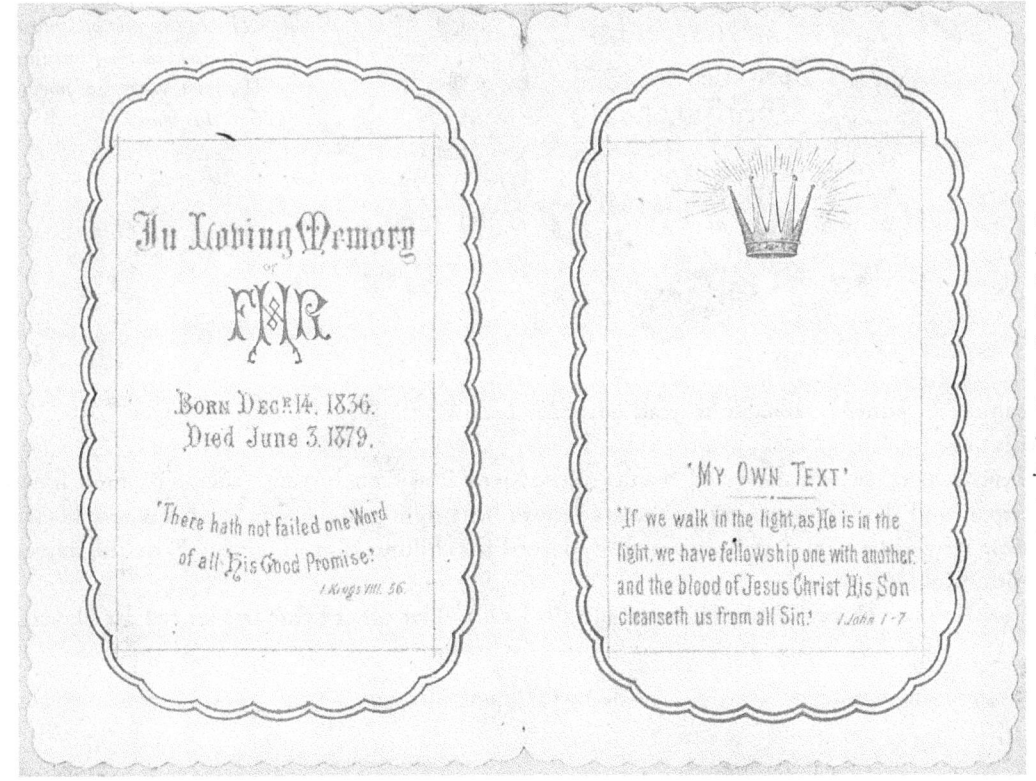

This memorial card (folded in the middle) was printed after F.R.H.'s death. (There was room for a small locket of her hair on the right side, which I think I remember seeing on one copy of this card.—David Chalkley) The two quotations are from I Kings 8:56 and I John 1:9. See pages 380, 388, 120, 153, 155, 162–163, and 170 of this book.

FRANCES RIDLEY HAVERGAL.

THE LAST WEEK.

SIXTY-FIFTH THOUSAND.

LONDON:

JAMES NISBET & CO., 21, BERNERS ST., W.

Frances said those words on June 3, 1879 (see pages 327, 380, and 381 of this book), quoted from I Kings 8:56. This was the plate that her dear friend, the Baroness Helga von Cramm, painted for F.R.H.'s coffin, photographed and publised as the frontispiece of The Last Week *(see page 126 of this book).*

Note: Maria's letter to Dr. Samuel B. James is valuable to read with *The Last Week*. This is found on pages 724–725 of Volume IV of the Havergal edition.

Maria gave copies of "Le beau Départ" (which she called "Fanny's little Memoir in French") and "the pretty French book for children called 'Le beau Départ de F. R. Havergal,' giving the account of her bright going home."[1] This is very likely or almost certainly Maria's *The Last Week* either translated (or possibly adapted for children) into French. Note the name in French of this account, "The Beautiful Departure."

Frances' brother in *The Last Week* was Francis Tebbs Havergal (1829–1890). Her other brother, Henry East Havergal, had died in 1875.

[1] *The Autobiography of Maria Vernon Graham Havergal* (London: James Nisbet & Co., 1887), pages 208 and 230. See pages 148 and 153 of this book.

FRANCES RIDLEY HAVERGAL.

THE LAST WEEK.

My Dear Cecilia:

Knowing that you and many others wish for some particulars of my beloved sister's last days, I write out for you some notes made at the time.

Your Aunt Frances had been unusually well for some weeks, and her dear friend, the Baroness Helga von Cramm, who was staying with us, remarked on her improved health and exceeding brightness. She lessened her desk work in order to show her friend the many walks on the sea-cliffs and in the valleys, which, even through the winter, had been her unfailing delight. On Saturday, May 17th, she watched attentively the Baroness finish on the sand-banks her sketch of the Mumbles Lighthouse.

On Sunday, the 18th, we went to our parish church of Oystermouth, and Frances afterward expressed the extreme pleasure she had derived from the exquisite and reverent playing of her friend, Arthur Batteson, the organist. When the afternoon service in the village school-room was over, we went to every house with tracts, giving notice (with our Vicar's consent) of an evangelistic and temperance meeting on the following Friday. Every child in the village, except two boys, had signed her pledge-book—also some whole families.

On Tuesday, May 20th, her Temperance Regiment came on our lawn, and with her own inexpressible vivacity she marshalled them. They marched and they sang, while recruits were brought up to sign her book in the porch. Every boy or girl who brought another to sign was at once called an "officer," and given something to do. When she dismissed the party, her "officers" clustered round her to receive papers wherewith to canvass the village for Friday's meeting. She came in to supper, bright but weary, saying, "Those dear boys! they are first-rate! And as for their eyes, they quite rivet me. I asked one boy why he was going to sign, and he said, 'Because Jesus Christ never got drunk, and I don't mean to.' Wasn't it capital?"

Wednesday, May 21st, was a rainy day, and Frances kept incessantly at her desk and typewriter, trying to keep pace with her daily flood of proofs and letters. For the last three years strangers and others constantly wrote to ask her opinion on all conceivable subjects, and for several months past the correction of some proofs was a great pressure on her over-wrought powers; as she said, "It is these proofs and business letters that hinder me from writing down flashes of hymns and poems, and Bible thoughts, that keep coming. What am I to do? If I don't answer it does not seem courteous, and yet the burden is so great I cannot sit down to my new papers after hard work at these proofs and letters."

It was a damp day, and I urged her not to keep her promise to meet some men and boys on the Newton village bank; but she went, and they swarmed round her while she pleaded with them not only to be temperate, but to "drink the water of life freely." She then, as always, spoke of the Lord Jesus as her living, loving Saviour. While on the exposed bank, strange-looking heavy clouds came up from the Channel, and she returned thoroughly wet and exhausted. She was chilly all night, but was at her desk soon after nine a.m. as usual. Being Ascension Day, she intended to go to the full morning service, but I persuaded her to go with Helga to the Communion only. There was no sermon, and all was so soon over that I met them at the church gate. Frances looked very tired, and she said she would take a donkey home. At dinner she told us that at the Stand she said, "Now, boys, I will be fair; which is the donkey I've never had?" "Mine, Miss." "Why, Fred Rosser, you are just the boy I am after! Do you know that you and Gwyn are the two boys in the village who have not signed?" "Then I had it all out with him, and he's all right! Marie, I had quite a procession through the village; nearly all my Regiment came after me." Helga said, "Of course you talked to them, and that is why you look so tired." Frances said, "Of course I flung words to them! Those dear fellows! they have twisted themselves around my heart entirely. When I got to our gate I ran for my temperance book, and turned the donkey-saddle into a desk, and then and there Rosser signed it; is it not good?" There was a fine young sailor, W. Llewellyn, going to sea on Friday; the rest of his family had signed, and Frances was extremely anxious for him to do so—"Think how it will save him from temptation, Marie dear; and you know I don't talk of temperance only, it is such a chance to get at them for Christ;" so, although evidently unfit to go out, she went with her last message—the last time her feet were

"Swift and beautiful for Thee!"

On Friday, May 23rd, she breakfasted in bed, but afterward went into her pretty study—"workshop," as she called it—and sat by the fire. Dr. J. came to see the Baroness that morning, and we persuaded Frances to let him prescribe for her also. He said she needed quiet rest in bed, and some medicine; and I begged him to come again. All that afternoon she was arranging for the meeting at seven, and put in order 150 temperance cards to be given away. Our Vicar and Mr. Bishop, from Swansea, had agreed to come. To them she sent her wishes for bright, short addresses, and for gospel truth to pervade the whole.

To me she said, "Marie dear, you will do it so much better than I could; meetings never were in my line. I wish you to give out the cards, and tell the people from me, I am not able to come, but I send two messages from my Bible: to those who have signed, 'Behold, God Himself is with us for our Captain' (2 Chronicles 13:12); to those who have not signed, 'Come thou with us, and we will do thee good'" (Numbers 10:29). The room was crowded, but the one brightest face was absent. A friend brought in a splendid bouquet of flowers. I said, "Who shall have these?" And every voice shouted, "Our Miss Frances." That evening she stitched a strong paper bag, and filled it with tracts for W. Llewellyn to take to sea.

Early on Saturday, May 24th, her silver whistle called me to her side. I found her feverish, and gave her some tea, and after a time, a cooling draught. The dear Baroness left us that afternoon. They then little thought their pleasant intercourse was over.

In a pencil note which she wrote that day to a friend, she said, "I am in bed again with another of those tryingly frequent feverish attacks. The fact is, I have knocked myself up with this temperance work; but having got the *whole* rising generation of the village into my Temperance Regiment, except four naughty little black sheep, seems to me quite worth being knocked up for!"

I have no account of Sunday, May 25th.

On Monday she could not attend to all that came by post, including a letter from the Church Congress inviting her to write a paper on Hymnology for its meeting at Swansea in October. She was pleased to get the first proof of "Morning Stars," her new book for children. She corrected the first page, on the text, "I am the Bright and Morning Star," and instructed me to explain to the printer that she wished spaces left for the little readers themselves to write in the verse of each reference. As with her feet, so now with her hands, the last time she employed them was in the service of her King. On Wednesday, May 28th, she had much internal pain, which did not yield to fomentation and other remedies. That night, after a short sleep, she awoke in extreme agony, poor darling; even screaming, and yet moaning, "Oh, I hope it's not wrong; but it is like sharp knives piercing, piercing!" As our able and careful doctor, who had been to see her three times, was suffering from toothache, she said, "Don't call him up; send to Swansea." So I aroused our good landlord to fetch a well-known and skilful medical man, and he returned in the early morning with Dr. Davis and her own doctor. A change of remedies was tried, and leeches and constant fomentation ordered. Before Dr. Davis left, Frances asked him to pray with her, which he did most beautifully. I then telegraphed for a most experienced nurse[1] whom, a year before, Frances had playfully engaged to come whenever she should be ill.

Instead of constantly mentioning her symptoms, let me tell you, dear Cecilia, that both doctors considered it a severe case of "peritonitis"—that is, universal internal inflammation—and that her extremely delicate organization intensified the severity of the pain. Ice in milk, and refreshing draughts were ordered to be frequently given, and pineapple water she took as her "treat." Opiates were taken, but failed to give ease or continuous sleep. Her sufferings throughout were *unusually and keenly severe;* and I believe God permitted this bodily agony to convince some dear, gloomy Christians that Frances' naturally sunny temperament was not the cause of her joy in life as now in death. "How will she do 'in the swellings of Jordan'?" said some. But her confident and joyful trust in God's promises never failed, and to the praise of His glory, I may say, she rejoiced in tribulation, and glorified God in the fires.

During Friday, May 30th, the dear sufferer said, "It would be very nice to go now, and not to go through all this again." "What vanity, if our assurance of salvation rested on our *own* obedience, as Mr. B. preached one Sunday; that doctrine of merit does away with the atoning blood of Christ." I repeated, "Unto Him that washed us from our sins in His own blood," etc. (Revelation 1:5).

F. "Yes, that's it!"

M. "Have you any fear to go, darling?"

F. "Why should I? Jesus said, 'It is finished'; and what was His precious blood shed for? Yes, I do trust Him and have perfect peace, but not so much joy as at other times. And, Marie dear, God is dealing differently with me in this illness; I do not know what He means by it. In other illnesses He always gave me new thoughts for my books, and I could always write a poem: now, nothing comes at all to me." She continued, "I have peace; but it is *Himself* I want."

---

[1] Sarah Calverly, from the Derby Institute.

M. "It is like the little boats on the stormy sea: they did not row back to Jesus, but Jesus came at last and drew nigh to them, and then He said, 'It is I; be not afraid.'"

F. "That's nice!"

Some time before this she said, "I have such an intense craving for the music of Heaven; nothing here ever satisfies me. I have a strong inborn love of harmony—part-singing—that was delicious with the Sankeys and Mr. Batteson—and last week singing with Helga and the two brothers—it was exquisite!"

Saturday, May 31st.—My poor darling said, "Marie, my tongue is strangely sore and dry; I know well now what that verse means, 'My tongue cleaveth to my gums.' I have had everything I could wish in this illness; and no one could nurse me better than you have done."

M. "Do you at all regret coming to live here?"

F. (*smiling*) "I should think not! The pleasantest time I ever had—delicious!"

In the afternoon Frances said, "Fetch me Mary Fay's card, 'Jesus Christ the same yesterday, to-day, and for ever,' and bring a nail. I can see those nice large letters, and put it quite straight under Helga's 'Glacier.'" And then she added, "Ask Jesus that it may not be long before He speaks to me Himself—some little love-token. If I am taken now I do not think it will be very long before you come; and be sure none of you put on crape for me, not one scrap!"

I had telegraphed for her sisters and brother. They came, but were not allowed to see her for some hours. When the nurse came, after a weary journey of two hundred and forty miles, Frances said, "Nursie, perhaps you have come to say 'Good-bye' to me. Do you think I am going?" Nurse told her she was very ill, but still she hoped she would be spared to us. Early on Whit-Sunday, June 1, she said, "Nurse, I feel a little better; I have got round the corner; I am disappointed—I want to go home." Her extreme consideration for us all was beautiful. She was tenderly anxious that I should not get overtired, and often begged me to go and rest. To our good maid also she showed much thoughtful kindness. Once she said, "Marie dear, you have been very brave, but don't force yourself; have a cry: but maybe I shall get well." Then she whispered softly, "I am sure 'I am not worthy to be called His son,' or His servant; but Jesus covers all. I never could make some friends understand, at the time of the 'holiness' movement, how tremendously I saw my unworthiness, but in Him completeness, and in Him strong to overcome sin."

M. "Not *our* worthiness, but 'Worthy is the Lamb'!"

F. "Yes, that is it!"

Again she said, "God is always right. I told my nice doctor that the Lord makes no mistakes; and, though this illness upsets all my Irish plans, it's all right! I asked him if there was a chance of my going now." On asking if she could see her sister she said, "Duckie! will it help you? Now you will take turns and rest yourself, Marie." When her brother came, on telling her that, through his carriage accident, he missed a train, and had been traveling all night, she said, "Frankie, I do love you dearly; so good and kind to come. Do you remember when we knelt together at dear papa's dying bed, what you said to me?—how that comforted me! Ever since I trusted Jesus *altogether* I have been so happy, so peaceful; I cannot tell you what Jesus has been to me, so good, so altogether lovely!"

She was extremely pleased with a letter from Frank's twins, and the verse Willie sent her, "Sorrow may endure for a night, but joy cometh in the morning," and said, "I hope Willie and Ethelbert will be ambassadors for Christ, even if they are not clergymen; oh, I hope they will win souls!"

The nurse repeatedly gave her milk, saying, "We must do all we can to keep you; but you want to go."

F. "I don't want to be impatient; God's time is best."

My sister Ellen reminded her that St. Paul said, "The will of the Lord be done, and let Christ be magnified whether by my life or death."

F. "Yes, that is it."

When E. spoke of the "Glory which Thou gavest Me I have given them," Frances said, "Perhaps to-night! I have not strength to send messages to *yours*. I should have liked my death to be like Samson's, doing more for God's glory than by my life; but He wills it otherwise."

Often through this Sunday she expressed a longing to go, and in the evening Frank said, "Do you feel your strength failing or increasing?"

F. "Failing. I am just waiting for Jesus to take me in. Frankie, it's so pleasant you are come; I felt I could not go without your giving me one kiss." Then she asked to be quite alone with him for some time.

The sickness was incessant every two or three minutes for the last forty-eight hours; she bore it so patiently, saying, "It comes more easily now: He is staying His rough wind in the day of His east wind." Kneeling by her and seeing her patient agony, I said, "My poor darling, this is dreadful! Marie will not wish you back once."

With the brightest smile she answered, "You darling! for saying that."

She awoke after a short sleep on Sunday night, exclaiming, "I am so disappointed; I thought I should awake in Heaven."

The nurse said, "Did you, dearie? but you are spared to us a little longer."

"Yes; I thought I was cowslipping."[1]

Craving for more air, she asked our good Mary to leave the room, but whispered, "Explain to her. She must not be hurt, but I want air; it is food to me." Window and door were

---

[1] cowslip: noun, a low-growing plant with drooping, fragrant yellow flowers in the spring. What Frances meant here is not certain. Possibly she thought that she was picking these flowers. Possibly she meant that she was drooping low like these flowers. We don't know. See page 382.

always open now; and sometimes fanning relieved the oppression. I forgot to mention that one day previously Dr. D. said, "Miss Havergal, we are anxious you should have all the aid possible."

F. "Do you mean divine aid?"

Dr. "No; that we have asked for. But if you or your sister have the least wish for another medical opinion, say so."

F. "Oh dear no, I have perfect confidence in you both; please do not: but tell me what is the element of danger?"

Dr. "You are very seriously ill; and the inflammation is increasing."

F. "I thought so. But if I am going it is too good to be true. I shall go just when Jesus likes." The night passed in pain and sickness, with an occasional doze.

Whit-Monday, June 2nd, about eight a.m., Frances said, "Call Frank." He was already at her door partly dressed, with the "Visitation of the Sick" in his hand. A strong impulse had come over him to see her without delay. He knelt and said, "Could you bear a few words of prayer?"

F. "Oh yes; I should so like it."

After one sentence she said, "Stop, let it be a sacramental service; sisters and all, kneel down."

In a moment I broke off some bread waiting for nurse's breakfast, and placed it on her own crystal stand. Dry champagne was at hand, which her brother poured into a wine-glass. All was ready, and we felt the Saviour also present.

She joined in the Confession, and also most emphatically in "It is meet and right so to do," and "Therefore with angels," etc. After the prayer of Consecration, and his own receiving of the elements, Frank began to say the words individually to each. Frances solemnly said, "Let the words be spoken *once* to *all*." After the Blessing she lay peacefully. Frank said, "It has been such a pleasure thus to join with you."

F. "Frank dear, it is not the performance of the rite—*no safety in that;* but I wished it in obedience to His command, and as a remembrance of His dying love."

Frank. "Quite so, dear, just as a memorial of His death."

An hour after she whispered to me, "I was delighted with the clear way Frank put it, and I'm glad he did not mind his shirtsleeves; I thought I was just going then, and no time to be lost. Why tarry His chariot wheels?"

M. "He really is coming for you, dear! and I quite say 'Thy will be done;' and I would not keep you back from Him."

F. "'*Not one thing hath failed,*' tell them all round; trust Jesus, it's simply trusting Jesus."

About ten a.m. her doctors came, and morphia was to be injected into her arm. The sleeve being tight, she said, "Let Maria do it—she knows how: cut it in the seam, not to spoil it for other people."

When Dr. D. was leaving, he knelt by her and said, "Goodbye; I shall not see you again."

F. "Then do you really think I am going?"

He said, "Yes."

F. "To-day?"

Dr. "Probably."

F. "Beautiful! too good to be true!"

Soon after she opened her eyes with such a smile! "How splendid it is to be so near the gates of Heaven!" My brother began to read "Rock of Ages." Frances said, "Sing 'Jerusalem, my happy home,' to dear papa's tune, 'St. Chrysostom,'[1] and play it on my harp-piano. You must sing from the copy that has 'Jesus, my Saviour, dwells therein.' Oh, it is Jesus that is so dear to me! I can't tell how precious!—how much He has been to me!" After that she sent to tell him to play the same tune again to "How sweet the name of Jesus sounds!" and that he was now to sing the bass part and her sisters the treble. He played other tunes, the soft notes floating in and around her. When he came back, she said, "Frank, do you think I shall be disappointed again, and not go to Jesus after all? I feel easier now."

As he could not speak just then, I answered, "Darling, we are quite sure you are going to Him, and we are glad for you."

She smiled, saying, "Jesus will be glad. Oh, He is so dear and so good!"

By and by she heard the Vicar of Swansea was downstairs, and said, "Ask him up." He took her hand. "You have talked and written a great deal about the King: now you will soon see Him in His beauty. Dear sister, is Jesus with you now?"

F. "*Of course!* It is splendid. I thought He would have left me here a long while; but He is so good to take me so soon. Give my love to dear Mrs. Morgan, and ask her to tell her dear girls of the Association[2] that what she and I have told them is all right—it is all true: tell them Jesus is a good big foundation to rest upon. Give my love to Mr. Aitken,[3] and tell him to speak plainly about Jesus. I want him to tell young clergymen to be faithful ambassadors, and win souls. I want all of you to speak *bright* words about Jesus—oh, do, *do!* And give my love to Dr. Wrenford, and say, I can never thank him enough for his help. It is all perfect peace: I am only waiting for Jesus to take me in."

"Tell Mrs. Morgan to come and look at me, but I can't speak out." When she came, Frances whispered, "There is no bottom to God's mercy and love; all His promises are true." To her sisters she said, "You don't think it wrong for me to be glad to go away and leave you? But I wish I could help groaning and screaming, is it wrong? This illness has been so painful all through."

---

[1] No. 53, Havergal's *Psalmody*.
[2] Young Women's Christian Association.
[3] Rev. W. H. Aitken.

I said, "You have been very, very patient, darling; the doctors noticed it, and said you were different to any one else, and so calm, they could tell you anything: you really are glorifying God now."

"Oh, I am so glad you tell me this. I did want to glorify Him every step of the way, and especially in suffering, even in this furnace."

She listened, though in agony, to her brother's singing "Christ for me!"[1] and your aunt Ellen repeated the verse—

> "On Christ the solid Rock I stand,
> All other ground is sinking sand"—

adding, "I want to rejoice more that you, dear Fanny, are on the Rock; and we are too, and we want no other."

Fanny answered, "It is the one God has laid for us."

About midnight her hands and feet became very cold; her sisters rubbed them, and her watchful nurse brought hot bottles.

Towards one o'clock a.m., Whit-Tuesday, June 3rd, a change came, and there were restless tossings after long inability to move. While we were endeavouring to refresh her, one of the sisters repeated, "When thou passest through the waters, I will be with thee." Frances immediately said, "He *must* keep His word." Another time when she was in distressing pain, one of us began, "Fear thou not; for I am with thee." (Isaiah 41:10). But neither of us repeated it correctly: our darling with her own accuracy set us right.

After a short doze she exclaimed, "I am lost in amazement! Not one thing of all His good promise hath failed; but I must not be impatient to be gone." The last thing she asked for was some coffee. "Marie, you make it your way; you always do things right." It was quickly brought, and with both hands she eagerly took the cup and drank it. "That's lovely! Now, Nursie, one little bit of bread and butter."

There were a few wandering words, such as "That arrangement about the meeting, it must stand over; I can't see to it." "That poor Welsh woman, she had no washstand or bookshelf!" "There is Miss Leigh's work in Paris, and Margaret C. working there all gratis! Strange I think of it now!" Then, with more consciousness, she whispered the names of many, H. C., Johnnie, Constance—poor Connie!—and Ellen's children—"I love them all."

[1] No. 493 in *Songs of Grace and Glory*.

With a yearning, loving look she said, "I want all to come to me in Heaven; don't disappoint me any of you. From great to small, trust Jesus!" Ellen repeated—

> "Jesus, I will trust Thee,
>   Trust Thee with my soul;
> Guilty, lost, and helpless,
>   Thou canst make me whole.
> There is none in Heaven
>   Or on earth like Thee;
> Thou hast died for sinners,
>   Therefore, Lord, for me."[2]

Then to our amazement Fanny sang the whole verse through to her own tune, Hermas.[3]

Then came a convulsive rush of sickness, Nurse saying, while gently supporting her, "My poor dearie, it will be home soon—can't be long now." Our very hearts bled to see that patient dear one in this agony, and we did cry, "Lord Jesus, take, oh take her!"

After this terrible time, Fanny said, "There, it is all over! Blessed rest!" She folded her hands most beautifully, and nestled down in the pillows. And now she looked up steadfastly, and her eyes shone gloriously as if she were looking at her King; and the glad expression of her face was as if she were already speaking to Him. This steadfast expectant gaze lasted some minutes: then, instead of her moans, came a glad, glad sound, "Oh! oh! oh!" and then she tried to sing. Only one high, sweet note came, "He!"—gently dying away. Still her eyes were unmoved, and shone with unearthly glory. Her brother commended her departing spirit into her Redeemer's hands. Gently, most gently, her breath ebbed away, and we saw that she was gone. I could only whisper,

"GLORIFIED."

And now, dear Cecilia, I am, as always, your affectionate aunt,

MARIA V. G. HAVERGAL.

Oakhampton,
　June 12, 1879.

[2] No. 569, *Songs of Grace and Glory*.
[3] No. 105, Havergal's *Psalmody*.

[Note: Please read the account of "notes from the sick chamber" immediately after the end of Rev. Snepp's memorial article on F.R.H., on pages 1068–1070 of Volume IV of the Havergal edition. These "notes from the sick chamber, sent to Rev. C. B. Snepp, by the dear sister of F.R.H." were very likely written by Ellen Prestage Havergal Shaw, because the writer said near the end: "About 1:40. I said, 'Jesus, I will trust Thee, trust Thee with my soul,' and immediately she began to sing it, faint and gaspingly, but each word of that one verse distinct (Maria helping her)." We know from Maria's account of *The Last Week* (on this page 381) that this was Ellen. That is a valuable account to be read with this one by Maria.]

POSTSCRIPT.

It is impossible to answer the many letters of deep sympathy. This printed letter must be accepted as the answer to many inquiries.

I will explain why I have not called her by her home name "Fanny." She always disliked it, and much preferred her baptismal name of Frances, and always signed it so. Only a month ago she was delighted to find in one of her dear father's letters describing her baptism, "I do not like the name of Fanny, but gave way to the general wish; but Frances is her baptismal name, and that I like."

When she died, the love of the whole village was stirred: her "Regiment" brought flowers; carriages brought white crowns of costly exotics: not only her room, but the house was one bower. We made wreaths, for Frances ever approved of such, and her oldest sister made a golden star (see Daniel 12:3) of Banksia roses, and a poet's wreath of laurel and bay; and these we left, with many white crowns, on her tomb.

In death she looked smiling and lovely, and many craved to see their "angel-friend." Many then bore testimony. To the dear nurse, one said, "It was Miss Frances led me to Christ." Another, "It was her words that brought me in."

Frances had written down four years ago, "Let my coffin be simply deal." Her brother added simple white with a chaste device of crown and stars, and the Baroness supplied the plate, painting roses and forget-me-nots around the inscription.

On Monday, June 9th, at six a.m., all the villagers and many others stood in order round the lawn, after walking reverently past the flower-crowned coffin, and the vicar of Swansea read from her well-marked Bible, and then addressed the crowd of over three hundred present.

My brother and I brought her to Worcestershire, where relatives and distant friends joined in following her to her father's tomb in Astley Churchyard.

There, within sight of her birth-room, in the Rectory, and under the branches of the fir her father planted—and away beyond the hills and valleys of her childhood's haunts—we laid our sister "in sure and certain hope of the resurrection to eternal life."

There had been heavy storms all day, but as the service ended the sunshine came, and a chorus of birds burst forth, and so her sunny life and death ended in a bright ALLELUIA! AMEN.

In Loving Remembrance of

Frances Ridley Havergal,

Born December 14th, 1836;
Entered into the King's Palace with exceeding joy,
at Caswell Bay, near Swansea, June 3rd, 1879.

She was the youngest Daughter of the late
Rev. W. H. Havergal,
Hon. Canon of Worcester Cathedral.

Buried at Astley, Worcestershire, the place of her birth, on
on Monday, June 9th.

This was a Christmas card published by Marcus Ward & Co. The flower is a cowslip. See page 379.

OUTLINE OF ADDRESS.

By Rev. S. C. Morgan, of Swansea,

To Sunday School Children and others, at 6.30 a.m., Monday, June 9th.

You have just seen your dear friend taken away; and I want you to think of her death, that you may die like her. Many persons hope it will be all right when they come to die; and, when they see a funeral, they say, "Let me die the death of the righteous,"—but the way to die is to *live* to Christ, and in Christ, as she did.

I want you each however, young or old, to say as her hymn says,

> "Take my life, and let it be
> Consecrated, Lord, to Thee."

She not only wrote it, but she did it—she gave her life to Him.

Each of you has a *life* now; it is that life He wants—it may be but short—what are you doing with your life? Give it to Him! — work for Him! — live to Him! She felt it a happy thing to live to Him! And then, when sickness came, she had nothing to do but die: her soul was safe—all was settled; she knew Jesus had done it all for her. He was "all her salvation and all her desire"—so hers was a happy death-bed. I have seen many death-beds—such different ones—some so dreadful in agony, for they knew not where they were going: one man cursed me for coming when he was dying. But hers was so happy. One of the doctors was much impressed by it, and said to me, "I never saw any one die so happily; she was quite delighted to go—it was so real—that happiness." It was not hard to die so. It was Jesus that made her happy—not what she was, or what she had done.

"I am not worthy," she said, "but Jesus is: His blood cleanses me." Think of your sins, "God requireth that which is past." Don't think *you* can cover them over. God sees them all. God must cover them. (1 John 1:7.)

As I stood by her bed, she looked so bright, and said, "God's love and mercy have no bottom to their depths—so deep—so high." Yes, He is full of love. His name is not "Terrible," but "Love." Think what His love did for you. (John 3:16.) He did not give what cost Him nothing, but His most precious, beloved Son. She wished to speak of Him. You have heard her speak of Him. And she wrote in her books about Him, about her King, and His Commandments, His Royal Bounty and Invitations. She delighted in Him; and He delighted in her—sustained and cheered her so consciously, so truly, that when I said, on taking my last leave of her, "The Lord is with you," her glad reply was, "Of course He is"—not *will* be—but like David she could say, "Thou *art* with me." (Psalm 23.)

Remember how she loved and cared for you; what interest she took in your Band of Hope; how she loved children and people. She did not say, "I am come here for rest and quiet;" but she was ever working among you for her Master's sake, trying to bring you to Him.

But she is gone now—her body is carried away and her soul is gone to glory: but if you love Jesus as she did, you are going to His palace, and you will see her there.

But while you are left here, what are you to do? Love Jesus! Live like Him! Work for Him as she did; and speak for Him, sing of Him. She was singing of Him *in death*—that beautiful hymn you have now sung—

> "Jesus, I will trust Thee!"

Don't *say* you will trust; but do it; go to *Him* and tell Him so; let there be no misunderstanding, no putting it off. Come to Jesus now! and say, "I come to touch the hem of Thy garment; I come for cleansing; I come to accept Thee—to be Thine forever."

Some day you will wish you had come. You will think of to-day and say, "He was calling me then, He was touching me." Oh then, come and touch Him now!—do it now!

Death has touched many here lately—but may God touch your hearts! Remember! it is happy to live *in* Jesus and for Him, and happy to die "in Him"—"living or dying" to be "the Lord's."

One Sunday I was preaching: some sailors dropped in, and the word came home to their hearts; and they told their wives they had given their hearts to the Lord. They soon had to go to sea—a storm came, and they were lost. When the news came to their wives, what could have comforted them—but knowing they had given themselves to Jesus!

Thank God! He gave His life for me! and I give mine to Him! His arms are the arms to die in—they are safe indeed!

These next five hymns are referred to in *The Last Week*.

SIHOR (River). [Havergal's Psalmody 158.]

Rock of Ages, cleft for me,
Let me hide myself in Thee!
Let the water and the blood,
From Thy riven side which flowed,
Be of sin the double cure,
Cleanse me from its guilt and power.

Not the labours of my hands
Can fulfill Thy law's demands:
Could my zeal no respite know,
Could my tears for ever flow,
All for sin could not atone:
Thou must save, and Thou alone!

Nothing in my hand I bring;
Simply to Thy cross I cling;
Naked, come to Thee for dress;
Helpless, look to Thee for grace;
Foul, I to the fountain fly:
Wash me, Saviour, or I die!

While I draw this fleeting breath—
When mine eyes shall close in death—
When I soar through tracts unknown—
See Thee on Thy judgment throne—

Rock of Ages, cleft for me,
Let me hide myself in Thee!

ST. CHRYSOSTOM. [Havergal's Psalmody 53.]

Jerusalem! my happy home!
    Name ever dear to me;
When shall my labours have an end,
    In joy, and peace, and thee?

When shall these eyes thy heaven-built walls
    And pearly gates behold?
Thy bulwarks with salvation strong,
    And streets of shining gold?

Oh when, thou city of my God,
    Shall I thy courts ascend,
Where congregations ne'er break up,
    And sabbaths have no end?

Apostles, martyrs, prophets there
    Around my Saviour stand;
And soon my friends in Christ below
    Will join the glorious band.

Jesus, my Saviour, dwells therein
    In glorious majesty;
And Him, through every stormy scene,
    I onward press to see.

ST. PETER [Havergal's Psalmody 263.]

MAMRE (Plain of). [Havergal's Psalmody 226.]

How sweet the name of Jesus sounds,
   In a believer's ear!
It soothes his sorrows, heals his wounds,
   And drives away his fear.

It makes the wounded spirit whole,
   And calms the troubled breast;
'Tis manna to the hungry soul,
   And to the weary, rest.

Dear Name! the rock on which I build,
   My shield and hiding-place;
My never-failing treasury, filled
   With boundless stores of grace.

By Thee my prayers acceptance gain,
   Although with sin defiled;
Satan accuses me in vain,
   And I am owned a child.

Jesus, my Shepherd, Husband, Friend,
   My Prophet, Priest, and King;
My Lord, my Life, my Way, my End,
   Accept the praise I bring.

Weak is the effort of my heart,
   And cold my warmest thought;
But when I see Thee as Thou art,
   I'll praise Thee as I ought.

Till then I would Thy love proclaim
   With every fleeting breath;
And may the music of Thy name
   Refresh my soul in death!

My hope is built on nothing less
Than Jesu's blood and righteousness:
I dare not trust the sweetest frame,
But wholly lean on Jesu's name:
   On Christ, the solid Rock, I stand,
   All other ground is sinking sand.

When darkness veils His glorious face,
I rest on His unchanging grace.
In every high and stormy gale,
My anchor holds within the veil:
   On Christ, etc.

His oath, His covenant, and His blood,
Support me in the sinking flood;
When all around my soul gives way,
He then is all my hope and stay:
   On Christ, etc.

When the last awful trump shall sound,
Oh, may I then in Him be found,
Clothed in His righteousness alone,
Faultless to stand before the throne:
   On Christ, etc.

HERMAS. [Havergal's Psalmody 105.]

Jesus, I will trust Thee, trust Thee with my soul;
Guilty, lost, and helpless, Thou canst make me whole.
There is none in heaven or on earth like Thee:
Thou hast died for sinners—therefore, Lord, for me.

Jesus, I may trust Thee, name of matchless worth
Spoken by the angel at Thy wondrous birth;
Written, and for ever, on Thy cross of shame,
Sinners read and worship, trusting in the name.

Jesus, I must trust Thee, pondering Thy ways,
Full of love and mercy all Thine earthly days:
Sinners gathered round Thee, lepers sought Thy face—
None too vile or loathsome for a Saviour's grace.

Jesus, I can trust Thee, trust Thy written word,
Though Thy voice of pity I have never heard.
When Thy Spirit teacheth, to my taste how sweet—
Only may I hearken, sitting at Thy feet.

Jesus, I do trust Thee, trust without a doubt:
"Whosoever cometh, Thou wilt not cast out,"
Faithful is Thy promise, precious is Thy blood—
These my soul's salvation, Thou my Saviour God!

This house was the comfortable lodgings on Caswell Bay Road, the Mumbles, on the ridge of the western horn of Swansea Bay, near Swansea, Wales, which Frances called "this quiet little nest," where she lived her last eight months and died. An undated, very old photograph is on the left (the title "Mumbles F.R.H." was written just above that photograph), and on the right is a photograph taken by David Marlow in 2009.

German Hymn, the End of the St. John Passion by J. S. Bach

This is the end of the St. John Passion by J. S. Bach.

Ach Herr, laß dein lieb Engelein	Ah, Lord, let Thy dear angels
Am letzten End die Seele mein	at my end, my soul
In Abrahams Schoß tragen;	in Abraham's bosom take;
Den Leib in seim Schlafkämmerlein	the body in its small sleeping chamber
Gar sanft, ohn ein'ge Qual und Pein,	fully gentle without one torment or pain,
Ruhn bis am jüngsten Tage!	rest till at the last day!
Alsdenn vom Tod erwecke mich,	Then from death awaken me,
Daß meine Augen sehen dich	that my eyes see Thee
In aller Freud, o Gottes Sohn,	in all joy, O God's Son,
Mein Heiland und Genadenthron!	my Saviour and throne of grace.
Herr Jesu Christ, erhöre mich, erhöre mich,	Lord Jesus Christ, hear me, hear me!
Ich will dich preisen ewiglich!	I will praise Thee for ever.

"I will praise Thee, O Lord my God, with all my heart, and I will glorify Thy name for evermore." Psalm 86:12

In Loving Memory

OF

F.R.H.

BORN DECR 14. 1836.
Died June 3. 1879.

"There hath not failed one Word of all His Good Promise."

I. Kings VIII. 56.

"MY OWN TEXT."

"If we walk in the light, as **He** is in the light, we have fellowship one with another, and the blood of **Jesus Christ His Son** cleanseth us from all Sin."

I. John i. 7.

M FAY.

This memorial page was found very near the front of Life Chords, *a posthumous collection of poetry by F.R.H. and her father, William Henry Havergal. See also a memorial card on F.R.H., on page 375 of this book. This was designed by Mary Fay, F.R.H.'s Irish friend, who also designed the card "Jesus Only" with Hebrews 13:8 shown on page 330 of this book. See pages 325–326, and 379–381 of this book.*

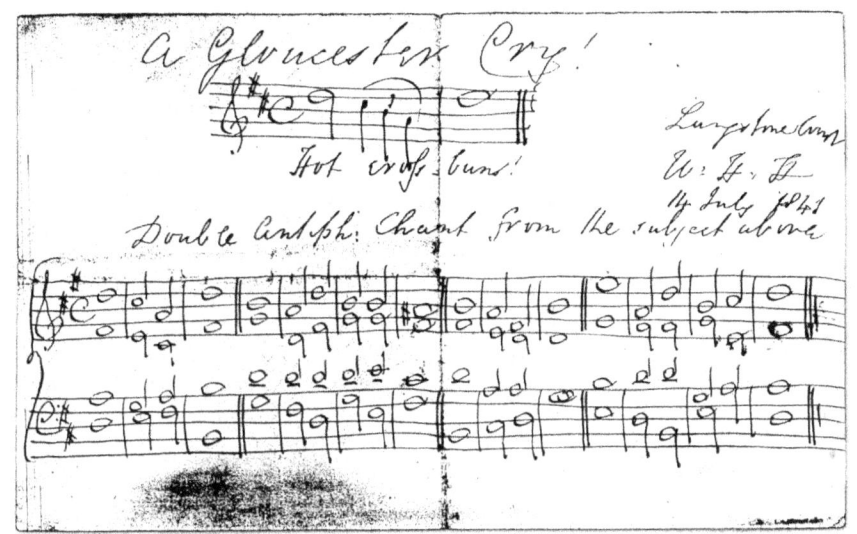

A manuscript score by William Henry Havergal, and a copy of his signature.

This next piece was written by Maria and was published as Chapter IV in her sister Miriam's biography of their father, William Henry Havergal, *Records of the Life of the Rev. William Henry Havergal, M.A.* (London: Home Words Publishing Office, 1883).

FOOTPRINTS OF MY FATHER WHEN CURATE OF COALEY, GLOUCESTERSHIRE, 1819–1822.[1]

Footprints — "The elders that outlived Joshua" — Eliza Workman — "Mr. Havergal is all music" — George's remembrances — "The way of transgressors is hard" — The fighting on Coaley Peak — The vicarage kitchen class — A cottage in Silver Street — "The doctrine to fill churches" — How he led "the rabble of Coaley" — Thomas Cam, the "musicianer" — The text in the "Pockrifa" — Work in the workhouse — "All the Dissenters turned to Church" — "Footprints" amongst the farmers — "His life preached."

FOOTPRINTS! Some never seen, some quickly erased, some shining indelibly, cheering and guiding others, pressing to the selfsame mark.

Soon after my dear father's death, in 1870, I determined to revisit my birthplace, Coaley, and if possible trace his footprints. The vicar kindly secured me lodgings just opposite the church and vicarage. Though my father was curate for only three years, his ministry, his life, and his visits were well remembered by many in both cottage and farm.

Sunday, July 17, 1870. The bells were chiming for church when I passed through the churchyard gate. The last time that gate opened for me I was in my christening robes! The old church is pulled down and beautifully rebuilt, the old tower remaining. Many of the tombstones bore the dates when my father must have stood there. I saw some Sunday-school children laying flowers on a grave; there were rails round it, but no stone. "Whose grave is that, dear child?" "It is our last clergyman; we bring flowers every Sunday, and when the cowslips come we put so many!"

After church I followed two aged women, hoping to find they were like "*the elders that overlived Joshua, and which had known all the works of the Lord that He had done for Israel*"

---

[1] This chapter has been written by my sister, Maria V. G. Havergal, who prepared the Memorials of F. R. H. for publication. (London: J. Nisbet & Co.)

(Joshua 24:31). In answer to my question, "Do you remember Mr. Havergal?" one said, "To be sure, and ha'n't never forgot him. Wasn't he kind to me and every one! I'm the widow Philamore. Dear Mr. Havergal!"

It was not kind to keep her tottering there, so I promised to call at her cottage.

It was soon known in the village that "a belonging of Mr. Havergal's" was come, and sundry visitors called, whose simple words shall now be given.

My name is Eliza Workman; you must have heard your dear father speak of me. I believe I was the first he spoke to. My mother was a dressmaker, and I remember Mrs. Havergal sending to know if she could go to work at the vicarage and sew a carpet for the study. My mother told me to go, but I was timid, and said, "Perhaps Mr. Havergal will be asking me questions I can't answer." But I went, and as soon as I saw him I was no more timid. He had such a way as won everybody. Dear Mr. Havergal! when my troubles came he was just everything to me. My mother died—his visits so comforted her. Then I went to live with grandmother, and was so cast down till Mr. Havergal called.

Mr. Havergal is printed on my mind, and will be till my dying day.

The congregations were wonderful. The church that was so empty hadn't even standing room. I've seen the road lined with horses, gigs, and carts from all parts. When the people knew he was going away they thickened to hear him; and the last sermon! not a dry eye in the church. I can show you the hymn-book Mr. Havergal made for us. We used to say, "Mr. Havergal is all music." Old Thomas Cam, the clerk, was so too; and they did have such talks. The new hymn-book was so liked that my little cousin George took some eggs to the vicarage to get one. Mr. Havergal was out, but George soon had one. The school children loved him dearly. He was the one to keep a parish right, for they took all their quarrels to him and he squared them all.

Another knock, and another visitor.

"Good evening, miss. Why, you features your father uncommon!"

"Perhaps you will tell me all you remember—it is so pleasant to find my dear father is not forgotten."

George.—I was a stiffish lad of fourteen when Mr. Havergal came to Coaley, and I went with my father to work at the vicarage garden. The vicarage was new, for the old one was pulled down after the last parson had hung himself in it. The garden was covered with rubbish. I remember Mr. Havergal would work along with us sometimes, and he could put his hand to anything. He was a lithesome man—not a lithesomer in England. Such a one to be up in the morning; and he'd set the vicarage windows open, to let out the night air. And to see him walk! why he'd be at Dursley in twenty-five minutes, and its three miles. He never touched the stiles; he'd go clean over them. When I heard you were come to the village, miss, I said to my missus, "Her father did what few would do now-a-days." There was a poor fellow, Joe Ford, convicted at Gloucester for horse-stealing. He was condemned to die, and when the 'Size was over Mr. Havergal travelled every day to see him, though it's fourteen miles, and he mostly walked it. From his condemnation to his execution Mr. Havergal saw him daily. His body was buried under the church tower; there were over three hundred at the funeral, and Mr. Havergal addressed them from the grave. The text of the sermon the next Sunday was, "The way of transgressors is hard."

I remember how people said "Mr. Havergal do be in and out of the houses all the week, and that fetched them to church on Sunday; and he do be as frequent to Dissenters as to the t'others." Why, the head man at the chapel turned over to the Church!

The old clerk, Thomas Cam, was a musicianer; he made pieces that were sung at Gloucester College. Mr. Havergal and he had mighty turns at it; and what seemed so curious to me was, that they both made tunes in their heads without stopping to play them.

Coaley Peak is one of the juttings of the Cotswold range. The long narrow lanes leading up to it are almost impassable in winter; not only "oxey" and clayey, but with water-springs overflowing the path. But through mud and water ankle deep did the pastor go after his flock. An old man remembered one night when, he said, "There was awful fighting highish up, quite at the hills. They ran to the vicarage and called him, though long past midnight. Up he went; he wasn't the sort to mind a journey night or day to do good, and he had some One to watch over him. They say when he got up to the fighting they soon dropped their hands, and he reasoned them into lambs, and got 'em all to shake hands and go home."

Returning down the lane, I saw a woman running after me, saying, "Will you please to stop, miss; there's a woman wants to see you; she says she went to his class in the kitchen."

Going into the cottage, the good woman exclaimed, "I heard talk there was some one belonging to Mr. Havergal up this hill. I never see that kitchen without remembering him."

"What kitchen?"

"The kitchen down at the vicarage."

"Who taught you there?"

"Who? him himself;" and she burst into tears. Then she continued: "He had the first class of girls every Wednesday to instruct in the Scriptures and in the answering. 'Twas him himself that tried to bring us to Christ, and if he had stopped longer we should all have come to the Lord's table. Mr. Havergal had such a sweet, lovely voice. Yes, I remember it, and the hymns and chapters he taught us. I never shall forget him. And is he gone?" And she cried afresh.

The woman went on telling how he always went to the opening and closing of the Sunday school. "And your mother, dear Mrs. Havergal, always came too; the girls were under her edication. I remember her well—such a pretty look; we thought her a lovely lady."

One of the Coaley lanes is called Silver Street. In one of the lonely cottages a woman asked me what my name was?

"Havergal."

"Havergal!" She burst into tears. "Then I count it must be him I did love; aye, I did love him well, and never heard of one as didn't. It's a few years back he called to see me; my sight was very dim, so he put out his hand and said, 'Don't you know me?' I could have fallen down before him! O I loved him, and he was so friendly to us all. I warrant he knew all the Scriptures by heart. He'd have his little Bible on the pulpit cushion, and take it up now and then, but I never saw a sarmint book in his hand."

Just then her husband came in.

"Tom, thee knowed Mr. Havergal?"

"Knowed him? aye, and loved him; and is he alive?"

"No; he's gone."

"Aye, gone to his Lord's kingdom. Many's the time I've heard him preach; but I was one of the giddy multitude, and then it took no effect of me; now I see the wall pulled down betwixt my soul and Christ. The wall must be pulled down before you can pluck roses on the t'other side. But I must give account of all his texts and sermons. Was he ill long, miss?"

"No, it was a very sudden call; he never opened his eyes to bless us, nor could he pray."

"That was done afore: he'd no need to pray then; he had lived in the Lord, and he died in the Lord, not a doubt."

They asked many questions, and listened, eagerly as I told how he sang and played that last Easter Even.

They said, "Ah, he was a musicianer; he drawed out music on paper; only he and old Cam the clerk could do that much."

Then asking them if I should sing one of my dear father's tunes, I sang "Evan," the old man joining in the tenor.

He said, "That tune is sung in all the churches and chapels round. I'll assure you we have some happy moments singing that sweet tune."

The dear old woman exclaimed, "I often think what I'll do when I get's to heaven; I'll be such a poor creatur up there! But I believe to see Jesus will be my first look out; and I shan't take any sin in with me, for the hymn says,

> 'Those holy gates for ever bar
> Pollution, sin, and shame;
> For none will gain admission there
> But followers of the Lamb.'"

Passing on to a wild common, I saw a man sitting on the trunk of a tree. I said, "What a beautiful view this is!"

"Yes, 'tis uncommon grand; not that many travels to see it."

"Do you go to Coaley church?"

"Sometimes; not as I did when a young 'un. The old church was crowded then. Mother told me she often stood three Sundays running. Mr. Havergal preached then; a good minister he was, beloved by all far and near. They travelled from Uley and Dursley and Kingscote to hear him. He preached the Gospel, and that's the doctrine to fill churches. Not that I'm a possessor, and I ain't going to make any profession till I has possession. Mr. Havergal and other parsons have talked at me, but the world, the flesh, and the devil are again me; and then the trials and troubles put out the amusements of religion from my heart. I had a book lent me lately, 'Four Last Things: Death, Judgment, Hell, Eternity.' Sommat in it striking, sommat in it encouraging; it's all my own disbelief that I'm not ready."

"Have you got a Bible?"

"Yes; it was my mother's, and Mr. Havergal gave it her; it's big print. My mother was an established Churchwoman. Often and often Mr. Havergal walked up to see her; and a smartish walker he was. One of his texts is plain afore me now, 'The way of transgressors is hard,' and many another comes round to me. Not that I'm religious, mind you, nor beint going to profess it, to please any one."

One more cottage stood far on the hillside. An old man was mending shoes; the wife looked very ill. Looking keenly at the stranger, he said—

I count as thee belongs't to Mr. Havergal; he brought her and me t'gether at Coaley church. But I didn't 'spect thee to travel so far. Mr. Havergal led the rabble of Coaley as asey as a shepherd leads his she'p dog. There was plenty of rabble when he çum'st to Coaley; and when he took to us, them that wudna hearken to nons't, ud hearken to him. There was one particular bad fellow, not over eighteen. Mr. Havergal got him put in the stocks a few hours, just as long as he thought needful to soften him. Then he took him to the vicarage, and gave him a good supper and good advice. He'd hearken to no one; but in course he hearkened to Mr. Havergal, for no one could go agen him. When my father was ill, that good parson came again and again, and he'd administer medicine to sowl as well as body—aye, a sight of medicine he guv for nothing—up till ten at night folks went for his mixtures. I remember Coaley church was cram full, not a standin' empty. He was a plain-spoken man, preaching the Gospel, and that "all our righteousness was as filthy rags." He's in my eye now—a very upstanding man, not his fellow in the pulpit, I knows.

Another day I called on the daughter of Thomas Cam, "the musicianer." She was not so communicative as some, but told me of the wonderful music her father made in his head. From her garden, just under Coaley Peak, the Severn looked almost like the sea, and she seemed pleased with my admiration of the view, exclaiming, "You may go hundreds of miles and not see such a sight! The tide comes up the Severn every twelve hours—it's ruled by the moon; it comes up like to the boil, and then lessens again; isn't it wonderful?"

I saw cottages still far away, and I knew my father's footprints would be "excelsior," and so I trudged on. Some women were churning at a cottage-door, so I could not hinder them; but I asked if they remembered Mr. Havergal.

"Yes, that I do, though I was only five years old. He preached a text mother could not find in all the Bible, so she said it must be in the 'Pockrifa;' and I remember her sending me across the fields to ask missus at the farm to please to find it out in the big Book."

"Can you tell me the words?"

"Yes: 'His head bare, and he shall put a covering upon his upper lip.'"

I assured her it was in Leviticus, but only carrying my Testament I failed to convince her it was not in the "Pockrifa."

Another footprint deep and clear! It is singular how the unobliterated track shines out unexpectedly. Returning Eliza Workman's call, she told me that my beloved father was voluntary chaplain at the workhouse. "Mr. Havergal went of his own free will to comfort and instruct them. He used to take a three-legged stool and sit down among them as freely as if he was in a palace. There was one poor creature, Kate Twirling, who had been excommunicated out of the Church. 'Twas stricter rules in those days. Poor thing! she had been a beautiful girl, but so bad. Mr. Havergal could not rest till he brought her back to the Church; and he knew that was not enough; ah, it was to Jesus he tried to bring us all. I remember after Kate died it was found that great property belonged to her. Never mind, Mr. Havergal showed her the true riches. All he did was out of love to God and free good-will to man."

Another man told me that when my father first came to Coaley, as soon as ever church was over the game of fives was played against the tower walls; but for shame they could not play after hearing such sermons. An old pilgrim, John Stiff by name, remarked: "Aye, he preached the Gospel and the marrow of the Gospel. There was mighty little of that in the Establishment then. I used to walk five miles to hear Mr. Havergal preach. And all the Dissenters turned to Church. Ah, he preached Christ and he lived Christ, and now he's with Christ for ever. He was the first to tell us about the missionaries."

Nor was it only amongst the cottagers, but in many farmhouses I found pleasant footprints. One farmer said: "I shall never forget Mr. Havergal's confirmation classes. He was beloved by all; such a nice spirited man, and no bigot. Never was a better churchman, and yet he never ran down Dissent. He was anxious to do good to every one's soul, and so won many. I remember how well he stood up in the pulpit; such a fine proportioned man, his head erect, his hand waving. And his voice! no one could ever forget it, and no one's like it. We gave him a silver teapot when he went away, though there was not a rich man in the parish. Oh, how, we wished to keep him! and as a lad I used to think I'd follow him to the ends of the earth."

An elderly lady told me of his voluntary lecture in Dursley Church on Sunday afternoons, walking four miles there and back just in time for his evening service. She said his preaching attracted large congregations, and most blessed results followed from his faithful preaching of Jesus Christ: "I was quite a child, about ten years old, when your dear father left Coaley. His sermons were the means of my dear father and mother's conversion, but I did not then know the Lord myself. I remember the effort made by my crippled father to go and hear him. How well I recollect your father's beaming face! He was so full of the love of Christ, it shone in every feature. Precious man! every one loved him, every one looked up to him, for his life preached. And it was not only his own parish he cared for, but many others; and it was Mr. Havergal who first held missionary meetings in Dursley, Uley, and other places. His correspondence was much blessed to me. For two years I had not heard from him. I used to stand before his portrait and think, 'I should like to know if you are in heaven.' I did not hear of his death for six weeks. Then I went to look at his picture, and thought, 'Now you *are* in the glory, and oh, what must your music be now!' And I knew my father would be with him, and both singing, 'Glory be to Thee, O God!' Yes, he has a glorious crown, and I can't tell you how sweetly I realize his glory."

Valley of Lauterbrunnen, with the Staubbach.

This color print was the frontispiece in F.R.H.'s bound manuscript volume of letters that she wrote in an earlier trip to Switzerland, written to her family back in England (letters posthumously published in Swiss Letters and Alpine Poems*). Below the print she wrote the caption, and on the page facing this frontispiece was Frances' handwritten title, "Encyclical Letter, specially for the benefit of Marie, Ellen & Frank 1869."*

This next piece was written by Maria and was published as Chapter XIII in the posthumously published *Swiss Letters and Alpine Poems* by Frances Ridley Havergal (edited by her sister Miriam, London: James Nisbet & Co., 1881).

MEMORANDA OF

A SWISS TOUR WITH F. R. H.

BY HER SISTER M. V. G. H.[1]

IT was on a calm evening in the beginning of July, 1876, that we crossed by steamer from Newhaven to Dieppe. Some Mildmay deaconesses were on board, and others, who were leaving their work for needful rest and change. Frances said: "Of course we shall have a delightful passage! I find these dear deaconesses have been praying for it, and so have the dear boys at Newport." And so it was, and we landed at Dieppe before the usual time.

Frances walked with me along the quaint old quays, and it was curious to see one of my own names, that of my godmother, "Vernon," on an ancient stone building.

No need to describe the journey through Normandy and Paris to Lausanne, where we slept at the Falcon Hotel.

July 13.—By steamer on the lake of Geneva to Montreux, where Frances landed and took a mule to "Les Avants," to call on Miss E. J. Whately. I went on to the castle of Chillon to wait for Frances, and after exploring it I sat down by the lake. A poor Italian woman came with clothes to wash. She told me her husband was dead, and so she was alone, "alone always," and far from her own country. So I spoke of the one Friend and Saviour, ever near, ever loving, and who said, "I will never, never leave thee." She readily learnt a text, and then went on with her work. It was very hot. I took off my hat and rested on a bank; presently two young women came running to see what was the matter: "O madame, nous croyions que vous etiez morte! vous vous reposiez si tranquillement."[2] I thanked them, and explained I was only tired and the washerwoman was within call. They sat down, and I gave them some biscuits, and they told me about their homes and their fruit gatherings. Then I drew a little parable from their running so kindly to help a stranger; how the Good Shepherd, Jesus, saw us really perishing; how He pitied us, and came down close to us in

[1] *Maria Vernon Graham Havergal (1821–1887).*

[2] French: O madame, we believed that you were dead, you were resting so peacefully.

our souls' sleep. That He would not leave us lying there, but would bring us to His own safe fold, if we were only willing to "follow Him." Let me not forget to pray for this kind Pauline and Adelaide.

Frances returned to me beaming, saying, "Miss Whately is all and more than I expected. Only it was tantalizing to meet her, and yet see so little of her; we only had time to find out how much there was to talk about. Anyhow she is no longer one of my unknown specials!"

We went on to Vernayaz. It was late, but I went through the Gorge du Trient. Strange crypt-like aisles and ceaseless water music.

July 14.—Frances awoke me at four a.m., and we were ready before our guide and mule; and then Frances gave me my first lesson in Swiss slow paces, so unlike the Havergal speed.

The vivid colouring of the flowers was new to me; they seem always in Sunday dress here, bright and fresh. Halting at the Pension du Mont Blanc in the village of Finshauts, Frances was charmed with the utter quiet of the valley, and decided to stay a week. Valerie Longfat proved a most attentive waitress. We began our Swiss holiday by very early "rising and setting," as Frances wished me to get into good training before real expeditions came on. Our usual morning walk brought us in time to see the sunrise on Mont Blanc. Frances' favourite evening stroll was to a fairy glen of flowers and ferns, and few could arrange its spoils with so much taste. The little chalets around looked tempting to me, and one evening's visit led to many more. Two very aged women were sitting in their shady porch; one of them said she was "la vieillarde de Finshauts," and able to walk about with her "bon baton." I answered: "*One* good stick is enough, a dozen would only throw you down; now just as you lean on *one* stick, so do lean upon the one Saviour, the mighty One, the strong One. Some lean on a dozen angels and saints and mediators, but the Bible says, 'There is one God and one Mediator.'" She seemed to catch my meaning, and presently several of her neighbours joined us; so I proposed they should bring their chairs, and I read a chapter. These little open air services are very pleasant.

Sunday, July 16.—A brilliant cloudless day. Many peasants came by, going to early mass. I sat down on some logs of wood, and made a seat for any one who would like to rest. All returned my salutations, one and another chatting awhile, and taking tracts. A woman asked me why I did not go with them to mass. I told her I could not join in worshipping the host; that Jesus Christ ascended into heaven; that His glorified body was at the right hand of God; that Stephen saw Him standing there; so His body could not be in heaven and in a wafer too. "But," she said, "I think you love Him." "Ah, yes! and in England I do take bread and wine in remembrance of His great love to me." She told me her name was Julie Zacharie, the familiar name of friends in Worcestershire; and it seems her ancestors were English!

After mass she called and invited me to see her home, a curious old chalet: thick stone walls, and the windows so narrow that I could only dimly see the variety of images and pictures. Julie showed me many of her old books. Before leaving I asked if I should kneel down and pray for God's blessing, that He would teach both of us.

"No, no, dear lady; I am just come from mass; I have taken Jesus there. Dear lady, you must believe our mass is a miracle; God can give our priest power to change the sign into the real body of Jesus."

"Show me in your Bible where God promises to do this."

"Oh, it is in our 'Instructions'! Madame, do you know them?"

"Yes, I was reading them to-day. The Epistles, Gospels, and Psalms are God's word, but not the 'Instructions.' Give me your book, and we will read exactly what the Lord Jesus said. Luke 22:19: 'Do this in remembrance of Me.' *What* did they then do? Ate bread, drank wine. The apostles could not *then* have eaten the Lord's body, for He was sitting alive by them; hence, as it was a sign, a memorial then, it must be the same now. Besides, whatever goes in my mouth never reaches my spirit, my affections; so, while taking bread, the outward sign, in my mouth, in my heart I feed on Him by faith with thanksgiving."

Julie listened and said: "Well, we do both love Him; will madame come with me this evening to my chalet by the river? I have cows there, and madame shall take cream."

I was resting upstairs in the evening, when a knock came at my door, and Julie appeared in my bedroom. We had a pleasant talk, and then she willingly knelt down with me: May the Spirit shine through all entangling webs!

Every day we found fresh walks, and the alpenrose blossomed where the snow was yet lingering. I tried crossing a snow slope, but gave it up, and watched Frances' agile steps, fearless and firm; now I can understand her glissades!

July 23.—Early this Sunday morning Frances wrote "Seulement pour Toi," and as our hostess and Valerie had often listened with pleasure to Frances singing, we told them they might invite any neighbours to assemble at three o'clock, for singing and Bible reading. But by two o'clock arrivals began, charming maidens and all the old peasants we had chatted with in the week. I would not disturb Frances, so produced pens and paper and the new French hymn for any who would like to copy it; this answered well. For the old women I proposed making some tea, but Valerie assured me no one ever cared for it! Lemonade seemed a more welcome idea, and was duly appreciated. There was one sprightly girl, Katrine, whose mischievous laughter betrayed her dislike to our plans. But even Katrine was interested when I produced the photographs of my Indian orphans in the Church Missionary school at Agurparah. The histories of little Daisy, Maria, and Monie (now called Frances, after Frances Ridley Havergal), and the novelty of some missionary information, awakened deep interest.

At three o'clock the room was full. Frances began by giving a free translation of her hymn, "Golden Harps," and singing it. Then came "Seulement pour Toi";[1] with Frances' lively encouragement, this was soon sung *en masse*. Frances read, in French, verses from the third, fourth, and fifth chapters of Romans, giving a few sweet linkings of the same, and then asked me to speak to them. I found it quite easy to address in French, and many thanked me afterwards.

No one seemed willing to kneel for the concluding prayer. I would not begin while all were sitting, so Valerie's father set the example, vigorously saying, "Mettez-vous tous à genoux." A few stayed to talk to us afterwards.

We welcomed our tea, though the old women did not. Frances said she wished she had a French Bible that she might put references to "Seulement pour Toi." M.: "Then I will go and ask monsieur the curè to lend us one, and certainly I shall give him your hymn." F.: "Whatever will you think of next! Marie, do you mean it?" M.: "I do; besides the curè has been on my mind all the week." F. (laughing): "Then ask him to correct my hymn."

Away I went to the priest's house, and who should open the door but the mischievous Katrine, evidently amused to see me! Giving my compliments to the curè and a request for the loan of a Bible, he returned with Katrine, inviting me to his study. He brought the Bible in four large volumes, inquiring which I required. I told him we had only French Testaments with us, and that my sister wished to put references to a hymn she had written that morning; possibly he would kindly correct it. After reading "Seulement pour Toi," he inquired if the writer was French, as only one idiom was incorrect. He was extremely pleasant, and I told him of our little service, adding a few words on the preciousness of Christ and the Holy Scriptures. Then he called Katrine and bade her carry the volumes home for me.

The next morning we walked to Argentière. While we were resting under a tree a lady, whom I had previously seen at our pension, and who wished to hear Frances sing, came by on her mule. She dismounted and joined us; and at my request Frances sang to her, thus ministering to one who seemed lonely and weary. I should like to have known the name of this solitary traveller. We stayed some days at Argentière; Mont Blanc was just opposite our windows. What variety of rose and golden crowns descend on that kingly mountain!

July 31.—Frances walked with me part of the way to La Flégere; she returned to Argentière. No need for a guide, she gives me such clear directions. Instead of sunset on Mont Blanc sheet lightning kept up illumination of its height, while the aiguilles flashed as if cased in steel armour. A young lady from Denmark walked with me up and down the terrace. I told her how we all loved our beautiful Princess of Wales. She was interested to hear of the Bible, given her by the maidens of England, and that led to her accepting one from me. Her loyalty was as lively as mine.

The next morning was dense mist, but I went on to the Bréven by breakfast time. Turning over the tourist's book I found my sister's entry, Aug. 2, 1871: "F. R. Havergal and Elizabeth Clay. Felt exceedingly triumphant over all the tourists at Chamouni, and especially over those who had been here in the heat of the day. For from seven to eight p.m., while they were in the dusk of the valley and probably at table d'hôte by candlelight, we were enjoying a glory of gold and rose upon the whole chain of Mont Blanc, and watching it die into that strange, pale, holy after-light, which is almost more thrillingly beautiful than any more glowing effect. Furthermore at 4.30 a.m. we saw the first touch of rose-fire on the crown of the monarch."

It was useless to wait in the clouds, so I went down to Chamouni; suddenly, through the pine woods, Mont Blanc unveiled in silver. I walked on to Argentière, and Frances commended me for pushing bravely through the mist, and says I have the bump of locality.

August 3.—We left Argentière, walking part of the way with the Rev. J. H. and Mrs. Rogers, to the Tête Noire, where we lunched. I rested, but Frances as usual found ministering work. Then away to the Col de Forclaz, a satisfactory distance! The next morning we walked to the Croix de Martigny, and then turned up the road towards St. Bernard, and slept at Lembranchier.

August 5.—By diligence to Orsière, interesting ride; all the travellers joined in singing "Seulement pour Toi," and even the driver tried to sing the bass, whereon Frances jumped up by him; I do think she would make any one sing.

We reached the Hospice of St. Bernard on Saturday, and were gracefully received by the good Father Hess.

Sunday, August 6.—Clear cloudless sunshine. Sat under the rocks with Frances, reading Exodus 33:21, 22, of that rock and that cleft in the rock, where the glory "passed by," connecting it with John 17:24, the glory which will not pass away, but which we shall behold for ever.

---

[1] We give the words and music, as published by Messrs. Nisbet & Co. in leaflet form. F. R. H. also arranged the same melody to "Precious Saviour, may I live," published by Hutchings & Romer. [See the next page, 396.]

Seulement pour Toi.

[Written for and sung by some Swiss peasants at a Sunday afternoon Bible reading, July 23rd, 1876.]

Que je sois, O cher Sauveur,
  Seulement à Toi !
	Hosea 3:1*	O that I be—May I be, O dear Saviour,
		  Only (wholly) Thine!

Soit l'amour de tout mon cœur
  Seulement pour Toi.
	Matt. 22:37	Be the love of all my heart
		  Solely for Thee.

Je reviens à mon Père
  Seulement par Toi,
	John 14:6	I come back to my Father
		  Only through Thee,

Ma confiance entière
  Sera en Toi,
    Seulement en Toi.
	Psalm 118:8	My confidence entire
		  Will be in Thee,
		    Only in Thee.

Le péché Tu as porté
  Seul, seul pour moi ;
	I Peter 2:24	The sin, Thou hast borne it
		  Alone, alone for me ;

Et Ton sang Tu as versé
  Seul, seul pour moi.
		And Thy blood Thou hast shed
		  Alone, alone for me.

Toute gloire, toute joie
  Sera pour Toi ;
	Rev. 5:12	All glory, all joy,
		  Will be for Thee ;

L'espérance et la foi
  Seront en Toi,
    Seulement en Toi.
	Acts 4:12	The hope and faith
		  Will be in Thee,
		    Only in Thee.

Aujourd'hui, O cher Seigneur,
  Acceptes-moi !
	II Cor. 6:2
	Eph. 1:6
		Today, O dear Lord,
		  Accept me !

Tu es seul mon grand Sauveur,
  Tu es mon Roi.
	Isaiah 19:20
	Psalm 44:4
		Thou art alone my great Saviour,
		  Thou art my King.

Tous mes moments, tous mes jours
  Seront pour Toi !
	II Cor. 5:15	All my moments, all my days
		  Will be for Thee !

Jésus, gardes-moi toujours
  Seulement pour Toi,
    Seulement pour Toi.
	Isaiah 27:3	Jesus, keep me always
		  Only for Thee,
		    Only for Thee.

Que je chante et que je pleure
  Seulement pour Toi !
	Psalm 21:13	O that I sing and that I weep
		  Only for Thee !

Que je vive et que je meure
  Seulement pour Toi !
	Romans 14:8	Let me live and let me die
		  Only for Thee !

Jésus, que m'as tant aimé,
  Mourant pour moi,
	Gal. 2:20	Jesus, how Thou hast loved me,
		  Dying for me,

Toute mon éternité
  Sera pour Toi,
    Seulement pour Toi.
	I Thess. 4:17	All my eternity
		  Will be for Thee,
		    Only for Thee.

July 23, 1876

*Note: In F.R.H.'s posthumously published *Under His Shadow*, these Scripture references were given on these lines.

[hymn in French by Frances Ridley Havergal, set to her tune "Onesimus," English translation by David Chalkley]

When the chapel bells tolled for mass, Frances said that *for once* she should like to try joining in the service. I did not go, having tried it, and felt utterly wretched and the clearest conviction I was grieving God. In half an hour Frances returned distressed with the service, and expressed her grief that Protestant tourists often join in that form which involves downright error and idolatry. Nor did she find the music soothing or elevating, it was "just aggravating and monotonous." Just then five St. Bernard dogs came out; they barked at me, but immediately caressed Frances: instinctive discernment! There were many groups of peasants scattered about; they seem to make this a picnic pilgrimage, receiving food and lodging. We made sundry friends; even a large group of card players put their cards away and thanked us for civil warnings. Leaflets and portions were gladly received. At four p.m. Frances, a traveller from Boston, and I enjoyed a service in the very hush of those rocky aisles and vast icy temples. Frances chose Psalm 22:31 and Psalm 23, also Zephaniah 3.

After dinner Frances sang, by request of Father Hess, "Comfort ye," then "Seulement pour Toi," in which many joined. Being asked to sing her own music she gave, "Whom having not seen ye love."[1] It was evidently thrilling to all, and Signor Luigi and others expressed their admiration to me. They didn't know how Frances had prayed that her song might be a King's message.

August 8.—Walked back to Orsière.

9th.—Explored the Val de Feri. I will detail an incident illustrative of many others. I always carry a tiny kettle and tea, for our refreshment. The wind blew out my pine cone fire, so we went to a chalet for boiling water. The little maiden put brown bread, which required chopping, and goat's cheese on the table. She had never tasted tea, and did not seem to like it at all.

I asked Constance[2] if there was any one ill in the village.

"Yes, little Aline; she used to lie alone all day long, till I asked her father to put the key under a stone, that I might get in. Aline has no mother."

I followed Constance up some dark stairs into a room like a hay loft. A little tired face looked up from the rough bed:

"Oh, Marie! I am so ill; is father come? He went away so early."

Alone, alone, locked up in that cold loft, some greasy soup in a can, and a hard crust! Dear little Aline! I sat down by her and fed her with some jelly and biscuits, and sent Constance for some new milk. I took the thin hot hand and said in French:

"Dear Aline, there is One who loves you very much; the kind, good Jesus; do you know Him?"

Yes, she knew the name of Jesus, and that He died on the cross; but she did not seem to know it really was for her, in her stead. She seemed to drink in all that was said, and learnt this prayer: "Lord Jesus, wash me in Thy blood; take me in Thy arms."

I don't think Aline will be hungry again, for it was easy to arrange for a supply of milk. And Victorine, the daughter of our hotel keeper at Orsière, promised to go often and take her nourishing food. Meanwhile Frances had been at work in a chalet; I cannot recount half she does!

August 10.—Walked up to the Lac de Champé, and the next morning Frances found the way through the Gorge du Durnand; we always enjoy unknown routes. Thence to Martigny, and by diligence to Champéry, where we remained till August 28th.

At Champéry the delightful ministrations of Mr. Rogers, the chaplain, new friendships, and Frances' incessant ministries, whether by song, or conversation, or Bible reading, filled up every day. One evening, after playing the Moonlight Sonata, an aged German lady assured me that it quite recalled Beethoven's own rendering of it.

After leaving Champéry, *viâ* Berne and Interlachen, we stayed at the Pension Schönfels. The pressure of letters seemed to follow Frances everywhere, and I remember how good-naturedly she corrected roll after roll of poetical compositions by a stranger, although she was suffering extremely from the effects of being caught in a thunderstorm in an excursion from Champéry. While staying at the Pension Schönfels, the Baroness von Cramm, and Miss Carmichael, joined us, from Champéry. Poor Frances could not join in any excursions, nor did she attempt writing any circular letters, as in former tours. She told me that in writing those circulars she rather avoided expressing either the spiritual or the poetical ideas suggested; so she wrote "Holiday Work," and "Our Swiss Guide," as glimpses of her practical work for Christ, and those celestial revelations, which Alpine scenery constantly unfolded to her mind. It was at this time, however, that she wrote the following sonnet to her friend the Baroness Helga von Cramm.

TO HELGA.

Come down, and show the dwellers far below
    What God is painting in each mountain place!
    Show His fair colours, and His perfect grace,
Dowering each blossom born of sun and snow:
His tints, not thine! Thou art God's copyist,
    O gifted Helga! His thy golden height,
    Thy purple depth, thy rosy sunset light,
Thy blue snow-shadows, and thy weird white mist.

---

[1] Published by Hutchings & Romer.
[2] Marie Constance Jodant, in the village of Isere près d'Orsière.

Reveal His works to many a distant land!
 Paint for His praise, oh paint for love of Him!
He is thy Master, let Him hold thy hand,
 So thy pure heart no cloud of self shall dim.
At His dear feet lay down thy laurel-store,
Which crimson proof of thy redemption bore.

September 19th, 1876.

A letter has been sent to me, written about this time, which may interest some.

PENSION SCHÖNFELS.

MY VERY DEAR MARGARET:

I can't tell you how your letter touched me. I never thought He would let me give you a lift, who were already so bright and devoted. I tried to help other folks at Champéry, but I did not try with you, only just said what came uppermost. Oh I am so glad you see the "only for Jesus" in its special power. Having seen it, one wants to live it out, simply and entirely, and we can only go on trusting the Lord Jesus hour by hour to show us how. I wonder what He is going to show us next, dear M.! for He has so many things to say to us, as we can bear them. We have been guided to a wonderfully quiet pension, off the usual beat. Seven Germans here, only one of whom can speak any English. In answer to your query: well, I'll see about it; and if I can get a chance of being decently photographed I will send you a copy; but I am sure you won't like it, because the prevailing tone of my results under photographic torture is, "resignation under afflictive dispensations!" which a cheerful friend suggested as the most suitable inscription on my photos, of which she declined to accept one! Query No. 3: "This is not your rest" really does seem to be written on every attempt I make to find a quiet perch (as for a nest, I don't dream of that). If one set of fatigues is done with, another arises, personal or postal; but I really stand as good a chance here as anywhere, I think, so that will be a relief to your mind. And it has been enforced the last two days, because I left Champéry with a sharp sore throat, which developed into that sort of cold that has made me totally stupefied yesterday and to-day, and I have been in bed a good many extra hours. It was such a pleasure to meet you and dear Edith at C——; it is such a pleasure to recollect it, and will be ditto if we can some fine day come over and see you again. I think Maria is more likely to be free to do so than I. I am not quite so freely situated as she is, and have far more arrears to make up too, of long promised visits, as my long invalidism has thrown me far behindhand in that respect; and being seldom strong enough for any winter travelling limits my time for getting through my visits.

Yours lovingly,

F. R. H.

When she was better, we went to the village of Eizenflou, hoping for a fine sunrise on the Jungfrau. A feverish cold detained me there. Frances went to the village schoolmaster and secured the use of his schoolroom for a service the next evening, as her spirit was stirred up by finding no pastor ever came near these villages, and they were five miles from church. The evening was wet, and I wanted Frances not to go; but she said, "I may never come here again; and no man cares for these scattered sheep." The room was quite full. Frances addressed them in German from 1 John 1:7, and also led the hymns from their chorale book. Our hostess' report was: "Never, no never, had any one told them what the dear young lady did; it was wonderful! They never could forget her words; and surely she must be a born German!"

From Schönfels, we went to the Pension Wengen, above Lauterbrunnen, for several weeks.

October 1.—Unclouded sunshine. The Jungfrau and Silberhorn were radiant. Frances remarked, "It will be one of the new delights of heaven to be able to express all one's thoughts." The next day we took horses to the Scheideck Hotel. After resting, we rode up the Lauberhorn, with Hans Lauener for our guide. He seemed such a nice fellow, and sang some French hymns with Frances, on the top of the mountain.

I had the audacity to sketch the Silberhorn for Mary Fay. In the evening Frances called me to watch the singular effect of the moon rising behind sharp jutting rocks; the silver rays of an invisible but coming presence were most striking.

Another day we went to the Mettlen Alp, which Frances thinks the finest view in Switzerland, through pine woods, and then I stood with her on the silver steps of the Jungfrau's throne. What then? Avalanches and our silent Alleluias! Here it may be of interest to quote copy of the entry in the visitors' book, at Pension Wengen:

Summer returned; cloudless sky. Thermometer from 90° to 100° during our stay. Obliging attentions, honest charges, and tried truthfulness. The Mettlen Alp stands out in picturesque beauty. "All Thy works praise *Thee*." Avalanche Alleluias will long echo in English homes.

MARIA V. G. HAVERGAL.
FRANCES RIDLEY HAVERGAL.

Sept. 23rd till Oct. 16th, 1876.

This was Frances' last excursion; her health entirely failed.

October 8.—Frances in acute pain all day, and could not get up at all. She wrote the hymn, "I take this pain, Lord Jesus." They brought lukewarm water for fomentations, so I dived into the kitchen, and secured a saucepan, gathered pine cones and wood, and got leave to use the salon stove night and day.

October 9 and 10.—Frances moaning all day, but so wonderfully patient, even in sleepless nights. I could not say "Thy will be done," till she spoke so sweetly of texts that hush and gladden her. She verily exults in that declaration, "I love, I love my Master" (Exodus 21:5), connecting it with Revelation 22:3, "shall serve Him for ever."

October 12.—Tried camomile fomentations, at midnight, and darling Frances so grateful; I never nursed any one so uncomplaining. Reading to her, "Let Thy judgments help me," I asked her what it meant. She said, "I think God's judgments prove our faith, forcing us to trust more, to lean more. 'Help,' because He comes so very close, helps us when no one else can."

Madame Lauener, the mother of our host, often came up to Frances' room. She is intensely fond of Frances, and repeats Scripture in German, and prays most soothingly by her.

October 13.—Mrs. Simpson (English Pension) came all the way from Interlachen, bringing remedies, fruit and jelly for Frances; so extremely kind, as we are comparative strangers.

Frances sent for me to hear Madame Lauener repeat from memory the seventh chapter of the Revelation. Such a picture! through the window the glisten of the snowy Silberhorn,[1] on the pillow dear Frances and her golden curls; by her side the aged woman, who with beaming eye and waving hand emphasized those wonderful words; truly it brought a glimpse of

"When robed in white before Thee,
Without one stain or tear,
Shall all Thy saints adore Thee,
'Midst wonder, love, and fear."
(Rev. W. H. H.)

Sunday, October 15.—Frances was decidedly better, and able to take a few steps in the sunshine. Her comment on "For His mercy endureth for ever," was, "that is, every day." It seemed uncertain if we could leave next day, but it is impossible to fidget about anything when with Frances. She playfully said, "Now, Marie, can't you leave me entirely to our Father!" Another time I was anxious, and she put her hand on mine: "Marie dear, just trust! Jesus *is* with us, all must come right."

October 16.—Frances better, and able to leave in a chaise à porteur to Lauterbrunnen, from whence she enjoyed the drive to Interlachen. From the lake of Thun the snowy mountains of the Bernese Oberland brightened into sunset glory, and we saw them no more.

October 18.—Left Basle through Alsace; the Vosges mountains were dimly outlined, and then we went through a pancake country with straight roads and fields, and straight poplars, to Strasbourg.

October 19.—Frances was too tired to go out, so I raced round Strasbourg. I was extremely interested in the flower market, and had sundry talks with the women. I took a diligence to get a sight of the Rhine, and, walking back by a short cut, got into the fortifications. The captain was most polite, and allowed me to speak to a few soldiers, giving them a rapid outline of what the Captain of our salvation did, and does.

The cathedral is magnificent, but it is so intensely grievous to see the shrines. One lady kept lighting little tapers at the Virgin's shrine, and another young girl seemed quite faint with kneeling; she came and sat by me, and I had an interesting talk with her.

We then left for Brussels, and arrived in England October 20th. The 21st from London to Winterdyne *viâ* Oxford. Just after leaving Oxford Frances startled me with: "Marie! I see it all; I can write a little book, 'My King!'"

That herald light was in her eye, which ever betokens some direct communication from her King. And the following letter to M. A. C. shows how prayerfully she afterwards wrote it, trusting for every word to be given her.

November 1, 1876. Oakhampton.

I really cannot let this be "gratis," though the next shall be. I am so delighted and thankful to hear that you really are going to give the whole winter to God's work, and that Miss de K. has joined you, and that you will be strengthening the hands of dear Miss Leigh, in Paris. Altogether, your letter has made me very happy and very grateful.

I am better now, but was far worse after you left us at Schönfels. Two attacks in succession, the second causing nearly a week of terribly prostrating pain. This day three weeks I could not even stand alone! So the only thing seemed to be to seize the very first day of being anyhow able to begin the journey from Pension Wengen, and get at least a stage or two nearer home, which we did; and though we had to take a week about it, and I was very ill on the way, we were brought safely to England. I am now at my eldest sister's, getting up my strength delightfully, and able for walks in the garden. Maria is quite renovated, and sleeps and eats properly, in spite of the really heavy strain upon her to have had to nurse me night and day while really very ill. Maria is not going to take to herself another wife at all! (since E. Clay's departure to India), so, after all, you won't have the pain of being superseded. She is going to live at Winterdyne for some time, and this is an immense satisfaction to us all.

Do you ever have time to pray for other people's work, now that you have so much before you? Because, if so, will

---
[1] See Frontispiece. [See page 276 of Volume IV of the Havergal edition.]

you ask that He would give me special help in a little book which I want to write, as He may give me strength. The title will be simply "My King," and it will be little daily thoughts for a month, (uniform with the "Bells" and "Pillows," only for grown up folk) on thirty-one texts, all from the Old Testament, about our King. It is such a delicious subject, and I have so enjoyed the mere looking out of the texts about it, while not yet strong enough for serious writing; but I am not sufficient for these things, and never felt more deeply my own insufficiency. Only the idea of the book came so *very* forcibly to my mind that I could not but think He had sent it me; and so I have done what I never did before, shelved the little work I already had on hand, to do this first. I will send you one of the texts, because possibly you might not have thought of it, and it seems so nice for use. 2 Samuel 19:20: the knowledge that Shimei had sinned being the very reason, not for keeping away, but for coming the first of all to meet the king. I took it as the text for a little talk with the servants here, and never found a more telling one. The 2nd Book of Samuel is full of exquisite typical texts. The headings of the little daily portions will be such as "The Friendship of the King," "Decision for the King," "The Business of the King," "The Banquet of the King," "Speaking to the King."

It is so utterly bumptious of me to think of writing for grown ups at all, much more on such a theme, that I feel more entirely shut up to asking and trusting for every word of it, than I ever did before.

Please give my love to dear Miss Leigh. I owe her ever such a debt of gratitude for her kindness, and most helpful influence, with one of my dear nieces.

Good bye, dearest Margaret; Paris is not "among plants and hedges," but may you there dwell with the King, for His work. Love to dear Edith when you write.

Yours ever,
F. R. H.

Two years passed away, and I again visited the Pension Wengen, in 1878, with Mrs. Usborne and Miss Cowan. Knowing how much my sister F. R. H. was loved there, I took care, when writing for rooms, to say she was not coming, lest they should be disappointed. But they did not notice it, and so the grandmother eagerly expected her beloved Fraulein Fannie. When I arrived, there she stood, smiling a welcome, but pointed up, saying, "O mein Hans!" Then she went to meet the other horses, searching for F., till seeing she was not come, her wail was quite touching: "O my beloved, my Fraulein Fannie, where are you? why are you not come to comfort me?" Her countenance was still beautiful, but there was now a far off look in her eyes, sorrow for some one gone. And so it was; her son Hans, our bright young guide to the Mettlen Alp and the Lauberhorn, had met with an accident and died. His mother and brother gave me the following particulars.

All the winter Hans had been most active in relieving the peasants and going to their scattered chalets with soup and food, often through deep snow. There is a society here for that purpose, and Hans was its most useful member.

Some of the mountain land and pine woods, adjoining the Pension Wengen, belonged to him and his brother Ulrich. These pines are thinned, cut down, and taken into the valley beneath, and there sawn into planks. After the branches are cut off, the pines are brought to the glissade, which is formed by the freezing of some mountain stream, over which lies a deep bed of frozen snow. On the morning of March 5th, 1878, Hans, his brother Ulrich, and twenty men were thus at work. It requires great skill to steer the pine and keep it steadily in its torrent slide. Hans was ever the first, enjoying the dash of power requisite to guide the giant pine down that icy path. But in a moment the pine swayed out of its course, Hans was struck down, the whole weight of the pine crushing his side and leg. A mattress and pillows were brought, his brother wisely taking him at once to Lauterbrunnen, where he would be nearer a doctor than at home. Skilfully was he carried to the Hotel Staubbach, and a telegram soon brought doctors from Interlachen. But nothing could be done, the loss of blood was too great to allow of amputation. Hans was calm and patient, though in agony. He told them that "he had his passport all ready, that he saw the path of life before him, and he was quite sure he was in it."

He lived three days, during which the pastor, who was rationalistic, visited Hans, and the words of the dying guide spoke of a better hope. Hans told him that no works, no merit, no good and noble life, gave him any comfort now, but it was the sacrifice of Jesus on the cross, and the precious blood there shed to put away sin, that was his "passport."

"It is believing in Jesus Christ brings me this joy. Without the blood that atones for sin, I could not stand accepted before the throne."

The pastor heard and believed; this testimony brought new light and life to him, and a crown to the dying Hans. (Since then his sermons are quite evangelistic.) His only sorrow was to leave his mother and brother, but even then he comforted them: "God has prepared a place also for you my brother. Mother, my mother, there is only a short course for you to run." Hans spoke of F. R. H., and more than once sang the hymn in which they had joined on the heights of the Lauberhorn.

> "Vers le ciel, vers le ciel,
>   J'entends, Jésus, Ton appel,
> O mon cœur, vers toi s'élance
> Dans la joyeuse espérance
>   De se voir, Emmanuel!"

And then with the ancient passport of "the blood," the young guide passed upward, and entered in " through the gates into the city." He died March 8th, 1878.

It is now October, 1881, and in F.R.H.'s study there lies her motto card, "My own text," identical with the dying guide's "passport," "The blood of Jesus Christ His Son cleans*eth* us from all sin" (1 John 1:7).

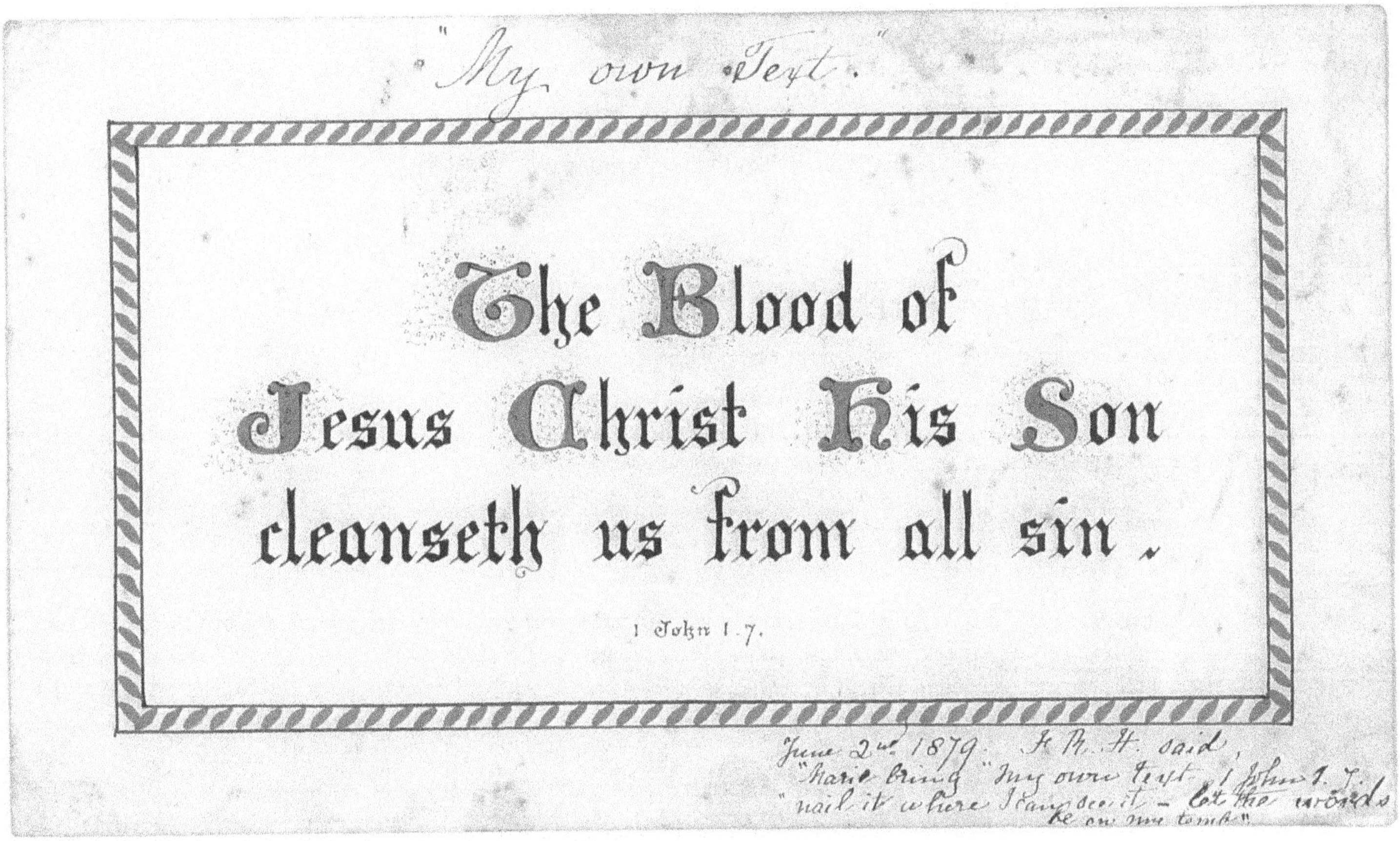

This hand-painted plaque was F.R.H.'s "My own Text." The handwritten title at the top and note in the bottom right corner are very likely or almost certainly her sister Maria's handwriting: June 2nd 1879. F.R.H. said, "Marie bring "My own text I John 1.7. "nail it where I can see it — let the words be on my tomb."

See page 326, the fifth paragraph of the left column.

Neither Frances Ridley Havergal nor any of those who knew her anticipated that she would die so soon, so young. After their stepmother Caroline Anne Havergal died on May 26, 1878, Maria invited Frances to come to live with her at Mumbles, a small village near Swansea on the coast of Wales, and Frances died there, only 42 and a half, on June 3, 1879. Maria realized the rare, rich value in her sister's works, and was a very diligent, faithful steward of her works not yet published, preparing and publishing her finished works and a number of her unfinished works, preserving and disseminating the treasure in her day and for future generations. Maria's Prefaces to the books by Frances that Maria posthumously published are given next, the first one being *Kept for the Master's Use* (on page 418 of Volume II of the Havergal edition).

PREFATORY NOTE.

My beloved sister Frances finished revising the proofs of this book shortly before her death on Whit Tuesday, June 3, 1879, but its publication was to be deferred till the Autumn.

In appreciation of the deep and general sympathy flowing in to her relatives, they wish that its publication should not be withheld. Knowing her intense desire that Christ should be magnified, whether by her life or in her death, may it be to His glory that in these pages she, being dead,

"Yet speaketh!"

Maria V. G. Havergal.

Oakhampton, Worcestershire,
11*th June* 1879.

Maria wrote this at the front of F.R.H.'s posthumously published *Morning Stars* (on page 257 of Volume III of the Havergal edition).

PREFATORY NOTE.

Just a week before my dear sister F. R. H. died, I took her letters up-stairs. Her pretty kittens Trot and Dot were playing on her bed. She was too ill to care about her letters, but was so pleased to get the first page of *this* book. She looked at it carefully, and with her pencil corrected mistakes. Then she was anxious every reader should have space to add the verses, and asked me to write about it. May I say that she hoped you would read one chapter daily! My dear sister intended writing another book for you, "Evening Stars; or, Promises for the Little Ones." But, though she is gone, the Promises are left. Will you not search them out in your Bibles every evening and just say, as she often did, "This promise is so bright, and it is for me."

Maria V. G. Havergal.

September, 1879.

This was the Preface to *Under His Shadow* The Last Poems of Frances Ridley Havergal, posthumously gathered and prepared by Maria (on pages 774–776 of Volume I of the Havergal edition).

PREFACE.

My dear sister Frances had intended writing an opening poem to this volume, showing *why* she chose its title of

"Under His Shadow."

Only these fragmentary lines, written in pencil, were found:—

> "Faint footsteps tracked the burning sand
>   Far o'er the wild white waste,
>   A thirsting band, lessening each hour;
>   Lost was all energy for hopeful haste,
>   Lost e'en despair's convulsive power,
>   Although the dangerous glare
>   Fell fiercely through heat-quivering air,
>   Although the way was strewn with bleaching bones,
>   And treasure dropped by hands that could not care,
>   For gold or precious stones;
>   When very life evaporated, and although
>   There was no safety in that terrible plain,
>   No point of pause but death. For swift or slow,
>   Advance or halt, seemed all alike in vain;—

. . . . . .

Happily I have preserved in writing the recollection of a conversation, in which she gave me an outline of what she intended the volume to be.

Three years ago, when we were in Switzerland, and she was recovering from illness, she said to me: "Marie, I think my third volume of poems will be my 'Nunc Dimittis'! Do you remember my poem, 'Three-fold Praise'? I think my first volume, 'Ministry of Song,' was like Haydn; then 'Under the Surface,' like Mendelssohn; and I want my third volume to be 'Messiah,' all to His praise!

"I should like the title to be 'Under His Shadow.' I seem to see four pictures suggested by that: under the shadow of a rock in a weary plain; under the shadow of a tree; closer still, under the shadow of His wing; nearest and closest, in the shadow of His hand. Surely that hand must be the pierced hand, that may oftentimes press us sorely, and yet evermore encircling, upholding, and shadowing!"

Only the day before my dear sister died she asked me to collect and publish all her MS. poems. I said, "Shall the title be 'Under His Shadow'?" and she answered: "Oh, yes; I am so glad you remembered it."

And now she more than realizes her own words:

> "As we fall o'erawed
> Upon our faces, and are lifted higher
> By His great gentleness, and carried nigher
> Than unredeemèd angels, till we stand
>   Even *in* the hollow of His hand:
> Nay, more! we lean upon His breast:
> There, there we find a point of perfect rest
>   And glorious safety!"

Maria V. G. Havergal.

Oakhampton, Stourport,
   November, 1879.

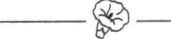

This is Maria's Preface to *Memorials of Frances Ridley Havergal* (London: James Nisbet & Co., 1880), original book pages v–vii, page 2 of Volume IV of the Havergal edition.

PREFACE.

It is with a reverent hand that these "hidden leaves" of my dear sister's life are now laid at the Master's feet, for His acceptance and blessing.

> "Leaves which grave Experience ponders,
>   Soundings for her pilot-charts;
> Leaves which God Himself is storing,
> Records which we read, adoring
>   Him, who writes on human hearts.
>
> Leaflets long unpaged and scattered
>   Time's great library receives;
> When eternity shall bind them,
> Golden volumes we shall find them,
>   God's light falling on the leaves."

No attempt has been made to write a Biography, but rather to allow her to relate her own life-story—a sister's loving touch uniting the several links. Her letters, so kindly lent to me by many friends, have furnished abundant materials for this purpose.

These pages will reveal, to some extent, her "true-hearted, whole-hearted" loyalty in the service of God. Often was it as unseen as the lonely watchfulness of the sentinel on some distant outpost; although in later years she seemed as one pacing the ramparts in the very presence of the King. And so—

> "The joy of loyal service to the King
>   Shone through her days, and lit up other lives
>   With the new fire of faith, that ever strives,
>   Like a swift-kindling beacon, far to fling
> The tidings of His victory, and claim
> New subjects for His realm, new honour for His Name."

May Christ be magnified by this record of her life and death! To her, Christ was indeed "all and in all"; and she did but describe her own experience in the words:

> "There were strange soul depths, restless, vast, and broad,
>   Unfathomed as the sea;
> An infinite craving for some infinite stilling:
> But now Thy perfect love is perfect filling,
> Lord Jesus Christ, my Lord, my God,
>   Thou, Thou art enough for me!"

Yes, she was satisfied with Him, and knew what it was to "rest *in* the Lord," whilst she worked *for* Him. May I not add that an equally joyous and blessed experience may be ours; and that His grace, which was sufficient for her, is sufficient for all who, possessing "like precious faith," "follow His steps."

Maria V. G. Havergal.

Caswell Bay Road, The Mumbles,
South Wales.
April, 1880.

This is Maria's Prefatory Note to F.R.H.'s *Loyal Responses* with music (London: Hutchings and Romer, 1881), an un-numbered page near the front of the original book, page 1177 of Volume V of the Havergal edition.

PREFATORY NOTE

Some of these melodies were the very last composed and sung by Frances Ridley Havergal. So rapidly did they occur to her that they were only pencilled down, but her hand was stayed from the chords of earth before the musical completion of "Loyal Responses." Other melodies by F.R.H. have therefore been chosen and fitted to her hymns, in order to complete the thirty-one days.

The following extract will express F.R.H.'s feeling on the subject of

SACRED SONG.

"I am delighted to have an opportunity of adding to the very meagre supply of Sacred Songs, and I hope they will be sufficiently tuneful and sufficiently easy for drawing-room singing. Some of those extant are very pathetic and dismal affairs! Why put off joyous singing till we reach the happier shore? Let us sing words which we feel and love, with clearness of enunciation, and looking up to meet His smile all the while we are singing. So shall we loyally sing for our King, yes for Him, Whose voice is our truest music." [F.R.H.]

MARIA V. G. HAVERGAL.

Caswell Bay Road,
Aug., 1881.

This is Maria's Preface to F.R.H.'s *Starlight Through the Shadows* (London: James Nisbet & Co., 1881), original book pages iii–v, page 504 of Volume II of the Havergal edition.

PREFACE.

"Work for 1879, if the Lord will. To write 'Starlight through the Shadows,' a daily book for Invalids." Such was the intention of my dear sister, F. R. H. Having herself passed through the shadows of sickness and sorrow, she sought to bring some "starry promise sure," which might be more welcome, to the feeble eye, than the dazzling rays of brighter promises.

In answer to a suggestion, that she should write on some other subjects, her characteristic reply was: "I don't think I have got any real commission to write anything at all for next autumn, except the invalid book. I believe I am going off the line of my especial calling if once I begin to think of writing as a matter of business and success and cheque, and all that; and I can't expect the same blessing in it. And so, though of course it stands to reason that the invalid book must have a very limited circulation compared to the others, I shall be much happier doing that; and I believe I shall have more real, *i.e.* spiritual results from it, than if I set myself to do any others, because I do think God gave me the thought to do this one. I have felt so very strongly and sweetly hitherto, that my pen was to be used *only* for the Master, that I am very fearful of getting the least out of the course in which I have felt His blessing." (*March* 1879.)

Only eleven chapters were written, when for her all shadows fled away, and were exchanged for the shadowless splendour of the very Light of Light!

To complete a seventh and last volume of F. R. H.'s Royal series, selections have been made from her unpublished manuscripts.

My beloved sister's life-long interest in all missionary work seems to culminate in her "Marching Orders." By request of Mr. Eugene Stock, she wrote these papers for the *Church Missionary Gleaner* of 1879.

Outlines of addresses given at various times, with other papers, show her diligent searchings in the Scripture of truth.

May the Holy Spirit's blessing cause them to be helpful Gleams from the King's Word.

Maria V. G. Havergal.

December 14th, 1881.

This is Maria's Prefatory Note to F.R.H.'s *Ben Brightboots* (London: James Nisbet & Co., 1882), original book pages vii–viii, page 318 of Volume III of the Havergal edition.

PREFATORY NOTE.

Many loving messages reached my dear sister, F. R. H., from the readers of "Little Pillows," and "Morning Bells," entreating for another book. Gladly would she have compiled such, from the treasures of her often-told merry stories; and it was her intention to write about "Percy," as a sequel to "Bruey."

But health and time failed her, and her ever busy pen has only left these fragments.

The true story of "Ben Brightboots" was written in 1869. Her beautiful allegory "The Spirit of Beauty" shows her youthful power in composition.

"Robin Redbreast and Brown Mousie," and two or three other papers, were written for the Children's Special Service Mission, and have been translated into many languages.

The unpublished "Talk with Philip the Boatman" was written January 24th, 1879. Its deeply precious teaching reflects the sunset glow of her own life.

May these pages bring true sunshine to every reader, and new praises to our Saviour King.

Maria V. G. Havergal.

Nov. 15th, 1882.

P.S.—Will the little friends of F. R. H. accept the lines which she wrote for *my* birthday as expressive of my wishes for *theirs*.

> The blessing of the trusting one,
>   Who knows her faithful Friend;
> The blessing of the waiting one,
>   Who trusts Him to the end;
> The blessing of the watching one
>   Whose eyes are on the Lord;
> The blessing of the chastened one,
>   That marvellous reward!
> These sweetest birthday blessings be
>   Abundantly bestowed on thee!

Dearest Marie,—Ever so much love. I enclose you birthday wishes.

F. R. H.

Nov. 15th, 1877.

This is Maria's Preface to F.R.H.'s *Life Echoes* (London: James Nisbet & Co., 1883), original book pages v–vi, pages 779–780 of Volume I of the Havergal edition. This was the complete title: "LIFE ECHOES." / By / Frances Ridley Havergal, / with a few selected pieces / by / William Henry Havergal, M.A. / "*A glimpse and an echo are given to-day / Of glory and music not far away.*" / With Twelve Illustrations / by / The Baroness Helga von Cramm.

PREFACE.

The echoes from some Alpine horn floating far upward on mountain heights can never be forgotten by the passing traveller; and all who will may pause on their journey, and be refreshed by the melody.

And thus also echoes from the pen of F. R. H. reach us still,—some from the glimmering distance of childhood, some from the far-away youthful mists of the valley, and some from the nearer "pastures," leading upwards to the golden heights.

All the known dates of the poems in this volume are given, as it may interest some readers to contrast the verses of her childhood with such lines as "The Thoughts of God," which "rise even to Miltonic grandeur."

The early dates of all her songs and secular poems conclusively show that she turned away from the opening path of earthly fame, and hereafter consecrated her talents wholly to Him who gave them. Truly did she look up to her King for every word she wrote, and literally were they messages from Him.

Many of her tiny but melodious echoes on Birthdays, Christmas, New Year, and other seasons, were originally written for, and published by, Messrs. Caswell and Marcus Ward, with floral entwinings, or Alpine illustrations by the Baroness von Cramm, and some of the mottoes on Scripture will be found in "Red Letter Days" (M. Ward & Co.). As the floral cards are evanescent, they are now by permission collectively given.

For the illustrations in this volume of Life Echoes, the pencil of F. R. H.'s friend has traced scenes from nature, where my dear sister's footstep often lightly trod. New decorative designs have also been prepared for this, the *concluding* volume of F. R. H.'s poems.

It will be observed that a few of the poems are by F. R. H.'s father, the Rev. W. H. Havergal. His lines will always be distinguished by his initials, W. H. H.

This is only carrying out F. R. H.'s own happy thought, expressed in the preface to "Red Letter Days":—"It is a pleasure to offer my readers the more valuable addition of verses by my sainted father." And thus the echoes of their lives and songs are blended still below, while—

> "From the great anthems of the crystal sea,
> Through the far vistas of eternity,
> Grand *echoes* of the word peal on for thee,
> Sweetest and fullest,
> Most blessèd for ever."—F. R. H.

Maria V. G. Havergal

September, 1883.

This is Maria's Prefatory Note to *The Poetical Works of Frances Ridley Havergal* (London: James Nisbet & Co., 1884), original book pages vii–ix, pages iii–iv of Volume I of the Havergal edition.

PREFATORY NOTE.

It is in answer to many requests that the various poems, hymns, and song of Frances Ridley Havergal are comprised in this library edition. It will be obvious, there was some difficulty in selecting the order of their sequence. We doubt not that the dear author's own arrangement in 'Ministry of Song,' 'Under the Surface,' and 'Loyal Responses' will be generally preferred, and consequently they remain intact. To group successfully poetic aspirations of such varied circumstances and ideas, ranging from the sweet simplicities of her songs for the little ones, to those higher soarings which seem to culminate in 'The Thoughts of God,' was indeed a problem. And it is due to my dear sister's memory to state distinctly that *she* never contemplated the publication of many impromptu verses, written to gratify young friends, or in the utterance of rapid imaginings. When F. R. H. was arranging a selection for the first illustrated volume, 'Life Mosaic,' she submitted her poems to her poet friend, the Rev. R. Wilton, earnestly soliciting him to prune away with unsparing keenness 'any of my weaker poems.' And we are aware that other poet critics would prefer only the finer chords to be lasting echoes of F. R. H.

But there are many, oh, so many, who lovingly treasure even the spray of her pen, as well as the nobler waves of thought, and so we open and unseal all the manuscripts in her study drawers. For some of her simpler utterances seem to go at once to the heart of those in humbler life, and their intellect can better grasp such thoughts than the loftier flights of her imagination. By them it is not as a feast of intellect, but as heart cheer for home sorrows, that F. R. H.'s lowliest lays are prized.

The arrangement is subjective, not chronological. But in the Index [page v of this Volume I] will be found the dates and places of her poems; we are aware this is unusual, but it would seem as if her sunny presence and springing footsteps may thus still linger in our midst. It is with pleasure that I entrust to my dear niece, Frances Anna Shaw, the entire arrangement and revision of this complete and final edition. It was no slight labour to prepare the various dates and subdivide the numerous subjects into their present order. In shattered health, I thankfully accept my niece's skilful labour. And we would bring these pages with loyal loving hand to the very feet of F. R. H.'s Master and King, re-echoing words, which seem to float down from the golden heights where now my sister stands amid the upper choir, joining the service of high praise in the 'Eternal Land:'

> 'I have no word to bring
> Worthy of Thee, my King,
> And yet one anthem in Thy praise
> I long, I long to raise.'

'*One* anthem'? Have they not been countless? has not her silver refrain echoed and re-echoed till many an isolated and trembling one has taken up in a gathering and rejoicing chorus, 'Unto Him that loved us, and washed us from our sins in His own blood, and hath made us kings and priests unto God and His Father; to Him be glory and dominion for ever and ever. Amen.'

And does not F. R. H.'s earliest prelude become a fitting closing chord to her life and poems,—

> 'AMID the broken waters of our ever-restless thought,
> Oh be my verse an answering gleam from higher radiance caught;
> That where through dark o'erarching boughs of sorrow, doubt, and sin,
> The glorious Star of Bethlehem upon the flood looks in,
> Its tiny trembling ray may bid some downcast vision turn
> To that enkindling Light, for which all earthly shadows yearn.
> Oh be my verse a hidden stream, which silently may flow
> Where drooping leaf and thirsty flower in lonely valleys grow;
> And often by its shady course to pilgrim hearts be brought
> The quiet and refreshment of an upward-pointing thought;
> Till, blending with the broad bright stream of sanctified endeavour,
> God's glory be its ocean home, the end it seeketh ever.'

MARIA V. G. HAVERGAL.

F.R.H.'s fair copy autograph of one of her "Verses on Texts" written in April, 1877, the single verse on Ezekiel 33:10 and Isaiah 53:6, on page 170 in her Manuscript Book Nº VIII begun November, 1873.

> XV Ezek. 33. 10.   Isa. 53. 6.
> On Thee, the Lord
> My mighty sins hath laid;
> And against Thee Jehovah's sword
> Flashed forth its fiery blade.
> The stroke of justice fell on Thee,
> That it might never fall on me.

This was Maria's last Preface on F.R.H., for her last compilation and edition of a book by F.R.H., the Preface to *Letters by the Late Frances Ridley Havergal* (London: James Nisbet & Co., 1885), original book pages v–vi, page 144 of Volume IV of the Havergal edition.

PREFACE.

"Such as we are in word by letters when we are absent, such will we be also in deed when we are present" (2 Corinthians 10:11). So, only those who saw St. Paul could verify his touchstone of deeds not words. And so with the beloved sister, whose letters are now unveiled; only those who saw her, could rightly estimate how truly her deeds of loving faithful labour for her Master were as golden seals to her words. Even these letters do not fully reveal all the wonderful submission of her home-life, or how the hand that takes the crown, may first be pierced with many a thorn.

It should be borne in mind that these letters were written chiefly to near and dear relatives and friends, who she knew would sympathize in the details of her service for the King.

Especial thanks are due to our eldest sister, J. Miriam Crane, for her valuable help in suggesting and revising.

Much gratitude is felt to those correspondents who now share their treasures with the ever-widening circle of F. R. H.'s readers. Attention has been given to their wishes in printing initials or names.

Her letters from Switzerland are not included, being already printed in *Swiss Letters*.

Frequent reference will be found to F. R. H.'s laborious editing of Havergal's *Psalmody*, containing her own and her father's tunes, which are now combined in one volume with the Rev. C. B. Snepp's selection of hymns, viz. *The New Musical Edition of Songs of Grace and Glory* (Nisbet & Co).

May these "Letters" cheer and guide some—

"Footsteps weak and weary
Through the desert dreary
Through the valley of the night."

Again her words may be quoted—

"Ye read *her* story,
Take home the lesson with a spirit smile:
Darkness and mystery a little while,
Then—light and glory,
And ministry mid saint and seraph band
And service of high praise in the Eternal Land."

This closing record of the loved and loving one is laid at her Master's glorious feet, praying that interwoven with her life-story, His praise and glory may shine forth.

August 1885.

Maria V. G. Havergal.

These are two poems by F.R.H., both involving Maria.

To M. V. G. H.

On her birthday.

The blessing of the trusting one,
  Who knows her faithful Friend;
The blessing of the waiting one,
  Who trusts Him to the end;
The blessing of the watching one,
  Whose eyes are on the Lord;
The blessing of the chastened one,
  That marvelous reward!—
These sweetest birthday blessings be
  Abundantly bestowed on thee!

  Blessing and blest
    May thy new year be,
  Brightest and best
    Of the years to thee,
    Awaiting the rest
    Of eternity!

Frances Ridley Havergal, November, 1877

Daily Strength.

"As thy days thy strength shall be!"
This should be enough for thee;
He who knows thy frame will spare
Burdens more than thou canst bear.

When thy days are veiled in night,
Christ shall give thee heavenly light;
Seem they wearisome and long,
Yet in Him thou shalt be strong.

Cold and wintry though they prove,
Thine the sunshine of His love,
Or, with fervid heat oppressed,
In His shadow thou shalt rest.

When thy days on earth are past,
Christ shall call thee home at last,
His redeeming love to praise,
Who hath strengthened all thy days.

Frances Ridley Havergal, January 1, 1859.

[See the first paragraph on page 281 of this book.]

Frances Ridley Havergal, one of eight photographs of her taken by Elliott and Frye on February 1, 1879.